RECOLLECTED WORDS
OF ABRAHAM LINCOLN

RECOLLECTED WORDS
OF ABRAHAM LINCOLN

Compiled and Edited by

Don E. Fehrenbacher and Virginia Fehrenbacher

STANFORD UNIVERSITY PRESS, STANFORD, CALIFORNIA

Stanford University Press
Stanford, California
© 1996 by the Board of Trustees of the
Leland Stanford Junior University
Printed in the United States of America

CIP data appear at the end of the book

Published with the support of the
National Endowment for the Humanities,
an independent federal agency

FOR THE THIRD GENERATION

Jennifer, Adrienne, Steven, Karen,
Caitlin, Peter, James, and Jesse

CONTENTS

INTRODUCTION

AT BALTIMORE in June 1864, the national convention of the Republican party (now calling itself the Union party) renominated Abraham Lincoln but then turned away from the incumbent vice president, Hannibal Hamlin, and awarded second place on the ticket to Andrew Johnson, the military governor of Tennessee. Consequently, when Lincoln died at the hands of an assassin ten months later, it would be a southern Democrat of proslavery background, rather than a New England Republican with radical leanings, who succeeded to the presidency.

In a communication intended for the chairman of the Illinois delegation, Lincoln had declared just before the convention that he did not want to interfere in any way with the vice-presidential nomination.* Nevertheless, many modern historians have been disposed to believe that the fateful selection of Johnson, whatever other influences may have come into play, was orchestrated from the White House. The story they tell is virtually one of political conspiracy, with the wily President maneuvering behind the scenes to achieve his purpose and, in the process, deceiving not only the American public but many of his closest associates as well.

Almost all the evidence of such a conspiracy comes from certain reminiscences, particularly those of a few men claiming to have been Lincoln's prime agents in imposing his will on the delegates at Baltimore. Two key figures were the Pennsylvania politician Alexander K. McClure and Lincoln's old friend Ward Hill Lamon, both of whom later wrote accounts of how they talked with the President on the eve of the convention and received his instructions for supporting Johnson. McClure recalled being told, among other things, that putting a southerner on the ticket would be the best way to prevent recognition of the Confederacy by England and France. According to Lamon, Lincoln refused to authorize the use of his name but then added that he would write a letter expressing his views, which was to be used only if "absolutely necessary."

The strong suspicion that neither McClure nor Lamon can be regarded as a reliable witness makes it all the more remarkable that the accepted explanation of this crucial political event should depend heavily upon words they attributed to Lincoln long after his death. Of course, recollective quotation has always been an important part of Lincoln biography. About his

* *Collected Works*, VII, 376.

mother, for instance, he never wrote anything beyond supplying a few routine facts, but he can be quoted as stating orally that she was the illegitimate daughter of a Virginia aristocrat, whose qualities she inherited and transmitted to her son. Similarly, there is no mention of Ann Rutledge in any of his writings, but he can be quoted as saying when he was president-elect, "I did honestly and truly love the girl and think often, often of her now."

Did Lincoln already have his eyes on the presidency in 1858? Did he make a conditional offer to evacuate Fort Sumter in April 1861? Was it he himself or his general in chief, Henry W. Halleck, who made the decision to restore George B. McClellan to army command in September 1862? To whom did he first reveal his intention to issue an emancipation proclamation? In the darker days of the war, did he ever consider suicide? Did he label the Gettysburg address a failure right after delivering it? Did he offer to support Governor Horatio Seymour for president in 1864 if that Democratic leader would give his full support to the war effort? As the conflict drew to a close, did he favor letting Jefferson Davis and other Confederate leaders flee the country? Did he, just a few days before his assassination, dream of a president lying dead in the White House? All of these questions arise from recollective quotations of Lincoln, and the answer in each instance depends upon how one appraises the reliability of such recollection.

In addition, much of what is known or believed about the man as a whole—about his temperament and cast of mind, his faith, wit, and social style—comes from utterances recalled piecemeal by hundreds of his contemporaries over a period of more than half a century. Scattered about in diaries, letters, newspaper interviews, and reminiscent writing of various kinds, these recollected words of Lincoln lie outside the Lincoln canon in the sense that they are not, with a few exceptions, included in his published "works." Unlike his speeches and writings, they have never been systematically collected; nor has their authenticity been more than randomly tested. Yet recollective quotation, such as that associated with the nomination of Andrew Johnson, is commonly cited as evidence, and in an array of footnotes it may appear to have the same standing as official public statements and private correspondence.

For a historian, as for a court of law, recollective testimony may be the only available source of essential facts. That is predominantly the case in the study of Lincoln's early life, which would not amount to much if it were limited to data derived from contemporary records. Recollective material can be of special value, however, even when other, more highly respected sources are plentiful. Remembered conversations with Lincoln as president, for instance, often have an element of spontaneity and lifelikeness that breaks through the barrier of formality and restraint in his written words. They reveal a wider range of moods and interests, a greater complexity of character, and sometimes they disclose secrets unmentioned in the other sources. But if such materials enrich Lincoln biography, they also tend to adulterate it and to pose difficult problems of authentication.

Lincoln's *written* words, as we know them, survive physically in original or nearly original documents, and their authenticity depends quite simply on the genuineness of those documents, something that can as a rule be conclusively determined. His *spoken* words, as we know them, are a different matter. With certain exceptions, they survive because they were recalled and written down by other persons, and their authenticity thus depends most critically, not on the genuineness of documents, but on the credibility of recollections, something that can seldom be determined beyond reasonable doubt.

At the heart of the matter lies the problem of how time affects memory in general and verbal recall in particular. An enormous amount of research on the processes of remembering and forgetting has not discredited the commonsense notion that a remark written down the same day by a diarist is probably more trustworthy than a remark recalled many years later in a memoir. It by no means follows, however, that reminiscences of the Lincoln presidency published in the 1870s are more reliable than those appearing in the 1880s. Lapse of time between utterance and recorded recollection is of limited value as a measure of accuracy because of all the other influences at work during the interval.

Memory, whether it is viewed as storage or as synthesis, begins with perception, the circumstances of which may significantly influence the memory process. For one thing, level of interest at the time of perception has been shown, not surprisingly, to affect the quantity and accuracy of what is remembered. A person having something at stake in an interview with Lincoln, such as one of his law clients in Springfield or a job applicant in Washington, was likely to retain a sharper-than-average memory of the occasion. Similarly, a conversation with Lincoln in the White House was for most people a memorable experience, recognized as such at the time, whereas conversation with the younger Lincoln on the legal circuit had a lower level of interest when it occurred and became memorable only in retrospect.

Bias and emotion can likewise affect the original perception and thus the memory of an experience. For instance, Charles Francis Adams's recollection of his unsatisfactory interview with Lincoln after being appointed minister to England was colored by the impression he took with him to the meeting that the awkward Illinoisan was poorly suited for the presidency. And when Jessie Benton Frémont met with Lincoln in September 1861, there was an antagonism between them that undoubtedly distorted their subsequent accounts of the confrontation.

For a longtime friend or associate, individual perceptions of Lincoln were so numerous that many of those not forgotten entirely tended to become blurred as separate data and to be organized by the memory into patterns of character and behavior. The Lincoln thus recalled had such and such an attitude, or he was accustomed to doing this, or he "used to say" that. Repetition of perceptions improves general knowledge but makes episodic knowledge increasingly confusable. William H. Herndon, law partner and biographer, who may have been right in claiming to "know" Lincoln better than anyone else, was frequently vague and sometimes demonstrably inaccurate in his recall of specific episodes and remarks.

Perceptions of Lincoln extended back to his boyhood, but recorded recollection of him did not begin until the days of his presidential candidacy. At that time, when he himself wrote two autobiographical sketches and when there was the customary exploration of the candidate's past in newspaper articles and campaign biographies, the first recollective quotations began to appear in print. One of them was the remark that he supposedly made just before the debate with Douglas at Freeport: "I am after larger game. The battle of 1860 is worth a hundred of this." Like many others to come, it had more quotability than credibility.

After his election, interest in Lincoln's antecedents subsided, and attention centered on how he looked, talked, and acted in the conduct of the presidency. This was pre-eminently the period of contemporaneous quotation—that is, recorded recollection of what he had said minutes, hours, or a day or two earlier—as found, for example, in the diaries of John Hay and Gideon Welles, in memoranda of John G. Nicolay, in letters of Charles Sumner and George Bancroft, and in dispatches of Noah Brooks to the Sacramento *Union*. Such material, although not uniform in quality, obviously constitutes the high-grade ore of recollective Lincoln quotation.

Reminiscences of Lincoln were relatively scarce during his lifetime, but they flowed copiously after his death, at first as part of the stream of funereal oratory that carried him toward apotheosis. Thus the Reverend Phineas D. Gurley in obsequies at the White House on April 19 quoted the martyred President as having said to a group of clergymen: "My hope of success in this struggle rests on that immutable foundation, the justness and the goodness of God." And Speaker of the House Schuyler Colfax, in one of the early political eulogies, recalled how Lincoln had explained the trembling of his hand when he signed the Emancipation Proclamation. The first person to combine his own recollections with others that he had deliberately gathered may have been the artist Francis B. Carpenter, whose *Six Months at the White House* appeared in 1866 and set the pattern for anecdotal writing about Lincoln.

The flow of reminiscence continued for more than half a century, with surges of newspaper interest every February and the crest reached in 1909, the centennial of Lincoln's birth. Remembrance of Lincoln was common, though often marginal, in the autobiographical writings of the time, such as the memoirs of Grant, Sherman, and Sheridan. As the years passed, however, it became increasingly fashionable to publish recollections centering on Lincoln and, if possible, revealing something new about him. Often, the revelations consisted of remarks that Lincoln had made to the author or in the author's presence. There were, to be sure, some counsels of restraint. Nicolay and Hay, the secretaries who became official biographers, declared somewhat disdainfully in one of their volumes: "It is not our custom to quote Mr. Lincoln's expressions from memory." * Such abnegation was extremely rare, however. Writings about Lincoln by persons who knew him are, as a whole, rich in recollective quotation.

But how reliable is the remembrance of words past, and especially of words long past? To what extent can we trust, for example, the recollection of Leonard W. Volk in 1881 that twenty-one years earlier, Lincoln had remarked: "When I hear a man preach, I like to see him act as if he were fighting bees." Or the recollection of centenarian Cornelius Cole in 1923 (as told to an interviewer) that sixty years earlier, Lincoln had said with respect to a lost white glove: "Never mind, Mrs. Cole, I shall have a search made for it tomorrow and shall reserve it as a souvenir."

Recall of discourse is a mental process only sketchily understood, having been studied for the most part under quasi-laboratory conditions that are far removed from the actualities of long-term reminiscence. People do undoubtedly retain certain past utterances in their memory, just as they remember certain other episodes of personal experience. The accuracy of such memory is what remains in dispute, partly because it seems to vary greatly, not only from individual to individual but from circumstance to circumstance. Every recollective quotation thus constitutes a unique problem in historical method.

One thing indicated by experimental research and reinforced by common sense is that quotation marks in reminiscence should not be taken very seriously. Verbatim recall ordinarily fades quickly, except where there is deliberate memorization. To be sure, brief remarks that are colorfully phrased or emotionally charged or especially significant may be remembered long afterward with considerable precision. But recollective quotation, like other functions of memory, is ultimately a constructive process in which bits and pieces of retrieved perception are fashioned into a satisfying whole. Most of the statements attributed to Lincoln in reminiscences

---

* Nicolay and Hay, VI, 13n. For a more extensive statement on this subject, see the quotation from Hay's letter to Charles Francis Adams, Dec. 19, 1903, in Tyler Dennett, *John Hay: From Poetry to Politics* (New York: Dodd, Mead & Co., 1934), 136–37.

should probably be regarded, not as literal reproduction, but as paraphrase at best.

Memory for the substance of discourse is generally better than memory for the surface form, and it can be very durable, lasting even across an entire life span. It can also be highly accurate—or wildly inaccurate—or a puzzling combination of the two. In reminiscence, it has been said, "truth and error dwell so closely together that one seems lost without the other." * The quality of "gist recall" is apparently affected less by the mere passage of time or the physical decline associated with aging than by other factors that intervene between the original perception and the recorded recollection.

For one thing, there is *rehearsal*, which perpetuates and strengthens the memory of a particular episode while often at the same time revising it. Thus Congressman Henry Bromwell, who had a chat with the President just a few weeks before the assassination, probably recalled the occasion and talked about it privately a number of times before providing an account for a newspaper in 1879; by then, however, his recollection of Lincoln's conversation appears to have been fortified with information otherwise acquired. As the years passed and the reminiscences accumulated, it was no doubt increasingly difficult to distinguish between what one remembered hearing Lincoln say and what one remembered reading or being told that Lincoln had said. Herndon was among those who had trouble doing so. More than once in *Herndon's Lincoln*, he presented, as though he had heard it himself, a quotation that had in fact been supplied to him by an interviewee or a correspondent. When the book was in the final stages of publication, he tried unsuccessfully to have the phrase "he [Lincoln] told me" stricken from one passage, confessing that he could not remember how the piece of information had come to him.

Another factor to consider is the context of recollection, which, like the context of original perception, may substantially affect the memory process. In Lincoln's case, the central fact is that an awareness of the manner of his death suffuses all retrospection of his life. One simple example is the large number of persons claiming to have talked with him at some time or other about the danger of assassination. In general, martyrdom and apotheosis tended to conventionalize Lincoln reminiscence. Whether fully conscious of it or not, every would-be author was under enormous pressure to conform his personal remembrance of Lincoln to the public image of the Great Emancipator. Leonard Swett, for instance, struck all reference to Lincoln's swearing from one of his letters before he would allow it to be published, declaring that the public did not want to hear such things.[†]

* Merrill D. Peterson, *Lincoln in American Memory* (New York: Oxford University Press, 1994), 84.
† Swett to Herndon, Aug. 30, 1887 (10:2197–2200), Herndon-Weik Collection.

Even Herndon, whose rule it was to "suppress no truth and suggest no falsehood," eventually chose to muffle his strong suspicion that Lincoln was illegitimate. After all, he reasoned to his partner, Jesse W. Weik, they had promised to tell the whole truth about *Lincoln*, not about his *mother*. "I want the book to be a success, a complete success," he wrote, "and I am in favor of putting the book on the safe side." *

Personal attitudes and motives are also part of the context of recollection and may be of crucial importance. In reminiscences of Lincoln, admiration and affection predominated, but there was animus too, however much it might be muted by discretion. Donn Piatt's rather unflattering portrait, for instance, should be read in the light of his belief that Lincoln held a grudge against him and blocked his promotion to brigadier general. Similarly, the derogatory remarks with which Herndon seasoned his generally favorable estimate of Lincoln may have reflected a lingering strain of resentment about the way he had been treated. Surely there was some personal feeling in his assertion to Weik that when Lincoln "used a man and sucked all the uses out of him, he would throw away the *thing* as an old orange peeling." †

Recollective writing about Lincoln was at least partly a pursuit of recognition and, to a more limited extent, of financial gain. Associating oneself in print with the great man of the age could scarcely be anything but nourishing for one's self-esteem and reputation. In the process, some persons stretched limited acquaintance into intimate friendship; some exaggerated the amount of time spent in Lincoln's company; some overstated their influence upon him; and more than a few supplemented memory with outright invention, especially in the reproduction of dialogue. Egocentric bias, a common feature of reminiscence, is especially prominent in certain recollections of Lincoln that are plainly self-serving in their accounts of conversations with him. As for the profit motive, it is perhaps best exemplified in the case of Henry C. Whitney, one of Lincoln's companions on the legal circuit, who self-admittedly viewed his rather belated entry into the field of Lincoln biography as a business venture. Notorious among Whitney's achievements was a reconstruction of the famous Bloomington "lost speech" of 1856 from notes allegedly taken at the time, which he sold to a gullible editor for five hundred dollars. His offer to produce four more documents of the same kind did not attract a buyer, however.

The basic guidelines for sensible use of recollective quotations would appear to be: that all such material is in some degree questionable; that the

---

* Herndon to Lamon, Mar. 15, 1870, Lamon Papers; Herndon, I, vii; Herndon to Weik, Dec. 1, 1888 (10:2410–17), Herndon-Weik Collection.

† Herndon to Weik, Jan. 15, 1886 (9:1936–39), Herndon-Weik Collection. This repeated an expression of the same feeling five days earlier (9:1928–31), when Herndon wrote that Lincoln would use his friends "to make himself successful or happy and then throw them away as old tools."

range of variations in credibility is extensive; and that a satisfactory estimation of credibility is often difficult and sometimes impossible. In addition
to these general hazards, there are other, more specific problems associated
with the compilation, evaluation, and presentation of a collection of utterances attributed to Lincoln by his contemporaries. Some of them are essentially matters of provenance, having to do, that is, with the identification
of sources; others are essentially matters of quality, having to do with the
critical evaluation of identified sources.

For more than a century, undocumented quotations have been attaching
themselves to Lincoln and gaining currency through repetition. Many of
them are undoubtedly spurious. There appears to be no credible evidence,
for example, that he ever said: "Tact [is] the ability to describe others as
they see themselves"; or "No man has a good enough memory to make a
successful liar"; or "I am in favor of animal rights as well as human rights";
or "The best thing about the future is that it comes only one day at a time." *
In addition, there are many quotations vaguely linked to him by anonymous narrative, contemporary gossip, family tradition, and other tenuous
connections. Such is the case, for instance, with his supposed greeting of
Harriet Beecher Stowe as "the little woman who made this great war";
and his supposed remark concerning the President of Haiti's impending
appointment of a diplomatic representative to the United States: "You can
tell Mr. Geffrard that I shan't tear my shirt if he does send a Negro here." †

In this volume, an effort has been made to raise the level of reliability by
including only quotations traceable to named *auditors* (persons claiming to
have heard the quoted words directly from Lincoln), plus quotations reported contemporaneously by anonymous newspaper correspondents. Even
within that compass, however, provenance is often a puzzling matter. Take,
for example, the well-known remark about fooling the people. At the time
of the centennial celebration in 1909, William P. Kellogg and Richard P.
Morgan independently recalled having heard Lincoln utter the epigram at
Bloomington in 1856. Here, then, are two auditors identified by name, their
recollections extending back more than half a century, to be sure, but ostensibly offering a measure of mutual corroboration. The trouble is that the
quotation had already appeared eight years earlier, without attribution, in
a collection of Lincoln's "yarns and stories," after which, some vigorous
efforts to discover its source had produced nothing more substantial than

---

* The first example is taken from Herbert V. Prochnow and Herbert V. Prochnow, Jr.,
eds., *A Treasury of Humorous Quotations* (New York: Harper & Row, 1969), 323; the second,
from Evan Esar, *The Dictionary of Humorous Quotations* (New York: Bramhall House, 1949),
131; the third, from Jon Wynne-Tyson, ed., *The Extended Circle: A Dictionary of Humane
Thought* (Fontwell, Eng.: Centaur Press, 1985), 179; the fourth, from Laurence J. Peter, *Peter's
Quotations: Ideas for Our Time* (New York: William Morrow & Co., 1977), 373.

† Fields A, 268–69; *Douglass' Monthly*, 5 (Sept. 1862): 719.

a few dubious recollections.* The origins of the epigram remain a mystery, but the evidence suggests that this is a case of reminiscence echoing folklore or fiction.

Another problem is that of secondhand quotation, for example: Horace Porter's recollection in the 1890s of Ulysses S. Grant's account in 1864 of an interview with the President seven weeks earlier in which Lincoln had said that he did not want to know the General's plans because "there was always a temptation to leak." Here, with Lincoln's spoken words transmitted through two intermediaries, we have something similar to what lawyers call "totem-pole hearsay." This kind of source material is generally considered to be not very reliable, but there are exceptions. Thus the entry in Salmon P. Chase's diary for April 15, 1865, includes an account of his conversation that same morning with Attorney General James Speed, during which Speed quoted Lincoln as having said the day before that he had "perhaps been too fast in his desires for early reconstruction." Quotations recorded contemporaneously, even if they are secondhand, inspire a certain amount of confidence.

The problem of secondhandness also arises whenever an auditor speaks through an interviewer, such as a newspaper reporter or a practitioner of oral history like Herndon. Since the statements made are usually noted down on the spot, an interview of this kind seems not very different from ordinary reminiscence. But the interviewer is in truth a second intermediary and not assumably passive or neutral. One must always consider the possibility of undue influence in his conduct of the interview, as well as the possibility of error or deliberate distortion in his write-up of it.

An added complication is that distinguishing between firsthand and secondhand quotation may be virtually impossible. Sometimes a writer quotes Lincoln without indicating whether he heard the remark himself or learned about it indirectly. That is the case with Francis Carpenter, for instance, as well as with Noah Brooks and certain other Washington newspaper correspondents. Any such doubt about the identity of the auditor obviously lowers the credibility of the quotation.

Generally speaking, estimation of credibility is a complex and often inconclusive enterprise. Special problems abound, such as that of recollections said to be based on contemporaneous notes. Unfortunately, these precious source materials seem never to have survived, and the list of persons assertedly using them includes some of the Munchausens of Lincoln literature. Yet not all such claims are dubious enough to be dismissed out of hand.

* "Abe" Lincoln's Yarns and Stories . . . with Introduction and Anecdotes by Colonel Alexander K. McClure (Chicago: Education Co., 1901), 184, where Lincoln is said to have made the remark to "a caller at the White House"; Albert A. Woldman, "Lincoln Never Said That," Harper's Magazine, 200 (May 1950): 74.

Another question that often arises is: how much should factual inaccuracy count against the overall credibility of a quotation? There is plenty of evidence to support the commonsense notion that the nub of a recollection may be right, even though the details are wrong, but even so, erroneous statements of fact seem to indicate that verbal recall from the same source will be only roughly accurate at best. And what about the author who in one or more instances proves to be, not just inaccurate, but demonstrably untruthful, perhaps even to the point of inventing conversations that never took place? Should the rest of this person's testimony be set aside according to the rule, *falsus in uno, falsus in omnibus*, or is it more reasonable to judge each quotation separately on the principle that even habitual liars tell the truth some of the time?

Where there are conflicting recollections, it might seem that giving credence to those on one side means withholding credence from those on the other. Such is not necessarily the case, however; for there can be little doubt that Lincoln the consummate politician sometimes spoke differently on the same subject to different people. That insight may be a useful approach to the debate over his role in the nomination of Andrew Johnson, as well as to the everlasting controversy over his religion.

In assessing the credibility of a recollective quotation, one looks, of course, for corroboration and sometimes finds it. For instance, Gideon Welles and Frederick Seward separately recalled how Lincoln, at his last cabinet meeting, described a recurrent dream in which he was aboard a strange vessel moving toward an unknown shore. More often, however, what appears to be independent corroboration is essentially echo, well exemplified in some of Ward Hill Lamon's reminiscences. Most often of all, satisfactory verification is impossible because the narrator was the only person present to hear what Lincoln said—or at least the only person to leave any record of what he said. The best one can do in such cases is make a judgment based on the auditor's general reputation, if that is known, plus the circumstantial and substantive verisimilitude of the quotation.

The material in this book is arranged alphabetically by auditor and, as far as possible, chronologically within each auditor's file. In addition to critical comment on a limited scale, every quotation has been given a letter grade that is not so much a judgment as a primitive guide to evaluation. A, B, and C are classificatory with evaluative implications. D and E are strictly evaluative.

A: A quotation cast in direct discourse and recorded contemporaneously—that is, within a few days after the words were spoken.

B: An indirect quotation recorded contemporaneously.

C: A quotation recorded noncontemporaneously.

D: A quotation about whose authenticity there is more than average doubt.

E: A quotation that is probably not authentic.

Why, it may be asked, are the more dubious quotations not simply omitted? First, because credibility is so difficult to gauge that learned opinions would differ about which ones to exclude. Second, because this book is designed not only as a collection of quotations but also as a step toward the evaluation of a great body of source material and toward a critique of its use by historians. Questionable quotations are germane to the evaluative process. Third, because the legendary Lincoln, created in part out of dubious recollective material, may have been, in the long run, as powerful an influence in American life as the historical Lincoln.

It must be emphasized that this is a collection of quotations, not of documents precisely transcribed in every respect. Spelling, capitalization, and punctuation have been standardized in the interest of reducing distraction. Abbreviations, with obvious exceptions like "Mr." and "Dr.," are spelled out. Suppressed letters, as in "d——d" for "damned," are restored. The ultimate quest, after all, is for what Lincoln *said*, not what the auditor *wrote*. Every effort has been made to reproduce exactly Lincoln's spoken words as they were attributed to him by each auditor. This includes following the auditor's use of direct or indirect discourse, but with quotation marks omitted. All quotations are set off from the reporting clause and other editorial matter by typographical contrast.

The distinction between direct and indirect discourse is useful in the case of contemporaneously recorded quotations because the one may well be verbatim recall or something close to it, while the other may be nothing more than paraphrase or summary. But in the case of quotations recorded noncontemporaneously, the distinction is less appropriate because verbatim recall is much less likely, and the employment of direct discourse may well be misrepresentative. Sometimes, indeed, a passage enclosed in quotation marks is accompanied by the auditor's acknowledgment that Lincoln's remarks have been recaptured only "in substance."

If a composite figure of Lincoln were pieced together from the totality of recollective quotations, it would probably not differ astonishingly from the image projected in his own writings and public speeches. There would be the same homely style, the same humane outlook and underlying strength of purpose, the same cautiousness that was sometimes labeled timidity, the same political shrewdness, verbal skill, and intellectual grasp. Yet the composite would also contain some interesting features of its own, including glimpses of a man who was less close-mouthed than Herndon pictured him to be, whose thought was occasionally streaked with religiosity or superstition, who, more than any other president, allowed himself to be cast in the role of national ombudsman, who complained frequently about the burdens of his office, and who was usually patient and kind but now and then surprisingly petulant or sarcastic or overwrought. But perhaps the most revealing difference between the Lincoln of *Collected Works* and the Lincoln of *Recollected Words* is the fact that only in the latter do we find that inveterate, even compulsive storyteller who seemed always ready to regale or pacify a visitor with the one about the noisy bullfrogs, or the one about the bridge to hell, or the one about the exploding dog, or the one about the hog that was on both sides of the creek, or the one about the preacher who was too lazy to stop writing his sermon, or the one about the man who was so short that his coattails wiped out his footprints, or the one about . . .

RECOLLECTED WORDS
OF ABRAHAM LINCOLN

WILLIAM A. AIKEN *Son-in-law of Governor William A. Buckingham of Connecticut and the state's quartermaster general, 1862–65.*

  1. *On April 25, 1861, a worried Lincoln, waiting for troops, said to Aiken:*

What is the North about? Do they know our condition? —*Aiken's narrative in Croffut and Morris, 840 (1868). {C}*

CYRUS ALDRICH (1808–1871) *Congressman from Minnesota during the first half of the Civil War.*

  1. *According to the New York* Tribune *reporter Adams S. Hill, Lincoln told Aldrich that:*

he didn't know that it wouldn't be better to have the Minnesota Indians lynched than executed by the authority of the government. —*Hill to Sydney Howard Gay, November 29, 1862, Gay Papers. {D}*

This secondhand quotation may have been the garbled version of a remark that mass executions would look worse than lynching. Of the 303 men condemned to death by a military commission after suppression of the Sioux uprising, Lincoln approved the execution of 39, selecting them because they had "participated in **massacres***, as distinguished from participation in* **battles***." One of the 39 was spared and subsequently pardoned.*[1]

JOHN B. ALLEY (1817–1896) *Republican congressman from Massachusetts throughout the Civil War.*

  1. *To Alley's suggestion that he had changed his mind completely on an important matter:*

Yes, I have; and I don't think much of a man who is not wiser today than he was yesterday. —*Rice AT, 576 (1886). {C}*

  2. *According to Alley, Lincoln once told him that:*

General Scott was responsible for the appointment of General McClellan to the head of the army—entirely so. —*588. {D}*

It is not clear whether the inaccuracy of this statement should be attributed to Lincoln or to Alley's recollection of it.[2]

  3. *When Alley and Charles Sumner sought the appointment of a certain Massachusetts man to a foreign post, Lincoln refused, saying that the position must go to an admittedly less able applicant from another state. He explained that:*

he could do nothing further in the way of appointments for Massachusetts because he could not afford to and she did not need it. Massachusetts was intelligent and patriotic. Her people would do right and support his administration, even if he offended scores of her most esteemed public men. But not so with this other state [he continued]. It is a close state. I can mention half a dozen of her public men, Republicans, who have influence enough combined, if I should seriously offend them, to carry the state over to the other side. For this reason, I cannot afford to disregard the wishes of these men. —578-79. {C}

4. *Alley recalled Lincoln's once telling him that:*

he had the greatest confidence in the judgment of our Massachusetts senator [Sumner] in everything pertaining to foreign relations. —579. {C}

5. *On some unspecified occasion, Lincoln remarked to Alley that:*

he felt assured the author of our being, whether called God or Nature (it mattered little which), would deal very mercifully with poor erring humanity in the other and, he hoped, better world. —591. {C}

6. *December 6, 1864, having just nominated Salmon P. Chase to be chief justice:*

Although I may have appeared to you and to Mr. Sumner to have been opposed to Chase's appointment, there never has been a moment since the breath left old Taney's body that I did not conceive it to be the best thing to do to appoint Mr. Chase to that high office; and to have done otherwise I should have been recreant to my convictions of duty to the Republican party and to the country. . . . As to his talk about me, I do not mind that. Chase is, on the whole, a pretty good fellow and a very able man. His only trouble is that he has "the White House fever" a little too bad, but I hope this may cure him and that he will be satisfied. —581-82. {C}

7. *In response to a petition for pardon of a man sent to prison for engaging in the slave trade:*

I believe I am kindly enough in nature and can be moved to pity and to pardon the perpetrator of almost the worst crime that the mind of man can conceive or the arm of man can execute; but any man, who, for paltry gain and stimulated only by avarice, can rob Africa of her children to sell into interminable bondage, I never will pardon, and he may stay and rot in jail before he will ever get relief from me. —583. {D}

Lincoln, in fact, did pardon more than one person involved in the slave trade.[3]

8. *To a man weeping because Lincoln had merely suspended his son's execution, rather than issuing a pardon:*

My dear man, if your son lives until I order him shot, he will live longer than ever Methuselah did. —585. {C}

EDWARD W. ANDREWS (1825–?)   *Lawyer and former Congregational minister, who entered the Union army as a captain of volunteers and later transferred to the Adjutant General's staff. Lincoln's words, as Andrews recalled them, do not always ring true.*

1. *November 18, 1863, on the train to Gettysburg, responding to a man who said that his only son had been killed in the battle there:*

You have been called upon to make a terrible sacrifice for the Union, and a visit to that spot, I fear, will open your wounds afresh. But oh! my dear sir, if we had reached the end of such sacrifices, and had nothing left for us to do but to place garlands on the graves of those who have already fallen, we could give thanks even amidst our tears; but when I think of the sacrifices of life yet to be offered and the hearts and homes yet to be made desolate before this dreadful war, so wickedly forced upon us, is over, my heart is like lead within me, and I feel, at times, like hiding in deep darkness. — *Rice AT, 511 (1886). {D}*

2. *At a stopping-place on the way to Gettysburg, after receiving a bouquet of rosebuds from a small child:*

You're a sweet little rosebud yourself. I hope your life will open into perpetual beauty and goodness. — *511 {C}*

3. *On the morning of the Gettysburg ceremonies, according to Andrews, he received this reply when he told Lincoln that New York's Governor Horatio Seymour had been serenaded the night before:*

I am glad Governor Seymour was specially honored. He deserves it. No man has shown greater interest and promptness in his cooperation with us. The New York soldiers may well admire and honor him. — *514. {D}*

It seems unlikely that Lincoln would have lavished such inaccurate praise (except, perhaps, in irony) on the man who had been a thorn in his flesh throughout the year.

RUFUS ANDREWS   *Surveyor of the port of New York during the Lincoln administration.*

1. *At a White House reception, Lincoln halted the procession to engage in a whispered conversation with Andrews. Later the same day, Andrews revealed to Chauncey M. Depew that the President had said:*

That capital story of yours has slipped my mind; give the point of it to me now. — *Depew in* Leslie's Illustrated Weekly, *February 4, 1909, p. 102. {D}*

A secondhand recollection.

ANONYMOUS NEWSPAPER REPORTERS AND CORRESPONDENTS   *The credibility of the following quotations is enhanced by their being contemporaneously recorded—that is, written down within minutes, hours, or a few days after the words were spoken. On the other hand, it is often not clear whether the reporter heard the words directly from Lincoln or from an intermediary.*

1. In the national House of Representatives on February 2, 1858, a quarrel between Galusha A. Grow of Pennsylvania and Laurence M. Keitt of South Carolina erupted into a general melee that reached its absurd climax when one southern member suffered separation from his wig. Several weeks later in Springfield, a group of congenial spirits gathered in the governor's room at the state house were talking about the affair, and Lincoln, under some prodding, remarked:

It reminds me of a case I once had up at Bloomington. Two old farmers living in the vicinity of Bloomington had, from time immemorial, been at loggerheads. They could never agree, except to disagree; wouldn't build division fences; and, in short, were everlastingly quarreling. One day, one of them got over on the land of the other; the parties met, and a regular pitched battle between them was the consequence. The one who came out second best sued the other for assault and battery, and I was sent for to come up and defend the suit.

Among the witnesses for the plaintiff was a remarkably talkative old fellow who was disposed to magnify the importance of the affair to my client's disadvantage. It came my turn to question him:

"Witness," said I, "you say you saw this fight?"

"Yes, stranger; I reckon I did."

"Was it much of a fight?" said I.

"I'll be darned if it wasn't, stranger; a right smart fight."

"How much ground did the combatants cover?"

"About an acre, stranger."

"About an acre," I repeated musingly. "Well, now, witness, just tell me, wasn't that just about the smallest crop of a fight off of an acre of ground that ever you heard of?"

"That's so, stranger; I'll be gol darned if it wasn't!"

The jury fined my client just ten cents. —*Peoria* Transcript, *reprinted in* Illinois State Journal *(Springfield), February 26, 1858.* {D}

It is not clear that the Peoria reporter heard Lincoln tell the story. Dickson, 63, and Conant, 516, claimed that Lincoln told them the same story in 1855 and 1860 respectively.

2. About a month after Lincoln's nomination for the presidency in 1860, a reporter asked him whether he was bored by all the visitors and correspondence coming his way. He replied that:

he liked to see his friends, and as to the letters, he took good care not to answer them.

Asked whether he was continuing his professional practice since his nomination, he answered that: he had attempted it, but pitied his clients. He had been arguing a case the day before, but the demands of his position made him an indifferent lawyer. —*Letter of June 21, 1860, from a correspondent of the* Utica (N.Y.) Herald, *reprinted in the Sacramento* Union, *August 15, 1860.*[4] {B}

3. *During the same interview, Lincoln spoke of corruption in American politics and said that:*

he could not respect, either as a man or a politician, one who bribed or was bribed. He was glad to know the people of Illinois had not yet learned the art of being venal. The whole expense of his campaign with Douglas did not exceed a few hundred dollars. —*Ibid.* {B}

4. *After acknowledging Douglas's hardihood, pertinacity, and magnetic power, Lincoln remarks to the same visitor that:*

of all men he has ever seen, he has the most audacity in maintaining an untenable position. Thus, in endeavoring to reconcile popular sovereignty and the Dred Scott decision, his argument, stripped of sophistry, is: "It is legal to expel slavery from a territory where it legally exists." And yet he has bamboozled thousands into believing him. —*Ibid.* {B, A}

5. *The same interviewer asked if he read any of the Democratic papers, and Lincoln replied that:*

some of his friends were kind enough to let him see the most abusive of them. He should judge the line of tactics which they intended to pursue was that of personal ridicule. The Chicago *Times* tried that in '58 and helped him amazingly. He was inclined to believe that the present effort of his enemies would be attended with like happy results. —*Ibid.* {B}

6. *Asked why no artist had managed to do him justice, Lincoln replied with a smile:*

It is impossible to get my graceful motions in—that's the reason why none of the pictures are like me. —*Correspondence of the Philadelphia* North American, *reprinted in the New York* Times, *August 23, 1860.* {A}

7. *On not responding to southern denunciation of his election:*

I know the justness of my intentions and the utter groundlessness of the pretended fears of the men who are filling the country with their clamor. If I go into the presidency, they will find me as I am on record—nothing less, nothing more. My declarations have been made to the world without reservation. They have been often repeated; and now, self-respect demands of me and of the party that has elected me that when threatened, I should be silent. —*Dispatch of November 14 in the New York* Post, *November 19, 1860.* {A}

8. *Concerning the rush for office:*

I have made up my mind not to be badgered about those places. I have promised nothing, high nor low, and will not. By and by, when I call somebody to me in character of an adviser, we will examine the claims to the most responsible posts and decide what shall be done. As for the rest, I shall have enough to do without reading recommendations for country postmasterships. These, and all others of the sort, I will turn over to the heads of departments and make them responsible for the good conduct of their subordinates. —*Ibid.* {A}

9. *With South Carolina on the verge of secession, he nevertheless declared:*

I think, from all I can learn, that things have reached their worst point in the South, and they are likely to mend in the future. If it be true, as reported, that the South Carolinians do not intend to resist the collection of the revenue, after they ordain secession, there need be no collision with the federal government. The Union may still be maintained. The greatest inconvenience will arise from the want of federal courts; as with the present feeling, judges, marshals, and other officers could not be obtained.

Of southern charges against the North, he said: If they were well defined, they could be fairly and successfully met. But they are so vague that they cannot be long maintained by reasoning men even in the southern states.

And of certain Republican newspapers that were calling secession good riddance: This tone was having a bad effect in some of the border states, especially in Missouri, where there was danger that it might alienate some of the best friends of the cause, if it were persisted in. In Missouri and some other states, where Republicanism has just begun to grow, and where there is still a strong proslavery party to contend with, there can be no advantage in taunting and bantering the South. Leading Republicans from those states had urged him to use his influence with the journals referred to, and induce them to alter their present tone towards the South. —*Correspondence of the Philadelphia* Bulletin, *December 14, reprinted in the New York* Times, *December 20, 1860.* {A, B}

10. *On traveling to Washington:*

I don't want to go before the middle of February, because I expect they will drive me insane after I get there, and I want to keep tolerably sane, at least until after the inauguration. —*Ibid.* {A}

11. *During a conversation with visitors one day in January 1861, Lincoln was asked whether he thought the Missouri Compromise line ought to be restored. He replied that:*

although the recent presidential election was a verdict of the people in favor of freedom upon all the territories, yet, personally, he would be willing for the sake of the Union to divide the territory we now own by that line, if in the judgment of the nation it would save the Union and restore harmony. But whether the acquisition of territory hereafter would not reopen the question and renew the strife, was a question to be thought of and in some way provided against. — *Correspondence of the* Missouri Democrat *(St. Louis), reprinted in the New York* Times, *January 14, 1861. {B}*

Such talk seems incompatible with the letters Lincoln sent to a number of Republican leaders in December expressing emphatic opposition to any compromise that would allow the extension of slavery. But there is other evidence of some softening in his attitude. Writing to William H. Seward on February 1, he reiterated his inflexibility on the territorial question, but then added that he did not care much about New Mexico if further extension were hedged against.[5]

12. *Lincoln then went on to review his answers to certain other questions that had been put to him:*

He had been inquired of whether he intended to recommend the repeal of the anti-fugitive-slave laws of the states. He replied that he had never read one of them, but that if they were of the character ascribed to them by southern men, they certainly ought to be repealed. Whether as president of the United States he ought to interfere with state legislation by presidential recommendation, required more thought than he had yet given the subject. He had also been asked if he intended to interfere or recommend an interference with slavery or the right of holding slaves in the dockyards and arsenals of the United States. His reply was, "Indeed, sir, the subject has not entered my mind." He was inquired of whether he intended to recommend the abolition of slavery in the District of Columbia. To which he replied, "Upon my word I have not given the subject a thought."

At this point, one of his listeners asked what he would do if these problems were not resolved before his inauguration. He replied: Well, I suppose I will have to run the machine as I find it. — *Ibid. {B, A}*

13. *On the subject of compromise, Lincoln said to the same group of men that:*

it was sometimes better for a man to pay a debt he did not owe, or to lose a demand which was a just one, than to go to law about it; but then, in compromising our difficulties, he would regret to see the victors put in the attitude of the vanquished, and the vanquished in the place of the victors. He would not contribute to any such compromise as that. — *Ibid. {B}*

14. *At a reception in New York City on February 20, 1861, one man spoke of Lincoln's winning re-election in 1864. He replied:*

I think when the clouds look as dark as they do now, one term might satisfy any man. — *New York* Herald, *February 21, 1861. {A}*

15. *On February 25, 1861, Lincoln told a delegation advocating compromise:*

that he was not their man; that he was distinctly elected on the principles of the Chicago platform, which he believed to be perfectly in harmony with the principles of the Constitution, and he intended to live up in good faith to the pledge he had given the people before the election; and he did not think the Union was to be saved in the way they suggested, but rather by supporting the Constitution and executing the laws. At all events, his duty lay in that direction.

Lincoln went on to hint that the Washington peace conference should adjourn, and he reiterated that: the Union could not be saved by nationalizing and extending slavery, as they proposed to do. — *Correspondence of February 26,* Chicago Tribune, *March 1, 1861. {B}*

16. *On April 26, 1861, Lincoln said to a company of Kansans who had been guarding the capital:*

The last hope of peace may not have passed away, but if I have to choose between the maintenance of the union of these states, of the authority of the government, and of the liberties of this nation, on the one hand, and the shedding of fraternal blood on the other, you need not be at a loss which course I shall take. — *Dispatch of April 28 in the Chicago* Tribune, *April 30, 1861. {A}*

A variant version, published by the New York Tribune *on May 1, is in* Collected Works, *IV, 345.*

17. *Concerning attacks on the administration, Lincoln said:*

We can afford to pass them by with the dying words of the Massachusetts statesman, "We still live." I am sure they don't worry me any, and I reckon they don't benefit the parties who write them. — *Correspondence of May 1 in the Chicago* Tribune, *May 4, 1861. {A}*

18. *During a review of New Jersey volunteers on May 7, 1861, Lincoln said in response to talk about dissolution of the Union:*

Gentlemen, the Union shan't be dissolved. — *Correspondence of May 7,* Chicago Tribune, *May 11, 1861. {A}*

19. *In the presence of a reporter and a senator on May 25, 1861, Lincoln burst into tears, grieving over the death of Elmer Ellsworth. After composing himself, he said:*

I will make no apology, gentlemen, for my weakness; but I knew poor Ellsworth well and held him in great regard. Just as you entered the room, Captain Fox left me, after giving me the painful details of Ellsworth's unfortunate death. The event was so unexpected, and the recital so touching, that it quite unmanned me. . . . Poor fellow, it was undoubtedly an act of rashness, but it only shows the heroic spirit that animates our soldiers, from high to low, in this righteous cause of ours. Yet who can restrain their grief to see them fall in such a way as this, not by the fortunes of war, but by the hand of an assassin? . . . There is one fact that has reached me, which is a great consolation to my heart and quite a relief after this melancholy affair. I learn from several persons, that when the Stars and Stripes were raised again in Alexandria, many of the people of the town actually wept for joy and manifested the liveliest gratification at seeing this familiar and loved emblem once more floating above them. This is another proof that all the South is not secessionist; and it is my earnest hope that as we advance we shall find as many friends as foes. — *New York* Herald, *May 25, 1861.* {A}

20. *Told in September 1861 that the Confederate army under Beauregard would soon be in Washington, Lincoln reportedly said:*

I wish they **would** come; it is so much easier to entertain our friends than to visit them. — *Washington* National Republican, *September 21, 1861.* {D}

21. *To delegates of several freedmen's associations who were concerned about the status of former slaves at Port Royal, South Carolina, Lincoln said:*

The slave of every rebel master who seeks protection of the flag shall have it and be free.

Two days later, the same correspondent, who may not have been present at the interview, reported that Lincoln's "precise words" had been: I am entirely satisfied that no slave who becomes for a time free within the American lines will ever be re-enslaved. Rather than have it so, I'd give up and abdicate. — *Dispatches of April 12 and 14 in the Chicago* Tribune, *April 14, 15, 1862.* {D}

22. *On July 21, 1862, according to a Washington correspondent, Lincoln declared:*

We are done throwing grass at the rebels.

He added that: henceforth he proposed trying stones. — *Chicago* Tribune, *July 22, 1862.* {D}

It is not clear that the reporter heard this remark directly from Lincoln.

23. *Concerning a wounded soldier who wanted to go home and raise a company but was prevented from doing so by military red tape, Lincoln said:*

The Corporal's case is a hard one and reminds me of a story told by Judge B. of Illinois, of the officers of some county town in Ireland who met and resolved: first, to build a new jail; second, to build it out of the old one; and third, to keep the prisoners in the old jail till the new one was built. — *Dispatch of August 11 in the New York* Herald, *August 12, 1862.* {D}

It is not clear that the reporter himself heard Lincoln make this remark.

24. *To an unidentified group of persons, Lincoln said in August 1862:*

McClellan must be a good military man. Everybody says he is. These military men all say so themselves, and it isn't possible that they all can be so completely deceived as some of you insist. He is well versed in military matters and has had opportunities of experience and observation. Still, there must be something wrong somewhere, and I'll tell you what it is. He never embraces his opportunities. That's where the trouble is. He always puts off the hour for embracing his opportunities. — *Cincinnati* Gazette, *August 11, 1862. {C}*

According to the correspondent, these thoughts were expressed "not a week ago."

25. *Concerning Eli Thayer's proposal that Florida be colonized with free laborers, Lincoln said to a delegation of German-Americans in January 1863:*

that Mr. Thayer's plan for Florida colonization had received the earnest and cordial attention of himself and cabinet, and that while recent military events had forced the postponement of this enterprise for the time by demanding the entire attention and power of the government elsewhere, yet he trusted the delay was but for a few days. — *Washington* Chronicle, *January 6, 1863. {B}*

26. *One evening in April 1863, according to an eyewitness account in the* Boston Gazette, *the Lincolns held a "spiritual soiree" to test the powers of a medium named Charles E. Shockle. Secretaries Stanton and Welles were among those in attendance, and the correspondent reported in all solemnity that one of them had his ears pinched and the other his beard twitched by the mischievous spirits present, who also moved tables about and raised two candelabras almost to the ceiling. When the séance began, there were some loud rappings and Shockle announced that an Indian wanted to communicate. The President said:*

I should be happy to hear what his Indian Majesty has to say. We have recently had a visitation from our red brethren, and it was the only delegation, black, white, or blue, which did not volunteer some advice about the conduct of the war.

Instead, however, a message came through from Henry Knox, the nation's first secretary of war, with some terse advice beginning: "Haste makes waste, but delays cause vexations." Lincoln said: I should like to ask General Knox if it is within the scope of his ability to tell us when this rebellion will be put down.

Knox responded that a discussion of that very question with Washington, Franklin, Napoleon, and others had produced various answers, which he summarized. Lincoln commented: Well, opinions differ among the saints as well as among the sinners. They don't seem to understand running the machines among the celestials much better than we do. Their talk and advice sound very much like the talk of my cabinet.

When Lincoln expressed concern about the Alabama, *the lights immediately dimmed and in the mirror over the mantelpiece there appeared a beautiful picture of the notorious Confederate raider with two burning merchantmen in the background. Then the picture changed and the vessel was shown riding at anchor in British custody. Said Lincoln:* So, England is to seize the *Alabama* finally? It may be possible, but, Welles, don't let one gunboat or monitor less be built. . . . Well, Shockle, I have seen strange things and heard rather odd remarks, but nothing which convinces me, except the pictures, that there is anything very heavenly about all this. I should like, if possible, to hear what Judge Douglas says about this war.

The arrangements with the spirit world having been made, Shockle rose and, in a voice recognizably that of Stephen A. Douglas, delivered an eloquent speech predicting some military successes and asserting that if victory were followed up by energetic action, all would be well. Lincoln remarked: I believe that, whether it comes from spirit or human. *With Shockle now utterly exhausted, the séance ended.* —Boston Gazette *correspondence of April 23, 1863, reprinted in Sacramento* Union, *June 19, 1863.* {E}

It is difficult to regard this piece as anything but a journalistic prank. More than one biographer has taken it more than half seriously, however, and there is a certain amount of soft evidence that Lincoln attended some séances, probably at the urging of his wife.[6]

27. *In May 1863, after Grant's brilliant campaign prior to the siege of Vicksburg, Lincoln said:*

I have had stronger influence brought against Grant, praying for his removal, since the battle of Pittsburg Landing, than for any other object, coming too from good men; and now look at his campaign since May 1. Where is anything in the Old World that equals it? It stamps him as the greatest general of the age, if not of the world. —May 25 *correspondence of the Philadelphia* Enquirer, *reprinted in the Chicago* Tribune, *May 29, 1863.*[7] {A}

28. *Concerning certain officers of black regiments who were prisoners of war, Lincoln said that:*

he would do all in his power to effect the release of these officers, and all others now prisoners, but he was not prepared, nor would he consent to make the release of officers of colored regiments an indispensable condition to a renewal of exchanges. The government was prepared to exchange man for man with the rebels, even should they refuse to release the officers of colored regiments. This would be done because the government considered it unfair to make the case of a few officers a test question, when a much larger number would be benefited by a resumption of exchanges, and the question of exchanging these officers left open for future consideration. He wished sincerely that they could be released speedily, but Jefferson Davis was a party to be consulted, and they could not be exchanged unless by some agreement with the rebel authorities. The question arising in regard to these officers was not covered by the cartel, and the officers of these regiments knew when they entered the service the peculiar risks incidental to their position and for the present must endure the disagreeable consequences.

The President added, however, that: any unusual or barbarous treatment of such officers, or of colored soldiers, would cause retaliation. — *Washington dispatch of September 8, New York* Times, *September 9, 1863. {B}*

According to a correspondent in the Chicago Tribune *of September 16, Lincoln declared that:* while exchanges would progress, a sufficient number of prisoners would be held back as hostages for colored soldiers in the hands of the rebels.

29. *The President said repeatedly to persons congratulating him on recent Republican victories in certain state elections:*

The people are for this war. They want the rebellion crushed and as quick as may be, too. — *Washington correspondence of November 4 in the New York* Post, *November 5, 1863. {A}*

30. *In November 1863, a committee of striking shipyard workers called at the White House and presented their case to Lincoln. He told them that:*

he could do nothing as president, but as Abraham Lincoln his sympathies were with us, and further, having been raised in a rural district, he had never participated in a strike. The only one he had ever beheld was a strike among the shoemakers of Haverhill, Massachusetts, some twelve or fifteen years ago, in which the shoemakers succeeded in worsting their bosses. As to the present strike, he considered the employers the first strikers, as they refused to accept the terms offered by the men and thereby compelled the latter to cease work or, as they term it, go on strike; and now that both were on a strike, the best blood would win. — *Correspondence of* Fincher's Trade Review *(Philadelphia), November 28, in New York* Times, *December 5, 1863. {D}*

The writer's emphatic pro-labor bias raises doubt about the accuracy of his report. There is, however, some evidence of Lincoln's bringing pressure for concessions to the workers.[8]

31. *While suffering from smallpox in the mild form of varioloid, Lincoln rejoices:*

that since he has been president, he has always had a crowd of people asking him to give them something, but that now he has something he can give them all. —*Correspondence of December 14, Chicago* Tribune, *December 15, 1863.* {B}

Although the reporter may not have heard Lincoln make this remark, it appears to have been made a number of times, and the joke quickly circulated. George Templeton Strong noted it in his diary on December 19, William Pitt Fessenden mentioned it in a letter written the same day, and the New York Post *put it in classic form on the following February 17: "I've got something now that I can give to everybody."* [9] *It was also reported that Lincoln had said to his physician: "There is one consolation about the matter, doctor. It cannot in the least disfigure me."* [10]

32. *On January 11, 1864, Lincoln explained to a reporter why he was counting greenbacks:*

This, sir, is something out of my usual line, but a president of the United States has a multiplicity of duties not specified in the Constitution or acts of Congress. This is one of them. This money belongs to a poor Negro who is a porter in one of the departments (the Treasury) and who is at present very bad with the smallpox. He did not catch it from me, however; at least I think not. He is now in hospital and could not draw his pay because he could not sign his name. I have been at considerable trouble to overcome the difficulty and get it for him and have at length succeeded in cutting red tape, as you newspaper men say. I am now dividing the money and putting by a portion labeled, in an envelope, with my own hands, according to his wish. —*Correspondence of January 14, Chicago* Tribune, *January 19, 1864.* {A}

33. *A Washington correspondent attributed this story to Lincoln early in 1864:*

My opinion as to who will be next president is very much the opinion that Pat had about the handsome funeral. You see, Pat was standing opposite the state house in Springfield, with a short, black pipe in his mouth and his hands deeply buried in his empty breeches pockets.

"Pat, who's funeral is that passing?" inquired Old Jake Miller, who seemed impressed with a belief that an Irishman must know everything.

"Plaize, yer honor," replied Pat, removing his pipe for a moment, "it isn't meself can say for sartin, but to the best o' my belief, the funeral belongs to the gentleman or lady that's in the coffin!"

Now, it's very much the same about the next presidency. I can't say for certain who will be the people's choice; but to the best of my belief it will be the successful candidate. —*New York* Herald, *February 21, 1864.* {D}

Lincoln may have told, but he did not originate, this venerable joke. It dates back at least to the fifteenth century.[11]

34. *On March 3, 1864, a delegation representing a thousand people of color of New Orleans submitted a petition for the right to vote.*[12] *According to the* New York Post *of the next day, Lincoln said to them that:*

an impression had gone abroad that he was acting irresponsibly in the elections in the rebel states; but it was wrong. He must finish the big job on his hands of crushing the rebellion, and in doing that, if it became necessary to prevent rebels from voting, he should do so. If the recognition of black men as having a right to vote was necessary to close the war, he would not hesitate. He saw no reason why intelligent black men should not vote, but this was not a military question, and he would refer it to the constitutional convention in Louisiana.

Similar in substance, though not in phrasing, was the New York Times *report on March 5. Lincoln, it said, took the ground:* that having the restoration of the Union paramount to all other questions, he would do nothing that would hinder that consummation or omit anything that would accomplish it; that therefore he did nothing in matters of this kind upon moral grounds, but solely upon political necessities. Their petition asking to become citizens and voters being placed solely on moral grounds did not furnish him with any inducement to accede to their wishes, but that he would do so whenever they could show that such accession would be necessary to the readmission of Louisiana as a state in the Union.[13] {B}

35. *On November 26, 1864, Lincoln was presented a buckhorn chair made by a western frontiersman named Seth Kinman. Invited by the spokesman, after his presentation speech, to "take the chair," the President said that:*

he was glad the speech concluded as it did, for while it deserved a response, the request that he should take the chair implied that a response was not expected of him.

Sitting down, he added that: it was the handsomest thing of the kind he had ever seen.

Inspecting Kinman's long-barreled flintlock, he remarked that: he had first learned to shoot with the long rifle. — *Washington* Chronicle, *November 27, 1864.* {B}

36. *To the Maryland presidential electors, who visited him in early December, Lincoln spoke of the recently approved state constitution, which abolished slavery:*

He felt convinced that even those who had opposed the adoption of the new constitution would live to approve of it and find themselves benefited by the change. —*Baltimore* American and Commercial Advertiser, *December 9, 1864.* {B}

37. *During the same interview, Lincoln responded to commendation of his nomination of Salmon P. Chase to be chief justice:*

He trusted that his appointment of chief justice was for the best. The country needed assurances in regard to two great questions, and they were assurances that could better be given by the character and well-known opinions of the appointee than by any verbal pledges. In the appointment of Mr. Chase, all holders of government securities in America and Europe felt assured that the financial policy of the government would be sustained by its highest judicial tribunal. In sustaining that policy Judge Chase would only be sustaining himself, for he was the author of it. His appointment also met the public desire and expectation as regarded the emancipation policy of the government. His views were well known upon both of these great questions, and while there were other distinguished gentlemen whose names had been suggested for this great trust whose views he believed were sound upon these important issues, yet they did not hold the same relations to them as did Mr. Chase. —*Ibid.* {B}

38. *On January 26, 1865, Lincoln responded to the plea of a committee of women employed in the Philadelphia arsenal by saying in their presence to Colonel Charles Thomas, the acting quartermaster general, that:*

if he could so administer his department as to secure employment for the women at the wages ordinarily paid, he would regard it as a personal favor, provided he could do so without interfering with the public interests or disturbing private contracts. — *Washington* Chronicle, *January 27, 1865.* {B}

39. *A southerner sought presidential endorsement of his claim for war damages, declaring that he was loyal to the Union. Lincoln responded:*

Yes, sir, and so are the men who stand up in front of Richmond to be shot, but they don't come here to plague me. . . . I know what you want—you are turning or trying to turn me into a justice of the peace to put your claims through. There are a hundred thousand men in the country, every one of them as good as you are, who have just such bills as you present, and you care nothing of what becomes of them so you get your money. . . . you know you can't prove what is in this paper by all the people of the United States, and you want me to prove it for you by writing my name on the back of it; yes, in plain words, you wish me to lie for you that you may get your money. I shall not do it. —*Washington correspondence of* The Methodist *(New York, N.Y.), reprinted in the St. Paul (Minn.) Press, April 6, 1865.* {C}

The writer did not specify the date on which he heard this exchange.

40. *On March 21, 1865, a friendly journalist, who described the President*

as in good spirits and looking "extremely well," heard him deal with a number of visitors. The first was an elderly man who had come to the capital in search of employment. Lincoln advised him to return home on the next train, declaring that:

Washington was the worst place in the country for anyone to seek to better their condition. He wished some species of saffron tea could be administered to produce an eruption of those already in Washington and make this migration fever strike out instead of striking in. —*Baltimore* American and Commercial Advertiser, *March 23, 1865. {B}*

41. *To a man concerned about Grant's prohibition of trade in cotton, Lincoln said that:*

in no case would he interfere with the wishes of General Grant. He held him responsible for inflicting the hardest blows possible on the enemy, and as desirable as it was to possess the cotton, if he thought that bacon was of more importance to the enemy at this moment than cotton was to us, why we must do without the cotton.[14] —*Ibid. {B}*

42. *To a Democratic congressman who had ventured to seek a minor appointment for one of his constituents, Lincoln remarked:*

That reminds me of my own experience as an old Whig member of Congress. I was always in the opposition, and I had no troubles of this kind at all. It was the easiest thing imaginable to be an opposition member—no running to the departments and the White House. —*Ibid. {A}*

43. *Next, Lincoln was asked to pardon a drayman sent to prison for stealing some pantaloons and shoes belonging to the government. The petitioner pointed out that one witness had testified to having sold the man a pair of shoes. Lincoln replied:*

Yes, so much for the shoes, but nothing about the pantaloons. The jury had the whole facts before them and convicted the man, and I am bound to regard him as guilty. I am sorry for his wife and children, sir, but the man must be punished. —*Ibid. {A}*

44. *The President responded encouragingly to the request of a young war widow that she be appointed postmistress of a small New York town, but he added that:*

he could not act on it at once; for, although he was president, she must remember that he was but one horse in the team, and if the others pulled in a different direction, it would be a hard matter for him to out-pull them. —*Ibid. {B}*

45. *To a wounded officer seeking a federal appointment in his home state, Lincoln replied:*

that he was disposed to favor the application, but that he must wait to hear from the member of Congress from that district. He would be forever in hot water if he did not pay some deference to the wishes of members on these appointments. —*Ibid.* {B}

46. *A petitioner for the release of a minor from military service named an officer who, he said, had endorsed the request as worthy of executive attention. Lincoln replied:*

Bring me his opinion to that effect in writing, and I will promptly discharge him. His word will be sufficient for me; I will require no argument on the subject. —*Ibid.* {A}

47. *Refusing to help a man avoid conscription, the President said:*

I don't know why it is that I am troubled with these cases, but if I were, by interfering, to make a hole through which a kitten might pass, it would soon be large enough for the old cat to get through also. —*Ibid.* {A}

HANNAH ARMSTRONG   *Friend from Lincoln's New Salem days, widow of Jack Armstrong.*

1. *In 1858, when asked about his fee for defending her son on a murder charge:*

Why, Hannah, I shan't charge you a cent, never. Anything I can do for you I will do for you willingly and freely without charges. —*Statement written down by Herndon in 1865 (11:2963-67), Herndon-Weik Collection.* {C}

2. *After the verdict of not guilty, Lincoln said:*

I pray to God that William may be a good boy hereafter, that this lesson may prove in the end a good lesson to him and to all. —*Ibid.* {C}

3. *February 1861, jokingly replying to her expression of fear for his safety:*

Hannah, if they kill me, I shall never die another death. —*Ibid.* {C}

JOHN ARMSTRONG (1814-?)   *A Springfield carpenter who was apparently active in local politics.*

1. *Armstrong corroborates the claim of William H. Herndon that he alone approved of the House-Divided speech when Lincoln gave it a preview reading before a group of political friends in June 1858. According to Armstrong, Lincoln said:*

I have thought about this matter a great deal, have weighed the question well from all corners and am thoroughly convinced the time has come when it should be uttered; and if it must be that I must go down because of this speech, then let me go down linked to truth—die in the advocacy of what is right and just. This nation cannot live on injustice. —*Armstrong's statement, enclosed with Herndon to Ward H. Lamon, February 19, 1870, Lamon Papers.* {D}

It is not clear that Armstrong was present at the reading of the speech, and, in any case, this pretentious talk is inconsistent with Lincoln's pragmatic approach to a campaign that he was determined to win. A substantial part of the quotation appeared in Herndon, II, 400, without attribution to Armstrong.[15]

2. *Armstrong recalled that after the House-Divided speech had been delivered, one critic told Lincoln that it would kill him politically. He replied:*

If I had to draw a pen across and erase my whole life from existence and all I did; and I had one poor gift or choice left, as to what I should save from the wreck, I should choose that speech and leave it to the world unerased. —*Ibid.* {D}

This passage, too, was quoted without attribution to Armstrong in Herndon, II, 401.

ISAAC N. ARNOLD (1815–1884)   *Republican congressman from Chicago during the Civil War and one of Lincoln's early biographers.*

1. *Of his covert trip through Baltimore as president-elect in February 1861, Lincoln much later told Arnold:*

I did not then, nor do I now, believe I should have been assassinated had I gone through Baltimore as first contemplated; but I thought it wise to run no risk where no risk was necessary. —*Arnold-1, 171 (1866).* {C}

2. *To Arnold and Owen Lovejoy on July 13, 1862, concerning his recent interview with border-state congressmen on the subject of gradual emancipation:*

Oh, if the border states would accept my proposition! Then you, Lovejoy and Arnold, and all of us, would not have lived in vain. The labor of your life, Lovejoy, would be crowned with success—you would live to see the end of slavery. —*Arnold-1, 287–88.* {C}

3. *On the first day of September in 1862, according to New York* Tribune *correspondent Adams S. Hill, Lincoln told Arnold that:*

the meaning of his letter to Mr. Greeley was this: that he was ready to declare emancipation when he was convinced that it could be made effective and that the people were with him.[16] —*Hill to Sydney Howard Gay, September 1, 1862, Gay Papers.* {D}

A secondhand quotation.

4. *On the bitter morning after the battle of Fredericksburg, Arnold found the President reading Artemas Ward and reproached him for it. Lincoln replied:*

Mr. Arnold, if I could not get momentary respite from the crushing burden I am constantly carrying I should die. —*Narrated by Arnold the same day to Congressman William A. Wheeler, and retold by him in the New York* Times, *May 10, 1885.* {D}

James M. Ashley and William H. Herndon (qq.v.) recalled Lincoln's making a similar remark.

5. *"With a pathos which language cannot describe," Arnold recalled, Lincoln said one day:*

I feel as though I shall never be glad any more. — *Arnold-3, 454 (1885). {C}*

Cordelia A. P. Harvey (q.v.) recalled a similar remark.

6. *Visiting the White House on January 1, 1864, Arnold expressed the hope and expectation that one year thereafter he would be able to congratulate Lincoln on three achievements: suppression of the rebellion, passage of the amendment abolishing slavery, and re-election to the presidency. Lincoln replied with a smile:*

I think I would be glad to accept the first two as a compromise. — *Arnold-2, 187 (1881). {C}*

JAMES M. ASHLEY (1824–1896) *Radical Republican congressman from the Toledo district of Ohio.*

1. *Ashley, wanting to talk about McClellan, expressed impatience when the President became anecdotal. Lincoln said:*

Ashley, I have great confidence in you and great respect for you, and I know how sincere you are. But if I couldn't tell these stories, I would die. Now you sit down. — *Ashley-1, 39 (1890). {C}*

Isaac N. Arnold and William H. Herndon (qq.v.) recalled Lincoln's making a similar remark.

2. *In July 1864, Ashley protested the authorization of Horace Greeley to negotiate with Confederate peace commissioners at Niagara Falls. Lincoln explained his reasons and then added:*

Don't you worry; nothing will come of it. — *Ashley-2, 13 (1891). {C}*

3. *After pardoning a condemned soldier in response to the appeal of his mother and other women of his household, Lincoln remarked:*

Well, I have made one family happy, but I don't know about the discipline of the army. — *Ashley-1, 39. {C}*

4. *As Ashley rose to go after a rather heated discussion of reconstruction policies, Lincoln congratulated him on his recent speech in Ohio. He crustily denied having made one, and Lincoln said:*

Well, I see Nasby says that in consequence of one speech made by Jim Ashley, four hundred thousand niggers moved into Wood County last week, and it must have taken a great speech to do that. — *Ashley-2, 15. {C}*

JOHN B. BALDWIN (1820–1873)   *Virginia lawyer and politician, a Unionist who voted against secession but subsequently served in the Confederate Congress.*

1. *On April 4, 1861, at a time when expeditions to Fort Pickens and Fort Sumter were being planned, Baldwin had a private meeting with Lincoln as spokesman for the Unionist majority in the Virginia convention, which had been in session since February 13. Baldwin's later testimony concerning that interview was largely an account of what he had said in lecturing the President on how to resolve the crisis. He did tell of being greeted with the words:*

I am afraid you have come too late; I wish you could have been here three or four days ago.

And then: Why do you not all adjourn the Virginia convention? . . . it is a standing menace to me which embarrasses me very much.

To Baldwin's argument that withdrawal from the forts would win him more friends than it would lose, Lincoln replied: That is not what I am thinking about. If I could be satisfied that I am right, and that I do what is right, I do not care whether people stand by me or not.

Baldwin recalled that Lincoln said "something about the withdrawal of the troops from Sumter on the ground of military necessity," and also "something or other about feeding the troops at Sumter." Baldwin warned against any course other than prompt withdrawal, saying that if a single gun were fired at the fort, Virginia would be out of the Union within forty-eight hours. Lincoln replied:

Oh, sir, that is impossible. —*Baldwin's testimony in* House Report 30, *pp. 102-4 (1866).* {D}

At one point, after quoting Lincoln, Baldwin said, "I do not pretend to recollect the language at all, but this is about the substance of it." The most striking feature of his testimony was his emphatic denial that Lincoln had offered to withdraw the troops from Fort Sumter if the Virginia convention would adjourn sine die. According to John Minor Botts and George Plumer Smith (qq.v.), Lincoln subsequently told each of them that he had made such an offer. Moreover, Smith's statement on the subject received corroboration from Lincoln himself. It is therefore difficult to escape the conclusion that Lincoln or Baldwin or both men later misrepresented what had passed between them.[17] A bizarre footnote to the controversy is the statement by Senator Jacob M. Howard of Michigan that Lincoln, speaking through a medium in the spring of 1866, had answered his question about the Baldwin interview by saying, "Senator, I never offered a bribe to treason in my life."[18]

RICHARD H. BALLINGER   *Ballinger, it is said, read law with Lincoln, but there appears to be no record of it. He was a member of the American (Know-Nothing) party in Springfield and later commanded a black regiment during the Civil War.*

He was the father of William Howard Taft's controversial secretary of the interior, Richard A. Ballinger.

1. *When he was notified in 1854 that the local Know-Nothing organization had nominated him for the state legislature, Lincoln replied that:*

he had belonged to the old Whig party and must continue to do so until a better one arose to take its place. He could not become identified with the American party. They might vote for him if they wanted to; so might the Democrats; yet he was not in sentiment with this new party.

Taking up the term "native Americans," he asked who they were and then went on to say: Do they not wear the breech-clout and carry the tomahawk? We pushed them from their homes and now turn upon others not fortunate enough to come over as early as we or our forefathers. Gentlemen of the committee, your party is wrong in principle. — *Ballinger's statement in Levering, 496 (1896). {C}*

2. *During the same discussion, Lincoln told a story:*

When the Know-Nothing party first came up, I had an Irishman, Patrick by name, hoeing in my garden. One morning I was there with him, and he said, "Mr. Lincoln, what about the Know-Nothings?" I explained that they would possibly carry a few elections and disappear, and I asked Pat why he was not born in this country. "Faith, Mr. Lincoln," he replied, "I wanted to be, but my mother wouldn't let me." —497. {C}

GEORGE BANCROFT (1800–1891)　*Noted historian and Democratic politician who served the Polk administration, first as secretary of the navy, and then as minister to Great Britain.*

1. *After a discussion with Lincoln on December 15, 1861, Bancroft writes to his wife the following day that the President thinks that:*

slavery has received a mortal wound . . . the harpoon has struck the whale to the heart. — *Howe, II, 147. {B}*

2. *More than two years later, Bancroft attended a large reception at the White House. Lincoln took his hand, trying to recall his name, and then cried out:*

Hold on—I know you; you are—History, History of the United States— Mr.—Mr. Bancroft, Mr. George Bancroft. — *To Mrs. Bancroft, February 24, 1864, Howe, II, 155–56. {A}*

T. B. BANCROFT　*A Pennsylvanian.*

1. *While waiting to talk to the President one day in the spring of 1862, Bancroft heard him answer a very young soldier's request to be made a captain:*

To be a captain you should have a company or something to be captain of. You know a man is not a husband until he gets a wife—neither is a woman a wife until she gets a husband. I might give you a commission as captain and send you back to the Army of the Potomac, where you would have nothing to be captain of, and you would be like a loose horse down there with nothing to do and no one having any use for you. My son, go back to the army, continue to do your duty as you find it to do, and, with the zeal you have hitherto shown, you will not have to ask for promotion. It will seek **you**. I may say that had we more like you in the army, my hopes of the successful outcome of this war would be far stronger than they are at present. Shake hands with me, and go back the little man and brave soldier that you came. —*Bancroft, 449 (1909).* {D}

A rather long speech (not all of which is given here) for a bystander to recall after nearly half a century.

JOHN G. BARNARD (1815–1882)   *Union general, chief engineer of the Army of the Potomac.*

   1. *Early in the war, when Lincoln asked McClellan why Washington had been fortified so strongly on its northern side, the General said that as a matter of military science, it was necessary to guard against every contingency, even the remote possibility of a Confederate attack from that direction. Lincoln then responded:*

The precaution is doubtless a wise one, and I'm glad to get so clear an explanation, for it reminds me of an interesting question once discussed for several weeks in our lyceum or moot court at Springfield, Illinois, soon after I began reading law. The question was, "Why does man have breasts?" After many evenings' debate the question was submitted to the presiding judge, who wisely decided "that if under any circumstances, however fortuitous, or by any chance or freak, no matter of what nature or by what cause, a man should have a baby, there would be the breasts to nurse it." —*Remarks of Barnard at a dinner in 1871, recalled by "S.S." in the New York Tribune, October 21, 1885.* {D}

JOHN S. BARNES   *Naval officer, commander of the* Bat, *which accompanied the* River Queen *when that vessel carried Lincoln to City Point in March 1865.*

   1. *In a discussion of the forthcoming trip on March 20, Lincoln said to Barnes:*

I'm only a freshwater sailor, and I guess I have to trust you saltwater folks when afloat. —*Barnes JS, 517 (1907).* {C}

   2. *After the Confederate attack of March 25 on Fort Stedman, Lincoln visited the scene of battle, where bodies still lay on the ground. He said:*

that he had seen enough of the horrors of war, that he hoped this was the beginning of the end and that there would be no more bloodshed or ruin of homes. —*522.* {C}

3. *Fixed in his memory, Barnes wrote, was what Lincoln had said at the historic moment when he seated himself in Jefferson Davis's chair in Richmond on April 5:*

I wonder if I could get a drink of water. —749. {C}

T. J. BARNETT *An official in the Department of the Interior.*

1. *Talking with Barnett late in 1862, Lincoln indicated:*

that he should **abate no jot** of his emancipation policy, but that by imperceptible (comparatively) degrees, perhaps, military law might be made to relent.

He goes on to say: that he highly appreciates the loyal sensibilities of the opposition . . . but that issues are swept away so fast by overtopping facts that no party will have time to mature until after the war.

He thinks: that the foundations of slavery have been cracked by the war, by the rebels, and that the masonry of the machine is in their own hands—that they have held its fate, and can't complain.

Deriding the notion that his emancipation policy will tend to stimulate servile insurrection, he thinks that: he will be able to make it clear that he usurps no power by the Proclamation.

Most troubled by the problem of providing for the freed blacks, he still thinks: that many of them will colonize and that the South will be compelled to resort to the apprentice system. —*Barnett to Barlow, November 30, 1862, Barlow Papers.* {B}

2. *During the same conversation, Lincoln commented on the public image of Seward, saying that:*

he seemed to share the fate of the ancient picture placed by the painter in the market-house to be retouched by all caviling critics.

Of Stanton, Lincoln says that: he is so utterly misjudged, that, at present, the man's public character is a public mistake.

As for Chase, he thought that: public sentiment was rather capricious in regard to him, to say the least of it.

In the end, however: The acts of the administration and all of its responsibilities belong to that unhappy wretch called Abraham Lincoln. —*Ibid.* {B}

CHARLES A. BARRY (1830–1892) *A drawing master in the Boston public schools, sent to Springfield by a printmaker in 1860 to do a portrait of the Republican presidential nominee.*[19]

1. *At their first meeting, Lincoln said:*

They want my head, do they? . . . Well, if you can get it you may have it, that is, if you are able to take it off while I am on the jump; but don't fasten me into a chair. I don't suppose you Boston folks get up at cock-crowing as we do out here. I am an early riser, and if you will come to my room at the state house on Monday at seven o'clock sharp, I will be there to let you in. —*Barry in the Boston* Transcript, *1902, reprinted in Wilson RR-2, 308. {C}*

WILLIAM O. BARTLETT   *New York lawyer and occasional editorial writer who acted as intermediary in a curious negotiation between Lincoln and James Gordon Bennett, editor of the New York* Herald.

    1. *On November 1, 1864, Bartlett called at the White House to discuss the appointment of Bennett as minister to France. Lincoln said that on the subject:*

he had been a shut pan to everybody and that he expected to do that thing as much as he expected to live.

He then reiterated: I expect to do it as certainly as I do to be re-elected myself. —*Bartlett to Bennett, November 4, 1864, in Carlson, 370. {B, A}*

Lincoln eventually offered the post to Bennett, who declined it.[20]

NEWTON BATEMAN (1822–1897)   *Illinois educator, a Jacksonville Republican who in 1858 won election as state superintendent of public instruction. After serving a total of fourteen years in that position, he became the president of Knox College.*

    1. *In introducing Bateman, Lincoln usually said something like:*

This is my little friend, the big schoolmaster of Illinois. —*Bateman, 21 (1899). {C}*

Bateman also remembered the phrasing as: my little friend, the big superintendent of state education. —*Bateman interview, January 22, 1895, Tarbell Papers.*

    2. *Bateman's office was in the state house, where Lincoln had a reception room after his election to the presidency. Bateman expressed fear that the noise of callers in his office would disturb Lincoln. Lincoln said:*

If you can stand my noise, I can stand yours. —*Bateman, 21. {C}*

    3. *In a draft of his letter dated May 23, 1860, accepting the Republican nomination for president, Lincoln used the phrase "to not violate." When Bateman suggested transposing the first two words, he replied:*

Oh, you think I'd better turn those two little fellows end for end, eh?[21] — *Bateman, 31. {C}*

    4. *Toward the end of October 1860, according to Bateman, he and Lincoln examined a book containing a list of Springfield voters with indications of how they were expected to cast their ballots in the approaching presidential election. Said Lincoln:*

Here are twenty-three ministers of different denominations, and all of them are against me but three; and here are a great many prominent members of the churches, a very large majority of whom are against me. Mr. Bateman, I am not a Christian—God knows I would be one, but I have carefully read the Bible, and I do not so understand this book [drawing forth a pocket New Testament]. These men well know that I am for freedom in the territories, freedom everywhere as far as the Constitution and laws will permit, and that my opponents are for slavery. They know this, and yet, with this book in their hands, in the light of which human bondage cannot live a moment, they are going to vote against me. I do not understand it at all.

His cheeks "wet with tears," Lincoln continued: I know there is a God, and that He hates injustice and slavery. I see the storm coming, and I know that His hand is in it. If He has a place and work for me—and I think He has—I believe I am ready. I am nothing, but truth is everything. I know I am right because I know that liberty is right, for Christ teaches it, and Christ is God. I have told them that a house divided against itself cannot stand, and Christ and reason say the same; and they will find it so. Douglas don't care whether slavery is voted up or voted down, but God cares, and humanity cares, and I care; and with God's help I shall not fail. I may not see the end; but it will come, and I shall be vindicated; and these men will find that they have not read their Bibles aright.

Doesn't it appear strange that men can ignore the moral aspects of this contest? A revelation could not make it plainer to me that slavery or the government must be destroyed. The future would be something awful, as I look at it, but for this rock on which I stand [alluding to the Testament in his hand], especially with the knowledge of how these ministers are going to vote. It seems as if God had borne with this thing [slavery] until the very teachers of religion have come to defend it from the Bible, and to claim for it a divine character and sanction; and now the cup of iniquity is full, and the vials of wrath will be poured out.

As the conversation went on at great length, Lincoln emphasized faith in Christianity's God as an element in statesmanship, declaring that: it gave that calmness and tranquillity of mind, that assurance of ultimate success, which made a man firm and immovable amid the wildest excitements.

He also stated his belief: in the duty, privilege, and efficacy of prayer,

and indicated that: he had sought in that way the divine guidance and favor.

As the two men parted, Bateman remarked that Lincoln's friends were ignorant of the sentiments he had just expressed. Lincoln replied: I know they are. I am obliged to appear different to them; but I think more on these subjects than upon all others, and I have done so for years; and I am willing that **you** should know it. —*Bateman's statement in Holland, 236–39 (1866).*[22] {D}

This well-known contribution to the apotheosis of Lincoln must be regarded as dubious biographical material, although it is not inconceivable that Lincoln had some kind of discussion with Bateman in which he revealed more religious feeling than had been his custom.²³

DAVID HOMER BATES (1843–1926)   *Clerk in the telegraph office of the War Department.*

1. *Asked for an explanation of his remark, as he finished reading telegrams, that he was "down to the raisins," Lincoln told the story of:*

the little girl who celebrated her birthday by eating very freely of many good things, topping off with raisins for dessert. During the night she was taken violently ill, and when the doctor arrived, she was busy casting up her accounts. The genial doctor, scrutinizing the contents of the vessel, noticed some small black objects that had just appeared, and remarked to the anxious parent that all danger was past, as the child was "down to raisins." So [Lincoln said] when I reach the message in this pile which I saw on my last visit, I know that I need go no further. —*Bates DH-1, 41 (1907).* {C}

Two fellow telegraphers, Albert Chandler and Charles A. Tinker, likewise recalled the raisins story, though with variations: Chandler-2, 32–33; Tinker, 444.

2. *Early in the war, General Robert C. Schenck sent a telegram from northern Virginia announcing a light skirmish in which thirty or forty prisoners were taken, all armed with Colt's revolvers. Lincoln said with a twinkle in his eye that:*

the newspapers were given to such exaggeration in publishing army news that we might be sure when General Schenck's dispatch appeared in print the next day all the little Colt's revolvers would have grown into horse-pistols. —*Bates DH-1, 113–14.* {C}

No record of the alleged telegram from Schenck has been found, but Albert Chandler also recalled Lincoln's joke, associating it with the minor engagement at Dranesville on December 20, 1861. Chandler-2, 33.

3. *Bates claimed to have noted in his diary a dissertation by Lincoln on the functions of the eye and brain while one is reading aloud. He said that:*

in his boyhood days, he had come across a book in which it was stated that as each letter of the alphabet and each word or sentence appeared before the eye, it was pictured upon the retina so that each particular word could be spoken aloud at the exact moment when its printed form in the volume was reflected upon the eye.

He went on to remark: that the eye is capable of receiving simultaneously several distinct impressions or a series of impressions constantly changing as

one continues to read across the page, and that these numerous and sometimes radically different impressions are communicated from eye to brain
and then back to the vocal organs by means of the most delicate nerves.
For instance, the eye may rest at the same instant not only upon a single
letter of the alphabet, but upon a series of letters forming a given word and
upon a moving procession of words in a sentence, and not only that, but the
resultant record of all these numerous and different impressions is translated by the brain into thought and sent back—telegraphed as it were—to
the organs of speech, each organ selecting its own particular message, the
whole sentence then being spoken aloud even while the eye is still resting
upon the printed page. The skilled accountant casts up a long column of
figures as fast as his eye moves down the page, and at the instant he reaches
the end of his column, his ready fingers jot down the total. In other words,
communications are being transmitted continuously and simultaneously in
both directions between the outer and inner senses. —*Bates DH-1, 218,
221–22.* {D}

*The fact that the passage contains some echoes of Lincoln's lecture on "Dis-
coveries and Inventions" could be viewed either as enhancing or as impairing
its credibility.*[24]

4. *Upon receiving telegraphed word of his renomination in 1864:*

Send it right over to the Madam. She will be more interested than I am. —
Bates DH-1, 267–68.[25] {C}

5. *Lincoln's comment on a signature partly obscured by the flourish with
which it ended:*

That reminds me of a short-legged man in a big overcoat, the tail of which
was so long it wiped out his footprints in the snow. —*Bates DH-2, 24
(1926).*[26] {C}

EDWARD BATES (1793–1869) *Missouri Whig-turned-Republican who was a
presidential candidate in 1860 and served as Lincoln's attorney general until
November 1864.*

1. *On December 15, 1860, Bates recorded in his diary, Lincoln told him
that if Seward did not agree to enter the cabinet:*

he would at once offer me the State Department—but failing that, he would
offer me the attorney-generalship, and urge my acceptance. . . . And further, if I thought, after consultation with friends, that it would be best to
let his offer be known and would write him so, he would stop conjectures
by letting it be known as a fact—but not the particular office. —*Bates E,
165.* {B}

John G. Nicolay (q.v.) provided a fuller account of this interview.

2. *On February 5, 1862, concerning the convicted slave-trader Nathaniel Gordon, Lincoln said that:*

he had no intention to pardon Gordon but was willing to give him a short respite, and that yesterday at cabinet council all the members present (though not asked **as a cabinet**) agreed to it. —*Bates E, 229. {B}*

Gordon was executed on February 21.

3. *Concerning Stanton's suggestion in February 1862 that Frank Blair be given command of the expedition down the Mississippi, Lincoln said that:*

that was the greatest business of all, and needed the highest general in that region.

He added: that it was generally thought that a man was better qualified to do a thing because he had learned how and that in this case it was Mr. Blair's misfortune not to have learned. —*Bates E, 232. {B}*

4. *At the beginning of a cabinet meeting on September 2, 1862, the day that McClellan was placed in command of the troops defending Washington, Lincoln, in great distress, exclaimed that:*

he felt almost ready to hang himself.

In response to the opposition of most cabinet members to the appointment, he said: that he was far from doubting our sincerity, but that he was so distressed, precisely because he knew we were earnestly sincere.

Fearing that defeat in the second battle of Bull Run had caused demoralization among the troops, he said that: if Pope's army came within the lines [of the forts] as **a mob,** the city would be overrun in 48 hours. —*Bates's undated note on a copy of a document opposing such an appointment, signed by four cabinet members.* Collected Works, V, 486n. *{B}*

5. *On December 19, 1862, Lincoln talked with the cabinet about a call for reconstruction of that body from the Republican senatorial caucus—the obvious purpose being to get rid of Seward. He said that:*

he had a long conference with the committee, who seemed earnest and sad, not malicious nor passionate, not denouncing anyone, but all of them attributing to Mr. Seward a lukewarmness in the conduct of the war and seeming to consider him the real cause of our failures. While they believed in the President's honesty, they seemed to think that when he had in him any good purposes, Mr. Seward contrived to suck them out of him unperceived. —*Bates E, 269. {B}*

6. *At a cabinet meeting on September 14, 1863, Lincoln spoke angrily about the increasing issue of writs of habeas corpus for soldiers and military prisoners. He said:*

that it was a formed plan of the Democratic Copperheads, deliberately acted out to defeat the government and aid the enemy; that no honest man did or could believe that the state judges have any such power. —*Bates E, 306.* {B}

7. *After talking to the delegation of Missouri and Kansas Radicals on September 30, 1863, Lincoln told Bates that:*

some of them were not as bad as he supposed. —*Bates E, 308.* {B}

8. *On February 13, 1864, in a discussion of the forthcoming presidential election, Lincoln said of the Radical leaders that:*

they were almost fiendish. —*Bates E, 333.* {B}

HIRAM W. BECKWITH   *Illinois lawyer and judge who studied law in Ward H. Lamon's office in Danville and was recommended for admission to the bar by Lincoln.*

1. *Speaking of courtroom practice, Lincoln said to Beckwith:*

Notes are a bother, taking time to make and more to hunt them up afterwards. Lawyers who do so soon get the habit of referring to them so much that it confuses and tires the jury. —*Beckwith's statement quoted in Tarbell, II, 45 (1907).* {C}

HENRY W. BELLOWS (1814–1882)   *Unitarian clergyman, founder and president of the Sanitary Commission, later a civil service reformer.*

1. *On April 18, 1862, Lincoln assured Bellows that Dr. William A. Hammond, the man of his choice, had been appointed surgeon-general of the United States. During their discussion, he said:*

I hain't been caught lying yet, and I don't mean to be. —*Bellows's account as apparently told to Dr. William Holme Van Buren and retold by him the next day to George Templeton Strong, who promptly recorded it in his diary, III, 218.* {D}

2. *When Bellows urged him to eat his meals at regular hours:*

Well, I cannot take my vittles regular. I kind o' just browze round. —*Ibid.* {D}

3. *Concerning the Secretary of War:*

Stanton's one of my team, and they must pull together. I can't have any one on 'em a-kicking out. —*Ibid.* {D}

H. B. BERRY   *Said to be a cousin of Lincoln's friend Leonard Swett, Berry was a telegrapher in Washington during the Civil War.*

1. *Berry and Swett were present one evening when a delegation of very large men from New Jersey called at the White House. Lincoln said in low tones to Swett:*

The state of New Jersey is a long, narrow state. These five men all come from the north end. I should think when they left, it would have tipped the state up. —*Ida M. Tarbell's interview with Berry, January 5, 1897, Tarbell Papers. {C}*

W. C. BIBB   *A resident of Montgomery, Alabama, who, with the approval of that state's governor, made his way to Washington and talked with Lincoln on April 12, 1865.*[27]

   1. *Asked if his proposed amnesty policy extended to Confederate leaders, Lincoln said:*

Yes, to all. It is universal in its application. I have consented to withhold it from publication for a few days for special reasons which have been urged, but which I regard as of little force, but I thought it better to pay that respect to the opinion of others. I love the southern people more than they love me. My desire is to restore the Union. I do not intend to hurt the hair of the head of a single man in the South if it can possibly be avoided. — *Bibb's account in the* Gulf Messenger *(San Antonio, Texas) for April and May 1893, transcription in the Sandburg Collection, folder 404. {C}*

   2. *Concerning requirements for the readmission of the southern states to the Union:*

All that I ask is that they shall annul their ordinance of secession and send their delegates to fill the seats in Congress which are now vacant, awaiting their occupation.

As for slavery: I am individually willing to grant either gradual emancipation, say running through twenty years, or compensated emancipation at the option of the southern people; but there are certain amendments to the Constitution now before the people for their adoption or rejection, and I have no power to do anything at present; but if it should so happen that I could control it, such would be my policy. —*Ibid. {C}*

Lincoln was perhaps dissembling here. Although gradual, compensated emancipation had been his original preference, he had strongly supported passage of the Thirteenth Amendment.

JOHN A. BINGHAM (1815–1900)   *Ohio congressman of the Civil War era, remembered especially for the part he played in the impeachment of Andrew Johnson and the framing of the Fourteenth Amendment.*

   1. *On April 11, 1861, the day before the attack on Fort Sumter, Lincoln told Bingham that:*

he had sent a message to Governor Pickens of South Carolina, acquainting him that it was his intention to send provisions to the fort. But [he continued] I added on my own hook if my effort to provision the garrison there is resisted, I will throw in supplies at all hazards. I hope good may come of it. —*Bingham, 282 (1866). {C}*

Actually, Lincoln's threat to use force, though plainly implied in the message to Pickens, was not explicitly stated.[28]

2. *As Lincoln stepped out of the White House one day during Early's raid in 1864, Bingham asked him whether he was leaving the city. He answered:*

Oh, no, but there is excitement among our boys, and I go out to encourage them. —282. {C}

JOSIAH BLACKBURN (1823–1890)   *Canadian editor, probably the author of an article written in the summer of 1864 for his newspaper, the London (Canada West) Free Press. "These words," he declared, "are given exactly as expressed by the President, written down a few moments after they were uttered."*

1. *Concerning the ease with which an interview had been arranged:*

Yes, this ready means of access is, I may say, under our form of government, the only link or cord which connects the people with the governing power; and however unprofitable much of it is, it must be kept up. As, for instance, a mother in a distant part, who has a son in the army who is regularly enlisted, has not served out his time, but has been as long as she thinks he ought to stay, will collect together all the little means she can to bring her here to entreat me to grant him his discharge. Of course, I cannot interfere and can only see her and speak kindly to her. —*London* Free Press, *reprinted in New York* Times, *August 1, 1864.* {A}

2. *During this same interview, Lincoln said:*

It is very strange that I, a boy brought up in the woods, and seeing, as it were, but little of the world, should be drifted into the very apex of this great event. —*Ibid.* {A}

FRANKLIN BLADES (1830–?)   *Illinois legislator, physician, lawyer, and judge.*

1. *In 1858, Blades wrote asking permission to use Lincoln's name as a reference on his professional card without explaining that he intended to switch from the practice of medicine to the practice of law. He received the following droll reply, which, he says, was later lost or stolen from his papers:*

I do not know whether you are Dr. Blades or not. If you are Dr. Blades, you may use my name; if you are not Dr. Blades, if Dr. Blades says you may use my name, you may do so. —*Phillips-2, 112 (1910).* {C}

ALBERT BLAIR   *A native of Pike County, Illinois, who was a classmate of Robert Todd Lincoln at Phillips Exeter Academy in 1859–60. He was later a lawyer in St. Louis.*

1. *While speaking at Exeter on March 3, 1860, Lincoln put a question to the audience and received no response. He said good-humoredly:*

You people here don't jaw back at a fellow as they do out West. —*Blair's statement in Stevens, 62 (1916).* {C}

2. *Attending a reception at the White House in February 1865, Blair heard Lincoln say to his friend Justice David Davis:*

Judge, I never knew until the other day how to spell the word "maintenance." I always thought it was m-a-i-n, main, t-a-i-n, tain, a-n-c-e, ance—maintainance, but I find that it is m-a-i-n, main, t-e, te, n-a-n-c-e, nance—maintenance. —62. *{C}*

FRANCIS PRESTON BLAIR, JR. (1821–1875)   *During the Civil War, alternately a member of Congress from Missouri and a military commander rising to the rank of major general.*

   1. *Concerning General Henry W. Halleck's announced policy, as commander in Missouri, of levying contributions from pro-Confederate sympathizers in St. Louis for the support of Unionist refugees from the southwestern part of the state, Lincoln told Blair to tell the General:*

that he had not given the subject much consideration, but that he was very much inclined to favor the policy you had announced in your order and that he heard nothing in regard to the matter from anyone that was not favorable to that policy.[29] —*Blair to Halleck, January 3, 1862, ISHL. {B}*

FRANCIS PRESTON BLAIR, SR. (1791–1876)   *Former editor of the Washington* Globe *and father of Montgomery Blair. A Jacksonian Democrat turned Republican, he had considerable influence on Lincoln during the first half of his presidency.*

   1. *November 6, 1862, to Blair's defense of General McClellan, Lincoln replied that:*

he had tried long enough to bore with an auger too dull to take hold.

After further entreaties from Blair, the President closed the discussion with these words: I said I would remove him if he let Lee's army get away from him, and I must do so. He has got the "slows," Mr. Blair. —*Blair to Montgomery Blair, November 7, 1862, in Smith WE, II, 144–45. {B, A}*

The order removing McClellan from command had in fact already been written on November 5. According to Gideon Welles (q.v.), Lincoln applied the word "slows" both to McClellan and to Samuel F. Du Pont.

   2. *In August 1864, concerning Radical Republican pressure for the dismissal of Montgomery Blair, Lincoln said that:*

nobody but enemies wanted Montgomery out of the Cabinet . . . he did not think it good policy to sacrifice a true friend to a false one or an avowed enemy. —*Blair to Francis Preston Blair, Jr., September 23, 1864, copied in Lee, 433. {B}*

   3. *About two weeks before the election of 1864, as Blair reportedly informed*

an army general, Lincoln made a startling suggestion with respect to McClellan's candidacy. He was quoted as saying:

Would it not be a glorious thing for the Union cause and the country, now that my re-election is certain, for him to decline to run, favor my election, and make speedy and certain termination of this bloody war?

According to the story, Blair actually delivered in person a letter from Lincoln asking McClellan to withdraw from the race and accept appointment as general of the army. —Blair's account supposedly told to General Alfred Pleasonton and retold by him to Ward H. Lamon, who recorded it many years later in a memorandum ("War Reminiscences," Lamon Papers) that was subsequently incorporated in Lamon-2, 208-10.[30] {E}

Here is a good example of tertiary quotation and its hazards. It is true that Blair undertook to arrange McClellan's return to an army command in 1864, but he did so six months before the election, and the initiative was his, not Lincoln's.[31]

4. *In November 1864, on appointing a chief justice:*

Although I may be stronger as an authority, yet if all the rest oppose, I must give way. Old Hickory, who had as much iron in his neck as anybody, did so some times. If the strongest horse in the team **would** go ahead, he **cannot,** if all the rest hold back. — *Blair to John A. Andrew, November 19, 1864, in* MHSP, *n.s., 63 (January 1930): 88-89. {A}*

MONTGOMERY BLAIR (1813-1883) *Lincoln's postmaster general, the son of Francis Preston Blair, Sr.*

1. *In March 1862, Blair apologized for his criticism of the President as feebly Whiggish in a private letter that had recently been made public.[32] Lincoln replied:*

Forget it and never mention or think of it again. I know what you meant; for you [were] very frank about your feelings and views at the time. General Scott was the Old Whiggism you meant—talked plainly enough—but the Old Hero has done his country noble service, and it was natural to trust him—but his vigor is past. —*Lee, 106. {D}*

This is secondhand as well as self-serving, being Blair's sister's report of what he told her Lincoln had said.

G. H. BLAKESLEE *Methodist minister at Binghamton, New York.*

1. *Visiting the White House on November 2, 1864, Blakeslee heard Lincoln say to a woman seeking release of her husband from prison:*

I can do nothing for you. . . . I am under no obligation to provide for the wives of disloyal husbands. —*Blakeslee's diary as quoted by his son in Blakeslee, 129. {A}*

J. S. BLISS   *A Wisconsin newspaper correspondent who visited the President-elect in July 1860.*

1. *Bliss asked the population of Springfield, and Lincoln answered:*

With those who want a large city, there are sixteen or seventeen thousand, but I suppose there is thirteen or fourteen thousand inhabitants. —*Bliss to Herndon, January 29, 1867 (9:1422-34), Herndon-Weik Collection.* {C}

2. *While the two men were talking, Willie Lincoln entered the office and asked his father for twenty-five cents to buy candy with. Lincoln, reaching into his vest pocket, replied:*

My son, I shall not give you twenty-five cents, but will give you five cents.

Willie scorned the offer and stormed out of the room. Lincoln said: He will be back after that in a few moments. . . . as soon as he finds I will give him no more, he will come and get it. *His prediction proved to be accurate.* —*Ibid.* {C}

HENRY W. BLODGETT (1821–1905)   *A lawyer, state legislator, and antislavery leader in antebellum Waukegan, Illinois, Blodgett later served more than twenty years as a federal judge.*

1. *During the presidential campaign of 1844, Blodgett told Lincoln that he was an abolitionist and would not vote for Henry Clay, a slaveholder. Lincoln responded that:*

he was himself opposed to slavery but didn't see how the abolitionists could reach it in the slave states.

Blodgett said that they could abolish the institution in the District of Columbia and put an end to the interstate slave trade. Lincoln replied: Well, you may do that if you get into power, but that will be very little toward getting rid of slavery in the states. —*Blodgett, 43-44 (1906).* {C}

2. *In an argument before the Illinois supreme court concerning a lien on his client's property, Lincoln pronounced the word "leen," but the presiding judge kept interrupting him to insist that the proper pronunciation was "lie-en." At last, Lincoln said:*

Certainly, your honor, certainly. I only desire to say that if my client had known there was a lion on his farm for so long a time, I'm sure he would not have stayed there even long enough to bring this suit, and I should not have the pleasure of appearing before this honorable court. —*Blodgett's account as reported in the Chicago* Mail, *reprinted in the New York* Tribune, *February 23, 1893.* {D}

JERIAH BONHAM   *Illinois editor and publisher.*

1. *Bonham called on Lincoln in the summer of 1860 and found him alone with Willie and Tad, helping the latter spin a top. He said that:*

he was having a little season of relaxation with the boys, which he could not always enjoy now, as so many callers and so much correspondence occupied his time. —*Bonham, 183 (1883). {C}*

ALEXANDER R. BOTELER (1815–1892) *Virginia congressman of Whig background. He was a unionist in the secession crisis but later served as a member of the Confederate Congress and as an aide to Stonewall Jackson and J. E. B. Stuart.*

1. *On March 1, 1861, Boteler urged Lincoln to use his influence against a pending "force bill," as he called it, that would have authorized the President to call out the militia for suppression of rebellion and to raise a force of volunteers. In the course of their conversation, Lincoln said:*

I'm really glad you have come and wish that more of you southern gentlemen would call and see me, as these are times when there should be a full, fair, and frank interchange of sentiment and suggestion among all who have the good of the country at heart. . . . Of course, I am extremely anxious to see these sectional troubles settled peaceably and satisfactorily to all concerned. To accomplish that, I am willing to make almost any sacrifice, and to do anything in reason consistent with my sense of duty. There is one point, however, I can never surrender—that which was the main issue of the presidential canvass and decided at the late election, concerning the extension of slavery in the territories.

Warned that passage of such legislation would drive Virginia out of the Union, Lincoln said: Well, I'll see what can be done about the bill you speak of. I think it can be stopped and that I may promise you it will be.

But when Boteler asked whether he might announce on the floor of the House that the President-elect was opposed to the measure, Lincoln replied: By no means, for that would make trouble. The question would at once be asked, what right I had to interfere with the legislation of this Congress. Whatever is to be done in the matter must be done quietly. —*Boteler, 223–26 (1879). {C}*

Boteler claimed to have made full notes of the interview immediately thereafter. Action on the bill was prevented that same night by an adjournment of the House. Lincoln's role in its defeat, if he had any, is not known, but there may be significance in the fact that his friend and fellow Illinoisan Elihu B. Washburne was a leader in the move to adjourn.[33]

JOHN MINOR BOTTS (1802–1869) *A Virginia lawyer and former Whig congressman, Botts was an outspoken Unionist during the secession crisis. Confederate authorities jailed him for a time in 1862.*

1. *Botts testified in 1866 that on April 7, 1861, he and Lincoln had a four-hour conversation during the course of which the President said:*

that he had, about a week or ten days before that, possibly a fortnight, written to Mr. Summers, with whom we had both served in Congress together, asking him to come to Washington without delay, as he had a most important proposition to make to him, and that if he could not come himself he would send some other prominent influential Union man of the convention to him; that he had not heard from Mr. Summers until the Friday preceding, which was the 5th; that on that day Mr. John B. Baldwin, a member of the convention, had presented himself to him as having been sent up by Mr. Summers . . .

Then, according to Botts, Lincoln repeated what he had said to Baldwin: Ah, Mr. Baldwin, why did you not come here sooner? I have been waiting and expecting some of you gentlemen of that convention to come to me for more than a week past. I had a most important proposition to make to you. I am afraid you have come too late. However, I will make the proposition now. Mr. Baldwin, we have in Fort Sumter with Major Anderson about eighty men, and I learn from Major Anderson that his provisions are nearly exhausted . . . I have not only written to Governor Pickens, but I have sent a special messenger to him to say that if he will allow Major Anderson to obtain his marketing at the Charleston market, or, if he objects to allowing our people to land at Charleston, if he will have it sent to him, that I will make no effort to provision the fort; but that if he does not do that, I will not permit these people to starve, and that I shall send provisions down . . . and that if he fires on that vessel, he will fire upon an unarmed vessel loaded with nothing but bread; but I shall at the same time send a fleet along with her, with instructions not to enter the harbor of Charleston unless that vessel is fired into; and if she is, then the fleet is to enter the harbor and protect her. Now, Mr. Baldwin, that fleet is now lying in the harbor of New York, and will be ready to sail this afternoon at five o'clock; and although I fear it is almost too late, yet I will submit, anyway, the proposition which I intended when I sent for Mr. Summers. Your convention in Richmond, Mr. Baldwin, has been sitting now nearly two months, and all that they have done has been to shake the rod over my head. You have recently taken a vote in the Virginia convention on the right of secession, which was rejected by ninety to forty-five, a majority of two-thirds, showing the strength of the Union party in that convention; and if you will go back to Richmond and get that Union majority to adjourn and go home without passing the ordinance of secession, so anxious am I for the preservation of the peace of this country, and to save Virginia and the other border states from going out, that I will take the responsibility of evacuating Fort Sumter, and take the chance of negotiating with the cotton states which have already gone out.

According to Botts, when he asked how Baldwin had received the proposal,

Lincoln replied: Sir, he would not listen to it for a moment; he hardly treated me with civility. He asked me what I meant by an adjournment; did I mean an adjournment *sine die.* "Why, of course, Mr. Baldwin," said I. "I mean an adjournment *sine die.* I do not mean to assume such a responsibility as that of surrendering that fort to the people of Charleston upon your adjournment, and then for you to return in a week or ten days and pass your ordinance of secession after I have given up the fort."

And when Botts then offered to carry the proposal himself to the convention, Lincoln said: Oh, it is too late; the fleet has sailed, and I have no means of communicating with it. —*Botts's testimony in* House Report *30, pp. 114-15 (1866). {D}*

The reliability of this recollective passage is subject to question because of its length and because of certain manifest inaccuracies (for instance, the Baldwin-Lincoln interview took place on April 4, not April 5). Furthermore, Baldwin (q.v.), testifying at the same time, flatly denied that Lincoln made any such proposal. Against that denial, however, one must place Lincoln's contrary account given to other persons besides Botts (see Garrett Davis and especially George Plumer Smith), together with the assertions of Botts and another member of the Virginia convention, John F. Lewis, that Baldwin on April 17, 1861, acknowledged to both of them that the offer to evacuate Sumter in exchange for adjournment of the convention had been made by Lincoln and rejected by him.[34]

2. During the same conversation, Lincoln said:

Botts, I have always been an old-line Henry Clay Whig, and if your southern people will let me alone, I will administer this government as nearly upon the principles that he would have administered it as it is possible for one man to follow in the path of another. —*Botts, 196 (1866). {C}*

GEORGE S. BOUTWELL (1818–1905) *Radical Republican congressman from Massachusetts, later secretary of the treasury and senator.*

   1. In February 1861, Boutwell and other Massachusetts members of the Washington peace convention called on the President-elect to urge the appointment of Salmon P. Chase as secretary of the treasury. Without committing himself, Lincoln said:

From what I hear, I think Mr. Chase is about one hundred and fifty to any other man's hundred. —*Boutwell-2, I, 275 (1902).*[35] *{C}*

   2. In a conversation with Boutwell and Charles Sumner at some time after the outbreak of war, Lincoln expressed:

regret that he had neglected to station troops in Virginia in advance of the occupation of the vicinity of Alexandria by the Confederates. —*Boutwell-2, II, 65. {C}*

3. *August 31, 1862, right after the Union defeat at Bull Run, Lincoln replied to Boutwell's suggestion that military success depended on emancipation:*

You would not have it done now, would you? Must we not wait for something like a victory? — *Rice AT, 124 (1886). {C}*

4. *October 1862, in response to a published assertion that he had issued the preliminary Emancipation Proclamation on September 22 under pressure from the impending conference of state governors at Altoona, Pennsylvania:*

I never thought of the meeting of the governors. The truth is just this: When Lee came over the river, I made a resolution that if McClellan drove him back I would send the proclamation after him. The battle of Antietam was fought Wednesday, and until Saturday I could not find out whether we had gained a victory or lost a battle. It was then too late to issue the proclamation that day, and the fact is I fixed it up a little Sunday, and Monday I let them have it. — *Rice AT, 126.*[36] *{C}*

5. *After his nomination of Chase for the chief justiceship in December 1864, Lincoln said to Boutwell:*

There are three reasons why he should be appointed and one reason why he should not be. In the first place, he occupies a larger space in the public mind, with reference to the office, than any other person. Then we want a man who will sustain the Legal Tender Act and the Proclamation of Emancipation. We cannot ask a candidate what he would do; and if we did and he should answer, we should only despise him for it. But he wants to be president, and if he doesn't give that up it will be a great injury to him and a great injury to me. He can never be president. — *Boutwell-1, 436 (1895). {C}*

HENRY C. BOWEN (1813–1896)   *New York merchant and for many years proprietor of the* Independent, *a weekly Congregational journal that was closely allied to the antislavery movement.*

1. *When Lincoln visited New York City in February 1860 to deliver an address to a local Republican organization, he twice refused Bowen's offers of hospitality, saying that:*

he was afraid he had made a mistake in accepting the call to New York and feared his lecture would not prove a success. He would have to give his whole time to it, otherwise he was sure he would make a failure, in which case he would be very sorry for the young men who had kindly invited him.

And the next day: Now, look here, Mr. Bowen, I am not going to make a failure at the Cooper Institute tomorrow night, if I can possibly help it. I am anxious to make a success of it on account of the young men who have so kindly invited me here. It is on my mind all the time, and I cannot be persuaded to accept your hospitality at this time. Please excuse me and let me go to my room at the hotel, lock the door, and there think about my lecture. — *Bowen, 432(1895). {C}*

2. *According to Bowen, Lincoln told him in March 1861 that:*

he was sure "from the word go," after his nomination that he would be elected. . . . In November, on the day of the election, he was calm and sure of the result.

That night, after informing his wife of his victory: I then went to bed, but before I went to sleep I selected every member of my cabinet save one. — *432. {D}*

Bowen's assertion that this conversation took place at the Soldiers' Home contributes to a general doubt about the accuracy of the recollection.[37]

ELIZABETH ALLEN BRADNER   *A resident of Bloomington, Illinois, whose father and brother-in-law both had associations with Lincoln.*

1. *On November 7, 1860, according to Mrs. Bradner, Lincoln told her and several other callers how he had waited for election returns at the telegraph office the night before. He added:*

My wife informed me that if I was not home by ten o'clock she would lock me out, and so she did. About midnight she heard music and looking out saw a great crowd coming to our door. Then she unlocked it in a hurry. — *Bradner's article in the Bloomington* Pantagraph, *February 6, 1909, reprinted in Wilson RR-2, 120-23. {D}*

JAMES T. BRADY (1815-1869)   *Noted Irish-American lawyer who lived and practiced in New York City.*

1. *When Brady, upon being asked to raise an Irish brigade, protested that he knew nothing of military matters, Lincoln replied:*

You know plenty of Irishmen who do know all about such matters, and as to the appointment of officers, did you ever know an Irishman who would decline an office, or refuse a pair of epaulets, or do anything but fight gallantly after he had them? — *Brady's account, given at the time to Senator Morton S. Wilkinson of Minnesota and published as part of the latter's reminiscences in the New York* Tribune, *July 12, 1885. {D}*

JAMES A. BRIGGS   *The New York lawyer with whom Lincoln made the arrangements for his address at Cooper Union in February 1860. He later wrote that he believed Briggs to be "an excellent man."*[38]

1. *On March 11, 1860, having returned to New York after his speaking trip into New England, Lincoln told Briggs:*

When I was East, several gentlemen made about the same remark to me that you did today about the presidency; they thought my chances were about equal to the best. —*Briggs's letter in the New York* Post, *August 16, 1867.* {C}

2. *Before leaving for home, Lincoln said:*

It is worth a visit from Springfield, Illinois, to New York to make the acquaintance of such a man as William Cullen Bryant. —*Ibid.* {C}

JOHNSON BRIGHAM (1846–1936) *As a youth, Brigham worked for the Sanitary Commission in Washington. He was later a journalist and the state librarian in Iowa.*

1. *At the age of ninety, Brigham recalled hearing Lincoln respond briefly to a serenade on April 10, 1865, and then remark to a reporter nearby that:*

he dared not say anything more, lest the reporter should fail to quote him right to the country.

He added with a smile: Such things have been done, you know. —*Typewritten interview titled "Living Lincoln Links," Lincoln Collection-Brown.* {D}

HENRY P. H. BROMWELL (1823–1903) *Illinois lawyer and Republican politician with whom Lincoln had some acquaintance. He was elected to Congress in 1864.*

1. *While Bromwell was calling on the President in late March 1865, an usher announced that a certain soldier was waiting to see him. Lincoln said:*

Tell him I can't see him any more about the matter. I've seen him as many times as I can. I wish that man would let me alone. I've seen him again and again, and I've done everything for him that I can do, and he knows it just as well as I do . . . There is no end of these cases of people that come to me for something or other that nobody else can do for them. I do everything I can for them, but I can't do everything; and some of them are so unreasonable about it, they won't let me off after I've talked it over with them time after time. It seems to me sometimes they will wear the very life out of me; but then all these other matters are nothing to these cases of life and death—and there are so many of them, and they all fall on me. I reckon there never was a man raised in the country, on a farm, where they are always butchering cattle and hogs and think nothing of it, that ever grew up with such an aversion to bloodshed as I have and yet I've had more questions of life and death to settle in four years than all the men who ever sat in this chair put together. But, I've managed to get along and do my duty, as I believe, and still save most of them, and there's no man knows the distress of my mind. But there have been some of them I couldn't save—there are some cases where the law must be executed. There was that man [Nathaniel Gordon] who was sentenced for piracy and slave trading on the high seas.

That was a case where there must be an example and you don't know how they followed and pressed to get him pardoned, or his sentence commuted; but there was no use of talking. It had to be done; I couldn't help him, and then there was that ——, who was caught spying and recruiting within Pope's lines in Missouri. That was another case. They besieged me day and night, but I wouldn't give way. We had come to a point where something must be done that would put a stop to such work. And then there was this case of [John Y.] Beall on the lakes. That was a case where there must be an example. They tried me every way. They wouldn't give up; but I had to stand firm on that, and I even had to turn away his poor sister when she came and begged for his life, and let him be executed, and he was executed, and I can't get the distress out of my mind yet. —*Interview in the Denver* Tribune, *May 18, 1879, reprinted in the New York* Times, *May 27, 1879.* {D}

A lengthy quotation transmitted through two intermediaries is bound to be questionable, although this one seems credible in its general substance.[39]

NOAH BROOKS (1830–1903) *Newspaper reporter and confidant of Lincoln in the later years of the Civil War. Brooks was born in Maine, began his career in Boston, and by 1856 had moved to Dixon, Illinois, where he met Lincoln during the political campaign of that year. He emigrated to California in 1859 but returned to the east coast in November 1862 as Washington correspondent for the* Sacramento Union. *A graceful and prolific writer, Brooks sent more than two hundred wartime dispatches to the* Union, *many of them centering on presidential activities. His later recollections of Lincoln, written over a period of four decades, were based in part upon those contemporary letters. His assertion that he saw the President "almost daily" is surely an overstatement, and corroborative evidence of the degree of intimacy that he described is rather thin. The very number of his quotations of Lincoln contributes to the doubt that he heard them all directly from Lincoln himself and to the suspicion that he may even have invented some of them.*[40] *Nevertheless, the two men did become friends, Brooks was a frequent visitor at the White House, and it appears that by 1865, Lincoln had fixed upon him to replace John G. Nicolay as his private secretary.*[41]

  1. *Campaigning for Frémont at Dixon, Illinois, on July 17, 1856, Lincoln was persistently annoyed by a heckler and finally said to him:*

Look here, my friend, you are only making a fool of yourself by exposing yourself to the ridicule which I have thus far succeeded in bringing upon you every time you have interrupted me. You ought to know that men whose business it is to speak in public, make it a part of their business to have something always ready for just such fellows as you are. You see you stand no show against a man who has met, a hundred times, just such flings as you seem to fancy are original with yourself; so you may as well, to use a popular expression, "dry up" at once. —*Brooks-1 (1860).*[42] {C}

2. *During a conversation with Brooks at Oregon, Illinois, in July or August 1856, Lincoln made it clear that he did not expect Frémont to win.*[43] *Expressing confidence in the eventual triumph of Republicanism if extremist doctrines were avoided, he declared that:*

the candidate for 1860 should be a national conservative man, unhackneyed by political tergiversations and untrammeled by party obligations, a man fresh from the people, who should be able to embody in himself the expression of the popular will.

Deploring the radicalism of some Illinois Republicans, he said that: such men and the false impressions they made would lose the state to [for] Frémont. —*Brooks-1.* {C}

A later version of the same discussion portrays Lincoln as less sanguine about victory in 1860. Brooks quoted him as saying: Well, I don't know. Everything depends on the course of the Democracy. There's a big antislavery element in the Democratic party, and if we could get hold of that, we might possibly elect our man in 1860. But it's doubtful—**very** doubtful. Perhaps we shall be able to fetch it by 1864; perhaps not. As I said before, the Free Soil party is bound to win in the long run. It may not be in my day; but it will in yours, I do really believe. —*Brooks-3, 562 (1878).* {C}

3. *One day in late March 1863, after talking with a group of Ohio soldiers who had survived an unsuccessful raid deep into Confederate territory, Lincoln said with much feeling that:*

their bearing, and their apparent unconsciousness of having taken their lives in their hands, with the chances of death all against them, presented an example of the apparent disregard of the tremendous issues of life and death which was so strong a characteristic of the American soldier. —*Brooks-5, 78 (1895).* {C}

4. *After telling two army stories, Lincoln said:*

It seems as if neither death nor danger could quench the grim humor of the American soldier. —*Brooks-5, 258.* {C}

5. *For Lincoln, a visit to the Army of the Potomac in early April 1863 seemed more relaxing than otherwise, though he said that:*

nothing could touch the tired spot within, which was all tired. —*Dispatch of April 12 in the Sacramento* Union, *May 8, 1863.* {B}

In a later version, responding to someone's remark that the excursion seemed to be a good rest for him: Well, yes I do feel some better, I think; but, somehow, it don't appear to touch the tired spot, which can't be got at. —*Brooks-2, 227 (1865).* {C}

And in a still later version: I don't know about the "rest," as you call it. I suppose it is good for the body. But the tired part of me is inside out of reach. —*Brooks-3, 673.* {C}

And later still: It is a great relief to get away from Washington and the politicians. But nothing touches the tired spot. —*Brooks-5, 55.* {C}

6. *One evening during that tour, Lincoln said to Brooks:*

I kept McClellan in command after I had expected that he would win victories, simply because I knew that his dismissal would provoke popular indignation and shake the faith of the people in the final success of the war. —*Brooks-5, 26.* {C}

7. *Respecting McClellan's successor, who spoke often of taking Richmond:*

That is the most depressing thing about Hooker. It seems to me that he is overconfident. —*Brooks-5, 56.* {C}

8. *To a driver who berated his mule team in colorful language and admitted to being a Methodist:*

Well, I thought you must be an Episcopalian, because you swear just like Governor Seward, who is a churchwarden. —*Brooks-5, 55.*[44] {C}

9. *During the same visit to the army in Virginia, Lincoln responded to a question from Brooks about his experience as a railsplitter:*

Now let me tell you about that. I am not a bit anxious about my reputation in that line of business; but if there is any thing in this world that I am a judge of, it is of good felling of timber, but I don't remember having worked by myself at splitting rails for one whole day in my life. . . . I recollect that, sometime during the canvass for the office I now hold, there was a great mass meeting, where I was present, and with a great flourish several rails were brought into the meeting, and being informed where they came from, I was asked to identify them, which I did, with some qualms of conscience, having helped my father to split rails, as at other odd jobs. I said if there were any rails which I had split, I shouldn't wonder if those were the rails. —*Brooks-2, 227.* {D}

Lincoln would surely have remembered that the rails incident was staged at the Republican state convention in Decatur on May 9, 1860.

10. *Probably during the same trip to Virginia, Lincoln looked out over the landscape and said that:*

he liked the trees best when they were not in leaf, as their anatomy could then be studied.

The next day, in a discussion of the difference between character and reputation, he said that: perhaps a man's character was like a tree, and his reputation like its shadow; the shadow is what we think of it; the tree is the real thing. —*Brooks-4, 586 (1879).* {C}

11. *Riding through a wood in Virginia at another time, Lincoln saw a luxuriant vine wrapped about a tree and said:*

Yes, that is very beautiful; but that vine is like certain habits of men; it decorates the ruin that it makes. —*Brooks-4, 586. {D}*

From the text, it appears that Brooks may not have heard this remark directly from Lincoln.

12. *Of the somewhat idealized portrait painted by Edward Dalton Marchant, Lincoln said that:*

he had no idea that a painter could make so good a picture of such excessively poor materials. —*Dispatch of April 20 in the Sacramento* Union, *May 18, 1863. {B}*

13. *One evening after the failure of the Union naval attack on Charleston in April 1863, Brooks was present when Lincoln asked Halleck:*

why it was not possible to land a strong infantry and artillery force upon Morris Island, under cover of the gunboats, to cooperate with the navy in the attack upon the works at Cummings Point; thus Sumter could be reduced, and, by gradual approaches, we could get within range of the city. —*Dispatch of January 1 in the Sacramento* Union, *February 4, 1864. {C}*

Halleck said the plan was impracticable, and Brooks later recalled that after the meeting, Lincoln expressed himself as discouraged by Halleck's "habitual attitude of demur." At another time, Lincoln remarked to Brooks that: he was Halleck's friend because nobody else was. —*Brooks-5, 43, 131. {C}*

14. *To a man who wanted a pass to Richmond:*

My dear sir, I would be most happy to oblige you if my passes were respected; but the fact is I have within the last two years given passes to more than 250,000 men to go to Richmond, and not one of them has got there yet in any legitimate way. —*Dispatch of May 2 in the Sacramento* Union, *May 27, 1863. {D}*

It is not clear whether Brooks heard this remark or merely read about it in the Washington Chronicle, *where it was reported on May 2 without identification of an auditor.*

15. *When Lincoln received word of Hooker's defeat at Chancellorsville in early May 1863, he exclaimed:*

What will the country say? Oh, what will the country say? —*Brooks-3, 674. {C}*

16. *Going with Brooks to Halleck's headquarters one evening in the spring of 1863, Lincoln carried a heavy walking stick, explaining:*

Mother has got a notion into her head that I shall be assassinated, and to please her I take a cane when I go over to the War Department at nights—when I don't forget it.

Later, on the way back to the White House, he said: I long ago made up my mind that if anybody wants to kill me, he will do it. If I wore a shirt of mail and kept myself surrounded by a bodyguard, it would be all the same. There are a thousand ways of getting at a man if it is desirable that he should be killed. Besides, in this case, it seems to me, the man who would come after me would be just as objectionable to my enemies—if I have any. —*Brooks-3, 674.* {C}

Another version, in Brooks-5, sets the conversation in early summer.

17. *On June 2, 1863, just as Lee was about to make the first moves in his invasion of the North, Brooks asked Lincoln about the possibility of a Confederate offensive, and he replied:*

that all indications were that there would be nothing of the sort and that an advance by the rebels could not possibly take place so as to place them on this side of the Rappahannock, unless Hooker was very much mistaken and was to be again outgeneraled. —*Dispatch of July 4 in the Sacramento* Union, *July 28, 1863.* {D}

This would be more credible if it had been written a month earlier.

18. *Lincoln is quoted as declaring in July 1863 that:*

the changes and promotions in the Army of the Potomac cost him more anxiety than the campaigns.

Also that: the ratio of men to generals in that army is now just 800 men to each general.

And that if Meade resigns, he, the President: will have a hole for which he has no peg. —*Dispatch of July 22 in the Sacramento* Union, *August 13, 1863.* {D}

It is not clear that Brooks himself heard these remarks.

19. *In the aftermath of the battle of Gettysburg, Lincoln expressed to Brooks his deep fear that:*

something would happen to prevent that annihilation of Lee's Army, which, as he thought, was then certainly within the bounds of possibility. —*Brooks-5, 91–92.* {C}

20. *Refusing to provide the Associated Press in advance with the text of his important letter of August 26, 1863, to James C. Conkling, Lincoln said that:*

though solemn promises not to publish had repeatedly been given, he had found the practice of furnishing advance copies to newspapers to be a source of endless mischief. —*Dispatch of October 2 in the Sacramento* Union, *October 29, 1863.* {D}

It is doubtful that Brooks was an auditor of this statement. In spite of all precautions, the New York Post *printed the letter before the time of its public reading in Illinois, and Lincoln, according to Brooks's later recollection, exclaimed that he was "mad enough to cry." —Brooks-5, 66.*

21. *On Sunday, November 14, 1863, Lincoln showed Brooks an advance printed copy of Edward Everett's address to be delivered on the 19th at Gettysburg. He said:*

It was very kind in Mr. Everett to send me this. I suppose he was afraid I should say something that he wanted to say. He needn't have been alarmed. My speech isn't long.

When Brooks asked whether it was written: Well, no, it is not exactly written. It is not finished, anyway. I have written it over, two or three times, and I shall have to give it another lick before I am satisfied. But it is short, short, short. —*Brooks-3, 565. {C}*

In Brooks-5, 253, Lincoln quotes Daniel Webster: "Solid men of Boston, make no long orations."

22. *Brooks recalled that one evening after seeing Edwin Booth in* The Merchant of Venice, *Lincoln remarked:*

It was a good performance, but I had a thousand times rather read it at home, if it were not for Booth's playing. A farce, or a comedy, is best played; a tragedy is best read at home. —*Brooks-3, 675. {D}*

According to Brooks, the two men attended the play at Ford's Theatre, sitting by themselves in a box directly below the one in which the assassination later took place; but according to a contemporary newspaper report, Lincoln saw Booth as Shylock on February 26, 1864, in his regular private box at Grover's Theatre, and there was no mention of his being accompanied by Brooks.[45]

23. *Respecting the Proclamation of Amnesty and Reconstruction, issued December 8, 1863, Lincoln is reported by Brooks as declaring soon thereafter that:*

if any construction can be placed upon his late proclamation so as to include persons who have been convicted of piracy or sedition by the courts, he will issue a supplemental proclamation disallowing such a construction.

A United States district judge in California nevertheless did rule that the proclamation applied to such a case in his court, and Lincoln, when he learned of it, indignantly remarked that: he would naturally expect that a judge, while placing his own construction upon the law, as given in the amnesty proclamation, might have had at least grace enough to place some weight or consideration upon the evident intentions of the framer of the proclamation. He wondered how a man with a thimbleful of brains could have so stretched that proclamation as to cover the case of a pirate, seized upon the coast of California, where no war or rebellion has ever existed. —*Dispatches of December 16, 1863, and March 16, 1864, in the Sacramento* Union, *January 20, April 16, 1864.*[46] {B}

24. *After his renomination by the Republican national convention at Baltimore on June 8, 1864, with Andrew Johnson as his running mate, Lincoln acknowledged to Brooks that he would have been gratified if Hannibal Hamlin could have been kept on the ticket. But then he added:*

Some of our folks had expressed the opinion that it would be wise to take a War Democrat as candidate for vice president, and that, if possible, a border-state man should be the nominee. . . . Andy Johnson, I think, is a good man. —*Brooks-5, 142.* {C}

25. *In the second week of June 1864, at a time when Grant was trying unsuccessfully to take Petersburg, Lincoln said to Brooks:*

I wish when you write and speak to the people you would do all you can to correct the impression that the war in Virginia will end right off victoriously. To me the most trying thing in all of this war is that the people are too sanguine; they expect too much at once. I declare to you, sir, that we are today further ahead than I thought one year and a half ago we should be, and yet there are aplenty of people who believe that the war is about to be substantially closed. As God is my judge I shall be satisfied if we are over with the fight in Virginia within a year. I hope we shall be "happily disappointed," as the saying is, but I am afraid not—I am afraid not. — *Dispatch of June 14 in the Sacramento* Union, *July 9, 1864.* {C}

Brooks wrote this dispatch a number of days after the conversation.[47] *Thirty years later, in Brooks-5, 138, he asserted that he immediately set Lincoln's words down on paper and that Lincoln read and approved what he had written, suggesting just one verbal change.*

26. *In the evening of July 1, 1864, Lincoln narrated the series of events precipitated by Chase's resignation the day before. Then he said to Brooks:*

When I finally struck the name of Fessenden as Governor Chase's successor, I felt as if the Lord hadn't forsaken me yet. —*Brooks-5, 122.* {C}

27. *Once or twice, says Brooks, Lincoln spoke of the religious change that had come upon him in the presidency. He declared that:*

after he went to the White House he kept up the habit of daily prayer. Sometimes it was only ten words, but those ten words he had. —*Brooks to James A. Reed, December 31, 1872, in Reed (1873), 340.* {C}

28. *Concerning the Wade-Davis bill, which he pocket vetoed on July 4, 1864, Lincoln said:*

that he had somewhere read of a robber tyrant who had built an iron bedstead on which he compelled his victims to lie. If the captive was too short to fill the bedstead, he was stretched by main force until he was long enough; and if he was too long, he was chopped off to fit the bedstead. This was the sort of reconstruction which the Wade-Davis plan contemplated. If any state coming back into federal relations did not fit the Wade-Davis bedstead, so much the worse for the state. —*Brooks-5, 156–57.* {C}

29. *After the raid of Jubal Early in July 1864, Lincoln said that:*

General Halleck's manifest desire to avoid taking any responsibility without the immediate sanction of General Grant was the main reason why the rebels, having threatened Washington and sacked the peaceful farms and villages of Maryland, got off scatheless. —*Brooks-5, 162.* {C}

30. *A day or two after the issuance of the Wade-Davis manifesto on August 5, 1864, Lincoln spoke lamentingly of the hostility that one of its authors, Maryland congressman Henry Winter Davis, had persistently displayed toward him:*

To be wounded in the house of one's friends is perhaps the most grievous affliction that can befall a man. I have tried my best to meet the wishes of this man and to do my whole duty by the country.

When Brooks remarked that it sometimes seemed as though Davis was mad, Lincoln replied: I have heard that there was insanity in his family; perhaps we might allow the plea in this case. —*Brooks-5, 156.* {C}

The last sentence, somewhat differently phrased and with Davis not identified, is in Brooks-2, 225.

31. *When the Democratic national convention of 1864 was about to begin in Chicago, Lincoln said:*

That convention must put a war man on a peace platform, or a peace man on a war platform, I don't care much which. —*Brooks-3, 679.* {C}

The wording is somewhat different in Brooks-5, 140, 164.

32. *Clement L. Vallandigham, who had been convicted by a military commission and banished from the country by Lincoln's order, returned to Ohio in June 1864. When Brooks mentioned his name about two months later, Lincoln said solemnly:*

What! has Vallandigham got back? . . . Dear me! I supposed he was in a foreign land. Anyhow, I hope I do not know that he is in the United States; and I shall not, unless he says or does something to draw attention to him. —*Brooks-5, 110.* {C}

According to Brooks, Lincoln then told him of a recent conversation with Fernando Wood on the subject, during the course of which, he, Lincoln, had said:

I don't believe that Vallandigham has returned; I never can believe it, and I never shall believe it until he forces himself offensively upon the public attention and upon my attention; then we shall have to deal with him. So long as he behaves himself decently he is as effectually in disguise as a slovenly man who went to a masquerade party with a clean face. —*Dispatch of August 24 in the Sacramento* Union, *October 1, 1864. {C}*

Brooks later asserted that Lincoln showed him "rough notes" of the Wood interview, but they have not come to light.

33. *Said Lincoln, commenting on Maryland's recent adoption of a new constitution that prohibited slavery:*

I had rather have Maryland upon that issue than have a state twice its size upon the presidential issue; it cleans up a piece of ground. —*Dispatch of October 19 in the Sacramento* Union, *November 25, 1864. {A}*

34. *A delegation of Jews from several cities called on Lincoln to assure him of their support in the approaching election. He thanked them and then added that:*

he was only the exponent of the wishes and opinions of a portion of the loyal states, and while he was president he had no right to seek personal political favors at the hands of any, but he believed that the support of the principles of the so-called Union party of the country, whoever might now be its nominee, was a more effectual way of putting down this rebellion than the contrary course. —*Ibid.*[48] *{B}*

35. *When Brooks told how a California politician had been coerced into telling the truth without knowing it, Lincoln said that:*

it reminded him of a black barber in Illinois, notorious for lying, who once heard some of his customers admiring the planet Jupiter rising in the evening sky. "Sho! I've seen dat star afore. I seen him way down in Georgy." Like your friend [Lincoln concluded], he told the truth, but he thought he was lying. —*Dispatch of October 24 in the Sacramento* Union, *November 23, 1864. {B}*

36. *Of his storytelling Lincoln once said:*

I do generally remember a good story when I hear it, but I never did invent anything original; I am only a retail dealer. —*Brooks-2, 228. {C}*

Brooks-3, 679, and Brooks-5, 255–56, have a different wording.

37. *Late one night, on being told by Brooks that James H. Hackett was waiting in the anteroom, Lincoln said:*

Oh, I can't see him; I can't see him. I was in hopes he had gone away. Now, this just illustrates the difficulty of having pleasant friends and acquaintances in this place. You know how I liked Hackett as an actor and how I wrote to tell him so. He sent me that book, and there I thought the matter would end. He is a master of his place in the profession, I suppose, and well fixed in it. But just because we had a little friendly correspondence, such as any two men might have, he wants something. What do you suppose he wants? Well, he wants to be consul to London. Oh, dear! — *Brooks-3, 675.* {C}

In Brooks-5, 254, Lincoln is quoted as adding that: it seemed impossible for him to have any close relations with people in Washington without finding that the acquaintance thus formed generally ended with an application for office.[49] {C}

38. *Concerning the threat of assassination, Lincoln once said in a sportive way that:*

he would not like to face death suddenly. . . . he thought himself a great coward physically, and was sure that he should make a poor soldier, for, unless there was something in the excitement of a battle, he was sure that he would drop his gun and run at the first symptom of danger.

He added: Moral cowardice is something which I think I never had. — *Brooks-2, 224.* {C}

39. *Lincoln, according to Brooks, once said:*

I have been driven many times upon my knees by the overwhelming conviction that I had nowhere else to go. My own wisdom and that of all about me seemed insufficient for that day. — *Brooks-2, 226.* {D}

The date and context of this remark are not specified, and it is not clear that Brooks was himself the auditor.

40. *Speaking of the ceaseless procession of importunate visitors to the White House, Lincoln said:*

I suppose I ought not to blame the aggregate, for each abstract man or woman thinks his or her case a peculiar one and must be attended to, though all others be left out; but I can see this thing growing every day.

And at another time: I sometimes fancy that every one of the numerous grist ground through here daily, from a senator seeking a war with France down to a poor woman after a place in the Treasury Department, darted at me with thumb and finger, picked out their especial piece of my vitality, and carried it off. When I get through with such a day's work there is only one word which can express my condition, and that is **flabbiness.** — *Brooks-2, 226-27.* {D}

Brooks may have heard these remarks from Lincoln, but date, context, and auditor are not specified.

41. *On October 24, 1864, greeting a regiment of New Yorkers on their way to the front, Lincoln made a little speech in which:*

he thanked them on behalf of the country for the service which they proposed to render the nation by fighting our battles, and he was glad to say that it would appear that the soldiers voted about right as well as fought right, though he supposed that many might differ with him as to their voting right, but that was his private opinion.

He added that: though it was important that there should be men at home to vote and to look after the soldiers' base of supplies, we could get along without them; but the soldiers we cannot get along without. *—Dispatch of October 24 [26?] in the Sacramento* Union, *November 23, 1864.*[50] *{B}*

42. *On November 1, 1864, black people of the District of Columbia held a celebration of emancipation in Maryland, and it ended with a procession to the White House. In response to repeated cheers, Lincoln went out and spoke to the crowd as follows:*

It is no secret that I have wished, and still do wish, mankind everywhere to be free. [Great cheering and cries of "God bless Abraham Lincoln."] And in the state of Maryland how great an advance has been made in this direction! It is difficult to realize that in that state, where human slavery has existed for ages, ever since a period long before any here were born—by the action of her own citizens—the soil is made forever free. [Loud and long cheering.] I have no feeling of triumph over those who were opposed to this measure and who voted against it, but I do believe that it will result in good to the white race as well as to those who have been made free by this act of emancipation, and I hope that the time will soon come when all will see that the perpetuation of freedom for all in Maryland is best for the interests of all, though some may thereby be made to suffer temporary pecuniary loss. And I hope that you, colored people, who have been emancipated, will use this great boon which has been given you to improve yourselves, both morally and intellectually; and now, good night. *— Dispatch of November 2 in the Sacramento* Union, *December 2, 1864. {A}*

This speech, though apparently not reported by any other journalist, probably should have been included in the Collected Works.[51]

43. *On election day, November 8, 1864, Lincoln did not conceal his anxiety, saying:*

I am just enough of a politician to know that there was not much doubt about the result of the Baltimore convention, but about this thing I am far from being certain; I wish I were certain. *—Dispatch of November 11 in the Sacramento* Union, *December 10, 1864. {A}*

44. *At about midnight, when it was more or less obvious that he had been re-elected, Lincoln said:*

that he was glad to be relieved of all suspense, and that he was grateful that the verdict of the people was likely to be so full, clear, and unmistakable that there could be no dispute. —*Brooks-5, 197. {C}*

45. *On November 9, he said:*

Being only mortal, after all, I should have been a little mortified if I had been beaten in this canvass before the people; but that sting would have been more than compensated by the thought that the people had notified me that all my official responsibilities were soon to be lifted off my back. —*Brooks-2, 226. {C}*

46. *On the same day, he said:*

I should be the veriest shallow and self-conceited blockhead upon the footstool if, in my discharge of the duties which are put upon me in this place, I should hope to get along without the wisdom which comes from God and not from men. —*Dispatch of November 11 in Sacramento* Union, *December 10, 1864. {A}*

The wording is the same in Brooks-5, 200, but substantially different in Brooks-2, 226.

47. *Lincoln refused to sign a telegram informing Anson G. Henry in Oregon of his victory in the election. He said to Brooks:*

I don't think it would look well for a message from me to go traveling around the country blowing my own horn. You sign the message and I will send it. —*Brooks-7, 403 (1888). {C}*

48. *On the night after his re-election, according to Brooks, Lincoln came into the White House parlor with "a roll of manuscript in his hand." He had written out a speech for an expected serenade and said regarding it:*

I know what you are thinking about; but there's no claptrap about me, and I am free to say that in the excitement of the moment I am sure to say something which I am sorry for when I see it in print; so I have it here in black and white, and there are no mistakes made. People attach too much importance to what I say anyhow. —*Brooks-2, 229-30. {D}*

*The speech in question was in fact delivered on November 10, **two** nights after the election. When Brooks repeated the story in later writings, he made what appears to be a mistake by changing the occasion to the last public speech of Lincoln's life, April 11, 1865.[52] Again the President was described as coming into the parlor with "a roll of manuscript in his hand," and Brooks quoted him as saying:* I know what you are thinking about. You think it mighty queer that an old stump-speaker like myself should not be able to address a crowd like this outside without a written speech. But you must remember I am, in a certain way, talking to the country, and I have to be mighty careful. Now, the last time I made an offhand speech, in answer to a serenade, I used the phrase, as applied to the rebels, "turned tail and ran." Some very nice Boston folks, I am grieved to hear, were very much outraged by that phrase, which they thought improper. So I resolved to make no more impromptu speeches if I could help it. —*Brooks-3, 567; Brooks-5, 226-27. {D}*

49. *Shortly after the election of 1864, Lincoln related an incident that had occurred four years earlier:*

It was just after my election in 1860, when the news had been coming in thick and fast all day, and there had been a great "Hurrah, boys!" so that I was well tired out, and went home to rest, throwing myself down on a lounge in my chamber. Opposite where I lay was a bureau, with a swinging-glass upon it, and, looking in that glass, I saw myself reflected, nearly at full length; but my face, I noticed, had **two** separate and distinct images, the tip of the nose of one being about three inches from the tip of the other. I was a little bothered, perhaps startled, and got up and looked in the glass, but the illusion vanished. On lying down again I saw it a second time—plainer, if possible, than before; and then I noticed that one of the faces was a little paler, say five shades, than the other. I got up and the thing melted away, and I went off and, in the excitement of the hour, forgot all about it—nearly, but not quite, for the thing would once in a while come up, and give me a little pang, as though something uncomfortable had happened. When I went home I told my wife about it, and a few days after, I tried the experiment again, when, sure enough, the thing came again; but I never succeeded in bringing the ghost back after that, though I once tried very industriously to show it to my wife, who was worried about it somewhat. She thought it was "a sign" that I was to be elected to a second term of office, and that the paleness of one of the faces was an omen that I should not see life through the last term. —*Brooks-2, 224-25. {C}*

Brooks enclosed the entire passage in quotation marks, although he acknowledged that he was merely trying to write "as nearly as possible" in Lincoln's own words. In a later account, Brooks asserted that when he discussed the incident with Mrs. Lincoln, she had expressed surprise that her husband was willing to talk about it with anyone. Yet John Hay, according to Brooks, confirmed having heard the story from Lincoln; Francis B. Carpenter (q.v.) described how he and Hay together heard Lincoln tell the story; and Ward Hill Lamon (q.v.) also claimed to have heard the story from Lincoln. The Brooks, Carpenter, and Lamon versions are discrepant in a number of ways.[53] Hay, it should be noted, did not mention the incident in his diary.

50. *In early December 1864, concerning the appropriateness of a semicolon in a paragraph that he had written for publication:*

With educated people, I suppose, punctuation is a matter of rule; with me it is a matter of feeling. But I must say that I have a great respect for the semicolon; it's a very useful little chap. —*Brooks-3, 566.* {C}

51. *Of a spectacular Union cavalry raid that did not achieve its primary purpose, Lincoln remarked:*

That was good circus-riding; it will do to fill a column in the newspapers, but I don't see that it has brought anything else to pass. —*Brooks-2, 227.* {D}

Date, circumstance, and auditor are unspecified.

52. *According to Brooks, Lincoln "often said" that:*

the worst feature about newspapers was that they were so sure to be "ahead of the hounds," outrunning events and exciting expectations which were sure to be disappointed. —*Brooks-2, 227–28.* {D}

*One wonders just **how** often, in Brooks's memory, Lincoln repeated himself on this subject and whether he varied his phrasing in doing so.*

53. *Once Lincoln declared that:*

the keenest blow of all the war was at an early stage, when the disaster of Ball's Bluff and the death of his beloved Baker smote upon him like a whirlwind from a desert. —*Brooks-2, 228.* {D}

It is not clear that Brooks himself heard Lincoln make this remark.

54. *Respecting objections to his conferring an appointment on a former opponent:*

Nobody will deny that he is a first-rate man for the place, and I am bound to see that his opposition to me personally shall not interfere with my giving the people a good officer. —*Brooks-2, 228.* {D}

The date, person in question, and auditor are all unspecified.

55. *One evening when Lincoln recited a long passage from the work of Petroleum V. Nasby, a visitor expressed surprise that he should commit such material to memory, and he replied:*

Oh, I don't. If I like a thing, it just sticks after once reading it or hearing it. —*Brooks-3, 564.* {C}

56. *Brooks quotes Lincoln as remarking cheerfully on one occasion:*

I am very sure that if I do not go away from here a wiser man, I shall go away a better man for having learned here what a very poor sort of a man I am. —*Brooks-2, 226.* {D}

The date, context, and auditor are not specified.

57. *Concerning his inner life, Lincoln is quoted as declaring that:*

he did not remember any precise time when he passed through any special change of purpose or of heart; but he would say that his own election to office, and the crisis immediately following, influentially determined him in what he called "a process of crystallization," then going on in his mind. — *Brooks-2, 226. {D}*

The date, context, and auditor are not specified.

58. *When asked why he did not have a letter-book and copying-press, Lincoln said:*

A letter-book might be easily carried off, but that stock of filed letters would be a back-load. — *Brooks-2, 229. {C}*

59. *When Brooks once mentioned his habit of not capitalizing days of the week, Lincoln laughed and said that:*

when he was a very young man, somebody persuaded him that that was the proper thing to do, and he pursued the practice for a short time; and now, when he did not intend to do it, he unconsciously slid into the old trick without noticing it. — *Brooks-6, 107 (1909). {C}*

60. *In a discussion of correspondence, Lincoln said that:*

he read with great regularity the letters of an old friend who lived on the Pacific coast until he received a letter of **seventy pages** of letter paper, when he broke down and never read another. — *Brooks-2, 229. {D}*

There is no such letter in Lincoln's file of correspondence.

61. *In a cynical mood one day, Lincoln said:*

Sitting here, where all the avenues to public patronage seem to come together in a knot, it does seem to me that our people are fast approaching the point where it can be said that seven-eighths of them were trying to find how to live at the expense of the other eighth. — *Brooks-2, 226. {D}*

The date, circumstance, and auditor are left unspecified.

62. *According to Brooks, Lincoln "often talked" with him about possibly moving to California after his presidency. He said that:*

he thought that country would afford better opportunities for his two boys than any of the older states. — *Brooks-5, 229. {C}*

63. *At some time between the death of Roger B. Taney on October 12, 1864, and the appointment of his successor on December 6, Lincoln said to Brooks:*

I have been all day, and yesterday and the day before, besieged by messages from my friends all over the country, as if there were a determination to put up the bars between Governor Chase and myself. But I shall nominate him for chief justice, nevertheless. — *Brooks-5, 122. {C}*

In Brooks-7, 436, Lincoln's concluding sentence is: Now, I know meaner things than any of those men can tell me, but I am going to nominate him. {D}

64. *After Edward Everett's death on January 15, 1865, Lincoln said to Brooks:*

Now, do you know, I think Edward Everett was very much overrated. He hasn't left any enduring monument. But there was one speech in which, addressing a statue of John Adams and a picture of Washington, in Faneuil Hall, Boston, he apostrophized them and said, "Teach us the love of liberty protected by law!" That was very fine, it seems to me. Still, it was only a good idea, introduced by noble language.[54] —*Brooks-3, 678.* {C}

65. *In a talk with Louis Agassiz the same day, Lincoln mentioned his own lecture on inventions and said:*

I think I can show, at least, in a fanciful way, that all the modern inventions were known centuries ago. —*Brooks-5, 269.* {C}

During the discussion, Lincoln said nothing about science but asked many questions about how Agassiz studied, how he prepared and delivered his lectures, and how different he found audiences throughout the country. When Brooks afterwards commented on this line of interrogation, Lincoln replied: Why, what we got from him isn't printed in the books; the other things are. — *Brooks-2, 224.* {C}

66. *Speaking of a member of his cabinet, Lincoln once quoted a saying of Sydney Smith that:*

"it required a surgical operation to get a joke into his head." —*Brooks-2, 229.* {D}

Neither the person in question nor the auditor is specified.

67. *When told that some newspapers had credited him with the authorship of his favorite poem, "Mortality," Lincoln said:*

I should not care much for the reputation of having written that, but would be glad if I could compose music as fit to convey the sentiment as the words now do. —*Brooks-2, 229.* {D}

It is not clear that Brooks himself was the auditor of these words. In 1846, Lincoln expressed a different feeling: "I would give all I am worth, and go in debt, to be able to write so fine a piece as I think that is."[55]

68. *As Lincoln was taking the oath of office on March 4, 1864, the sun broke through the clouds. He said to Brooks the next day that:*

he was just superstitious enough to consider it a happy omen. —*Brooks-5, 74.* {C}

69. *Concerning applicants for federal jobs, Lincoln said that he did not see why:*

because a man has been defeated for renomination or re-election for Congress, he should be returned on his [Lincoln's] hands, like a lame duck, to be nursed into something else. —*Dispatch of March 22 in Sacramento* Union, *April 19, 1865.* {B}

70. *Speaking of Tad:*

Let him run; there's time enough yet for him to learn his letters and get pokey. Bob was just such a little rascal, and now he is a very decent boy. —*Brooks-5, 249.* {C}

71. *A western senator who had failed to win re-election introduced his successor to the President. After the exchange of greetings, Lincoln said:*

I hate to have old friends like Senator W[ilkinson] go away. And another thing, I usually find that a senator or representative out of business is a sort of lame duck. He has to be provided for.

Later, Lincoln said to Brooks: You thought I was almost rude to Senator W[ilkinson] the other day. Well, now he wants Commissioner Dole's place.[56] —*Brooks-3, 679.* {C}

72. *In answer to criticisms of his amnesty policy:*

How many more lives of our citizen soldiers are the people willing to give up to insure the death penalty to Davis and his immediate coadjutors? —*Dispatch of April 1 in Sacramento* Union, *May 8, 1865.* {D}

In this instance, too, Brooks is not clearly the auditor.

73. *Twice on April 10, in response to crowds celebrating Lee's surrender at Appomattox, Lincoln promised to speak more formally the following evening. He closed his first response with a request for the band to play "Dixie," suggesting that the song had become a "lawful prize."*[57] *During the performance, he said to Brooks:*

I just feel like marching, always, when that tune is played. —*Brooks to Edward Everett Hale, November 29, 1865, Lincoln Collection-Brown.* {C}

74. *Immediately afterward, thinking of what he would say the following day, Lincoln told Brooks:*

that he should not make a jubilant speech at the celebration of the victories. . . . that the political situation was now very critical. He wanted to give his views on reconstruction as early and as frequently as possible. —*Brooks letter to the editor,* Scribners Monthly, *15 (April 1878): 885.*[58] {C}

Many years later, Brooks also quoted Lincoln as remarking at this time that: a speech in reply to a serenade was the most difficult job that he undertook in the line of speechmaking. For [he continued] while I am glad to congratulate the people on our victories, I do not like even to seem to glorify ourselves at the expense of a fallen foe. And besides, after you have said you are glad, what more is there to say? — *Brooks-7, 389.* {D}

75. *Brooks tells of holding a candle for Lincoln as the latter stood at a White House window and read his last public speech on April 11, 1865. Afterwards, he said to Brooks:*

That was a pretty fair speech, I think, but you threw some light on it. — *Brooks-3, 567.* {C}

76. *According to Brooks, writing just two days after the assassination, he and Schuyler Colfax were at the White House when the Lincolns left for Ford's Theatre shortly after 8:00 P.M. on April 14, 1865, and the President's last words as he went out to the carriage were:*

Grant thinks that we can reduce the cost of the army establishment at least a half million a day, which, with the reduction of expenditures of the navy, will soon bring down our national debt to something like decent proportions, and bring our national paper up to a par, or nearly so, with gold; at least so they think. — *Dispatch of April 16 in Sacramento* Union, *May 17, 1865.* {E}

This passage appears to have been a journalist's invention. Colfax, in his fairly detailed description of Lincoln's last half-hour in the White House, made no mention of Brooks. Furthermore, Brooks himself, in a later account, told of visiting Lincoln **late in the afternoon** *of April 14 and of meeting Colfax on his way home. Then he added: "The evening being inclement, I stayed within doors to nurse a violent cold with which I was afflicted."*[59]

WILLIAM BROSS (1813–1890)   *Chicago journalist who was elected lieutenant-governor of Illinois in 1864.*

　　1. *At Freeport on August 27, 1858, as he rose to reply to Douglas, Lincoln threw his "immense shawl" into the lap of another man sitting on the platform and said:*

There, Father Brewster, hold my clothes while I stone Stephen. — *Bross to John G. Nicolay, December 31, 1886, Nicolay Papers.* {D}

It was a damp, chilly day in Freeport, but other accounts of the debate do not mention Lincoln's using a shawl, and Bross seems to have been under the mistaken impression that Douglas led off the speaking on that occasion.

JOHN BROUGH (1811–1865)   *Ohio journalist and Democratic politician, elected governor in 1863 on the Union ticket.*

　　1. *Talking with Brough on June 29, 1864, the day that Chase submitted his resignation as secretary of the treasury, Lincoln said:*

This is the third time he has thrown this at me, and I do not think I am called on to continue to beg him to take it back, especially when the country would not go to destruction in consequence. —*Memorandum dictated by Brough, July 12, 1864, Smith Papers, volume 20. {C}*

2. *When Brough proposed to mediate his dispute with Chase, the President replied:*

I know you doctored the matter up once, but on the whole, Brough, I reckon you had better let it alone this time. —*Ibid. {C}*

3. *Concerning his letter written to Chase the day before, in which he explained his stand on New York patronage politics, Lincoln asked:*

Don't you think I had him? —*Ibid.*[60] *{C}*

BENJAMIN GRATZ BROWN (1826–1885)   *A leader of the radical wing of the Republican party in Missouri, Brown was elected to the United States Senate in 1863.*

1. *Speaking of proposed legislation in aid of compensated emancipation in Missouri, Lincoln told Brown on December 11, 1863, that:*

he would put his hand in and see if he could not push the compensation bill through.[61]

With reference to the commanding general in Missouri, John M. Schofield, whom the Radicals disliked, he expressed an inclination: to order Schofield elsewhere and substitute in his place Rosecrans. —*Brown to Norman B. Judd, December 11, 1863, Lincoln Collection-Brown. {B}*

CHRISTOPHER C. BROWN (1834–1904)   *Springfield attorney who in October 1859 married the daughter of John T. Stuart, Lincoln's first law partner.*

1. *On the morning after the wedding, Lincoln posed a riddle:*

Brown, why is a woman like a barrel?

Answer: You have to raise the hoops before you put the head in. —*Undated statement of Brown recorded by Herndon (11:2980–81), Herndon-Weik Collection. {C}*

2. *Replying to an eastern newspaper proprietor who wanted to propose his name as a candidate for president or vice president:*

Well, my friend, I am much obliged to you. I guess either position is big and high enough for me.[62] —*Ibid. {C}*

GEORGE W. BROWN (1812–1890)   *Mayor of Baltimore at the beginning of the Civil War. Arrested in September 1861, Brown was held in federal prisons for fourteen and one-half months. He later served many years on the supreme court of Maryland.*

1. *At a conference with Brown and three companions on April 21, 1861, Lincoln spoke of:*

the absolute, irresistible necessity of having a transit through the state for such troops as might be necessary for the protection of the federal capital.

He declared that: the protection of Washington was the sole object of concentrating troops there, . . . none of the troops brought through Maryland were intended for any purposes hostile to the state, or aggressive as against the southern states. Being now unable to bring them up the Potomac in security, the government must either bring them through Maryland or abandon the capital.

After General Scott had outlined two alternative routes bypassing the center of the city, Lincoln told Brown that: no more troops should be ordered through Baltimore if they were permitted to go uninterrupted by either of the other routes suggested.[63]

The Brown delegation returned to the White House later the same day after receiving word that a contingent of Union troops was approaching Baltimore. Lincoln protested that: he had no idea they would be there today.

He immediately made arrangements with General Scott to have them turned back, saying that he did so: lest there should be the slightest suspicion of bad faith on his part in summoning the Mayor to Washington, and allowing troops to march on the city during his absence. —*Brown's statement dated April 21, in the* National Intelligencer *(Washington), April 23, 1861; reprinted in Moore F, I, 123-24.*[64] *{B}*

At one point during the first interview, according to a later account by Brown, he declared that the people of Maryland regarded the presidential proclamation calling for 75,000 volunteers as an act of war on the South and a violation of its constitutional rights. Lincoln sprang to his feet and exclaimed: Mr. Brown, I am not a learned man! I am not a learned man!

He went on to say: that his proclamation had not been correctly understood; that he had no intention of bringing on war, but that his purpose was to defend the capital, which was in danger of being bombarded from the heights across the Potomac. —*Brown, 74 (1887). {C}*

In his diary, John Hay made note of these interviews from a different perspective, referring to Brown and his companions as the "whining traitors from Baltimore."[65]

ROBERT S. BROWN (Born 1850) *Washington resident and property-owner, a former slave whose father Peter Brown was the White House butler during the Civil War years.*

1. *When Robert, in response to a question, acknowledged that he was always hungry, Lincoln said:*

Well, that's a terrible state for a boy to be in. We'll have to see about that! . . .
Peter, I want you to feed this boy. He looks hungry and admits it. Fill up
his legs too; if he is like my boys, his legs are hollow. — *Brown's statement
in the Washington* Star, *February 12, 1928. {C}*

ROBERT H. BROWNE (1835–?) *A schoolboy and office boy in Bloomington, Illinois, during the early 1850s.*

1. *Speaking of slavery one evening, Lincoln said to Browne:*

I saw it all myself when I was only a little older than you are now, and the
horrid pictures are in my mind yet. — *Browne RH, I, 506 (1901). {C}*

2. *In 1852, Lincoln remarked:*

Robert, the less I support that very obnoxious fugitive-slave law, I think, is
all the better for me. I have imagined that I am to be something of a leader
against slavery encroachments, and that I consider as striking and positive
an example as I need to begin with. — *517. {D}*

*Lincoln did not react strongly to the Fugitive Slave Act of 1850 and did not
cast himself as an antislavery leader until after the enactment of the Kansas-
Nebraska bill in 1854.*

3. *Browne recalled Lincoln's saying in 1854 (presumably early in the year):*

The slavery question often bothered me as far back as 1836–40. I was
troubled and grieved over it; but after the annexation of Texas I gave it up,
believing as I now do, that God will settle it, and settle it right, and that he
will, in some inscrutable way, restrict the spread of so great an evil; but for
the present it is our duty to wait. — *285. {C}*

*This statement, which more or less contradicts the one preceding, is not out of
line with Lincoln's passive attitude toward the slavery question on the eve of
the Kansas-Nebraska controversy.*

ORVILLE H. BROWNING (1806–1881) *Lincoln's Illinois friend and White
House confidant was briefly United States senator (1861–63) and later secretary
of the interior under Andrew Johnson. Militantly Republican at the beginning of
the war, he turned conservative as public policy moved toward emancipation.*

1. *The entry in Browning's diary for July 3, 1861, is a Lincoln document of
critical importance. The President, he wrote, told him:*

that the very first thing placed in his hands after his inauguration was a letter
from Major Anderson announcing the impossibility of defending or relieving Sumter; that he called the cabinet together and consulted General Scott;
that Scott concurred with Anderson, and the cabinet, with the exception
of himself and Postmaster General Blair, were for evacuating the fort; and
that all the troubles and anxieties of his life had not equaled those which
intervened between this time and the fall of Sumter. He himself conceived

the idea and proposed sending supplies without an attempt to reinforce, giving notice of the fact to Governor Pickens of South Carolina. The plan succeeded. They attacked Sumter. It fell and thus did more service than it otherwise could. — *Browning, I, 476. {B}*

John G. Nicolay (q.v.) was apparently present for at least the first part of this discussion.

2. *On July 28, 1861, when Browning asked whether there was any danger that the outbreak of civil war would plunge the United States into trouble with foreign powers, Lincoln acknowledged that there was. He said:*

that in his opinion, they were determined to have the cotton crop as soon as it matured; that our coast was so extensive that we could not make the blockade of all the ports effectual; and that England was now assuming the ground that a nation had no right, whilst a portion of its citizens were in revolt, to close its port or any of them against foreign nations; that we had passed a law at this session of Congress authorizing him, in his discretion, to close our ports, but if he asserted the right of closing such as we could not blockade, he had no doubt it would result in foreign war; and that under the circumstances, we had better increase the navy as fast as we could and blockade such ports as our force would enable us to and say nothing about the rest. — *Browning, I, 489. {B}*

3. *Browning later recalled saying to Lincoln in the summer or fall of 1861 that there could be no hope for the blessing of God on the efforts of the Union armies until a decisive blow was struck against slavery. Lincoln replied:*

Browning, suppose God is against us in our view on the subject of slavery in this country and our method of dealing with it. — *John G. Nicolay interview with Browning, June 17, 1875, Hay Collection-Brown. {C}*

4. *By December 1, 1861, Lincoln was already beginning to lay plans for emancipation. He talked of:*

paying Delaware, Maryland, Kentucky, and Missouri $500 apiece for all the Negroes they had according to the census of 1860, provided they would adopt a system of gradual emancipation which should work the extinction of slavery in twenty years . . . It would require only about one third of what was necessary to support the war for one year.

He agreed with Browning that: there should be connected with it a scheme of colonizing the blacks somewhere on the American continent. — *Browning, I, 512. {B}*

5. *After a dinner at the White House Christmas evening, Lincoln talked with Browning about the* Trent *crisis, telling him:*

that they had a cabinet meeting about British affairs today and had agreed not to divulge what had occurred, but that there would be no war with England; that whilst the cabinet was in session the French minister sent them a letter he had just received from his government saying that the European powers were against us on the question of international law and desired that we should settle the controversy amicably. Also, Sumner sent three letters which he had just received from England, one from Bright and two from Cobden, both of whom are our friends, and both urging a settlement, and both saying that the dispositions of the English are friendly—that England does not want war with us, and that if this trouble is settled they will not interfere in our domestic troubles, but leave us to deal with the rebellion as we think proper. —*Browning, I, 518-19. {B}*

6. *On January 12, 1862, setting forth a war strategy expounded more fully the next day in a letter to General Don Carlos Buell,*[66] *Lincoln said that he was thinking of taking the field himself, and he suggested several plans of operation:*
One was to threaten all their positions at the same time with superior force, and if they weakened one to strengthen another, seize and hold the one weakened. Another was to shell them out of their entrenchments with guns that would throw very large shell over two miles, the enemy having none of that size. —*Browning, I, 523. {B}*

7. *On April 2, 1862, at a time when the President's patience with McClellan was running out, Browning asked whether he still had confidence in the man's fidelity. Lincoln replied:*
that he had never had any reason to doubt it; that he [McClellan] had now gone to Fortress Monroe with his command, with orders to move on Richmond without delay; and that only on yesterday when McClellan came to take leave of him preparatory to marching, he shed tears when speaking of the cruel imputations upon his loyalty, and defending himself against them.
Lincoln added: that General Scott and all the leading military men around him had always assured him that McClellan possessed a very high order of military talent and that he did not think they could all be mistaken; yet he was not fully satisfied with his conduct of the war; that he was not sufficiently energetic and aggressive in his measures; that he had studied McClellan and taken his measure as well as he could; that he thought he had the capacity to make arrangements properly for a great conflict, but as the hour for action approached, he became nervous and oppressed with the responsibility and hesitated to meet the crisis, but that he had given him peremptory orders to move now, and he must do it. —*Browning, I, 537-38. {B}*

8. *Lincoln on April 14, 1862, received the bill abolishing slavery in the District of Columbia and expressed his partial dissatisfaction with it. He also revealed a personal reason for waiting two days before signing the measure. He said that:*

he would sign the bill, but would return it with a special message recommending a supplemental bill making savings in behalf of infants, etc., and also some other amendments.[67]

He said: that he regretted the bill had been passed in its present form; that it should have been for gradual emancipation; that now families would at once be deprived of cooks, stable boys, etc., and they of their protectors without any provision for them.

He said further: that he would not sign the bill before Wednesday; that old Governor Wickliffe had two family servants with him who were sickly and who would not be benefited by freedom, and wanted time to remove them, but could not get them out of the city until Wednesday; and that the Governor had come frankly to him and asked for time. —*Browning, I, 541.* {B}

9. *On April 25, 1862, after reading poems of Thomas Hood to Browning for over an hour, Lincoln said that:*

a crowd was buzzing about the door like bees, ready to pounce upon him as soon as I should take my departure and bring him back to a realization of the annoyances and harassments of his position. —*Browning, I, 542-43.* {B}

10. *On June 18, 1862, as the Peninsular campaign approached its climax, the President stated:*

that his opinion always had been that the great fight should have been at Manassas; that he had urged it upon McClellan that if the enemy left Manassas he would entrench at Yorktown, and we would have the same difficulties to encounter there; that McClellan was opposed to fighting at Manassas, and he [the President] then called a council of twelve generals and submitted his proposition for fighting at Manassas to them; and that eight of them decided against him, and four concurred with him, of whom Heintzelman was one. The majority being so great against him, he yielded, but subsequent events had satisfied him he was right. —*Browning, I, 552.* {B}

11. *On July 1, 1862, Lincoln read to Browning a paper, hastily drafted for presentation to the cabinet, in which he set forth his views on the war as it related to slavery:*

No Negroes necessarily taken and escaping during the war are ever to be returned to slavery. No inducements are to be held out to them to come into our lines; for they come now faster than we can provide for them and are becoming an embarrassment to the government. At present, none are to be armed. It would produce dangerous and fatal dissatisfaction in our army and do more injury than good. Congress has no power over slavery in the states, and so much of it as remains after the war is over will be in precisely the same condition that it was before the war began and must be left to the exclusive control of the states where it may exist. — *Browning, I, 555.* {B}

12. *Lincoln, according to his own account, spoke as follows on about July 4, 1862, to General Randolph B. Marcy, who had reportedly suggested that McClellan, after failing to take Richmond, might himself have to capitulate:*

General, I understand you have used the word "capitulate." That is a word not to be used in connection with our army. — *Browning, I, 559.* {C}

Written July 14.

13. *On July 24, 1862, after pointing out that blacks greatly outnumbered whites along the Mississippi from Memphis southward, Lincoln declared:*

I will tell you, I am determined to open it, and, if necessary will take all these Negroes to open it and keep it open. — *Browning, I, 562.* {A}

14. *During the same interview, Browning advised the President to make his decisions carefully and then adhere to them firmly, allowing himself to be neither bullied nor cajoled into changing them. Lincoln replied:*

that he had done so to a greater extent than was generally supposed; that when he made up his mind to send supplies to Fort Sumter he was sustained by only two members of his cabinet, Blair and Chase; and that when he determined to give the rebels at Charleston notice of his purpose, the entire cabinet was against him, though they all now admitted that he was right. — *Browning, I, 563.* {B}

15. *Lincoln said on July 25, 1862:*

that General Halleck had gone to the army at James River and was to have supreme command of the entire army; that he was satisfied McClellan would not fight and that he had told Halleck so and that he could keep him in command or not as he pleased; that if by magic he could reinforce McClellan with 100,000 men today, he would be in an ecstasy over it, thank him for it, and tell him that he would go to Richmond tomorrow; but that when tomorrow came, he would telegraph that he had certain information that the enemy had 400,000 men and that he could not advance without reinforcements. — *Browning, I, 563.* {B}

16. *In the same conversation, he said that:*

England wanted us to permit her to get $50 million worth of cotton from the South and that the matter was being considered, but that we could not let the cotton out without letting its value in, and in this way we would never succeed in crippling them much in their resources. — *Browning, I, 563-64.* {B}

17. *Concerning a letter of complaint that Browning had received from a treasury official in New Orleans about the radical antislavery policies of John Wolcott Phelps, one of the generals governing occupied Louisiana, Lincoln said:*

that the people there were making false pretenses; that there was but little union sentiment; they wanted the government to protect them, their property, and institutions whilst they sympathized with and aided treason and rebellion; that it should not be done. If they were tired of General Phelps's administration they knew how to get rid of it by returning to their allegiance and submitting to the authority of the government, and if they did not do so, and he could send any heavier scourge upon them than General Phelps, they had better be looking out for it.[68] —*Browning, I, 564. {B}*

18. *Responding on November 29, 1862, to Browning's question whether General John Pope, who had lost the second battle of Bull Run in August, was truly a failure or the victim of treacherous subordinates, Lincoln replied:*

that he knew no reason to suspect any one of bad faith except Fitz-John Porter, and that he very much hoped an investigation would relieve **him** from suspicion, but that at present he believed his disobedience of orders and his failure to go to Pope's aid in the battle of Friday [August 29] had occasioned our defeat and deprived us of a victory which would have terminated the war. . . .

That after the last battle fought by Pope, the army was much demoralized, and it was feared the enemy would be down on Washington. In this emergency, he had called McClellan here to take upon him the defense of the city. That he soon brought order out of chaos and got the army in good condition. That for such work McClellan had great talents. Indeed, for organizing, disciplining, and preparing an army for the field and handling it in the field, he was superior to any of our generals. That when the rebels crossed into Maryland he sent for Burnside and told him he must take command of our army, march against the enemy, and give him battle. Burnside declined—said the responsibility was too great, the consequences of defeat too momentous. He was willing to command a corps under McClellan, but was not willing to take the chief command of the army. Hence, McClellan was reinstated. The battles of South Mountain and Antietam were fought with ability, as well as any general could have fought them, but McClellan was too slow in his movements. He could and ought to have prevented the loss of Harpers Ferry but was six days marching forty miles, and it was surrendered. He did not follow up his advantages after Antietam. The army of the enemy should have been annihilated, but it was permitted to recross the Potomac without the loss of a man, and McClellan would not follow. He coaxed, urged, and ordered him, but all would not do. At the expiration of two weeks after a peremptory order to that effect, he had only three-fourths of his army across the river and was six days doing that, whereas the rebel army had effected a crossing in one day. —*Browning, I, 589-90.* {B}

19. *On December 12, 1862, Lincoln said:*

that there was never an army in the world, so far as he could learn, of which so small a percentage could be got into battle as ours; that eighty percent was what was usual, but that we could never get to exceed sixty; that when he visited the army after the battles of South Mountain and Antietam, he made a count of the troops, and there were only 93,000 present, when the muster rolls showed there should be 180,000. —*Browning, I, 594-95.* {B}

20. *Asked during the same conversation for his opinion of Cassius M. Clay, the antislavery Kentuckian who had been minister to Russia until replaced by Simon Cameron, the President answered:*

that he had a great deal of conceit and very little sense, and that he did not know what to do with him, for he could not give him a command—he was not fit for it. He had asked to be permitted to come home from Russia to take part in the war, and as he wanted some place to put Cameron to get him out of the War Department, he consented and appointed Clay a major general, hoping the war would be over before he got home. When he came, he was dissatisfied and wanted to go back and was not willing to take a command unless he could control everything, conduct the war on his own plan, and run the entire machine of government. That could not be allowed, and he was now urging to be sent back to Russia. What embarrassed him was that he had given him his promise in writing to send him back if Cameron resigned. —*Browning, I, 595.* {B}

21. *December 18, 1862, concerning the severe criticism of his administration by a Republican senatorial caucus after the disastrous defeat at Fredericksburg:*

They wish to get rid of me, and I am sometimes half disposed to gratify them. . . . We are now on the brink of destruction. It appears to me the Almighty is against us, and I can hardly see a ray of hope. —*Browning, I, 600.* {A}

22. *Responding on December 22, 1862, to Browning's suggestion of cabinet changes along what amounted to more conservative lines, the President declared that:*

he could not afford to make a new cabinet. If he did, the new one would be immediately assailed as the old one was, and it would give no additional strength to our cause.

After further discussion, he added that: a cabinet composed of the class of men I had suggested would give him trouble and be in his way on the Negro question. —*Browning, I, 603.* {B}

23. *To Browning and Senator John P. Hale of New Hampshire on January 9, 1863, Lincoln said:*

that since the Proclamation, the Negroes were stampeding in Missouri, which was producing great dissatisfaction among our friends there, and that the Democratic legislatures of Illinois and Indiana seemed bent upon mischief, and the party in those states was talking of a union with the lower Mississippi states. That we could at once stop that trouble by passing a law immediately appropriating $25 million to pay for the slaves in Missouri; that Missouri being a free state, the others would give up their scheme; that Missouri was an empire of herself, could sustain a population equal to half the population of the United States and pay the interest on all of our debt, and we ought to drive a stake there immediately.

He said particularly to Hale: You and I must die, but it will be enough for us to have done in our lives if we make Missouri free. — *Browning, I, 611-12.* {B, A}

24. *After transferring command of the Army of the Potomac from Burnside to Hooker on Monday, January 26, 1863, Lincoln explained to Browning:*

that on Saturday, Burnside was here and informed him that various causes had contributed to lose him the confidence of the army, and that he was satisfied the service would suffer by it if he continued longer in command, and he desired to relinquish it, which he did. That he did not know what better to do than to appoint Hooker, although he was not satisfied with his conduct (for he was one of those who had thwarted Burnside), but he appointed him, and knowing that Sumner and Franklin did not wish to be under his command and would not probably cooperate heartily with him, he had simply relieved them of their commands, but that they had not been arrested.

To Browning's suggestion that McClellan possessed the confidence of the army to a greater extent than any other man, Lincoln replied that: McClellan stood very high with all educated military men, but the fact was he would not fight. — *Browning, I, 619.* {B}

25. *Lincoln told Browning on December 14, 1863, that:*

his sister-in-law, Mrs. Helm, was in the house, but he did not wish it known. She wished an order for the protection of some cotton she had at Jackson, Mississippi. He thought she ought to have it, but he was afraid he would be censured if he did so. — *Browning, I, 651.*[69] {B}

26. *Several times, Browning later recalled, Lincoln talked with him about his domestic troubles, confiding that:*

he was constantly under great apprehension lest his wife should do something which would bring him into disgrace. —*Nicolay interview, June 17, 1875, Hay Collection-Brown.* {C}

27. *Several days after his visit to the army at City Point in June 1864, Lincoln quoted Grant as promising that he would surely take Richmond. He added that:*

Grant told him that in the Wilderness he had completely routed Lee, but did not know it at the time, and that had he known it, he could have ruined him and ended the campaign. —*Browning, I, 673–74.* {B}

As a quotation of Grant, this is, of course, secondhand testimony.

28. *On October 17, 1864, Lincoln confided to Browning that:*

Attorney General Bates had personally solicited the chief justiceship of him. —*Browning, I, 688.* {B}

29. *Lincoln said on November 14, 1864, that:*

General Canby and General Hurlbut in Louisiana were doing all they could to break down the state government, organized under the new constitution, and to deprive the Negroes of all benefit they had expected to derive from it.[70] —*Browning, I, 692.* {B}

30. *On the same day, speaking of his annual message to Congress, Lincoln told Browning that:*

[he] had not yet written a word of his message and thought he would close doors tomorrow and go to work at it. —*Browning, I, 693.* {B}

31. *December 24, 1864, after showing Browning his correspondence with Horace Greeley regarding the latter's peace negotiations in July with Confederate agents at Niagara Falls, Lincoln said:*

that he had been misrepresented and misunderstood, and that he had never entertained the purpose of making the abolition of slavery a condition precedent to the termination of the war and the restoration of the Union. —*Browning, I, 699.* {B}

According to Browning, Lincoln had previously made a similar statement to James W. Singleton (q.v.). In this seemingly startling pronouncement, which is filtered to us through Browning's paraphrasing, Lincoln was apparently clinging to a technical distinction that he had made in his annual message to Congress on December 6. The fact is that he had explicitly laid down "restoration of the Union and abandonment of slavery" as the two necessary conditions of any peace settlement.[71]

32. *Early in 1865, Browning talked repeatedly with the President about plans that he and Singleton had for trading in cotton and tobacco. Lincoln told him that:*

he wanted to get out all he could and send in all the greenbacks he could in exchange, and that he would do for us all that he could.

When Browning expressed concern about opposition from the Secretary of War, Lincoln replied: Oh, no, Stanton is not going to do anything desperate; he has always heretofore been as much in favor of the trade as I am. — *Browning, II, 5, 12. {B}*

ORESTES A. BROWNSON (1803–1876)   *Clergyman, editor, and author, who in middle age converted to Catholicism.*

1. *In an interview with Brownson on August 23, 1862, Lincoln said that:*

he was not fully persuaded that it was yet time to proclaim emancipation.

Brownson inferred from the conversation that such an edict would follow immediately if there were a major Union victory on the Virginia front. — Presumably Brownson's account to a reporter soon after the interview, New York Tribune, *August 25, 1862. {D}*

M. L. BUNDY   *Indiana politician who was in 1861 a member of the state legislature.*

1. *One of Lincoln's Illinois friends, Robert L. Wilson, had been appointed an army paymaster but was informed that his bond could not be approved because his sureties had not testified as to their property. Upon being told of the problem, Lincoln promptly walked with him to the office of the paymaster general, Benjamin F. Larned, and in Bundy's presence said:*

Colonel Larned, I know this gentleman well, and all his securities, and I know them to be perfectly responsible, and while I do not desire to interfere with the rules of your office, I should be much gratified if you could approve this bond. — *Bundy's statement in the Indianapolis* Journal, *reprinted in the New York* Times, *April 24, 1887.[72] {C}*

JOHN W. BUNN (1831–1920)   *Springfield businessman, acquainted with Lincoln from about 1847 on.*

1. *October 4, 1854, concerning the reply that he would deliver in Springfield that evening to Stephen A Douglas's speech of the day before:*

I will answer that speech without any trouble, because Judge Douglas made two misstatements of fact, and upon these two misstatements he built his whole argument.[73] I can show that his facts are not facts, and that will refute his speech. — *Phillips-2, 147–48 (1910). {C}*

2. *In the mid-1850s, one of Lincoln's cases involved the patent for a self-rocking cradle, which tickled his habitual interest in mechanical devices. Asked by Bunn how the contraption, once started, could be stopped, he said:*

There's the rub, and I reckon I'll have to answer you as I did the judge who asked the same question. The thing's like some of the glib and interesting talkers you and I know, John; when it gets to going it doesn't know when to stop. —*Related to Jesse K. Weik c. 1920, Weik-2, 159.*[74] *{D}*

3. *In 1857, when told that Bunn, a candidate for city treasurer, had not gone out and asked people to vote for him:*

If you don't think enough of your success to ask anybody to vote for you, it is probable they will not do it and that you will not be elected. —*Phillips-2, 161. {C}*

4. *In January 1861, responding to Bunn's warning that Chase regarded himself as the bigger man of the two:*

Well, do you know of any other men who think they are bigger than I am? . . . I want to put them all in my cabinet. —*Phillips-2, 163–64. {C}*

W. T. BURGESS   *A resident of Kansas.*

1. *Burgess recalled that as a youngster visiting his brother in Ohio, he talked with a man who proved to be Abraham Lincoln about a huge contraption on display at the state fair. The man said:*

How many yoke of oxen, my boy, do you think it takes to drag this machine? Well, they haul it with eight yoke, but when heavy ditching is to be done, they generally use twelve. —*Burgess as quoted in the New York Tribune, October 4, 1903. {C}*

Lincoln did in fact attend the county fair while speaking at Columbus, Ohio, on September 16, 1859.

AMBROSE E. BURNSIDE (1824–1881)   *Union general, briefly commander of the Army of the Potomac.*

1. *A week after the battle of Fredericksburg, Burnside informed Lincoln that he intended to publish a letter taking full responsibility for the defeat. The President replied that:*

he [Burnside] was the first man he had found who was willing to relieve him [Lincoln] of a particle of responsibility. —*As told to Henry J. Raymond on January 22, 1863, Raymond-2, 424. {D}*

LUMAN BURR   *In the late 1850s, a young lawyer in Bloomington, Illinois.*

1. *In a law office one day, while studying a book on the German language, Lincoln said:*

Here is a curious thing; the Germans have no word for thimble; they call it a finger-hat. They have no word for glove; they call it a hand-shoe. —*Signed statement, January 25, 1909, Centennial Reminiscences. {C}*

SILAS W. BURT   *Colonel on the military staff of New York's Civil War governors; later a civil service reformer.*

1. *June 26, 1863, in response to the request of a boorish army major for one of his "good stories":*

I believe I have the popular reputation of being a storyteller, but I do not deserve the name in its general sense; for it is not the story itself, but its purpose, or effect, that interests me. I often avoid a long and useless discussion by others or a laborious explanation on my own part by a short story that illustrates my point of view. So, too, the sharpness of a refusal or the edge of a rebuke may be blunted by an appropriate story, so as to save wounded feeling and yet serve the purpose. No, I am not simply a storyteller, but storytelling as an emollient saves me much friction and distress. —*Burt (1907), 502. {C}*

Burt added, "These are almost his exact words, of which I made a record that very night." Even so, the verbal accuracy of the quotation seems questionable.

CORNELIUS S. BUSHNELL *Connecticut industrialist and shipbuilder, associated with John Ericsson in the construction of the* Monitor.

　　1. *At a conference in September 1861 with Secretary Welles and some members of the Naval Board, Lincoln, holding a pasteboard model of the* Monitor *in his hand, closed the meeting with the remark:*

All I have to say is what the girl said when she stuck her foot into the stocking: "It strikes me there is something in it." —Bushnell to Welles, c. March 1877 in Battles and Leaders, I, 748. {C}

BENJAMIN F. BUTLER (1818–1893) *Democratic politician and controversial Civil War general. In at least some instances, Butler's recollections of Lincoln lack credibility. Thoroughly discredited, for example, is his story that in the spring of 1865, Lincoln asked him to develop a plan for shipping blacks out of the country.*[75]

　　1. *May 1861, replying to Butler's remark that as a Democrat he might not be able to support administration policy:*

I do not care whether you do or not if you will fight for the country. —*Rice AT, 140 (1886). {C}*

　　2. *In a different account of the same interview:*

When you see me doing anything that for the good of the country ought not to be done, come and tell me so. —*Butler-2, 242 (1892). {D}*

　　3. *In February 1862, just before Butler's departure as commander of the land forces in the expedition against New Orleans, Lincoln said:*

Good-bye, General; get into New Orleans if you can, and the backbone of the rebellion will be broken. It is of more importance than anything else that can now be done; but don't interfere with the slavery question as Frémont has done at St. Louis. —*Rice AT, 142. {C}*

4. *Responding in 1863 to Butler's urgent recommendation that all deserters be shot:*

God help me, how can I have a butcher's day every Friday in the Army of the Potomac? — *Rice AT, 144; Butler-2, 296. {C}*

Leonard Swett (q.v.) likewise recalled Lincoln's using the phrase "butcher-day."

5. *In the summer of 1863, on the peril of riding alone at night to the Soldiers' Home, where Lincoln often slept during hot weather:*

Oh, assassination of public officers is not an American crime. But perhaps it would relieve the anxiety of anxious friends which you express if I had a guard. — *Rice AT, 144. {C}*

6. *November 1863, at the time of Butler's appointment to command the Department of Virginia and North Carolina:*

Yes, General, I believe in you, but not in shooting deserters. As a commander of a department, you can now shoot them for yourself. . . . I wish you would give all the attention you can to raising Negro troops; large numbers of Negroes will probably come in to you. . . . Don't let Davis catch you, General; he has put a price on your head; he will hang you sure. — *Rice AT, 145. {D}*

7. *On a visit to Butler's command in 1864, Lincoln made a laughing reply to the proposal that he screen himself from enemy fire while riding along the lines:*

Oh, no, the commander in chief of the army must not show any cowardice in the presence of his soldiers, whatever he may feel. — *Rice AT, 147. {D}*

It is not clear when this visit is supposed to have taken place.

8. *During a dinner at Fort Wool, Virginia, in 1864:*

Would to God this dinner or provisions like it were with our poor prisoners in Andersonville. — *Rice AT, 148. {C}*

9. *April 11, 1865:*

General Butler, I am troubled about the Negroes. We are soon to have peace. We have got some one hundred and odd thousand Negroes who have been trained to arms. When peace shall come I fear lest these colored men shall organize themselves in the South, especially in the states where the Negroes are in preponderance in numbers, into guerrilla parties, and we shall have down there a warfare between the whites and the Negroes. In the course of the reconstruction of the government it will become a question of how the Negro is to be disposed of. Would it not be possible to export them to some place, say Liberia or South America, and organize them into communities to support themselves? Now, General, I wish you would examine the practicability of such exportation. —*Rice AT, 150-51.* {E}

A longer version of similar substance but different wording is in Butler-2, 903.

SALOME BUTLER   *Daughter of William Butler.*

1. *As Lincoln was about to leave for his wedding on November 4, 1842, a child in the Butler family asked where he was going, and he said jokingly:*

To the devil. —*So Butler recalled in Hunt, 238.*

Speaking to another interviewer, she quoted Lincoln as saying: To Hell, sonny. —*Roberts, 28.*[76] {D}

WILLIAM BUTLER   *Illinois businessman, active in Whig and Republican politics, with whom Lincoln boarded for several years after moving to Springfield.*

1. *On the way home to New Salem after adjournment of the legislature, presumably in February 1835, Lincoln said to Butler:*

All the rest of you have something to look forward to, and all are glad to get home, and will have something to do when you get there. But it isn't so with me. I am going home, Butler, without a thing in the world. I have drawn all my pay I got at Vandalia and have spent it all. I am in debt. I am owing Van Bergen, and he has levied on my horse and compass, and I have nothing to pay the debt with and no way to make any money. I don't know what to do.

To Butler's suggestion that he study law, Lincoln replied: How can I study law when I have nothing to pay my board with? *According to Butler, he paid off Lincoln's debts and invited him to board at his house.* —*John G. Nicolay interview with Butler, June 1875, in Hay Collection-Brown.* {D}

Factual inaccuracy reinforces a general doubt about this recollection, which repeats in greater detail and with some discrepancy a statement made to an interviewer in 1860.[77]

DANIEL BUTTERFIELD (1831–1901)   *Union general from New York, a division and corps commander who twice served as Joseph Hooker's chief of staff.*

1. *One day in the spring of 1863, Butterfield heard Senator Charles Sumner complain to the President that in South Carolina, Rufus Saxton was about to be placed in a position of subordination to another brigadier general whom he outranked, namely, Quincy Adams Gillmore.*[78] *Sumner suggested that Saxton was being discriminated against because of an abolitionist order that he had issued. Lincoln responded with a description of how Gillmore's plan for an attack on Charleston had been brought to his attention and discussed with his advisers. Then he said:*

It seemed to us a wise thing to do, and it was decided to give the order to place General Gillmore in command. No one ever thought of any orders given by General Saxton. There was no intended disapprobation of them. The subject was not thought of or talked of in connection with putting General Gillmore in command. You are at liberty to say [that] to all of our people and to the newspaper men and the press generally. Let the explanation go out in semiofficial manner. I will fully confirm it. There is no feeling with regard to the course General Saxton has pursued, and such a thing was not thought of.

Sumner nevertheless continued to press the problem of rank. Lincoln asked: Will it be entirely satisfactory to you, Mr. Senator, and all our friends, and General Saxton, if the ranking officer is in command?

Receiving an affirmative answer, he declared: Very well, I will arrange it. I will have General Gillmore made a major general.

When the discomfited Sumner had left, Lincoln said to Butterfield: We have to manage all sorts of ways to get along with this terrible war position. — *Undated statement in Butterfield, 156-58. {C}*

Gillmore was indeed soon promoted to major general.

A. HOMER BYINGTON   *A correspondent for the New York* Tribune.

1. *Concerning the failure of the attack on Fort Fisher, North Carolina, in December 1864 by forces under General Benjamin F. Butler and Admiral David Dixon Porter, the President remarked:*

that Wilmington was a fizzle because both parties fooled away the first three days after starting of most beautiful weather, that Grant telegraphed him this would be the result when he heard they had failed to move to an immediate attack. — *Byington to Sydney Howard Gay, December 30, 1864, Gay Papers. {B}*

SYLVANUS CADWALLADER (c. 1825–?)   *War correspondent with Grant's army, first for the Chicago* Times *and then for the New York* Herald.

1. *On April 1, 1865, according to Cadwallader, he delivered, at Grant's request, several Confederate flags captured that day in the battle of Five Forks. Lincoln unfurled them one by one and said:*

Here is something material—something I can see, feel, and understand. This means victory. This is victory. — *Cadwallader, 307 (c. 1890). {C}*

SIMON CAMERON (1799–1889)   *Pennsylvania Republican leader, a candidate for the presidential nomination in 1860. He served relatively brief terms as secretary of war and minister to Russia in the Lincoln administration.*

1. *Lincoln once told Cameron that:*

he was more indebted to Judd than any other one man for his nomination. —*Interview with John G. Nicolay, February 20, 1875, Nicolay Papers.* {C}

2. *After the battle of Gettysburg, Lincoln agreed with Cameron in regretting that General Meade had not followed it with an attack on Lee's army, but then he added:*

We cannot blame him, Mr. Cameron; we cannot censure a man who has done so much because he did not do more. —*Interview in the New York Times, June 3, 1878.* {C}

3. *One day in late 1863, Lincoln said:*

Cameron, I don't like the idea of having Chase and Wade against me. I'm afraid I can't be nominated if they continue to oppose me.[79] —*Ibid.* {C}

JAMES H. CAMPBELL (1820–1895) *Republican congressman from Pennsylvania, appointed minister to Sweden in 1864.*

1. *On March 3, 1862, Campbell expressed dissatisfaction with the military situation. Lincoln replied that:*

if General Washington, or Napoleon, or General Jackson was in command on the Potomac, they would be obliged to move or resign the position.

He added: One thing I can say, that the army will move, either under General McClellan or some other man, and that very soon. —*Campbell to his wife, March 4, 1862, in Peskin, 158.* {A}

JOHN A. CAMPBELL (1811–1889) *Alabama lawyer, associate justice of the United States Supreme Court, and assistant secretary of war in the Confederate government. Campbell, one of the three southern commissioners to the Hampton Roads peace conference in February 1865, conferred with Lincoln on April 4 and 5 at Richmond, seeking to arrange terms for an end to hostilities and the restoration of Virginia to the Union.*

1. *To Campbell and Richmond attorney Gustavus A. Myers (q.v.), Lincoln read a memorandum setting forth the "indispensable" terms of peace, one of which was: no recession by him from the position on slavery that he already assumed in various public documents.[80] This meant, he explained:*

that the executive action on the subject of slavery, so far as it had been declared in messages, proclamations, and other official acts, must pass for what they are worth; that he would not recede from his position, but that this would not debar action by other authorities of the government.

To this somewhat indeterminate statement on the postwar status of slavery, Campbell attached the equally tentative comment: "I suppose that if the proclamation of the President of the United States be valid as law that it has already operated and vested rights." —Campbell to Joseph R. Anderson and others, April 7, 1865, OR, Series I, Volume 46, Part III, 656. {B}

2. Lincoln then added:

that he had said nothing in the paper as to pains and penalties; that he supposed that it would not be proper to offer a pardon to Mr. Davis—whom we familiarly call Jeff Davis—who says he won't have one; but that most anyone can have most anything of the kind for the asking.

Further on in the discussion, he stated: that he had been thinking of a plan for calling the Virginia legislature that had been sitting in Richmond together, and to get them [to] vote for the restoration of Virginia to the Union; that he had not arranged the matter to his satisfaction and would not decide upon it until after his return to City Point, and he would communicate with General Weitzel. He deemed it important that that very legislature that had been sitting in Richmond should vote upon the question. That he had a government in northern Virginia—the Pierpont government—but it had but a small margin, and he did not desire to enlarge it; that the Virginia legislature was in the condition of a tenant between two contending landlords and that it should attorn to the party that had established the better claim. —*Campbell to James S. Speed, August 31, 1865, SHSP-ns, IV, 68-69.*[81] {C}

JOSEPH G. CANNON (1836–1926) *Illinois political leader who served forty-six years in Congress, ten of them as Speaker.*

1. When Lincoln took hold of Orlando B. Ficklin and drew him to the front of the platform during the debate with Douglas at Charleston, Illinois, in 1858, he said:

I am not going to hurt Colonel Ficklin; I only call him as a witness. Now, the Colonel and I were in Congress together, and I want him to tell the whole truth about this Mexican business. —*Speech by Cannon in* House Document 1056 (1916), 42. {C}

Though undoubtedly less accurate than the reportorial transcripts of the debate,[82] Cannon's recollection may very aptly reflect the atmosphere created by Lincoln's action.

2. In May 1860, as an onlooker at the Republican state convention in Decatur, which instructed Illinois delegates to vote for him at the approaching national convention in Chicago, Lincoln said:

I'm most too much of a candidate to be here and not enough of one to stay away. —*Cannon to an interviewer in Aubere, 8528 (1907).* {C}

According to Leonard Swett (q.v.), writing in 1860, Lincoln made such a statement about attending the Chicago convention. Of course, he may have liked the quip so much that he used it more than once.

LE GRAND B. CANNON (1815–1906) *Army colonel on the staff of General John E. Wool; later a banker.*

1. *At Fortress Monroe around 11 P.M. on May 10, 1862, General Wool arrived in a dusty uniform with word that Norfolk had been captured. Stanton, in his nightshirt, rushed impetuously to embrace Wool, and Lincoln said:*

Look out, Mars! If you don't, the General will throw you. — *Cannon, 162 (1895). {C}*

2. *At breakfast the next morning, with the Secretary of the Treasury also present:*

Now Mr. Chase, you know we have been solicited by artists to fill the panels at the Capitol with pictures illustrative of this war. I don't think anything has been done on our side until the capture of Norfolk worthy of illustration. But now you can send for artist Leitze, and tell him to illustrate the taking of Norfolk. It should be illustrated by a picture showing the meeting of the Secretary of War and General Wool, on the announcement of the capture. —167. {C}

3. *One evening during his visit to Fortress Monroe, Lincoln asked to borrow Cannon's hairbrush, but when it was handed to him, he said:*

Why, I can't do anything with such a thing as that. It wouldn't go through my hair. Now, if you have anything you comb your horse's mane with, that might do. —169. {C}

At this point, according to Cannon, Lincoln told a story about newsboys and his unruly hair, one that Albert B. Chandler (q.v.) likewise recalled hearing from him.

4. *At another time, Lincoln read from Shakespeare, finishing with the passage in* King John *where Constance bewails the loss of her son. Then he said:*

Did you ever dream of some lost friend and feel that you were having a sweet communion with him, and yet have a consciousness that it was not a reality? . . . That is the way I dream of my lost boy Willie. —174.[83] {C}

STEPHEN R. CAPPS   *A merchant in Jacksonville, Illinois.*

1. *Capps, who heard Lincoln speak on "Discoveries and Inventions" before an Illinois College audience in February 1859, recalled that toward the end of the lecture, he quoted a Horace Greeley statement that truly great men never indulged in levity. After which he added:*

If Mr. Greeley's definition of a great man is correct, then farewell, a long farewell to all my hopes of greatness. — *Capps to James R. B. Van Cleave, July 17, 1908, Centennial Reminiscences. {D}*

It is impossible to say whether this quotation corroborates or merely echoes a similar one supplied 43 years earlier by William H. Herndon (q.v.).

FRANCIS B. CARPENTER (1830–1900)   *A portrait painter already well established in his profession before the Civil War, Carpenter lived at the White House from February to July 1864 while he painted the famous picture of Lincoln reading a draft of the Emancipation Proclamation to his cabinet. Soon after Lincoln's death, Carpenter began assiduously to publish anecdotal material about him. It appeared in newspapers and magazines, as an appendix in a volume by Henry J. Raymond, and in his own book,* Six Months at the White House with Abraham Lincoln. *He probably exaggerated the extent of his intimacy with Lincoln, and, if Mary Lincoln can be believed, eventually wore out his welcome with presumptuous intrusions upon the President's time.*[84] *Carpenter's recollected words of Lincoln are a mixture of what he himself heard and what he heard secondhand from others, and it is not always easy to tell the difference.*

1. *At their first interview on February 6, 1864, Lincoln said:*

Well, Mr. Carpenter, we will turn you in loose here, and try to give you a good chance to work out your idea.

He then proceeded to give the artist an account of how emancipation came to be adopted as government policy: It had got to be midsummer, 1862. Things had gone on from bad to worse, until I felt that we had reached the end of our rope on the plan of operations we had been pursuing; that we had about played our last card and must change our tactics or lose the game. I now determined upon the adoption of the emancipation policy, and, without consultation with, or the knowledge of the cabinet, I prepared the original draft of the proclamation, and, after much anxious thought, called a cabinet meeting upon the subject. This was the last of July, or the first part of the month of August, 1862. This cabinet meeting took place, I think, upon a Saturday. All were present, excepting Mr. Blair, the postmaster general, who was absent at the opening of the discussion, but came in subsequently. I said to the cabinet that I had resolved upon this step and had not called them together to ask their advice but to lay the subject matter of a proclamation before them, suggestions as to which would be in order after they had heard it read. Mr. Lovejoy was in error when he informed you that it excited no comment, excepting on the part of Secretary Seward. Various suggestions were offered. Secretary Chase wished the language stronger in reference to the arming of the blacks. Mr. Blair, after he came in, deprecated the policy on the ground that it would cost the administration the fall elections. Nothing, however, was offered that I had not already fully anticipated and settled in my own mind, until Secretary Seward spoke. Said he:[85] "Mr. President, I approve of the proclamation, but I question the expediency of its issue at this juncture. The depression of the public mind, consequent upon our repeated reverses, is so great that I fear the effect of so important a step. It may be viewed as the last measure of an exhausted government—a cry for help—the government stretching forth its hands to Ethiopia, instead of Ethiopia stretching forth her hands to the government." His idea was that it would be considered our last **shriek**, on the retreat. "Now," continued Mr. Seward, "while I approve the measure, I suggest, sir, that you postpone its issue until you can give it to the country supported by military success, instead of issuing it, as would be the case now, [following] upon the greatest disasters of the war!" The wisdom of the view of the Secretary of State struck me with very great force. It was an aspect of the case that, in all my thought upon the subject, I had entirely overlooked. The result was that I put the draft of the proclamation aside, as you do your sketch for a picture, waiting for a victory. From time to time I added or changed a line, touching it up here and there, waiting the progress of events. Well, the next news we had was of Pope's disaster at Bull Run. Things looked darker than ever. Finally, came the week of the battle of Antietam. I determined to wait no longer. The news came, I think, on Wednesday, that the advantage was on our side. I was then staying at the Soldiers' Home. Here I finished writing the second draft of the preliminary proclamation; came up on Saturday, called the cabinet together to hear it, and it was published the following Monday.

It was a somewhat remarkable fact that there were just one hundred days between the dates of the two proclamations, issued upon the twenty-second of September and the first of January. I had not made the calculation at the time.

The Proclamation as Lincoln first read it to the cabinet, after designating which slaves were to be "forever free," declared that the executive government of the United States, including the military forces, would "recognize the freedom" of such persons and do nothing to repress them or hinder their efforts to become free in actuality. When I finished reading this paragraph [Lincoln continued in his narration to Carpenter], Mr. Seward stopped me, and said: "I think, Mr. President, that you should insert after the word 'recognize' in that sentence the words 'and maintain.'" I replied that I had already fully considered the import of that expression in this connection, but I had not introduced it, because it was not my way to promise what I was not entirely sure that I could perform, and I was not prepared to say that I thought we were exactly able to 'maintain' this. But Mr. Seward insisted that we ought to take this ground; and the words finally went in. —*Carpenter-1, 760–62 (1865), reprinted in Carpenter-2, 20–24 (1866), with one paragraph moved to a different position. {C}*

Carpenter's assertion that he wrote down Lincoln's statement "soon afterward" improves the credibility of this lengthy quotation but seems too vague to qualify it as a contemporary account. Which man was responsible for the chronological inaccuracies is anyone's guess. Lincoln broached the subject of emancipation to the cabinet on Tuesday (not Saturday), July 22 (not the end of July or early August), and the historic cabinet meeting at which he announced his intention to issue the Proclamation took place on Monday (not Saturday), September 22.

2. *On February 9, 1864, as he worked through court-martial cases with Joseph Holt, the judge advocate general, Lincoln remarked:*

Does your mind, Judge Holt, associate events with dates? Every time this morning that I have had occasion to write the day of the month, the thought has come up: "This was General Harrison's birthday." —*Carpenter-2, 32.* {C}

3. *On February 10, the White House stables burned, and the next day, according to Carpenter, Robert Lincoln approached his father with a legal problem that he and John Hay had been debating. A coachman had lost some greenbacks in the fire, and the question was whether the government remained liable for them in such circumstances. Said Lincoln:*

The payment of a note presupposes its presentation to the maker of it. It is the sign or symbol of value received. It is not **value** itself; that is clear. At the same time the production of the note seems a necessary warrant for the demand, and while the moral obligation is as strong without this, governments and banking institutions do not recognize any principle beyond the strictly legal. It is an established rule that the citizen cannot sue the government; therefore, I don't see but that it is a dead loss for Jehu. —*Carpenter-2, 45.* {D}

Carpenter does not indicate whether he heard these words directly from Lincoln or at second hand from his son. In any case, the fact that Hay was in Florida at this time throws doubt upon the credibility of the whole story.

4. *At a sitting on March 2, 1864, after some talk about newspaper attacks upon him, Lincoln told this story:*

A traveler on the frontier found himself out of his reckoning one night in a most inhospitable region. A terrific thunderstorm came up to add to his trouble. He floundered along until his horse at length gave out. The lightning afforded him the only clue to his way, but the peals of thunder were frightful. One bolt, which seemed to crash the earth beneath him, brought him to his knees. By no means a praying man, his petition was short and to the point,—"O Lord, if it is all the same to you, give us a little more light and a little less noise!" —*Carpenter-2, 49.* {C}

5. *At the same sitting, conversation turned to Shakespeare, about whom Carpenter quotes Lincoln as having "once remarked":*

It matters not to me whether Shakespeare be well or ill acted; with him the thought suffices. —*Carpenter-2, 49.* {D}

Whether Carpenter heard these words directly from Lincoln or from an intermediary source, is not clear.

6. *Looking ahead to seeing Edwin Booth play Hamlet that very evening and Richard III on March 10, Lincoln remarked:*

There is one passage of the play of "Hamlet" which is very apt to be slurred over by the actor or omitted altogether, which seems to me the choicest part of the play. It is the soliloquy of the king, after the murder. It always struck me as one of the finest touches of nature in the world.

He proceeded to recite the speech of Claudius that begins "O, my offence is rank." Then he said: The opening of the play of "King Richard the Third" seems to me often entirely misapprehended. It is quite common for an actor to come upon the stage, and, in a sophomoric style, to begin with a flourish:

> "Now is the winter of our discontent
>   Made glorious summer by this sun of York,
>   And all the clouds that lowered upon our house,
>   In the deep bosom of the ocean buried!"

Now, this is all wrong. Richard, you remember, had been, and was then, plotting the destruction of his brothers, to make room for himself. Outwardly, the most loyal to the newly crowned king, secretly he could scarcely contain his impatience at the obstacles still in the way of his own elevation. He appears upon the stage, just after the crowning of Edward, burning with repressed hate and jealousy. The prologue is the utterance of the most intense bitterness and satire.

Whereupon, says Carpenter, he again repeated from memory the entire soliloquy under discussion, "rendering it with a degree of force and power that made it seem like a new creation." — Carpenter-2, 50-52. {C}

7. *One evening several weeks later, after some more talk about Shakespeare, Lincoln remarked:*

There is a poem which has been a great favorite with me for years, which was first shown to me when a young man by a friend, and which I afterwards saw and cut from a newspaper and learned by heart. I would give a great deal to know who wrote it, but I have never been able to ascertain.

The poem he then recited was, of course, William Knox's "Mortality," better known by its first line: "O, why should the spirit of mortal be proud?" Following which, he said: There are some quaint, queer verses, written, I think, by Oliver Wendell Holmes, entitled "The Last Leaf," one of which is to me inexpressibly touching. . . . For pure pathos, in my judgment, there is nothing finer than those six lines in the English language.[86] *— Carpenter-1, 728-30 (dating the discussion March 22); Carpenter-2, 58-59 (dating it March 25). {C}*

8. *In late March 1864, discussing a report of a Confederate plan to abduct or assassinate him:*

Well, even if true, I do not see what the rebels would gain by killing or getting possession of me. I am but a single individual, and it would not help their cause or make the least difference in the progress of the war. Everything would go right on just the same. Soon after I was nominated at Chicago, I began to receive letters threatening my life. The first one or two made me a little uncomfortable, but I came at length to look for a regular installment of this kind of correspondence in every week's mail, and up to inauguration day I was in constant receipt of such letters. It is no uncommon thing to receive them now; but they have ceased to give me any apprehension. . . . there is nothing like getting **used** to things! — *Carpenter-2, 62–63.* {C}

9. *Told that the author of the play* Richelieu, *scheduled for presentation at Ford's Theatre, was Edward Bulwer-Lytton, Lincoln said:*

I knew Bulwer wrote novels, but I did not know he was a play-writer also. It may seem somewhat strange to say, but I never read an entire novel in my life. . . . I once commenced *Ivanhoe,* but never finished it. —*Carpenter-2, 114–15.* {C}

10. *On April 7, 1864, Lincoln received George Thompson and a group of his friends at the White House, having the night before heard an address by this noted British antislavery orator. When Thompson spoke of class divisions in England with respect to the Civil War, Lincoln responded:*

Mr. Thompson, the people of Great Britain, and of other foreign governments, were in one great error in reference to this conflict. They seemed to think that the moment I was president, I had the power to abolish slavery, forgetting that before I could have any power whatever, I had to take the oath to support the Constitution of the United States and execute the laws as I found them. When the rebellion broke out, my duty did not admit of a question. That was, first, by all strictly lawful means to endeavor to maintain the integrity of the government. I did not consider that I had a **right** to touch the state institution of slavery until all other measures for restoring the Union had failed. The paramount idea of the Constitution is the preservation of the Union. It may not be specified in so many words, but that this was the idea of its founders is evident; for, without the Union, the Constitution would be worthless. It seems clear, then, that in the last extremity, if any local institution threatened the existence of the Union, the executive could not hesitate as to his duty. In our case, the moment came when I felt that slavery must die that the nation might live. I have sometimes used the illustration, in this connection, of a man with a diseased limb and his surgeon. So long as there is a chance of the patient's restoration, the surgeon is solemnly bound to try to save both life **and** limb; but when the crisis comes, and the limb must be sacrificed as the only chance of saving the life, no honest man will hesitate.

Many of my strongest supporters urged emancipation before I thought it indispensable, and, I may say, before I thought the country ready for it. It is my conviction that, had the Proclamation been issued even six months earlier than it was, public sentiment would not have sustained it. Just so as to the subsequent action in reference to enlisting blacks in the border states. The step, taken sooner, could not, in my judgment, have been carried out. A man watches his pear tree day after day, impatient for the ripening of the fruit. Let him attempt to **force** the process, and he may spoil both fruit and tree. But let him patiently **wait**, and the ripe pear at length falls into his lap. We have seen this great revolution in public sentiment slowly but surely progressing, so that, when final action came, the opposition was not strong enough to defeat the purpose. I can now solemnly assert, that I have a clear conscience in regard to my action on this momentous question. I have done what no man could have helped doing, standing in my place. —*Carpenter-2, 76–77.* {C}

The length of this passage casts extra doubt upon its authenticity as a reproduction of Lincoln's words, but its substance seems credible enough.

11. *Lincoln took the group to see Carpenter's painting in progress, and on the way, he remarked to Thompson:*

Your folks made rather sad work of this mansion when they came up the Potomac in 1812. Nothing was left of it but the bare walls. —*Carpenter-2, 79.* {C}

There is no way of knowing whether the factual errors in this statement were Lincoln's or Carpenter's.

12. *April 25, 1864, as he showed the painting to Governor Andrew G. Curtin of Pennsylvania:*

You see, Curtin, I was brought to the conclusion that there was no dodging this Negro question any longer. We had reached the point where it seemed that we must avail ourselves of this element or in all probability go under.

Curtin mentioned the impression prevailing in some quarters that Seward had opposed the Proclamation. Lincoln replied: That is not true; he advised postponement at the first meeting, which seemed to me sound. It was Seward's persistence which resulted in the insertion of the word "maintain," which I feared under the circumstances was promising more than it was quite probable we could carry out. —*Carpenter-2, 83–84.* {C}

13. *When they turned to the subject of government finances, Lincoln exclaimed:*

Curtin, what do you think of those fellows in Wall Street, who are gambling in gold at such a time as this? . . . For my part, I wish every one of them had his devilish head shot off! —*Carpenter-2, 84.* {C}

14. *At another time, when asked by Carpenter about the cabinet's attitude toward his emancipation policy:*

Mr. Blair thought we should lose the fall elections and opposed it on that ground only. . . . He proved right in regard to the fall elections, but he is satisfied that we have since gained more than we lost. — *Carpenter-1, 764.* {C}

15. *April 30, 1864, discussing his amnesty policy with Elizabeth Cady Stanton and her brother-in-law:*

When a man is sincerely penitent for his misdeeds and gives satisfactory evidence of the same, he can safely be pardoned, and there is no exception to the rule. — *Carpenter-1, 746; Carpenter-2, 102.* {C}

16. *On the same occasion, or soon thereafter, Lincoln responded to some remark of Carpenter's by narrating how he and the Secretary of War received word of the capture of Norfolk in May 1862:*

Chase and Stanton had accompanied me to Fortress Monroe. While we were there, an expedition was fitted out for an attack on Norfolk. Chase and General Wool disappeared about the time we began to look for tidings of the result, and after vainly waiting their return till late in the evening, Stanton and I concluded to retire. My room was on the second floor of the Commandant's house, and Stanton's was below. The night was very warm; the moon shining brightly; and, too restless to sleep, I threw off my [bed]clothes and sat for some time by the table, reading. Suddenly hearing footsteps, I looked out of the window, and saw two persons approaching whom I knew by their relative size to be the missing men. They came into the passage and I heard them rap at Stanton's door and tell him to get up, and come upstairs. A moment afterward they entered my room. "No time for ceremony, Mr. President," said General Wool. "Norfolk is ours!" Stanton here burst in, just out of bed, clad in a long nightgown, which nearly swept the floor, his ear catching, as he crossed the threshold, Wool's last words. Perfectly overjoyed, he rushed at the General, whom he hugged most affectionately, fairly lifting him from the floor in his delight. The scene altogether must have been a comical one, though at the time we were all too greatly excited to take much note of mere appearances. — *Carpenter-2, 104-5.* {C}

Le Grand B. Cannon (q.v.) was present and later recalled some of Lincoln's contemporary comments on the incident.

17. *During the battle of the Wilderness in early May 1864, Carpenter asked how Grant compared with other Union commanders, and Lincoln replied:*

The great thing about Grant, I take it, is his perfect coolness and persistency of purpose. I judge he is not easily excited, which is a great element in an officer, and he has the grit of a bulldog! Once let him get his teeth in, and nothing can shake him off. — *Carpenter-2, 283.* {C}

18. *An officer who had been dismissed from the service repeatedly sought the President's intervention and ended by accusing him of failure to do justice. Lincoln, his patience exhausted, replied:*

Sir, I give you fair warning never to show yourself in this room again. I can bear censure, but not insult! — *Carpenter-2, 105-6.* {D}

Carpenter may or may not have heard this exchange himself.

19. *In Carpenter's presence, Lincoln once said to the New York clergyman and editor, Henry M. Field, that he thought:*

there was not upon record, in ancient or modern biography, so **productive** a mind, as had been exhibited in the career of Henry Ward Beecher. — *Carpenter-2, 135.* {C}

20. *To Carpenter's remark that no president since Washington had so won the hearts of the people, Lincoln replied that:*

in such a crisis as the country was then passing through, it was natural that the people should look more earnestly to their leaders than at other periods. . . . Their regard for any man in his position who should sincerely have done his best to save the government from destruction would have been equally as marked and expressive. — *Carpenter-2, 143-44.* {C}

21. *This, according to Carpenter, is a story Lincoln "used to tell." That he himself heard Lincoln tell it, is not explicitly stated:*

In the days when I used to be on the circuit, I was once accosted in the cars by a stranger, who said, "Excuse me, sir, but I have an article in my possession which belongs to you." "How is that?" I asked, considerably astonished. The stranger took a jackknife from his pocket. "This knife," said he, "was placed in my hands some years ago with the injunction that I was to keep it until I found a man uglier than myself. I have carried it from that time to this. Allow me now to say, sir, that I think you are fairly entitled to the property." [87] — *Carpenter-2, 148-49.* {D}

22. *Mrs. Gideon Welles, viewing the picture with friends, said that newspaper reports had led her to believe it was nearly finished. Carpenter replied that the papers were not always reliable, and Lincoln quickly added:*

That is to say, Mrs. Welles, they **lie**, and then they **re-lie**! — *Carpenter-2, 156.* {C}

23. *While showing the picture one evening to his biographer, Joseph H. Barrett, the President was somehow reminded of a man who exemplified a certain kind of legal mind:*

Judge —— held the strongest ideas of rigid government and close construction that I ever met. It was said of him, on one occasion, that he would hang
a man for blowing his nose in the street, but he would quash the indictment
if it failed to specify which hand he blew it with. —*Carpenter-1, 753–54.
There is a slightly different version in Carpenter-2, 254.*[88] {C}

24. *On May 31, 1864, Lincoln watched a parade of Sunday-school children
past the White House and was reminded of a story he had recently heard about
Daniel Webster:*

When quite young, at school, Daniel was one day guilty of a gross violation
of the rules. He was detected in the act and called up by the teacher for
punishment. This was to be the old-fashioned "feruling" of the hand. His
hands happened to be very dirty. Knowing this, on his way to the teacher's
desk he spit upon the palm of his right hand, wiping it off upon the side of
his pantaloons. "Give me your hand, sir," said the teacher, very sternly. Out
went the right hand, partly cleansed. The teacher looked at it a moment,
and said, "Daniel, if you will find another hand in this schoolroom as filthy
as that, I will let you off this time." Instantly from behind his back came
the left hand. "Here it is, sir," was the ready reply. "That will do," said
the teacher, "for this time; you can take your seat, sir!" —*Carpenter-1, 748.*
{C}

*Chittenden, 333–34, gives a more elaborate version, allegedly told by Lincoln
after having watched a procession of colored Sunday-school children in May
1862. John A. Dahlgren and Byron Berkeley Johnson likewise recalled hearing
Lincoln make use of this joke (Dahlgren, 364; Johnson BB, 17). The same story,
unassociated with Daniel Webster, appeared in a Joe Miller jokebook in 1845.*

25. *When Carpenter admired an elaborately decorated pen-and-ink representation of the Emancipation Proclamation, Lincoln said:*

Yes, it is what I call **ingenious nonsense.** —*Carpenter-2, 158.* {C}

26. *On June 8, 1864, the day of his renomination for the presidency, Lincoln
said to Carpenter and Hay:*

A very singular occurrence took place the day I was nominated at Chicago
four years ago, of which I am reminded tonight. In the afternoon of the day,
returning home from downtown, I went upstairs to Mrs. Lincoln's sitting
room. Feeling somewhat tired, I lay down upon a couch in the room, directly opposite a bureau upon which was a looking-glass. As I reclined, my
eye fell upon the glass, and I saw distinctly **two** images of myself, exactly
alike, except that one was a little paler than the other. I arose and lay down
again, with the same result. It made me quite uncomfortable for a few moments, but some friends coming in, the matter passed out of my mind. The
next day, while walking in the street, I was suddenly reminded of the cir-

cumstance, and the disagreeable sensation produced by it returned. I had never seen anything of the kind before and did not know what to make of it. I determined to go home and place myself in the same position, and if the same effect was produced, I would make up my mind that it was the natural result of some principle of refraction or optics which I did not understand, and dismiss it. I tried the experiment, with the same result, and as I had said to myself, accounting for it on some principle unknown to me, it ceased to trouble me. But some time ago, I tried to produce the same effect here by arranging a glass and couch in the same position, without success. — *Carpenter-1, 751; and, with one minor verbal change, Carpenter-2, 163–64. {C}*

According to Carpenter, the account of this mysterious phenomenon was already "going the rounds of the newspapers" in 1865. Noah Brooks and Ward Hill Lamon (qq.v.) provided variant versions, placing the incident and Lincoln's telling of it at different times. The effect of the three recollections is partly corroboration and partly contradiction. Hay made no mention in his diary of Lincoln's describing the incident on June 8.

27. *Without remembering the context, Carpenter recalled that Lincoln once told him this story:*

Some years ago, a couple of emigrants fresh from the Emerald Isle, seeking labor, were making their way toward the West. Coming suddenly one evening upon a pond of water, they were greeted with a grand chorus of bullfrogs, a kind of music they had never before heard. "B-a-u-m! B-a-u-m!" Overcome with terror, they clutched their shillelaghs and crept cautiously forward, straining their eyes in every direction to catch a glimpse of the enemy, but he was not to be found. At last a happy idea seized the foremost one; he sprang to his companion and exclaimed, "And sure, Jamie, it is my opinion it's nothing but a noise." — *Carpenter-2, 155. {D}*

The story had already been attributed to Lincoln in an 1864 jokebook. Later, Ward Hill Lamon, Shelby M. Cullom, and Benjamin R. Cowen all claimed to have heard him tell it.[89]

28. *In late July 1864, Lincoln took a last look at the painting, now virtually finished. Asked for criticism, he said that:*

he could suggest nothing whatever as to the portraiture—the likenesses seemed to him absolutely perfect.

But the presence of William Whiting's The War Powers of the President *among the accessories in the picture did inspire one suggestion:* Now, Whiting's book is not a regular law book. It is all very well that it should be there; but I would suggest that you change the character of the binding. It now looks like an old volume of United States Statutes.

Otherwise, he saw nothing to change: All else is perfectly satisfactory to me. In my judgment, it is as good a piece of work as the subject will admit of. And I am right glad you have done it! — *Carpenter-1, 763–64; Carpenter-2, 353–54, slightly variant, and with the parting words:* Carpenter, I believe I am about as glad over the success of this work as you are. {C}

29. *Visiting the White House soon after the Hampton Roads conference of February 3, 1865, Carpenter asked the President about a story he had reportedly told the Confederate peace commissioners. Lincoln replied:*

Why, yes, but has it leaked out? I was in hopes nothing would be said about it, lest some oversensitive people should imagine there was a degree of levity in the intercourse between us. You see, we had reached and were discussing the slavery question. Mr. Hunter said, substantially, that the slaves, always accustomed to an overseer and to work upon compulsion, suddenly freed, as they would be if the South should consent to peace on the basis of the Emancipation Proclamation, would precipitate not only themselves but the entire southern society into irremediable ruin. No work would be done, nothing would be cultivated, and both blacks and whites would starve. I waited for Seward to answer that argument, but as he was silent, I at length said: "Mr. Hunter, you ought to know a great deal better about this matter than I, for you have always lived under the slave system. I can only say, in reply to your statement of the case, that it reminds me of a man out in Illinois by the name of Case, who undertook, a few years ago, to raise a very large herd of hogs. It was a great trouble to feed them, and how to get around this was a puzzle to him. At length he hit on the plan of plant-ing an immense field of potatoes, and, when they were sufficiently grown, he turned the whole herd into the field, and let them have full swing, thus saving not only the labor of feeding the hogs, but also that of digging the potatoes. Charmed with his sagacity, he stood one day leaning against the fence, counting his hogs, when a neighbor came along. 'Well, well,' said he, 'Mr. Case, this is all very fine. Your hogs are doing very well just now, but you know out here in Illinois the frost comes early, and the ground freezes for a foot deep. Then what are they going to do?' This was a view of the matter Mr. Case had not taken into account. Butchering time for hogs was 'way on in December or January. He scratched his head and at length stammered, 'Well, it may come pretty hard on the snouts, but I don't see but that it will be root, hog, or die.'" — *Carpenter-1, 745–46; Carpenter-2, 210–11.* {D}

A briefer version, supposedly provided by Alexander H. Stephens and perhaps more reliable than this long-drawn narrative, appeared in a Georgia newspaper in June 1865.[90]

30. *With the Thirteenth Amendment having just been passed by Congress,*

Carpenter spoke of the Emancipation Proclamation as a great moral event. Said Lincoln:

Yes, as affairs have turned, it is the central act of my administration and the great event of the nineteenth century. —*Carpenter-1, 764. {C}*

31. *Carpenter recalled being present the evening of March 18, 1865, when a group of politicians visited the President on business. Surprised to find that none of them had ever heard of* The Nasby Papers, *Lincoln said:*

There is a chap out in Ohio who has been writing a series of letters in the newspapers over the signature of Petroleum V. Nasby. Someone sent me a pamphlet collection of them the other day. I am going to write to "Petroleum" to come down here, and I intend to tell him if he will communicate his talent to me, I will swap places with him. —*Carpenter-1, 744. {D}*

There are several reasons for doubting the accuracy or authenticity of this recollection, including the testimony of Nasby himself (real name, David Ross Locke, q.v.).[91]

32. *According to Carpenter, one of the last stories he heard from Lincoln was about John Tyler, generally considered by Whigs to be a party traitor:*

A year or two after Tyler's accession to the presidency, contemplating an excursion in some direction, his son went to order a special train of cars. It so happened that the railroad superintendent was a very strong Whig. On Bob's making known his errand, that official bluntly informed him that his road did not run any special trains for the president. "What," said Bob, "did you not furnish a special train for the funeral of General Harrison?" "Yes," said the superintendent, stroking his whiskers, "and if you will only bring your father here in **that** shape, you shall have the best train on the road." —*Carpenter-2, 278. {C}*

33. *Very likely it was Carpenter who provided a newspaper's account of a conversation in which Lincoln said of the new vice president, Andrew Johnson:*

He is too much of a man for the American people to cast him off for a single error. —*New York* Post, *April 15, 1865.*[92] *{D}*

HUMPHREY W. CARR   *A New Jersey businessman who visited Lincoln in the summer of 1860.*

1. *Learning that Carr stood six feet, two and one-half inches, Lincoln said:*

When I get the kinks all out, I am six feet, four inches. Now, Mr. Carr, doesn't that entitle me to your vote? —*Carr's recollection in Whipple W, 337. {C}*

ANNA ELLA CARROLL (1815–1893)   *A Maryland woman who wrote several pamphlets in defense of the Union war effort and made some extravagant claims about her influence on military policy.*

1. *When Miss Carroll requested payment of $50,000 for her pamphleteering work, Lincoln replied that her proposition was:*

the most outrageous one ever made to any government upon earth. — *Carroll to Lincoln, August 14, 1862, Lincoln Papers.* {A}

JOHN D. CATON (1812–1895) *A longtime member of the Illinois supreme court and its chief justice from 1855 to 1864.*

1. *In 1857, it came to light that all three members of the court were from Oneida County, New York. Lincoln asked Caton if this was true and then said:*

I could never understand before why this was a One-i-dea court. —*Caton, 185 (1893).* {C}

MARQUIS DE CHAMBRUN (1831–1891) *Charles Adolphe Pineton, French liberal royalist, who was a member of the presidential party that visited City Point and Petersburg, Virginia, April 6–9, 1865.*

1. *Concerning Petersburg, Lincoln said:*

Animosity in the town is abating. The inhabitants now accept accomplished facts, the final downfall of the Confederacy, and the abolition of slavery. There still remains much for us to do, but every day brings new reason for confidence in the future. —*Chambrun, 29 (1893).* {C}

2. *On the possibility of an American response to the French occupation of Mexico:*

There has been war enough. I know what the American people want, but, thank God, I count for something, and during my second term there will be no more fighting. —*34.* {C}

3. *On the mention of Springfield as the returning steamer passed Mount Vernon:*

How happy, four years hence, will I be to return there in peace and tranquillity! —*35.* {C}

Lincoln expressed the same desire to John T. Stuart (q.v.) at about the same time.

4. *In the carriage approaching Washington, Mrs. Lincoln said, "That city is filled with our enemies." Lincoln responded somewhat impatiently:*

Enemies! We must never speak of that. —*35.* {C}

ALBERT B. CHANDLER (1840–1923) *Telegrapher in the War Department during the latter part of the Lincoln administration, later president of the Postal Telegraph Company.*

1. *One day, Lincoln told a story about a traveler passing a farmhouse at night:*

A man, apparently struggling with the effects of bad whisky, thrust his head out of the window and shouted loudly, "Hullo! hullo!" The traveler stopped and asked what was wanted. "Nothing of you," was the reply. "Well, what in the devil do you shout hullo for when people are passing?" angrily asked the traveler. "Well, what in the devil are you passing for when people are shouting hullo?" replied the inebriate. —*Chandler-1, 448 (1895)*. {C}

For antecedents, see Zall, 109.

   2. *Another story that Chandler remembered went like this:*

Boys, did I ever tell you the joke the Chicago newsboys came on me? Well, soon after I was nominated for president at Chicago, I went up one day, and one of the first really distinguished men who waited on me was a picture-man, who politely asked me to favor him with sitting for my picture. Now at that time there were less photographs of my phiz than at present, and I went straightway with the artist, who detained me but a moment and took one of the most really life-like pictures I have ever seen of myself, from the fact that he gave me no **fixing** nor **positions**. But this stiff, ungovernable hair of mine was all sticking every way, very much as it is now, I suppose; and so the operation of his camera was but "holding the mirror up to nature." I departed and did not think of pictures again until that evening I was gratified and flattered at the cry of newsboys who had gone to vending the pictures: " 'Ere's yer last picter of Old Abe! He'll look better when he gets his hair combed." —*Chandler's account as given to a writer for* Harper's Monthly, *32 (February 1866): 405*. {D}

In the version that Chandler himself wrote much later (Chandler-1, 448), Lincoln dated the incident shortly before, rather than soon after, his nomination, but he was not in Chicago at either time. Le Grand B. Cannon (q.v.) likewise recalled hearing the story from Lincoln and located the incident more credibly in Springfield. The photograph in question had been taken in 1857. It was indeed widely used during the presidential campaign, and Lincoln wrote one letter about it mentioning the "disordered condition of the hair."[93]

   3. *Lincoln was asked whether he had, as reported, sought to learn where Grant got his liquor, saying that he would like to send some to his other generals. He replied:*

that he had heard the story before, and that it would have been very good if he had said it, but that he didn't. He supposed it was charged to him to give it currency. . . . the original of the story was in King George's time. Bitter complaints were made to the King against his General Wolfe in which it was charged that he was mad. The King replied angrily: "I wish he would bite some of my other generals then." —*Chandler-1, 448*. {C}

Lincoln may likewise have disowned the Grant story in a conversation with Moses F. Odell (q.v.). John Eaton and John M. Thayer (qq.v.) were among those who claimed to have heard him tell it. John A. Dahlgren (q.v.) is another person who recalled hearing Lincoln tell the King George story. Chandler-1, 449, also includes the exploding dog story, told earlier by Joseph Medill (q.v.) and others.

4. Commenting on Colonel Benjamin H. Grierson's 600-mile cavalry raid from Memphis to Baton Rouge in April 1863, Lincoln said that:

it reminded him of a story he once heard, of a person who had run a needle into his hand and never knew anything of it again till it came out of one of his feet fifteen years afterward. —*Chandler-2, 34 (c. 1903). {C}*

Chandler-2, 32–33, also includes the raisins and Colt revolvers stories recalled by his fellow telegrapher, David Homer Bates (q.v.).

5. On July 12, 1863, after receiving a message from General Meade about his plans for attack, Lincoln expressed his fear that Lee's army would escape across the Potomac:

They will be ready to fight a magnificent battle when there is no enemy there to fight. —*Chandler-2, 34. {C}*

6. According to Chandler, the President "often said" to him:

I come here to escape my persecutors. Hundreds of people come in and say they want to see me for only a minute. That means if I can hear their story and grant their request in a minute, it will be enough. —*Chandler interview with Ida M. Tarbell, September 16, 1898, typescript in the Tarbell Papers. {C}*

7. When Norman B. Judd, home from his post as minister to Prussia, complained that the government was not sufficiently stern and retaliatory in its prosecution of the war, Lincoln told a story and then added:

You see, Judd, that it is always possible for the other fellow to retaliate, and we have had to think of that in this war. —*Ibid. {C}*

WILLIAM E. CHANDLER (1835–1917) *New Hampshire legislator during the Civil War, later secretary of the navy and United States senator. In 1865, Lincoln appointed him solicitor and judge advocate general of the Navy Department.*

1. On Chandler's motion, the New Hampshire Republican convention in February 1864 struck a blow at Salmon P. Chase's presidential hopes by passing a resolution in favor of Lincoln's renomination. In December of that year, Lincoln said to him:

If Chase or any of his friends makes a raid upon you for what you have done, call upon me. —*Colby Memorandum (1911), 4–5.*

According to an earlier Chandler recollection, Lincoln's words were: If they pursue you for supporting me, call on me and I'll take care of you. —*Chandler interview in the Boston* Globe, *May 9, 1897. {C}*

2. *During the same conversation, Lincoln said concerning his appointment of Chase as chief justice:*

that Mr. Chase had participated in all the acts of the government which the Supreme Court would have to pass upon if they were assailed and that his consistency would make him support all those measures. — *Boston* Globe *May 9, 1897.*[94] {C}

3. *According to a note by Gideon Welles in his diary, Lincoln told a protesting Chandler that:*

he would rather have swallowed his buckhorn chair than to have nominated Chase. — *Welles-1, II, 196.* {D}

AUGUSTUS H. CHAPMAN   *Civil War officer, husband of Harriet Hanks Chapman.*

1. *While visiting his stepmother at the end of January 1861, Lincoln tells Chapman that:*

she has been his best friend in this world and that no son could love a mother more than he loves her.

When they parted, she expressed fear that she would never see him again— that his enemies would assassinate him. He replied: No, no, Mama, they will not do that. Trust in the Lord and all will be well. We will see each other again. — *Chapman to Herndon, October 8, 1865 (7:419-24), Herndon-Weik Collection.* {C}

HARRIET HANKS CHAPMAN   *Daughter of Dennis Hanks and granddaughter of Lincoln's stepmother, Sarah Bush Lincoln. She lived with the Lincolns for perhaps as much as eighteen months in the 1840s.*

1. *Lincoln, according to Mrs. Chapman, once said that:*

he would have killed Douglas if he had not released Mary Todd from their engagement. — *Interview with Jesse W. Weik, October 16, 1914, Weik Papers.* {D}

There is no credible evidence of any such engagement or of any such fierceness in Lincoln's love for Mary Todd, but of course he could have been joking.

2. *Asked by his wife whether Douglas, whom he had met on the street, thought their baby son was pretty, Lincoln replied that:*

he failed to notice or ask about Bob. *Mary was indignant.* — *Ibid.* {C}

SALMON P. CHASE (1808–1873)   *Ohio senator and governor, one of the country's leading antislavery politicians, who served as secretary of the treasury until 1864 and then was appointed chief justice. Chase, who had sought the presidency in 1860, was the choice of many Radical Republicans opposed to the re-election of Lincoln.*

1. *On August 3, 1862, according to Chase's diary, Lincoln spoke of the treaty reportedly signed between the Cherokees and the Confederate government. He suggested:*

the expediency of organizing a force of whites and blacks, in separate regiments, to invade and take possession of their country. — *Chase, 357. {B}*

2. *During the same meeting, in a discussion of slavery and possible steps toward emancipation, Lincoln said that:*

he was pretty well cured of objections to any measure except want of adaptedness to put down the rebellion. — *358. {B}*

3. *At a great war meeting in front of the Capitol on August 6, 1862, Lincoln remarked when the crowd called for him to speak:*

Well, hadn't I better say a few words and get rid of myself? — *360. {A}*

4. *In a cabinet session on September 2, following Pope's defeat at Bull Run, Lincoln discussed the new assignment given McClellan, declaring that:*

he had set him to putting these troops into the fortifications about Washington, believing that he could do that thing better than any other man.

In answer to criticism from Chase and Stanton, he repeated that: the whole scope of the order was simply to direct McClellan to put the troops into the fortifications and command them for the defense of Washington.

When the criticism continued, he said that: it distressed him exceedingly to find himself differing on such a point from the Secretary of War and Secretary of the Treasury; that he would gladly resign his place, but he could not see who could do the work wanted as well as McClellan. — *368-69. {B}*

5. *Concerning one general's conduct in the recent battle, Lincoln told Chase on September 5 that:*

the clamor against McDowell was so great that he could not lead his troops unless something was done to restore confidence. — *370. {B}*

Lincoln suggested that McDowell ask for a court of inquiry, which he did.

6. *On September 22, 1862, Lincoln read the text of his preliminary Emancipation Proclamation to the cabinet. Here is Chase's approximation of what he said before doing so:*

I have, as you are aware, thought a great deal about the relation of this war to slavery; and you all remember that, several weeks ago, I read to you an order I had prepared on this subject, which, on account of objections made by some of you, was not issued. Ever since then, my mind has been much occupied with this subject, and I have thought all along that the time for acting on it might very probably come. I think the time has come now. I wish it were a better time. I wish that we were in a better condition. The action of the army against the rebels has not been quite what I should have best liked. But they have been driven out of Maryland, and Pennsylvania is no longer in danger of invasion. When the rebel army was at Frederick, I determined, as soon as it should be driven out of Maryland, to issue a proclamation of emancipation such as I thought most likely to be useful. I said nothing to anyone; but I made the promise to myself and [hesitating a little] to my Maker. The rebel army is now driven out, and I am going to fulfill that promise. I have got you together to hear what I have written down. I do not wish your advice about the main matter; for that I have determined for myself. This I say without intending anything but respect for any one of you. But I already know the views of each on this question. They have been heretofore expressed, and I have considered them as thoroughly and carefully as I can. What I have written is that which my reflections have determined me to say. If there is anything in the expressions I use, or in any other minor matter, which any one of you thinks had best be changed, I shall be glad to receive the suggestions. One other observation I will make. I know very well that many others might, in this matter as in others, do better than I can; and if I were satisfied that the public confidence was more fully possessed by any one of them than by me, and knew of any constitutional way in which he could be put in my place, he should have it. I would gladly yield it to him. But though I believe that I have not so much of the confidence of the people as I had some time since, I do not know that, all things considered, any other person has more; and, however this may be, there is no way in which I can have any other man put where I am. I am here. I must do the best I can and bear the responsibility of taking the course which I feel I ought to take. —393-94. {A}

A statement of this length, even though written down soon after it was made and cast in direct speech, should probably be regarded as in some part paraphrase.

7. *On September 27, in response to a question from Chase about General John A. McClernand, the President said that:*

he thought him brave and capable, but too desirous to be independent of everybody else. —403. {B}

8. *After visiting the Antietam battlefield, Lincoln told the cabinet on October 7 that:*

he was fully satisfied that we had not over 60,000 men engaged.

Concerning strength of position, he said that: [the] enemy's [was] much the best, his wings and center communicating easily by the Sharpsburg road parallel with [the] stream. —415. {B}

9. *At a cabinet meeting on January 23, 1863, while discussing Grant's canal project near Vicksburg and the hazards involved, Lincoln told a story of:*

the man with the mill supplied from a lake at the top of the hill on the side of which the mill was built. He opened the sluice a trifle and the water rushed out, widening the passage until its volume swept off mill and miller. —425. {B}

10. *A little later, in another connection, the President told the story of:*

the man at the muster who sold cider at one end of his barrel while a rogue who had tapped it at the other end outside the shanty was underselling him from his own barrel. —425. {B}

11. *Concerning the resignation of General Ambrose E. Burnside, received on September 10, 1863, Lincoln said to Chase that:*

he was not willing to accept it at present, at any rate, as Burnside was now doing very well and was very loyal and true-hearted. He proposed to say to him that he could not be spared at present, but that after a while, should success still attend us and his private affairs should make his retirement necessary, his resignation would be accepted.[95] —439. {B}

12. *Concerning proposed new regulations of trade with occupied portions of the South, Lincoln remarked to Chase, as he signed his approval:*

You understand these things; I do not. —440. {A}

13. *To the cabinet on September 14, 1863, the President said that:*

the applications for discharges by drafted men and deserters were very numerous and were granted under circumstances which show that the judges are disposed to defeat the objects of the law.

He expressed the opinion that: state courts had no authority to issue a writ of habeas corpus for any person in the custody of United States officers claiming to act under the national law.

He proposed, therefore: to direct officers holding persons in such custody, to make a return of the fact that they were so held and to refuse to obey the writ, and if force should be used, to overcome it by force. —441. {B}

14. *To Chase's urging on September 17 that he revoke the exception of southeastern Virginia from the Emancipation Proclamation, Lincoln replied by reading the unfinished draft of a letter discussing the subject.[96] Then he added that:*

the revocation, at all events, was not expedient at present and should be deferred until after the fall elections. —447. {B}

15. *On September 23, 1864, after some discussion of Stanton's proposal to send reinforcements from the Army of the Potomac to General Rosecrans in Chattanooga, Lincoln said that:*

he would telegraph Meade in the morning and if he did not propose an immediate movement, the order for the two corps to move should be given at once by General Halleck. —452. {C}

Retrospective comment in this journal entry indicates that at least part of it was written at a later date.

CHARLES P. T. CHINIQUY (1809–1889)   *A Catholic priest who left the Church in 1860 and became one of the country's most prominent anti-Catholic propagandists. He was the principal source of the charge that Jesuits were responsible for the assassination of Lincoln. Chiniquy did retain Lincoln in 1856 as one of his defense counsel in a slander suit, but the account in his autobiography of several conversations with Lincoln in the White House have earned him recognition as perhaps the biggest liar in Lincoln literature. More than one reputable biographer has nevertheless placed some credence in Chiniquy's writings, and they served as ready ammunition for a number of later campaigns against Catholicism.[97] It therefore seems appropriate to provide a sampling from the lengthy harangues that he attributed to Lincoln.*

   1. *In August 1861, Lincoln supposedly said:*

You see that your friends, the Jesuits, have not yet killed me. But they would have surely done it when I passed through their most devoted city, Baltimore, had I not defeated their plans by passing incognito a few hours before they expected me. We have the proof that the company which had been selected and organized to murder me was led by a rabid Roman Catholic called Byrne. It was almost entirely composed of Roman Catholics. More than that, there were two disguised priests among them, to lead and encourage them. . . . It is evident that it is to the intrigues and emissaries of the Pope that we owe, in great part, the horrible civil war which is threatening to cover the country with blood and ruins. —*Chiniquy, 691–92 (1885). {E}*

   2. *And in June 1864:*

This war would never have been possible without the sinister influence of the Jesuits. We owe it to Popery that we now see our land reddened with the blood of her noblest sons. . . . The New York riots were evidently a Romish plot from beginning to end. We have the proofs in hand that they were the work of Bishop Hughes and his emissaries. . . . From the beginning of our civil war, there has been, not a secret, but a public alliance between the Pope of Rome and Jeff Davis. —*699, 703. {E}*

LUCIUS E. CHITTENDEN (1824–1902)   *Vermont lawyer and politician who was a delegate to the Washington peace conference in February 1861 and served as register of the treasury throughout the Lincoln administration. Chittenden's recollections, which he introduced with the assertion that they were based on contemporary notes,[98] have often been cited as authority (in* Lincoln Day by Day, *for instance), but many scholars consider them to be dubious material. One critic classified him among those men "who colored their memories with their imagination until their accounts became wholly unsafe as historical data."*[99]

1. In the evening of February 23, 1861, the very day of Lincoln's arrival in Washington, the members of the peace convention paid him a formal visit at Willard's Hotel. According to Chittenden, he called on the President-elect earlier in the day to tell him something in advance about the men whom he would be meeting. Lincoln said that:

he was pleased to have an opportunity of meeting so many representative men from different sections of the Union; the more unjust they were in their opinions of himself, the more he desired to make their acquaintance. He had been represented as an evil spirit, a goblin, the implacable enemy of southern men and women. He did not set up for a beauty, but he was confident that, upon a close acquaintance, they would not find him so ugly nor so black as he had been painted. He hoped every delegate from the slave states would be present, especially those most prejudiced against himself. — *Chittenden, 69 (1891). {D}*

There is no other evidence that Chittenden had a private interview with Lincoln on the latter's very busy first day in Washington.

2. A special correspondent of the New York Herald *reported that Lincoln, in greeting the peace convention delegates, displayed "a most wonderful memory" for their names and personal histories. He offered just one example. To Alexander W. Doniphan of Missouri the President said: "Is this Doniphan, who made that splendid march across the plains, and swept the swift Comanches before him?"*[100] *For a fuller account of Lincoln's remarks at this, his first reception in Washington, historians have had to rely on Chittenden, who recalled, for instance, that the President said to William C. Rives of Virginia:*

You are a smaller man than I supposed—I mean in person. Everyone is acquainted with the greatness of your intellect. It is, indeed, pleasant to meet one who has so honorably represented his country in Congress and abroad.

And to James B. Clay, son of a famous father: Your name is all the endorsement you require. From my boyhood, the name of Henry Clay has been an inspiration to me.

And to George W. Summers of western Virginia: You cannot be a disunionist, unless your nature has changed since we met in Congress.

And to Felix K. Zollicoffer: Does liberty still thrive in the mountains of Tennessee?

"Everything now depends upon you," said Rives at one point. Lincoln replied: I cannot agree to that. My course is as plain as a turnpike road. It is

marked out by the Constitution. I am in no doubt which way to go. Suppose now we all stop discussing and try the experiment of obedience to the Constitution and the laws. Don't you think it would work?

Answering a Virginian's complaint that northerners failed to suppress the likes of John Brown and William Lloyd Garrison: I believe John Brown was hung and Mr. Garrison imprisoned. You cannot justly charge the North with disobedience to statutes or with failing to enforce them. You have made some which were very offensive, but they have been enforced, notwithstanding.

Replying to the more specific assertion that the Fugitive Slave Act went unexecuted in the free states: You are wrong in your facts again. Your slaves have been returned, yes, from the shadow of Faneuil Hall in the heart of Boston. Our people do not like the work, I know. They will do what the law commands, but they will not volunteer to act as tipstaves or bumbailiffs. The instinct is natural to the race. Is it not true of the South? Would you join in the pursuit of a fugitive slave if you could avoid it? Is such the work of gentlemen?

And in response to even more savage charges from the same Virginian: No northern newspaper, not the most ultra, has advocated a slave insurrection or advised the slaves to cut their masters' throats. A gentleman of your intelligence should not make such assertions. We do maintain the freedom of the press—we deem it necessary to a free government. Are we peculiar in that respect? Is not the same doctrine held in the South?

When a New Yorker warned of impending economic disaster and asked whether he would make concessions to the South in order to prevent it, Lincoln spoke of his inaugural oath: I shall swear that I will faithfully execute the office of president of the United States, of **all** the United States, and that I will, to the best of my ability, preserve, protect, and defend the Constitution of the United States. This is a great and solemn duty. With the support of the people and the assistance of the Almighty, I shall undertake to perform it. I have full faith that I **shall** perform it. It is not the Constitution as I would like to have it, but as it **is**, that is to be defended. The Constitution will not be preserved and defended until it is enforced and obeyed in every part of every one of the United States.

To a New Jersey delegate who asked whether concessions should not be made in order to avoid civil war, Lincoln replied: In a choice of evils, war may not always be the worst. Still, I would do all in my power to avert it, except to neglect a constitutional duty. As to slavery, it must be content with what it has. The voice of the civilized world is against it; it is opposed to its growth or extension. Freedom is the natural condition of the human race in which the Almighty intended men to live. Those who fight the purposes of the Almighty will not succeed. They always have been, they always will be, beaten. —72-76. {D}

It is extremely difficult to believe that there could have been so much heated argument and so much oratory from Lincoln during the half hour or so in which he greeted perhaps as many as a hundred men. Furthermore, Chittenden's credibility suffers from his assertion that he stood at Lincoln's side and introduced the delegates one by one. The Herald's *correspondent on the scene wrote that Salmon P. Chase performed that function.*[101]

3. The story of William Scott, the sleeping sentinel, had been part of the Lincoln tradition for nearly three decades when Chittenden insinuated himself into it with what he offered as the true account.[102] *It was he, we are told, who, in September 1861, took a group of Vermont soldiers to see Lincoln in the hope of obtaining a pardon for their friend Scott, sentenced to death for falling asleep while on sentry duty at a Potomac bridge. Chittenden suggested a presidential order suspending the execution and offered to carry it to the War Department. But Lincoln said:*

No, I do not think that course would be safe. You do not know these officers of the regular army. They are a law unto themselves. They sincerely think that it is good policy occasionally to shoot a soldier. I can see it, where a soldier deserts or commits a crime, but I cannot in such a case as Scott's. They say that I am always interfering with the discipline of the army and being cruel to the soldiers. Well, I can't help it, so I shall have to go right on doing wrong. I do not think an honest, brave soldier, conscious of no crime but sleeping when he was weary, ought to be shot or hung. The country has better uses for him. . . . I will have to attend to this matter myself. I have for some time intended to go up to the Chain Bridge. I will do so today. I shall then know that there is no mistake in suspending the execution. —272-73. {E}

Scott was indeed sentenced to death by a court-martial on September 4 and then pardoned on September 8 by General McClellan in an order stating that, along with various other considerations, "the President of the United States has expressed a wish that as this is the first condemnation to death in this army for this crime, mercy may be extended to the criminal." There is, however, no contemporary evidence of Chittenden's association with the case or of Lincoln's having gone himself to the army camp to prevent the execution.[103]

4. Chittenden recalled that on March 7, 1862, he accompanied Gustavus Fox, assistant secretary of the navy, on a visit to the President. "I cannot now undertake to give the precise words used," he wrote, "but the substance of the conversation I shall probably never forget." Whereupon he proceeded to quote

the two men directly and extensively. Fox was apprehensive about the Con-
federate ironclad Merrimac *(renamed the* Virginia*), which was known to be*
ready for action. When Lincoln minimized the danger, Fox expressed fear that
the vessel would destroy the wooden warships opposing it and move up the Poto-
mac to Washington. Who then, he asked, could prevent the Merrimac *from*
battering down the walls of the Capitol itself? Lincoln replied:

The Almighty, Captain. I expect setbacks, defeats; we have had them, and
shall have them. They are common to all wars. But I have not the slightest
fear of any result which shall fatally impair our military and naval strength,
or give other powers any right to interfere in our quarrel. The destruction
of the Capitol would do both. I do not fear it, for this is God's fight, and
he will win it in his own good time. He will take care that our enemies do
not push us too far.

Lincoln also reminded Fox that the Union now had its own ironclad: The Monitor was one of my inspirations. I believed in her firmly when that energetic
contractor first showed me Ericsson's plans. Captain Ericcson's plain but
rather enthusiastic demonstration made my conversion permanent. It was
called a floating battery then; I called it a raft. I caught some of the inventor's enthusiasm, and it has been growing upon me. I thought then, and I
am confident now, it is just what we want. I am sure that the *Monitor* is
still afloat, and that she will yet give a good account of herself. Sometimes
I think she may be the veritable sling with a stone that shall yet smite the
Merrimac Philistine in the forehead. —*219-21.* {E}

The conviction that Lincoln never uttered any of these words is reinforced by
the absence of other evidence that such an interview took place at the White
House on March 7. Instead, it appears that Lincoln visited Fox's residence that
day and, finding him absent, chatted for half an hour with his wife Virginia
(q.v.).

5. *After hearing from John L. Worden, commander of the* Monitor, *a de-*
scription of the encounter with the Merrimac, *Lincoln said:*

Some uncharitable people say that old bourbon is an indispensable element
in the fighting qualities of some of our generals in the field. But, captain,
after the account that we have heard today, no one will say that any Dutch
courage is needed on board the *Monitor*. —*233-34.* {C}

6. *Toward the end of February 1862, Lincoln talked with Chittenden about*
the new law declaring treasury notes (greenbacks) to be legal tender:

Here is a committee of great financiers from the great cities who say that,
by approving this act, I have wrecked the country. . . . I say to these gentlemen, "Go to Secretary Chase; he is managing the finances." They persist
and have argued me almost blind. . . . We owe a lot of money which we

cannot pay; we have got to run in debt still deeper. Our creditors think we are honest and will pay in the future. They will take our notes, but they want small notes which they can use among themselves. So far, I see no objection, but I do not like to say to a creditor: You shall accept in payment of your debt something that was not money when it was contracted. That doesn't seem honest, and I do not believe the Constitution sanctions dishonesty. —307-8. {D}

Without expressing any qualms, Lincoln signed the legal tender bill on the same day that it was presented to him, and the measure seems to have had more support than opposition from the financial community.[104]

7. During the same conversation, Chittenden quoted from a ballad that included the phrase "conversation in sweet solitude." Lincoln cheered up and said with a "musical laugh" as he departed:

A good Irish bull is medicine for the blues. —309. {D}

This would have been no more than two or three days after the funeral of Willie Lincoln, which Chittenden does not mention.

8. On May 3, according to Chittenden, Lincoln sent him to Annapolis to investigate the condition of recently exchanged Union soldiers who had been prisoners of war at Belle Island, near Richmond. He returned the next day with a horror story of men reduced to skeletons by cruelty and neglect. Lincoln exclaimed:

Can such things be possible? And you are the fourth who has given me the same account. I cannot believe it! There must be some explanation for it. The Richmond people are Americans—of the same race as ourselves. It is incredible! . . . Nothing has occurred in the war which causes me to suffer like this. I know it seems impossible to account for the treatment of these poor fellows, except on the theory that somebody is guilty. But the world will be slow to believe that the Confederate authorities intend to destroy their prisoners by starvation. We should be slow to believe it ourselves. It must be that they have some claim of excuse. Why, the Indians torture their prisoners, but I never heard that they froze them or starved them. . . . We shall have enough to answer for if we survive this war. Let us hope, at least, that the crime of murdering prisoners by exposure and starvation may not be fastened on any of our people. —327-29. {D}

Though cited twice in Lincoln Day By Day, *this story lacks the corroboration that one would like to have whenever Chittenden is the source. Furthermore, there is no explanation of why Lincoln should have chosen the register of the treasury for such a mission or why, after receiving three concordant reports on the subject, he should have felt the need for a fourth.*

9. *Early in the winter of 1862-63, Lincoln came into Chittenden's office and said:*

Do you know any energetic contractor? One who would be willing to take a large contract, attended with some risk? . . . There will be profit and reputation in the contract I may propose. It is to remove the whole colored race of the slave states into Texas. If you have any acquaintance who would take that contract, I would like to see him. —*337. {E}*

Chittenden tells us that Lincoln was much impressed with John Bradley of Vermont, the contractor whom he recommended, but that nothing eventuated from their two-hour interview. There appears to be no other evidence that Lincoln gave even that much consideration to such a scheme.

10. *According to Chittenden, Lincoln consulted him on June 29, 1864, about Chase's resignation, which grew out of a disagreement over an appointment for Maunsell B. Field (q.v.). When Chittenden insisted that Chase's continuance in office was a national necessity, Lincoln replied:*

How mistaken you are! Yet it is not strange. I used to have similar notions. No, if we should all be turned out tomorrow and could come back here in a week, we should find our places filled by a lot of fellows doing just as well as we did, and in many instances better. As the Irishman said, "In this country one man is as good as another and, for the matter of that, very often a great deal better." No, this government does not depend upon the life of any man.

Later in their discussion, the President remarked: I will tell you how it is with Chase. It is the easiest thing in the world for a man to fall into a bad habit. Chase has fallen into two bad habits. One is that to which I have often referred. He thinks he has become indispensable to the country, that his intimate friends know it, and he cannot comprehend why the country does not understand it. He also thinks he ought to be president; he has no doubt whatever about that. It is inconceivable to him why people have not found it out, why they don't as one man rise up and say so. He is, as you say, an able financier. As you think without saying so, he is a great statesman and, at the bottom, a patriot. Ordinarily he discharges a public trust, the duties of a public office, with great ability—with greater ability than any man I know. Mind, I say **ordinarily**, for these bad habits seem to have spoiled him. They have made him irritable, uncomfortable, so that he is never perfectly happy unless he is thoroughly miserable and able to make everybody else just as uncomfortable as he is himself. He knows that the nomination of Field would displease the Unionists of New York, would delight our enemies and injure our friends. He knows that I could not make it without seriously offending the strongest supporters of the government in New York and that the nomination would not strengthen him anywhere or with anybody. Yet he resigns because I will not make it. He is either determined to annoy me or that I shall pat him on the shoulder and coax him to stay. I don't think I ought to do it. I will not do it. I will take him at his word. . . . And yet there is not a man in the Union who would make as good a chief justice as Chase. And if I have the opportunity, I will make him chief justice of the United States. —377-80. {D}

11. *Chittenden was at the White House, he says, early in the morning of July 1, 1864, when William P. Fessenden arrived to protest that he could not accept appointment as Chase's replacement. Lincoln is quoted as replying:*

Fessenden, since I have occupied this place, every appointment I have made upon my own judgment has proved to be a good one. I do not say the best that could have been made, but good enough to answer the purpose. All the mistakes I have made have been in cases where I have permitted my own judgment to be overruled by that of others. Last night I saw my way clear to appoint you secretary of the treasury. I do not think you have any right to tell me you will not accept the place. I believe that the suppression of the rebellion has been decreed by a higher power than any represented by us, and that the Almighty is using his own means to that end. You are one of them. It is as much your duty to accept as it is mine to appoint. Your nomination is now on the way from the State Department, and in a few minutes it will be here. It will be in the Senate at noon. You will be immediately and unanimously confirmed, and by one o'clock today you must be signing warrants in the Treasury. —382. {D}

Chittenden emphasizes that the words in this passage and the passage above were written down at the time in his "journal," but that alleged primary source has never come to light. There is no corroborative evidence that he was present at the Fessenden-Lincoln interview, and his account differs in significant detail from those of Fessenden (q.v.) and of Lincoln as recorded by John Hay (q.v.).

12. *Later that summer, Chittenden says, he managed to draw Lincoln into a discussion of God's role in the affairs of mankind. Here are some of the statements he attributes to the President:*

That the Almighty does make use of human agencies and directly intervenes in human affairs, is one of the plainest statements of the Bible. I have had so many evidences of his direction, so many instances when I have been controlled by some other power than my own will, that I cannot doubt that this power comes from above. I frequently see my way clear to a decision when I am conscious that I have no sufficient facts upon which to found it. But I cannot recall one instance in which I have followed my own judgment, founded upon such a decision, where the results were unsatisfactory; whereas, in almost every instance where I have yielded to the views of others, I have had occasion to regret it. I am satisfied that when the Almighty wants me to do or not to do a particular thing, he finds a way of letting me know it. I am confident that it is his design to restore the Union. He will do it in his own good time. We should obey and not oppose his will. . . .

I know by my senses that the movements of the world are those of an infinitely powerful machine, which runs for ages without a variation. A man who can put two ideas together knows that such a machine requires an infinitely powerful maker and governor. Man's nature is such that he cannot take in the machine and keep out the maker. This maker is God—infinite in wisdom as well as in power. Would we be any more certain if we saw him? . . . I decided a long time ago that it was less difficult to believe that the Bible was what it claimed to be than to disbelieve it. It is a good book for us to obey—it contains the ten commandments, the golden rule, and many other rules which ought to be followed. No man was ever the worse for living according to the directions of the Bible. —*448-50.* {D}

THOMAS M. CLARK (1812–1903) *Episcopal Bishop of Rhode Island and a member of the Sanitary Commission during the Civil War.*

1. *In the spring of 1861, when Clark questioned the wisdom of summoning Congress into special session, Lincoln replied:*

I have called this Congress because I must have money. There is Chase; sometimes he calls for a million of dollars in the course of twenty-four hours, and I can assure you that it is not an easy matter to raise that amount in a day. The result of this war is a question of resources. That side will win in the end where the money holds out longest; but if the war should continue until it has cost us five hundred millions of dollars, the resources of the country are such that the credit of the government will be better than it was at the close of the War of the Revolution, with the comparatively small debt that existed then. —*Clark, 141 (1895).* {C}

2. *At a later time, Clark visited him to urge an exchange of prisoners, and Lincoln said:*

I feel just as you do about this matter. I don't like to think of our men suffering in the southern prisons; neither do I like to think that the southern men are suffering in our prisons; but you don't want me to recognize the Southern Confederacy, do you? Well, I can't propose an exchange of prisoners without recognizing the existence of the Confederate government.

Clark asked why he could not initiate an exchange policy informally and unilaterally by sending some men to the South with the expectation that a like number of northerners would be returned. Lincoln replied: I will tell you why it can't be done at present; I haven't capital enough on hand to discount. —142-43. {C}

3. *On some occasion when cabinet members, diplomats, and other dignitaries were present, Clark suggested playfully that labels on their backs would help onlookers to identify them. Lincoln responded in the same spirit:*

I do not think that I should need any label; they would know me by my height. Here is Stanton; he supposes that he has more weight of character than I have, but I stand much higher in society than he does. —143. {C}

ENOS CLARKE   *A St. Louis resident, one of the large delegation of Missouri and Kansas Radicals who presented an "address" to the President on September 30, 1863.*

1. *Clarke later recalled that in the ensuing discussion Lincoln said:*

You gentlemen must bear in mind that in performing the duties of the office I hold I must represent no one section of the Union, but I must act for all sections of the Union in trying to maintain the supremacy of the government. . . . I desire to so conduct the affairs of this administration that if, at the end, when I come to lay down the reins of power, I have lost every other friend on earth, I shall at least have one friend left, and that friend shall be down inside of me. —*Clarke's statement in Tarbell, III, 175 (1907). {C}*

Clarke told substantially the same story to another interviewer, Walter B. Stevens.[105]

CASSIUS M. CLAY (1810–1903)   *Spirited, erratic antislavery Kentuckian whom Lincoln twice appointed minister to Russia.*

1. *In 1860, when Clay pursued the subject of emancipation, Lincoln said:*

I always thought that the man who made the corn should eat the corn. —*Rice AT, 297 (1886). {C}*

2. *In August 1862, after Clay's return from Russia, there was this presidential response to his complaint that Lincoln had promised to make him secretary of war and then given the place to Simon Cameron instead:*

Who ever heard of a reformer reaping the rewards of his work in his lifetime? I was advised that your appointment as secretary of war would have been considered a declaration of war upon the South. I have no objection to your return to St. Petersburg. I thought that you had desired to return home; at least, Seward so stated to me. —*Clay, 302-3 (1886).*[106] *{C}*

A slightly different version is in Rice AT, 303.

3. *During the same conversation, Clay urged Lincoln to emancipate southern slaves. Later, Lincoln sent for him and said:*

I have been thinking of what you said to me, but I fear if such proclamation of emancipation was made, Kentucky would go against us; and we have now as much as we can carry. . . . The Kentucky legislature is now in session. Go down and see how they stand and report to me. — *Clay, 310.* {D}

According to Clay, he made his report on about September 1, and three weeks later, the Emancipation Proclamation was issued. His claim to have been the primary influence on Lincoln's action is not credible.

4. *Clay recalled that when he returned from Kentucky, Lincoln said to him:*

Don't be uneasy about yourself and your return to St. Petersburg. Seward and no other man can hurt you. We have no confidence in Seward's friendship, and he is kept in office only for reasons of state. — *Rice AT, 304.* {D}

This alleged statement, which reflects Clay's abiding hatred of Seward, is inconsistent with what is otherwise known about Lincoln's attitude toward his secretary of state.

HENRY CLAY COCHRANE (1842–1913) *Naval volunteer in the first half of the Civil War and then a career Marine Corps officer. He accompanied the Marine band to Gettysburg.*

1. *On the train, Lincoln accepted Cochrane's offer of a copy of the New York* Herald, *saying:*

I like to see what they say about us.

After reading for awhile, he began to converse, remarking among other things that: when he had first passed over that road on his way to Congress in 1847, he noticed square-rigged vessels up the Patapsco River as far as the Relay House, and now there seemed to be only small craft.

Later, as the train arrived atHanover, Pennsylvania, he rose and said: Gentlemen, this is all very pleasant, but the people will expect me to say something to them tomorrow, and I must give the matter some thought. — *Cochrane, 9-10 (1907).* {C}

Cochrane believed that Lincoln, having written a substantial portion of the address before leaving Washington, finished it on the train, but Hanover is only about a dozen miles from Gettysburg.[107]

TITIAN J. COFFEY (1824–1867) *Pennsylvania lawyer and politician who served as assistant attorney general during Lincoln's first term.*

1. *In Philadelphia on February 21, 1861, a group of Pennsylvanians urged the appointment of Simon Cameron to the cabinet. Coffey, like James Millikin (q.v.), wrote to Cameron reporting Lincoln's reply that:*

all along, the preponderance in Pennsylvania was so largely in your favor that he did not consider the opposition from Pennsylvania to you sufficient to prevent your appointment.

But then he added: The kind of hostility expressed to General Cameron by those who opposed him in Pennsylvania has spread to other states, and it is from those states that the greatest opposition is made.

He said that: the question would be settled when he reached Washington, and there were some questions which might have to be considered then, arising out of the state of the country. For instance [he continued], it may become expedient to retain in the cabinet some of those who are now doing well, and if any of them be retained, some of those whose claims are pressed on me must be kept out. I merely suggest this, without saying it will be done. — *Coffey to Cameron, February 22, 1861, in Pratt-2, 61.* {A, B}

Among possible holdovers from the Buchanan administration, Lincoln named Secretary of War Joseph Holt, but it was Cameron whom he appointed to that position.

2. *Speaking to Attorney General Edward Bates in November 1861, after receiving word that Captain Charles Wilkes had forcibly removed two Confederate diplomats from the* Trent, *a British ship:*

I am not getting much sleep out of that exploit of Wilkes, and I suppose we must look up the law of the case. I am not much of a prize lawyer, but it seems to me pretty clear that if Wilkes saw fit to make that capture on the high seas he had no right to turn his quarter-deck into a prize court. — *Rice AT, 245 (1886).* {D}

It is not clear whether Coffey heard these words spoken by Lincoln or was told about it later by Bates.

3. *When Bates asked that a captured Confederate soldier be sent home to his father, a loyal Union man, Lincoln said:*

I have an almost parallel case. The son of an old friend of mine in Illinois ran off and entered the rebel army. The young fool has been captured, is a prisoner of war, and his old broken-hearted father has asked me to send him home, promising of course to keep him there. I have not seen my way clear to do it, but if you and I unite our influence with this administration I believe we can manage it together and make two loyal fathers happy. Let us make them our prisoners. — *Rice AT, 244–45.* {D}

Again, it is not clear that Coffey was present and heard this exchange.[108]

4. *Coffey reported that federal marshals challenged in court for certain arrests and seizures were now seeking legal defense money from a fund recently appropriated by Congress, rather than asking, as they had in the past, to be defended by United States district attorneys. Lincoln said:*

Yes, they will now all be after the money and be content with nothing else. They are like a man in Illinois whose cabin was burned down, and, according to the kindly custom of early days in the West, his neighbors all contributed something to start him again. In his case, they had been so liberal that he soon found himself better off than before the fire, and he got proud. One day, a neighbor brought him a bag of oats, but the fellow refused it with scorn. "No," said he, "I'm not taking oats now. I take nothing but money." —*Rice AT, 239. {C}*

5. *To Coffey after the resignation of Bates in November 1864:*

My cabinet has **shrunk up** North, and I must find a southern man. I suppose if the twelve apostles were to be chosen nowadays the shrieks of locality would have to be heeded. — *Rice AT, 241. {C}*

CHARLES CARLETON COFFIN (1823–1896) *Civil War journalist and later a prolific author.*

1. *At City Point, on March 28, 1865, Coffin told the President about a southern planter who had come down the Savannah River with his cotton crop and his entire family—wife, children, Negro woman and her children, of whom he was the father. Lincoln said:*

Oh, yes, I see, I see. Patriarchal times once more. Abraham, Sarah, Isaac, Hagar, and Ishmael, all in one boat. I reckon they'll accept the situation now that they can sell their cotton. — *Rice AT, 177 (1886). {C}*

ISAAC COGDAL *A longtime acquaintance of Lincoln in New Salem and Springfield, Cogdal was a farmer and brick mason who rather late in life became a lawyer.*

1. *In about 1859, according to Cogdal, Lincoln responded to a question about his religious thought by asserting that:*

he did not nor could not believe in the endless punishment of anyone of the human race. He understood punishment for sin to be a Bible doctrine; that the punishment was parental in its object, aim, and design, and intended for the good of the offender; hence it must cease when justice is satisfied. All that was lost by the transgression of Adam was made good by the atonement; all that was lost by the fall was made good by the sacrifice.

He added that: punishment being a provision of the gospel system, he was not sure but the world would be better off if a little more punishment was preached by our ministers, and not so much pardon for sin.

When Cogdal advised him not to talk about such beliefs because they amounted to the unpopular doctrine of Universalism, Lincoln replied that: he never took any part in the argument or discussion of theological questions. — *Cogdal to Benjamin F. Irwin, April 10, 1874 in* Illinois State Journal *(Springfield), May 16, 1874. {D}*

The final statement stands in contrast to the preceding discussion and to Cogdal's assertion in an earlier letter that over a twenty-five-year period, he had "often talked" with Lincoln about religion. The effect of this recollection and the one following is to place Cogdal on such terms of intimacy with Lincoln that the latter was willing to talk with him about matters he would discuss with no one else. There is little corroborating evidence of such a relationship.[109]

2. *Cogdal recalled asking Lincoln as president-elect whether it was true that he had loved and courted Ann Rutledge. Lincoln replied:*

It is true—true, indeed I did. I have loved the name of Rutledge to this day. I have kept my mind on their movements ever since and love them dearly.

Asked whether it was also true that he had "run a little wild" over her death, he said: I did really. I ran off the track; it was my first. I loved the woman dearly and sacredly. She was a handsome girl, would have made a good loving wife, was natural and quite intellectual, though not highly educated. I did honestly and truly love the girl and think often, often of her now. — *Undated statement (probably about 1866) taken down by William H. Herndon (11:3000–3001), Herndon-Weik Collection. {D}*

The confessional style is not the only reason for doubting the substance of this recollection. Whatever the relationship between Lincoln and Ann Rutledge may have been, he was silent about her after leaving New Salem in 1837. Her name does not appear in any of his correspondence, and none of his close friends— not even Herndon or Joshua Speed—ever testified to having heard him mention her. Cogdal alone claimed to have done so, and Cogdal was not by any reliable evidence the likely confidant of this reticent man on such a delicate subject at such a critical moment in his career.[110]

CORNELIUS COLE (1822–1924)   *Representative and later senator from California.*

1. *During a reception in 1863, Lincoln noticed that Mrs. Cole had lost one of her white gloves and said:*

Never mind, Mrs. Cole, I shall have a search made for it tomorrow and shall reserve it as a souvenir. —*Cole-2, 29 (1923). {D}*

This is the recollection of a 100-year-old man as told to an interviewer.

2. *In declining some request from Cole and another California congressman, Lincoln told a story about a Presbyterian minister who preached against the establishment of a Universalist church in his town:*

He began by reminding his hearers how happily they were getting along in Springfield, spiritually and otherwise. "And now," he said, "there comes among us a stranger to establish a church on the belief that all men are to be saved, but my brethren, let us hope for better things." —*Cole-1, 173 (1908). {C}*

3. *In the latter part of the war, responding to Cole's expression of fear for his safety:*

Well, I determined when I first came here, that I would not be dying all the while. I have always observed that one man's life is as dear to him as another's, and no one would take my life without expecting to lose his own. Besides, if anyone wanted to kill me, he could shoot me from a window on Seventh Street any day when I am riding out to the Soldiers' Home. I do not believe it is my fate to die in this way. —*Cole-1, 214-15*.[111] *{C}*

4. *On April 14, 1865, according to Cole, Lincoln commented on an address to the people of Richmond by General Godfrey Weitzel. He said:*

that Weitzel's proclamation was a little too good and that he had already directed some modifications of it. —*Cole-1, 229. {D}*

Cole may have been thinking vaguely of a lenient order for the opening of Richmond's churches, but Lincoln more or less approved of Weitzel's policy.[112]

SCHUYLER COLFAX (1823–1885) *Indiana Republican congressman who was elected Speaker in 1863 and later served one term as vice president.*

1. *One night in the telegraph room of the War Department, Lincoln discussed the idiosyncrasies of several political leaders and then added:*

A peculiarity of his own life from his earliest manhood had been that he habitually studied the opposite side of every disputed question, of every law case, of every political issue, more exhaustively, if possible, than his own side. He said that the result had been, that in all his long practice at the bar he had never once been surprised in court by the strength of his adversary's case—often finding it much weaker than he had feared. —*Rice AT, 333-34 (1886). {C}*

2. *Lincoln signed the final Emancipation Proclamation on January 1, 1863, after having shaken many hands at his New Year's Day reception. That evening, he said to Colfax and several other men:*

The signature looks a little tremulous, for my hand was tired, but my resolution was firm. I told them in September if they did not return to their allegiance and cease murdering our soldiers, I would strike at this pillar of their strength. And now the promise shall be kept, and not one word of it will I ever recall. —*Colfax-1, 16-17 (1865). {C}*

A variant version of Colfax's account is in Carpenter-2, 87. Another account sometimes quoted was provided in 1865 by John W. Forney, who presumably had heard it from William H. Seward or his son Frederick, both of whom were present at the signing.[113] *Frederick Seward (q.v.) wrote his own account many years later.*

3. *After bad news and a sleepless night in 1863:*

How willingly would I exchange places today with the soldier who sleeps on the ground in the Army of the Potomac. —*Colfax-1, 14, repeated in Rice AT, 337.*[114] {C}

4. *Following the battle of the Wilderness in May 1864, Lincoln exclaimed to Colfax:*

Why do we suffer reverses after reverses? Could we have avoided this terrible, bloody war? Was it not forced upon us? Is it ever to end?

But then he recovered himself and said: Grant will not fail us now. He says he will fight it out on that line, and this is now the hope of our country. —*Rice AT, 337.*[115] {C}

5. *In response to Colfax's request for pardon of a soldier sentenced to be shot:*

Some of my generals complain that I impair discipline and subordination in the army by my pardons and respites, but it makes me rested, after a day's hard work if I can find some good excuse for saving a man's life, and I go to bed happy as I think how joyous the signing of my name will make him and his family and friends. —*Colfax-1, 18.* {C}

A variant version is in Rice AT, 339.

6. *On being told that Confederate raiders had struck a nearby Virginia community and carried off a Union general, as well as a dozen mules:*

How unfortunate; I can fill his place with one of my generals in five minutes, but those mules cost us two hundred dollars apiece. —*Rice AT, 339.* {D}

A contemporary version with somewhat different details and the auditor not identified appeared in the New York Times, *March 11, 1863.*

7. *Colfax, soon to leave on a trip to the Pacific coast, visited the White House in the morning of April 14, 1865, and again early in the evening. Lincoln said:*

You are going to California, I hear. How I would rejoice to make that trip, but public duties chain me down here, and I can only envy you its pleasures. —*Colfax to Isaac N. Arnold, May 1, 1867 (copy), Hay Collection-Brown.* {C}

8. *Lincoln asked him to take a message to western miners:*

I have very large ideas of the mineral wealth of our nation. I believe it practically inexhaustible. It abounds all over the western country from the Rocky Mountains to the Pacific, and its development has scarcely commenced. During the war, when we were adding a couple of millions of dollars every day to our national debt, I did not care about encouraging the increase in the volume of our precious metals. We had the country to save first. But now that the rebellion is overthrown and we know pretty nearly the amount of our national debt, the more gold and silver we mine makes the payment of that debt so much easier. Now, I am going to encourage them in every possible way. We shall have hundreds of thousands of disabled soldiers, and many have feared that their return home in such great numbers might paralyze industry by furnishing suddenly a greater supply of labor than there will be demand for. I am going to try to attract them to the hidden wealth of our mountain ranges, where there is room enough for all. Immigration, which even the war has not stopped, will land upon our shores hundreds of thousands more per year from overcrowded Europe. I intend to point them to the gold and silver that waits for them in the West. Tell the miners for me that I shall promote their interests to the utmost of my ability, because their prosperity is the prosperity of the nation, and we shall prove in a very few years, that we are indeed the treasury of the world. —*Colfax-2 (1865).* {C}

Declaring that he put this message on paper a few days after Lincoln's death, Colfax added, "I think I wrote it down in nearly his own words."

9. *In the same conversation, Lincoln repeated this report from his son, a member General Grant's staff:*

Bob has just returned home and breakfasted with us. He was at the surrender of Lee, and told me that some of the rebel officers told him they were very glad the contest was over at last. —*Colfax to Arnold, May 1, 1867.* {C}

10. *Also in conversation on that last day:*

I have been criticized for authorizing General Weitzel to allow the rebel legislature of Virginia to come together again at Richmond and am not sure that it was wise. It was an idea entirely my own. Lee's army was then in existence; I thought it could be demoralized by the legislature formally withdrawing from it the Virginia troops, who would probably be glad to obey their order of recall. I thought that it was for the best—that it would hasten the ending of this bloody war and save life. But, since Lee's army has surrendered, it became needless. It was a doubtful experiment at best, and I have revoked the authority. —*Ibid.* {C}

11. *Colfax asked Lincoln what he could do about the Confederate leaders, and he replied:*

that he did not want their blood, but that we could not have peace or order in the South, he feared, while they remained there with their great influence to poison public opinion.

After Colfax repeated his question, the President said: Scare them out of the country by having our generals inform them if they stay, they will be punished for their crimes, but if they leave, no attempt will be made to hinder them. Then we can be magnanimous to all the rest and have peace and quiet in the whole land. —*Ibid.* {C}

12. *When Colfax told him how uneasy many people had been about his recent visit to the Confederate capital, Lincoln said:*

Why, if anyone else had been president and had gone to Richmond, I would have been alarmed too, but I was not scared about myself a bit. —*Colfax-1, 10. {C}*

CHARLES H. T. COLLIS (1838–1902)   *Irish-born Union officer who eventually received the Medal of Honor for his performance at Fredericksburg.*

1. *Introduced in April 1865 to a captured Confederate general, Rufus Barringer, with whose brother he had served in Congress, Lincoln wrote a note to Stanton asking that his detention be made "as comfortable as possible." He remarked as he did so:*

I suppose they will send you to Washington, and there I have no doubt they will put you in the old Capitol prison. I am told it isn't a nice sort of a place, and I am afraid you won't find it a very comfortable tavern; but I have a powerful friend in Washington—he's the biggest man in the country—and I believe I have some influence with him when I don't ask too much. Now, I want you to send this card of introduction to him, and if he takes the notion he may put you on your parole or let up on you that way or some other way. Anyhow, it's worth while trying. —*Collis's account in his wife's book: Collis, 68–69 (1889). {C}*

Barringer was not released until July.

SEPTIMA M. COLLIS (1842–1917)   *Wife of Charles H. T. Collis.*

1. *When Lincoln explained that her husband was too young for promotion to brigadier general, Mrs. Collis responded that he was not too young to be killed and make her a widow. Said Lincoln, in what she regarded as a mildly flirtatious vein:*

Well, you would have no trouble in finding promotion **then**. —*Collis, 21 (1889). {C}*

2. *During Lincoln's extended visit to City Point in late March and early April 1865, General Collis asked him how long he intended to remain there with the army. He replied:*

Well, I am like the western pioneer who built a log cabin. When he commenced he didn't know how much timber he would need, and when he had finished, he didn't care how much he had used up. So you see I came down among you without any definite plans, and when I go home I shan't regret a moment I have spent with you. —*60. {C}*

LUCY N. COLMAN (1817–1906)   *Schoolteacher and antislavery lecturer whose home was Rochester, New York. She accompanied Sojourner Truth (q.v.) on her visit to the White House, October 29, 1864.*

1. While the two women were waiting to see Lincoln, Mrs. Colman heard the President's response to a delegation seeking his intervention in behalf of a Baltimore man who had been arrested for trading with the enemy:

Gentlemen, this government is a big machine, even in times of peace. It is no small thing to keep it in good running order, but now, when added to the usual duties of my position, I have on my hands this great rebellion (which is to be put down), I have no time to waste. I have been visited already more than once by parties from Baltimore urging my interference in this case. You protest that this man is innocent; then let him await his trial when he can easily prove it.

Responding to the assertion that they were Lincoln voters: Can't help it; it is not so essential that I have votes as that the rebellion be crushed. To what purpose is it that you vote for me, that you pay a small sum of money to soldiers, as a cover-up, while you supply the rebels with goods or arms? I tell you, gentlemen, it will not do. Already has the War Department declared to me that it could not and would not stand by me in this work of subduing the rebels if every time they catch a rascal, I let him loose. Gentlemen, I ain't going to do it.

The spokesman for the group then announced that he was a fighting man, who had once paid three hundred dollars for knocking a man down. Lincoln good-naturedly replied: Let me beg you not to try that on me.

Whereupon the man changed his tune and appealed to Lincoln's goodness of heart, insisting: "Mr. President, you can do this thing." Said Lincoln: Certainly I can, and I can end this war and let the rebels have their own way, but I'm not going to do it. —*Colman's letter of November 1 in the Rochester (N.Y.) Express, November 10, as reprinted in the Sacramento Union, December 14, 1864. {A}*

2. When Sojourner Truth, during her conversation with Lincoln, said that he was the only president who had ever done anything for her people, he replied:

And the only one who ever had such opportunity. Had our friends in the South behaved themselves, I could have done nothing whatever. —*Ibid. {A}*

In an account written much later, one that contains some factual inaccuracies, Mrs. Colman quoted Lincoln as replying more unpleasantly: I'm not an abolitionist; I wouldn't free the slaves if I could save the Union in any other way. I'm obliged to do it. —*Colman, 67 (1891). {C}*

3. In her later account, Mrs. Colman recalled that at the same interview, she also introduced an ailing black woman who was in dire financial distress because her husband, a Union soldier, had not yet been paid. Lincoln, after reading the woman's letter, said privately to Colman:

'Tis a hard case, but what can I do? I have no more money than she has. Can't you take her off my hands?

Mrs. Colman's response, we are given to understand, shamed the President into writing on the envelope: "I think this is a worthy object." —Colman, 67. {C}

ALBAN JASPER CONANT (1821–1915)   *Artist recently settled in St. Louis who painted Lincoln's portrait in the late summer of 1860. The many factual errors in Conant's reminiscences (for instance, he quotes Lincoln as describing the debates with Douglas as nighttime events) do not inspire confidence in his memory of their conversations.*

    1. *Concerning the debates:*

In all my life, I never engaged in any enterprise with such reluctance and grave apprehension as in that contest. Douglas was the idol of his party, and justly so, for he was a man of great ability. He was reckless in many of his statements, but "Judge Douglas said so" clinched the argument and ended the controversy. I soon found that my simple denial carried no weight against the imperious and emphatic style of his oratory. —*Conant, 513 (1909). {E}*

    2. *About the charge that he had engaged in the whiskey trade:*

When I was in the grocery business at New Salem, money was scarce, and I was obliged to receive in exchange all kinds of produce. When enough had accumulated, I loaded it on a flatboat, took it to New Orleans, and traded it off for supplies. On one of these trips a neighbor of mine asked me to take along three barrels of whiskey with my freight, and sell them for him. This I did, and that was the only whiskey transaction of my life. —*514. {E}*

Lincoln's second and last flatboat trip to New Orleans took place more than a year before his ill-fated venture into the grocery business. Egbert L. Viele (q.v.) offered another version of this story.

    3. *In response to Conant's question about his net worth:*

Well, I pay taxes on $15,000, but I'm not worth $20,000. —*514. {D}*

JOHN CONNESS (1821–1909)   *Senator from California for one term beginning in 1863.*

    1. *On June 30, 1864, Lincoln talked with Conness and other members of the Senate finance committee about his acceptance of Salmon P. Chase's resignation as secretary of the treasury. Of Maunsell B. Field (q.v.), Chase's overruled choice for a treasury position in New York, he said:*

I could not appoint him. He had only recently at a social gathering, in presence of ladies and gentlemen, while intoxicated, kicked his hat up against the ceiling, bringing discredit upon us all and proving his unfitness.

As for the Secretary's presidential aspirations, Lincoln said that: he had no ob-

jection to the candidacy of Mr. Chase—he had a right to be a candidate—
but there had grown such a state of feeling that it was unpleasant for them
to meet each other; and now Mr. Chase had resigned, and he had accepted
the resignation.

He added: I am ready and willing to resign the office of president, and let
you have Mr. Hamlin for your president, but I will no longer endure the
state I have been in. —*Rice AT, 564 (1886). {D}*

*Two years earlier, according to a newspaper report and according to the recol-
lection of Senator James Harlan (q.v.), Lincoln had mentioned the possibility
of resigning in favor of the Vice President, Hannibal Hamlin. It seems most
unlikely that he would have talked that way in late June 1864, just three weeks
after the Republican national convention had renominated him but not Hamlin.*

MONCURE D. CONWAY (1832–1907)   *Virginia-born preacher, writer, and antislavery leader, regarded as erratic even by some of his fellow abolitionists.[116] Conway was bitterly critical of the Lincoln presidency but changed his tone after the
assassination.*

   1. *Conway heard Lincoln speak in Cincinnati on September 17, 1859, and
recalled the following passages:*

Be sure that no compromise, no political arrangement with slavery, will be
satisfactory or will ever last which does not deal with it as a great wrong.
Every man that comes into this world has a mouth to be fed and a back to
be clothed; by a notable coincidence, every man has two hands; I infer that
those hands were meant to feed that mouth and clothe that back; and—
mark it, brother Kentuckians—any institution which interferes with the
right of those hands so to do will be sure, sooner or later, to come tumbling
about those who uphold it. There is room for us all to be free. It cannot
wrong the white man that the Negro should be free, but it does the majority
of white men that the Negro should not be free. —*Conway reminiscence in
the New York* Tribune, *August 30, 1885, reproduced with considerable change
in Conway-2, I, 318 (1904). {D}*

*Except for the statement that slavery was wrong and must be treated as a
wrong, these quotations are not corroborated in the complete newspaper report
of the speech, which was revised by Lincoln himself.[117]*

   2. *Early in 1862, when urged by Conway and William H. Channing to move
toward emancipation:*

We grow in this direction daily, and I am not without hope that some great
thing is to be accomplished. When the hour comes for dealing with slavery,
I trust I shall be willing to act, though it costs my life; and, gentlemen, lives
will be lost. —*Conway-1, 61 (1865). {C}*

In his autobiography, published many years later, Conway expanded Lin-

coln's remarks considerably: Perhaps we may be better able to do something in that direction after a while than we are now. . . . . I think the country grows in this direction daily, and I am not without hope that something of the desire of you and your friends may be accomplished. Perhaps it may be in the way suggested by a thirsty soul in Maine who found he could only get liquor from a druggist; as his robust appearance forbade the plea of sickness, he called for soda, and whispered, "Couldn't you put a drop o' the creeter into it unbeknownst to yourself?" In working in the antislavery movement you may naturally come in contact with a good many people who agree with you and possibly may overestimate the number in the country who hold such views. But the position in which I am placed brings me into some knowledge of opinions in all parts of the country and of many different kinds of people, and it appears to me that the great masses of this country care comparatively little about the Negro and are anxious only for military successes. We shall need all the antislavery feeling in the country and more. You can go home and try to bring the people to your views, and you may say anything you like about me, if that will help. Don't spare me! When the hour comes for dealing with slavery, I trust I will be willing to do my duty, though it cost my life. And, gentlemen, lives will be lost. — *Conway-2, I, 345–46. {D}*

The story of the thirsty soul, which had already been attributed to Lincoln in different contexts by Grant, Sherman (qq.v.), and several other persons, does not seem very apposite in this instance.

3. *During the same conversation in 1862, Lincoln spoke feelingly of southerners, who, he said:*

had become at an early day, when there was at least a feeble conscience against slavery, deeply involved commercially and socially with the institution. He pitied them heartily, all the more that it had corrupted them; and he earnestly advised us to use what influence we might have to impress on the people the feeling that they should be ready and eager to share largely the pecuniary losses to which the South would be subjected if emancipation should occur. It was the disease of the entire nation, and all must share the suffering of its removal. — *Conway-1, 61. {C}*

4. *January 25, 1863, speaking to an abolitionist delegation that included Conway and Wendell Phillips:*

I fear that some of the severity with which this administration is criticized results from the fact that so many of us have had so long to act with minorities that we have got an uncontrollable habit of criticizing. — *Conway-1, 62. {C}*

The recollection in Conway's autobiography is somewhat different: My own impression, Mr. Phillips, is that the masses of the country generally are only dissatisfied at our lack of military successes. Defeat and failure in the field make everything seem wrong. Most of us here present have been long working in minorities and may have got into a habit of being dissatisfied. At any rate, it has been very rare that an opportunity of "running" this administration has been lost. — *Conway-2, I, 379. {C}*

5. *During the same meeting in 1863, when the subject of a second term in the presidency was raised:*

Oh, Mr. Phillips, if I have ever indulged **that** hope, and I do not say I have not, it has long ago been beaten out of me. — *Conway-1, 62. {C}*

In the autobiography: Oh, Mr. Phillips, I have ceased to have any personal feeling or expectation in that matter,—I do not say I never had any,—so abused and borne upon as I have been. — *Conway-2, I, 379. {C}*

6. *Responding to a suggestion by one member of the delegation that John C. Frémont be appointed military governor in North Carolina:*

I have great respect for General Frémont and his abilities, but the fact is that the pioneer in any movement is not generally the best man to carry that movement to a successful issue. It was so in old times, wasn't it? Moses began the emancipation of the Jews but didn't take Israel to the promised land after all. He had to make way for Joshua to complete the work. It looks as if the first reformer of a thing has to meet such a hard opposition and gets so battered and bespattered that afterward, when people find they have to accept his reform, they will accept it more easily from another man. — *New York* Tribune, *August 30, 1885, repeated in Conway-2, I, 380. {C}*

7. *To a question from Phillips about the effect achieved by the Emancipation Proclamation, the President replied that:*

he had not expected much from it at first and consequently had not been disappointed. He had hoped, and still hoped, that something would come of it after a while.

Later in the interview, after reminding the delegation that he had been elected by a minority of the people, he said that: he felt convinced that his administration would not have been supported by the country at any earlier stage of the war in a policy of emancipation.

Then he added: All I can say now is that I believe the Proclamation has knocked the bottom out of slavery, though at no time have I expected any sudden results from it. — *New York* Tribune, *August 30, 1885, reproduced with minor changes in Conway-2, I, 378, 380-81. {C}*

RUSSELL H. CONWELL (1843-1925)   *Soldier and lawyer, who eventually became a clergyman and writer, famous for his lecture "Acres of Diamonds." One suspects that there is far more invention than recollection in Conwell's account of a meeting with Lincoln in December 1864, which, as he described it, would have had to go on for hours.*[118]

1. *Concerning the impending military execution about which Conwell had called, Lincoln said that he should write to the soldier's mother and:*

tell her the President told you that he never did sign an order to shoot a boy under twenty years of age and that he never will! —*Conwell, 33 (1922).* {D}

2. *Indicating that it was his ambition to carry on a farm, with Tad for a partner, Conwell's Lincoln said:*

that he had bought a farm at New Salem, Illinois, where he used to dig potatoes at twenty-five cents a day, and that Tad and he were to have mule teams and raise corn and onions. —*35.* {E}

Lincoln had no personal interest in farming and never bought farmland for himself in New Salem or anywhere else.

3. *When he learned that Conwell had been brought up on a farm in the Berkshires:*

I hear that you have to sharpen the noses of the sheep up there to get them down to the grass between the rocks. —*36.* {D}

4. *In a long discourse on the humorist Artemus Ward and the nature of his appeal:*

Ward rests me more than any living man. —*37.* {D}

JAY COOKE (1821–1905)   *Philadelphia banker and financial adviser to the Lincoln administration, whose banking house served as principal agent for the sale of United States bonds.*

1. *During a carriage ride, Cooke ventured to ask Attorney General Edward Bates why his whiskers were white and his hair still dark. Lincoln, with a quizzical look at Bates, remarked that the problem was easy to solve:*

It is because he uses his jaws more than he uses his brain. —*Cooke, 11 (1890).* {C}

JOHN W. CRISFIELD (1806–1897)   *Unionist congressman from Maryland.*

1. *On March 10, 1862, Lincoln talked to a delegation of border-state congressmen about his recent message to Congress, in which he had recommended an initiatory step toward federal support for gradual emancipation by state action. After expressing some fear that the import of the message had been misunderstood, the President disclaimed any intent to injure the interests or wound the sensibilities of the slave states. He said:*

that on the contrary, his purpose was to protect the one and respect the other; that we were engaged in a terrible, wasting, and tedious war; immense armies were in the field, and must continue in the field as long as the war lasts; that these armies must, of necessity, be brought into contact with slaves in the states we represented and in other states as they advanced; that slaves would come to the camps and continual irritation was kept up; that he was constantly annoyed by conflicting and antagonistic complaints; on the one side, a certain class complained if the slave was not protected by the army; persons were frequently found who, participating in these views, acted in a way unfriendly to the slaveholder; on the other hand, slaveholders complained that their rights were interfered with, their slaves induced to abscond and protected within the lines; these complaints were numerous, loud, and deep, were a serious annoyance to him and embarrassing to the progress of the war; that it kept alive a spirit hostile to the government in the states we represented; strengthened the hopes of the Confederates that at some day the border states would unite with them and thus tend to pro-long the war; and he was of opinion, if this resolution should be adopted by Congress and accepted by our states, these causes of irritation and these hopes would be removed and more would be accomplished towards short-ening the war than could be hoped from the greatest victory achieved by Union armies; that he made this proposition in good faith and desired it to be accepted, if at all, voluntarily, and in the same patriotic spirit in which it was made; that emancipation was a subject exclusively under the control of the states and must be adopted or rejected by each for itself; that he did not claim nor had this government any right to coerce them for that purpose; that such was no part of his purpose in making this proposition, and he wished it to be clearly understood; that he did not expect us there to be pre-pared to give him an answer, but he hoped we would take the subject into serious consideration, confer with one another, and then take such course as we felt our duty and the interest of our constituents required of us. — *Crisfield memorandum in McPherson, 210 (1864). {B}*

Crisfield wrote his summary of the discussion immediately after it ended. Two other members of the delegation attested to its substantive accuracy.

2. *In the same meeting, when the subject of his own attitude toward slavery was raised, he said:*

that he did not pretend to disguise his antislavery feeling; that he thought it was wrong and should continue to think so; but that was not the question we had to deal with now. Slavery existed, and that, too, as well by the act of the North as of the South; and in any scheme to get rid of it, the North, as well as the South, was morally bound to do its full and equal share. — *211. {B}*

WILLIAM A. CROFFUT (1835-1915) *Connecticut-born journalist and author. He took the initiative in organizing a series of public lectures at the Smithsonian in the winter of 1861-62.*

1. *Asked by Croffut whether he would attend Horace Greeley's lecture on January 3, Lincoln said:*

Yes, I will. I can get away, can't I, Hay? I never heard Greeley, and I want to hear him. In print, every one of his words seems to weigh about a ton. I want to see what he has to say about us. — *Croffut, 58.* {C}

2. *On January 17, 1862, at the conclusion of a talk with Senator James H. Lane of Kansas and others about fugitive slaves, Lincoln reportedly said:*

Yes, General, I understand you. And the only difference between you and me is that you are willing to surrender fugitives to loyal owners in case they are willing to return; while I do not believe the United States government has any right to give them up in any case. And if it had, the people would not permit us to exercise it. — *Croffut's dispatch of January 19 in the New York* Tribune, *January 21, 1862.* {B}

Croffut may not have been himself an auditor of this statement, but its accuracy was substantially confirmed by a correspondent of the Chicago Tribune, *who differed only in recalling that Lincoln had said "United States army" instead of "United States government."*[119] *Croffut later wrote that he was "authorized by those who were present at the conversation" to reiterate the substance of the President's remarks as follows: "That the rebel states having, by their own insane action, abolished slavery in all its relations with our government by repudiating our protection, they can make no claim on us for fugitives, and that therefore the United States cannot return them, either with the military or civil arm, without enslaving free men."*[120]

3. *At a White House reception in 1864, Croffut heard a woman ask whether the incessant handshaking was not harder work than what he did in his office. The President replied:*

Oh, no — no. Of course, this is tiresome physically; but I am pretty strong, and it rests me, after all, for here nobody is cross or exacting, and no man asks me for what I can't give him. — *Croffut, 63.* {C}

WILLIAM H. CROOK (1839–1915) *Washington policeman detailed as a guard at the White House beginning in January 1865. His recollections come to us at second hand, having been written out by an interviewer.*

1. *In his first conversation with Crook after a White House reception on January 9, Lincoln said:*

Yes, it does tire me to shake hands with so many people. Especially now when there is so much other work to do. And most of the guests come out of mere curiosity. — *Crook, 9 (1910).* {C}

2. *Summoned one day to Lincoln's room, Crook found him sewing a button on his trousers. The President said:*

All right, just wait until I repair damages. — *14.* {C}

3. *When friends ventured to tease him about yielding to his wife's authority on a small matter, he said:*

If you knew how little harm it does me and how much good it does her, you wouldn't wonder that I am meek. —16. {C}

4. *Late in March, according to Crook, Lincoln said to Thaddeus Stevens concerning prosecution of the war:*

Stevens, this is a pretty big hog we are trying to catch and to hold when we do catch him. We must take care that he doesn't slip away from us. — 28–29. {D}

There is no indication that Crook was present at this interview.

5. *At City Point, when he was told that Vice President Johnson had arrived in the area, Lincoln said:*

Well, I guess he can get along without me. —44. {C}

Mary Lincoln and David Dixon Porter (qq.v.) had similar recollections.

6. *On April 10, a delegation presented Lincoln a portrait of himself in an elaborate silver frame. To the spokesman's remarks he responded:*

Gentlemen, I thank you for this token of your esteem. You did your best. It wasn't your fault that the frame is so much more rare than the picture. — 63. {C}

7. *The afternoon of April 14, 1865, on the way to the War Department:*

Crook, do you know, I believe there are men who want to take my life? And I have no doubt they will do it. . . . I have perfect confidence in those who are around me, in every one of you men. I know no one could do it and escape alive. But if it is to be done, it is impossible to prevent it. —66. {D}

It seems rather pat that Lincoln should have spoken of assassination just a few hours before it happened.[121]

8. *On attendance at the theater that evening:*

It has been advertised that we will be there, and I cannot disappoint the people. Otherwise I would not go. I do not want to go. —67. {D}

T. J. CROWDER   *In the early twentieth century, superintendent of the Illinois Society Park Association.*

1. *At a temperance meeting in 1844 or 1845, Lincoln remarked:*

Some of you boys may have said, "I would like to get drunk once to see how it seems." Better stick your big toe out and let a rattlesnake bite it and see how that seems. —*Crowder to James R. B. Van Cleave, undated but probably 1908, Centennial Reminiscences.*[122] {D}

SHELBY M. CULLOM (1829–1914)   *Illinois lawyer and legislator, elected to Congress in 1864, later governor and United States senator.*

1. *In early 1862, discussing injuries suffered at the hands of the government, Lincoln pointed to an injustice that was not remedied until the twentieth century:*

There is this difference between dealing with the government and dealing between individuals. If you deal with an individual and he doesn't do right you can sue him in court and make him pay damages. But if you are dealing with the government you are helpless. — *Cullom interview in New York* Times, *March 22, 1908; repeated with verbal changes in Cullom-2, 97–98 (1911).* {C}

2. *In the summer of 1862, although complaining about the man's chronic unreadiness for battle, Lincoln said that:*

he would rather trust McClellan to get his army out of a tight place than any other general that he had. — *Cullom-2, 93.* {C}

3. *Responding to Cullom's suggestion in February 1864 that he turn Chase out of the cabinet:*

Let him alone; he can do no more harm in here than he can outside. — *Cullom-2, 94.* {C}

4. *Cullom was at the White House in late March 1864 when news of Owen Lovejoy's death arrived. Lincoln said:*

He was one of the best men in Congress. If he became too radical, I always knew that I could send for him and talk it over, and he would go back to the floor and do about as I wanted. — *Cullom-1, 503 (1910).* {C}

5. *Also in 1864:*

There is a young man by the name of Blaine now serving in Congress who seems to be one of the brightest men in the House. His speeches are always short, always full of facts, and always forcible. I am very fond of him. He is one of the coming men of the country. — *Cullom-2, 115.* {D}

This seems a little too prophetic, considering that James G. Blaine had entered Congress just the year before.

JOHN L. CUNNINGHAM   *New York soldier, detailed to duty in Washington for several months in 1863.*

1. *Cunningham visited the White House in the company of his newly elected congressman, Orlando Kellogg, who had served with Lincoln in the Thirtieth Congress. Lincoln said to Kellogg:*

I am glad to see that you know the kind of company to keep. I hardly feel respectable these days if I haven't a soldier for a companion. Citizen's dress doesn't amount to much nowadays. — *Cunningham JL, 50 (1920).* {C}

2. *At the close of the interview, Lincoln told Kellogg:*

I have enjoyed your call and this revival of our experiences in that Congress. We thought then that our responsibilities were considerable, but compare them with what confronts us now!

Then, turning to Cunningham, he said: I count you and every soldier a friend. I trust you will survive the war and see a reunited country and be happy in the fact that you did your part to make it so. —*51. {C}*

3. *Concerning rank and priorities at Mathew Brady's photographic studio, where Cunningham chanced to meet the President again:*

Soldiers come first everywhere, these days. Black-coats are at a discount in the presence of the blue, and I recognize the merit of the discount. —*52. {C}*

4. *When the photographer suggested a full-length picture, Lincoln asked whether it could be done with a single negative, explaining:*

that he had lately seen a very long, or rather, a very wide landscape photograph and that he wondered if there was a camera large enough to take in such an area; but on close examination he found that it had been taken in parts and nicely joined together, and he thought perhaps this method might be necessary for his full-length "landscape." —*52. {C}*

5. *To the suggestion, as he was being posed, that he "just look natural," Lincoln said:*

That is what I would like to avoid.

After developing the negative, the photographer remarked that it did indeed look natural, and Lincoln replied: Yes, that is my objection. These cameras are painfully truthful. —*52, 53. {C}*

6. *On the art of storytelling:*

Mr. Seward is limited to a couple of stories which from repeating he believes are true. —*53. {C}*

JOSEPH O. CUNNINGHAM (1830–1917) *Journalist, lawyer, and judge in Urbana, Illinois.*

1. *In 1905, Cunningham wrote out a brief recollection of the main theme in the famous "lost speech," delivered on May 29, 1856, at Bloomington, Illinois, on the occasion of the formation of the Republican party as a statewide organization. Lincoln argued:*

the unwisdom of disunion and the direful consequences to the country of an attempt of any party at dissolution.

He assured his audience that: northern men had no desire for a separation and would never consent to it.

And he closed this part of the speech with the words: We won't go out of the Union and you shan't! *— Cunningham JO, 108. {C}*

ANDREW G. CURTIN (1815?–1894) *Republican war-time governor of Pennsylvania.*

1. *After the disastrous battle of Fredericksburg, when Curtin reported graphically on the carnage and expressed a wish that the war could somehow be ended, a distressed Lincoln eventually roused himself by telling a story about a farmer's prize hog that was let loose by his two mischievous sons:*

The hog went straight for the boys and drove John up a tree. Then the hog went for the seat of James's trousers, and the only way the boy could save himself was by holding on to the hog's tail. The hog would not give up his hunt nor the boy his hold. After they had made a good many circles around the tree, the boy's courage began to give out, and he shouted to his brother, "I say, John, come down, quick, and help me let this hog go!" Now, Governor, that is exactly my case. I wish some one would come and help me let this hog go! *— Rice AT, xxvi (1886). {C}*

This is Curtin's account as told to Rice. He repeated the story with somewhat different details in Wilson RR-1, 200, and Mowry, 1068. In Herndon, II, 329, it is said that Lincoln used the anecdote to illustrate his argument during a murder trial. For other versions, see Zall, 41.

2. *In the 1890s, Curtin recalled that Lincoln, soon after his arrival at Gettysburg in November 1863, said to other people in the hotel parlor:*

I believe, gentlemen, the committee are expecting me to say something here today. If you will excuse me I will go into this room here and prepare it.

After a time, says Curtin, the President returned with his speech written on a large yellow government envelope. — Curtin to an interviewer, Mowry, 1069 (1897). {D}

Despite its flawed chronology (Lincoln traveled to Gettysburg the day before the ceremony), this contribution to a familiar myth is perhaps not entirely without foundation; for there is other evidence that Lincoln, at the very least, put the finishing touches on his masterpiece after arriving in Gettysburg.[123]

3. *Having offered in May 1864 to supply additional 100-day troops from Pennsylvania, Curtin subsequently reminded Lincoln that he had declined on the ground that:*

you did not desire, without actual necessity, to further exhaust her laboring population on which . . . the government depended so largely for coal, iron, and other material aid. *— Curtin to Lincoln, June 6, 1864, Lincoln Papers. {C}*

GEORGE WILLIAM CURTIS (1824–1892)   *Author, orator, and for many years editor of* Harper's Weekly.

1. *Curtis visited Lincoln one evening in the first winter of the war, and as they parted, the weary-looking President said:*

We shall beat them, my son—we shall beat them. —*Curtis GW, 429 (1895).*[124] {C}

JOHN A. DAHLGREN (1809–1870)   *Career naval officer who served during the Civil War as commandant of the Washington Navy Yard and chief of the Bureau of Ordnance. In 1863, he was made an admiral and took command of the South Atlantic blockading squadron.*

1. *While driving to the Navy Yard on January 2, 1862, Lincoln spoke of the bare possibility of there being two nations. He added that:*

he could not see how the two could exist so near to each other. —*Extract from Dahlgren's diary in Nicolay Papers.* {B}

2. *Looking back in April 1862 to the outbreak of civil war a year earlier, Lincoln said that:*

when he received the nomination he had forebodings as to the trouble which might ensue. This passed away before a resolution to abide the consequences, whatever they might be. —*Dahlgren's diary in Dahlgren, 365.* {B}

3. *Lincoln remarked on May 24, 1862, that:*

Shields was said to be crazy, which put him in mind that George III had been told the same of one of his generals, namely, that he was mad. The King replied he wished he would bite his other generals. —*Dahlgren, 375.* {B}

General James Shields was the man with whom Lincoln had very nearly fought a duel in 1842. Albert B. Chandler (q.v.) also recalled hearing Lincoln relate this anecdote.

4. *Speaking of the Army of the Potomac after the close of the Peninsular campaign, Lincoln said that:*

its total had been 160,000, but it was only 91,000 now—35,000 accounted for [in] casualties, but 34,000 absent who should not be. He was adverse to the Peninsular campaign, but would have given McClellan all the men he asked for had he had them. —*Diary entry for August 7, 1862, in Nicolay Papers.* {B}

5. *On August 19, as McClellan was completing his withdrawal from the James River area, Lincoln said:*

Now I am to have a sweat of five or six days. The Confederates will strive to gather on Pope before McClellan can get around, and his first corps is not in the Potomac yet. —*Dahlgren, 379. {A}*

6. *Told by Halleck that the promotion he desired for Dahlgren's son would be contrary to the rules, Lincoln said that:*

he was only the lead horse in a team, and must not kick out of traces. —*Dahlgren, 382, entry for November 13, 1862. {B}*

7. *During the same conversation, Lincoln said that:*

he knew his proclamation would not make a single Negro free beyond our military reach. —*Dahlgren, 382. {B}*

8. *On December 22, 1862, speaking to John W. Forney in Dahlgren's presence about the recently proffered resignations of Seward and Chase, Lincoln said:*

If one goes, the other must; they must hunt in couples. —*Dahlgren, 383. {A}*

Referring to the senatorial group that precipitated the cabinet crisis, he said that: it was very well to talk of remodeling the cabinet, but the caucus had thought more of **their** plans than of **his** benefit, and he had told them so. —*Dahlgren, 384. {B}*

9. *On March 29, 1863, Dahlgren found the President in a nervous and complaining mood. He said that:*

they were doing nothing at Vicksburg or Charleston. Du Pont was asking for one ironclad after another as fast as they were built. . . . the canal at Vicksburg was of no account, and [he] wondered that a sensible man would do it. —*Dahlgren, 389. {B}*

10. *Visiting the Navy Department on April 21, 1863, Lincoln was in good humor and said as he left:*

Well, I will go home; I had no business here; but, as the lawyer said, I had none anywhere else. —*Dahlgren, 390. {A}*

11. *Speaking of David Hunter, Samuel F. Du Pont, and the unsuccessful attempt to force the entrance of Charleston harbor on April 7, the President said that:*

he had written a joint letter to the General and Admiral, giving discretion as to an attack on Charleston or Savannah, but did not suppose they would give up Charleston after a fight of forty minutes. —*Dahlgren, 390, entry for April 26, 1863.*[125] *{B}*

CHARLES A. DANA (1819-1897)   *One of the great American newspaper editors of the later nineteenth century. Managing editor of the New York* Tribune *at the beginning of the war, he became a troubleshooter for the War Department in 1862 and was its assistant secretary, 1864-65. Dana's* Recollections of the Civil War *were ghostwritten by Ida M. Tarbell following a series of interviews in the winter of 1896-97.*[126]

1. *Shortly after his inauguration in 1861, Lincoln said to a group of anti-Seward New Yorkers who feared that they would be discriminated against in appointments:*

One side shall not gobble up everything. Make out a list of the places and men you want, and I will endeavor to apply the rule of give and take. — *Rice AT, 364 (1886). {C}*

2. *In March 1864, according to Dana's later recollection, Lincoln was eager for the admission of Nevada to statehood, believing that it would facilitate ratification of the proposed Thirteenth Amendment, which in turn would presumably shorten the war and save many lives. Speaking of the Nevada enabling bill then before the House of Representatives, he said:*

Dana, I am very anxious about this vote. It has got to be taken next week. The time is very short. It is going to be a great deal closer than I wish it was.

He then asked Dana to approach three congressmen offering patronage rewards if they would support the measure: It makes no difference, though, what they want. Here is the alternative: that we carry this vote or be compelled to raise another million, and I don't know how many more, men, and fight no one knows how long. It is a question of three votes or new armies. — *Dana, 175-76 (1898). {E}*

For a number of reasons, this story wholly lacks credibility. If not an outright fabrication, it resulted from Dana's confusing events in March 1864 with events in January 1865.[127]

3. *Concerning the problem of how to confiscate a letter from Clement C. Clay in Canada to Judah P. Benjamin in Richmond without compromising the Union spy who carried it, Lincoln said:*

Oh, I think you can manage that. Capture the messenger, take the dispatch from him by force, put him in prison, and then let him escape. If he has made Benjamin and Clay believe his lies so far, he won't have any difficulty in telling them new ones that will answer for this case. — *Rice AT, 374. {C}*

4. *April 1865: With Richmond in Union hands, Lincoln offered to allow the Virginia legislature to meet, provided that it would recall Virginia troops from the field. To Dana he said, however, that:*

Sheridan seemed to be getting Virginia soldiers out of the war faster than this legislature could think. —*Dana to Edwin M. Stanton, April 7, 1865, Stanton Papers.* {B}

5. *April 14, 1865, on the question of whether to arrest Jacob Thompson, former secretary of the interior, who had been a Confederate agent in Canada:*

Well, I rather guess not. When you have an elephant on hand, and he wants to run away, better let him run. — *Rice AT, 376.* {C}

The wording was somewhat different in Dana's later version: Well, no, I rather think not. When you have got an elephant by the hind leg, and he's trying to run away, it's best to let him run. —*Dana, 274.*

DAVID DAVIS (1815–1886) *Illinois circuit judge, one of Lincoln's closest associates in law and politics, whom he appointed to the United States Supreme Court in 1862.*

1. *Davis recalled a case in which Lincoln and Leonard Swett each represented one of two men on trial for murder. In the hotel one evening, Lincoln said:*

Now we have been engaged in this trial for two days, and I am satisfied that our clients are guilty and that the witnesses for the state have told the truth. It is my opinion that the best thing we can do for our clients is to have them come in tomorrow morning and plead guilty to manslaughter and let Davis give them the lowest punishment.

Swett disagreed and the trial continued, but Lincoln withdrew from participation, saying: I cannot argue this case because our witnesses have been lying, and I don't believe them.

Swett made the defense argument alone, and the jury acquitted both men. Lincoln then offered to turn his fee over to Swett, but the latter refused to accept it. —*Davis's account to Ratcliffe Hicks in 1881, recalled in Hicks's letter to* Century Magazine, *November 10, 1893, 47 (1893–94): 638.* {D}

2. *According to an interview with Davis, Lincoln spoke up as follows during a discussion of presidential candidates for 1860:*

Why don't you run me? I can be nominated, I can be elected, and I can run the government. — *Unlabeled clipping in the Lincoln clipping file, Lincoln Collection-Brown.*[128] {D}

3. *Of William S. Wood as a possible commissioner of public buildings, Lincoln told Davis that:*

it would be ruinous to appoint him. —*Davis to Ward H. Lamon, May 6, 1861, Lamon Papers.* {C}

Nevertheless, Lincoln did appoint Wood, but the Senate failed to confirm him.[129]

4. *After his visit to the Army of the Potomac in October 1862, Lincoln apparently confided to Davis that he had told McClellan:*

he would be a ruined man if he did not move forward, move rapidly and effectually. — *Davis to Leonard Swett, November 26, 1862, Davis Papers.* {C}

5. *In November 1862, Lincoln expresses the belief:*

that if Congress will pass a law authorizing the issuance of bonds for the payment of the emancipated Negroes in the border states, Delaware, Maryland, Kentucky, and Missouri will accept the terms. — *Ibid.* {C}

6. *In January 1863, after considerable urging from Davis, Lincoln recommended their mutual friend William W. Orme for promotion to brigadier general. Davis then sought presidential approval of Orme's request for a leave of absence.*[130] *Lincoln was "much annoyed," saying:*

that the whole thing was full of trouble on account of the constant pressure on that account — that if leave was granted to Orme, he would have to grant leave to others. — *Davis to Leonard Swett, January 23, 1863, Davis Papers.* {B}

7. *When Davis warned that military trials in the northern and border states were unconstitutional, Lincoln said:*

that he was opposed to hanging; that he did not love to kill his fellow men; that if the world had no butchers but him, he guessed the world would go bloodless. — *Davis statement, September 19-20, 1866 (8:886-99), Herndon-Weik Collection.*[131] {C}

8. *In response to a question, Lincoln said that:*

he never consulted his cabinet; they all disagreed so much he would not ask them. — *Ibid.* {D}

Whether Lincoln misstated or Davis misunderstood, this assertion was far from the truth.

9. *In February 1864, when Davis asked what he would do if Chase should dismiss Treasury clerks not supporting his presidential aspirations, Lincoln reportedly answered:*

The head, I guess, would have to go with the tail. — *Samuel Wilkeson to Sydney Howard Gay, February 18, 1864, Gay Papers.* {D}

It is not clear that Wilkeson heard this story directly from Davis.

10. *Davis, after showing Lincoln a letter from Thurlow Weed, reported to the latter that Lincoln had replied:*

that he has the highest esteem for you, knows that you are patriotic, and that it hurts him when he cannot do what you think advisable. — *Davis to Weed, March 21, 1864, in Barnes TW, 444.* {B}

GARRETT DAVIS (1801-1872) *Kentucky senator, 1861-72.*

1. *On about April 23, 1861, Davis sought an interview with Lincoln, who said:*

that neither he, nor any other president who had been elected by a party could administer the government in exact accordance with his own opinions and judgment, but must make some departure to satisfy those who had placed him in power. That before the Carolinians had made their attack on Fort Sumter, he had decided not to reinforce or to attempt to reinforce its garrison, but merely, and only, to supply its handful of famishing men with food, and that he had distinctly communicated these purposes to the authorities of the southern confederation. That he had also determined that until the meeting of Congress he would make no attempts to retake the forts, etc., belonging to the United States, which had been unlawfully seized and wrested from their possession, but would leave the then existing state of things to be considered and acted upon by Congress, unless he should be constrained to depart from that purpose by the continued military operations of the seceded states.

The President went on to declare: that events had now reached a point when it must be decided whether our system of federal government was only a league of sovereign and independent states, from which any state could withdraw at pleasure, or whether the Constitution formed a government invested with strength and powers sufficient to uphold its own authority, and to enforce the execution of the laws of Congress; that he had no doubt of the truth of the latter proposition, and he intended to make it good in the administration of the government to the extent that he should be sustained by the people of the United States. . . . That he had expected all the states upon which he had made a requisition for military aid to enable him to execute the laws to respond to that call, and particularly the state of Kentucky, which had been so loyal to the Union and faithful in the performance of all her duties. That he greatly regretted she had not acted up to the principle of her great statesmen now no more, and for which she cast her vote in the late presidential election, "The Union, the Constitution, and the enforcement of the laws."

That he intended to make no attack, direct or indirect, upon the institutions or property of any state, but, on the contrary, would defend them to the full extent with which the Constitution and laws of Congress have vested the president with the power. And that he did not intend to invade with an armed force, or make any military or naval movement against any state, unless she or her people should make it necessary by a formidable resistance of the authority and laws of the United States. That if Kentucky or her citizens should seize the post of Newport, it would become his duty, and he might attempt to retake it, but he contemplated no military operations that would make it necessary to move any troops over her territories, though he had the unquestioned right at all times to march the United States troops into and over any and every state. That if Kentucky made no demonstration of force against the United States, he would not molest her. That he regretted the necessity of marching troops across Maryland, but forces to protect the seat of the United States government could not be concentrated there without doing so, and he intended to keep open a line of communication through that state to Washington City, at any risk, but in a manner least calculated to irritate and inflame her people. — *Davis to George D. Prentice, April 28, 1861, Congressional Globe, 37th Congress, 2nd session, Appendix, 82. {C}*

Despite its length, this is a credible account written no more than a week after the interview.

2. *Probably in the same discussion, Lincoln stated to Davis that:*

when Mr. Baldwin and one or two other gentlemen came here from the Virginia convention he had made the proposition to Mr. Baldwin and his colleagues distinctly that if the Virginia convention would adjourn without doing anything he would withdraw the troops from Fort Sumter. — Congressional Globe, 40th Congress, 2nd session, 1207 (February 17, 1868). {C}

Baldwin (q.v.) was not accompanied by anyone else when he conferred secretly with Lincoln on April 4, 1861.

HENRY WINTER DAVIS (1817-1865) *Maryland politician of Whig antecedents who became one of Lincoln's bitterest critics in Congress.*

1. *On May 2, 1863, Davis went to see the President about a Baltimore newspaper's criticism of Admiral Samuel F. Du Pont after the failure of the naval attack on Charleston in April.[132] Writing to Du Pont the same day, he reported Lincoln's saying:*

that no one stood higher than you with him and the department; that you were the idol of the navy and the favorite of Mr. Welles and enjoyed their full confidence; neither had ever felt the slightest abatement of it; they knew you had done all that in your opinion was possible, and they had never dropped a word of censure or discontent respecting you. That the attack on Charleston had been noised abroad from last fall as always imminent and his expectations and the country's raised to a high pitch, and the delay became oppressive, when finally you announced that you would try your ironclads on Fort McAllister and then on or about the latter part of February would be ready to attack Charleston. He was looking to that time for the attack and expecting to have the city, when you sent up Stimers for plates to strengthen the decks of the ironclads and to say that you must

have three more monitors; this did not cause any change of feeling, no discontent, but he did not understand how it was that you made no reference
to the postponement of the attack involved in the application, and that it
occasioned some surprise that there was no mention of the attack, which
he had been informed was to have come off at that time. That then the
plates were furnished and it seemed possible that the delay in making the
attack might arise from an opinion on your part that you could not succeed, and, if that was so, it was useless to keep the vast iron fleet idle at
Port Royal, an order was sent you from the Navy Department to the effect
that if you doubted the ability of the force at your disposal to take Sumter
and Moultrie, you might abandon the attack and order the ironclads round
to the Mississippi or elsewhere; and that you proceeded to make the attack, but after a further and considerable delay which he did not entirely
understand; and respecting the attack, he said there was no disapproval of
what you had done either in making or desisting from the attack, but that
he had been under the impression that the attack might last for days and
even weeks and be a gradual process, and when he learned that it had been
made and closed in two or three hours, it was a matter of **surprise**, not
of **blame** or **censure**, nor a cause of discontent, but simply an **unexpected
shape** of the matter; and when he heard at the same time that the fleet was
actually about to be withdrawn, an order was telegraphed by him to you on
the 13th April which . . . was not intended in the slightest degree to censure
or reflect on either the attack or retreat but merely to secure a continued
menace of Charleston while other operations proceeded elsewhere; and for
fear the telegram might seem abrupt and possibly capricious, he wrote you
and Hunter a joint letter explaining the telegram in **that** sense [133] . . . he felt
sure there could be no intention in the Navy Department to allow you to
be injured; for the Secretary and Fox both were friendly and really felt the
utmost confidence in your disposition and ability to render service.

*To Welles (q.v.) on April 2, however, Lincoln had already compared Du Pont
to McClellan in his reluctance to take offensive action.*

*Later in the conversation, when Davis reiterated Du Pont's belief that a
joint sea and land force was necessary for a successful attack on Charleston,
Lincoln said that:* he had begun to suspect that the enterprise was a department **pet**—something which had been kept for the **navy** alone. —*Du Pont,
III, 80–82.*[134] {B}

HENRY L. DAWES (1816–1903) *For thirty-five years, beginning in 1857, a member of Congress from Massachusetts, first in the House and then in the Senate.*

1. *Soon after the appointment of Stanton as secretary of war in January
1862, Dawes called at the White House to voice his approval. The President
replied:*

that it was an experiment which he had made up his mind to try, and that whenever a Union man was willing to break away from party affiliations and stand by the government in this great struggle, he was resolved to give him an opportunity and welcome him to the service. . . . that he had been warned against this appointment and had been told that it never would do; that Stanton would run away with the whole concern; and that he would find that he could do nothing with such a man unless he let him have his own way.

Lincoln then told a story of a preacher who was in the habit of going off on such high flights at camp meetings that they had to put bricks in his pockets to keep him down. He added: I may have to do that with Stanton, but if I do, bricks in his pocket will be better than bricks in his hat. I'll risk him for a while without either.[135] *—Dawes, 163 (1894). {C}*

JOHN D. DEFREES (1811–1882) *Indiana journalist and Republican leader, superintendent of public printing during the Lincoln administration.*

   1. *When Defrees objected to the term "sugar-coated" in the message to Congress of July 4, 1861, declaring that it was undignified:*

Defrees, that word expresses precisely my idea, and I am not going to change it. The time will never come in this country when the people won't know exactly what **sugar-coated** means! *—Defrees statement reported in Carpenter-2, 127 (1866). {D}*

   2. *On the day after the first battle of Bull Run, Lincoln said:*

John, if hell is any worse than this, it has no terror for me. *— Told by Defrees to George P. Goff soon afterward, and related in Goff to John G. Nicolay, February 9, 1889, Nicolay Papers. {D}*

   3. *According to a newspaper report circulated in the summer of 1866, Defrees had gone to the Indiana Republican state convention in 1864 with a letter from Lincoln urging delegates to support Andrew Johnson for vice president. Defrees denied the story, declaring that he had attended the convention solely to work for the renomination of Lincoln and adding that he had never heard the President express a preference for Johnson or anyone else. Defrees had heard him say instead that:*

on that question he would say nothing. *—Defrees to Herndon, August 21, 1866 (8:807–8), Herndon-Weik Collection. {C}*

HENRY C. DEMING (1815–1872) *Connecticut political leader and Civil War officer, briefly the mayor of occupied New Orleans. Deming was elected to Congress in 1862.*

   1. *Deming once asked Lincoln if he had ever despaired of the country. He answered:*

When the Peninsular campaign terminated suddenly at Harrison's Landing, I was as nearly inconsolable as I could be and live. —*Deming, 40 (1865).* {C}

2. *During the same conversation, Deming asked whether there had been times when he thought that better management by the commanding general would have brought the war to an end. Lincoln replied:*

that there were three; that the first was at Malvern Hill, where McClellan failed to command an immediate advance upon Richmond; that the second was at Chancellorsville, where Hooker failed to reinforce Sedgwick, after hearing his cannon upon the extreme right; and that the third was after Lee's retreat from Gettysburg, when Meade failed to attack him in the bend of the Potomac.

Then, by way of palliation, he added: I do not know that I could have given different orders had I been with them myself. I have not fully made up my mind how I should behave when minié balls were whistling and these great oblong shells shrieking in my ear. I might run away. —*40-41.* {C}

3. *Without specifying the occasion, Deming recalled a discussion of religion during which Lincoln said that:*

he had never united himself to any church because he found difficulty in giving his assent, without mental reservation, to the long, complicated statements of Christian doctrine which characterize their articles of belief and confessions of faith. When any church [he continued] will inscribe over its altar, as its sole qualification for membership, the Savior's condensed statement of the substance of both law and gospel, "Thou shalt love the Lord thy God with all thy heart, and with all thy soul, and with all thy mind, and thy neighbor as thyself," that church will I join with all my heart and all my soul.[136] —*42.* {C}

CHAUNCEY M. DEPEW (1834–1928) *A New York legislator and public official during the Civil War, Depew later became a railroad president, United States senator, and celebrated after-dinner speaker.*

1. *In 1864, Lincoln remarked:*

They say I tell a great many stories. I reckon I do, but I have found in the course of a long experience that common people, take them as they run, are more easily influenced and informed through the medium of a broad illustration than in any other way, and as to what the hypercritical few may think, I don't care. . . . I have originated but two stories in my life, but I tell tolerably well other people's stories. —*Rice AT, 427-28 (1886).* {C}

A slightly different version is in Depew, 57-58 (1924).

2. *Asked where he got all his stories, Lincoln replied that:*

for many years he traveled the circuit when Illinois was sparsely settled. The judge, counsel, clients, witnesses, and jurymen would be at the same hotel. They were all storytellers. The experiences of a virile frontier people in new and original environment furnished more and better anecdotes than were ever invented. —*Depew's reminiscence in* Leslie's Illustrated Weekly, *February 4, 1909, p. 102.* {C}

3. *On one visit to the White House, Depew said that he wanted nothing but had called just to pay his respects. Lincoln replied:*

Well, it is such a luxury to have somebody here who does not want anything, that if you will wait until I dispose of these cases I would like to talk with you. —*Ibid., 114.* {C}

4. *Concerning the Niagara Falls peace negotiation initiated by Confederate agents in the summer of 1864, Lincoln said:*

This effort was to inflame the peace sentiment of the North, to embarrass the administration, and to demoralize the army, and in a way it was successful. Mr. Greeley was hammering at me to take action for peace and said that unless I met these men, every drop of blood that was shed and every dollar that was spent I would be responsible for, that it would be a blot upon my conscience and soul. I wrote a letter to Mr. Greeley and said to him that those two ex-United States senators were Whigs and old friends of his, personally and politically, and that I desired him to go to Niagara Falls and find out confidentially what their credentials were and let me know.

Instead of Mr. Greeley doing it that way, he went there as an ambassador and with an array of reporters established himself on the American side and opened negotiations with these two alleged envoys across the bridge. I had reason to believe from confidential information which I had received from a man I trusted and who had interviewed Jefferson Davis, the president of the Confederacy, that these envoys were without authority, because President Davis had said to this friend of mine and of his that he would treat on no terms whatever but on absolute recognition of the independence of the Southern Confederacy.[137] The attention of the whole country and of the army centered on these negotiations at Niagara Falls, and to stop the harm they were doing I recalled Mr. Greeley and issued my proclamation "To Whom It May Concern," in which I stated if there was anybody or any delegation at Niagara Falls, or anywhere else, authorized to represent the Southern Confederacy and to treat for peace, they had free conduct and safety to Washington and return. Of course, they never came, because their mission was a subterfuge. But they made Greeley believe in them, and the result is that he is still attacking me for needlessly prolonging the war for purposes of my own. —*Depew, 61-63.* {D}

This long statement contains a number of inaccuracies that are more reasonably attributable to Depew writing in the 1920s than to Lincoln speaking in 1864.[138]

CHARLES M. DERICKSON *A Pennsylvania soldier whose company was on guard duty at the Soldiers' Home and then at the White House in 1862.[139] He was later a hardware merchant in Mercer, Pennsylvania.*

1. *Discussing a minor carriage accident in which he had recently been involved, Lincoln said that:*

he had been in several runaways and was never frightened by horses, but about the worst scared he ever was, was when he was a young man. He had been hauling wood with a yoke of steers, and, going through the woods with an empty wagon, sitting on the hounds with his legs hanging down on either side, something frightened the steers. They started to run, and every time the wheels would strike the root of a tree he would bound up in the air. He held on the best he could. They finally got out into an open field, where he got them stopped. —*Derickson's handwritten statement, December 15, 1897, Tarbell Papers.* {C}

EDWARD DICEY (1832–1911) *English journalist who during 1862–63 spent six months in the United States as a special correspondent for two British magazines.*

1. *On having no vices:*

I recollect once being outside a stage in Illinois, and a man sitting by me offered me a cigar. I told him I had no vices. He said nothing, smoked for some time, and then grunted out, "It's my experience that folks who have no vices have plaguy few virtues." —*Dicey, 24 (1862).* {C}

William H. Herndon, John B. Henderson, and Newton Bateman each later claimed to have heard Lincoln tell a variant version of the same story.[140]

2. *On staying technically within the law:*

That reminds me of an hotel-keeper down at St. Louis who boasted that he never had a death in his hotel, and no more he had; for whenever a guest was dying in his house he carried him out to die in the street. —24.[141] {C}

3. *During discussion of the Missouri Compromise:*

It used to amuse me some to find that the slaveholders wanted more territory, because they had not room enough for their slaves, and yet they complained of not having the slave trade, because they wanted more slaves for their room. —24. {C}

4. *On American oratory:*

It is very common in this country to find great facility of expression and less common to find great lucidity of thought. The combination of the two in one person is very uncommon; but whenever you do find it, you have a great man. —24. {C}

T[HEOPHILUS] LYLE DICKEY (1812–1885)   *Lincoln's longtime friend, an Illinois lawyer, judge, and conservative Whig politician who supported Douglas in 1858 and 1860. He was a Union colonel of cavalry in the earlier years of the Civil War.*

1. *After a long argument about slavery one night in 1855, Lincoln said the next morning:*

I tell you, Dickey, I am right. It is not possible for slavery to continue to exist in the nation; it's got to go. —*Told by Dickey to William Pitt Kellogg in 1860, Kellogg, 326 (1909).* {D}

2. *In a speech at Bloomington on September 12, 1856, according to Dickey, Lincoln expressed the opinion:*

that our government could not last, part slave and part free; that either slavery must be abolished everywhere, or made equally lawful in all the states, or the Union would be dismembered.

At their hotel afterwards, Dickey's vigorous remonstrations proved persuasive. Lincoln said: I don't see any necessity for teaching this doctrine, and I don't know but it might do harm. At all events, from respect for your judgment, Dickey, I'll promise you I won't say so again during this campaign. —*Dickey to Herndon, December 8, 1866 (8:1243–45), Herndon-Weik Collection.* {D}

Dickey was certainly present on this occasion, but the brief newspaper report of Lincoln's speech makes no mention of his using the house-divided argument and no one else seems to have remembered that he did so.[142]

3. *In the fall of 1862:*

Now there's Joe Hooker. He can fight—I think that point is pretty well established—but whether he can "keep tavern" for a large army is not so sure. —*Dickey as interviewed by John G. Nicolay, October 20, 1876, Nicolay Papers.* {C}

ANNA ELIZABETH DICKINSON (1842–1932)   *Youthful antislavery orator whom Lincoln heard speak at the Capitol on January 16, 1864. She was later an actress, novelist, and playwright, as well as a public lecturer and reformer.*

1. *At the beginning of their interview in late March or early April 1864, Lincoln said:*

They tell me you are on my side. I want to know how it is.

Miss Dickinson proceeded to a severe criticism of his reconstruction policy as administered in Louisiana. He closed the conversation with these words: All I can say is, if the Radicals want me to lead, let them get out of the way and let me lead. —*Dickinson's lecture of April 27 as reported in the Boston Courier, April 28, 1864.* {C}

WILLIAM M. DICKSON   *Cincinnati lawyer whose wife was a cousin of Mary Lincoln. For about a week, during the McCormick-Manny reaper trial in September 1855, Lincoln stayed with the Dicksons.*

1. *Dickson later recalled Lincoln's talking at some length about Douglas and especially about the political campaign of 1854 in Illinois:*

After having spoken at a number of places, I was surprised one evening, before the speaking began, at Mr. Douglas entering my room at the hotel. He threw himself on the bed and seemed in distress. "Abe, the tide is against me," said he. "It is all up with me. I can do nothing. Don't reply to me this evening. I cannot speak, but I must, and it is my last. Let me alone tonight." I saw he was in great distress—he could not bear adversity—and I acquiesced in his request and went home. —*Dickson, 64 (1884). {D}*

This recollection may be a garbled explanation of what happened at Lacon on October 17, when, it appears, both men, although scheduled to speak, refrained from doing so.[143]

2. *Of Douglas as a debater, Lincoln acknowledged:*

It is impossible to get the advantage of him. Even if he is worsted, he so bears himself that the people are bewildered and uncertain as to who has the better of it. —*64. {C}*

3. *Not having been allowed by the other Manny attorneys (including Edwin M. Stanton) to play any part in the trial, Lincoln said to Dickson on his departure:*

You have made my stay here most agreeable, and I am a thousand times obliged to you; but in reply to your request for me to come again I must say to you I never expect to be in Cincinnati again. I have nothing against the city, but things have so happened here as to make it undesirable for me ever to return here. —*62. {D}*

Dickson and Ralph Emerson (q.v.) disagreed sharply about how Lincoln spent his time in Cincinnati.

ROLAND W. DILLER   *Co-owner of the Springfield drugstore where Lincoln had an account in the 1850s.*

1. *Asked why Willie and Tad were both crying as hard as they could, Lincoln replied:*

Just what's the matter with the whole world. I've got three walnuts and each of them wants two. —*Ida M. Tarbell's memorandum of an interview with Diller, probably in 1894, Tarbell Papers. {C}*

2. *On a visit to the White House, Diller told the President that he worked hard and should get more rest, transacting no business in the evening. Lincoln said:*

Well, now, Rollie, see here. I can put off war governors and secretaries and senators and all that, but there's the women. What would you do about the women? The other night a woman called to see me, and they told her I was resting. She wouldn't go away, and Mrs. Lincoln said I couldn't go down, but she wouldn't go, and I got up and went down, and Rollie, that woman was a mother, and her boy eighteen years old was to be shot next morning at six o'clock for neglect of duty. Would you have gone down, Rollie, would you? —*Ibid.* {D}

MARY DINES *A former slave who had fled from Maryland to Washington and during the Civil War lived at a "contraband camp" near the future site of Howard University.*

1. *According to Dines, Lincoln sometimes stopped at the camp on his way to the Soldiers' Home, and even joined in the singing. On one occasion, he said:*

Well, Mary, what can the people sing for me today? I've been thinking about you all since I left here and am not feeling so well. I just want them to sing some more good old hymns for me again. Tell Uncle Ben [a slave preacher, the oldest man in the camp] to pray a good old-fashioned prayer. —*Washington, 86–87 (1942).* {D}

This is a secondhand recollection, told to a young friend and later recorded by him.

ABRAM J. DITTENHOEFER (1836–1919) *A New York lawyer born in South Carolina, whose claim to have had frequent interviews with Lincoln is not corroborated by other evidence.*[144]

1. *In the summer of 1861, Dittenhoefer visited the White House in the company of Congressman Reuben Fenton, and as they approached Lincoln, he said:*

The storm is upon us; it will be much worse before it is better. I suppose there was a divine purpose in thrusting this terrible responsibility upon me, and I can only hope for more than human guidance. I am only a mortal in the hands of destiny. I am ready for the trial and shall do my best, because I know I am acting for the right. —*Dittenhoefer, 57 (1916).* {D}

Such pompous effusion was not Lincoln's style in greeting visitors.

2. *Concerning criticism of his reconstruction policy:*

I do the best I can, and I mean to keep doing so until the end. If the end brings me out all right, what is said against me won't amount to anything. If the end brings me out wrong, ten angels swearing I was right would make no difference. —*67.* {D}

3. *Asked by Dittenhoefer at the end of the war what he thought should be done with Jefferson Davis, Lincoln said that:*

if he had his way, he would let him die in peace on his southern plantation. —*52.* {D}

Lincoln seems to have told Ulysses S. Grant (q.v.) and others that he preferred to have Davis leave the country.

GRENVILLE M. DODGE (1831–1916) *Civil War general and railroad builder who served as chief engineer of the Union Pacific during the years of its construction.*

1. *While visiting Council Bluffs, Iowa, in August 1859, Lincoln said to Dodge that:*

there was nothing more important before the nation than the building of the railroad to the Pacific coast. —*Dodge, 11 (1914).* {C}

2. *The Pacific Railway Act of 1862 proved ineffective because the financial arrangements were not attractive for investors. Discussing the problem with Lincoln in the spring of 1863, Dodge declared that the government should itself build the railroad. Lincoln replied:*

that the government of the United States had all it could care for then, but that he and the government were willing to do anything they could to aid any company who would take this matter up in earnest and raise the money and go forward with the work. . . . he was perfectly willing to have the law changed so that the government should take the second mortgage and the promoters of the road should take the first. —*16.* {C}

Congress passed legislation to that effect in 1864.

DILLARD C. DONNOHUE *Law partner of John P. Usher in Greencastle, Indiana, and a member of that state's pro-Lincoln delegation to the Republican national convention in 1860.*

1. *After the Charleston debate on September 18, 1858 (according to Donnohue as recalled by Jesse K. Weik), Lincoln spoke acidly of Adele Douglas's continuing presence on the campaign trail:*

I flatter myself that thus far my wife has not found it necessary to follow me around from place to place to keep me from getting drunk. —*Weik-2, 236.* {D}

FREDERICK DOUGLASS (1817–1895) *Escaped slave who became a distinguished editor and author and the leading black abolitionist of his generation.*

1. *Douglass first visited Lincoln on August 10, 1863, and described the meeting in speeches delivered soon thereafter. The President received him, he told his audience, "just as you have seen one gentleman receive another: with a hand and a voice well-balanced between a kind cordiality and a respectful reserve." Early in the discussion, Lincoln responded to the complaint of Douglass and others that he had been following a hesitant and vacillating policy:*

I do not think that charge can be sustained; I think it cannot be shown that when I have once taken a position, I have ever retreated from it. —*Speech, January 15, 1864, printed in the* Liberator, *January 29, 1864.* {C}

2. *In the same meeting, when Douglass suggested that he had been rather slow in proclaiming equal protection for colored soldiers and prisoners of war, Lincoln said that:*

the country needed talking up to that point. He hesitated in regard to it when he felt that the country was not ready for it. He knew that the colored man throughout this country was a despised man, a hated man, and he knew that if he at first came out with such a proclamation, all the hatred which is poured on the head of the Negro race would be visited on his administration. There was preparatory work needed, and that preparatory work had been done.

He added: Remember this, Mr. Douglass. Remember that Milliken's Bend, Port Hudson, and Fort Wagner are recent events; and that these were necessary to prepare the way for this very proclamation of mine.[145] —*Ibid.* {C}

3. *Douglass's later account of the meeting is much fuller and in some respects probably less reliable. He recalled laying out several demands with respect to the treatment of colored troops—namely, that they be paid the same as white soldiers; that they be promoted, like white soldiers, for meritorious service; that the Confederate government be compelled to treat captured black soldiers as prisoners of war; and that the federal government retaliate in kind if the Confederates should execute any such captives. Lincoln listened to the little speech, says Douglass, and then "replied to each point in his own peculiar, forcible way." First he spoke of:*

the opposition generally to employing Negroes as soldiers at all, of the prejudice against the race, and of the advantage to colored people that would result from their being employed as soldiers in defense of their country. He regarded such an employment as an experiment.

He emphasized: the advantage it would be to the colored race if the experiment should succeed.

He said: that he had difficulty in getting colored men into the United States uniform; that when the purpose was fixed to employ them as soldiers, several different uniforms were proposed for them; and that it was something gained when it was finally determined to clothe them like other soldiers.

Now, as to the pay [Lincoln continued], we had to make some concession to prejudice. There were threats that if we made soldiers of them at all, white men would not enlist, would not fight beside them. Besides, it was not believed that a Negro could make a good soldier, as good a soldier as a white man, and hence it was thought that he should not have the same pay as a white man. But I assure you, Mr. Douglass, that in the end they shall have the same pay as white soldiers.

As to Confederate treatment of captured black soldiers, Lincoln said that he would insist upon their being entitled to all privileges of such prisoners. He also admitted the justice of the demand for promotion of colored soldiers for good conduct in the field, but on the matter of retaliation he differed from Douglass entirely: Once begun, I do not know where such a measure would stop.

He said that: he could not take men out and kill them in cold blood for what was done by others. If he could get hold of the persons who were guilty of killing the colored prisoners in cold blood, the case would be different, but he could not kill the innocent for the guilty. *— Rice AT (1886), 187–89. {D}*

Lincoln had, in fact, already signed a draconian order of retaliation on July 30, 1863, but it was never put into practice.[146]

4. *In their last interview, Lincoln said:*

Douglass, I hate slavery as much as you do, and I want to see it abolished altogether. *—Speech at Rochester, N.Y., April 18, 1865, in Washington* Chronicle, *April 27, 1865. {C}*

JESSE K. DUBOIS (1811–1876) *A longtime associate of Lincoln in the Whig and Republican parties of Illinois, Dubois was state auditor from 1857 to 1865.*

1. *Dubois recalled that during the legislative session of 1836-37 in Vandalia, Lincoln came to his room one evening and said:*

that he was whipped, that his career was ended, that he had traded off everything he could dispose of, and still had not got strength enough to locate the seat of government at Springfield. And yet [he continued], I can't go home without passing that bill. My folks expect that of me, and that I can't do—and I am finished forever.

According to Dubois, he then outlined a strategy for achieving their purpose, and Lincoln said: By jings, I reckon that will do it. *—John G. Nicolay interview with Dubois, July 4, 1875. {E}*

This self-serving recollection is not in accord with the history of the legislation transferring the state capital from Vandalia to Springfield.

2. *In June 1858, a few days after the state Republican convention nominated him for the Senate and he responded with one of his most famous speeches, Lincoln met Dubois on the street and said:*

Now, Dubois, I will tell you what I was doing when you came into my office and why I would not show you what I was doing. . . . This passage in the speech about the house divided against itself, I would not read to you because I knew you would make me change it, modify and modify, and I was determined to read it—had willed it so. —*Undated Dubois statement writ-ten down by William H. Herndon (11:3010-11), Herndon-Weik Collection. A more polished version is in Herndon, II, 397n. {D}*

This story does not square with Herndon's own recollection that before deliver-ing the speech, Lincoln read it to a group of local Republican leaders and asked for their comments.[147]

HENRY E. DUMMER   *Lawyer in Beardstown, Illinois, with whom Lincoln had both professional and political associations.*

1. *Dummer, who said that Lincoln was a man of "purity" but had an "in-sane love" for dirty stories, remembered an occasion in 1859 when someone asked him why he did not assemble his stories into a book. Lincoln replied:*

Such a book would stink like a thousand privies. —*Dummer's undated state-ment written down by Herndon (11:3024A-24B), Herndon-Weik Collection. {C}*

THOMAS H. DUVAL (1813-1880)   *Unionist federal judge in Texas, who traveled to Washington in 1863 seeking nearly three years of back pay and offering a plan to reestablish federal authority in his state.*

1. *November 18, the day of the departure for Gettysburg, in response to Duval's proposal of a certain line of action, Lincoln said:*

that while the destruction of slavery was a necessary incident of war, he was well aware that its sudden extinction would be attended with great ruin; that for his own part, he saw nothing inconsistent with the gradual eman-cipation of slavery and his proclamation; that while he would be glad to see a majority of the people of Texas act as I hoped they would in reference to this proposition, yet if we could only succeed in inaugurating a . . . state government in Texas, inside of the Union, he would recognize and protect [it] with all the power of the government of the United States. —*Duval's diary in Marten, 85. {B}*

ERNEST DUVERGIER DE HAURANNE (1843-1876)   *Young Frenchman who visited the United States in 1864-65 and published a two-volume record of his impressions.*

1. *During their ten-minute meeting on January 20, 1865, Lincoln made some comments on:*

the unrealistic hopes the Democratic party entertained four years ago that it could impose its policies on the victorious Republicans. —*Duvergier, 351. {B}*

CHARLES V. DYER (1808-1878)   *Chicago physician and early antislavery leader, whom Lincoln chose to be a judge on the mixed court for suppression of the slave trade.*

1. *Lincoln said to Dyer that:*

it was a great pleasure to him to appoint old abolitionists to office. *—Dyer's statement, presumably, to Zebina Eastman, reported in Eastman to Herndon, January 2, 1866 (8:472-75), Herndon-Weik Collection. {D}*

JOHN EATON (1829-1906) *Teacher, army chaplain, superintendent of freedmen for Grant.*

1. *In July 1863, the President remarked:*

that there were some people who thought the work on the Capitol ought to stop on account of the war, people who begrudged the expenditure, and the detention of the workmen from the army. . . . In his judgment, the finishing of the Capitol would be a symbol to the nation of the preservation of the Union. If [said he] people see the Capitol going on, it is a sign we intend the Union shall go on. *—Eaton, 89 (1907). {C}*

2. *During the same interview, Lincoln said:*

You know, a raid in Washington is different from what you military men mean by a raid. With you, it is an attack by the enemy—the capture of soldiers and supplies. With us, it is an attack by our friends in Congress seeking to influence a change in policy. A company of congressmen came to me to protest that Grant ought not to be retained as a commander of American citizens. I asked what was the trouble. They said he was not fit to command such men. I asked why, and they said he sometimes drank too much and was unfit for such a position. I then began to ask them if they knew what he drank, what brand of whiskey he used, telling them most seriously that I wished they would find out. They conferred with each other and concluded they could not tell what brand he used. I urged them to ascertain and let me know, for if it made fighting generals like Grant, I should like to get some of it for distribution. *—90. {D}*

This familiar story, told also by John M. Thayer (q.v.), appeared as early as 1864 in a Democratic jokebook and was a recycling of a witticism attributed to George III.[148] *Albert B. Chandler and Moses F. Odell (qq.v.) quoted Lincoln as denying that he had told the story.*

3. *About a year later, in response to a remark by Eaton concerning the Secretary of State, Lincoln declared:*

Seward knows that I am his master.

He then went on to tell how: he had pushed the prompt surrender of Mason and Slidell as an act of justice toward England, realizing that in the light of international law the *Trent* affair might justly have given ground for reprisal. Seward would have temporized, and so risked a most unwelcome complication with England. —*178.* {D}

This statement is inaccurate, and the boastfulness does not sound like Lincoln, but there is other recollective quotation of a similar kind from James R. Gilmore and Benson J. Lossing (qq.v.).

4. *Upon hearing the sound of rifles from across the Potomac:*

This is the day when they shoot deserters. I am wondering whether I have used the pardoning power as much as I ought. I know some of our officers feel that I have used it with so much freedom as to demoralize the army and destroy the discipline. . . . I feel that the picket who sleeps at his post is imperiling, it may be, the entire army, and I know how serious that is. But the officers only see the force of military discipline; perhaps it is right, but I see other things. I feel how the man may have been exposed to long watches with no opportunity for proper rest, and so sleep steals upon him unawares. I would not relax the discipline of the army, but I do want to be considerate of every case. —*180.* {C}

5. *On talk of Grant as a possible presidential candidate:*

The disaffected are trying to get him to run, but I don't think they can do it. If he is the great general we think he is, he must have some consciousness of it, and know that he cannot be satisfied with himself and secure the credit due for his great generalship if he does not finish his job. I do not believe that they can get him to run. —*186.* {C}

6. *After asking Eaton to sound out the General regarding the presidency, Lincoln said:*

Before Grant took command of the eastern forces we did not sleep at night here in Washington. We began to fear the rebels would take the capital, and once in possession of that, we feared that foreign countries might acknowledge the Confederacy. Nobody could foresee the evil that might come from the destruction of records and of property. But since Grant has assumed command on the Potomac, I have made up my mind that whatever it is possible to have done, Grant will do, and whatever he doesn't do, I don't believe is to be done. And now we sleep at night. —*186-87.* {C}

ELIZABETH TODD EDWARDS (1813–1888) *Sister of Mary Lincoln and wife of Ninian W. Edwards, a prominent figure in Springfield society and Illinois politics.*
    1. *Mrs. Edwards, who stayed at the White House for an extended period after Willie's death in February 1862, took Lincoln to the conservatory one day and exclaimed over the beauty of the roses. Lincoln said:*

I never was in here before; how spring-like it looks! I don't care for flowers, have no natural and educated taste for such things. —*Undated statement in the Herndon-Weik Collection (11:3025–32). The wording is altered in Herndon, III, 509. {C}*

2. *To a servant girl who proposed to seek other employment because Mary Lincoln would not raise her pay to $1.50 a week, the President said:*

Don't leave. Tell Mrs. Lincoln you have concluded to stay at $1.25, and I'll pay the odd 25¢ to you. —*Undated statement (11:3025–32). {C}*

NINIAN W. EDWARDS (1809–1889) *Springfield lawyer, politician, and social leader who was married to Mary Todd Lincoln's older sister, Elizabeth.*

1. *During his campaign for re-election to the legislature in 1840, Lincoln responded to the demagogic oratory of Edmund D. Taylor, a well-dressed local Democrat, who insisted that Whigs were the party of aristocracy and wealth. He said that:*

whilst Colonel Taylor had his stores over the county and was riding in a fine carriage, wore his kid gloves, and had a goldheaded cane, he was a poor boy hired on a flatboat at eight dollars a month and had only one pair of breeches and they were of buckskin. Now if you know the nature of buckskin when wet and dried by the sun, they would shrink, and mine kept shrinking until they left for several inches my legs bare between the top of my socks and the lower part of my breeches; and whilst I was growing taller they were becoming shorter and so much tighter that they left a blue streak around my legs which you can see to this day. If you call this aristocracy, I plead guilty to the charge. —*Edwards's statement as noted down by Herndon, no date, but probably 1865 (7:408), Herndon-Weik Collection. A heavily copyedited version is in Herndon, I, 195. {D}*

It is not clear that Edwards heard the speech himself.

2. *Soon after James Smith (q.v.) became pastor of Springfield's First Presbyterian Church in the early 1850s, Lincoln said to Edwards:*

I have been reading a work of Dr. Smith on the evidences of Christianity, and have heard him preach and converse on the subject, and I am now convinced of the truth of the Christian religion. —*Edwards to James A. Reed, December 24, 1872, in Reed, 338–39. {C}*

THOMAS S. EDWARDS *A farmer living near New Salem for whom Lincoln was a bondsman in 1833 and from whom he bought two Springfield lots in 1836.[149]*

1. *During an interview with a newspaper correspondent in September 1860, Edwards asserted that he had been the person who in 1857 approached Lincoln about defending William Armstrong in his trial for murder. According to Edwards, when he raised the question of a fee, Lincoln replied:*

You, Edwards, you ought to know me better than to think I'd take a fee from any of Jack Armstrong's blood. Why, bless your soul, I've danced that boy on my knee a hundred times in the long winter nights by his father's fire down in old Menard.[150] I wouldn't be worthy to take your hand, Tom, if I turned on him now. Go back and tell old Hannah to keep up a good heart, and we will see what can be done. —*Providence (R.I.)* Journal, *October 19, 1860. {D}*

Factual errors cast doubt on Edwards's recollection, which, in any case, does not agree with that of Armstrong's mother, Hannah.[151]

MRS. WILLIAM A. ELDERKIN *Daughter of a Washington clergyman who in 1861 became the bride of a lieutenant fresh out of West Point.*

   1. *Mrs. Elderkin told a reporter nearly fifty years later that Lincoln attended her wedding and gave her this advice:*

If it's only one room with a stove in one corner and a bed in the other, have a home of your own. A man needs a wife as much in war as he does in peace. I think he needs her more. Stay with your husband when you can. Don't let a third party interfere between you two; stay by yourselves. Never trouble trouble till trouble troubles you. —*New York* Times, *February 12, 1909. {D}*

Questionable statements in other parts of the story cast added doubt on the credibility of this quotation.

ABNER Y. ELLIS *A longtime acquaintance of Lincoln, who helped him secure the Springfield postmastership in 1849, but did not satisfy his desire to regain that position in 1861.*

   1. *As a candidate for the legislature in 1832, Lincoln made a speech at Pappsville, a village west of Springfield. In 1865, Ellis ventured to reproduce it for Herndon:*

Fellow citizens, I presume you all know who I am. I am humble Abraham Lincoln. I have been solicited by many friends to become a candidate for the legislature. My politics are short and sweet, like the old woman's dance. I am in favor of a national bank. I am in favor of the internal improvement system and a high protective tariff. These are my sentiments and political principles. If elected, I shall be thankful; if not, it will be all the same. —*Ellis's statement (14:1629–41), Herndon-Weik Collection; dated 1865 by Herndon and published in Herndon, I, 104.*[152] *{D}*

There is some reason to believe that the speech was synthesized rather than reconstructed from memory. At about the same time, Herndon received a suspiciously similar version from another source, but he seems to have regarded it as corroboration.[153]

   2. *Speaking of Bowling Green, a fatherly friend of his New Salem days, Lincoln, according to Ellis, used to say that:*

he owed more to Mr. Green for his advancement than any other man. — *Ellis to Herndon, December 6, 1866 (8:1220-26). {C}*

3. During the contest for the Whig congressional nomination in the spring of 1843, Lincoln was accused of belonging to a proud and aristocratic family—presumably a reference to the Todds and Edwardses. According to Ellis, he remarked:

Well, that sounds strange to me, for I do not remember of but one that ever came to see me, and while he was in town, he was accused of stealing a jew's-harp. —*Ellis to Herndon, February 14, 1866 (8:620-22).*[154] *{D}*

4. Asked in 1844 whether he was a Mason, Lincoln replied:

I do not belong to any society except it be for the good of my country. — *Ellis to Herndon, January 30, 1866 (8:533-35). {C}*

5. Ellis recalled that Lincoln used to tell "with embellishments" the story of a Millerite with five sons who insisted that he and his wife must confess their failings before the day of ascension:

"Well, dear," said she, "our little Sammy is not your child." "Well," said the husband, "whose is he?" "Oh dear," said she, "he is the one-eyed shoe-maker's. He came to see me once when you was away and in an evil hour I gave way." "Well," said the husband, "is the rest mine?" "No," said she, "they belong to the neighborhood." "Well," said the old man, "I am ready to leave; Gabriel, blow your horn." —*Ellis's 1865 statement (14:1629-41). {C}*

6. Speaking of religious denominations, Lincoln said that:

he thought baptism by immersion was the true meaning of the word; for John baptized the Savior in the River Jordan because there was much water and they went down into it and came up out of it. —*Ibid. {D}*

ELMER E. ELLSWORTH (1837-1861) *Spirited young officer and friend of the Lincolns, whose death at the hands of a Confederate sympathizer in Alexandria, Virginia, made him one of the early heroes of the Civil War.*

1. In March 1861, on establishing Ellsworth as head of a bureau of militia:

Well, I am pressed to death for time and don't pretend to know anything of military matters. Fix the thing up so that I shan't be treading on anybody's toes or carrying anybody across lots, and then come to me and I'll finish it. —*Ellsworth to Mrs. Charles H. Spafford, mother of his fiancée, March 22, 1861, Ellsworth Papers.*[155] *{A}*

RALPH EMERSON (1831-1914) *Business associate of John H. Manny, a reaper manufacturer in Rockford, Illinois, whose firm was sued for patent infringement by Cyrus H. McCormick. Lincoln was one of several lawyers retained for the defense, but his services were not used during the trial, held at Cincinnati in September 1855.*

1. *Lincoln, according to Emerson, attended the entire proceedings and was so impressed by the knowledge and ability of counsel on both sides that he at last exclaimed:*

Emerson, I'm going home. I am going home to study law. . . . I do occupy a good position there now. But these college-trained men who have devoted their whole lives to study are coming west, don't you see? They study on a single case perhaps for months, as we never do. We are apt to catch up the thing as it goes before a jury and trust to the inspiration of the moment. They have got as far as Ohio now. They will soon be in Illinois. . . . I'm going home to study law! I am as good as any of them, and when they get to Illinois I will be ready for them. —*Emerson R (1909), 7-8. {D}*

The fact that many Illinois lawyers of that time had college educations is only one reason why this story inspires as much doubt as Emerson's claim to be an "intimate friend" of Lincoln. William M. Dickson (q.v.), with whom Lincoln stayed in Cincinnati, maintained that he took little interest in the case and spent most of his time elsewhere.

2. *At one point during their time together, Emerson recalled, Lincoln held forth on the debilitating social effect of slavery:*

Here is this fine city of Cincinnati, and over there is the little town of Covington. Covington has just as good a location as Cincinnati, and a fine country back of it. It was settled before Cincinnati. Why is it not a bigger city? Just because of slavery and nothing else. My people used to live over there, and I know. Why the other day I went to ship my family on a little railroad they have got down there from Covington back into the country. I went to the ticket office and found a lank fellow sprawling over the counter, who had to count up quite a while on his fingers how much two and one-half fares would come to. While over here in Cincinnati, when I shove my money through the window, the three tickets and the change would come flying back at me quick. And it is just the same way in all things through Kentucky. That is what slavery does for the white man. —*9. {D}*

There is no record of any such trip by Mary Lincoln and the children.

RALPH WALDO EMERSON (1803-1882) *Essayist and poet, probably America's most famous literary figure when he visited Lincoln in February 1862.*

1. *Emerson recorded in his journal that after he was introduced, Lincoln remarked:*

I once heard you say in a lecture that a Kentuckian seems to say by his air and manners, "Here am I; if you don't like me, the worse for you." —*Emerson RW, 187. {A}*

2. *Concerning an appeal for clemency from the slave-trader Nathaniel Gordon, he said that:*

he was not quite satisfied yet and meant to refresh his memory by looking again at the evidence. —*187.* {B}

Gordon was executed several weeks later.

3. *In a discussion of the recent* Trent *crisis:*

France, on the moment of hearing the surrender of the prisoners, had ordered a message of gratification to be sent. . . . Spain also had sent a message of the same kind. He was glad of this that Spain had done. For he knew, that, though Cuba sympathized with secession, Spain's interest lay the other way. Spain knew that the secessionists wished to conquer Cuba. —*195.* {B}

WILLIAM ENDICOTT (1826-?) *A Boston dry goods merchant.*

1. *After his visit to the Army of the Potomac in early October 1862, Lincoln talked to Endicott about McClellan, expressing the opinion that:*

he should have prevented Lee from escaping into Virginia and should have pursued him vigorously without giving his army time to recuperate.

The President went on to say: that Fitz-John Porter had a large reserve corps which was not ordered into action at the battle, that he had supposed that the object of a reserve was to be ordered in at a critical moment, but that Porter did nothing. —*Endicott, 225 (1912).* {C}

In a later interview, according to Endicott, 226, Lincoln discussed the Vicksburg campaign and told the same story of hogs and a crooked log that John H. Littlefield (q.v.) recalled hearing at about the same time.

JAMES S. EWING (1835-1918) *Lawyer in Bloomington, Illinois, later minister to Belgium and law partner of Adlai E. Stevenson.*

1. *In 1854, on being teased by Douglas when he refused to take a drink:*

No, I am not a member of any temperance society; but I am temperate in this that I don't drink anything. —*Phillips-2, 55 (1910).* {C}

ROSE EYTINGE (1835-1911) *Temperamental but highly successful American actress, described as "a handsome brunette with brilliant dark eyes."*

1. *When Eytinge was presented to Lincoln, he said:*

So this is the little lady that all us folks in Washington like so much. Don't you ever come 'round here asking me to do some of those impossible things you women always ask for, for I would have to do it, and then I'd get into trouble. —*Eytinge, 76-77 (1905).* {C}

JESSE W. FELL (1808–1887)   *Lawyer, politician, land speculator, civic leader in Bloomington, Illinois. Fell was secretary of the Republican state central committee and one of the inner circle of men who secured Lincoln's nomination for the presidency in 1860.*

1. *In September 1854, several months after passage of the Kansas-Nebraska Act, Douglas was scheduled to speak at a Democratic meeting in Bloomington.[156] Fell tried to arrange a debate between him and Lincoln but was told by the latter:*

Fell, this is not our meeting; it is Judge Douglas's meeting; he called it, and he and his friends have a right to control it. Notwithstanding all you say about our country people and the great desire I have to talk to them, we must do nothing to defeat his object in calling it. He has heard of the great racket the passage of his bill has kicked up, and he wants to set himself right with his people, a job not very easily done, you and I being the judges. Partly on this ground and partly to keep me from speaking, he will no doubt consume so much of the time that I'll have no chance till in the evening. I fully appreciate all you say about our country friends and would like mighty well to talk to them on this subject. If Judge Douglas will give me a chance I will follow him out in the grove, but as he won't do this, I guess you may give it out, after he is done, that I will reply to him after candle lighting in the court house. —*Oldroyd, 471 (1882). {C}*

This wordy passage seems more credible in its general substance than as a reproduction of Lincoln's language. An extensive newspaper report of the speech that he delivered on this occasion is in Collected Works, *II, 234–40.*

2. *In the fall of 1858, after the close of the senatorial contest with Douglas, Fell broached the subject of his becoming a presidential candidate, and Lincoln replied:*

Oh, Fell, what's the use of talking of me for the presidency, whilst we have such men as Seward, Chase, and others, who are so much better known to the people and whose names are so intimately associated with the principles of the Republican party. Everybody knows them; nobody, scarcely, outside of Illinois, knows me. Besides, is it not, as a matter of justice, due to such men, who have carried this movement forward to its present status, in spite of fearful opposition, personal abuse, and hard names? I really think so.

When Fell persisted and asked for information about his earlier life, Lincoln said: I admit the force of much that you say, and admit that I am ambitious and would like to be president. I am not insensible to the compliment you pay me and the interest you manifest in the matter, but there is no such good luck in store for me as the presidency of these United States. Besides, there is nothing in my early history that would interest you or anybody else, and, as Judge Davis says, "It won't pay." — *Oldroyd, 474, 476. {C}*

REUBEN E. FENTON (1819–1885) *Republican congressman who was elected governor of New York in 1864.*

1. *In December 1861, concerning public dissatisfaction over military inaction, Lincoln said that:*

Providence, with favoring sky and earth, seemed to beckon the army on, but General McClellan, he supposed, knew his business and had his reasons for disregarding these hints of Providence. And as we have got to stand by the General [he continued], I think a good way to do it may be for Congress to take a recess for several weeks, and by the time you get together again, if McClellan is not off with the army, Providence is very likely to step in with hard roads and force us to say, "The army can't move." You know, Dickens said of a certain man that if he would always follow his nose, he would never stick fast in the mud. Well, when the rains set in, it will be impossible for even our eager and gallant soldiers to keep their noses so high that their feet will not stick in the clay mud of Old Virginia. — *Rice AT, 74–75 (1886). {C}*

2. *In August 1864, Lincoln talked with Fenton about the coming political campaign and the problem posed by a dissatisfied Thurlow Weed:*

You are to be nominated by our folks for governor of your state. Seymour, of course, will be the Democratic nominee. You will have a hard fight. I am very desirous that you should win the battle. New York should be on our side by honest possession. There is some trouble among our folks over there, which we must try and manage. Or, rather, there is one man who may give us trouble, because of his indifference, if in no other way. He has great influence, and his feelings may be reflected in many of his friends. We must have his counsel and cooperation if possible. This, in one sense, is more important to you than to me, I think, for I should rather expect to get on without New York, but you can't. But in a larger sense than what is merely personal to myself, I am anxious for New York, and we must put our heads together and see if the matter can't be fixed. — *68–69. {C}*

WILLIAM PITT FESSENDEN (1806–1869) *Republican senator from Maine who served as secretary of the treasury for approximately eight months beginning in July 1864.*

1. *Speaking to Fessenden in February 1862, apparently about the military operations in Tennessee under Grant's command and Henry Halleck's general supervision, Lincoln says:*

that he has warned Halleck to be cautious. . . . there was too much at stake on the battle; that no hazard must be run which could be avoided. —

Fessenden to a member of his family, February 15, 1862, in Fessenden, I, 261. {B}

2. *On December 18, 1862, to a committee of the Republican senatorial caucus seeking a reconstruction of the cabinet, Lincoln said that:*

it was Mr. Seward's habit to read his dispatches to him before they were sent, but they were not usually submitted to a cabinet council. — *Fessenden's undated recollection in Fessenden, I, 242.* {C}

3. *At a meeting the next day with the committee and members of the cabinet except Seward, the President opened with a speech admitting that the cabinet had not been very regular in its consultations and pleading lack of time. He thought that:*

most questions of importance had received a reasonable consideration, was not aware of any divisions or want of unity. Decisions had, so far as he knew, received general support after they were made. He thought Mr. Seward had been earnest in the prosecution of the war and had not improperly interfered, had generally read him his official correspondence and had sometimes consulted with Mr. Chase. He called on the members of the cabinet present to say whether there had been any want of unity or of sufficient consultation. — *Fessenden, I, 243-44.* {C}

Chase responded that questions of importance had generally received the cabinet's consideration and that there had been no want of unity among its members.

4. *Talking with some of the senators after the meeting, Lincoln said that:*

he had reason to fear a general smashup if Mr. Seward was removed, and he did not see how he could get along with an entire change in his cabinet. . . . He thought Mr. Chase would seize the occasion to withdraw, and it had been intimated that Mr. Stanton would do the same, and he could not dispense with Mr. Chase's services in the Treasury just at this time. — *Fessenden, I, 248.* {C}

5. *After Lincoln accepted Chase's resignation in June 1864, he said to Fessenden:*

that he had great respect for Mr. Chase, and that if the chief justiceship of the Supreme Court was now vacant he would appoint him to that place; that previously, when it was thought the Chief Justice was near his end, he had made up his mind, in the event of his death, to appoint Mr. Chase, and that he had not changed his mind and would appoint him now if the place was vacant. — *Fessenden's recollection several months later as recorded in Orville H. Browning's diary, I, 687.* {D}

6. *The nomination of Fessenden as secretary of the treasury was sent to the Senate on July 1, 1864, and promptly confirmed. When Fessenden declared that he could not accept the appointment, Lincoln insisted, saying:*

that the crisis was such as demanded any sacrifice, even life itself; that Providence had never deserted him or the country; and that his choice of me was a special proof that Providence would not desert him.[157] —*Fessenden, I, 317-18.* {C}

7. *On July 4, Lincoln agreed that Fessenden should have a free hand in filling Treasury vacancies, with the reservation that:*

should he himself desire any particular appointment made that his wishes in that regard should be fully considered.

He added that: he hoped Mr. Fessenden would not, without a real necessity, remove any friends of Governor Chase. —*Chase, 476.* {B}

MAUNSELL B. FIELD (1822–1875) *Lawyer, public official, and author who served as assistant secretary of the treasury from 1863 to 1865.*

1. *In June 1864, when Lincoln refused, on political grounds, to appoint Field as assistant treasurer of the United States in New York City, Salmon P. Chase submitted another of his resignations, and this time it was accepted.[158] Discussing the matter with the President about two months later, Field expressed at some length his belief that he had been discriminated against because of his Democratic antecedents. Lincoln listened "laughingly, but impatiently, shaking his head all the time," and then replied:*

You are altogether on the wrong track. Why, didn't I nominate, as Chase's successor, Dave Tod, who has been all his life a Democrat, and who worked and voted for Douglas and against me? No, sir; I will tell you all about it. The Republican party in your state is divided into two factions, and I can't afford to quarrel with either of them. By accident, rather than by any design of mine, the Radicals have got possession of the most important federal offices in New York. I care nothing whatever about your personal politics. You were pressed by Mr. Chase and opposed by Senator [Morgan]. Had I, under these circumstances, consented to your appointment, it would have been another Radical triumph, and I couldn't afford one. That is all that there is about it, so far as you are concerned. But I'll tell you what happened at the time between myself and Chase. One day, early in June, Chase came to me and said, "Mr. President, Cisco has resigned at New York, and I am going on there to see who is the best man to put into his place." . . . Well, Chase went to New York, and in due time returned, I suppose, but he did not come near me. In the meantime there was the fiercest contest waging for the vacant office that I remember since I have been in this place. I must confess that you were the most numerously endorsed, but [Morgan] opposed you. The next time that I heard from Chase upon the subject was when he wrote to me requesting me to nominate you. I answered his communication and asked him to come and see me and talk over the matter. Instead of doing so, he wrote me again, saying that he would have you and nobody else. And so we fired letters at each other for two or three days. I offered to nominate either of three gentlemen who happened to be acceptable to Senator [Morgan], but Chase objected to all of them. Finally, as I was sitting here at my desk one morning, with the room full of people, a letter from the Treasury Department was brought to me. I opened it, recognized Chase's handwriting, read the first sentence, and inferred from its tenor that this matter was in the way of satisfactory adjustment. I was truly glad of this, and, laying the envelope with its enclosure down upon the desk, went on talking. People were coming and going all the time till three o'clock, and I forgot all about Chase's letter. At that hour it occurred to me that I would go down stairs and get a bit of lunch. My wife happened to be away, and they had failed to call me at the usual time. While I was sitting alone at table, my thoughts reverted to Chase's letter, and I determined to answer it just as soon as I should go upstairs again. Well, as soon as I was back here, I took pen and paper and prepared to write; but then it occurred to me that I might as well read the letter before I answered it. I took it out of the envelope for that purpose, and, as I did so, another enclosure fell from it upon the floor. I picked it up, read it, and said to myself, "Halloo, this is a horse of another color!" It was his resignation. I put my pen into my mouth and grit my teeth upon it. I did not long reflect. I very soon decided to accept it, and I nominated Dave Tod to succeed him.

But there is a history behind all this which I don't mind telling you. Are you aware that this was the **fourth** time that Chase had tendered me his resignation? No? Well, it was. I will tell you how it all happened. The first occasion was when Seward tendered his, after the Republican senators had passed resolutions hostile to him. Chase soon followed suit, and by so doing rendered me a great favor, which I shall ever hold in grateful remembrance. Matters were fixed up, and neither of them left the cabinet.

Some time after this there was a collector of customs on the Pacific coast, one of Chase's men, who was represented to me to be a worthless vagabond and even a defaulter. I spoke to Chase about him; but he had entire confidence in him and refused to listen to anything to his disadvantage. While matters stood thus, Chase one day told me that he felt overworked, and proposed taking a little trip down the Potomac, but that he would not be gone longer than two days. I said, "All right, Mr. Secretary," and we shook hands and parted. As luck would have it, I was waited upon the very next day by a delegation of all the gentlemen from the Pacific coast, both official and unofficial, who then happened to be in Washington. They filed formal charges with me against the Collector to whom I have referred and demanded his immediate removal. I told them that the Secretary of the Treasury was out of town, that it would be discourteous to him if I acted upon the matter in his absence, but that he would return in one or two days at the latest, and I invited them to call upon me again in about a week, when I promised, under all circumstances, a definite answer to their request. A week passed. No Chase. The delegation returned, and as I was thoroughly convinced of not only the propriety of, but even the necessity for the act, I removed the Collector, and appointed another in his stead. The first notice that I received of Chase's return was about three days afterward, when I found his resignation lying upon my table. I waited until evening, and then ordered my carriage and drove to his house. I found him in the office to the left as you enter the door. I went directly up to him with the resignation in my hand, and, putting my arm around his neck, said to him, "Chase, here is a paper with which I wish to have nothing to do. Take it back and be reasonable." I then explained to him what had occurred while he was away. I told him that the man whom I had appointed happened to have been dead several weeks; that I couldn't replace the person whom I had removed—that was impossible—but that I would appoint anyone else whom he should select for the place. It was difficult to bring him to terms; I had to plead with him a long time, but I finally succeeded and heard nothing more of **that** resignation.

You remember that when Hiram Barney was appointed, at the beginning of this administration, collector of the port of New York, everybody supposed that he was Chase's selection and nobody else's. Now Barney was as much my choice as he was Chase's; and when (Chase, Seward, and myself standing round that table) Barney's appointment was decided upon, I believe that I was the most gratified person then present. Well, I have just as great confidence in Mr. Barney's integrity and patriotism now as I had then. But after a time things got **very mixed** in the New York custom house, and the establishment was being run almost exclusively in the interest of the Radicals. I felt very great delicacy in doing anything that might be offensive to my friend Barney. And yet something had to be done. There was no use in attempting to bring Chase over to my views. But I tried it, and failed. Then I waited for a time. At last I made up my mind to take action, hoping to be able to afterward reconcile Chase to it. So I sent for Seward and told him that he must find a diplomatic position in Europe for Barney. Seward said that it was not an easy thing to do, but I was peremptory, and told him it **must** be done. After two or three days, Seward came back, and reported to me that he had found the place. Just then Chase became aware of my little conspiracy. He was very angry, and he told me that the day that Mr. Barney left the New York custom house, with or without his own consent, he, Chase, would withdraw from the secretaryship of the treasury. Well, I backed down again. Now I ask you, as a reasonable man, whether, when the resignation with which you are concerned came, I could, with any self-respect, hesitate to accept it? —*Field, 300-304 (1874). {D}*

This, according to Field, is the "substance" of what Lincoln said, based on notes written down that same evening. Yet, it seems unlikely that Lincoln would have confided so elaborately in Field, a Chase favorite, especially if there was any truth in the testimony of John Conness (q.v.).

2. After some discussion of religious denominations, Lincoln remarked with a twinkle in his eye that:

he preferred the Episcopalians to every other sect, because they are equally indifferent to a man's religion and his politics. —*310.* {C}

HAMILTON FISH (1808–1893)   *Senator from New York in the 1850s and later secretary of state in the Grant administration.*

1. Discussing with Fish and Charles Sumner the Burnside expedition to the North Carolina coast in 1862, Lincoln said:

Well, I am no military man, and of course, I cannot tell about these matters—and indeed if I did know, the interests of the public service require that I should not divulge them. But now see here [pointing to a map]. Here are a large number of inlets, and I should think a fleet might perhaps get in there somewhere. And if they were to get in here, don't you think our boys would be likely to cut some flip-flaps? I think they would. —*Fish interview, April 10, 1874, in Nicolay Papers.* {C}

STEPHEN R. FISKE (1840–1916)   *A reporter for the New York* Herald *during the Civil War.*

1. As he arrived in New York City on February 19, 1861, Lincoln remarked:

I haven't any speech ready. I shall have to say just what comes into my head at the time. —*Fiske S, 7 (1897).* {C}

2. At New Brunswick, New Jersey, on February 21, as Fiske was shaking hands with a number of his Rutgers College friends, Lincoln playfully demanded:

Is this your reception or mine?

After Fiske explained, he said: Ah, that is what I have always regretted—the want of a college education. Those who have it should thank God for it. —*8.* {C}

3. At the inaugural ball, March 4, 1861:

This handshaking is harder work than rail-splitting. —*8.* {C}

4. When Fiske asked whether he had any news to send James Gordon Bennett, editor of the Herald, *Lincoln replied:*

Yes, you may tell him that Thurlow Weed has found out that Seward was not nominated at Chicago. —*8.* {C}

GEORGE P. FLOYD *Briefly a hotel keeper in Quincy, Illinois, during the 1850s.*

1. *According to Floyd, Lincoln nearly collapsed from fatigue after his debate with Douglas at Quincy on October 23, 1858. Taken to his room in the hotel, he spoke of having to "quit and give up the race." Mrs. Floyd recommended a "rum sweat," a treatment requiring him to sit wrapped in blankets over a pan of flaming rum, the vapors of which induced profuse perspiration. Lincoln responded:*

Well, if you think it will do me any good, just crack your whip and go ahead. Any port in a storm, and, I tell you, I am mighty near overboard.

The next morning, Lincoln rose early and said: I am feeling like a two-year-old. I can jump a five-rail fence right now, I swanny! I've heard of folks drinking liquor and rubbing their bodies with the bottle for ailments, but I never yet heard of driving the stuff through the pores of the hide to get a man full. If Mrs. Floyd would only join us in this campaign and prescribe for me, I think we could beat out Judge Douglas slick and clean. —*Floyd, 303-6 (1908). {E}*

This story appears to be a good example of fictional reminiscence. No contemporary evidence supports the assertion that Lincoln suffered from excessive fatigue after the Quincy debate. On the other hand, there is evidence that Lincoln stayed the night at the home of Orville H. Browning, rather than at the Quincy House, and that by the time of the debate, Floyd was no longer the hotel's proprietor.[159]

JOHN W. FORNEY (1817–1881) *Philadelphia journalist and Buchanan Democrat turned Republican, who was secretary of the Senate during Lincoln's administration.*

1. *Speaking in July 1861 to Kentucky commissioners protesting against any movement of Union troops through their state, Lincoln said:*

Gentlemen, my position in regard to your state is like that of the woodman, who, returning to his home one night, found coiled around his beautiful children, who were quietly sleeping in their bed, several poisonous snakes. His first impulse was to save his little ones, but he feared that if he struck at the snakes he might strike the children, and yet he dared not let them die without an effort. So it is with me. I know Kentucky and Tennessee are infested with the enemies of the Union, but I know also that there are thousands of patriots in both who will be persecuted even unto death unless the strong hand of the government is interposed for their protection and rescue. We must go in. The old flag must be carried into Tennessee at whatever hazard. —*Forney, I, 265 (1874). {C}*

2. *Addressing a political convention at Harrisburg on July 17, 1862, Forney reported that Lincoln had very recently said to him:*

that henceforth his policy should be as stringent as the most enthusiastic could desire. That hereafter there will be no restriction in the employment of all men to put down this rebellion. No more doubting about the confiscation of rebel property. No longer need the northern people be frightened with the cry of Negro equality and emancipation. He thought it proper to put arms in their hands to save the lives of the whites. He thought we might as well terminate the war today if it was not to be fought with the aid of the colored men of the South. General Washington, in the Revolutionary War, used them, and at the battle of Red Bank, 1777, near Philadelphia, a Rhode Island regiment of blacks turned the fortunes of the day. *—Printed in the New York Tribune, July 19, 1862, and in other newspapers throughout the country under the heading: "The President's Policy." {D}*

Although Lincoln at about this time was revealing his plans for emancipation, first to secretaries Seward and Welles, and then to the entire cabinet, he told a deputation of citizens on August 4 that he was prepared to accept blacks only as laborers and not as soldiers.[160]

LAFAYETTE S. FOSTER (1806–1880)   *Republican senator from Connecticut for twelve years beginning in 1855.*

    1. *When Foster requested suspension of the execution of a soldier sentenced for desertion:*

Why don't you men up there in Congress repeal the law requiring men to be shot when they desert, instead of coming here to me and asking me to override the law and practically make it a dead letter? . . . I shall grant your request. But you know that when I have once suspended the sentence of that man I can't afterwards order him to be shot. *—Foster interview, October 23, 1878, in Nicolay Papers. {C}*

    2. *On December 6, 1864, the day that Chase was appointed chief justice:*

Mr. Chase will make a very excellent judge if he devotes himself exclusively to the duties of his office and don't meddle with politics. But if he keeps on with the notion that he is destined to be president of the United States, and which in my judgment he will never be, he will never acquire that fame and usefulness as a chief justice which he would otherwise certainly attain. *— Ibid. {C}*

GUSTAVUS V. FOX (1821–1883)   *Naval officer, brother-in-law of Montgomery Blair, who served as assistant secretary of the navy throughout the Civil War.*

    1. *At a council of war held on March 6, 1862, to discuss McClellan's plan for moving his army down the Chesapeake to the mouth of the Rappahannock, Lincoln declared that:*

taking the whole army first to Annapolis, to be embarked in transports, would appear to the extremely sensitive and impatient public opinion very much like a retreat from Washington. It would be impolitic to explain that it was merely a first step by way of the Chesapeake Bay and Fort Monroe towards Richmond. Could not 50,000 men or even 10,000 men be moved in transports directly down the Potomac? This would be a self-evident forward movement, which the public would comprehend without explanation.[161] *—Nicolay and Hay, V, 221, citing undated Nicolay memorandum of interview with Fox.* {C}

2. *In December 1862, Lincoln remarked to Fox:*

that he was very anxious to have us take Sumter, and that he would man it with Negroes. *—Fox to John Murray Forbes, December 19, 1862, in Forbes, I, 343.* {B}

3. *On February 12, 1863, speaking of the proposed attack on Charleston by Du Pont's fleet, Lincoln said to Fox:*

I should be very anxious about this job if you did not feel so sure of your people being successful. *—Fox to Samuel F. Du Pont, February 12, 1863, in Fox, I, 178.* {A}

4. *A few weeks after the election of 1864, Fox told Alexander Rice (q.v.) that on election night, when a message announced Rice's re-election by 4,000 votes, Lincoln declared that it must be wrong, adding:*

Rice has one of the closest districts in the country, and those figures are more likely to be 40 or perhaps 400.

After confirmation of the larger margin arrived, he said: If the doubtful districts come in this shape, what may we expect from the certain ones? — Rice's reminiscence in the Boston Journal, *reprinted in the Washington* Post, *September 24, 1889.* {D}

5. *Fox told his wife that Lincoln felt compelled to give Chase the chief justiceship and said that:*

he would sooner have eat flatirons than do it. *—Fox Diary, December 10, 1864.* {D}

It is not clear that Fox was an auditor of this remark.

VIRGINIA WOODBURY FOX *Wife of Assistant Secretary of the Navy Gustavus V. Fox.*

1. *On March 7, 1862, the day before he had a confrontational meeting with General McClellan, Lincoln said to Mrs. Fox:*

We won't mention names, and I'll tell you how things are, state a proposition to you. Suppose a man whose profession it is to understand military matters is asked how long it will take him and what he requires to accomplish certain things, and when he has had all he asked and the time comes, he does nothing. *—Fox Diary.* {A}

JESSIE BENTON FRÉMONT (1824–1902)   *Daughter of Thomas Hart Benton and wife of General John C. Frémont, Union commander in Missouri, where, on August 30, 1861, he issued a proclamation establishing military rule in the state and emancipating the slaves of all persons who supported the Confederacy. Requested by Lincoln to modify the order, Frémont sent his wife to Washington with a letter declining to do so.*

1. *In an interview the evening of September 10, Lincoln said:*

The General ought not to have done it; he never would have done it if he had consulted Frank Blair. I sent Frank there to advise him and to keep me advised about the work, the true condition of things then, and how they were going. Frank never would have let him do it. The General should never have dragged the Negro into the war. It is a war for a great national object, and the Negro has nothing to do with it.

At one point in the discussion, after Mrs. Frémont had spoken sharply in defense of her husband, the President remarked: You are quite a female politician. — *Frémont, 266 (1891). {D}*

The tone throughout this recollection is too hostile to inspire complete confidence in its accuracy, and the same can probably be said for Lincoln's account of the confrontation as recorded in December 1863 by John Hay (q.v.).

A. W. FRENCH   *A Springfield dentist.*

1. *French recalled this remark by Lincoln when his first son was born:*

I'm glad it is all over and that he is such a fine-looking little fellow. I was afraid he might have one of my long legs and one of Mary's short ones, and he'd have had a terrible time getting through the world. —*French's statement in the Chicago* Times-Herald, *August 25, 1895. {D}*

According to the accompanying biographical passage, French became a resident of Springfield in 1848, five years after the birth of Robert Todd Lincoln.

BENJAMIN BROWN FRENCH (1800–1870)   *Jacksonian Democrat turned Republican who served as commissioner of public buildings during the Lincoln administration.*

1. *On December 14, 1861, at Mary Lincoln's request, French talked with the President about her excess of expenditure in refurnishing the White House and the need for an additional congressional appropriation of about $7,000. Lincoln was adamant, declaring that:*

it would stink in the land to have it said that an appropriation of $20,000 for furnishing the house had been overrun by the President when the poor freezing soldiers could not have blankets. . . he would never approve the bills for flub dubs for that damned old house! It was furnished well enough when they came—better than any house **they** had ever lived in. —*French, 382. {B}*

To this account, written in his journal on December 16, French added a some-what expanded version in a letter to his sister, Pamela French, dated December 24: It never can have my approval—I'll pay it out of my own pocket first—it would stink in the nostrils of the American people to have it said that the President of the United States had approved a bill overrunning an appropriation of $20,000 for flub dubs for this damned old house, when the soldiers cannot have blankets. . . . It was all wrong to spend one cent at such a time, and I never ought to have had a cent expended. The house was furnished well enough, better than any one we ever lived in, and if I had not been overwhelmed with other business, I would not have had any of the appropriation expended, but what could I do? I could not attend to everything. —*French Papers.* {C}

2. *On March 5, 1865, in a discussion of the fact that Congress had adjourned two days earlier without making the needed appropriations for public buildings and grounds, Lincoln said:*

We must **pick** along in some way. —*French, 466.* {A}

JAMES B. FRY (1827–1894) *West Point graduate who distinguished himself as a staff officer and in 1863 became provost-marshal-general in charge of army recruitment.*

1. *On his desire for a second term as president:*

No man knows what that gnawing is till he has had it. —*Rice AT, 390 (1886).* {C}

According to General James Harrison Wilson, Lincoln once said to James Russel Jones, the United States marshal for northern Illinois: "No man knows how deeply that presidential grub gnaws till he has had it himself."[162]

2. *During a discussion with Edwin M. Stanton about the selection of brigadier generals, the President said:*

The only point I make is, that there has got to be something done that will be unquestionably in the interest of the Dutch, and to that end, I want Schimmelfennig appointed.

When the Secretary suggested that some other German officer might be more highly recommended, Lincoln replied: No matter about that, his name will make up for any difference there may be, and I'll take the risk of his coming out all right. —*391–92.* {C}

Alexander Schimmelfennig (whose name Fry consistently misspelled "Schemmelfinnig") was promoted to brigadier general in November 1862.

3. *To a soldier making a complaint and persisting in his plea for Lincoln's intervention:*

Now, my man, go away, **go away**! I cannot meddle in your case. I could as easily bail out the Potomac River with a teaspoon as attend to all the details of the army. —*393.* {C}

The same outburst, with somewhat different wording, is described in Hay-3 (1890), 33–34.

4. *Concerning an interview with an angry governor who complained about military conscription and the demands upon his state:*

I did not concede anything. You know how that Illinois farmer managed the big log that lay in the middle of his field. To the inquiries of his neighbors one Sunday, he announced that he had got rid of the big log. "Got rid of it," said they, "how did you do it? It was too big to haul out, too knotty to split, and too wet and soggy to burn. What did you do?" "Well, now, boys, if you won't divulge the secret, I'll tell you how I got rid of it—**I plowed around it.**" Now, don't tell anybody, but that's the way I got rid of Governor ——. I plowed around him, but it took me three mortal hours to do it, and I was afraid every minute he'd see what I was at. —*Rice AT, 400.* {C}

5. *Commenting on General Meade's congratulatory order after the victory at Gettysburg, in which he spoke of the need to "drive from our soil every vestige of the presence of the invader":*

Drive the invaders from our soil! My God! Is that all? —*402.* {C}

FRANK FULLER　*An acquaintance of Robert Lincoln at Phillips Exeter Academy in 1859–60.*

1. *Robert would not agree to read the Declaration of Independence at a Fourth of July celebration without his father's approval. Fuller sent a telegram to Springfield and received this reply:*

Tell Bob to read that immortal document every chance he has, and the bigger the crowd, the louder he must holler. —*Fuller, 1 (c. 1905?).* {D}

◆◆◆◆◆◆

ALEXANDER T. GALT (1817–1893)　*Member of the Canadian cabinet who visited Washington in December 1861.*

1. *Responding to Galt's assertion at the time of the* Trent *crisis that Canadians feared the intentions and military power of the United States, the President said that:*

he had implicit faith in the steady conduct of the American people even under the trying circumstances of the war, and though the existence of large armies had in other countries placed successful generals in positions of arbitrary power, he did not fear this result, but believed the people would quietly resume their peaceful avocations and submit to the rule of the government. . . . He pledged himself as a man of honor that neither he nor his cabinet entertained the slightest aggressive designs upon Canada, nor had any desire to disturb the rights of Great Britain on this continent. — *Galt memorandum, December 5, 1861, in Skelton, 315.* {B}

HENRY J. GARDNER (1818–1892) *A Boston merchant who entered politics as a Whig, then became the Know-Nothing governor of Massachusetts in the mid-1850s.*

1. *As president, Lincoln once talked with Gardner about his speaking tour of Massachusetts in 1848 and especially about a dinner he attended at the home of Levi Lincoln in Worcester. He said:*

I had been chosen to Congress then from the wild West, and with hayseed in my hair, I went to Massachusetts, the most cultured state in the Union, to take a few lessons in deportment. That was a grand dinner, a superb dinner—by far the finest I ever saw in my life. And the great men who were there too! Why, I can tell you just how they were arranged at table. — *Gardner's statement in Herndon-2nd, I, 291.*[163] {C}

ROBERT GARDNER *A California delegate to the national convention of the Union (Republican) party in June 1864.*

1. *To Gardner's question shortly before the convention whether he had any preference for vice president, Lincoln replied:*

I see no reason for a change. — *Gardner's letter of July 12 in the San Francisco Bulletin, July 13, 1891.* {C}

SYDNEY HOWARD GAY (1814–1888) *Garrisonian abolitionist, editor of the* American Anti-Slavery Standard, *and during the Civil War, managing editor of the New York* Tribune.

1. *During a conversation with Gay on August 12, 1862, Lincoln said:*

I regard General Banks as one of the best men in the army. He makes me no trouble; but, with a large force or a small force, he always knows his duty and does it. — *New York* Tribune, *August 13, 1862.* {A}

JOHN GIBBON (1827–1896) *Civil War general, a professional soldier who for a time led the famous "Iron Brigade" and subsequently became a corps commander.*

1. *Upon being introduced to Gibbon in 1862, Lincoln asked:*

Is this the man who wrote the *Decline and Fall of the Roman Empire?*

When Gibbon looked confused, he added: Never mind, General, if you will write the decline and fall of this rebellion, I will let you off. — *Gibbon, 32 (c. 1885).* {C}

2. *Reviewing some sharp-looking black regiments near Petersburg in March 1865, Lincoln said:*

I wonder how Jeff would like to have such colored troops in his army! — 291. {C}

JOSEPH GILLESPIE (1809–1885)   *Lawyer in Edwardsville, Illinois, who was Lincoln's personal, professional, and political friend.*

1. *Lincoln once told Gillespie that:*

he could not avoid believing in predestination, although he considered it a very unprofitable field of speculation because it was hard to reconcile that belief with responsibility for one's acts. — *Gillespie to William H. Herndon, December 8, 1866 (8:1247–56), Herndon-Weik Collection.* {C}

2. *At another time, Lincoln remarked that:*

he never could reconcile the prescience of Deity with the uncertainty of events.

He went on to say that: he thought it was unprofitable to discuss the dogmas of predestination and free will. — *Oldroyd, 457 (1882).* {C}

3. *On one occasion, Lincoln confessed to Gillespie that:*

he never felt his own utter unworthiness so much as when in the presence of a hotel clerk or waiter. — *Oldroyd, 462.* {C}

4. *Speaking of state sovereignty, Lincoln said that:*

the advocates of that theory always reminded him of the fellow who contended that the proper place for the big kettle was inside of the little one. — *Gillespie to Herndon, January 31, 1866 (8:536–55).*[164] {C}

Herndon later asserted, without any reference to the Gillespie letter, that Lincoln made use of this analogy during a conversation with **him** *in 1859. — Herndon, III, 622.*

5. *According to Gillespie, Lincoln had faith in the curative power of madstones, though acknowledging that their use looked like superstition. He said that:*

he found the people in the neighborhood of these stones fully impressed with a belief in their virtues from actual experiment, and that was about as much as we could ever know of the properties of medicines. — *Gillespie to Herndon, January 31, 1866 (8:536–55).* {C}

6. *Asked why he did not speculate in land, Lincoln said that:*

he had no capacity whatever for speculation and never attempted it. — *Ibid.* {C}

7. *Gillespie recalled Lincoln's saying with respect to analysis of the nature of wit that:*

the first impression would be that the thing was of easy solution, but the varieties of wit were so great that what would explain one case would be wholly inapplicable to another. — *Gillespie to Herndon, December 8, 1866 (8:1247–56). {C}*

8. *Lincoln "used to say" with respect to slavery that:*

it was singular that the courts would hold that a man never lost his right to his property that had been stolen from him but that he instantly lost his right to himself if he was stolen. — *Gillespie to Herndon, January 31, 1866 (8:536–55). {C}*

9. *When the Illinois legislature elected a United States senator in February 1855, Lincoln led on the first ballot, but it soon became apparent that he could not win and that the contest lay between Democrat Joel Matteson and free-soil Democrat Lyman Trumbull. Gillespie, then a state senator, asked Lincoln what to do, and he replied:*

You ought to drop me and go for Trumbull. That is the only way you can defeat Matteson.

To Stephen T. Logan, who expressed a determination to continue supporting him, Lincoln said: If you do, you will lose both Trumbull and myself, and I think the cause in this case is to be preferred to men. — *Ibid.*[165] *{C}*

10. *At Shelbyville, Illinois, perhaps on August 9, 1856, Lincoln expressed his concern about the expansion of slavery:*

This thing is spreading like wildfire over the country. In a few years we will be ready to accept the institution in Illinois, and the whole country will adopt it.

He went on to say: that slavery was a great and crying injustice, an enormous national crime, and that we could not expect to escape punishment for it. — *Ibid. {C}*

11. *In the senatorial campaign of 1858, Lincoln spoke at Edwardsville on September 11, and Gillespie asked afterward why he did not make use of his talent for storytelling. Lincoln replied that:*

he thought the occasion was too grave and serious. — *Ibid. {C}*

12. *During the same conversation, Lincoln confided to Gillespie that:*

the principal complaint he had to make against Mr. Douglas was his continual assumption of superiority on account of his elevated position. — *Ibid. {C}*

13. *When Gillespie visited Springfield in January 1861, the President-elect said to him:*

Stay with me tonight. I can take no refusal. I have learned the value of old friends by making many new ones. — *Recollections published in the Cincinnati* Commercial Gazette *in 1888, reprinted in Wilson RR-2, 332. {C}*

14. *Expressing a wish that he could take the oath of office immediately, Lincoln said:*

Every hour adds to the difficulties I am called upon to meet, and the present administration does nothing to check the tendency toward dissolution. I, who have been called to meet this awful responsibility, am compelled to remain here, doing nothing to avert it or lessen its force when it comes to me. . . . It is not of myself I complain, but every day adds to the difficulty of the situation and makes the outcome more gloomy. Secession is being fostered rather than repressed, and if the doctrine meets with general acceptance in the border states, it will be a great blow to the government. — *Wilson RR-2, 333. {C}*

15. *On avoiding a war:*

It is only possible upon the consent of this government to the erection of a foreign slave government out of the present slave states. — *Wilson RR-2, 333. {C}*

16. *An analogy:*

I suppose you will never forget that trial down in Montgomery County, where the lawyer associated with you gave away the whole case in his opening speech. I saw you signaling to him, but you couldn't stop him. Now, that's just the way with me and Buchanan. He is giving away the case, and I have nothing to say and can't stop him. — *Wilson RR-2, 334. {C}*

17. *On cabinet-making:*

I wish I could take all you lawyers down there with me, Democrats and Republicans alike, and make a cabinet out of you. I believe I could construct one that would save the country, for then I would know every man and where he would fit. I tell you there are some Illinois Democrats whom I know well I would rather trust than a Republican I would have to learn, for I'll have no time to study the lesson. — *Wilson RR-2, 334. {C}*

18. *On changing the date of inauguration:*

When you were here last, you spoke of amending the Constitution for the benefit of some man who will be caught, in the future, in the same fix that I am in now. I think it had better be left alone, Joe. I have thought a good deal about that since you spoke of it, and while it might answer the present purpose, the fixing of an inaugural day too soon after the election might, if the result was disputed, plunge the country into civil war before party passion could cool or means of settlement be adopted. — *Wilson RR-2, 335. {C}*

19. *Shortly before the departure for Washington on February 11, 1861, Lincoln remarked:*

It seems to me that Douglas got the best of it at the election last fall. I am left to face an empty treasury and a great rebellion, while my own party endorses his popular sovereignty idea and applies it in legislation. . . . I only wish I could have got there to lock the door before the horse was stolen. But when I get to the spot, I can find the tracks. — *Wilson RR-2, 336.* {C}

20. *At some time after he became president, Lincoln told Gillespie that:*

circumstances had happened during the war to induce him to a belief in "special providences." — *Oldroyd, 457.* {C}

21. *In the spring of 1864, Lincoln declared that:*

the people were greatly ahead of the politicians in their effort for and confidence in putting down the rebellion. . . . The government had been driven by the public voice into the employment of means and the adoption of measures for carrying on the war which they would not have dared to put into practice without such backing.

He went on to say that: he had no doubt whatever of our success in overthrowing the rebellion at the right time. God was with us, and the people were behaving so nobly that all doubt had been removed from his mind as to our ultimate success. The army and the navy were in the right trim and in the right hands. — *Gillespie to Herndon, January 31, 1866 (8:536-55).* {C}

22. *On the way to the Soldiers' Home, accompanied by a cavalry escort, Lincoln said:*

that the escort was rather forced upon him by the military men, that he could see no certain protection against assassination if it was determined to take away his life. . . . It seemed to him like putting up the gap in only one place when the fence was down all along. — *Ibid.* {C}

Joseph Holt (q.v.) recalled Lincoln's making a similar remark.

23. *Concerning paroled Confederate soldiers who had been returned to active duty in the field:*

These men are liable to be put to death when recaptured for breach of parole. If we do not do something of that sort, this outrage will be repeated on every occasion. . . . It is indeed a serious question, and I have been more sorely tried by it than any other that has occurred during the war. It will be an act of great injustice to our soldiers to allow the paroled rebels to be put into the field without exchange. Such a practice would demoralize almost any army in the world if played off upon them. It would be nearly impossible to induce them to spare the lives of prisoners they might capture. On the other hand, these men were no doubt told by their superiors that they had been exchanged and it would be hard to put them to death under such circumstances. On the whole, my impression is that mercy bears richer fruits than any other attribute. — *Ibid.* {D}

*The death penalty for violation of military parole was rarely imposed, and the
question of how to deal with such violators as might be recaptured was scarcely
Lincoln's most trying problem of the war.*[166] *In a later writing, Gillespie placed
the final clause in an entirely different context and quoted it as follows:* I have
always found that mercy bears richer fruits than strict justice. — *Letter to
the St.* Louis Republican, *reprinted in the New York* Times, *February 23,
1876 (also in Oldroyd, 459).*

24. *Near the end of the war, when Gillespie asked what was to be done
with the rebels, Lincoln replied:*

Well, some people think their heads ought to come off, but there are too
many of them for that, and for one, I would not know where to draw the
line between those whose heads, it might be said, ought to come off or
stay on.

*He then recalled the story of how David, as he pardoned Shimei, exclaimed,
"Shall there any man be put to death this day in Israel?" — New York* Times,
February 23, 1876 (modified in Oldroyd, 458). {C}

JAMES R. GILMORE (1822–1903) *A New York businessman turned writer
under the pseudonym Edmund Kirke. Gilmore became involved with James F.
Jaquess, a Methodist preacher commanding his own regiment of Illinois volunteers,
in two private efforts to negotiate peace terms with the Confederate government.
First, in June 1863, Jaquess alone passed through enemy lines and met some southern leaders, but he failed to obtain an interview with Jefferson Davis. Then, in
July 1864, with Lincoln's unofficial approval, the two men went to Richmond and
returned with a statement from Davis that seemed to make recognition of southern
independence an absolute condition of any peace settlement. Gilmore subsequently
inflated his brief acquaintance with Lincoln into a sustained friendship. "It was
my good fortune," he wrote, "to know him well, and to be, at an early period in
his administration, the depositary of his confidential views on national policy, and
also his trusted agent in the attempted carrying out of some of his more important
plans in connection with the Civil War." The extravagance of this claim does not
improve the credibility of the statement that follows it: "All conversations with
Mr. Lincoln it was my habit to write down in my note-book within twenty-four
hours after they occurred, and hence I am able to reproduce, after the lapse of more
than thirty years, his very words, and his peculiarities of speech and manner."*[167]
*Thus, if Gilmore could be trusted, his recollected words of Lincoln would have
a status similar to those of a diarist. Instead, they belong, with a few exceptions,
among the curiosities of Lincoln literature.*[168]

1. *From 1861 to 1863, Gilmore was associated in a magazine venture with
Robert J. Walker, the northern-born Mississippi slaveholder who had been a
United States senator, a cabinet member, and the governor of Kansas Territory.
Walker, according to Gilmore, had a powerful influence on Lincoln, especially*

at the time of the Trent *crisis. Here are Lincoln's remarks on the subject as Gilmore supposedly recorded or recalled them:*

I lay awake all night, contriving how to get out of the scrape without loss of national dignity. Seward was for fight and went so far as to concoct a savage dispatch to Adams, but I told him that one war at a time was enough and sent for the Governor. He reminded me that we fought the War of 1812 in denial of the right of search and that in this *Trent* affair we had violated our own principles. Then my course was as clear as noonday. I could disown the act of Wilkes with perfect consistency. Until the Governor gave me that idea I could see no way out of the difficulty but by an open avowal that the real issue between the North and the South was slavery, and by issuing an immediate proclamation declaring free every slave in the states now in rebellion. Of course, the proclamation, so far as the South is concerned, would be a Pope's bull against the comet, inoperative except within the lines of our armies, but it would tie the hands of England; for no British government could stand for a day that sided with the slave-owners after the issue between slavery and freedom had been distinctly stated. . . . I got so enamored of the idea from intently brooding upon it that I was disposed to take the bull by the horns and make the proclamation at once, at the same time that I disavowed the blunder of Wilkes, but the Governor said: "You must not do it. It would be premature. You don't know how it would affect the North. Keep this in reserve; the disavowal of Wilkes will serve your present purpose." — *Gilmore-3, 57-58 (1898). {E}*

This account is inaccurate with respect to Seward's attitude and conduct. Furthermore, there is no evidence that Lincoln consulted Walker during the Trent *crisis or that he considered issuing an emancipation proclamation at that time.*

2. Late in May 1863, according to Gilmore, he had an interview of more than three hours with Lincoln about the Jaquess proposal and returned the next night, at the President's request, for another long discussion that lasted till midnight. In Gilmore's first published account of these meetings, Lincoln is quoted as saying:

I can't talk with you about that Jaquess matter. . . . We can make no overtures to the rebels. If they want peace, all they have to do is to lay down their arms.

Eventually, however, he came round to the point of discussing the terms he was willing to offer the Confederate government, while at the same time reiterating that he could not be a part of any negotiations. Summing up those terms, he said: The country will do everything for safety, nothing for revenge. — *Gilmore-1, 243-45 (1864). {D}*

In another account written much later, Gilmore was more expansive. Here are some of the remarks he attributed to Lincoln: As to Stanton, you know that it is hard to teach old dogs new tricks. He is terribly in earnest, and he does not always use the most conciliatory language. He very sensibly feels the need we have of victories, and he would take almost any means to get them. . . . His bark is a great deal worse than his bite.

On Jaquess: I've about concluded to let him go. My only fear is that he may compromise me, but I don't see how he can if I refuse to see him and he goes altogether on his own responsibility. But he must understand distinctly that I have nothing to do with his project, either directly or indirectly. If the impression should go abroad that I had, it might complicate matters badly. . . . The Copperheads would be sure to say I had shown the white feather and resorted to back-door diplomacy to get out of a bad scrape. This, whether true or not, would discourage loyal people. You see, I don't want to be like the dog that crossed the brook with a piece of meat in his mouth and dropped it to catch its enlarged shadow in the water. I want peace; I want to stop this terrible waste of life and property; and I know Jaquess well and see that, working in the way he proposes, he may be able to bring influences to bear upon Davis that he cannot well resist and thus pave the way for an honorable settlement; but I can't afford to discourage our friends and encourage our enemies, and so, perhaps, make it more difficult to save the Union.

On compensated emancipation: The feeling is against slavery, not against the South. The war has educated our people into abolition, and they now deny that slaves can be property. But there are two sides to that question. One is ours, the other, the southern side; and those people are just as honest and conscientious in their opinion as we are in ours. They think they have a moral and legal right to their slaves, and until very recently the North has been of the same opinion. For two hundred years the whole country has admitted it and regarded and treated the slaves as property. Now, does the mere fact that the North has come suddenly to a contrary opinion give us the right to take the slaves from their owners without compensation? The blacks must be freed. Slavery is the bone we are fighting over. It must be got out of the way to give us permanent peace, and if we have to fight this war till the South is subjugated, then I think we shall be justified in freeing the slaves without compensation. But in any settlement arrived at before they force things to that extremity, is it not right and fair that we should make payment for the slaves? *— Gilmore-2, 437, 438 (1887); Gilmore-3, 155–57, 159. {D}*

3. *In July 1863, Gilmore wrote to Lincoln offering evidence from an informer that the recent draft riots in New York City had been planned by Governor Horatio Seymour and a small group of fellow conspirators with the*

purpose of starting a Copperhead revolution against the federal government. Apparently with the approval of Horace Greeley, he proposed the appointment of a New York judge, John W. Edmonds (his future father-in-law), as special commissioner to investigate the origin of the riots.[169] Receiving no answer to his letters, Gilmore went to Washington and asked Lincoln the reason why. Lincoln replied:

Well, you see if I had said no, I should have admitted that I dare not enforce the laws and consequently have no business to be president of the United States. If I had said yes and had appointed the judge, I should—as he would have done his duty—have simply touched a match to a barrel of gunpowder. You have heard of sitting on a volcano. We are sitting upon two. One is blazing away already, and the other will blaze away the moment we scrape a little loose dirt from the top of the crater. Better let the dirt alone, at least for the present. One rebellion at a time is about as much as we can conveniently handle. —*Gilmore-3, 199.* {C}

If Gilmore did indeed query Lincoln face-to-face on the subject, this seems like the sort of response he might have received.

4. In March 1864, Gilmore and a companion allegedly met with Lincoln to discuss plans for arranging a separate peace with Governor Zebulon B. Vance of North Carolina—a project in which he, Gilmore, was to be the President's negotiator. They found Lincoln in good spirits after having placed Grant in command of all Union armies. He said:

Oh, yes! I feel better, for now I'm like the man who was blown up on a steamboat and said, on coming down, "It makes no difference to me; I'm only a passenger." —*Gilmore-3, 227.* {D}

It is doubtful that this conversation ever took place, for there appears to be no contemporary evidence supporting Gilmore's story of having the central role in a proposed mission to North Carolina. It has nevertheless been given credence in Collected Works, VI, 330–31.[170]

5. On May 18, 1864, Lincoln told Gilmore:

that the announcement made by the *World* of this morning of a proclamation calling for 400,000 men was a fabrication; that he had decided to call for 300,000 in July, not before. Signed a paper to that effect last night.[171] —*Gilmore to Sydney Howard Gay, May 18, 1864, Gay Papers.* {B}

6. During the same interview, which, according to Gilmore's probably inflated estimate, lasted two hours, Lincoln spoke of Grant's Spotsylvania campaign:

When my wife had her first baby, the doctor from time to time reported to me that everything was going on as well as could be expected under the circumstances. That satisfied me **he** was doing his best, but still I felt anxious to hear the first squall. It came at last, and I felt mightily relieved. I feel very much so about our army operations at this moment. —*Ibid. {A}*

7. *In an interview on July 6, 1864, according to Gilmore, he urged a reluctant Lincoln to endorse another Jaquess peace venture, presenting it as a clever stratagem for eliciting from Jefferson Davis a refusal to negotiate on any basis other than southern independence. That, Gilmore explained to the President, would unite the North, re-elect him, and save the Union. Lincoln, after some thought, replied:*

There is something in what you say. But Jaquess couldn't do it. He couldn't draw Davis's fire; he is too honest. You are the man for that business. . . . He feels that he is acting as God's servant and messenger, and he would recoil from anything like political finesse. But if Davis should make such a declaration, the country should know of it, and I can see that, coming from him now, when everybody is tired of the war and so many think some honorable settlement can be made, it might be of vital importance to us. But I tell you that not Jaquess, but **you,** are the man for that business.

It was eventually settled that Gilmore and Jaquess should undertake the mission together. Gilmore tells us that he returned to the White House that same evening, accompanied at Lincoln's request by Salmon P. Chase, with whom he had consulted and then dined.[172] The three men conferred on the project for several hours, and Lincoln dictated a seven-point statement of peace terms:

First. The immediate dissolution of the southern government and disbandment of its armies, and the acknowledgment by all the states in rebellion of the supremacy of the Union.

Second. The total and absolute abolition of slavery in every one of the late slave states and throughout the Union. This to be perpetual.

Third. Full amnesty to all who have been in any way engaged in the rebellion and their restoration to all the rights of citizenship.

Fourth. All acts of secession to be regarded as nullities and the late rebellious states to be, and be regarded, as if they had never attempted to secede from the Union. Representation in the House from the recent slave states to be on the basis of their voting population.

Fifth. The sum of five hundred millions in United States stock to be issued and divided between the late slave states, to be used by them in payment to slave-owners, loyal and disloyal, for the slaves emancipated by my proclamation. This sum to be divided among the late slave-owners, equally and equitably, at the rate of one half the value of the slaves in the year 1860; and if any surplus should remain, it to be returned to the United States treasury.

Sixth. A national convention to be convened as soon as practicable, to ratify this settlement and make such changes in the Constitution as may be in accord with the new order of things.

Seventh. The intent and meaning of all the foregoing is that the Union shall be fully restored as it was before the rebellion, with the exception that all slaves within its borders are, and shall forever be, freemen. — *Gilmore-2, 443–46; also in Gilmore-3, 240–44.* {E}

Although some highly respected historians have accepted Gilmore's account, it is difficult to believe that Lincoln so facilely extemporized a document of such importance and such detail, or that he consulted Chase in this way just a few days after accepting his resignation from the cabinet. Moreover, the silence of Chase's diary on the subject leads one to suspect that the whole story of the evening conference is a fabrication.[173]

8. *In a discussion with Gilmore after he and Jaquess returned from Richmond, Lincoln said:*

It is important that Davis's position should be known at once. It will show the country that I didn't fight shy of Greeley's Niagara business without a reason . . . This may be worth as much to us as half a dozen battles. — *Gilmore-3, 289.*[174] {C}

LAWRENCE A. GOBRIGHT (1816–1879) *A journalist resident many years in Washington, D.C.*

1. *When Gobright called to ask about the siege of Vicksburg, Lincoln said:*

I have nothing new. I am much concerned about affairs. I can't sleep tonight without hearing something; come, go with me to the War Department. Perhaps Stanton has something.

Handed a dispatch containing a report (which turned out to be false) that Union forces had been badly defeated, the President exclaimed: Bad news, bad news!

Then he admonished Gobright: Don't say anything about this. Don't mention it. — *Gobright, 335–36 (1869).* {C}

GRANT GOODRICH (1812–1889) *Chicago lawyer and judge who, according to Herndon, once offered Lincoln a partnership.*[175]

1. *In July 1850, Lincoln represented the defendant in the two-week trial of* Parker v. Hoyt, *a patent-infringement case in the federal district court at Chicago. While the jury was deliberating, one of its members signaled to Lincoln from a window that he was standing alone against the other eleven. Lincoln remarked that:*

if he was like a juryman he had in Tazewell County, the defendant was safe. . . . He was then employed to prosecute a suit for a divorce. His client was a very pretty, refined, interesting woman in court. The defendant was a rather gross, morose, querulous, fault-finding, cross, and uncomfortable person, entirely unfitted for the husband of such a woman. . . . He was able to prove the use of very offensive and vulgar epithets applied by him to his wife and all sorts of annoyances, but no such acts of personal violence as required by the statute to justify divorce. He did the best he could and appealed to the jury to have compassion on the woman and not bind her to such a man and such a life as awaited her as the wife of such a man. The jury took about the same view of it in their deliberations. They desired to find for her but could find no evidence which would really justify a verdict for her and drew up a verdict for the defendant, and all signed but one, who, when asked to do so, said: "Gentlemen, I am going to lie down to sleep and when you get ready to give a verdict for that woman, wake me up, for before I will give a verdict against her, I will be here until I rot and the pismires carry me out of the keyhole." Now [Lincoln continued], if that juryman will stick like that man, we are safe. — *Goodrich to Herndon, December 9, 1866 (8:1258-65), Herndon-Weik Collection. {C}*

The Chicago jury found for Hoyt. In a speech many years later, Goodrich told the same story, using somewhat different language and casting his quotation of Lincoln in direct discourse. —New York Times, *March 25, 1883.*

2. *Shortly before his departure for Washington in 1861, Lincoln said to Goodrich:*

Do you believe any man ever lived who had responsibilities laid upon him and saw great difficulties before him he could not see his way out of who did not look to some wiser and stronger being for help and wisdom to support and guide him? That is my condition. — *New York* Times, *March 25, 1883. {C}*

JAMES GORDON   *A resident of Illinois.*

1. *After helping an emigrant family pull their wagon out of a slough, Lincoln said:*

Those people are going to the Far West and by and by will have a home, and should I ever pass their way, tired and hungry, I imagine they would divide their last loaf of bread with me. — *Gordon's recollection reported in the* Logan County Republican *(Lincoln, Ill.), undated clipping, Tarbell Papers. {D}*

JOHN FRANKLIN GOUCHER (1845–1922)   *Methodist clergyman, a founder and the longtime president of the institution that came eventually to be named Goucher College.*

1. *At Pittsburgh's Monongahela House on February 14 or 15, 1861, young Goucher accosted Lincoln in order to shake his hand. Nearly fifty years later he recalled that the President-elect said:*

God bless you, my son. Love God, obey your parents, and serve your country, and you will give the world cause to remember and honor you. —

Goucher's reminiscence in the Christian Advocate, *84 (February 4, 1909): 165-66. {C}*

JAMES GOURLEY *A Springfield shoemaker who for a time lived near the Lincolns.*

1. *Respecting the low ceiling in Gourley's house, Lincoln "used to say" that:*

little people had some advantages; it did not take quite so much wood and wool to make their house and clothes. — *Undated statement to Herndon in Herndon-Weik Collection (11:3051-58). {C}*

ULYSSES S. GRANT (1822-1885) *Like Lincoln an Illinoisan, Grant first met the President in March 1864 when he became general in chief, commanding all armies of the United States.*

1. *In their first consultation, Lincoln said to Grant that:*

he had never professed to be a military man or to know how campaigns should be conducted, and never wanted to interfere in them; but that procrastination on the part of commanders, and the pressure from the people at the North and Congress, which was always with him, forced him into issuing his series of military orders . . . He did not know but they were all wrong and did know that some of them were. All he wanted or had ever wanted was someone who would take the responsibility and act and call on him for all the assistance needed, pledging himself to use all the power of the government in rendering such assistance. . . . He did not want to know what I proposed to do. — *Grant, II, 122-23 (1886). {C}*

2. *In another, more extensive version of the same interview, Grant told Horace Porter on April 30, 1864, what the President had said some seven weeks earlier:*

that he did not pretend to know anything about the handling of troops, and it was with the greatest reluctance that he ever interfered with the movements of army commanders, but he had common sense enough to know that celerity was absolutely necessary; that while armies were sitting down waiting for opportunities to turn up which might, perhaps, be more favorable from a strictly military point of view, the government was spending millions of dollars every day; that there was a limit to the sinews of war, and a time might be reached when the spirits and resources of the people would become exhausted. He had always contended that these considerations should be taken into account, as well as purely military questions, and that he adopted the plan of issuing his "executive orders" principally for the purpose of hurrying the movements of commanding generals; but that he believed I knew the value of minutes, and that he was not going to interfere with my operations.

He said further: that he did not want to know my plans; that it was, per-haps, better that he should not know them, for everybody he met was trying to find out from him something about the contemplated movements, and there was always a temptation "to leak." — *Porter H-1, 26 (1897). {D}*

A secondhand recollection.

3. *Perhaps also in their first consultation, Lincoln issued a warning in the form of a story:*

At one time there was a great war among the animals, and one side had great difficulty in getting a commander who had sufficient confidence in himself. Finally, they found a monkey by the name of Jocko, who said that he thought he could command their army if his tail could be made a little longer. So they got more tail and spliced it on to his caudal appendage. He looked at it admiringly and then thought he ought to have a little more still. This was added, and again he called for more. The splicing process was repeated many times, until they had coiled Jocko's tail around the room, filling all the space. Still he called for more tail, and, there being no other place to coil it, they began wrapping it around his shoulders. He continued his call for more, and they kept on winding the additional tail about him until its weight broke him down. — *Rice AT, 1–2 (1886).*[176] *{C}*

This fable caricaturing McClellan, which came from a poem by Orpheus C. Kerr, had been related by Lincoln to Gideon Welles (q.v.) and others nearly a year earlier.

4. *On April 20, 1864, when Grant explained his policy of having even defensive troops advance:*

Oh, yes! I see that. As we say out West, if a man can't skin he must hold a leg while somebody else does. — *Grant, II, 143. {C}*

Lincoln apparently repeated this remark to John Hay, who quoted it more succinctly in his diary on April 30: "Those not skinning can hold a leg." — Hay-1, 179.

5. *In February 1865, speaking of the big overcoat worn by undersized Alex-ander H. Stephens at the Hampton Roads conference:*

Didn't you think it was the biggest shuck and the littlest ear that ever you did see? — *Grant, II, 423. {C}*

6. *During one of Lincoln's visits to City Point, Virginia, in the spring of 1865, Grant showed him the work on the Dutch Gap Canal and the results of a miscalculated explosion. Lincoln said that it reminded him of a blacksmith out in Springfield:*

One day, when he did not have much to do, he took a piece of soft iron that had been in his shop for some time, and for which he had no special use, and, starting up his fire, began to heat it. When he got it hot, he carried it to the anvil and began to hammer it, rather thinking he would weld it into an agricultural implement. He pounded away for some time until he got it fashioned into some shape, when he discovered that the iron would not hold out to complete the implement he had in mind. He then put it back into the forge, heated it up again, and recommenced hammering, with an ill-defined notion that he would make a claw hammer, but after a time he came to the conclusion that there was more iron there than was needed to form a hammer. Again he heated it and thought he would make an axe. After hammering and welding it into shape, knocking the oxidized iron off in flakes, he concluded there was not enough of the iron left to make an axe that would be of any use. He was now getting tired and a little disgusted at the result of his various essays. So he filled his forge full of coal, and, after placing the iron in the center of the heap, took the bellows and worked up a tremendous blast, bringing the iron to a white heat. Then with his tongs he lifted it from the bed of coals and thrusting it into a tub of water near by, exclaimed with an oath, "Well, if I can't make anything else of you, I will make a fizzle, anyhow." — *Rice AT, 2–4. {C}*

According to Horace Porter, Lincoln told this story on the River Queen *in late March 1865, associating it with the failures of a "prominent general," perhaps Frémont. According to David Dixon Porter, he told it during the trip from Richmond back to City Point on April 5.*[177]

7. *Even as he forced the evacuation of Petersburg on April 2, Grant was taking vigorous steps to prevent Lee's retreating army from linking up with that of Joseph E. Johnston. Lincoln said to Grant the next day:*

Do you know, General, that I have had a sort of sneaking idea for some days that you intended to do something like this.

When Grant declared that as a matter of sectional morale, it would be better if the Army of the Potomac could capture Lee's force without help from Sherman's westerners, the President replied that: he saw that now but had never thought of it before, because his anxiety was so great that he did not care where the aid came from so the work was done. — *Grant, II, 459, 460–61. {C}*

8. *Soon after the surrender of Lee at Appomattox, Grant arrived in Washington and there received a letter from William Smith, the Confederate governor of Virginia, asking whether he would be permitted to go abroad without interference. Grant consulted Lincoln, who replied that:*

his position was like that of a certain Irishman he knew in Springfield, who was very popular with the people, a man of considerable promise and very much liked. Unfortunately he had acquired the habit of drinking, and his friends could see that the habit was growing on him. These friends determined to make an effort to save him, and to do this they drew up a pledge to abstain from all alcoholic drinks. They asked Pat to join them in signing the pledge, and he consented. He had been so long out of the habit of using plain water as a beverage that he resorted to soda-water as a substitute. After a few days this began to grow distasteful to him. So, holding the glass behind him, he said: "Doctor, couldn't you drop a bit of brandy in that, unbeknownst to myself." — *Grant, II, 533.* {C}

According to William T. Sherman, the President told this story to him, in Grant's presence, some two weeks earlier at City Point, Virginia, in response to the question whether Jefferson Davis should be allowed to flee the country.[178] *There is also testimony that Lincoln repeated the story to the cabinet, perhaps at its last meeting before his death.*[179]

THOMAS THATCHER GRAVES (1841–1893) *Aide to General Godfrey Weitzel, who commanded the Union troops that occupied Richmond near the end of the war. Later a physician of dubious reputation, he was convicted of murder and committed suicide in a Denver jail.*

    1. *During the presidential visit to Richmond on April 4, 1865, Weitzel asked how the conquered people were to be treated. Lincoln indicated that he did not want to give any specific orders, but then added:*

If I were in your place, I'd let 'em up easy, let 'em up easy. — *Graves manuscript, "Our Occupation of Richmond," 1889, Nicolay Papers.* {C}

HORACE GREELEY (1811–1872) *Founder and editor of the New York* Tribune *and one of the leading figures in the antislavery movement.*

    1. *In February 1863, Lincoln spoke to Greeley:*

of the emancipation policy as not having yet effected so much good here at home as had been promised or predicted.

He added, however, that: it had helped us decidedly in our foreign relations. — *Greeley, 380 (c. 1868).* {C}

DUFF GREEN (1791–1875) *Kentucky-born journalist, politician, and entrepreneur who operated ironworks for the Confederacy.*

    1. *In early April 1865, Green visited Lincoln at City Point and asked about peace terms. The President replied:*

If you desire peace, all that will be required of you is to acknowledge the authority of the United States. If you wish to keep your slaves, vote against the amendments to the Constitution. I cannot recall my proclamations. Whether they are binding or not will be a question for the courts. — *Green, 232 (1866).* {D}

Green's description of the interview as a friendly one is contradicted by David Dixon Porter (q.v.) and in Crook, 56–57.

HORACE GREEN (1802–1866)   *Noted New York physician, a specialist in diseases of the throat.*

1. *On June 16, 1862, Dr. Green and a companion called on the President to urge that the house and lawn of Robert E. Lee's estate at Arlington Heights be made available for use as a military hospital. Lincoln responded:*

Gentlemen, I understand all this matter perfectly well. It is only a political raid against General McClellan. General McClellan does not choose to give up these grounds, and a political party is determined that he shall be compelled to do it. There is no necessity that this property should be used for this purpose.

Persuaded, however, by Green's further argument, he declared: I will tell you the truth of the case. General McClellan promised Mrs. General Lee that those grounds should be protected from all injury, and that is the reason he doesn't want them used. . . . McClellan has made this promise, but I think it is wrong; I believe what you say in reference to this matter. He doesn't want to break the promise he has made, and I will break it for him. —*Excerpt from Green's journal in* Century Magazine, *81 (February 1911): 594–96. {A}*

GILBERT J. GREENE (1835–1906)   *A typesetter who, as a youth in the winter of 1850–51, assertedly walked the length of Illinois from south to north and on the way delivered some legal papers to Lincoln from a client in a nearby county.*[180]

1. *Since Greene had recently tried teaching on a Tennessee plantation, conversation soon turned to the great issue of the day, and Lincoln said:*

Slavery exists only by the tolerance of Christian people; but its advocates are determined that Christianity shall not only tolerate but approve it. It was a conflict [he continued] that could not last forever, and it could have but one ending. It must cease to exist. If during the last twenty years its advocates had held an annual convention to determine upon something they would do in the following year to annoy or incense their opponents, they would have proposed about what they had done, and if it were continued, as it had been in the past, there were plenty of people then living who would see the end of human slavery. He was quite sure it would not outlive the century. It seemed to him that gradual emancipation and governmental compensation, would bring it to an end. —*Greene, 13. {D}*

Lincoln did not begin to talk along these lines until 1854. Furthermore, this account of a discussion of slavery in mid-January 1851 contains no mention of the great compromise enacted by Congress just a few months earlier.

LYNN M. GREENE   *Lawyer in Petersburg, Illinois, brother of William G. Greene.*

1. *One day in the early 1830s, Lincoln said to Greene that:*

all his folks seemed to have good sense but none of them had become distinguished, and he believed it was for him to become so—had talked with men who had the reputation of being great men, but could not see that they differed from other men. —*Greene's statement in 1860, Howard JQ, 393.* {C}

WILLIAM G. GREENE (1812–?) *A friend of Lincoln from his New Salem days, Greene was a farmer and man of various business interests in central Illinois.*

1. *In April 1832, soon after his enlistment in the state militia for the Black Hawk War, Lincoln was pitted against one Lorenzo Dow Thompson in a wrestling match. He lost in two straight falls, the second of which was disputed by his supporters. Lincoln said:*

Boys, give up your bet; if he has not thrown me fairly, he could.

When Greene paid a visit to the White House during the Civil War, Lincoln recalled the incident and said playfully of Thompson that: if he knew where he was living, he would give him a post office by way of showing him that he bore him no ill will. —*Oldroyd, 516–17 (1882). {C}*

Greene mistakenly placed the match at Rock Island, rather than at Beardstown where it actually took place, but his account is substantially corroborated by Risdon M. Moore (q.v.).

2. *Also during the Black Hawk War, a friendly Indian came into camp, and the soldiers were disposed to shoot him. As Greene's recollection of the affair was noted down by an interviewer in 1860, Lincoln opposed them, declaring that:*

barbarians would not kill a prisoner.

When several men accused him of cowardice, he said: Try me.

He swore that: if the Indian was slaughtered it must be done over his dead body.

He invited them: to come out and fight him if they thought he was cowardly. —*Howard JQ, 398–99. {C}*

The Indian was not killed.[181]

3. *After the death of Ann Rutledge in 1835, according to Greene, Lincoln said:*

I can never be reconciled to have the snow, rains, and storms to beat on her grave. —*Greene to Herndon, May 30, 1865 (7:91–103), Herndon-Weik Collection. {C}*

Another New Salem friend, Elizabeth Abell, wrote of his remarking on a rainy day "that he could not bear the idea of its raining on her grave." To Herndon, February 15, 1867 (9:1449–50).

4. *Visiting his old friend in the White House, Greene protested when he was introduced to William H. Seward as the man who had taught Lincoln grammar. Lincoln said:*

Bill, don't you recollect when we stayed in the Offut store in New Salem, that you would hold the book and see if I could give the correct definitions and accurate answers to the questions? . . . That was all the teaching of grammar I ever had. —*From an interview of Greene around 1893 in Reep, 30–31. {C}*

WILLIAM GRIGSBY   *A resident of Spencer County, Indiana, brother of Lincoln's brother-in-law, Aaron Grigsby.*

1. *Grigsby told his brother Nathaniel that after he had whipped Lincoln's stepbrother John Johnston, Lincoln (then about twenty years old) challenged him to a fight. He proposed a duel instead, and Lincoln replied that:*

he was not a-going to fool his life away with one shot. —*Nathaniel Grigsby to Herndon, October 25, 1865 (7:427–28), Herndon-Weik Collection. {D}*

[JOSEPH] JACKSON GRIMSHAW (1820–1875)   *Illinois attorney, a resident of Pittsfield and then Quincy, with whom Lincoln was associated in law and politics. In 1860, he was a member of the Republican state central committee.*

1. *Just before the Chicago convention, Grimshaw asked whether Lincoln, if he failed to win the presidential nomination, would accept the nomination for vice president. Lincoln authorized him to say that:*

his name having been used for the office of president, he would not permit it to be used for the other office, however honorable it might be. —*Grimshaw to Herndon, April 28, 1866 (8:720–23), Herndon-Weik Collection. {C}*

ELIZABETH TODD GRIMSLEY (1825–1895)   *Cousin of Mary Lincoln and for six months in 1861 a resident in the White House.*

1. *Watching as Willie silently pondered a problem and then at last smiled as though he had solved it, Lincoln said to a visitor:*

I know every step of the process by which that boy arrived at his satisfactory solution of the question before him, as it is by just such slow methods I attain results. —*Grimsley, 54 (1895). {C}*

JOSIAH B. GRINNELL (1821–1891)   *Clergyman and lawyer, railroad promoter and town founder, member of Congress from Iowa, 1863–67. Grinnell's claim that he was the person to whom Horace Greeley said "Go west, young man" may be a pretty accurate indication of the reliability of his reminiscences in general.*[182]

1. *Grinnell wrote that on his first visit to the White House in 1861, he took notice of a volume by Orpheus C. Kerr lying on the mantel and that Lincoln said:*

Don't judge your friend by that book of fun and romance. I read it when my brain is weary, and I seek relief by diversion, which this promotes. I have hours of depression, and I must be unbent. When a boy, the owner of a bow and arrow, I found one must let up on the bow if the arrow is to have force. Read Kerr and then pity me chained here in the Mecca of office-seekers. You flaxen men with broad faces are born with cheer and don't know a cloud from a star. I am of another temperament. But, drop the book, and if the country will get up as much fever in enlistments as there is strife for the offices, the rebel leaders will soon have a collapse. — *Grinnell, 171 (1891).* {D}

Kerr's writings did not begin to appear in book form until 1862.

2. *Some months after that first meeting, says Grinnell (meaning, presumably, sometime in late 1861 or early 1862), he called on the President to urge promotion of Iowan Elliott W. Rice to brigadier general. Stanton, he complained, would not give the matter serious consideration. Lincoln said:*

Yes, I know the cases like yours are hundreds, and it disturbs him, even my hint that we may move up the boys and encourage enlistments. It is a very delicate question. Don't be impatient, but get on the right side of a very good officer.

When Grinnell subsequently renewed his efforts, Lincoln remarked that: Stanton was fairly mad on the suggestion of promotion by civilians or members of Congress.

Approached a third time, he declared: I cannot attempt to make Stanton over at this stage. You will win, if patient.

But then, according to Grinnell, he promptly reversed himself and wrote a note to Stanton ordering Rice's promotion "without an if or an and." —172.[183] {D}

Whatever else may be said, Grinnell's chronology is confused; for Rice did not even become a colonel until April 1862, and his promotion to brigadier general took place in June 1864.

3. *When Grinnell called at the White House to air some grievances, Lincoln said:*

Don't mention them. I meet insults, standing between two fires, and the constant blazes of anger. Why, not an hour ago, a woman, a lady of high blood, came here, opening her case with mild expostulation, but left in anger flaunting her handkerchief before my face, and saying, "Sir, the General will try titles with you. He is a man and I am his wife." I will tell you before you guess. It was Jessie, the daughter of old Bullion, and how her eye flashed! Young man, forget your annoyances! They are only as flea-bites to mine. They are serious comedy, while I am in the focus of tragedy and fire. You folks up on the hill must aid me in placating those congenital Democrats, whom we want to keep fighting for us if they will. We must coyly give rope if we have to make a short turn later. I remember, of the New York "Barnburners" it was charged that to get clear of the rats they burned the barn. We must put up with vermin intrusion, to save the barn. —174. {E}

The flaws in this account are all too obvious. Jessie Benton Frémont's famous confrontation with Lincoln took place around midnight on September 10, 1861. It is highly unlikely that the President received Grinnell or any other caller within an hour afterwards. Furthermore, Lincoln speaks of "you folks up on the hill," and yet Grinnell did not take his seat in Congress until December 1863.

4. *At another time, Grinnell presented the petty complaint of a constituent against a Democrat employed as a clerk in one of the departments. Lincoln laid a hand on his shoulder and said:*

Don't ask me to strike so low; I have to do with those whom I despise; for we are at war. Democratic aid we must have if possible, and I conciliate to avoid all friction. —174. {C}

5. *Several times during 1863, Lincoln attended performances of James H. Hackett in the role of Falstaff. When Grinnell mentioned having seen him at the theater, he said:*

Yes, and they said my coarse laugh was very audible. But what did you think, Grinnell, was the best thing there last night? I will tell you what convulsed me. "Lord, how this world is given to lying." We had some good war news yesterday, and I was glad to unbend and laugh. The acting was good, and true to the case, according to my experiences, for each fellow tells his own story and smirches his rival. —173-74. {C}

6. *On February 1, 1864, Grinnell introduced a resolution in the House calling for a more vigorous policy of enlisting blacks in the army. Shortly after, Lincoln said to him:*

That resolution implies that we are not doing all we could, but I am glad that Congress has endorsed the policy of actively enlisting black men. It implies that if they are enlisted and fight for the country it must do something more for them. It is a great day for the black man when you tell him he shall carry a gun. Now, tell your people in Iowa, and your friends in Congress if you choose, that the time has come when I am for everybody fighting the rebels. Let Indians fight them; let the Negroes fight them; and if you have got any strong-legged jackasses in Iowa that can kick rebels to death, they have my hearty consent. When you give the Negro these rights, when you put a gun in his hands, it prophesies something more: it foretells that he is to have the full enjoyment of his liberty and manhood. — *Grinnell speech on January 17, 1867, in* Congressional Globe, *39th Congress, 2nd session, 537.* {D}

There would appear to be more Grinnell than Lincoln in this passage.

7. *In the autumn of 1864, when Grinnell and several other Iowans urged the appointment of Chase to the Supreme Court:*

Are you sure the seat of a chief justice will not heighten rather than banish political ambition? It ought to banish it; so high and honorable a place should satisfy and engross any American. Well, you are of good hope on the outside, but I must do the right thing in this critical hour. — *Grinnell, 173. {C}*

ALONZO J. GROVER (1828–?)   *Lawyer and abolitionist of Earlville, near Ottawa, Illinois.*

1. *Talking with Grover early in 1860, several months after a slave rescue at Ottawa, Lincoln said of the Fugitive Slave Law:*

It is ungodly; it is ungodly; no doubt it is ungodly! But it is the law of the land, and we must obey it as we find it.

Pressed further on the subject, he replied: Grover, it's no use to be always looking up these hard spots. — *Grover's account as presented in Browne FF, 355 (1886).*[184] *{C}*

LEONARD GROVER (1835–1926)   *An upstate New Yorker who, after some experience as an impresario and editor, became the manager of the National Theatre (soon known as "Grover's Theatre") in Washington, D.C. His assertion that Lincoln attended his theater "probably more than a hundred times" and Ford's Theatre not once until the night of the assassination, contributes to doubt about his recollective accuracy in general.*[185]

1. *As President-elect, Lincoln compared some Baltimore Republicans seeking appointments to crusaders of old, scaling the ramparts of a walled city. Then he said to them:*

But, gentlemen, those heroic soldiers who were first on top of the walls didn't get the offices. — *Grover, 944 (1909). {C}*

2. *On one occasion, Lincoln remarked:*

Do you know, Mr. Grover, I really enjoy a minstrel show. — *944. {C}*

3. *On June 8, 1864, Lincoln was renominated by the National Union Convention at Baltimore. That evening, according to Grover, Lincoln came alone to his theater, saying:*

There is a convention, as I suppose you know, Mr. Grover, and I thought I would get away for a little while, lest they make me promise too much.

During the performance, he received a telegram and, after reading it, said to Grover: Well, they have nominated me again. . . . but I am a little bit curious to know what man they are going to harness up with me. Still, I reckon I'll stay a little while longer and look at the play. — *947. {D}*

This story, although given the imprint of acceptance in Lincoln Day by Day, *seems improbable in itself and is contradicted by other accounts of how Lincoln was informed of his renomination and how he spent the evening.*[186]

4. *In the fall of 1864, when questioned about political sentiment in New York and New England, Grover said that Stanton's presence in the cabinet was widely regarded as a handicap. Lincoln replied:*

Mr. Grover, many people tell me that. I feel that Mr. Stanton is not generally popular. And if they'll find me a man who will do his **work**, I'll dismiss him.

In another conversation after his re-election, the President said: Well, they stood for the handicap. When they were advising me against Stanton, I knew that my term of office did not expire till next March. I felt that with Grant and Stanton's help we would have the rebellion subdued by that time. And I still believe we shall. So I took whatever chance there might have been with Stanton, rather than take any part of a chance for defeat in a purpose much greater than my election. I thought in the emergency it was bad policy to swap horses. —948. {D}

JOHN P. GULLIVER (1819–1894) *Minister in Norwich, Connecticut, later president of Knox College. His article published during the war (and reprinted two years later in Francis B. Carpenter's* Six Months at the White House) *is an excellent early example of pretended reminiscence at work constructing the Lincoln myth.*

1. *In a conversation on the train from Norwich to Bridgeport during his New England tour in 1860, Lincoln pondered the reasons for his remarkable success as a public speaker. Gulliver attributed it to the clarity of his style and reasoning, along with the aptness of his illustrations, then asked about his education. Lincoln, we are told, replied:*

The newspapers are correct. I never went to school more than six months in my life. But, as you say, this must be a product of culture in some form. I have been putting the question you ask me to myself, while you have been talking. I can say this, that among my earliest recollections I remember how, when a mere child, I used to get irritated when anybody talked to me in a way I could not understand. I don't think I ever got angry at anything else in my life. But that always disturbed my temper and has ever since. I can remember going to my little bedroom, after hearing the neighbors talk of an evening with my father, and spending no small part of the night walking up and down and trying to make out what was the exact meaning of some of their, to me, dark sayings. I could not sleep, though I often tried to, when I got on such a hunt after an idea, until I had caught it; and when I thought I had got it, I was not satisfied until I had repeated it over and over, until I had put it in language plain enough, as I thought, for any boy I knew to comprehend. This was a kind of passion with me, and it has stuck by me, for I am never easy now, when I am handling a thought, till I have bounded it north, and bounded it south, and bounded it east, and bounded it west. Perhaps that accounts for the characteristic you observe in my speeches, though I never put the two things together before. —*Gulliver, 1 (1864)*. {D}

2. *Asked how he prepared himself for his profession, Lincoln said:*

Oh, yes, I "read law," as the phrase is; that is, I became a lawyer's clerk in Springfield, and copied tedious documents and picked up what I could of law in the intervals of other work. But your question reminds me of a bit of education I had, which I am bound in honesty to mention. In the course of my law reading I constantly came upon the word "demonstrate." I thought at first that I understood its meaning, but soon became satisfied that I did not. I said to myself, "What do I do when I **demonstrate** more than when I **reason** or **prose**? How does **demonstration** differ from any other proof?" I consulted Webster's *Dictionary*. That told of "certain proof," "proof beyond the possibility of doubt," but I could form no idea what sort of proof that was. I thought a great many things were proved beyond a possibility of doubt, without recourse to any such extraordinary process of reasoning as I understood "demonstration" to be. I consulted all the dictionaries and books of reference I could find, but with no better results. You might as well have defined "blue" to a blind man. At last I said, "Lincoln, you can never make a lawyer if you do not understand what **demonstrate** means," and I left my situation in Springfield, went home to my father's house, and stayed there till I could give any proposition in the six books of Euclid at sight. I then found out what "demonstrate" means and went back to my law studies. —*Ibid.* {E}

In a devastating critique of this article, Herndon pointed out a number of factual errors. For instance, Lincoln was never a law clerk and never visited his parents for any extended period of time.[187]

JOHN A. GURLEY (1813–1863) *Ohio congressman who died soon after being appointed governor of Arizona Territory.*

1. *After the failure of the Peninsular campaign, Lincoln said to Gurley:*

I have given McClellan 160,000 men. I cannot discover where nearly half have gone. Burnside can tell me where every man in his army is. —*Gurley's statement as reported in Adams S. Hill to Sydney Howard Gay, July 12, 1862, Gay Papers*. {D}

2. *During the same conversation, Lincoln also said that:*

he was much troubled at these attacks on Stanton making him the scapegoat for the presidential blunders. —*Ibid.* {D}

PHINEAS D. GURLEY (1816–1868) *Pastor of the New York Avenue Presbyterian Church in Washington, which the Lincolns regularly attended. Gurley
preached the funeral sermon in the White House on April 19, 1865, and in another
sermon soon thereafter, he drew from Lincoln's assassination the lesson that "the
theater is one of the last places to which a good man should go and among the very
last in which his friends would wish him to die."*[188]

1. *To Gurley and a member of the cabinet on the art of storytelling:*

Well, there are two ways of relating a story. If you have an auditor who has
the time and is inclined to listen, lengthen it out, pour it out slowly as if
from a jug. If you have a poor listener, hasten it, shorten it, shoot it out of
a popgun. — *Gurley manuscript quoted in Chapman, II, 502. {C}*

2. *Denying reports circulated after the death of his son Willie that he had
taken up spiritualism:*

A simple faith in God is good enough for me, and beyond that I do not
concern myself very much. — *Chapman, II, 506. {C}*

3. *To a group of clergymen who called on him to pay their respects:*

Gentlemen, my hope of success in this great and terrible struggle rests on
that immutable foundation, the justness and goodness of God; and when
events are very threatening and prospects very dark, I still hope that in
some way which man cannot see, all will be well in the end, because our
cause is just and God is on our side. — *Gurley's funeral sermon at the White
House, April 19, 1865, published the following day in the* National Intelligencer *(Washington). {C}*

4. *In the latter part of his presidency, Gurley recalled, Lincoln said with
tears in his eyes:*

that he had lost confidence in everything but God, and that he now believed his heart was changed, and that he loved the Savior, and if he was
not deceived in himself, it was his intention soon to make a profession of
religion. — *Gurley's statement to the Reverend James A. Reed, in Reed, 339
(1873). {D}*

*This is secondhand testimony that probably reflects some wishful thinking by
both clergymen.*

5. *After discussion of a pardoning case in which the father of the culprit
had been driven to petitioning the President by fear for his wife's sanity:*

Ah, doctor, these wives of ours have the inside track on us, don't they?
— *From an anecdote told by Gurley soon after the war, as related by D. H.
Mitchell in the* Independent *and reprinted in the New York* Tribune, *Decem-
ber 16, 1894. {D}*

6. *Toward the end of his life, according to Gurley, Lincoln used to say:*

While others are asleep, I think. Night is the only time I have to think. — *Chapman, II, 507. {C}*

7. *On his visit to Richmond in April 1865 and the friendliness of his reception there:*

Why, Doctor, I walked alone on the street, and anyone could have shot me from a second-story window. —*Chapman, II, 500. {C}*

ALEXANDER B. HAGNER (1826–1915)   *A Maryland lawyer who supported the Bell-Everett presidential ticket in 1860. He was later a federal judge in the District of Columbia.*

1. *Seeking the release of his wife's uncle, an elderly Presbyterian minister charged with disloyal conduct, Hagner explained that the trouble stemmed from a discussion of the doctrine of states' rights. Lincoln said:*

Oh, yes, I understand—the big tub ought to go into the little one.

When Hagner argued that a retired clergyman could scarcely be a threat to the Union, he received this answer: Sir, you are mistaken, the parsons and the women made this war.

Upon being informed, however, that the man's wife was in very delicate health, Lincoln wrote out the order for his release.[189] —*Hagner, 46 (1915). {C}*

JAMES HAINES (1822–?)   *Lawyer in Pekin, Illinois.*

1. *In 1850, at the beginning of his legal career, Haines was associated with Lincoln in the defense of Gideon Hawley, indicted for the obstruction of a public road in Tazewell County. When Lincoln proposed that Haines make the opening speech, the latter expressed surprise and some reluctance. Said Lincoln, laying a hand on the young man's shoulder:*

I want you to open the case, and when you are doing it, talk to the jury as though your client's fate depends on every word you utter. Forget that you have any one to fall back upon, and you will do justice to yourself and your client. —*Haines's statement in Hill FT, 186–87 (1906). {C}*

ALBERT HALE (1799–1891)   *Pastor of the Second Presbyterian Church in Springfield.*

1. *Responding to a question from Hale four weeks after his nomination in 1860, Lincoln said that:*

he had made no pledge of office, honor, or patronage in any way, to any man or party, on the condition of his election to the presidency, and he was most happy to say that very little of the kind had been sought, and that so unimportant as to draw from him no reply. For instance [he continued], some few rather silly persons have by letter applied, saying that in case of my election they would like the appointment of postmaster in their places—all of them very unimportant places—and I have not replied to one of them. I have made no pledges, and the Lord helping me, I shall make none. I shall go to Washington, if at all, as an unpledged man.

But he added as the minister was leaving: Mr. Hale, I have read my Bible some, though not half as much as I ought, and I have always regarded Peter as sincere when he said he would never deny his master. Yet he did deny Him. Now I think I shall keep my word and maintain the stand I have taken, but then I must remember that I am liable to infirmity and may fall. —*Hale to Theron Baldwin, June 15, 1860, copy in Nicolay Papers. {B, A}*

2. *In mid-January 1861, with secession under way, Hale asserted that Lincoln had said to him "again and again":*

Compromise is not the remedy, not the cure. The South (that is, the leaders) don't want it—won't have it—no good can come of it. The system of compromise has no end. Slavery is the evil out of which all our other national evils and dangers have come. It has deceived and led us to the brink of ruin, and it must be stopped. It must be kept where it now is. —*Hale to Baldwin, January 16, 1861, copy in Nicolay Papers. {C}*

One may doubt that in those busy days, Hale had as many conversations with Lincoln as his letter implied.

HENRY W. HALLECK (1815–1872)   *Union general, first a commander in the West, then general in chief from 1862 to 1864, and finally army chief of staff.*

1. *On September 2, 1862, the President, accompanied by Halleck, called on McClellan and said to him:*

General, you will take command of the forces in the field. —*Halleck testimony, March 7, 1863, before the Joint Committee on the Conduct of the War, Senate Report 108. {C}*

Halleck added: "Until that moment, I did not know who was to take command." This conflicts with Lincoln's own statements recorded in Welles-1, I, 105, 116.

CHARLES G. HALPINE (1829–1868)   *Irish-American journalist who served as a staff officer during the Civil War and, using the pseudonym "Miles O'Reilly," wrote some highly popular pieces from the viewpoint of an army private.*

1. *Lincoln to Halpine after bowing an elderly woman out the door:*

What odd kinds of people come in to see me, and what odd ideas they must have about my office. Would you believe, Major, that the old lady who has just left came in here to get from me an order for stopping the pay of a Treasury clerk who owes her a board bill of about seventy dollars? She may have come in here a loyal woman, but I'll be bound she has gone away believing that the worst pictures of me in the Richmond press only lack truth in not being half black and bad enough. —*Halpine, 103-4 (1866).* {C}

2. *When Halpine expressed surprise that the President did not follow the example of military commanders and cause visitors to be filtered through a screen of subordinates:*

Ah, yes! such things do very well for you military people, with your arbitrary rule, and in your camps. But the office of president is essentially a civil one, and the affair is very different. For myself, I feel, though the tax on my time is heavy, no hours of my day are better employed than those which thus bring me again within the direct contact and atmosphere of our whole people. Men moving only in an official circle are apt to become merely official, not to say arbitrary, in their ideas, and are apter and apter, with each passing day, to forget that they only hold power in a representative capacity. Now this is all wrong. I go into these promiscuous receptions of all who claim to have business with me twice each week, and every applicant for audience has to take his turn as if waiting to be shaved in a barber's shop. Many of the matters brought to my notice are utterly frivolous, but others are of more or less importance, and all serve to renew in me a clearer and more vivid image of that great popular assemblage, out of which I sprang, and to which at the end of two years I must return. I tell you, Major, that I call these receptions my public-opinion baths; for I have but little time to read the papers and gather public opinion that way, and though they may not be pleasant in all their particulars, the effect as a whole is renovating and invigorating to my perceptions of responsibility and duty. It would never do for a president to have guards with drawn sabres at his door, as if he fancied he were, or were trying to be, or were assuming to be, an emperor. —*105-7.* {C}

3. *On the danger of his being killed, either by enemies or by a lunatic:*

Now as to political assassination, do you think the Richmond people would like to have Hannibal Hamlin here any better than myself? In that one alternative, I have an insurance on my life worth half the prairie-land of Illinois. And besides, if there were such a plot, and they wanted to get at me, no vigilance could keep them out. We are so mixed up in our affairs, that no matter what the system established, a conspiracy to assassinate, if such there were, could easily obtain a pass to see me for any one or more of its instruments. To betray fear of this by placing guards, and so forth, would only be to put the idea into their heads and perhaps lead to the very result it was intended to prevent. As to the crazy folks, Major, why I must only take my chances—the worst crazy people I at present fear being some of my own too zealous adherents. That there may be such dangers as you and many others have suggested to me, is quite possible, but I guess it wouldn't improve things any to publish that we were afraid of them in advance. — *108-9. {C}*

4. *Concerning the detachment detailed to guard his carriage on its way to and from the Soldiers' Home, Lincoln protested, half jocularly, half in earnest:* that he and Mrs. Lincoln couldn't hear themselves talk for the clatter of their sabres and spurs; and that, as many of them appeared new hands and very awkward, he was more afraid of being shot by the accidental discharge of one of their carbines or revolvers than of any attempt upon his life, or for his capture by the roving squads of Jeb Stuart's cavalry. —*110. {C}*

JAMES A. HAMILTON (1788-1878) *New York lawyer and politician, son of Alexander Hamilton. He was an influential Jacksonian Democrat who turned Whig and then Republican.*

  1. *On or about April 22, 1861, Hamilton asked whether Lincoln intended to give blows as well as receive them, and he replied:*

I intend to **give** blows. The only question at present is, whether I should first retake Fort Sumter or Harpers Ferry. —*Hamilton, 477 (1869). {C}*

In a letter to the New York Post, *written and published April 29, 1861, Hamilton writes that he is authorized by the President to say that:* he is determined to prosecute the war begun against the government of the United States with all the energy necessary to bring it to a successful termination. He will call for a large additional force, relying upon Providence and the loyalty of the people to the government they have established. *{B}*

  2. *On September 10, 1862, Hamilton was part of a committee of New Yorkers, who, speaking also for five New England governors, called at the White House to urge changes in the administration. Lincoln, without concealing his vexation, declared "in substance":*

It is plain enough what you want—you want to get Seward out of the cabinet. There is not one of you who would not see the country ruined, if you could turn out Seward. —*Hamilton, as quoted the same day in Chase, 378. {B}*

In a self-serving memorandum said to have been written immediately after the interview, Hamilton himself quoted Lincoln as saying: You gentlemen, to hang Mr. Seward, would destroy this government. —*Hamilton, 530. {A}*

SCHUYLER HAMILTON (1822-1903) *Grandson of Alexander Hamilton, Union officer who, after serving on the staffs of Winfield Scott and Henry W. Halleck, became a brigadier general of volunteers.*

  1. *In July 1861, upon being introduced to an army staff surgeon, Lincoln said:*

Doctor, although you do not know me, I know you. You are getting up a hospital for those who may fall sick or be wounded in the defense of the Union. I have been there and have seen you at work, although you were not aware of it. I want to aid you in your preparations for taking care of the poor fellows who will need all that we can do for them. When you need anything don't let there be any red tape. Come to me at once without hesitation, and you shall have anything you want if I can get it for you.

Promptly overruled by General Scott, who lectured him on the need to maintain discipline and follow proper procedures, Lincoln acquiesced, saying: You are the only man in Washington who gives me backbone. —*Hamilton reminiscence in the New York* Tribune, *June 20, 1889.* {C}

2. *Upon being presented with Confederate flags from the battle of Rich Mountain (July 11, 1861), Lincoln said:*

How sad it is to think that our southern fellow citizens, so highly educated and their women so accomplished, as this beautiful embroidery shows, should be so misguided. It is the baneful fruit of their institutions and slavery. . . . I reckon, boys, that it did not take you nearly so long to win these flags as it did the ladies to make them. —*Hamilton in the New York* Tribune, *July 7, 1889.* {C}

3. *It was mid-afternoon on another day in July 1861 that Lincoln entered Scott's office, settled wearily into a chair, and said:*

Since nine o'clock this morning, I have been trying to get a hearing from some clerk in the Pension Bureau. I believe that I have tried them all, but in vain. They have sent me up and down those stairs, from the ground floor to the attic and back again, until I am about tired out. . . . I haven't a doubt that the claim is a just one, for I have examined it carefully. You see, General, the poor woman who makes this application for a pension lost her husband . . . at the hands of some bloody Indian twenty-five years ago. Nobody seems to have taken any friendly interest in the case, and she has been haunting the White House for weeks, until, between ourselves, I'm afraid Mrs. Lincoln is getting a little jealous. I thought I had better end the matter up in some way or other today, and I have promised the poor woman an answer at four o'clock. She's waiting over there now. Between the two of them, I don't know that I dare go home without having the job finished. —*Hamilton as quoted in the New York* Tribune, *March 24, 1889.* {D}

A rather unlikely story.

4. *Speaking of his prospects for re-election in August 1864, Lincoln said to Hamilton:*

You think I don't know I am going to be beaten, but I do, and unless some great change takes place, **badly beaten**. . . . The people promised themselves when General Grant started out that he would take Richmond in June. He didn't take it, and they blame me, but I promised them no such thing, and yet they hold me responsible. —*Hamilton's account retold in J. K. Herbert to Benjamin F. Butler, August 11, 1864, Butler-1, V, 35. {D}*

CHARLES HAMLIN (1837-1911) *Maine lawyer and Union officer, son of Hannibal Hamlin.*

1. *To a wounded officer asking for a staff appointment but lacking a request from a commanding general, Lincoln, after examining the relevant act of Congress, declared:*

It cannot be done without such a request. I have no more power to appoint you in the absence of such request than I would have to marry a woman to any man she might desire for her husband without his consent. Bring me such an application and I will make it at once, for I see you deserve it. — *Hamlin, 450 (1895). {C}*

HANNIBAL HAMLIN (1809-1891) *Senator from Maine and Lincoln's first vice president.*

1. *Meeting with Hamlin at Chicago in November 1860, Lincoln said to him:*

I think I have never met you before, Mr. Hamlin, but this is not the first time I have seen you. I have just been recalling the time when, in '48, I went to the Senate to hear you speak. Your subject was not new, but the ideas were sound. You were talking about slavery, and I now take occasion to thank you for so well expressing what were my own sentiments at that time.[190] —*Hamlin's account told to C. J. Prescott, in Tarbell, II, 191-92. {D}*

DENNIS HANKS (1799-1892) *Lincoln's mother's cousin, who lived with the Lincoln family in Indiana and married Lincoln's stepsister, Sarah Elizabeth Johnston.*

1. *Hanks recalled that the boy Lincoln would say:*

Denny, the things I want to know is in books. My best friend's the man who'll get me one. —*Atkinson, 364. {D}*

These recollections, taken down in 1889, are suspect for several reasons, not the least of which is doubt about the reliability of Hanks's memory at any age, let alone at the age of ninety.[191]

2. *Asked where he got so many lies:*

Denny, when a story learns you a good lesson, it ain't no lie. God tells truth in parables. They're easier for common folks to understand and recollect. —*364-65. {D}*

3. *Hanks also quoted Lincoln as saying:*

Pap thinks it ain't polite to ask folks so many questions. I reckon I wasn't born to be polite. There's so darned many things I want to know. And how else am I going to get to know them? —*366. {D}*

JOHN HANKS (1802–1889)   *Lincoln's mother's cousin, notable as the man primarily responsible for creating the image of Lincoln the rail-splitter.*

    1. *In his autobiographical sketch written in 1860, Lincoln recalled the sewing up of some hogs' eyes at the beginning of his flatboat trip to New Orleans in 1831.[192] According to Hanks, when it came to doing the work, Lincoln said:*

I can't sew the eyes up.

Instead, he held the hogs' heads while others did the sewing. —*Hanks to Herndon, June 13, 1865 (7:156–60), Herndon-Weik Collection.[193] {C}*

    2. *After watching a slave auction in New Orleans, Lincoln supposedly said:*

By God, boys, let's get away from this. If ever I get a chance to hit that thing, I'll hit it hard. —*Told by Hanks to Herndon in 1865, according to Herndon, I, 76. {E}*

The credibility of this famous quotation is triply impaired: first, by the fact that it does not appear in any extant statement of Hanks; second, by Hanks's assertion (as recorded by Herndon) that when Lincoln saw slaves being maltreated in New Orleans, he "said nothing much, was silent from feeling"; and third, by Lincoln's assertion in his autobiography that Hanks was on the flatboat trip only as far as St. Louis. Concerning the unpleasant experience of seeing a slave auction, however, Herndon noted that he himself had heard Lincoln speak of it.[194]

WILLIAM H. HANNA   *Lawyer of Bloomington, Illinois, with whom Lincoln had professional and political associations in the 1850s.*

    1. *Lincoln told Hanna:*

that he was a kind of Universalist;[195] that he never could bring himself to the belief in eternal punishment; that man lived but a little while here, and that if eternal punishment were man's doom that he should spend that little life in vigilant and ceaseless preparation by never-ending prayer. —*Hanna's undated statement taken down by Herndon (11:3085), Herndon-Weik Collection. {C}*

SIMON P. HANSCOM   *A New York* Herald *correspondent who in 1863 became editor of the Washington* National Republican.

    1. *In interviews with Hanscom on July 3 and 5, 1862, Lincoln explained why he would not order a transfer of troops from the western theater to reinforce McClellan in his advance on Richmond. He said:*

that we had better put Richmond off six months than have any backward movement in the West; that the river must be kept open; and that the closing of the river would have a bad moral effect abroad. —*Hanscom to Sydney Howard Gay, July 6, 1862, Gay Papers.* {B}

JAMES HARLAN (1820–1899) *Republican senator from Iowa, whom Lincoln appointed secretary of the interior in 1865. Three years later, Harlan's daughter Mary was married to Robert Todd Lincoln.*

1. *To Harlan and some other Republican senators who called on Lincoln early in the summer of 1862 to urge the enrollment of freed slaves in the Union army:*

Gentlemen, I do not see my way clear to do as you advise me. Some time ago representative Union men from Kentucky, eastern Tennessee and western North Carolina called on me and said: "If the government will furnish us arms and ammunition, we will not only protect ourselves, but will also drive the enemies of the Union into the gulf states." I believed that they were in earnest and would undertake to do what they promised, and I have put 200,000 muskets and rifles into their hands. I still think them honest, earnest, courageous Union men. But I fear if I should now do what you advise, the major part of these 200,000 muskets and rifles would be turned against us and that, if it should occur, that would do us more harm than the Negroes could do us good. But you may be right, and I may be wrong, and although I cannot do as you think I should, perhaps Mr. Hamlin could. I am willing to get out of the way and let him try it. —*Harlan, 14 (1898).*[196] {C}

Although Harlan insisted that the offer to resign was made with "the utmost seriousness," it is difficult to believe that Lincoln's words were anything but banter or a conversational ploy.

2. *In Harlan's presence, Lincoln once said:*

Everyone, admitting that his neighbor's ability may be equal in size to a silver dollar, thinks his own as large as a cart wheel. —*Harlan, 12.* {C}

3. *Speaking of Horace Greeley's peace efforts at Niagara Falls in July 1864, Lincoln said:*

Greeley kept abusing me for not entering into peace negotiations. He said he believed we could have peace if I would do my part, and when he began to urge that I send an ambassador to Niagara to meet Confederate emissaries, I just thought I would let him go up and crack that nut for himself. —*Tarbell, III, 198, presumably from an interview with Harlan.* {C}

IRA HARRIS (1802–1875) *New York jurist who served as United States senator during the Civil War era.*

1. *On December 20, 1862, Lincoln, shortly after having received Chase's resignation to match that of Seward, said cheerfully to Harris:*

Now I can ride; I have a pumpkin in each end of my bag. —*Harris's statement the same day as recalled by Frederick W. Seward in an interview on January 9, 1879, with John G. Nicolay, Nicolay-Hay Papers. Quoted with a slight verbal change in Nicolay and Hay, VI, 271. {D}*

Senator William P. Fessenden heard on "entirely reliable authority" that Lincoln remarked, "Now I have the biggest half of the hog. I shall accept neither resignation." —Fessenden, I, 251.

SAMUEL HART   *Father of the Philadelphia lawyer and art critic, Charles H. Hart.*

   1. *During a conversation in February 1863, Lincoln said to Hart:*

My dear sir, never aspire to the presidential chair. I have neither rest by day nor sleep by night. I am surrounded by people of such clashing ideas—for instance, in regard to Grant. I have testimony from men who, I am told, are most usually honorable men, that Grant is a drunkard, very immoral, and everything that is bad; on the other hand, I have the same amount of testimony from men of the same station saying he is everything that can be wanted, of a high moral character; and now I have to weigh each in my own mind and pass my judgment upon it. I have decided in his favor, and time will show who is right. So it is with every appointment I make. After every small victory, I am crowded by men of every rank from a colonel down to a corporal, each one claiming the honor to themselves . . . and of course demanding promotion. —*Presumably Hart's account to his son, reported in the latter's letter to William H. Herndon, March 3, 1866, ISHL. {D}*

   2. *Of his election to the presidency, Lincoln was quoted by Hart as saying:*

that he did not feel suited to the position; that he filled it because it had been thrown upon him; for when he was informed of his nomination, he was as much surprised as many others must have been.

He continued: I only accepted it as I considered it was my duty; for I know very little of public life. I have only been twice in the state legislature and once in Congress. I was then so disgusted, I made up my mind to retire to private life and practice my profession. —*Ibid. {D}*

The inaccuracies in this passage could be attributed to one man's faulty memory or the other's disingenuousness.

CORDELIA A. P. HARVEY (1824–1895)   *Wife of the governor of Wisconsin, who, after her husband's accidental death in 1862, persuaded Lincoln to endorse the establishment of a hospital in Madison for Wisconsin soldiers. Her account of several interviews with him in September 1863 apparently originated as a letter written soon thereafter to a Union officer stationed in Tennessee. Though summarized at great length by J. G. Holland in his biography of Lincoln (1866), it was not published as a complete document until the twentieth century.[197]*

1. *At one point in their discussions, Lincoln spoke of the number of men available for the battle of Antietam:*

This war might have been finished at that time if every man had been in his place that was able to be there, but they were scattered hither and thither over the North, some on furloughs, and in one way and another, gone; so that out of 170,000 that the government was paying, only 83,000 could be got for action. The consequence, you know, proved nearly disastrous. —*Harvey to Colonel James H. Howe, September 13, 1863, typescript copy in Civil War Manuscripts Collection, Manuscripts and Archives, Yale University Library. {C}*

2. *Returning to the White House the next day, Harvey heard the President's response to a man urging someone's promotion:*

My friend, let me tell you something about that. You are a farmer, I believe; if not, you will understand me. Suppose you had a large cattle yard full of all sorts of cattle, cows, oxen, and bulls, and you kept selling and killing your cows and oxen, taking good care of your bulls. Bye and bye you would find out you had nothing but a yard full of old bulls, good for nothing under heaven. Now it will be just so with my army if I don't stop making brigadier generals. —*Ibid. {C}*

3. *During their conversation that day, Lincoln said to her:*

I shall never be glad any more. . . . the springs of life are wearing away. —*Ibid. {C}*

Isaac N. Arnold (q.v.) recalled a similar remark.

4. *Asked if he slept well, Lincoln replied that:*

he never was a good sleeper. He of course slept less now than ever before. —*Ibid. {C}*

OZIAS M. HATCH (1814–1893) *One of Lincoln's political associates in the 1850s and Illinois secretary of state throughout the Civil War.*

1. *On a visit to the military front after the battle of Antietam, Lincoln pointed to the vast encampment before them and asked what it was. Hatch said he supposed it was the Army of the Potomac, to which Lincoln replied:*

No, you are mistaken; that is General McClellan's bodyguard. —*Hatch interview, undated but probably c. 1876–78, in Nicolay Papers. {C}*

Hatch apparently told this story a number of times, with variations in the wording.[198]

HERMAN HAUPT (1817–1905) *Railroad engineer and Civil War general. For more than a year, beginning in April 1862, he was in charge of construction and transportation on United States military railroads.*

1. *According to Haupt, Lincoln had sabbatarian sensitivities. When Gen-*

eral McDowell told him on May 23, 1862, that his unit would not be ready until Sunday to begin its scheduled march southward, he said:

Take a good ready and start Monday morning. —*Haupt, 298 (1901).* {C}

2. *On one gloomy occasion when Congressman John Covode of Pennsylvania was talking at length about dissatisfaction in the army and public criticism of administration policy, Lincoln interrupted:*

Covode, stop! Stop right there! Not another word! I am full, brim full up to here [drawing his hand across his neck]. —*298.* {C}

RUSH C. HAWKINS (1831–1920)   *Contentious organizer and commander of the 9th New York Volunteers ("Hawkins' Zouaves"), later a noted collector of incunabula.*

1. *Hawkins visited the White House in November 1861 at the direction of his commanding officer, General John E. Wool, to urge the holding of the Hatteras Inlet. During the discussion, he also told the President about a quarrel he was having with Governor Edwin D. Morgan over the assignment of an officer to the 9th New York without his consent. Lincoln listened patiently and then said:*

You are clearly in the right and I sympathize with you in your desire for a clean reputation for your regiment. But we are in the midst of a great war and have a terrible business before us, and I cannot afford to enter into a controversy with the governor of a state that I rely upon more than any other to assist in putting down this terrible rebellion, and you must say as much to General Wool, and tell him that I say he must fix it up with Governor Morgan so that justice will be done to you, and in such a way as to avoid irritation in the future. —*Hawkins manuscript (1893).* {C}

2. *In December 1861, with Wool's blessing, Hawkins was back in Washington, this time to talk with congressmen and the President about McClellan's deficiencies and to promote a plan for combining a movement from Fortress Monroe toward Richmond with a simultaneous attack by the main army at Manassas. Lincoln said that:*

the generals in command at different points were urging the importance of moves in their departments; these importunities were embarrassing to the government.

He spoke of the difficulties in organizing a great army out of raw material; the time needed for drilling, the seasoning of soldiers in the field, and so forth. Then he closed with "about these words": But General Wool knows more about army matters than we do, and it has seemed to me that McClellan ought to do something, and I wish you would see him and talk to him as you have to me. —*Ibid.* {C}

Even though Hawkins carried with him a note from Lincoln, McClellan refused to talk with him.[199]

3. *At a meeting in May 1864, Lincoln said to others present:*

This is the colonel who in the fall of 1861 tried to induce me to remove McClellan from the command of the army. At one time I thought I would have to arrest him for a traitorous conspiracy. . . . Poor George, you knew him better than any of us. I did all I could for him but he could do nothing for himself. —*Ibid.*[200] {C}

IRA HAWORTH   *A resident of Vermilion County, Illinois.*

1. *In 1860, according to Haworth, Lincoln gave him a cane, saying it was for use in his old age and adding:*

You know, the wicked generally do live to become old. —*Haworth's statement to Walter B. Stevens in Stevens, 25 (1916). {D}*

Various inaccuracies in the statement seriously weaken its credibility.[201]

2. *On one occasion, Lincoln told Haworth that:*

he had never in his life been really angry. —*26. {D}*

NATHANIEL HAWTHORNE (1804–1864)   *The novelist went to the White House in the spring of 1862 as part of a Massachusetts delegation that presented Lincoln an ivory-handled buggy whip. He wrote an account of the visit a few weeks later.*

1. *Responding to a broad hint in the presentation speech that the whip was symbolic of the proper treatment for rebels, Lincoln said that:*

he accepted the whip as an emblem of peace, not punishment. —*Fields JT, 512.*[202] {C}

JOHN HAY (1838–1905)   *Lincoln's assistant private secretary throughout his presidency and afterwards coauthor with John G. Nicolay of the ten-volume "official" biography,* Abraham Lincoln: A History *(1890). Hay was born in Indiana but grew up in the little Mississippi River town of Warsaw, Illinois. He attended Brown University and in 1859 entered the law office of an uncle in Springfield. There, he renewed an earlier friendship with Nicolay, through whose intercession he was invited to accompany Lincoln to Washington as a second member of his secretarial staff. Hay's wartime diary, kept intermittently, is a rich source of informal remarks by Lincoln, although its lengthier passages in particular raise some question about the part that literary creativity played in his reproduction of the President's words. More sophisticated than profound, this gifted American Victorian was in later life a journalist, poet, novelist, diplomat, and secretary of state.*

1. *In the summer of 1859, after reading Douglas's article on popular sovereignty in* Harper's Magazine, *Lincoln said to Hay:*

This will never do. He puts the moral element out of this question. It won't stay out. —*Hay-2, 4. {C}*

2. *On April 19, 1861, the day of the riots against Union troop movements through Baltimore, two men from that city called on Lincoln and expressed fear that there would be a wave of northern retaliation against Maryland. He replied:*

Our people are easily influenced by reason. They have determined to prosecute this matter with energy but with the most temperate spirit. You are entirely safe from lawless invasion. —*Hay-1, 4. {A}*

3. *On April 21, Lincoln yielded to the plea of Marylanders that no more federal troops be sent through Baltimore for the time being. Afterwards, he said:*

that this was the last time he was going to interfere in matters of strictly military concernment; that he would leave them hereafter wholly to military men.

Later the same day, he spoke of certain troops to Major David Hunter, declaring that: that order commanding their return to Pennsylvania was given at the earnest solicitation of the Maryland conservatives, who avowed their powerlessness in Baltimore but their intention to protect the federal troops elsewhere—granted them as a special extension, as an exhaustion of the means of conciliation and kindness. Hereafter, however, he would interfere with no war measures of the army. —*Hay-1, 6, 7. {B}*

4. *Told of the resignation of Captain John B. Magruder, a Virginian who soon became a Confederate general, Lincoln said:*

Only three days ago, Magruder came voluntarily to me in this room and with his own lips and in my presence repeated over and over again his asseverations and protestations of loyalty and fidelity. —*Nicolay and Hay, IV, 142. {C}*

This wordy quotation was synthesized from the following diary entry: "I spoke of the intended resignation of Col. Magruder. The Tycoon was astonished. Three days ago, Magruder had been in his room making the loudest protestations of undying devotion to the Union." —Hay-1, 6. In the summer of 1862, Lincoln talked to General Samuel D. Sturgis (q.v.) about the Magruder incident.

5. *Waiting anxiously for more troops, Lincoln said on April 24 to some of the Massachusetts volunteers who had already arrived:*

I don't believe there is any North. The Seventh Regiment is a myth. Rhode Island is not known in our geography any longer. You are the only northern realities. —*Hay-1, 11.*[203] *{A}*

6. *Lincoln's plan of action as stated to Hay on April 25, 1861:*

I intend at present, always leaving an opportunity for change of mind, to fill Fortress Monroe with men and stores, blockade the ports effectually, provide for the entire safety of the capital, keep them quietly employed in this way, and then go down to Charleston and pay her the little debt we are owing her. —*Hay-1, 11.* {A}

7. *When three Potawatomi Indians called at the White House, Hay was amused by Lincoln's notion of how to communicate with them, thus:*

Where live now? When go back Iowa? —*Hay-1, 14.* {A}

8. *Talking on May 1 to a half-dozen members of New York's Seventh Regiment and responding especially to a recent critical article in the New York* Times, *Lincoln said that:*

the government had three things to do: defend Washington, blockade the ports, and retake government property. All possible dispatch was to be used in these matters, and it would be well if the people would cordially assist in these matters before clamoring for additional work.

He added: The proclamation calling out the troops is only two weeks old. No people on earth could have done what we have in that time.[204] —*Hay-1, 16.* {B, A}

It is possible that the final sentence was a record of Hay's thought, rather than of Lincoln's words.

9. *On May 3, 1861, when he read a letter from Governor Isham G. Harris of Tennessee protesting the seizure of a steamboat suspected of carrying munitions for the Confederacy, Lincoln said quietly:*

He be damned. —*Hay-1, 17–18.*[205] {A}

10. *A Maryland delegation called on May 4 to oppose the military occupation of their state. They implored Lincoln not to act in a spirit of revenge for the Union soldiers already killed. He replied that:*

he never acted from any such impulse and as to their other views he should take them into consideration and should decline giving them any answer at present. —*Hay-1, 18.* {B}

11. *On May 6, Lincoln told Nicolay and Hay that he had written to Hannibal Hamlin in New York, asking that he report daily troop departures and other related information.*[206] *He said:*

it seemed there was no certain knowledge on these subjects at the War Department, that even General Scott was usually in the dark in respect to them. —*Hay-1, 19.* {B}

12. *When told by Hay that James W. Singleton, a onetime Whig turned Democrat, was causing trouble in Illinois, Lincoln replied that:*

Singleton was a miracle of meanness. —*Hay-1, 19.* {A}

Yet, near the end of the war, Lincoln supported Singleton in a scheme to make money trading in southern produce across military lines.[207]

13. *Concerning the idea of turning the South into a black republic after the war, Lincoln said:*

Some of our northerners seem bewildered and dazzled by the excitement of the hour. Doolittle seems inclined to think that this war is to result in the entire abolition of slavery. Old Colonel Hamilton, a venerable and most respectable gentleman, impressed upon me most earnestly the propriety of enlisting the slaves in our army.

When Hay remarked that the incoming correspondence contained many such suggestions, he replied: For my part, I consider the central idea pervading this struggle is the necessity that is upon us of proving that popular government is not an absurdity. We must settle this question now, whether in a free government the minority have the right to break up the government whenever they choose. If we fail, it will go far to prove the incapability of the people to govern themselves. There may be one consideration used in stay of such final judgment, but that is not for us to use in advance. That is, that there exists in our case, an instance of so vast and far-reaching a disturbing element, which the history of no other free nation will probably ever present. That, however, is not for us to say at present. Taking the government as we found it, we will see if the majority can preserve it. —*Hay-1, 19–20.* {A}

14. *In a talk on August 22, 1861, with two commissioners seeking a neutral status for Kentucky, the President said that:*

professed Unionists gave him more trouble than rebels. —*Hay-1, 25.* {B}

15. *On October 10, 1861, after listening to General Frederick W. Lander's talk about dying somewhere with a corporal's guard in order to offset the shame of Bull Run, Lincoln remarked:*

If he really wanted a job like that, I could give it to him. Let him take his squad and go down behind Manassas and break up their railroad. —*Hay-1, 26–27.* {A}

16. *At McClellan's quarters on the night of October 10, a gangly youth introduced as Captain Orleans went upstairs to summon the General, and Lincoln remarked:*

One doesn't like to make a messenger of the King of France, as that youth, the Count of Paris, would be if his family had kept the throne. —*Hay-1, 27.* {A}

17. *When McClellan asked on October 10 that he not be hurried, the President answered:*

You shall have your own way in the matter, I assure you. —*Hay-1, 27.* {A}

18. *During a discussion of Daniel Webster and other past statesmen, Lincoln disagreed with Seward in maintaining that:*

Webster will be read forever. —*Hay-1, 28.* {B}

19. *Vexed by General Thomas W. Sherman's request that additional troops be assigned to the expedition against Port Royal, Lincoln said on October 17, 1861:*

I think I will telegraph to Sherman that I will not break up McClellan's command and that I haven't much hope of his expedition anyway. *Seward persuaded Lincoln to omit the final clause.*[208] —*Hay-1, 29.* {A}

20. *At Seward's the night of October 22, Lincoln talked about secession and told of:*

a committee of southern pseudo-Unionists coming to him before inauguration for guarantees and so forth. He promised to evacuate Sumter if they would break up their convention without any row or nonsense. They demurred. Subsequently, he renewed [the] proposition to Summers, but without any result. —*Hay-1, 30.* {B}

Charles S. Morehead (q.v.), one of the southerners in question, provided a more extensive and somewhat conflicting account of the meeting. There is no evidence, other than this passage in Hay's diary, that Lincoln subsequently renewed through George W. Summers of Virginia his offer to evacuate Fort Sumter in exchange for adjournment of the Virginia convention. Lincoln or Hay may simply have gotten the name wrong; for there is some controversial evidence that the same proposal was made to John B. Baldwin (q.v.) in early April.

21. *In a conference with McClellan on October 26, the President, while deprecating the popular impatience for military action, said that it was a reality and should be taken into account. Then he added:*

At the same time, General, you must not fight till you are ready. . . . I have a notion to go out with you and stand or fall with the battle. —*Hay-1, 31.* {A}

22. *Early in the war, a temperance committee told Lincoln that the army could not win because it drank so much whiskey as to bring down the curse of the Lord upon it. He replied that:*

it was rather unfair on the part of the aforesaid curse, as the other side drank more and worse whiskey than ours did. —*Hay to Herndon, September 5, 1866 (8:843–51), Herndon-Weik Collection.* {C}

23. *Lincoln talked with Hay on November 7 about the advisability of opening the cotton trade in the southern coastal area under Union control. He said:*

that it was an object to show the world we were fair in this matter, favoring outsiders as much as ourselves; that it was by no means sure that they would bring their cotton to the port after we opened it, but it would be well to show Europe that it was secession that distressed them and not we; that the chief difficulty was in discovering how far the planters who bring us their cotton can be trusted with the money they receive for it. —*Hay-1, 33. {B}*

24. *In a famous incident on November 13, 1861, McClellan ignored the President, who was waiting to see him, and went upstairs to bed. When Hay spoke of the discourtesy on the way home, Lincoln said that:*

it was better at this time not to be making points of etiquette and personal dignity. —*Hay-1, 35. {B}*

25. *By presidential order on March 11, 1862, McClellan was removed as commander in chief but continued in command on the Virginia front.*[209] *Discussing the change with Seward the same evening, Lincoln said that:*

though the duty of relieving General McClellan was a most painful one, he yet thought he was doing General McClellan a very great kindness in permitting him to retain command of the Army of the Potomac and giving him an opportunity to retrieve his errors. —*Hay-1, 37. {C}*

26. *On August 30, 1862, without yet knowing the outcome of the battle then in progress at Bull Run, Lincoln said to Hay that:*

it really seemed to him that McClellan wanted Pope defeated.

He mentioned: a dispatch of McClellan in which he proposed, as one plan of action, to "leave Pope to get out of his own scrape, and devote ourselves to securing Washington."[210]

He spoke of: McClellan's dreadful cowardice in the matter of Chain Bridge, which he had ordered blown up the night before, but which order had been countermanded; and also of his incomprehensible interference with Franklin's corps, which he recalled once and then, when they had been sent ahead by Halleck's order, begged permission to recall them again and only desisted after Halleck's sharp injunction to push them ahead till they whipped something or got whipped themselves. —*Hay-1, 45. {B}*

This diary entry, which was apparently written two days after the conversation, reflects Hay's bias against McClellan, as well as Lincoln's feelings in the matter. It may be doubted, for instance, that the President used the phrase "dreadful cowardice" to characterize the man whom he was about to place in charge of the defense of Washington.

27. *Asked during the same conversation whether Halleck, now the general in chief, had any prejudices, Lincoln replied:*

No, Halleck is wholly for the service. He does not care who succeeds or who fails, so the service is benefited. —*Hay-1, 45.* {A}

28. *On Sunday morning, August 31, Lincoln called Hay from his room and said:*

Well, John, we are whipped again, I am afraid. The enemy reinforced on Pope and drove back his left wing, and he has retired to Centreville, where he says he will be able to hold his men. I don't like that expression. I don't like to hear him admit that his men need "holding."

Later, he repeated several times: We must hurt this enemy before it gets away.

And on Monday morning, when Hay made a gloomy remark, he replied: No, Mr. Hay, we must whip these people now. Pope must fight them. If they are too strong for him, he can gradually retire to these fortifications. If this be not so, if we are really whipped and to be whipped, we may as well stop fighting. —*Hay-1, 46.* {A}

29. *Walking over to the War Department on the morning of September 5, Lincoln said to Hay:*

McClellan is working like a beaver. He seems to be aroused to doing something by the sort of snubbing he got last week. I am of the opinion that this public feeling against him will make it expedient to take important command from him. The cabinet yesterday were unanimous against him. They were all ready to denounce me for it, except Blair. He has acted badly in this matter, but we must use what tools we have. There is no man in the army who can man these fortifications and lick these troops of ours into shape half as well as he. . . . Unquestionably he has acted badly toward Pope. He wanted him to fail. That is unpardonable, but he is too useful just now to sacrifice.

At another time, presumably during the same day, Lincoln said of McClellan: If he can't fight himself, he excels in making others ready to fight. —*Hay-1, 47.* {A}

30. *After the issuance of the preliminary Emancipation Proclamation on September 22, 1862, Hay spoke to Lincoln about the newspaper editorials on the subject, and he replied that:*

he had studied the matter so long that he knew more about it than they did. —*Hay-1, 50.* {B}

This may have been the basis for Hay's later extravagant assertion: "He read very little. Scarcely ever looked into a newspaper unless I called his attention to an article on some special subject. He frequently said: 'I know more about that than any of them.'" Hay to Herndon, September 5, 1866 (8:843-51).

31. *While riding to the Soldiers' Home on September 25, eight days after the battle of Antietam, Lincoln told Hay that:*

he had heard of an officer who had said they did not mean to gain any decisive victory but to keep things running on so that they, the army, might manage things to suit themselves. . . . He should have the matter examined, and if any such language had been used, his head should go off. —*Hay-1, 50-51.* {B}

The officer in question, Major John J. Key, was dismissed from the service.[211] *For Lincoln's later statement to Hay about the dismissal, see item 107 below.*

32. *On the same ride, when Hay tried to discuss the so-called McClellan conspiracy, Lincoln made no answer, except to say that:*

McClellan was doing nothing to make himself either respected or feared. —*Hay-1, 51.* {B}

33. *Sometime in 1863, Lincoln said that:*

the army dwindled on the march like a shovelful of [live] fleas pitched from one place to another.[212] —*Hay-1, 53.* {B}

Mary A. Livermore and Richard Cunningham McCormick (qq.v.) recalled hearing Lincoln use such a simile.

34. *Captain James Madison Cutts, brother of Mrs. Stephen A. Douglas, was charged with several offenses against propriety, one of which was spying on a woman while she was undressing. Lincoln issued a rather kindly reprimand but commented privately that:*

he should be elevated to the peerage for it with the title of Count Peeper. —*Hay-1, 53.*[213] {A}

Full appreciation of this double pun depends upon knowing that the Swedish minister in Washington was Count Piper.

35. *One summer afternoon, Lincoln said to an importunate soldier:*

Now, my man, go away! I cannot attend to all these details. I could as easily bail out the Potomac with a spoon. —*Hay-3 (1890), 33-34.* {D}

It is not clear that Hay was an auditor of this remark. He may have heard about it from James B. Fry (q.v.) or read about it in Fry's reminiscence of Lincoln, published two years earlier.

36. *On July 14, 1863, when Lincoln learned that Lee's army had crossed the Potomac back into Virginia, he said:*

We had them within our grasp. We had only to stretch forth our hands and they were ours. And nothing I could say or do could make the army move.

Lincoln was especially depressed by Meade's order calling on his troops to "drive from our soil every vestige of the presence of the invader."[214] *Hay quotes him as saying:* This is a dreadful reminiscence of McClellan. The same spirit that moved McClellan to claim a great victory because Pennsylvania and Maryland were safe. The hearts of ten million people sunk within them when McClellan raised that shout last fall. Will our generals never get that idea out of their heads? The whole country is our soil. —*Hay-1, 67. {A}*

37. *Considering court martial cases on July 18, Lincoln was especially reluctant to impose the death penalty for cowardice. He said that:*

it would frighten the poor devils too terribly to shoot them.

Of a man who had been convicted of desertion and then had escaped into Mexico, he said: We will condemn him as they used to sell hogs in Indiana: "as they run." —*Hay-1, 68-69. {A}*

38. *Talking with Hay again on July 19 about Lee's escape across the Potomac, he said:*

Our army held the war in the hollow of their hand, and they would not close it. We had gone through all the labor of tilling and planting an enormous crop, and when it was ripe, we did not harvest it. Still, I am very grateful to Meade for the great service he did at Gettysburg. —*Hay-1, 69. {A}*

39. *On August 1, Lincoln said to the adjutant general, Lorenzo Thomas, who had been placed in charge of raising black troops in the Mississippi Valley:*

General, you are going about a most important work. There is a draft down there which can be enforced. —*Hay-1, 74. {A}*

40. *In early August 1863, at the time of the diplomatic crisis over the Laird rams, Lincoln says that:*

there is no foundation for the rumor of war with England. —*Hay-1, 75. {A}*

41. *Told of a defendant who said that he could bring a man to prove an alibi, Lincoln remarked:*

I have no doubt you can bring a man to prove a lie by. —*Undated entry in the front of a Hay manuscript diary, Hay Collection-Brown. {A}*

42. *On August 6, 1863, having received a long letter from Governor Horatio Seymour on the draft, Lincoln says that:*

he [Lincoln] is willing and anxious to have the matter before the courts. —*Hay-1, 75. {B}*

43. *During a trip to a photographer's studio on August 9, Lincoln expressed the belief that rebel power was beginning to disintegrate. He commented on a reported disagreement within the Confederate government:*

Davis is right. His army is his only hope, not only against us, but against his own people. If that were crushed the people would be ready to swing back to their old bearings. —*Hay-1, 77.* {A}

44. *Hay's diary summarizes these presidential remarks made during the same outing:*

He is very anxious that Texas should be occupied and firmly held in view of French possibilities. He thinks it just now more important than Mobile. He would prefer that Grant should not throw his army into the Mobile business before the Texas matter is safe. —*Hay-1, 77.* {B}

45. *In a discussion of Seymour's conduct and the political wisdom of supporting one's country at war, Lincoln said:*

Butterfield of Illinois was asked at the beginning of the Mexican War if he were not opposed to it; he said, "No, I opposed one war. That was enough for me. I am now perpetually in favor of war, pestilence, and famine." —*Hay-1, 80.* {A}

46. *Speaking of an Illinois Democrat who had become a very successful general, Lincoln said that:*

John Logan was acting so splendidly now that he absolved him in his own mind for all the wrong he ever did and all he will do hereafter. —*Hay-1, 82.* {B}

47. *Early in the morning of September 21, 1863, Lincoln informed Hay of the outcome at Chickamauga:*

Well, Rosecrans has been whipped, as I feared. I have feared it for several days. I believe I feel trouble in the air before it comes. Rosecrans says we have met with a serious disaster, extent not ascertained. Burnside, instead of obeying the orders which were given him on the 14th and going to Rosecrans, has gone up on a foolish affair to Jonesboro to capture a party of guerrillas who are there. —*Hay-1, 92.* {C}

It appears that Hay wrote this entry on September 27.

48. *The precise context is not given for Lincoln's remark on September 27:*

Whenever trouble arises, I can always rely on Hooker's magnanimity. —*Hay-1, 94.* {A}

49. *On September 29, as he prepares to receive a large delegation of Radical Republicans from Missouri and Kansas, the President remarks that:*

they come, he supposes, to demand principally the removal of Schofield, and if they can show that Schofield has done anything wrong and has interfered to their disadvantage with state politics or has so acted as to damage the cause of the Union and good order, their case is made. But on the contrary, he thinks that it will be found that Schofield is a firm, competent, energetic, and eminently fair man, and that he has incurred their ill will by refusing to take sides with them in their local politics; that he does not think it in the province of a military commander to interfere with the local politics or to influence elections actively in one way or another.

After further discussion, he said: John, I think I understand this matter perfectly and I cannot do anything contrary to my convictions to please these men, earnest and powerful as they may be. —*Hay-1, 95-96.* {B, A}

50. *The next morning, at a meeting of more than two hours with the Missouri-Kansas delegation, Hay took full notes as Lincoln responded to the formal statement read by their leader:*

I suppose the committee now before me is the culmination of a movement inaugurated by a convention held in Missouri last month and is intended to give utterance to their well-considered views on public affairs in that state. The purpose of this delegation has been widely published and their progress to this city everywhere noticed. It is not therefore to be expected that I shall reply hurriedly to your address. It would not be consistent, either with a proper respect for you or a fair consideration of the subject involved, to give you a hasty answer. I will take your address, carefully consider it, and respond at my earliest convenience. I shall consider it without partiality for, or prejudice against, any man or party. No painful memories of the past and no hopes for the future personal to myself shall hamper my judgment. There are some matters which you have discussed upon which my impressions are somewhat decided, in regard to which I will say a few words, reserving the privilege of changing my opinion even upon these, upon sufficient evidence. —*Hay's memorandum, presumably written from his notes that same day or soon afterward, Nicolay-Hay Papers; partly printed in Nicolay and Hay, VIII, 215-19.* {A}

51. *Lincoln began by talking about a phrase of his that had caused much anger:*

You have alluded to an expression I used in a letter to General Schofield characterizing your troubles in Missouri as a "pestilent factional quarrel." You do not relish the expression, but let me tell you that Governor Gamble likes it still less. He has written me a letter complaining of it so bitterly that on the representation of my private secretary, I declined reading it and sent a note to him informing him that I would not.

You have much to say in regard to Governor Gamble's position. You will remember that at the very beginning of the war, your own governor being disloyal, you elected a convention, a large majority of whom were Union members, for whom I suppose you yourselves voted. There were at that time no dissensions among Union men in your state. Your convention elected Mr. Gamble governor in place of the disloyal incumbent, seemingly with the universal assent of the Union people of the state. At that time, Governor

Gamble was considered, and naturally so, the representation of the loyalty of Missouri. As such, he came to Washington to request the assistance and support of the general government in the organization of a state militia force. It was considered here a matter of importance. It was discussed in a meeting of the cabinet, and an arrangement which seemed satisfactory was finally made. No one doubted the proper intentions of those who planned it. The only doubt was whether the arrangement could be properly carried out—whether their *imperium in imperio* would not breed confusion. Several times since that, Governor Gamble has endeavored to have the troops raised on this basis transferred to the exclusive control of the state. This I have invariably refused. If any new arrangement has been made of enrolling state troops independently of the general government, I am not yet aware of it. Such organizations exist in some of the states. I have no more right to interfere with them in Missouri than elsewhere. If they are consistent with your state laws, I cannot prevent them. If not, you should redress your proper wrong. I will, however, give this subject, as presented by you, careful consideration. —*Ibid.* {A}

52. *Lincoln then turned to the complaints about the army commander in Missouri:*

I am sorry you have not been more specific in the statements you have seen fit to make about General Schofield. I had heard in advance of your coming that a part of your mission was to protest against his administration, and I thought I should hear some definite statements of grievances instead of the vague denunciations which are so easy to make and yet so unsatisfactory. But I have been disappointed. If you could tell me what General Schofield has done that he should not have done, or what omitted that he should have done, your case would be plain. You have, on the contrary, only accused him vaguely of sympathy with your enemies. I cannot act on vague impressions. Show me that he has disobeyed orders; show me that he has done something wrong, and I will take your request for his removal into serious consideration. He has never protested against an order, never neglected a duty with which he has been entrusted, so far as I know. When General Grant was struggling in Mississippi and needed reinforcement, no man was so active and efficient in sending him troops as General Schofield. I know nothing to his disadvantage. I am not personally acquainted with him. I have with him no personal relations. If you will allege a definite wrongdoing and, having clearly made your point, prove it, I shall remove him.

You object to his order on my recent proclamation suspending the privilege of the writ of habeas corpus. I am at a loss to see why an order executing my own official decree should be made a ground of accusation to me against the officer issuing it. You object to its being used in Missouri.

In other words, that which is right when employed against your opponents is wrong when employed against yourselves. Still, I will consider that. You object to his muzzling the press. As to that, I think when an officer in any department finds that a newspaper is pursuing a course calculated to embarrass his operations and stir up sedition and tumult, he has the right to lay hands upon it and suppress it, but in no other case. I approved the order in question after the *Missouri Democrat* had also approved it. —*Ibid.* {A}

53. *Next, Lincoln took up the subject of friendship in politics:*

You have spoken of the consideration which you think I should pay to my friends as contradistinguished from my enemies. I suppose, of course, that you mean by that those who agree or disagree with me in my views of public policy. I recognize no such thing as a political friendship personal to myself. You insist upon adherence to the policy of the proclamation of emancipation as a test of such political friendship. You will remember that your state was one excluded from the operation of that decree by its express terms. The proclamation can therefore have no direct bearing upon your state politics. Yet you seem to insist that it shall be made as vital a question as if it had. You seem to be determined to have it executed there. . . . You are then determined to make an issue with men who may not agree with you upon the abstract question of the propriety of that act of mine. Now let me say that I, who issued that proclamation, after more thought on the subject than probably any one of you have been able to give it, believe it to be right and expedient. I am better satisfied with those who believe with me in this than with those who hold differently. But I am free to say that many good men, some earnest Republicans and some from very far North, were opposed to the issuing of that proclamation, holding it unwise and of doubtful legality. Now, when you see a man loyally in favor of the Union, willing to vote men and money, spending his time and money and throwing his influence into the recruitment of our armies, I think it ungenerous, unjust, and impolitic to make his views on abstract political questions a test of his loyalty. I will not be a party to this application of a pocket Inquisition.

You are aware of movements in the North of a different character — interfering with the draft, discouraging recruiting, weakening the war spirit, striving in all possible ways to weaken the government merely to secure a partisan triumph. I do not take the party of your opponents in Missouri to be engaged in this line of conduct. In a civil war, one of the saddest evils is suspicion. It poisons the springs of social life. It is the fruitful parent of injustice and strife. Were I to make a rule that in Missouri, disloyal men were outlawed and the rightful prey of good citizens, as soon as the rule should begin to be carried into effect, I would be overwhelmed with affidavits to prove that the first man killed under it was more loyal than the one who killed him. It is impossible to determine the question of the motives that govern men or to gain absolute knowledge of their sympathies.

To a delegate's interruption, "Let the loyal people judge," Lincoln replied: And who shall say who the loyal people are? You ask the disfranchisement of all disloyal people, but difficulties will environ you at every step in determining the questions which will arise in that matter. A vast number of Missourians who have at some time aided the rebellion will wish to return to their homes and resume their peaceful avocations. Even if you would, you cannot keep them all away. You have your state laws regulating the qualifications of voters. You must stand by those till yourselves alter them. —*Ibid. {A}*

54. *Delegates returned to discussion of Schofield, and Lincoln responded to the charge that the General in his "imbecility" was responsible for the guerrilla massacre at Lawrence, Kansas, some six weeks earlier:*

It seems to me that is a thing which could be done by anyone making up his mind to the consequences and could no more be guarded against than assassination. If I make up my mind to kill you, for instance, I can do it, and these hundred gentlemen could not prevent it. They could avenge but could not save you. —*Ibid. {A}*

At this point, Hay left the meeting, and William O. Stoddard noted down and subsequently wrote out Lincoln's further remarks.[215]

55. *On October 18, 1863, respecting Chase's maneuvers toward the presidency, Lincoln said:*

that it was very bad taste, but that he had determined to shut his eyes to all these performances; that Chase made a good secretary and that he would keep him where he is. If [Lincoln continued] he becomes president, all right. I hope we may never have a worse man. I have all along clearly seen his plan of strengthening himself. Whenever he sees that an important matter is troubling me, if I am compelled to decide it in a way to give offense to a man of some influence, he always ranges himself in opposition to me and persuades the victim that he has been hardly dealt by and that he [Chase] would have arranged it very differently. It was so with General Frémont, with General Hunter when I annulled his hasty proclamation, with General Butler when he was recalled from New Orleans, with these Missouri people when they called the other day. I am entirely indifferent as to his success or failure in these schemes, so long as he does his duty as the head of the Treasury Department. —*Hay-1, 100-101. {B, A}*

56. *In a discussion of the military situation, Lincoln said:*

Lee probably came up the other day thinking our army weaker than it is and, finding his mistake from the fight at Bristoe, is holding off at present. —*Hay-1, 101. {A}*

The reference is to the engagement at Bristoe Station, Virginia, October 14, 1863.

57. *On October 19, 1863, Lincoln removed Rosecrans from command of the Army of the Cumberland. He said:*

Rosecrans has seemed to lose spirit and nerve since the battle of Chickamauga. —*Hay-1, 102.* {A}

58. *Concerning Montgomery Blair's desire to run a candidate against Maryland's Radical Republican congressman, Henry Winter Davis, Lincoln said:*

Davis is the nominee of the Union convention and as we have recognized him as our candidate, it would be mean to do anything against him now. —*Hay-1, 105.* {A}

59. *Speaking of General Robert C. Schenck and his aggressive program for enlistment of blacks in the Baltimore area, Lincoln said:*

Schenck is wider across the head in the region of the ears and loves fight for its own sake better than I do. —*Hay-1, 105.* {A}

60. *On October 24, the President told of Rosecrans's apparently needless anxiety over food supplies and added:*

He is confused and stunned like a duck hit on the head, ever since Chickamauga. —*Hay-1, 106.* {A}

61. *October 28, speaking of the political struggle in Missouri:*

I believe, after all, those Radicals will carry the state, and I do not object to it. They are nearer to me than the other side in thought and sentiment, though bitterly hostile personally. They are utterly lawless, the unhandiest devils in the world to deal with, but after all, their faces are set Zionwards. —*Hay-1, 108.* {A}

62. *When Hay suggested that Chase would try to make capital out of the removal of Rosecrans, Lincoln laughed and replied:*

I suppose he will, like the bluebottle fly, lay his eggs in every rotten spot he can find. —*Hay-1, 110.* {A}

63. *Of Chase's run for the presidency, Lincoln says that:*

it may win. He hopes the country will never do worse. —*Hay-1, 110.* {B}

64. *On the night of October 30, 1863, Lincoln got to talking with Hay about the cabinet crisis of the preceding December. After describing the affair in detail, he said:*

I do not now see how it could have been done better. I am sure it was right. If I had yielded to that storm and dismissed Seward, the thing would all have slumped over one way and we should have been left with a scanty handful of supporters. When Chase sent in his resignation, I saw that the game was in my own hands, and I put it through. When I had settled this important business at last with much labor and to entire satisfaction, into my room one day walked D. D. Field and George Opdyke and began a new attack upon me to force me to remove Seward. For once in my life I rather gave my temper the rein, and I talked to those men pretty damned plainly. Opdyke may be right in being cool to me. —*Hay-1, 111-12.* {A}

Field and Opdyke, both prominent New Yorkers, subsequently played leading roles in the effort to prevent Lincoln's renomination.

65. *During the same conversation, he said:*

I wish they would stop thrusting that subject of the presidency into my face. I don't want to hear anything about it. —*Hay-1, 112.* {A}

66. *In a discussion on November 1 of Montgomery Blair's speech delivered some four weeks earlier at Rockville, Maryland, the President declared:*

Really, the controversy between the two sets of men, represented by him and by Mr. Sumner, is one of mere form and little else. I do not think Mr. Blair would agree that the states in rebellion are to be permitted to come at once into the political family and renew the very performances which have already so bedeviled us. I do not think Mr. Sumner would insist that when the loyal people of a state obtain the supremacy in their councils and are ready to assume the direction of their own affairs, that they should be excluded. I do not understand Mr. Blair to admit that Jefferson Davis may take his seat in Congress again as a representative of his people. I do not understand Mr. Sumner to assert that John Minor Botts may not. So far as I understand Mr. Sumner, he seems in favor of Congress taking from the executive the power it at present exercises over insurrectionary districts and assuming it to itself. But when the vital question arises as to the right and privilege of the people of these states to govern themselves, I apprehend there will be little difference among loyal men. The question at once is presented in whom this power is vested, and the practical matter for decision is how to keep the rebellious populations from overwhelming and outvoting the loyal minority. —*Hay-1, 112-13.* {A}

67. *Asked about Rosecrans, Lincoln replies:*

that he sees no immediate prospect of assigning him to command; that he had thought, when the trouble and row of this election in Missouri is over, and the matter will not be misconstrued, of sending Rosecrans to Missouri and Schofield into the field; that it was because of Grant's opposition that Rosecrans is not in the Army of the Cumberland. When it was decided to place Grant in command of the whole military division, two sets of orders were made out, one contemplating Rosecrans's retention of the command of his own army and the other, his relief. Grant was to determine that question for himself. He said at once that he preferred Rosecrans should be relieved, that he never would obey orders. —*Hay-1, 115.* {B}

68. *On November 24, 1863, speaking of the great influx of slaves into the Gulf states, Lincoln said:*

It creates in those states a vast preponderance of the population of a servile and oppressed class. It fearfully imperils the life and safety of the ruling class. Now, the slaves are quiet, choosing to wait for the deliverance they hope from us, rather than endanger their lives by a frantic struggle for freedom. The society of the southern states is now constituted on a basis entirely military. It would be easier now than formerly to repress a rising of unarmed and uneducated slaves. But if they should succeed in secession, the Gulf states would be more endangered than ever. The slaves, despairing of liberty through us, would take the matter into their own hands, and, no longer opposed by the government of the United States, they would succeed. When the Democrats of Tennessee continually asserted in their canvass of '56 that Frémont's election would free the Negroes, though they did not believe it themselves, their slaves did; and as soon as the news of Frémont's defeat came to the plantations the disappointment of the slaves flashed into insurrection. —*Hay-1, 126.* {A}

69. *Later the same day, Lincoln said that:*

he was much relieved at hearing from Foster that there was firing at Knoxville yesterday. . . . anything showing Burnside was not overwhelmed was cheering. Like Sally Carter, when she heard one of her children squall, would say, "There goes one of my young 'uns, not dead yet, bless the Lord." —*Hay-1, 127.* {B}

70. *In a discussion with Hay, Nicolay, John P. Usher, and Norman B. Judd on December 9, 1863, Lincoln talked at length about the Blair-Frémont feud:*

The Blairs have to an unusual degree the spirit of clan. Their family is a close corporation. Frank is their hope and pride. They have a way of going with a rush for anything they undertake, especially have Montgomery and the old gentleman. When this war first began, they could think of nothing but Frémont. They expected everything from him, and upon their earnest solicitation he was made a general and sent to Missouri. I thought well of Frémont. Even now I think well of his impulses. I only think he is the prey of wicked and designing men, and I think he has absolutely no military capacity. He went to Missouri the pet and protégé of the Blairs. At first they corresponded with him and with Frank, who was with him, fully and confidently thinking his plans and his efforts would accomplish great things for the country. At last, the tone of Frank's letters changed. It was a change from confidence to doubt and uncertainty. They were pervaded with a tone of sincere sorrow and of fear that Frémont would fail. Montgomery showed them to me and we were both grieved at the prospect. Soon came the news that Frémont had issued his emancipation order and had set up a bureau of abolition, giving free papers and occupying his time apparently with little else. At last, at my suggestion, Montgomery Blair went to Missouri to look at and talk over matters. He went as the friend of Frémont. I sent him as Frémont's friend. He passed on the way Mrs. Frémont coming to see me. She sought an audience with me at midnight and taxed me so violently with many things that I had to exercise all the awkward tact I have to avoid quarreling with her. She surprised me by asking why their enemy, Montgomery Blair, had been sent to Missouri. She more than once intimated that if General Frémont should conclude to try conclusions with me he could set up for himself. The next we heard was that Frémont had arrested Frank Blair and the rupture has since never been healed.

During Frémont's time the *Missouri Democrat*, which had always been Blair's organ, was bought up by Frémont and turned against Frank Blair. This took away from Frank, after his final break with Frémont, the bulk of the strength which had always elected him. This left him ashore. To be elected in this state of things he must seek for votes outside of the Republican organization. He had pretty hard trimming and cutting to do this consistently. It is this necessity, as it appears to me, of finding some ground for Frank to stand on that accounts for the present somewhat anomalous position of the Blairs in politics. —*Hay-1, 133-34.* {A}

71. *During the same conversation, Judd raised the question whether Lincoln's annual message to Congress of December 8 would not, as a platform, compel Blair and Bates to "walk the plank." Lincoln replied:*

Both of these men acquiesced in it without objection. The only member of the cabinet who objected to it was Mr. Chase. —*Hay-1, 134.* {A}

72. *Talking the next evening with Hay and Isaac N. Arnold about reconstruction policy, the President reiterates what he has "often said before," that:*

there is no essential contest between loyal men on this subject if they consider it reasonably. The only question is who constitutes the state? When that is decided the solution of subsequent questions is easy. He wrote in the message originally that he considered the discussion as to whether a state has been at any time out of the Union as vain and profitless. We know that they were, we trust that they shall be, in the Union. It does not greatly matter whether in the meantime they shall be considered to have been in or out. But he afterwards considered that the fourth section, fourth article, of the Constitution empowers him to grant protection to states *in* the Union, and it will not do ever to admit that these states have at any time been out. So he erased that sentence as possibly suggestive of evil. He preferred to stand firmly based on the Constitution rather [than] to work in the air. — *Hay-1, 135. {B}*

73. *Turning then to the political troubles in Missouri, he said:*

I know these Radical men have in them the stuff which must save the state and on which we must mainly rely. They are absolutely uncorrosive by the virus of secession. It cannot touch or taint them. While the Conservatives, in casting about for votes to carry through their plans, are tempted to affiliate with those whose record is not clear. If one side **must** be crushed out and the other cherished, there could be no doubt which side we would choose as fuller of hope for the future. We would have to side with the Radicals.

But just there is where their wrong begins. They insist that I shall hold and treat Governor Gamble and his supporters—men appointed by loyal people of Missouri as representatives of Missouri loyalty, and who have done their whole duty in the war faithfully and promptly, who, when they have disagreed with me, have been silent and kept about the good work— that I shall treat these men as Copperheads and enemies to the government. This is simply monstrous.

I talked to these people in this way when they came to me this fall. I saw that their attack on Gamble was malicious. They moved against him by flank attacks from different sides of the same question. They accused him of enlisting rebel soldiers among the enrolled militia and of exempting all the rebels and forcing Union men to do the duty—all this in the blindness of passion. I told them they were endangering the election of senator, that I thought their duty was to elect Henderson and Gratz Brown, and nothing has happened in our politics which has pleased me more than that incident.

He went on to point out the dubious past records of some Missouri Radicals: Not that he objected to penitent rebels being radical; he was glad of it, but fair play; let not the pot make injurious reference to the black base of the kettle. He was in favor of short statutes of limitations. —*Hay-1, 135-36. {A, B}*

On August 23, 1864, Hay wrote in his diary: "It seems utterly impossible for the President to conceive of the possibility of any good resulting from a rigorous and exemplary course of punishing political dereliction. His favorite expression is, 'I am in favor of short statutes of limitations in politics.'" —*Hay-1, 239.*

74. *When the subject changed to the state of affairs in Kentucky, the President said:*

that he had for a long time been aware that the Kentuckians were not regarding in good faith the proclamation of emancipation and the laws of Congress but were treating as slaves the escaped freedmen from Alabama and Mississippi; that this must be ended as soon as his hands grew a little less full. —*Hay-1, 136. {B}*

75. *Speaking again about Missouri matters on December 13, Lincoln said:*

that he had heard some things of Schofield which had very much displeased him; that while Washburne was in Missouri he saw or thought he saw that Schofield was working rather energetically in the politics of the state, and that he approached Schofield and proposed that he should use his influence to harmonize the conflicting elements so as to elect one of each wing, Gratz Brown and Henderson. Schofield's reply was that he would not consent to the election of Gratz Brown. Again, when Gratz Brown was about coming to Washington, he sent a friend to Schofield to say that he would not oppose his confirmation if he would, so far as his influence extended, agree to a convention of Missouri to make necessary alterations in her state constitution. Schofield's reply, as reported by Brown. . . ,was that he would not consent to a state convention. These things [Lincoln continued], are obviously transcendent of his instructions and must not be permitted. —*Hay-1,* *137-38. {B}*

76. *In a discussion of Shakespeare's* King Henry IV *with the actor James H. Hackett, Lincoln asks:*

why one of the best scenes in the play, that where Falstaff and Prince Hal alternately assume the character of the King, is omitted in the representation.

Hackett replies that the passage is admirable to read but ineffective on stage. *—Hay-1, 138. {B}*

77. *After seeing the play on December 19, Lincoln criticized Hackett's reading of one line and labeled:*

the dying speech of Hotspur an unnatural and unworthy thing. —*Hay-1,* *139. {B}*

78. *On December 23, Lincoln told of having a dream the night before:*

He was in a party of plain people, and as it became known who he was, they began to comment on his appearance. One of them said, "He is a very common-looking man." The President replied, "Common-looking people are the best in the world; that is the reason the Lord makes so many of them." —*Hay-1, 143. {B, A}*

The more familiar version of this quotation originated with Alexander K. McClure (q.v.). James Grant Wilson (q.v.) claimed to have heard a similar utterance.

79. *On Christmas day, 1863, Lincoln said:*

that he thought Chase's banking system rested on a sound basis of principle, that is, causing the capital of the country to become interested in the sustaining of the national credit; that this was the principal financial measure of Mr. Chase, in which he had taken an especial interest. Mr. Chase had frequently consulted him in regard to it. He had generally delegated to Mr. Chase exclusive control of those matters falling within the purview of his department. This matter he had shared in to some extent. —*Hay-1, 144–45.* {B}

80. *After visiting General Gilman Marston and the camp for Confederate prisoners at Point Lookout, Maryland, on December 27, Lincoln reports that:*

General Marston represents a strong feeling of attachment to the Union or rather, disgust for the rebellion, existing among his prisoners, a good many of whom are northern men and foreigners, the victims of conscription. From one-third to one-half ask that they may not be exchanged and about one-half of this number desire to enter our army, having, poor devils, nowhere else to go and nothing else to do. The bill just introduced in the rebel Congress which will probably become a law, holding permanently all soldiers now in the army, will doubtless greatly increase the disaffection. —*Hay-1, 145.* {A}

It is hard to say whether the final sentence is a record of Lincoln's words or an expression of Hay's thought.

81. *At one of the White House receptions, a man from Buffalo said, "Up our way, we believe in God and Abraham Lincoln," and the President replied:*

My friend, you are more than half right. —*Hay-3, 35.* {D}

It is not clear that Hay himself heard this remark.

82. *On March 24, 1864, Lincoln said:*

Grant is commander in chief and Halleck is now nothing but a staff officer. In fact, when McClellan seemed incompetent to the work of handling an army and we sent for Halleck to take command, he stipulated that it should be with the full power and responsibility of commander in chief. He ran it on that basis till Pope's defeat, but ever since that event, he has shrunk from responsibility wherever it was possible. —*Hay-1, 167.* {A}

See item 85 below.

83. *After reading a letter dated April 2 from General Nathaniel P. Banks, who had launched his Red River campaign, Lincoln said:*

I am sorry to see this tone of confidence; the next news we shall hear from there will be of a defeat. —*Nicolay and Hay, VIII, 291, citing Hay's diary, where it is not to be found.* {C}

84. *April 24, after reading an editorial attack on Jefferson Davis by the* Richmond *Examiner:*

Why, the *Examiner* seems about as fond of Jeff as the *World* is of me. — *Hay-1, 172.* {A}

The New York World, *edited by Manton Marble, was persistently and often acrimoniously critical of the Lincoln administration.*

85. *Recalling how Montgomery Meigs, the quartermaster-general, urged a hasty retreat from Harrison's Landing in the summer of 1862, Lincoln said:*

Thus, often I, who am not a specially brave man, have had to sustain the sinking courage of these professional fighters in critical times. When it was proposed to station Halleck here in general command, he insisted, to use his own language, on the appointment of a general in chief who should be held responsible for results. We appointed him, and all went well enough until after Pope's defeat, when he broke down—nerve and pluck all gone—and has ever since evaded all possible responsibility—little more since that than a first-rate clerk. —*Hay-1, 176.* {A}

The repetition with respect to Halleck (see item 82 above) was presumably Lincoln's, but possibly Hay's.

86. *Lincoln showed Hay a letter from Greeley written eight days after the first battle of Bull Run, in which he had named as one of Lincoln's alternatives making peace with the rebels on their terms. Nicolay remarked that James Gordon Bennett, editor of the New York* Herald, *would probably pay $10,000 for the letter. Lincoln replied:*

I need $10,000 very much, but he could not have it for many times that. —*Hay-1, 178.* {A}

87. *One day, after reading some lines of Robert Burns, Lincoln remarked that:*

Burns never touched a sentiment without carrying it to its ultimate expression and leaving nothing further to be said. —*Hay-3, 36.* {C}

88. *During Grant's Spotsylvania offensive in May 1864, Lincoln said:*

How near we have been to this thing before and failed. I believe if any other general had been at the head of that army it would have now been on this side of the Rapidan. It is the dogged pertinacity of Grant that wins. —*Hay-1, 180.* {A}

89. *May 14, 1864, speaking of the recent deaths of two generals, John Sedgwick and James Wadsworth:*

Sedgwick's devotion and earnestness were professional. But no man has given himself up to the war with such self-sacrificing patriotism as General Wadsworth. He went into the service not wishing or expecting great success or distinction in his military career and profoundly indifferent to popular applause, actuated only by a sense of duty which he neither evaded nor sought to evade. —*Hay-1, 182.* {A}

90. *Responding on May 22 to Hay's remark that power would be dangerous in Frémont's hands if he had more ability and energy:*

Yes, he is like Jim Jett's brother. Jim used to say that his brother was the damndest scoundrel that ever lived, but in the infinite mercy of Providence he was also the damndest fool. —*Hay-1, 183.* {A}

91. *Concerning dispatches from General Rosecrans, now the commander in Missouri, warning of a great conspiracy against the government, Lincoln said to Hay on June 9:*

I am inclined to think that the object of the General is to force me into a conflict with the Secretary of War and to make me overrule him in this matter. This at present I am not inclined to do. I have concluded to send you out there to talk it over with Rosecrans and to ascertain just what he has. I would like you to start tomorrow. —*Hay-1, 187.* {C}

Written eight days later, after his return from Missouri.

92. *When Hay, in making his report on June 17, communicated Rosecrans's suggestion of the importance of secrecy, Lincoln commented that:*

a secret which had already been confided to Yates, Morton, Brough, Bramlette, and their respective circles of officers could scarcely be worth the keeping now.

Lincoln was referring to four western governors. He viewed: the northern section of the conspiracy as not especially worth regarding, holding it a mere political organization, with about as much of malice and as much of puerility as the Knights of the Golden Circle.

Concerning Vallandigham, who had returned from exile and was allegedly the leader of the conspiracy, he said: The question for the government to decide is whether it can afford to disregard the contempt of authority and breach of discipline displayed in Vallandigham's unauthorized return; for the rest, it cannot but result in benefit to the Union cause to have so violent and indiscreet a man go to Chicago as a firebrand to his own party. —*Hay-1, 192–93.* {B, A}

93. *During the same discussion, Lincoln declared:*

The opposition politicians are so blinded with rage seeing themselves unable to control the politics of the country that they may be able to manage the Chicago convention for some violent end, but they cannot transfer the people, the honest though misguided masses, to the same course. —*Hay-1, 193.* {A}

94. *On the morning of June 30, 1864, the President alerted Hay for a trip to the Capitol, saying:*

It is a big fish. Mr. Chase has resigned, and I have accepted his resignation. I thought I could not stand it any longer.

Asked who was to be Chase's successor, he replied: Dave Tod. He is my friend, with a big head full of brains. . . . He made a good governor, and has made a fortune for himself. I am willing to trust him. —*Hay-1, 198.* {A}

95. *Later in the day, Lincoln told Hay:*

that Chase was perfectly unyielding in this whole matter of Field's appointment; that Morgan objected so earnestly to Field that he could not appoint him without embarrassment and so told the Secretary, requesting him to agree to the appointment of Gregory Blatchford or Hillhouse or some other good man that would not be obnoxious to the senators. The Secretary still insisted but added that possibly Mr. Cisco would withdraw his resignation. The President answered that he could not appoint Mr. Field but would wait Mr. Cisco's action. Yesterday evening, a letter came from the Secretary announcing first the intelligence that Mr. Cisco had withdrawn his resignation. This was most welcome news to the President. He thought the whole matter was happily disposed of. Without waiting to read further he put the letters in his pocket and went at his other work. Several hours later, wishing to write a congratulatory word to the Secretary, he took the papers from his pocket and found to his bitter disappointment the resignation of the Secretary. He made up his mind to accept it. It meant, "You have been acting very badly. Unless you say you are sorry and ask me to stay and agree that I shall be absolute and that you shall have nothing, no matter how you beg for it, I will go." The President thought one or the other must resign. Mr. Chase elected to do so. —*Hay-1, 198-99.* {B}

Chase demanded and Senator Edwin D. Morgan opposed the appointment of Maunsell B. Field as assistant treasurer in New York. In his memoirs, Field (q.v.) told of a subsequent meeting with Lincoln in which the latter gave a lengthy account of the controversy.

96. *After talking that same day with members of the Senate finance committee about the resignation of Chase and the appointment of Tod, Lincoln reported to Hay that:*

Fessenden was frightened, Conness was mad, Sherman thought we could not have gotten on together much longer anyhow, Cowan and Van Winkle did not seem to care anything about it.

The senators, Lincoln continued, had objected to the appointment and he had told them: that he had not much personal acquaintance with Tod, had nominated him on account of the high opinion he had formed of him while governor of Ohio; but that the Senate had the duty and responsibility of considering and passing upon the question of fitness, in which they must be entirely untrammeled. He could not in justice to himself or Tod withdraw the nomination. —*Hay-1, 199.* {B}

97. *Also on June 30, Lincoln told Hay that:*

he had a plan for relieving us to a certain extent financially: for the government to take into its own hands the whole cotton trade and buy all that [was] offered; take it to New York, sell for gold, and buy up its own greenbacks. —*Hay-1, 203.* {B}

98. *At 10:30 A.M. on July 1, the President handed Hay a nomination, saying:*

I have determined to appoint Fessenden himself.

Told that Fessenden was waiting to see him, he said: Send him in and go at once to the Senate. —*Hay-1, 201.* {A}

99. *Later the same day, Lincoln held forth at some length on the subject:*

It is very singular, considering that this appointment of Fessenden's is so popular when made, that no one ever mentioned his name to me for that place. Thinking over the matter, two or three points occurred to me. First, he knows the ropes thoroughly; as chairman of the Senate committee on finance, he knows as much of this special subject as Mr. Chase. Second, he is a man possessing a national reputation and the confidence of the country. Third, he is a Radical—without the petulant and vicious fretfulness of many Radicals. On the other hand I considered the objections: the vice president and secretary of the treasury coming from the same small state— though I thought little of that. Then, that Fessenden, from the state of his health, is of rather a quick and irritable temper, but in this respect he should be pleased with this incident; for, while for some time he has been running in rather a pocket of bad luck—such as the failure to renominate Mr. Hamlin, which makes possible a contest between him and the Vice President, the most popular man in Maine, for the election which is now imminent; and the fact of his recent spat in the Senate where Trumbull told him his ill-temper had left him no friends—this thing has developed a sudden and very gratifying manifestation of good feeling in his appointment, his instant confirmation, the earnest entreaties of everybody that he may accept and all that. It cannot but be very grateful to his feelings. This morning he came into this room just as you left it. He sat down and began to talk about other things. I could not help being amused by seeing him sitting there so unconscious and you on your way to the Capitol. He at last began to speak of this matter, rather supporting McCulloch for secretary. I answered, "Mr. Fessenden, I have nominated you for that place. Mr. Hay has just taken the nomination to the Senate." "But it hasn't reached there—you must withdraw it—I can't accept." "If you decline," I replied, "you must do it in open day, for I shall not recall the nomination." We talked about it for some time, and he went away less decided in his refusal. I hope from the long delay that he is making up his mind to accept. If he would only consent to accept and stay here and help me for a little while, I think he would be in no hurry to go. —*Hay-1, 202-3.* {*A*}

100. *Also on July 1, Lincoln said:*

What Chase ought to do is to help his successor through his installation (as he professed himself willing to do in his letter to me), go home without making any fight, and wait for a good thing hereafter—such as a vacancy on the supreme bench or some such matter. —*Hay-1, 203.* {*A*}

101. *That evening, when Hay asked whether he might prepare a correction of certain misstatements in the New York* Tribune, *Lincoln replied:*

Let 'em wriggle. —*Hay-1, 203.* {*A*}

According to the Welles diary (Welles-1, II, 95), he used the same phrase on August 6 with respect to the Wade-Davis manifesto, which had been published the day before. It was the punch line of comment on the manifesto in the form of a story about animalcules in cheese, recounted in Carpenter-2, 145 (1866).[216]

102. *At the Capitol on July 4, 1864, as Congress prepared for adjournment, the President was busy examining and signing various last-minute bills. One of the Radical Republican leaders, Senator Zachariah Chandler of Michigan, expressed concern about his intentions with respect to the Wade-Davis reconstruction bill. Lincoln responded:*

Mr. Chandler, this bill was placed before me a few minutes before Congress adjourns. It is a matter of too much importance to be swallowed in that way.

Referring to one section of the measure that emancipated all slaves in the rebel states, he said: That is the point on which I doubt the authority of Congress to act.

When Chandler remarked that it was no more than he himself had done, Lincoln replied: I conceive that I may in an emergency do things on military grounds which cannot be done constitutionally by Congress.

After Chandler's departure, he continued: I do not see how any of us now can deny and contradict all we have always said, that Congress has no constitutional power over slavery in the states. . . .

This bill and this position of these gentlemen seems to me to make the fatal admission (in asserting that the insurrectionary states are no longer in the Union) that states whenever they please may of their own motion dissolve their connection with the Union. Now, we cannot survive that admission, I am convinced. If that be true, I am not president, these gentlemen are not Congress. I have laboriously endeavored to avoid that question ever since it first began to be mooted and thus to avoid confusion and disturbance in our own counsels. It was to obviate this question that I earnestly favored the movement for an amendment to the Constitution abolishing slavery, which passed the Senate and failed in the House. I thought it much better, if it were possible, to restore the Union without the necessity of a violent quarrel among its friends as to whether certain states have been in or out of the Union during the war—a merely metaphysical question and one unnecessary to be forced into discussion. —*Hay-1, 204-5. {A}*

103. *Concerning how his attitude toward the Wade-Davis bill might affect his relations with the Radicals, Lincoln said:*

If they choose to make a point upon this I do not doubt that they can do harm. They have never been friendly to me, and I don't know that this will make any special difference as to that. At all events, I must keep some consciousness of being somewhere near right; I must keep some standard of principle fixed within myself. —*Hay-1, 205-6. {A}*

104. *On July 14, 1864, after Jubal Early's raid on Washington had been turned back by Union troops under the command of General Horatio Wright, Lincoln remarked sarcastically:*

Wright telegraphs that he thinks the enemy are all across the Potomac but that he has halted and sent out an infantry reconnaissance, for fear he might come across the rebels and catch some of them. —*Hay-1, 210. {A}*

105. *On September 24, having accepted Montgomery Blair's resignation as postmaster general, Lincoln said:*

If he will devote himself to the success of the national cause without exhibiting bad temper towards his opponents, he can set the Blair family up again. —*Hay-1, 216. {A}*

106. *Concerning the personal hostility of Maryland congressman Henry Winter Davis:*

If he and the rest can succeed in carrying the state for emancipation, I shall be very willing to lose the electoral vote. —*Hay-1, 216. {A}*

107. *Nicolay sent word from New York that Thurlow Weed had gone to Canada. Lincoln said to Hay on September 25:*

I think I know where Mr. Weed has gone. I think he has gone to Vermont, not Canada. I will tell you what he is trying to do. I have not as yet told anybody.

Some time ago the governor of Vermont came to see me "on business of importance," he said. I fixed an hour and he came. His name is Smith. He is, though you would not think it, a cousin of Baldy Smith. Baldy is large, blond, florid. The Governor is a little dark feisty sort of man. This is the story he told me, giving General Baldy Smith as his authority.

When General McClellan was here at Washington, Baldy Smith was very intimate with him. They had been together at West Point and friends. McClellan had asked for promotion for Baldy from the President and got it. They were close and confidential friends. When they went down to the Peninsula, their same intimate relations continued, the General talking freely with Smith about all his plans and prospects, until one day Fernando Wood and one other politician from New York appeared in camp and passed some days with McClellan. From the day that this took place, Smith saw, or thought he saw, that McClellan was treating him with unusual coolness and reserve. After a little while he mentioned this to McClellan who after some talk told Baldy he had something to show him. He told him that these people who had recently visited him, had been urging him to stand as an opposition candidate for president; that he had thought the thing over, and had concluded to accept their propositions and had written them a letter (which he had not yet sent) giving his idea of the proper way of conducting the war, so as to conciliate and impress the people of the South with the idea that our armies were intended merely to execute the laws and protect their property, and pledging himself to conduct the war in that inefficient, conciliatory style. This letter he read to Baldy, who, after the reading was finished, said earnestly, "General, do you not see that looks like treason and that it will ruin you and all of us?" After some further talk the General destroyed the letter in Baldy's presence and thanked him heartily for his frank and friendly counsel. After this, he was again taken into the intimate confidence of McClellan. Immediately after the battle of Antietam, Wood and his familiars came again and saw the General, and again Baldy saw an immediate estrangement on the part of McClellan. He seemed to be anxious to get his intimate friends out of the way and to avoid opportunities of private conversation with them. Baldy, he particularly kept employed on reconnaissances and such work. One night, Smith was returning from some duty he had been performing, and seeing a light in McClellan's tent, he went in to report. Several persons were there. He reported and was about to withdraw when the General requested him to remain. After everyone was gone, he told him those men had been there again and had renewed their proposition about the presidency—that this time he had agreed to their proposition and had written them a letter acceding to their terms and pledging himself to carry on the war in the sense already indicated. This letter he read then and there to Baldy Smith. Immediately thereafter Baldy Smith applied to be transferred from that army. At very nearly the same time, other prominent men asked the same—Franklin, Burnside, and others.

Now, that letter must be in the possession of Fernando Wood, and it will not be impossible to get it. Mr. Weed has, I think, gone to Vermont to see the Smiths about it.

Hay expressed surprise that McClellan, whose principal fault was timidity, should have been involved in any such scheme, and Lincoln replied: After the battle of Antietam, I went up to the field to try to get him to move and came back thinking he would move at once. But when I got home, he began to argue why he ought not to move. I peremptorily ordered him to advance. It was nineteen days before he put a man over the river. It was nine days longer before he got his army across, and then he stopped again, delaying on little pretexts of wanting this and that. I began to fear he was playing false—that he did not want to hurt the enemy. I saw how he could intercept the enemy on the way to Richmond. I determined to make that the test. If he let them get away I would remove him. He did so, and I relieved him. I dismissed Major Key for his silly, treasonable talk because I feared it was staff talk, and I wanted an example. —*Hay-1, 217-19. {A}*

108. *Concerning the retirement of Edward Bates from the attorney-generalship, Lincoln said on October 2 that:*

he would be troubled to fill his place in the cabinet from Missouri, especially from among the Radicals.

Hay suggested Joseph Holt of Kentucky, the army's judge advocate general, and Lincoln replied: That would do very well. That would be an excellent appointment. I question if I could do better than that. I had always thought, though I had never mentioned it to anyone, that if a vacancy should occur on the supreme bench in any southern district, I would appoint him. But giving him a place in the cabinet would not hinder that. —*Hay-1, 222. {B, A}*

Instead, however, he appointed another Kentuckian: James Speed, the brother of his old friend, Joshua F. Speed.

109. *In the state elections held on October 11, the Republican margin of victory was less impressive in Pennsylvania than in Ohio and Indiana. With the national election just four weeks away, Lincoln said that:*

he was anxious about Pennsylvania because of her enormous weight and influence, which, cast definitely into the scale, would close the campaign and leave the people free to look again with their whole hearts to the cause of the country. —*Hay-1, 229-30. {B}*

110. *After Chief Justice Taney's death on October 12, Lincoln tells Hay that with respect to a successor:*

he does not think he will make the appointment immediately. He will be rather "shut pan" in the matter at present. —*Hay-1, 231. {B}*

111. *On November 8, election day, Lincoln said to Hay:*

It is a little singular that I, who am not a vindictive man, should have always been before the people for election in canvasses marked for their bitterness—always but once; when I came to Congress it was a quiet time. But always besides that, the contests in which I have been prominent have been marked with great rancor. —*Hay-1, 233.* {A}

112. *Thoughts of one earlier election in particular:*

For such an awkward fellow, I am pretty surefooted. It used to take a pretty dexterous man to throw me. I remember the evening of the day in 1858 that decided the contest for the Senate between Mr. Douglas and myself was something like this: dark, rainy, and gloomy. I had been reading the returns and had ascertained that we had lost the legislature and started to go home. The path had been worn hog-back and was slippery. My foot slipped from under me, knocking the other one out of the way, but I recovered myself and lit square, and I said to myself, "It's a slip and not a fall." —*Hay-1, 234.* {A}

113. *One member of the group waiting for returns at the War Department expressed special pleasure at the defeat of two critics of the administration, Senator John P. Hale and Congressman Henry Winter Davis. Lincoln said to him:*

You have more of that feeling of personal resentment than I. Perhaps I may have too little of it, but I never thought it paid. A man has not time to spend half his life in quarrels. If any man ceases to attack me, I never remember the past against him. It has seemed to me recently that Winter Davis was growing more sensible to his own true interests and has ceased wasting his time by attacking me. I hope for his own good he has. He has been very malicious against me but has only injured himself by it. His conduct has been very strange to me. I came here, his friend, wishing to continue so. I had heard nothing but good of him. He was the cousin of my intimate friend, Judge Davis. But he had scarcely been elected when I began to learn of his attacking me on all possible occasions. It is very much the same with Hickman. I was much disappointed that he failed to be my friend. But my greatest disappointment of all has been with Grimes. Before I came here, I certainly expected to rely upon Grimes more than any other one man in the Senate. I like him very much. He is a great strong fellow. He is a valuable friend, a dangerous enemy. He carries too many guns not to be respected in any point of view. But he got wrong against me, I do not clearly know how, and has always been cool and almost hostile to me. I am glad he has always been the friend of the navy and generally of the administration. —*Hay-1, 234-35.*[217] {A}

114. *On the night of November 10, after reading from a White House window the response to a serenade that he had written out beforehand, Lincoln said:*

Not very graceful, but I am growing old enough not to care much for the manner of doing things. —*Hay-1, 239.* {A}

115. *On December 18, 1864, Lincoln talked with Montgomery Blair and Nathaniel P. Banks about the reconstruction bill recently introduced in the House of Representatives by James M. Ashley of Ohio.*[218] *He said that:*

he liked it with the exception of one or two things which he thought rather calculated to conceal a feature which might be objectionable to some. The first was that under the provisions of that bill, Negroes would be made jurors and voters under the temporary governments.

That provision, Banks said, would be stricken, and Lincoln continued: The second is the declaration that all persons heretofore held in slavery are declared free. This is explained by some to be not a prohibition of slavery by Congress but a mere assurance of freedom to persons actually there in accordance with the proclamation of emancipation. In that point of view it is not objectionable, though I think it would have been preferable to so express it. —*Hay-1*, 244-45. {B, A}

116. *During the same conversation, Blair vehemently attacked the conduct and purposes of the Radical leaders in Congress. Lincoln said:*

It is much better not to be led from the region of reason into that of hot blood by imputing to public men motives which they do not avow. —*Hay-1*, 246. {A}

117. *In 1904, Hay recalled that Lincoln had said to him not many days before his assassination:*

A man who denies to other men equality of rights is hardly worthy of freedom; but I would give **even to him** all the rights which I claim for myself. —*Hay-4*, 40. {C}

The first half of this sentence echoes a statement in Lincoln's letter of April 6, 1859, to Henry L. Pierce and others, Collected Works, *III, 376.*

MILTON HAY (1817–1893) *Springfield lawyer, the uncle of John Hay.*

1. *Some years after the Lincoln-Shields duel, one of the men associated with it sought to rehearse the details of the affair. After he had left, Lincoln said:*

That man is trying to revive his memory of a matter that I am trying to forget. —*Hay to Thomas Vennum, January 26, 1892, published in* Lincoln Lore, *no. 653 (October 13, 1941).* {C}

GEORGE P. A. HEALY (1813–1894) *Noted portrait painter who established himself in Chicago for a decade beginning in 1855. He painted Lincoln as the Republican presidential nominee in 1860.*

1. *Lincoln, glancing through his mail during a sitting, burst out with a laugh and said:*

As a painter, Mr. Healy, you shall be a judge between this unknown correspondent and me. She complains of my ugliness. It is allowed to be ugly in this world, but not as ugly as I am. She wishes me to put on false whiskers to hide my horrible lantern jaws. Will you paint me with false whiskers? No? I thought not. I tell you what I shall do: give permission to this lover of the beautiful to set up a barber's shop at the White House. —*Healy, 69-70 (1894).* {D}

In her letter of October 15, 1860, suggesting that Lincoln let his whiskers grow, Grace Bedell said merely that he would look better because his face was so thin.[219] *In an earlier version, reported by the Chicago lawyer and civic leader Charles B. Bryan, Lincoln allegedly exclaimed:* The saucy hussy! Why, Healy, she may be right after all, but go ahead and paint me now as I am. Some of these days, when the whiskers have sprouted, you can come to the White House and beard the lion in his den. —*From a paper read by Bryan, November 14, 1889, before the Illinois Commandery of the Military Order of the Loyal Legion, transcript in the Sandburg Collection, folder 179.* {D}

OTTO L. HEIN (1847–1933)   *After the Civil War, a career army officer who eventually became the commandant of cadets at West Point.*

1. *At 5:30 P.M. one day in late autumn 1864, Hein visited the White House with two sponsors, seeking appointment to West Point. After greeting them, the President asked:*

Gentlemen, won't you please let me have a cup of tea?

He disappeared for a few minutes, then returned, listened to the sponsors, received the application papers, and said: Gentlemen, all that I can do at present is to place this application on file with the other three hundred. *Not until 1866 did Hein obtain the coveted appointment.* —*Hein, 32-33 (1925).* {C}

EMILIE TODD HELM (1836–1930)   *Mary Lincoln's half-sister, whose husband, a Confederate general, was killed at the battle of Chickamauga in September 1863.*

1. *Emilie Helm was a guest at the White House in December 1863. In her diary she wrote of Lincoln's saying to her on one occasion:*

Little Sister, I hope you can come up and spend the summer with us at the Soldiers' Home. You and Mary love each other; it is good to have you with her. I feel worried about Mary; her nerves have gone to pieces; she cannot hide from me that the strain she has been under has been too much for her mental as well as her physical health. —*Helm, 225.* {A}

2. *Mrs. Lincoln expressed great fear that if their son Robert went into the army, he would never come back. Lincoln sadly replied:*

Many a poor mother, Mary, has had to make this sacrifice and has given up every son she had—and lost them all. —*227-28.* {A}

Elizabeth Keckley (q.v.) recalled a similar response to Mary's fears.

JOHN B. HENDERSON (1826–1913) *Civil War senator from Missouri. It was Henderson, a Unionist of Democratic antecedents, who introduced the resolution for the Thirteenth Amendment in 1864.*

1. *In the Senate chamber on March 4, 1865, after the new Vice President's embarrassing harangue during the swearing-in ceremony, Lincoln said to the marshal:*

Don't let Johnson speak outside. —*Henderson JB, 198 (1912). {C}*

2. *Later in the same month, Henderson sought clemency for a number of Confederate sympathizers in Missouri. Lincoln said:*

Henderson, I am deeply indebted to you and I want to show it, but don't ask me at this time to pardon rebels.

To further pleading he replied: I can't do it! People are continually blaming me for being too lenient. Don't encourage such fellows by inducing me to turn loose a lot of men who perhaps ought to be hanged.

In the end, however, the Senator won his argument by agreeing to accept responsibility for the persons freed. After signing the release papers, Lincoln remarked: Now, Henderson, remember that you are responsible to me for these men; and if they don't behave, I shall have to put you in prison for their sins. —*200.*[220] *{C}*

THOMAS J. HENDERSON (1824–1911) *In the 1850s, a lawyer and state legislator living in Toulon, Illinois; later, a Civil War colonel and ten-term congressman.*

1. *Having been chosen to introduce Lincoln when he spoke at Toulon, Henderson asked whether there was anything in particular that he should say. Lincoln replied:*

Well, Tom, if you have a nice little speech all ready, you may deliver it, but if not, I would a good deal rather have the time.

After a delegation of women greeted him with a wreath of flowers for his head, Lincoln remarked to Henderson: I don't like this nonsense. —*Ida M. Tarbell's notes of an interview with Henderson, July 15, 1895, Tarbell Papers. {C}*

The notes date the speech 1856, but a later, presumably corrected version places it more credibly in 1858, when Lincoln spoke at Toulon on October 8.[221]

2. *According to Henderson, he mentioned some statements that Douglas had made at Toulon the day before, and Lincoln declared:*

Well, Tom, the truth is Douglas is a liar. —*Ibid. {D}*

Douglas did not speak at Toulon until October 26, 1858. On October 7, he and Lincoln were engaged in their seventh and final debate at Galesburg.

3. *Before the Republican National Convention in 1860, Henderson asked Lincoln whether he would accept a nomination for vice president and received this answer:*

Well, Tom, the truth is I have been a little too prominently mentioned for the first place to think of accepting a second. —*Ibid.* *{C}*

4. *After his nomination in 1860, Lincoln said at the close of a conversation with Henderson and several other men:*

Hold on, boys, I want to talk with you a moment. We are going to have a terrible struggle. I do not know that I shall survive it. We have been friends for years in politics. I do not believe this arising trouble will be settled by arms but by the ballot. Pledge yourselves that if I fall before it is over, you will carry this in by the ballot. —*Ibid.* *{D}*

The later version places the time of this remark in February 1861.

ANSON G. HENRY (1804–1865)   *Lincoln's physician, friend, and associate in the Whig party. He moved to Oregon in 1852, and in 1861, Lincoln appointed him surveyor general of Washington Territory.*

1. *In March 1863, when Lincoln learned of Grant's decision in the Vicksburg campaign to send an expedition up the Yazoo River via Steele's Bayou, he said to Henry, who was a visitor in the White House:*

that it would do no good, but that we run a great risk of losing all our transports and steamers. —*Henry to his wife, April 12, 1863, Henry Papers.* *{C}*

The expedition did prove to be a failure. John H. Littlefield (q.v.) recalled a more extensive statement by Lincoln on an earlier phase of Yazoo strategy.

2. *Henry returned to Washington in 1865 seeking a better position, and his hopes came to center on the commissionership of Indian affairs, held by William P. Dole. Lincoln would say only that he was undecided about the appointment, explaining:*

The thing that troubles me most is that I dislike the idea of removing Mr. Dole, who has been a faithful and devoted personal and political friend. —*Henry to his wife, March 13, 1865, published in Pratt-2, 116–20.* *{A}*

J. ROWAN HERNDON   *Cousin of William H. Herndon and the man from whom Lincoln in 1832 bought a half-interest in a New Salem general store.*

1. *In an anecdote of a boyhood adventure with a companion who was probably his stepbrother, John D. Johnston, Lincoln told Herndon that:*

he used to be very fond of coon hunting, and his father used to oppose their hunting. But he would slip out of a night after the old man had gone to bed and take a hunt. But they had a small fist [mongrel] dog that would detect them when they would return. So one night they took the fist along. They caught a coon and skinned him and then stretched it over the little dog and sewed him up and turned him loose and put the other dogs on the track, and they ran him home and caught him in the yard, and the old man jumped up and sicked the dogs on the fist, thinking it was a coon, and they killed the fist. They couldn't come up to his relief. The next morning when the old man went to examine the coon, it was the little dog. They were called up and were both thrashed, but the little dog never told on them any more when they went a-coon hunting. —*Herndon to William H. Herndon, June 21, 1865 (7:181-83), Herndon-Weik Collection. {C}*

2. *As a candidate for the state legislature in 1832, Lincoln made several speeches, in one of which, according to Herndon, he declared:*

I have been told that some of my opponents have said that it was a disgrace to the county of Sangamon to have such a looking man as I am stuck up for the legislature. Now, I thought this was a free country. That is the reason I address you today. Had I have known to the contrary, I should not have consented to run, but I will say one thing. Let the shoe pinch where it may, when I have been a candidate before you some five or six times and have been beaten every time, I will consider it a disgrace and will be sure never to try it again. —*Herndon to Herndon, May 28, 1865 (7:68-73). {C}*

WILLIAM H. HERNDON (1818-1891) *Lincoln's law partner and biographer. Born in Kentucky, he lived nearly all of his life in Springfield or its vicinity and was city attorney and mayor in the 1850s. The Lincoln-Herndon partnership, formed in 1844, lasted nominally until Lincoln's death but ended effectively with his departure for Washington in February 1861. During those seventeen years, Herndon, the better read and more radically antislavery of the two, undoubtedly had some influence on Lincoln's political thought and action, though not as much as he later claimed. With Lincoln the president he was generally out of touch and at times out of sympathy. The assassination, by swelling public interest in every detail of Lincoln's origins and rise to national prominence, restored him to the center of Herndon's life.*

Plied with requests for information about his partner and vexed by the tendency of memorialists and early biographers to idealize him beyond recognition, Herndon resolved to write a truthful life of the real Lincoln—one that would examine the elements of his greatness without concealing his imperfections. Two significant products of this resolve took shape before the end of 1865, as Herndon began to accumulate statements about Lincoln from other persons, while himself undertaking a series of lectures in Springfield. The fourth of those lectures, which unveiled Ann Rutledge as the one great love of Lincoln's life, provoked a storm of criticism. Thereafter, for a number of reasons, work on the biography languished.

A few years later, Herndon sold copies of his Lincoln materials to Ward Hill Lamon (q.v.), and they were used extensively in Lamon's Life of Abraham Lincoln, *a book that appeared in 1872 and scandalized many people because of what it had to say about Lincoln's parentage, character, religion, and marriage. Herndon's own project was not revived until the 1880s, when his friendship with a young Indianian, Jesse W. Weik, ripened into a collaboration that at last produced* Herndon's Lincoln: The True Story of a Great Life. *Put into its final form by Weik, the book was nevertheless almost entirely Herndon's in substance, resting largely on the materials that he had gathered in the 1860s and on scores of letters, replete with his own reminiscences, that he wrote to Weik in the 1880s. Criticism of the work has often been severe, but after more than a century it remains the most influential biography of Lincoln ever published.*

A leading Lincoln authority once declared that "when Herndon relates a fact as of his own observation, it may generally be accepted without question."[222] This pronouncement is itself questionable, however, and especially so with respect to Herndon's recollected words of Lincoln, most of which were written down more than a quarter of a century after he supposedly heard them. By then, what he really remembered despite the erosive effects of time was intermingled with all that he had read and been told about Lincoln, as well as with certain inferences and speculations that he had elevated to the status of fact. Faulty memory, bias, and self-inflation—all tended to compromise his essentially honest intent.

Herndon's quotations of Lincoln often sound more like Herndon himself than his partner, most noticeably in flurries of redundancy such as "go along with and accompany" and "toil, work, and labor." Some of them must have been invented outright or synthesized from exceedingly dim recollections. A few were appropriated from contemporaries, and in at least one instance, the remarks of another man were erroneously attributed to Lincoln.[223] Still, much of Herndon's quotation of Lincoln seems credible enough in substance, and it appears that he may have managed sometimes to recapture bits of phrasing with considerable precision.

1. Describing his family's journey from Kentucky to Indiana, Lincoln told of a pet dog left behind on the bank of a stream:

But I could not endure the idea of abandoning even a dog. Pulling off shoes and socks, I waded across the stream and triumphantly returned with the shivering animal under my arm. His frantic leaps of joy and other evidences of a dog's gratitude amply repaid me for all the exposure I had undergone. —Herndon, I, 68n (1889). {E}

In the book, Herndon offered this story as one told to him by Lincoln, but in a letter to Weik he said that he got it from Jesse K. Dubois, who had heard it from Lincoln "when the two were young men."[224] The incident itself may have taken place, but the quoted words of Lincoln are apparently a fabrication.

2. Herndon remembered that Lincoln once told him of drawing an angry response from Stephen A. Douglas during the campaign of 1840 with his assertion that Martin Van Buren had voted for Negro suffrage. Lincoln said further that:

Douglas was always calling the Whigs "Federalists," "Tories," "aristocrats," and so forth, [charging] that the Whigs were opposed to freedom, justice, and progress.

Lincoln said that he replied: "This is a loose assertion, I suppose to catch votes. I don't like to catch votes by cheating men out of their judgments, but in reference to the Whigs being opposed to liberty, let me say that that remains to be seen and demonstrated in the future. The brave don't boast. A barking dog don't bite." — *Herndon addendum to a statement by James H. Matheny, May 3, 1866 (8:746), Herndon-Weik Collection.*[225] {D}

The reply is doubly recollective.

3. *On the stump in the 1840s, Democrats were often called "Locofocos," referring to a radical branch of the party centered in New York. Lincoln, according to Herndon, "frequently" emphasized the connection by telling the story of a farmer who found a polecat in his henhouse and prepared to shoot it:*

The polecat demurred as well as he could in his own language, saying that he was no such brute as charged but an innocent animal and a friend of the farmer just come to take care of his chickens. The farmer to this replied: "You look like a polecat, just the size of a polecat, act like one" —and snuffing up his nose—"and smell like one, and you are one, by God, and I'll kill you, innocent and as friendly to me as you say you are." These Locofocos claim to be true Democrats, but they are only Locofocos. They look like Locofocos, just the size of Locofocos, act like Locofocos, and [turning up his nose and backing away from the stand] are Locofocos, by God. — *Herndon to Weik, undated (11:2877-78). {C}*

4. *On his decision to volunteer for another few weeks of service in the Black Hawk War after his original term ended:*

I was out of work, and there being no danger of more fighting, I could do nothing better than enlist again. — *Herndon, I, 100. {C}*

5. *Speaking of his ability to throw a hammer or cannonball farther than anyone else in New Salem, Lincoln did not attribute it simply to physical strength but contended that:*

because of the unusual length of his arms, the ball or projectile had a greater swing and therefore acquired more force and momentum than in the hands of an average man. — *Herndon, I, 83n. {C}*

6. *When Lincoln asked Herndon to become his law partner, he said:*

Billy, I can trust you, if you can trust me. — *Herndon, II, 266. {C}*

7. *When Herndon, for strategic purposes, once filed a plea that was not in accord with known fact, Lincoln asked:*

Hadn't we better withdraw that plea? You know it's a sham, and a sham is very often but another name for a lie. Don't let it go on record. The cursed thing may come staring us in the face long after this suit has been forgotten. —*Herndon, II, 327.* {C}

8. *According to Herndon, Lincoln thus concluded his legal argument in behalf of the widow of a Revolutionary War soldier whose pension had been partially withheld:*

Time rolls by; the heroes of '76 have passed away and are encamped on the other shore. The soldier has gone to rest, and now, crippled, blinded, and broken, his widow comes to you and to me, gentlemen of the jury, to right her wrongs. She was not always thus. She was once a beautiful young woman. Her step was as elastic, her face as fair, and her voice as sweet as any that rang in the mountains of old Virginia. But now she is poor and defenseless. Out here on the prairies of Illinois, many hundreds of miles away from the scenes of her childhood, she appeals to us, who enjoy the privileges achieved for us by the patriots of the Revolution, for our sympathetic aid and manly protection. All I ask is, shall we befriend her? — *Herndon, II, 341-42.* {D}

One suspects that this quotation is more a product of imagination and literary artifice than of recollection.[226]

9. *When Herndon, as city attorney in the early 1850s, asked Lincoln's opinion on the voting rights of foreign-born residents not yet naturalized, he received this reply:*

The question is a doubtful one, and the foreigner is taxed by the city, and it is but justice that they should vote on all questions of city policy or interest. —*Herndon to Weik, February 11, 1887 (10:2102-9).* {C}

10. *Herndon also recalled that at about the same time, Lincoln refused to join him in arguing a suffrage case before the state supreme court, saying:*

I am opposed to the limitation, the lessening of the right of suffrage; am in favor of its extension, enlargement; want to lift men up and broaden them; don't intend by no act of mine to crush or contract. —*Herndon's notation on an undated statement by Charles S. Zane (11:3226); the phrasing is made more graceful in Herndon, III, 625.* {C}

11. *During a professional trip to Menard County in the early 1850s, Lincoln confided to Herndon:*

Billy, I'll tell you something, but keep it a secret while I live. My mother was a bastard, was the daughter of a nobleman, so called, of Virginia. My mother's mother was poor and credulous, and she was shamefully taken advantage of by the man. My mother inherited his qualities and I hers. All that I am or hope ever to be I get from my mother, God bless her. Did you never notice that bastards are generally smarter, shrewder, and more intellectual than others? Is it because it is stolen?

This repeated more elaborately what Herndon had written to Lamon nine days earlier: "Lincoln himself told me that his mother was a bastard, that she was an intellectual woman, a heroic woman, that his mind he got from his mother, etc."
—Herndon to Lamon, February 25, March 6, 1870, Lamon Papers. In Herndon, I, 3-4, Lincoln's wording was considerably changed, and he was said to have argued that from the seducer, his grandfather (now described as a "well-bred" and "broad-minded" Virginian), he got "his power of analysis, his logic, his mental activity, his ambition, and all the qualities that distinguished him from the other members and descendants of the Hanks family."[227] *{D}*

Nancy Lincoln's parentage is indeed obscure. She may have been illegitimate, or at least Lincoln may have believed that she was. Such a revelation, even to his partner, is not consistent, however, with Herndon's repeated assertion that Lincoln was the most reticent and secretive of men. Furthermore, writing in 1889, Herndon declared that Lincoln was "always mum about his mother," and that he, Herndon, never dared mention "Hanks" in Lincoln's presence.[228]

12. *During a discussion of the nation and its troubles in about 1851, Lincoln exclaimed:*

How hard—oh, how more than hard—it is to die and leave one's country no better for the life of him that lived and died her child! —*Herndon-3L, 188-89 (1866). {C}*

This remark echoes sentiment expressed by Lincoln in 1841 to Joshua Speed (q.v.). In a letter written four years later, Herndon recalled that the conversation took place on a trip to Petersburg, probably in 1850, and he expanded Lincoln's remarks as follows: How hard, oh, how hard it is to die and leave one's country no better than if one had never lived for it! The world is dead to hope, deaf to its own death struggles made known by a universal cry. What is to be done? Is anything to be done? Who can do anything and how can it be done? Did you ever think of these things? —*Herndon to Lamon, March 6, 1870, Lamon Papers. {D}*

The effusion after the first sentence sounds more like Herndon than Lincoln.

13. *Speaking of human motivation, Lincoln said:*

At bottom, the snaky tongue of selfishness will wag out. —*Herndon-2L, 411 (1865). {C}*

14. *According to Herndon, Lincoln once remarked in a lecture in Springfield that:*

it was a common notion that those who laughed heartily and often never amounted to much—never made great men.

To which he then added: If this be the case, farewell to all my glory. — *Herndon-2L, 420. {C}*

The substance of this quotation was either corroborated or echoed by Stephen R. Capps (q.v.).

15. *Lincoln gave as his reason for choosing the profession of law that:*

it was the grandest science of man; it was the best profession to develop the logical faculty and the highest platform on which man could exhibit his powers in a well-trained manhood. —*Herndon-2L, 425. {D}*

At best, this disorderly sentence may roughly approximate something that Lincoln said.

16. *Concerning legal fees collected on the judicial circuit, Herndon once queried Lincoln about his habit of dividing them and labeling Herndon's half before putting them in his pocketbook. Lincoln explained:*

Well, Billy, I do it for various reasons: first, unless I did as I do, I might forget that I collected money or had money belonging to you; second, I explain to you how and from whom I got it so that you have not to dun the men who paid; third, if I were to die, you would have no evidence that I had your money, and you could not prove that I had it. By marking the money, it becomes yours, and I have not in law or morality a right to use it. I make it a practice never to use any man's money without his consent, first obtained. —*Herndon to Weik, January 27, 1888 (10:2258-61); repeated with different wording February 13, 1891 (10:2780-83). {C}*

17. *To the argument that a lawyer owed complete loyalty to his client without regard to conscience, Lincoln replied:*

No client ever had money enough to bribe my conscience or to stop its utterance against wrong and oppression. My conscience is my own—my creator's—not man's. I shall never sink the rights of mankind to the malice, wrong, or avarice of another's wishes, though those wishes come to me in the relation of client and attorney. —*Herndon-2L, 431. {D}*

18. *During the same conversation about legal practice, Lincoln declared:*

I cannot read generally. I never read text books; for I have no particular motive to drive and whip me to it. As I am constituted, I don't love to read generally, and as I do not love to read, I feel no interest in what is thus read. I don't and can't remember such reading. When I have a particular case in hand, I have that motive and feel an interest in the case, feel an interest in ferreting out the questions to the bottom, love to dig up the question by the roots and hold it up and dry it before the fires of the mind. I know that general reading broadens the mind, makes it universal, but it never makes a precise, deep, clear mind. The study of particular cases does do that thing, as I understand it. General reading has its advantages and its disadvantages. Special case reading has its advantages and its disadvantages. —*Herndon-2L, 431. {D}*

Here is another Herndon effusion that may incorporate a simpler statement made by Lincoln.

19. *After listening to his partner's argument in a case, Herndon suggested that he had spent too much time rehearsing the history of the law, with which the judge was undoubtedly already familiar. Lincoln replied:*

That's where you're mistaken. I dared not trust the case on the presumption that the court knows everything. In fact, I argued it on the presumption that the court didn't know anything. —*Herndon, II, 338. {C}*

20. *At the law office one day, a certain Colonel King asked for advice on how to conduct himself in his new role as a justice of the peace. Lincoln replied:*

There is no mystery in this matter. King, when you have a case between neighbors before you, listen well to all the evidence, stripping yourself of all prejudice, if any you have, and throwing away, if you can, all technical law knowledge. Hear the lawyers make their argument as patiently as you can; and after the evidence and the lawyers' arguments are through, then stop one moment and ask yourself: what is justice in this case, and let that sense of justice be your decision. Law is nothing else but the best reason of wise men applied for ages to the transactions and business of mankind.[229] —*Undated Herndon statement (11:3575). {C}*

21. *In a civil case in Coles County, the jury had much trouble understanding the phrase "preponderance of evidence." Finally, Lincoln tried his hand at explaining:*

Gentlemen of the jury, did you ever see a pair of steel yards or a pair of store scales? If you did I can explain, I think, to your satisfaction the meaning of the word. If the plaintiff has introduced any evidence, put that in the scales and have it weighed. Say it weighs sixteen ounces. If the defendant has introduced any evidence in the case, put that in the scales; and if that evidence weighs sixteen ounces, the scales are balanced and there is no preponderance of evidence on either side. There are four witnesses on each side of this case. If the plaintiff's evidence weighs one grain of wheat more than the defendant's, then the plaintiff has the preponderance of evidence—his side of the scales go[es] down, is the heaviest. If the defendant's evidence weighs one grain of wheat more than the plaintiff's, then the defendant's side of the scales goes down, is the heaviest; and that movement of the scales tell[s] what is the preponderance of evidence. Now apply this illustration to the state of your mind on weighing the evidence for the plaintiff and defendant. —*Herndon to Weik, November 11, 1885 (9:1807-8). {D}*

There is no assurance that Herndon himself heard these remarks. He did not ordinarily accompany Lincoln on the circuit.

22. *Speaking of John Calhoun, the Springfield Democrat who hired him as a surveyor but opposed him on the stump, Lincoln said that:*

Calhoun gave him more trouble in his debates than Douglas ever did, because he was more captivating in his manner and a more learned man than Douglas. —*Herndon, I, 119.* {C}

23. *Discussing temperance one day in the office, Lincoln declared:*

All such questions must first find lodgment with the most enlightened souls, who stamp them with their approval. In God's own time, they will be organized into law and thus woven into the fabric of our institutions. —*Herndon, I, 167.* {C}

24. *Herndon quoted Lincoln as saying often in substance:*

that universal education should go along with and accompany the universal ballot in America; that the very best, firmest, and most enduring basis of our republic was the education, the thorough and the universal education of the great American people; and that the intelligence of the mass of our people was the light and life of the republic. —*Letter to John C. Henderson, published in the* Independent, *47 (April 4, 1895): 431.* {C}

25. *According to Herndon, Lincoln believed in women's rights but thought that the American public was not yet ready for the idea. Herndon quoted him as saying:*

This question is one simply of time. —*Ibid.*[230] {C}

26. *"A dozen or more times," Herndon recalled, he had heard Lincoln say:*

that a woman had the same right to play with her tail that a man had and no more nor less, and that he had no moral or other right to violate the sacred marriage vow. —*Herndon to Weik, January 23, 1890 (10:2629-32).*[231] {C}

27. *After his wife had bored visitors with exhaustive praise of their children, Lincoln (according to Herndon) would smooth things over by saying:*

These children may be something sometimes, if they are not merely rare-ripes, rotten-ripes, hothouse plants. I have always noticed that a rare-ripe child quickly matures but rots as quickly. —*Herndon to Weik, January 8, 1886 (9:1902-5).* {E}

Since Herndon was never present on such occasions, this quotation is either retailed gossip or pure invention. In both language and substance it has a Herndonian ring.

28. *In a discussion one day, Lincoln declared:*

There are no accidents in my philosophy. Every effect must have its cause. The past is the cause of the present, and the present will be the cause of the future. All these are links in the endless chain stretching from the finite to the infinite.

When Herndon contended that man was free and could act without a motive, Lincoln replied that: it was impossible, because the motive was born before the man. —*Herndon, III, 438. {C}*

29. *According to Herndon, Lincoln "often said":*

What is to be will be, and no efforts nor prayers of ours can change, alter, modify, or reverse the decree. —*Herndon to Weik, February 6, 1887 (10:2092-95). {C}*

The younger Lincoln's leaning toward fatalism was self-acknowledged,[232] though the style of this remark, with redundancy used for emphasis, is peculiarly Herndon's.

30. *Concerning his religious code, Lincoln once said that:*

it was like that of an old man named Glenn in Indiana, whom he heard speak at a church meeting and who said: "When I do good I feel good; when I do bad I feel bad, and that's my religion." —*Herndon, III, 439. {C}*

31. *Whenever Herndon complained of Lincoln's conservatism on the slavery question, Lincoln would say:*

Billy, you're too rampant and spontaneous. —*Herndon, II, 362-63. {C}*

32. *After passage of the Kansas-Nebraska Act in 1854, Lincoln in office conversations with Herndon began to speak more boldly of the coming struggle between freedom and slavery. He said:*

The day of compromise has passed. These two great ideas have been kept apart only by the most artful means. They are like two wild beasts in sight of each other, but chained and held apart. Some day these deadly antagonists will one or the other break their bonds, and then the question will be settled. —*Herndon, II, 366. {C}*

33. *With Douglas in the audience, Lincoln delivered a three-hour speech at the State Capitol on October 4, 1854. According to Herndon, he said during his introductory remarks:*

I willingly give Senator Douglas, who now sits in front of me, the privilege of correcting me where I am wrong in the facts about the whole matter of the Kansas-Nebraska bill, which was introduced by the Senator himself and which is the offspring of the ambition and greed of slavery. I say that I extend to him the privilege of correcting me in my facts and not in my inferences, as they are subject of dispute among men and would cause too many collateral issues to be raised and of no value to the main subject.

But when Douglas (who, according to Herndon, was "a little 'cocked' at the time") began to interrupt frequently, the partisan crowd grew angry, and Lincoln finally declared: I revoke, I withdraw what I have said to the honorable Senator as to privilege and shall assert what I do assert on my own responsibility. *—Herndon to Weik, September 24, 1890 (10:2717-20); repeated with somewhat different wording December 4, 1890 (10:2753-56). {D}*

Contemporary reports of the speech, including one by Herndon himself, do not corroborate this belated recollection beyond the fact that there were indeed some interruptions by Douglas.[233]

34. According to Herndon, II, 355-56, after Lincoln returned in 1855 from the McCormick reaper trial in Cincinnati, he told his partner:

that he had been roughly handled by that man Stanton; that he overheard the latter from an adjoining room, while the door was slightly ajar, referring to Lincoln, inquire of another, "Where did that long-armed creature come from, and what can he expect to do in this case?" *{E}*

The wording was different in the letter on which this passage was based. Herndon quoted Lincoln as having heard Stanton say: "Why did you bring that damned long-armed ape here for? He does not know anything and can do you no good." But in letters written two years later when the book was in press, Herndon tried unsuccessfully to have the words "He told me" struck out, admitting that he could not remember who had told him the story.[234]

35. Herndon recalled that Lincoln, presumably in 1855, spoke to a meeting of Springfield abolitionists about the turmoil in Kansas and counseled against violence:

You can better succeed with the ballot. You can peaceably then redeem the government and preserve the liberties of mankind through your votes and voice and moral influence. . . . Let there be peace. Revolutionize through the ballot box and restore the government once more to the affections and hearts of men by making it express, as it was intended to do, the highest spirit of justice and liberty. Your attempt, if there be such, to resist the laws of Kansas by force is criminal and wicked, and all your feeble attempts will be follies and end in bringing sorrow on your heads and ruin the cause you would freely die to preserve. *—Herndon, II, 380. {D}*

The sentiments are certainly Lincoln's, but there appears to be no other evidence that he made such a speech.

36. Sometime in the mid-1850s, Herndon bought and read a biography of Edmund Burke, then offered it to Lincoln, who said:

No, I do not wish to read his life, nor any man's life as now written. You and I have talked over life-writing many and many times, and you know that biographies are eulogistic, one-sided, colored, and false. The dead man's glories are painted hugely, brightly, and falsely; his successes are held up to eulogy, but his failures, his shortcomings, his negatives, his errors, slips, and foibles, and the like are kept in the dark. You don't get a peep at them. You don't get a true understanding of the man, only see one side and that colored and hence false. I have no confidence in biographies. Why do not book sellers have blank biographies ready printed and piled on their shelves and published for sale, so that when a man dies, his heirs or admirers or those who wish it can find a life of the dead ready-made and at hand, and all that has to be done is to buy the eulogistic thing, fill up the blanks, and call it the life and writings of the admired and loved dead. This would economize time and save strains on the brain. This is my opinion of biographies as now written. I want none of them and will not read them. —*Herndon to Weik, December 1885 (9:1875-76). {D}*

Whatever kernel of authenticity there may be in this harangue attributed to Lincoln, it is more recognizably a defense by Herndon of his strategy as a biographer. In another letter to Weik written February 16, 1887 (10:2120-21), Herndon quoted Lincoln somewhat differently and this time remembered that he had read a few pages here and there before making his pronouncement.[235] In Herndon, III, 437n (1889), Lincoln goes further and reads enough to criticize the book itself, as well as biographies in general. Then he concludes with a statement not to be found in the earlier versions: "History is not history unless it is the truth." Significantly, Herndon added the comment: "This emphatic avowal of sentiment from Mr. Lincoln not only fixes his estimate of ordinary biography, but is my vindication in advance if assailed for telling the truth."

37. After buying a set of volumes about science sometime in the mid-1850s, Lincoln made "substantially" the following remarks:

I have wanted such a book for years because I sometimes make experiments and have thoughts about the physical world that I do not know to be true nor false. I may, by this book, correct my errors and save time and expense. I can see where scientists and philosophers have failed and avoid the rock on which they split or can see the means of their success and take advantage of their brains, toil, and knowledge. Men are greedy to publish the successes of efforts, but meanly shy as to publishing the failures of man. Many men are ruined by this one-sided practice of concealment of blunders and failures. —*Herndon to Weik, December 16, 1885 (9:1855-56).[236] {C}*

38. According to Herndon, soon after the famous Bloomington convention of May 1856 organized the Illinois Republican party, he and Lincoln called a meeting in Springfield to ratify its actions. Only one other man showed up, and Lincoln said to his audience of two:

that the meeting was larger than he **knew** it would be, and that while he knew that he himself and his partner would attend, he was not sure anyone else would, and yet another man had been found brave enough to come out.

He then continued: While all seems dead, the age itself is not. It liveth as sure as our Maker liveth. Under all this seeming want of life and motion, the world does move nevertheless. Be hopeful, and now let us adjourn and appeal to the people. —*Herndon, II, 385–86. {E}*

This story is absurd on its face and contradicted by contemporary newspaper reports.[237]

39. *In the three-man presidential contest of 1856, some of Lincoln's old Whig friends established a Fillmore paper in Springfield. This was bad news for the Republican supporters of Frémont, and Lincoln said bitterly to Herndon:*

These men are stool pigeons for the Democracy—bought up like cattle and hogs in the market.[238] The *Conservative* is run by the Democrats in fact. —*Herndon to Weik, January 8, 1889 (10:2452–55). {C}*

40. *"Why are you so fair and scrupulously honest in all your debates with men?" According to Herndon, he "often" asked Lincoln this question and received "universally" the following reply (which makes one wonder why he kept asking):*

I want no disputes and fusses with men about simple unimportant facts. I must conciliate. I want to argue the principles that lie at the foundation of our differences. You well know, that I can't argue a question of principles with one half of the proposition suppressed in the mind and the other half uttered to the people. It's impossible, and besides, it is morally wrong. —*Herndon-3L, 179. {D}*

41. *Herndon recalled in 1866 that about nine years earlier, Lincoln had sent him to ask Governor William H. Bissell's intervention in behalf of a young black Illinoisan who had been jailed in New Orleans. When Herndon returned and reported that the Governor said he had no authority in the case, Lincoln exclaimed:*

By God, before I've done, I'll make the road so hot that he shall find authority! —*Herndon's statement recorded in Dall, 415 (1867).*

As the story was told in Herndon, II, 378–79, both men went to see Governor Bissell, and it was to him that Lincoln exclaimed: By God, Governor, I'll make the ground in this country too hot for the foot of a slave, whether you have the legal power to secure the release of this boy or not. *{D}*

42. *Concerning the duel that he had come close to fighting with James Shields in 1842, Herndon once heard Lincoln say:*

I did not intend to hurt Shields unless I did so in perfect self-defense. I could have split him from the crown of the head to the end of his backbone. — *Herndon to Weik, December 24, 1887 (10:2243-44). {C}*

43. *Returning from a trip to the East in 1858, Herndon reported to Lincoln that many people asked about the Shields duel. Lincoln said regretfully:*

If all the good things I have ever done are remembered as long and well as my scrape with Shields, it is plain I shall not soon be forgotten. *—Herndon, II, 231. {C}*

44. *Thrilled by a visit to Niagara Falls in 1858, Herndon asked Lincoln about his reaction to the spectacle ten years earlier. Lincoln replied:*

The thing that struck me most forcibly when I saw the Falls was, where in the world did all that water come from? *— Herndon, II, 297. {C}*

Unaware that his leg was being pulled, Herndon treasured this remark as convincing evidence that Lincoln had no eye for the beauty and grandeur of nature.[239]

45. *Lincoln once sought to have an article printed in the* Prairie Beacon *of Paris, Illinois, but the editor, Jacob Harding, replied that it was his policy to publish nothing as editorial matter not written by himself. To Herndon, Lincoln commented:*

That editor has a rather lofty but proper conception of true journalism. *—Herndon, II, 376. Herndon dates this incident in 1855, but other evidence indicates that it probably took place in 1858.*[240] *{C}*

46. *After some of his friends told him that he had acted foolishly, Lincoln said to Herndon:*

Well, I suppose it's a damned good thing that I was not born a woman. — *Herndon to Weik, December 22, 1888 (10:2436-39).*

In Herndon, II, 325n, Lincoln is quoted as saying that: he thanked God that he was not born a woman, because he could not refuse any request if it was not apparently dishonest.

Repeated in Herndon II, 374, as follows: It's a fortunate thing I wasn't born a woman, for I cannot refuse anything, it seems. *{C}*

47. *Herndon told Weik that he had "often" asked Lincoln why he habitually did his reading aloud and that this was the "invariable" reply:*

I catch the idea by two senses; for when I read aloud, I hear what is read and I see it, and hence two senses get it, and I remember it better, if I do not understand it better. *—Herndon to Weik, October 21, 1885 (9:1799-1800). {C}*

A more succinct version, provided February 18, 1887 (10:2110-13), was used in Herndon, II, 332, and made more credible as a one-time-only statement: "I once asked him why he did so. This was his explanation: 'When I read aloud, two senses catch the idea: first, I see what I read; second, I hear it, and therefore I can remember it better.'"

48. *In about 1858, when Herndon complained that Lincoln was not energetic enough in his work on a certain case, he received this reply:*

Billy, I am like a long, strong jackknife doubled up in the handle. The extreme point of the blade has to move through a wider space before it is open than your little short woman's knife, which you hold in your hand, but when the jackknife is open, it cuts wider and deeper than your little thing. I am six feet, two inches high, and it takes me a good while to open and to act, so be patient with me. To change the figure, these long convolutions of my poor brain take time, sometimes a long time, to open and gather force, but like a long, well-platted, heavy, and well-twisted ox lash, when swung around and around high in the air on a good whip stalk, well seasoned, by an expert ox-driver and popped and cracked and snapped at a lazy ox shirking duty, it cuts to the raw, brings blood, opens a gash that makes the lazy ox sting with pain, and so, when these long convolutions are opened and let off on something, are they not a power and a force in action, as you say? You yourself have often complimented me on my force of expression and now in part you have the desired **why.** —*Herndon to Weik, January 1, 1886 (9:1877-80). {D}*

It is difficult to believe Herndon's concluding assurance that this outpouring was Lincoln's, not only in substance, but in much of its wording. A shorter version, with the whip-and-ox analogy removed, appeared in Herndon, II, 33-39.

49. *Early in 1858, Lincoln said to Herndon:*

I think Greeley is not doing me, an old Republican and a tried antislavery man, right. He is talking up Douglas, an untrue and untried man, a dodger, a wriggler, a tool of the South once and now a snapper at it—hope he will bite 'em good—but I don't feel that it is exactly right to pull me down in order to elevate Douglas. I like Greeley, think he intends right, but I think he errs in this hoisting up of Douglas, while he gives me a downward shove. I wish that someone could put a flea in Greeley's ear—see Trumbull, Sumner, Wilson, Seward, Parker, Garrison, Phillips, and others, and try and turn the currents in the right directions. These men ought to trust the tried and true men. —*Herndon to Weik, December 23, 1885 (9:1857-60). {C}*

This, Herndon added, was what Lincoln said "in substance," and there is no reason to doubt it; for Lincoln made the same complaint to other persons. Herndon's wording, no doubt a far cry from Lincoln's, was severely edited by Weik for the biography.[241]

50. *Before he delivered his House-Divided speech on June 16, 1858, Lin-*

coln read it privately to Herndon, pausing to ask for comment on the opening section. Herndon questioned whether such a statement was politic, and Lincoln responded:

That makes no difference. That expression is a truth of all human experience: a house divided against itself cannot stand, and he that runs may read. The proposition is indisputably true and has been true for more than six thousand years, and I will deliver it as written. I want to use some universally known figure, expressed in simple language as universally known, that it may strike home to the minds of men in order to rouse them to the peril of the times. I would rather be defeated with this expression in the speech and it held up and discussed before the people than to be victorious without it. —*Herndon-3L, 184; repeated with some changes in Herndon, II, 398. {D}*

There is other evidence that Lincoln rejected prior criticism of the house-divided passage, but this histrionic pronouncement does not ring true and would have been inconsistent with his dominant purpose of winning Douglas's seat in the Senate. Furthermore, Herndon's several accounts of this discussion are to some extent contradictory.[242]

51. According to Herndon, he not only stood alone in giving prior approval to the House-Divided speech but even predicted that it would make Lincoln president. After the election of 1858 ended in defeat, "hundreds of friends" flocked into the office and said: "I told you that that speech would kill you." To their complaints Lincoln would reply:

You don't fully comprehend its importance, but I suppose you all have or will desert me for that speech. There is one man who will stick to me to the end. He understands it and its importance, and that man is Billy Herndon, my good old and longtime friend. —*Herndon to Weik, October 29, 1885 (9:1805-6). {D}*

A self-serving recollection, but it should be noted that Henry C. Whitney (q.v.) likewise recalled Lincoln's paying such a tribute to Herndon, dating it about two months later.

52. Lincoln was informed on July 8, 1858, that the Buchanan Democrats in Illinois intended to run a full slate of candidates for office in opposition to the Douglas wing of the party. He told Herndon immediately afterward that he had responded:

If you do this, the thing is settled—the battle is fought. —*Herndon to Lyman Trumbull, July 8, 1858, Trumbull Papers. {A}*

53. During an office discussion in 1859 about the possibility of civil war, Herndon expressed a fear that in such a crisis, the North would not have the great leader it needed. Lincoln answered with an analogy:

Go to the river bank with a coarse sieve and fill it with gravel. After a vigorous shaking, you will observe that the small pebbles and sand have sunk from view and fallen to the ground. The next larger in size, unable to slip between the wires, will still be found within the sieve. By thorough and repeated shakings you will find that, of the pebbles still left in the sieve, the largest ones will have risen to the top. Now, if, as you say, war is inevitable and will shake the country from center to circumference, you will find that the little men will fall out of view in the shaking. The masses will rest on some solid foundation, and the big men will have climbed to the top. Of these latter, one greater than all the rest will leap forth armed and equipped — the people's leader in the conflict. — *Herndon, III, 622-23.* {C}

54. *Herndon recalled in 1885 that Lincoln had "once" said to him:*

I feel as if I should meet with some terrible end.

A few weeks later he wrote that Lincoln had made the remark "more than once." After another fourteen months had passed, he remembered having heard it "more than a dozen times," — Herndon to Weik, November 14, 1885 (9:1815-16); February 6, 1887 (10:2092-95); Herndon to the editor of the Religio-Philosophical Journal, *December 4, 1885, in Hertz, 110.*[243] {C}

55. *Lincoln, according to Herndon, was a gloomy man who loved mirth as therapy, saying:*

If it were not for these stories, jokes, jests, I should die; they give vent — are the vents — of my moods and gloom. — *Herndon to Weik, November 17, 1885 (9:1819-20). See also January 10, 1891 (10:2768-71).* {C}

This is another substantively credible quotation wrapped in Herndonian redundancy. Isaac N. Arnold and James M. Ashley (qq.v.) recalled Lincoln's making similar remarks.

56. *"Many times," according to Herndon, Lincoln advised him:*

Billy, don't shoot too high; shoot low down, and the common people will understand you. They are the ones which you wish to reach; at least, they are the ones whom you ought to reach. The educated ones will understand you anyhow. If you shoot too high, your bullets will go over the heads of the mass and only hit those who need no hitting. — *Herndon to Weik, January 9, 1886 (9:1920-23).*[244] {C}

57. *Lincoln, according to Herndon, was not a teetotaler; he "sometimes drank liquor."*[245] *But he was "often heard to say":*

I never drink much and am entitled to no credit therefor, because I hate the stuff.

A friend once asked him if he did not like liquor, and he said: No, it is unpleasant to me and always makes me feel flabby and undone. — *Herndon to Weik, February 5, 1887 (10:2088-90).* {D}

It is not clear from this letter that Herndon was present to hear either of these remarks.

58. *When he returned home after delivering his Cooper Union address in February 1860, Lincoln told Herndon that:*

for once in his life he was greatly abashed over his personal appearance. The new suit of clothes which he donned on his arrival in New York were ill-fitting garments and showed the creases made while packed in the valise; and for a long time after he began his speech and before he became warmed up, he imagined that the audience noticed the contrast between his western clothes and the neat-fitting suits of Mr. Bryant and others who sat on the platform. —*Herndon, III, 454–55n.* {C}

59. *As president-elect, Lincoln said:*

that he felt himself under no promise or obligation to appoint anyone; that if his friends made any agreements for him, they did so over his expressed direction and without his knowledge. —*Herndon, III, 473.* {C}

60. *At another time after his election, Lincoln confided to Herndon:*

that he wanted to give the South, by way of placation, a place in his cabinet; that a fair division of the country entitled the southern states to a reasonable representation there, and if not interfered with, he would make such a distribution as would satisfy all persons interested.

Less apprehensive than the public as a whole, he said that: he could not in his heart believe that the South designed the overthrow of the government. —*Herndon, III, 473.* {C}

61. *About December 1860, as Herndon recalled it, Lincoln said to him concerning the secession crisis:*

I shall attempt to defend and preserve this Union and will make one vast grave yard of the valley of the Mississippi—yes of the whole South, if I must—to maintain, preserve, and defend the Union and Constitution in all their ancient integrity. —*Herndon-3L, 193–94.* {D}

If Lincoln did emit such a remark, it was more savage than any other statement reliably attributed to him during the secession winter. Interestingly, Herndon himself used the phrase "make a grave yard of the South" in a letter written at that time.[246]

62. *Writing in February 1861, Herndon said that Lincoln's answer to would-be compromisers was in substance:*

Away—off—begone! If the nation wants to back down, let it—not I. —*Herndon to Wendell Phillips, February 1, 1861, Bartlett, 161.* {B}

63. *In his last talk with Herndon before leaving for Washington, Lincoln spoke of the signboard at the entrance to their office:*

Let it hang there undisturbed. Give our clients to understand that the election of a president makes no change in the firm of Lincoln and Herndon. If I live, I'm coming back sometime, and then we'll go right on practicing law as if nothing had ever happened. —*Herndon, III, 483-84.* {C}

64. *On the same occasion, Lincoln said:*

I am sick of officeholding already, and I shudder when I think of the tasks that are still ahead.

He added that: the sorrow of parting from his old associations was deeper than most persons would imagine, but it was more marked in his case because of the feeling which had become irrepressible that he would never return alive. —*Herndon, III, 484.* {C}

65. *According to Herndon, Lincoln's very last words to him before departing for Washington as president-elect were, in substance:*

I am decided; my course is fixed; my path is blazed. The Union and the Constitution shall be preserved and the laws enforced at every and at all hazards. I expect the people to sustain me. They have never yet forsaken any true man. —*Herndon to Edward L. Pierce, February 18, 1861 (7:29-31); published in Pratt-2, 51-52.* {B}

66. *In January 1862, while Herndon was paying a visit of several days to his friend in the White House,*[247] *Lincoln complained about the never-ending pressures for patronage. He said:*

If ever American society and the United States government are demoralized and overthrown, it will come from the voracious desire of office—this struggle to live without toil, work, and labor—from which I am not free myself. —*Herndon-2L, 406-7. The same remark, with somewhat different phrasing and the final clause omitted, was quoted in Herndon, III, 507, and again at 605.* {C}

67. *One day during his visit, Herndon heard Lincoln's response to a warning from Congressman Horace Maynard of Tennessee that there was danger ahead if he tried to move too fast:*

I know that, but I shall go just so fast and only so fast as I think I'm right and the people are ready for the step. —*Herndon, III, 508.* {C}

68. *When Herndon urged Lincoln to act more boldly in the manner of Andrew Jackson, he received this answer:*

I can't do it. I am moving slowly outward, as if pressing iron rings [were] riveted on me. Traitors are under me, around me, and above me. I do not know whom to trust and must move slowly and cautiously. I think I have my foot on the rebellion, nevertheless. —*Herndon-3L, 180.* {C}

ABRAM S. HEWITT (1822–1903) *Iron manufacturer closely associated with his father-in-law, Peter Cooper, in the establishment and operation of Cooper Institute. In later life, he was also a member of Congress and mayor of New York City.*

    1. *Lincoln met Hewitt for the first time in 1862 and said to him:*

Why, you're not such a hell of a fellow after all. . . . From what they told me of you and from the fact that you furnished those mortar beds in thirty days when everybody else said it would take ninety, I thought you must be at least seven feet tall. — *Ida M. Tarbell's notes of an interview with Hewitt, March 8, 1901, Tarbell Papers.* {C}

THOMAS HICKS (1823–1890) *New York artist who in June 1860 traveled to Springfield and painted a portrait of Lincoln for reproduction as a campaign lithograph.*[248]

    1. *Concerning a very dark photograph of himself:*

Parson Brownlow says I am a nigger, and if he had judged alone from that picture, he would have had some ground for his assertion. — *Rice AT, 597 (1886).* {C}

    2. *After being visited by two young men who did not announce their names:*

I had never seen them before, and I had to beat about the bush till I found who they were. It was uphill work, but I topped it at last. — *599.* {C}

    3. *This was the first painting of Lincoln from life, and as the work progressed, he said:*

It interests me to see how, by adding a touch here and a touch there, you make it look more like me. I do not understand it, but I see it is a vocation in which the work is very fine. — *599.* {C}

    4. *Of the finished portrait:*

I think the picture has a somewhat pleasanter expression than I usually have, but that, perhaps, is not an objection. — *602.* {C}

ADAMS S. HILL (1833–1910) *Washington correspondent for the New York Tribune, later professor of rhetoric at Harvard. Hill often quoted remarks made by Lincoln to other persons (see, for example, Isaac N. Arnold, Alexander Ramsey, Charles Sumner). He may or may not have heard the following words directly from the President's lips.*

    1. *On July 5, 1862, the President said that:*

had it not been for Lovejoy's resolution he would have removed McClellan. — *Hill to Sydney Howard Gay, July 8, 1862, as quoted in Starr, 151n.*[249] {D}

Owen Lovejoy's resolution of thanks to McClellan passed the House of Representatives on May 9, 1862.[250]

    2. *After the second battle of Bull Run, Lincoln says that:*

he has heard before of "knocking a person into the middle of next week," but the rebels have knocked us into the middle of last year. — *Hill to Gay, September 4, 1862, Gay Papers. {D}*

3. *Speaking of the eccentric writer and promoter George Francis Train, Lincoln said that:*

he reminded him of the Irishman's description of soda water: "It was a tumbler of piss with a fart in it". — *Hill to Gay, September 18, 1862, Gay Papers. {D}*

4. *Edward Everett, a former secretary of state, was invited to a consultation with the President, who said that:*

it was not with the view of superseding Seward but because he had understood that his views touching foreign affairs materially differed from Seward's, and [he] wished to hear all sides. — *Hill to Gay, October 1, 1862. {D}*

5. *Commenting on the second ride around the Army of the Potomac by Confederate cavalry leader J. E. B. Stuart, Lincoln said:*

Three times round and out is the rule in baseball. Stuart has been twice around McClellan. The third time, by the rules of the game, he must surrender. — *Hill to Gay, undated, but probably mid-October 1862. {D}*

6. *At about the same time, Lincoln complained:*

that McClellan couldn't account for 90,000 men that ought to be with him. — *Hill to Gay, undated, but probably October 1862. {D}*

7. *Returning in a discouraged mood from a conference with General Burnside, Lincoln said that:*

when McClellan failed to get between [the] rebels and Richmond, **the** great chance was lost. — *Hill to Gay, November 29, 1862. {D}*

8. *Speaking of Du Pont's unsuccessful attack on Charleston in April 1863, Lincoln said that:*

the six months' preparation for Charleston was a very long grace for the thin plate of soup served in the two hours of fighting. — *Hill to Gay, April 14, 1863. {D}*

9. *Concerning two New York* Tribune *correspondents being held as Confederate prisoners, Lincoln said that:*

he would do all in his power to effect their release. — *Hill to Gay, June 4, 1863.*[251] *{B}*

J. J. HILL *Orderly for the commander of the 29th Connecticut Colored Infantry, one of the regiments that entered Richmond on April 3, 1865.*

1. *Hill recalled two years afterward that Lincoln, when he visited Richmond*

on April 4, spoke as follows to a crowd gathered in front of the Confederate capitol:

In reference to you, colored people, let me say God has made you free. Although you have been deprived of your God-given rights by your so-called masters, you are now as free as I am, and if those that claim to be your superiors do not know that you are free, take the sword and bayonet and teach them that you are; for God created all men free, giving to each the same rights of life, liberty, and the pursuit of happiness. —*Aptheker, I, 490. {D}*

David Dixon Porter (q.v.) likewise recalled Lincoln's telling Richmond blacks that they were free, but it seems very unlikely that he advised them to take up arms against anyone who denied that freedom.

JOHN HILL (1839–?) *Democratic editor in Petersburg, Illinois, a town near New Salem. He was the first person to print an account of Lincoln's alleged romance with Ann Rutledge.*

1. *When he was about to leave for the Democratic national convention at Charleston in April 1860, Hill met Lincoln, who said:*

I am glad I met you. I am a candidate for vice president on the Seward ticket. Charleston is too hot for any of my party to be there, and I guess you are the best friend I will have down there. When anybody is nominated for president, I wish you would telegraph it to me. —*Hill to Ida M. Tarbell, February 6, 1896, Tarbell Papers. {D}*

It is unlikely that Lincoln would have labeled himself a vice-presidential candidate, and Hill's general credibility is somewhat dubious.[252]

LOIS NEWHALL HILLIS *Member of a company of singers that toured Illinois in the 1850s.*

1. *In a hotel one evening, a group of lawyers present called upon Lincoln to sing some of the songs for which he was famous, and Miss Newhall, sitting at a melodeon, urged him to do so. Lincoln replied:*

Why, Miss Newhall, if it would save my soul, I couldn't imitate a note that you would touch on that instrument. I never sang in my life, and those fellows know it. They are simply trying to make fun of me. But I'll tell you what I am willing to do. Inasmuch as you and your sister have been so kind and entertained us so generously, I shall try to return the favor. Of course I can't produce music, but if you will be patient and brave enough to endure it, I will repeat for your benefit several stanzas of a poem of which I am particularly fond.

According to Mrs. Hillis, as she told it to William J. Anderson in the late 1880s, Lincoln then recited lines from "O, Why Should the Spirit of Mortal Be Proud?" —Weik-2, 78–79.[253] *{D}*

ETHAN ALLEN HITCHCOCK (1798–1870)   *Union general who served princi-*
pally as a staff officer and as commissioner for the exchange of prisoners.

   1. *Concerned about McClellan's slowness on the Virginia front, Lincoln in*
March 1862 expressed the wish to have the benefit of Hitchcock's experience,
adding that he, Lincoln:

was the depository of the power of the government and had no military
knowledge. —*Hitchcock, 439 (1909). {C}*

R. M. HOE   *Perhaps Richard March Hoe (1812–1886), inventor and manufac-*
turer of the very successful Hoe rotary printing press.

   1. *According to Hoe, he and Simon Cameron were present one evening*
in the summer of 1864 when Thaddeus Stevens demanded Lincoln's promise
that if re-elected, he would reorganize the cabinet, leaving Blair out of it. The
President replied:

Mr. Stevens, I am sorry to be compelled to deny your request to make such
a promise. If I were even myself inclined to make it, I have no right to do
so. What right have I to promise you to remove Mr. Blair, and not make
a similar promise to any other gentleman of influence to remove any other
member of my cabinet whom he does not happen to like? The Republican
party, wisely or unwisely, has made me their nominee for president without
asking any such pledge at my hands. Is it proper that you should demand it,
representing only a portion of that great party? Has it come to this, that the
voters of this country are asked to elect a man to be president—to be the
executive, to administer the government—and yet that this man is to have
no will or discretion of his own? Am I to be the mere puppet of power—
to have my constitutional advisers selected for me beforehand, to be told I
must do this or leave that undone? It would be degrading to my manhood
to consent to any such bargain; I was about to say it is equally degrading
to your manhood to ask it.

   I confess that I desire to be re-elected. God knows I do not want the
labor and responsibility of the office for another four years. But I have the
common pride of humanity to wish my past four years' administration endorsed; and besides, I honestly believe that I can better serve the nation in
its need and peril than any new man could possibly do. I want to finish
this job of putting down the rebellion and restoring peace and prosperity
to the country. But I would have the courage to refuse the office rather than
accept it on such disgraceful terms as not really to be the president after I
am elected. —*Undated statement by Hoe in Nicolay Papers. {D}*

OLIVER WENDELL HOLMES (1841–1935)   *Civil War officer who became the*
most famous associate justice of the United States Supreme Court.

   1. *General Jubal Early's Washington raid reached the outskirts of the city*

on July 11, 1864. That day and the next, Lincoln visited nearby Fort Stevens to watch the fighting. At one point, Holmes became fearful for the President's safety and shouted, "Get down, you fool!" Lincoln obeyed, saying:

Colonel Holmes, I am glad you know how to talk to a civilian. —*Holmes's statement to Laski in 1931, as reported by Laski in 1946, Cramer, 105. {D}*

There are good reasons to doubt this story, although Holmes apparently told it to more than one person, including Justice Felix Frankfurter.[254]

JOSEPH HOLT (1807–1894) *A Kentucky unionist who had served in Buchanan's cabinet, Holt was appointed in 1862 as chief legal officer of the army with the title judge advocate general.*

1. *Upon being urged to take greater precautions for his personal safety:*

What is the use of putting up the bars when the fence is down all around? —*Interview with Holt, October 29, 1875, in Nicolay Papers. {C}*

Joseph Gillespie (q.v.) recalled hearing a similar remark from Lincoln.

2. *When Holt advised him not to intervene in an execution:*

I don't believe it will make a man any better to shoot him, while if we keep him alive, we may at least get some work out of him. You have no doubt heard the story of the soldier who was caught and asked why he had deserted. "Well, Captain," said the man, "it was not my fault. I have got just as brave a heart as Julius Caesar, but these cowardly legs of mine will always run away with me when the battle begins." I have no doubt that is true of many a man who honestly meant to do his duty but who was overcome by a physical fear greater than his will. —*Ibid.*

Holt added: "They came to be familiarly known between us as his 'leg cases.'" {C}

If Holt's recollection is to be believed, Lincoln was repeating a story that he had told as early as 1839 in a public speech.[255] *Daniel W. Voorhees (q.v.) likewise recalled hearing Lincoln talk about "leg cases."*

SAMUEL HOOPER (1808–1875) *Massachusetts merchant and a Republican congressman from 1861 until his death.*

1. *On June 30, 1864, the day that Salmon P. Chase's resignation as secretary of the treasury was accepted, Hooper called on Chase and told him of a conversation he had had with the President a few days earlier. This is Chase's account in his diary of what he understood Lincoln to have said, namely that:*

he had intended in case of vacancy in the chief justiceship to tender it to me and would now, did a vacancy exist. This he said to show his real sentiments toward me; for he remembered that not very long after we took charge of the administration, I had remarked one day that I preferred judicial to administrative office and would rather, if I could, be chief justice of the United States than hold any other position that could be given me. —*Chase, 471.* {D}

BUSHROD E. HOPPIN (Born c. 1830) *A resident of Sangamon County from 1855 to December 1860.*

1. *Asked how he felt after an unspecified Republican defeat, Lincoln said:*

I'm worked and down, but ready for another fight. —*Hoppin's recollection in the Arlington (Massachusetts)* Herald, *reprinted in the Waverly (Iowa)* Journal, *February 16, 1923, from a clipping in the Lincoln Reminiscences file,* ISHL. {D}

2. *A few days before his election to the presidency, Lincoln said with respect to southern attitudes:*

that he could only execute the laws as he found them; that he recognized their legal rights and had no disposition to interfere with them. —*Hoppin's letter in the Chicago* Tribune, *February 7, 1909.* {C}

3. *In December 1860, when Mrs. Hoppin exclaimed at the lightness of a model log cabin that Lincoln had been given, he thought for a moment and then replied:*

I hope it may be symbolic of the chain that binds the union—light but strong. —*Ibid.* {C}

JAMES QUAY HOWARD (1836–1912) *A law student who went to Springfield in the summer of 1860 to gather material for William Dean Howells's campaign biography.*

1. *Lincoln's statement, as recorded in Howard's notes, explaining his conduct in January 1849, when, as a member of Congress, he presented a plan for gradual abolition in the District of Columbia but did not actually introduce legislation to that purpose:*

Before giving notice to introduce a bill to abolish slavery in the District of Columbia, I visited [the] Mayor, senators, and others whom I thought best acquainted with the sentiment of the people, to ascertain if a bill such as I proposed would be endorsed by them according to its provisions.

Being informed that it would meet with their hearty approbation I gave notice in Congress that I should introduce a bill. Subsequently I learned that many leading southern members of Congress, had been to see the Mayor and the others who favored my bill and had drawn them over to their way of thinking. Finding that I was abandoned by my former backers and having little personal influence, I dropped the matter, knowing that it was useless to prosecute the business at that time. My mind has been in process of education since that time. [I] do not know that I would now approve of the bill, but in the main, think that I would. —*Howard JQ, 395.* {A}

2. *In the same interview:*

The tariff subject must be touched lightly. My speeches in favor of a protective tariff would please Pennsylvania and offend William Cullen Bryant in the same degree. It is like the case of three men who had nothing to cover them but a blanket only sufficient to cover two. When Number One pulled it **on** himself, he pulled it **off** Number Three. —*395. {A}*

JOSEPH HOWARD, JR. (1833–1908) *Journalist with more talent than scruples, whose various employers during the Civil War era included the New York* Times *and the Brooklyn* Eagle. *In 1864, he was held in prison for three months after forging a presidential proclamation that was published by two New York papers.*[256]

1. *In the spring of 1861, according to Howard, he asked whether it was true that Douglas had been offered an appointment as brigadier general, and Lincoln replied:*

No, sir, I have not done so; nor had I thought of doing so until tonight, when I saw it suggested in the paper. I have no reason to believe Mr. Douglas would accept it. He has not asked it, nor have his friends. But I must say that if it is well to appoint brigadier generals from the civil list, I can imagine few men better qualified for such a position than Judge Douglas. For myself, I know I have not much military knowledge, and I think Douglas has. It was he who first told me I should have trouble at Baltimore, and, pointing on the map, showed me the route by Perryville, Havre de Grace, and Annapolis, as the one over which our troops must come. He impressed on my mind the necessity of absolutely securing Fortress Monroe and Old Point Comfort, and, in fact, I think he knows all about it. —*Howard JJr, 212 (1861). {C}*

OLIVER O. HOWARD (1830–1909) *Civil War general from Maine, later head of the Freedmen's Bureau and founder of Howard University.*

1. *At a White House gathering, a senator declared: "I believe that, if we could only do right as a people, the Lord would help us, and we should have a decided success in this terrible struggle."*[257] *Lincoln heard the remark and said:*

My faith is greater than yours. I am confident that God will make us do sufficiently right to give us the victory. —*Howard OO, 876 (1908). {C}*

James F. Wilson (q.v.) provided a more inflated version of Lincoln's remarks on this occasion.

2. *In September 1863, pointing to Cumberland Gap on the map:*

Could you not, General Howard, with your corps pass through that gap and seize Knoxville and deliver those people of east Tennessee? They are loyal there, General, they are loyal. —*877. {C}*

3. *In a newspaper interview, Howard quoted Lincoln as saying at the same time:*

General, if you come out of this horror and misery alive, and I pray to God that you may, I want you to do something for those mountain people who have been shut out of the world all these years. I know them. If I live, I will do all I can to aid, and between us, perhaps we can do the justice they deserve. Please remember this, and if God is good to us we may be able to speak of this later. —*New York* Globe and Commercial Advertiser, *October 27, 1909, reprinted in Kinkaid, 342. {D}*

Howard's quotation of Lincoln in this way was related to his promotion of Lincoln Memorial University in Harrogate, Tennessee, which he helped to found.

JOHN W. HOYT (1831–1912)   *A Wisconsin agricultural leader who arranged for Lincoln to speak at the state fair in Milwaukee on September 30, 1859, Hoyt was later governor of Wyoming Territory and the first president of the University of Wyoming.*

1. *Upon finding that no room had been held for him at the hotel:*

Oh, my dear sir, don't be unhappy on my account. I see there is vacant space enough right here, at the end of the counter. Just bring a cot and a clothes-rack, with sheet for a screen, and I'll sleep like a top. —*Hoyt, 1306 (1910). {D}*

GURDON S. HUBBARD (1802–1886)   *Chicago pioneer and businessman, long acquainted with Lincoln.*

1. *In 1861, soon after the firing on Fort Sumter, Lincoln said to Hubbard:*

Douglas and myself have studied this map very closely. I am indebted to him for wise counsel. I have no better adviser and feel under great obligations to him. —*Oldroyd, 306 (1882). {C}*

HENRY S. HUIDEKOPER (1839–1918)   *Army officer from northwestern Pennsylvania who suffered the loss of an arm at Gettysburg and received the Medal of Honor; later postmaster of Philadelphia.*

1. *In September 1864, at the urging of Huidekoper and Congressman Solomon N. Pettis, Lincoln endorsed a plan for enlisting certain Confederate prisoners of war in the Union army.*[258] *Having written out the order, he said:*

Now we will take this into the Secretary of War's office, and I wish you to notice how they treat me in there. They do not think I know anything in their line of business or should ever give them any direction concerning it. —*Huidekoper, 16 (1896). {C}*

DAVID HUNTER (1802–1886)   *Civil War general whose military order in May 1862 emancipating the slaves of South Carolina, Georgia, and Florida was revoked by Lincoln.*

1. *After being removed from command of the Department of the South in June 1863, Hunter protested vigorously, first by letter and then in a visit to the*

White House.[259] *Lincoln assured the General that he held him in high respect and explained the appointment of Quincy A. Gillmore in his place as a special effort to achieve the capture of Charleston:*

Well, now, General Hunter, I will tell you all about how that happened. Greeley wrote me, or telegraphed me, I forget which, that he had found a man who would "do the job," and asked me to send for General Gillmore and talk to him and try him. So I sent for Gillmore and talked it over with him and with Fox, Halleck, and Mr. Stanton. Gillmore thought he could do it, and I thought it was best to try him. I told Halleck that he must write such an order about it as not to offend General Hunter, and he said he would do it, but the next day when he brought the order, he told me he did not think Gillmore could do anything there, but if we were determined to try him and have him act independent of you, there would be trouble, and that if we would send him, we had better relieve General Hunter. So you were relieved temporarily to give Gillmore a chance to do the job. — *Hunter to Charles G. Halpine, July 21, 1863, Halpine Papers. {C}*

Hunter's account of the interview (the exact date of which is not known) was colored by his anger and abundant self-esteem.

ELIZABETH G. HUTCHINS   *On the eve of the Civil War, an Illinoisan teaching school in Missouri.*

1. *When Hutchins was introduced to Lincoln, he said:*

Well, well, little Betty the schoolteacher. If I had a teacher like you, I would be in school yet.

Noting her embarrassment, he added: Never mind, Chestnut Curls, teaching is the most important work to be done in the world; keep at it.

When she told him she hoped one day to teach in a seminary (meaning an upper-level girls' school), he said: Then you'll have to study while you teach. You know, you can't fly a high kite unless you have a long string. — *Interview in the* Dearborn Independent, *February 7, 1925, p. 14. {D}*

This charming incident took place, according to Hutchins, in 1861 at the Palmer House in Chicago, but Lincoln did not visit that city in 1861, and the Palmer House did not open for business until 1870. It is possible that she was thinking of the Tremont House, where Lincoln as president-elect spent the better part of a week in November 1860.

2. *During the war, Hutchins delivered some papers from her father to Secretary Stanton. Lincoln, coming in just as Stanton remarked that they were not important and could wait, was reminded of a story, one that he had heard from General Clinton B. Fisk:*

It seems that Fisk started out as a colonel in Missouri, and when he had enlisted a regiment, he informed the men that he would do all the swearing done in that organization. They agreed, as they had to, and for some time no one heard any profanity around that camp. Then, one day, John Todd, a teamster, encountered several miles of mudholes, each one worse than the one before. About midway along this road, Todd let go a flood of cussing that reached even Fisk's ears. The Colonel called John into his tent and said: "Look here, John, didn't you agree to let me do all the cussing for this regiment?" "Yes, Colonel, I did," John answered, "but this job of cussing had to be done right there and then, and I couldn't see you anywhere around to do it." The point of that story is, Stanton, that anything which comes up today in this war must be done today in order to finish this war. —*Ibid.* {C}

Fisk, a Methodist, was indeed noted for his aversion to profanity and drink.

WALDO HUTCHINS (1822–1891)   *Lawyer and park commissioner in New York City during the Civil War; later a member of Congress.*

1. *One day during the presidential campaign of 1864, Lincoln explained to Hutchins that Horace Greeley could not be appointed to the cabinet as long as Seward, another New Yorker, remained a member of it. Then he continued:*

When this war closes we will have great need for a diplomat at the Court of St. James. We have a long account to settle with Great Britain. Seward has performed great service as secretary of state. I believe he could perform better service as ambassador to the Court of St. James.[260] By the by, Franklin perhaps was the greatest man that ever lived in this country—philosopher, statesman, scientist. He was postmaster general under the Confederation. Franklin was a printer. Greeley is a printer. Do you know, I believe Greeley would make a good postmaster general. I think I am right in saying that is the position he would rather occupy than any other . . . Mind you, I am not making a promise to bind me in the constitution of my cabinet. I am telling you how I feel toward him personally. I am honest about it. —*Hutchins as quoted by Joseph G. Cannon on the floor of Congress,* House Document *1056* (1916), 48. {D}

Although Lincoln at about this time was speaking of Greeley as "so rotten that nothing can be done with him," it is not beyond belief that he might have sought to tempt him in the same way that he tempted James Gordon Bennett.[261] Some five years after publication of Cannon's speech, an article in an upstate New York newspaper told substantially the same story, associating it with an upstate New York politician, George G. Hoskins, instead of with Hutchins. This later account has been used by a number of writers.[262]

JOHN W. HUTCHINSON (1821–?)   *Member of a family singing group.*

1. *The Hutchinsons performed at the White House in 1862, and Lincoln said:*

I remember one song that you sung when you were in Springfield. It was a good while ago—ten years, perhaps—but I never have forgotten it. It was about a ship on fire, and I want to hear it again. —*Hutchinson's undated letter to Charles C. Coffin, in Coffin, 293-94 (1893).* {C}

HANNAH SLATER JACOBS *Daughter of a New Jersey soldier.*

1. *When told that her father had been wounded at Fredericksburg, Lincoln exclaimed:*

Oh, what a terrible slaughter that was! Those dreadful days! Shall I ever forget them? No, never, never. —*Jacobs, 119 (1932).* {D}

This is secondhand reminiscence from Jacobs by way of her daughter.

JOHN J. JANNEY (1812-1908) *Local political leader and longtime state official in Columbus, Ohio.*

1. *During a conversation in the summer of 1864 about the Ohio Democratic congressman Samuel S. ("Sunset") Cox, Lincoln said that:*

Sunny was claiming to be a good friend of his and a good Democrat at the same time. Sunny appeared to him like Jacob Straus's old sow. She had been missing several days, when the old man said to his two boys, Jake and Sam, that the old hog was down the creek somewhere, for he saw where she had been rooting among the ironweeds, and he was going to find her. "Now you go over the creek and go down that side of it, and I'll go down this side and we'll find her, for I believe she is on both sides of the creek." I believe [Lincoln concluded] Sunny is trying to be on both sides of the creek. —*Janney, 34.* {C}

Robert Livingston Stanton (q.v.) recalled hearing Lincoln tell the same story at about the same time, but in a different context.

2. *Later the same year, while waiting to see the President in behalf of his son-in-law, who had been dismissed from army service, Janney heard him deal with a number of other callers. He declined to help an obviously pro-Confederate woman who wanted to go to Richmond, adding somewhat mischievously:*

I'll compromise with you. I don't know but I would be willing to give you a pass to Richmond if you will promise to not come back again.

To a man seeking appointment as a paymaster, he said: I have more paymasters than I have any use for. I need money much worse than paymasters. . . . I would like to trade some paymasters for some money.

A woman seeking pardon for her son was told: Now, Madam, I do not think you are treating me fairly. Your son has been tried by a sworn court and convicted upon the testimony of sworn witnesses of giving aid and comfort to the rebels by furnishing them with quinine, percussion caps, and other such things which they can't make and must have, and now you ask me to pardon him and set the verdict aside just as a matter of humanity and kindness to you. I do not think that fair to me, and while I would like to gratify you, I suspect if I should do so, it would not be two weeks before he would be doing the same thing again; and I am not at all sure but that is just what you would like to have him do.

After Lincoln had spent half an hour with a mute young woman who did her talking with a pencil and tablet, he said to Janney: That girl had no favor to ask, but she will live happier all her life because she met the President, and it is better at times to let a woman have her way and so he let her talk.

He added that: he heard everybody that wanted to be heard and usually heard all they had to say. —*Janney, 35.* {C}

WILLIAM JAYNE (1826–1916) *Springfield physician and Republican politician, brother-in-law of Lyman Trumbull. In 1861, Lincoln appointed him governor of Dakota Territory.*

1. *It is said that on the eve of the Republican state convention in June 1858, a group of party leaders was given a preview reading of the House-Divided speech and that most of them took exception to its radical quality. According to Jayne, Lincoln responded:*

My dear friends, the time has come when these sentiments should be uttered, and if it is decreed that I shall go down because of this speech, then let me go down linked to the truth; let me die in the advocacy of what is just and right. In taking this position, I do not suspect that any one of you disagree [agree?] with me as to the doctrine which I will announce in that speech; for I am sure you would all like to see me defeat Douglas.[263] It may be inexpedient for me to announce such principles at this time, but I have given the subject matter the most patient, honest, and intelligent thought that I am able to command, because I have felt at times, and now feel, that we are standing on the advanced line of a political campaign which in its results will be of more importance than any political event that will occur during the nineteenth century. I regret that my friend Herndon is the only man among you who coincides with my views and purposes in the propriety of making such a speech to the public as I have indicated to you, but I have determined in my own mind to make this speech, and in arriving at this determination, I cheerfully admit to you that I am moved to this purpose by the noble sentiments expressed in those beautiful lines of William Cullen Bryant in his poem on "The Battlefield."

Here, Lincoln quoted six verses of the poem and then continued: I am aware that many of our friends, and all of our political enemies, will say that like

Scipio I am "carrying the war into Africa"; but that is an incident of politics which none of us can help, but it is an incident which in the long run will be forgotten and ignored. We all believe that every human being, whatever may be his color, is born free, and that every human soul has an inalienable right to life, liberty, and the pursuit of happiness. The Apostle Paul said that "The just shall live by faith." This doctrine, laid down by St. Paul, was taken up by the greatest reformer of the Christian era, Martin Luther, and was adhered to with a vigor and fidelity never surpassed until it won a supreme victory, the benefits and advantages of which we are enjoying today. I will lay down these propositions in the speech I propose to make and risk the chance of winning a seat in the United States Senate because I believe the propositions are true and that ultimately we shall live to see, as Bryant says, "the victory of endurance born." —*Jayne, 39-42 (1900). {E}*

This recollection, probably stemming from one by Herndon (q.v.), is a splendid example of Lincoln myth in the process of elaboration and decoration.

2. *On Jayne's election to the state legislature in 1860:*

You seem to succeed in politics as you have succeeded in pills. If I were as lucky as you are in politics and strong enough to beat as good a man as Murray McConnell in a Democratic district for state senator, I would change my sign so that it read: "Dr. William Jayne, Purveyor of Pills and Politics. I guarantee the care of Democratic headaches and all the ailments of popular sovereignty cranks. No cure, no pay!" —*45. {C}*

3. *As president-elect in the midst of a disunion crisis, Lincoln said that:*

he would rather be hung by the neck till he was dead on the steps of the Capitol, before he would buy or beg a peaceful inauguration. —*Jayne to Lyman Trumbull, January 28, 1861, in Pratt-2, 46-47. {D}*

It is not clear whether Jayne heard Lincoln make this remark or heard about it from someone else.

JANE MARTIN JOHNS   *Wife of Dr. Harvey C. Johns of Piatt and Macon counties, Illinois.*

1. *Prosecuted by Lincoln before Judge David Davis on a charge that no one took very seriously, Johns was fined one cent and costs. When asked for an explanation, Lincoln said:*

Well, he was guilty of assault, wasn't he? And he did get battered, and, well, we needed the costs. —*Johns, 69 (1912). {E}*

An example of family folklore. Although court records reveal two cases in which Dr. Johns was accused of assault and battery, there is no evidence that Lincoln was involved in either of them or that he ever acted as prosecutor before Davis in that particular county.[264]

ANDREW JOHNSON (1808–1875)   *Pro-Union Tennessee Democrat who served as military governor of his state and in 1865 became Lincoln's second vice president.*

1. *In a speech defending his presidency on February 22, 1866, Johnson recalled that shortly before inauguration day the year before, Lincoln had said to him:*

When the amendment of the Constitution now proposed is adopted by three-fourths of the states, I am pretty near done, or, indeed, quite done, in favor of amending the Constitution, if there was one other adopted. . . .I have labored to preserve this Union. I have toiled during the four years I have been subjected to calumny and misrepresentation. My great and sole desire has been to presume these states intact under the Constitution as they were before.

When asked to specify what he proposed, his answer was: Why, it is that there should be an amendment added to the Constitution which would compel the states to send their senators and representatives to the Congress of the United States. —Johnson Papers, *X, 153. {D}*

This recollection is self-serving, and there appears to be no corroborating evidence of such a conversation.

ANNA EASTMAN JOHNSON (Born 1842)   *Daughter of a Springfield businessman who lived near the Lincolns.*

1. *In very old age, Mrs. Johnson recalled for an interviewer that Lincoln once came to see her father and said:*

Mary is having one of her spells, and I think I had better leave her for a few days. I didn't want to bother her, and I thought as you and I are about the same size, you might be kind enough to let me take one of your clean shirts. I have found that when Mrs. Lincoln gets one of these nervous spells, it is better for me to go away for a day or two. —Fiske AL, *494 (1932). {D}*

BYRON BERKELEY JOHNSON (1833–?)   *An employee of the War Department during the Civil War.*

1. *At a military hospital where a woman had been handing out moralistic tracts, one soldier with both legs amputated at the knees displayed a leaflet titled "The Sin of Dancing." Lincoln said to Johnson:*

That's the best evidence I ever saw of misapplied philanthropy. —*Johnson BB, 16 (1914). {C}*

2. *At the annual parade of the Sunday School Union, Lincoln said:*

I never see boys like those but what I wonder what is in their heads; you never can tell.

Then, according to Johnson, the President launched into the story of Daniel

Webster's dirty hands, the telling of which had already been recalled in print by Francis B. Carpenter (q.v.) and others. —17. {D}

This is one of those instances where it is impossible to distinguish between corroboration and echo.

RICHARD W. JOHNSON (1827–1897) *A Union general from Kentucky.*

  1. *Soon after the beginning of the war, Lincoln remarked to Johnson:*

that military necessity demanded the construction of a railroad from Louisville to Knoxville, passing through Cumberland Gap; that if Knoxville could be taken, it would break the backbone of the rebellion. —*Johnson RW, 50. {C}*

PRINCE DE JOINVILLE (1818–1900) *Younger son of Louis Philippe and uncle of the Comte de Paris, Orleanist claimant to the French throne. Joinville spent considerable time in the United States during the Civil War and in 1862 published a book on the Army of the Potomac.*

  1. *Perhaps on September 20, 1861, when Joinville and members of his family are known to have visited the White House, he asked Lincoln what his policy was and received this reply:*

I have none. I pass my life in preventing the storm from blowing down the tent, and I drive in the pegs as fast as they are pulled up. —*Related by Joinville at a banquet in Langres, undated clipping in the Nicolay Papers. {C}*

John M. Palmer (q.v.) also quoted Lincoln as saying that he had no policy.

EDWARD F. JONES (1828–1913) *The colonel commanding the Sixth Massachusetts militia regiment, which marched into Washington on April 19, 1861, after suffering casualties while passing through a riotous Baltimore.*

  1. *In greeting Jones upon his arrival, Lincoln said:*

If you had not arrived tonight, we should have been in the hands of the rebels before morning. —*Jones to Daniel Butterfield, April 19, 1901, in Butterfield, 29. {C}*

THOMAS D. JONES (1811–1881) *Ohio sculptor who made two busts of Lincoln from life, the first during the secession winter of 1860–61 and the second in 1864. In March 1865, Lincoln indicated a desire that Jones should have one of "those moderate sized consulates which facilitate artists a little [in] their profession."*[265]

  1. *In late December 1860, as Jones was setting to work:*

I like your mode. When Mr. Volk of Chicago made a bust of me, he took a plaster cast of my face, a process that was anything but agreeable. —*Jones TD, 5 (1871). {C}*

  2. *To a visitor who asked "Don't you know me?" Lincoln replied:*

I may have met you before, as I have thousands, but I cannot recall your former face at present. —*Jones TD, 7.* {C}

3. *Asked for his opinion of the bust as it began to take shape:*

I think it looks very much like the critter. —*Jones TD, 12.* {C}

"Those," Jones adds, "were the exact words."

4. *Upon examining a very long letter of application for a position, Lincoln remarked:*

That man ought to be sent to the penitentiary or lunatic asylum. —*Jones to William Linn McMillen, February 11, 1861, in Temple, 450.* {A}

5. *When Jones presented him a friend's gift of a whistle made from a pig's tail, Lincoln said:*

Tell Russell I thank him for his valuable present. When I get to Washington, I will use it to call my cabinet together. —*Presumably related by Jones in a letter to A. P. Russell, quoted in Russell AP, 6.* {D}

ADELINE JUDD   *Wife of Norman B. Judd.*

1. *Lincoln spent a midsummer evening in the late 1850s with the Judds at their lakefront home in Chicago.*[266] *As they sat on the porch looking at the stars, Lincoln began to speak:*

of the mystery which for ages enshrouded and shut out those distant worlds above us from our own; of the poetry and beauty which was seen and felt by seers of old when they contemplated Orion and Arcturus as they wheeled, seemingly around the earth, in their nightly course; of the discoveries since the invention of the telescope, which had thrown a flood of light and knowledge on what before was incomprehensible and mysterious; of the wonderful computations of scientists who had measured the miles of seemingly endless space which separated the planets in our solar system from our central sun, and our sun from other suns, which were now gemming the heavens above us with their resplendent beauty.

He speculated on: the possibilities of knowledge which the increased power of the lens would give in the years to come; and then the wonderful discoveries of late centuries as proving that beings endowed with such capabilities as man must be immortal and created for some high and noble end by Him who had spoken those numberless worlds into existence and made man a little lower than the angels that he might comprehend the glories and wonders of his creation.

Turning to a broader discussion of other discoveries, he gave a summary of all the inventions referred to in the Old Testament, and when Mrs. Judd expressed surprise at his biblical knowledge, he explained: that, discussing with some friend the relative age of the discovery and use of the precious metals, he went to the Bible to satisfy himself, and became so interested in his researches that he made a memoranda of the different discoveries and inventions; that soon after, he was invited to lecture before some literary society. . . in Bloomington; that the interest he had felt in the study convinced him that the subject would interest others, and he therefore prepared and delivered his lecture on the "Age of Different Inventions." —*Oldroyd, 521–23 (1882). {D}*

Mrs. Judd's vagueness about the date and circumstances casts some doubt upon the reliability of this interesting recollection.

NORMAN B. JUDD (1815–1878) *Illinois Republican leader who played a leading role in securing Lincoln the presidential nomination and whom Lincoln appointed minister to Prussia.*

 1. Before the Freeport debate on August 27, 1858, Lincoln prepared his replies to the seven questions propounded by Douglas in their first encounter at Ottawa. Judd later recalled that when he suggested some verbal changes in order to make the answers more palatable to Republicans in the northern part of the state, Lincoln refused to budge, saying:

Now, gentlemen, that is all. I wouldn't tomorrow mislead any gentleman in that audience to be made president of the United States. —*Judd interview, February 28, 1876, in Nicolay Papers. {D}*

The circumstances of this alleged exchange, as described by Judd, do not fit other evidence.[267]

 2. It is said that a group of advisers urged Lincoln not to ask his famous second question at Freeport and that he replied:

I am after larger game. The battle of 1860 is worth a hundred of this. —*Judd's statement to William H. Herndon, recalled in Herndon to Weik, October 2, 1890 (10:2721–24), Herndon-Weik Collection. {D}*

According to Herndon, several other men besides Judd told him that Lincoln made such a statement, but contemporary evidence casts doubt upon the whole story, and Herndon himself expressed reservations about it. The quotation first appeared in an 1860 campaign biography by one of the editors of the Chicago Press and Tribune.[268]

 3. On February 21, 1861, at Philadelphia, Lincoln responded to the advice that he leave for Washington sooner than scheduled in order to foil a rumored plot to assassinate him:

I cannot go tonight. I have promised to raise the flag over Independence Hall tomorrow morning and to visit the legislature at Harrisburg. Beyond that, I have no engagements. Any plan that may be adopted that will enable me to fulfill these two promises I will carry out, and you can tell me what is concluded upon tomorrow.

The next morning, when it was suggested that the other members of the traveling party should be informed of the change in schedule, Lincoln replied: I reckon they will laugh at us, Judd, but you had better get them together.

After the group had assembled and heard the information gathered by detective Allan Pinkerton, Lincoln said: I have thought over this matter considerably since I went over the ground with Pinkerton last night. The appearance of Mr. Frederick Seward, with warning from another source, confirms my belief in Mr. Pinkerton's statement. Unless there are some other reasons, besides fear of ridicule, I am disposed to carry out Judd's plan. *—Judd to Pinkerton, November 3, 1867, in Pinkerton, 19, 21, 22. {C}*

At about the same time, Judd told approximately the same story, with variant quotations, in an undated statement to Herndon (11:3131-40).

GEORGE W. JULIAN (1817-1899)   *Radical Republican congressman from Indiana.*

1. *In 1861, when Julian protested the selection of a fellow Indiana politician, David P. Holloway, as commissioner of patents, arguing that he was incompetent and unworthy:*

There is much force in what you say, but in the balancing of matters, I guess I shall have to appoint him. *—Julian, 183 (1884). {C}*

2. *After hearing a speech by Horace Greeley at the Smithsonian in the winter of 1861-62:*

That address is full of good thoughts, and I would like to take the manuscript home with me and carefully read it over some Sunday. *—Rice AT, 60 (1886). {C}*

3. *In March 1863, on the problem of finding another command for Frémont, Lincoln said that:*

he did not know where to place him, and that it reminded him of the old man who advised his son to take a wife, to which the young man responded, "Whose wife shall I take?"

When Julian remarked that restoration of Frémont to duty would stir the country as no other appointment could, Lincoln replied: It would stir the country favorably on one side and stir it the other way on the other. It would please Frémont's friends and displease the conservatives; and that is all I can see in the **stirring** argument. My proclamation was to stir the country; but it has done about as much harm as good. *—Rice AT, 55-56. {C}*

According to Alexander K. McClure (q.v.), Lincoln used the same story when urged to make a certain diplomatic appointment.

4. *In the summer of 1864, responding to Julian's complaint that a Hollo-*

way newspaper in his district was refusing to recognize his renomination for Congress:

Your nomination is as binding on Republicans as mine, and you can rest assured that Mr. Holloway shall support you, openly and unconditionally, or lose his head. —*Julian, 244-45. {C}*

5. *Asked on July 2, 1864, about confiscating the landed estates of rebels, Lincoln replied:*

that when he prepared his veto of our law on the subject two years before, he had not examined the matter thoroughly, but that on further reflection, and on reading Solicitor Whiting's law argument, he had changed his opinion, and thought he would now sign a bill striking at the fee, if we would send it to him. —*Julian, 245. {C}*

JOHN LANGDON KAINE *A Springfield youngster in the 1850s.*

  1. *On the art of delivering an oration:*

Try to think they're your own words and talk them as you would talk them to me. —*Kaine, 557 (1913). {C}*

  2. *On the oratorical uses of literature:*

It is a pleasure to be able to quote lines to fit any occasion. . . . the Bible is the richest source of pertinent quotations. —557. {C}*

ELIZABETH KECKLEY (1818-1907) *Dressmaker, a former slave who bought her freedom in the 1850s and became Mary Lincoln's closest confidante in the White House. The fact that her memoirs were ghostwritten tends to diminish their credibility.*

  1. *Concerning a dress with a long train and a low neckline:*

Whew! our cat has a long tail tonight. Mother, it is my opinion, if some of that tail was nearer the head, it would be in better style. —*Keckley, 101 (1868). {C}*

  2. *During one of her outbursts after the death of their son Willie, Lincoln led his wife to a window, pointed to the insane asylum, and said:*

Mother, do you see that large white building on the hill yonder? Try and control your grief, or it will drive you mad, and we may have to send you there. —104-5. {D}*

This story is suspect because the building in question was not visible from the White House.[269]

3. *On Stonewall Jackson:*

He is a brave, honest Presbyterian soldier; what a pity that we should have to fight such a gallant fellow! If we only had such a man to lead the armies of the North, the country would not be appalled with so many disasters. — *137. {D}*

4. *When Mary, worried about his safety, urged him not to go out alone:*

All imagination. What does any one want to harm me for? Don't worry about me, mother, as if I were a little child, for no one is going to molest me. —*121. {C}*

5. *On the two White House goats:*

I believe they are the kindest and best goats in the world. See how they sniff the clear air and skip and play in the sunshine. Whew! what a jump. . . Madame Elizabeth, did you ever before see such an active goat? . . . He feeds on my bounty, and jumps with joy. Do you think we could call him a bounty-jumper? But I flatter the bounty-jumper. Mr. Goat is far above him. I would rather wear his horns and hairy coat through life than demean my-self to the level of the man who plunders the national treasury in the name of patriotism. The man who enlists into the service for a consideration and deserts the moment he receives his money but to repeat the play, is bad enough; but the men who manipulate the grand machine and who simply make the bounty-jumper their agent in an outrageous fraud are far worse. They are beneath the worms that crawl in the dark, hidden places of earth. —*179-80. {D}*

6. *Fiercely opposed to Robert's entering military service, Mary said that the loss of one son was as much as she could bear. Lincoln replied:*

But many a poor mother has given up all her sons, and our son is not more dear to us than the sons of other people are to their mothers. . . . The services of every man who loves his country are required in this war. You should take a liberal instead of a selfish view of the question, Mother. — *121-22. {C}*

Emilie Todd Helm (q.v.) recorded a similar remark in her diary.

7. *When Mary told him to beware of Chase:*

Mother, you are too suspicious. I give you credit for sagacity, but you are disposed to magnify trifles. Chase is a patriot, and one of my best friends. . . . True, I receive letters daily from all parts of the country telling me not to trust Chase, but then these letters are written by the political enemies of the Secretary, and it would be unjust and foolish to pay any attention to them. —*129. {D}*

It is doubtful that Lincoln at any time would have called the Secretary one of his best friends, and it is most unlikely that in late 1863 or early 1864, when this conversation supposedly took place, he would have brushed aside warnings about Chase's political intentions.[270]

8. *Replying to Mary's assertion that Seward was even worse than Chase because he had no principle:*

Mother, you are mistaken; your prejudices are so violent that you do not stop to reason. Seward is an able man, and the country, as well as myself, can trust him. —*131.* {C}

9. *On the day of his assassination, looking at a picture of Robert E. Lee:*

It is a good face; it is the face of a noble, noble, brave man. I am glad that the war is over at last. —*137.* {D}

WILLIAM D. KELLEY (1814–1890) *Pennsylvanian elected fifteen times to Congress, beginning in 1860. A Radical Republican during the Civil War and Reconstruction, he came to be called "Pig Iron" Kelley because of his enthusiasm for protective tariffs.*

1. *Many bitter Republicans blamed Lincoln for the party's defeats in the state and congressional elections of 1862. They were especially angry about his retention of McClellan in command of the Army of the Potomac. One Pennsylvania politician was quoted as saying he would be glad to hear some morning that the President had been found hanging from a lamppost at the door of the White House. Lincoln commented:*

You need not be surprised to find that that suggestion has been executed any morning; the violent preliminaries to such an event would not surprise me. I have done things lately that must be incomprehensible to the people, and which cannot now be explained. —*Rice AT, 276 (1886).* {C}

2. *Several weeks after the battle of Antietam, Lincoln spoke of McClellan as a man who had been reappointed for a limited purpose:*

Whatever the troops and people may think and say of his failure to capture Lee's army and supplies, my censure should be tempered by the consciousness of the fact that I did not restore him to command for aggressive fighting, but as an organizer and a good hand at defending a position.

Acknowledging that McClellan, by his incessant complaints, had damaged the morale of his troops and that he had sacrificed Pope in the second Bull Run campaign, Lincoln said that: to entrust to him the rescue of the army from its demoralization was a good deal like curing the bite with the hair of the dog.

He went on to declare that: he regarded his position at the time of McClellan's restoration as a striking and noteworthy illustration of the dangers to which republican institutions were subjected by wars of such magnitude as might produce ambitious and rival commanders; for it must be admitted that the civil power of the government was then subordinate to the military, and though he acted as commander in chief, he found himself in that season of insubordination, panic, and general demoralization consciously under military duress. McClellan, even while fighting battles which should produce no result but the expenditure of men and means, had contrived to keep the troops with him, and by charging each new failure to some alleged dereliction of the Secretary of War and President, had created an impression among them that the administration was hostile to him and withheld vital elements of success that should have been accorded to him, and which, in some instances, he falsely represented as having been promised to him. He [Lincoln] believed the restoration to command of McClellan, Porter, and other of his chiefs, in the face of the treasonable misconduct of which they had been so flagrantly guilty in the sacrifice of Pope's army, was the greatest trial and most painful duty of his official life. Yet, situated as he was, it seemed to be his duty, and in opposition to every member of his cabinet, he performed it and felt no regret for what he had done.

I am now [he continued] stronger with the Army of the Potomac than McClellan. The supremacy of the civil power has been restored, and the executive is again master of the situation. The troops know that if I made a mistake in substituting Pope for McClellan, I was capable of rectifying it by again trusting him. They know, too, that neither Stanton nor I withheld anything from him at Antietam and that it was not the administration but their own former idol who surrendered the just results of their terrible sacrifices and closed the great fight as a drawn battle, when, had he thrown Porter's corps of fresh men and other available troops upon Lee's army, he would inevitably have driven it in disorder to the river and captured most of it before sunset. —*Kelley, 73-75 (1885). {D}*

This lengthy recollective quotation, part of Kelley's response to an article by McClellan, was undoubtedly colored by his hostility to the General.

3. In discussion of a successor to McClellan, Kelley favored Hooker over Burnside because the situation, he said, called for a determined fighter rather than a housekeeper. Lincoln replied:

I am not so sure that we are not in search of a housekeeper. I tell you, Kelley, the successful management of an army requires a good deal of faithful housekeeping. More fight will be got out of well-fed and well-cared-for soldiers and animals than can be got out of those that are required to make long marches with empty stomachs, and whose strength and cheerfulness are impaired by the failure to distribute proper rations at proper seasons. —*Rice AT, 278. {C}*

4. The actor John McDonough visited the White House one evening in Kelley's company, and Lincoln said to him:

I am very glad to see you, sir, for I want to learn something of Shakespeare. I don't get much time to study his writings, and I want to put some questions to you that I put to Mr. Hackett. I will tell you frankly that Mr. Hackett's replies on one or two of the points were very unsatisfactory to me; they almost impressed me with a doubt as to whether he studies Shakespeare thoroughly, or only the acting plays.

Turning to an army chaplain also present, Lincoln said: Probably you do not know that the acting plays are not the plays as Shakespeare wrote them. *Richard III*, for instance, begins with passages from *Henry VI*; then you get a portion of *Richard III*; then more of *Henry VI*; and then there is one of the best known soliloquies, which is not Shakespeare's at all, but was written by quite another man—by Colley Cibber, was it not, Mr. McDonough? — *Kelley's speech, April 26, 1865, in Philadelphia* Telegraph, *April 26, 1865.* {C}

A variant account is in Rice AT, 265-67.

WILLIAM PITT KELLOGG (1830-1918) *Illinois lawyer and politician whom Lincoln twice appointed to federal office. He later became a United States senator and the Reconstruction governor of Louisiana.*

1. *Present at the Republican state convention in Bloomington on May 29, 1856, Kellogg later recalled that Lincoln, in the course of his famous "lost speech," uttered the words:*

You can fool all the people some of the time; you can fool some of the people all the time; but you can't fool all the people all the time. — *Kellogg, 323 (1909).* {D}

Historians are generally disposed to doubt that this epigram originated with Lincoln or that he used it at Bloomington in 1856, but Richard Price Morgan (q.v.) lent partial support to Kellogg's recollection.[271]

2. *Concerning the same speech, Kellogg agreed with other persons who remembered that it reached a climax with the words:*

We say to the southern disunionists, we **won't** go out of the Union, and you **shan't.** —*323.* {C}

3. *After the last speech of his life on April 11, 1865, Lincoln said with respect to reconstruction and the situation in Louisiana:*

I am trying to blaze a way through the swamp. —*333.* {C}

4. *During the same conversation, he remarked:*

Finances will rule the country for the next fifty years. —*334.* {C}

JOSEPH P. KENT *A carpenter's son who, as a youth in the late 1850s, lived near the Lincolns on Eighth Street in Springfield.*

1. *Having obtained permission to use the Lincoln horse one Sunday in 1859,*

Kent ventured to ask whether he might also borrow the family carriage. Lincoln said with a smile:

No, Joseph, there are two things I will not loan, my wife and my carriage. —*Kent's recollections published in the* Illinois State Journal *(Springfield), January 28, 1909.*[272] {C}

ELISHA W. KEYES (1828–1910)   *Wisconsin Republican who eventually became one of the dominant figures in state politics.*

  1. *In the company of Congressman Luther Hanchett, Keyes visited the White House and secured appointment as postmaster at Madison. During the interview, Lincoln remarked concerning patronage:*

The fact is, Hanchett, I have got more pigs than I have teats. —*Keyes statement in a newspaper clipping, Lincoln Collection-Brown.*[273] {C}

ERASMUS D. KEYES (1810–1895)   *Career army officer who became a corps commander and major-general of volunteers.*

  1. *According to Keyes, his journal for March 29, 1861, recorded the President as saying that:*

his administration would be broken up unless a more decided policy was adopted, and if General Scott could not carry out his views, some other person might. —*Keyes, 378.* {B}

JAMES W. KEYES   *Springfield tailor who served terms as postmaster and justice of the peace.*

  1. *Lincoln gave as his reason for belief in a creator:*

that in view of the order and harmony of all nature which we behold, it would have been more miraculous to have come about by chance than to have been created and arranged by some great thinking power.

With respect to the divinity of Jesus, he said: that it had better be taken for granted, for by the test of reason we might become infidels on that subject, for evidence of Christ's divinity came to us in somewhat doubtful shape; but that the system of Christianity was an ingenious one, at least, and perhaps was calculated to do good. —*Keyes statement, undated but probably c. 1866, Herndon-Springer, II, 439.*[274] {C}

EDWARD N. KIRK (1802–1874)   *A Congregational minister in Massachusetts.*

  1. *In July 1864, a time when his political prospects seemed dim, Lincoln told Kirk:*

I have faith in the people. They will not consent to disunion. The danger is, they are misled. Let them know the truth, and the country is safe.

To Kirk's suggestion that he was wearing himself out with work, he responded: I can't work less, but it isn't that. Work never troubles me. Things look badly, and I can't avoid anxiety. Personally, I care nothing about a re-election, but if our divisions defeat us, I fear for the country.

When Kirk said that he had never despaired of eventual victory, the President replied: Neither have I, but I may not live to see it. I feel a presentiment that I shall not outlast the rebellion. When it is over, my work will be done. — *Kirk to the Boston* Journal, *reprinted in the* Liberator, *May 19, 1865.*[275] {D}

The final sentences here, like all such talk recalled after the assassination, should probably be viewed with a certain amount of skepticism.

JOSEPH KIRKLAND (1830–1894)   *Union officer from Chicago, later a lawyer, editor, and novelist in the vein of midwestern realism.*

1. *One day in the fall of 1862, when Kirkland visited the White House and was chatting away merrily with the presidential secretaries, Lincoln looked into the room and said:*

I thought you were laughing pretty loud in here and that I should like to come in and laugh too. — Prairie Chicken, *July 1865, as reprinted in Mabbott, 166.*[276] {C}

HENRY W. KNIGHT   *A wounded soldier assigned to guard duty at the War Department in 1864.*

1. *One rainy night, Lincoln said as he was about to leave:*

Don't come out in this storm with me tonight, boys. I have my umbrella and can get home safely without you.

When Knight protested that they dared not disobey orders, he replied: No, I suppose not; for if Stanton should learn that you had let me return alone, he would have you court-martialed and shot inside of twenty-four hours. — *Knight, 446 (1895).* {C}

2. *On another night, Lincoln looked at two fire axes on the wall and remarked:*

Well, now, I wonder if I could lift one of those axes up by the end of the handle.

He proceeded to do so, holding it at arm's length for several seconds, after which he said: When I used to split rails, thirty years ago in Illinois, I could lift two axes that way, and I believe I could do it now, and I will try it some other time. — *446.* {C}

Egbert L. Viele (q.v.) also told of Lincoln's performing this feat.

GUSTAVE P. KOERNER (1809–1896)   *German-American political leader in Illinois whom Lincoln appointed minister to Spain in 1862.*

1. *January 6, 1861, in a discussion of cabinet appointments, when Koerner and Norman B. Judd urged him not to include Cameron, Lincoln said:*

There has been delegation after delegation from Pennsylvania, hundreds of letters, and the cry is "Cameron, Cameron!" Besides, you know I have already fixed on Chase, Seward, and Bates, my competitors at the convention. The Pennsylvania people say: "If you leave out Cameron you disgrace him." Is there not something in that?

To Koerner's protest that Cameron had the reputation of being a corrupt politician, he replied: I know, I know, but can I get along if that state should oppose my administration? —*Koerner, II, 114 (1909).* {C}

2. *In September 1864, after the nomination of McClellan by the Democrats, Lincoln remarked uneasily to Koerner:*

that the General was very strong with the army and that General Frémont would make such a division in New York and some of the northern states as to defeat him. He thought from what he could learn of the Cleveland convention which had nominated Frémont that he would lose . . . the German element, which held the balance of power in Missouri, Wisconsin, and Illinois. —432. {C}

JULIAN KUNE   *A Hungarian exile who settled in Chicago and became a lawyer.*
    1. *Talking with Kune in Springfield before the election of 1860, Lincoln said:*

No man has the right to keep his fellow man in bondage, be he black or white, and the time will come, and must come, when there will not be a single slave within the borders of this country. —*Kune, 87–88 (1911).* {C}

2. *After the firing on Fort Sumter, Kune and several other Illinoisans consulted Lincoln about a proposed regiment of foreign-born volunteers from Chicago. He said:*

I see that Cameron is opposed to accepting any more regiments. I am afraid I cannot help you, for my influence with this administration don't amount to much. . . . we have 75,000 men already in the field, and if we should accept any more we would not be able to feed them. —98. {C}

According to Kune, he nevertheless persuaded Lincoln to order acceptance of this, the 24th Illinois, known as the [Friedrich] Hecker Regiment.

JOHN W. LAMAR   *A neighbor of the Lincolns in Indiana.*
    1. *A man bragged that his horse had been run a great distance in record speed and "never fetched a long breath." Lincoln replied:*

I presume, sir, he fetched a good many short ones. —*Lamar to Herndon, May 18, 1867 (9:1464–66) Herndon-Weik Collection; also in Herndon, I, 46, with a different date assigned.*[277] {D}

Remembering words spoken by Lincoln as president was one thing, but here the question is whether the bright remark of a youth so impressed a small boy that he remembered it some forty years afterward.

WARD HILL LAMON (1828–1893) *Virginia-born lawyer in Danville, Illinois, the one friend of his circuit-riding days who accompanied Lincoln to Washington and remained closely associated with him throughout his presidency. Lamon was Lincoln's only companion on the covert trip through Baltimore in February 1861. Appointed United States marshal for the District of Columbia, he continued to assume at times the role of presidential bodyguard. No one appears to have worried as much as he did about Lincoln's safety, and he later asserted that but for him, the assassination would have occurred much earlier than it did.*[278] *At the same time, Lamon became involved with Leonard Swett and others in certain business ventures that seem to have depended in some part upon his influence with the President. In July 1864, several days after Lincoln refused to veto a bill reducing his fees as marshal, Lamon wrote to the governor of Illinois that for three years he had been a "slave" to his friends at the cost of much money and some self-respect.*[279]

After Lincoln's death, Lamon returned to the private practice of law in a firm headed by Jeremiah S. Black, who had been a member of Buchanan's cabinet. In 1872, he published a biography of Lincoln covering only the prepresidential years—one that many people considered scandalous because of its treatment of Lincoln's parentage, marriage, and religion. Based in considerable part on material purchased from William H. Herndon, the book was actually written by Black's son Chauncey, a silent partner in the enterprise. It contained virtually nothing in the way of reminiscence by Lamon himself and has long since fallen into almost total disuse. A second book, Recollections of Abraham Lincoln, *appeared two years after Lamon's death, having been stitched together by his daughter from letters, newspaper articles, and fragments of manuscript that he left behind. This work, though not without its skeptical critics among Lincoln scholars, has been widely accepted and quoted as source material. Yet there is good reason to believe that more than a few of its supposedly firsthand anecdotes of Lincoln were derived from Lamon's reading, rather than his experience, and that more than a little of its quotation of Lincoln was simply invented.*[280]

1. According to Lamon, it was at Danville in the fall of 1847 that he first met Lincoln, who said to him:

Going to try your hand at the law, are you? I should know at a glance that you were a Virginian, but I don't think you would succeed at splitting rails. That was my occupation at your age, and I don't think I have taken as much pleasure in anything else from that day to this.

When Lamon protested that he had done a good deal of hard manual labor, Lincoln said with amusement: Oh, yes, you Virginians shed barrels of perspiration while standing off at a distance and superintending the work your slaves do for you. It is different with us. Here it is every fellow for himself, or he doesn't get there. —*Lamon-2, 14–15 (1895, 1911). {D}*

This alleged reference to rail-splitting and slavery in the first few minutes of their acquaintance is a little too pat to inspire credence.

2. Upbraided by his fellow attorneys and by Judge David Davis for returning half of a legal fee, Lincoln declared:

That money comes out of the pocket of a poor, demented girl, and I would rather starve than swindle her in this manner. —*Lamon-2, 19. {C}*

3. During the debate at Charleston, Illinois, in 1858, Lincoln initiated a brief exchange with Orlando B. Ficklin, a former Democratic congressman, whom he laid hold of and drew to the front of the platform. Afterward, Lamon recalled, Ficklin complained of having had all the Democracy nearly shaken out of him. Lincoln replied:

That reminds me of what Paul said to Agrippa, which in language and substance I will formulate as follows: I would to God that such Democracy as you folks here in Egypt have were not only almost but altogether shaken out of, not only you, but all that heard me this day, and that you would all join in assisting in shaking off the shackles of the bondmen by all legitimate means, so that this country may be made free as the good Lord intended it.

When Ficklin then suggested that Lincoln and his party might soon be advocating a war to kill off proslavery people, Lincoln answered: No, I will never advocate such an extremity, but it will be well for you folks if you don't force such a necessity on the country. —*Lamon-2, 25–26. {E}*

Lamon's account of the public exchange between Lincoln and Ficklin is so inaccurate as to cast added doubt on his recollection of their ensuing private conversation, if they had one.[281]

4. During the journey from Springfield to Washington in February 1861, Lincoln remarked to Lamon that:

he had done much hard work in his life, but to make speeches day after day, with the object of speaking and saying nothing, was the hardest work he ever had done.

He added: I wish that this thing were through with and I could find peace and quiet somewhere. —*Lamon-2, 33–34. {C}*

5. According to Lamon, Lincoln said to him in Harrisburg, Pennsylvania, on February 22:

I guess I have lost my certificate of moral character, written by myself. Bob has lost my gripsack containing my inaugural address. I want you to help me to find it. I feel a good deal as the old member of the Methodist Church did when he lost his wife at the camp meeting and went up to an old elder of the church and asked him if he could tell him whereabouts in hell his wife was. In fact, I am in a worse fix than my Methodist friend; for if it were nothing but a wife that was missing, mine would be sure to pop up serenely somewhere. That address may be a loss to more than one husband in this country, but I shall be the greatest sufferer. —*Lamon-2, 36-37. {E}*

Such inane loquacity (supposedly indulged in at a moment of crisis) is more Lamon's style than Abraham Lincoln's. Furthermore, an account of the incident, purportedly as related by Lincoln to Benjamin Perley Poore (q.v.) and with details similar to those supplied by Lamon, had already been published. The story of the temporarily lost inaugural address has also been associated with Cleveland, but Robert Lincoln himself declared that the incident took place in Indianapolis.[282]

6. After the missing bag had been found, Lincoln decided to keep the inaugural address on his person. He said that:

he knew a fellow once who had saved up fifteen hundred dollars and had placed it in a private banking establishment. The bank soon failed, and he afterward received ten percent of his investment. He then took his one hundred and fifty dollars and deposited it in a savings bank, where he was sure it would be safe. In a short time, this bank also failed, and he received at the final settlement ten percent on the amount deposited. When the fifteen dollars was paid over to him, he held it in his hand and looked at it thoughtfully; then he said, "Now, darn you, I have got you reduced to a portable shape, so I'll put you in my pocket." —*Lamon-2, 37. {D}*

7. When it was decided that Lincoln would go to Willard's Hotel, instead of to a private house, on his arrival in Washington, he remarked:

This arrangement, I fear, will give mortal offense to our friends, but I think the arrangement a good one. I can readily see that many other well-meant plans will "gang aglee," but I am sorry. The truth is, I suppose I am now public property and a public inn is the place where people can have access to me. —*Lamon Papers: Recollections of Abraham Lincoln, Drafts and Anecdotes, folder 2 (c. 1887). {C}*

8. Lamon recalled that when Lincoln proposed to send him to Charleston in early April 1861, Seward argued against it, saying that the South Carolinians might kill him. Lincoln replied:

Mr. Secretary, I have known Lamon to be in many a close place and he has never been in one that he didn't get out of. By jing, I'll risk him. Go, Lamon, and God bless you! Bring back a palmetto, if you can't bring us good news. —*Lamon-2, 70. {D}*

9. According to Lamon, the President gave him "private instructions" to execute the fugitive-slave laws in the District of Columbia until they were modified or repealed. He added:

In doing this, you will receive much adverse criticism and a good deal of downright abuse from members of Congress. This is certain to come, but it will be not so much intended for you as for me. —*Lamon-2*, 255. {D}

From the evidence, it appears that Lamon's controversial policy with respect to fugitive slaves was largely his own and that Lincoln sought to mediate between the Marshal and his antislavery critics.

10. *After the issuance of legal tender notes or "greenbacks" had begun in 1862, Lamon warned Lincoln about the danger of fraud, and Lincoln called in the Secretary of the Treasury, saying:*

Mr. Chase, this marshal of ours has been frightening me nearly out of my boots.

In the discussion that followed, Chase insisted that enough checks against dishonesty had been installed. Lincoln said: Don't think, Mr. Chase, I could have any doubt about your integrity or that of Mr. Spinner, but you are both known to me and the country.[283] Others who are great factors in this money-making business are not so well known, and I can see that they have the power, if corrupt enough, to use it to bankrupt the country. —*Lamon Papers: Drafts and Anecdotes, folder 9 (c. 1889). A revised and expanded version is in Lamon-2*, 219. {D}

11. *On one occasion, Lincoln said to Lamon:*

In God's name, if anyone can do better in my place than I have done, or am endeavoring to do, let him try his hand at it, and no one will be better contented than myself. —*Lamon-2*, 182. {C}

12. *According to Lamon, he "often heard" Lincoln say with respect to Republican attacks on him:*

I would rather be dead than, as president, thus abused in the house of my friends. —*Lamon-2*, 261. {C}

13. *At another time, we are told, Lincoln unburdened himself as follows:*

You know better than any man living that from my boyhood up, my ambition was to be president. I am president of one part of this divided country at least, but look at me! I wish I had never been born. It is a white elephant on my hands and hard to manage. With a fire in my front and rear, having to contend with the jealousies of the military commanders and not receiving that cordial cooperation and support from Congress which could reasonably be expected, with an active and formidable enemy in the field threatening the very life-blood of the government, my position is anything but a bed of roses. —*Lamon-2*, 182–83. {D}

It is not easy to believe that Lincoln was responsible for this cluster of clichés.

14. *With reference to those Republicans who led a congressional move to drive Lamon out of the marshal's office in 1862, Lincoln is quoted as saying:*

I have great sympathy for these men, because of their temper and their weakness, but I am thankful that the good Lord has given to the vicious ox short horns; for if their physical courage were equal to their vicious dispositions, some of us in this neck of the woods would get hurt. —*Lamon-2, 260. {D}*

Although Lincoln was no doubt unhappy about the attack on Lamon, this recollection is obviously self-serving, and its language reflects Lamon's bitter hostility to antislavery radicals.

15. *One morning in August 1862, the loquacious Lincoln of Lamon's* Recollections *described an adventure he had had the night before. He began by saying:*

You know I have always told you I thought you an idiot that ought to be put in a strait jacket for your apprehensions of my personal danger from assassination. You also know that the way we skulked into this city in the first place has been a source of shame and regret to me; for it did look so cowardly. . . . Well, I don't now propose to make you my father-confessor and acknowledge a change of heart; yet I am free to admit that just now I don't know what to think; I am staggered. Understand me, I do not want to oppose my pride of opinion against light and reason, but I am in such a state of "betweenity" in my conclusions that I can't say that the judgment of this court is prepared to proclaim a reliable decision upon the facts presented.

Finally, he got to the point: Last night, about eleven o'clock, I went out to the Soldiers' Home alone, riding "Old Abe," as you call him, and when I arrived at the foot of the hill on the road leading to the entrance of the Home grounds, I was jogging along at a slow gait, immersed in deep thought, contemplating what was next to happen in the unsettled state of affairs, when suddenly I was aroused—I may say the arousement lifted me out of my saddle, as well as out of my wits—by the report of a rifle, and seemingly the gunner was not fifty yards from where my contemplations ended and my accelerated transit began. My erratic namesake, with little warning, gave proof of decided dissatisfaction at the racket, and with one reckless bound he unceremoniously separated me from my eight-dollar plug hat, with which I parted company without any assent, expressed or implied, upon my part. At a breakneck speed, we soon arrived in a haven of safety. Meanwhile I was left in doubt whether death was more desirable from being thrown from a runaway federal horse or as the tragic result of a rifle ball fired by a disloyal bushwhacker in the middle of the night. . . .

Now, in the face of this testimony in favor of your theory of danger to me, personally, I can't bring myself to believe that anyone has shot or will deliberately shoot at me with the purpose of killing me, although I must acknowledge that I heard this fellow's bullet whistle at an uncomfortably short distance from these headquarters of mine. I have about concluded that the shot was the result of accident. It may be that someone on his return from a day's hunt, regardless of the course of his discharge, fired off his gun as a precautionary measure of safety to his family after reaching his house.

I tell you there is no time on record equal to that made by the two Old Abes on that occasion. The historic ride of John Gilpin and Henry Wilson's memorable display of bareback equestrianship on the stray army mule from the scenes of the battle of Bull Run a year ago are nothing in comparison to mine, either in point of time made or in ludicrous pageantry. My only advantage over these worthies was in having no observers. I can truthfully say that one of the Abes was frightened on this occasion, but modesty forbids my mentioning which of us is entitled to that distinguished honor. This whole thing seems farcical. No good can result at this time from giving it publicity. It does seem to me that I am in more danger from the augmentation of imaginary peril than from a judicious silence, be the danger ever so great; and, moreover, I do not want it understood that I share your apprehensions. I never have.[284] —*Lamon-2, 266–69.* {D}

Although the burlesque style must undoubtedly be charged to Lamon, John W. Nichols (q.v.) recalled just such an incident, declaring that Lincoln's hat was later found with a bullet hole in it. However, his testimony, though unclear, seems to place the adventure in August 1864, rather than August 1862.

16. *Lamon quotes Lincoln as saying in August 1862:*

I am determined to borrow no trouble. I believe in the right and that it will ultimately prevail, and I believe it is the inalienable right of man, unimpaired even by this dreadful distraction of our country, to be happy or miserable at his own election, and I for one make choice of the former alternative. —*Lamon-2, 269.* {D}

Pursuit *of happiness was the inalienable right that Lincoln believed in; there is no evidence that he thought* **being** *happy was such a right.*

17. *After repeating without attribution a story first told in the New York* Times *of January 15, 1866, about how Lincoln had refused a woman's request that a certain church in Alexandria be released from its use as a military hospital, Lamon recalled that afterwards, Lincoln said the incident reminded him:*

of the story of the young man who had an aged father and mother owning considerable property. The young man, being an only son and believing that the old people had lived out their usefulness, assassinated them both. He was accused, tried, and convicted of the murder. When the judge came to pass sentence upon him and called upon him to give any reason he might have why the sentence of death should not be passed upon him, he with great promptness replied that he hoped the court would be lenient upon him because he was a poor orphan. —*Lamon Papers: Drafts and Anecdotes, folder 7 (c. 1889); published in Lamon-2, 89–90. {D}*

Here is another example of Lamon's habit of appropriating and elaborating on recollections of other persons.

18. *After the battle of Antietam in September 1862, Lincoln said to Lamon:*

Well, I suppose our victory at Antietam will condone my offense in re-appointing McClellan. If the battle had gone against us, poor McClellan (and I, too), would be in a bad row of stumps. —*Lamon-2, 289. {C}*

19. *In early October 1862, Lincoln visited McClellan's headquarters in Maryland. Sometime afterward, certain opposition newspapers began to accuse him of having called upon Lamon to sing a ribald song while they were crossing the Antietam battlefield, where the bodies of many fallen soldiers still awaited burial. When Lamon urged him to issue a refutation, Lincoln replied:*

No, Hill, there has already been too much said about this falsehood. Let the thing alone. If I have not established character enough to give the lie to this charge, I can only say that I am mistaken in my own estimate of myself. In politics, every man must skin his own skunk. These fellows are welcome to the hide of this one. Its body has already given forth its unsavory odor. —*Lamon-2, 145. {C}*

The substance of this quotation, if not its phrasing, seems credible enough.

20. *After dealing with the problem of an ex-governor's washerwoman whose husband had gone off to join the rebel army, Lincoln said to Lamon:*

This case of our old friend the governor and his Betsy Ann is a fair sample of the trifles I am constantly asked to give my attention to. I wish I had no more serious questions to deal with. If there were more Betsy Anns and fewer fellows like her husband, we should be better off. She seems to have laundered the governor to his full satisfaction, but I am sorry she didn't keep her husband washed cleaner. —*Lamon-2, 85. {C}*

21. *When he learned that the two stepsons of his friend and former client, Dr. William Fithian, had fallen in battle, Lincoln broke into tears and exclaimed:*

Here, now, are these dear, brave boys killed in this cursed war? My God, my God! It is too bad! They worked hard to earn money enough to educate themselves, and this is the end. I loved them as if they were my own.[285] — *Lamon-2, 105. {C}*

22. *In January 1863, Lamon warned the President of a scheme to depose him and put a military dictator in his place. Lincoln responded:*

I think, for a man of accredited courage, you are the most panicky person I ever knew. You can see more dangers to me than all the other friends I have. You are all the time exercised about somebody taking my life—murdering me—and now you have discovered a new danger; now you think the people of this great government are likely to turn me out of office. I do not fear this from the people any more than I fear assassination from an individual. —*Lamon-2, 193–94.* {C}

23. *After the battle of Chancellorsville in early May 1863, Lamon suggested that Lincoln's situation was somewhat like that of Richelieu, and he replied:*

Far from it, Richelieu never had a fire in his front and rear at the same time, as I have. Besides, he had a united constituency; I never have had. If ambition in Congress and jealousy in the army could be allayed, and all united in one common purpose, this infernal rebellion would soon be terminated. —*Lamon Papers, Drafts and Anecdotes, folder 6 (c. 1888).* {C}

In Lamon-2, 183, 191, these two sentences are presented as separate quotations, both revised, and the following passage is added to the first: If I can only keep my end of the animal pointed in the right direction, I will yet get him through this infernal jungle and get my end of him and his tail placed in their proper relative positions. I have never faltered in my faith of being ultimately able to suppress this rebellion and of reuniting this divided country, but this improvised vigilant committee to watch my movements and keep me straight, appointed by Congress and called the "committee on the conduct of the war," is a marplot, and its greatest purpose seems to be to hamper my action and obstruct the military operations. {D}

24. *Shortly before the fall of Vicksburg, Lamon recalled, Lincoln said to him:*

I fear I have made Senator Wade of Ohio my enemy for life. . . . Wade was here just now urging me to dismiss Grant, and in response to something he said, I remarked, "Senator, that reminds me of a story." "Yes, yes!" Wade petulantly replied, "It is with you, sir, all story, story! You are the father of every military blunder that has been made during the war. You are on your road to hell, sir, with this government, by your obstinacy, and you are not a mile off this minute." I good-naturedly said to him: "Senator, that is just about the distance from here to the Capitol, is it not?" He was very angry and grabbed up his hat and cane and went away. —*Lamon-2, 185.* {D}

This familiar anecdote had appeared in print as early as 1864. One may doubt that Lamon heard it directly from Lincoln himself.

25. *During the same conversation, Lincoln remarked:*

Grant assures me he will take Vicksburg by the Fourth of July, and by jing, he shall have a chance, but I believe I am the only friend he seems to have left. —*Lamon Papers: Memorandum on Lincoln and Grant, p. 6.*

A revised version in Lamon-2, 185, includes the statement: Even Washburne, who has always claimed Grant as his by right of discovery, has deserted him and demands his removal. {E}

There is no communication from Grant to Lincoln specifying July 4 as a target date, and there is no evidence of Washburne's turning against Grant.[286]

26. *In a chapter purporting to be the "true history" of the Gettysburg address, Lamon recalled that a day or two before the ceremony, Lincoln told him:* that he would be expected to make a speech on the occasion; that he was extremely busy and had no time for preparation; and that he greatly feared he would not be able to acquit himself with credit, much less to fill the measure of public expectation.

On the platform, after he finished speaking, Lincoln said: Lamon, that speech won't scour! It is a flat failure, and the people are disappointed.

When they had returned to Washington, he reiterated: I tell you, Hill, that speech fell on the audience like a wet blanket. I am distressed about it. I ought to have prepared it with more care. —*Lamon-2, 172–73, 175.* {E}

In the memorandum on which this passage was based, the phrasing is somewhat different, and it is Lamon himself, not Lincoln, who describes the speech as falling on the audience "like a wet blanket." —Lamon Papers: Drafts and Anecdotes, folder 8 (c. 1889). There is, in fact, reason to suspect that the whole story is invention. Lamon's chronically weak credibility is not improved in this instance by his accompanying assertion that Edward Everett and William H. Seward exchanged derogatory comments on the speech immediately after its delivery, or by his insistence that the merit of the Gettysburg Address went totally unrecognized in the United States until after Lincoln's death.[287]

27. *Concerning the double image of himself that he had seen in his bedroom mirror in 1860, Lincoln "more than once" told Lamon:* that he could not explain this phenomenon; that he had tried to reproduce the double reflection at the Executive Mansion, but without success; that it had worried him not a little; and that the mystery had its meaning, which was clear enough to him. To his mind, the illusion was a sign, the lifelike image betokening a safe passage through his first term as president; the ghostly one, that death would overtake him before the close of the second. —*Lamon-2, 113.* {D}

Lamon was here associating himself with a familiar incident that had been recounted many years before by Noah Brooks and Francis B. Carpenter (qq.v.).

28. *With reference to the presidential contest, Lamon wrote, "There was at no time during the campaign a reasonable doubt of the election of Mr. Lincoln over General McClellan." He recalled that one night early in the campaign, Lincoln welcomed him gleefully, saying:*

I am glad you have come in. Lamon, do you know that we have met the enemy, and they are ourn? I think the cabal of obstructionists am busted! I feel certain that if I live, I am going to be re-elected. Whether I deserve to be or not, it is not for me to say, but on the score even of remunerative chances for speculative service, I now am inspired with the hope that our disturbed country further requires the valuable services of your humble servant. Jordan has been a hard road to travel, but I feel now that, notwithstanding the enemies I have made and the faults I have committed, I'll be dumped on the right side of that stream. I hope, however, that I may never have another four years of such anxiety, tribulation, and abuse. My only ambition is and has been to put down the rebellion and restore peace, after which I want to resign my office, go abroad, take some rest, study foreign governments, see something of foreign life, and in my old age, die in peace with the good will of all of God's creatures. —*Lamon-2, 207–8. {E}*

At about the time that he was supposedly indulging in this babble, Lincoln was actually writing a memorandum beginning: "This morning, as for some days past, it seems exceedingly probable that this Administration will not be re-elected."[288]

29. *The story of singing at Antietam was revived during the presidential campaign, and in September 1864, Lamon prepared a response that he asked the President to read. Lincoln said:*

I would not publish this; it is too belligerent in its tone. You are at times too fond of a fight. There is a heap of wickedness mixed up with your usual amiability. If I were you, I'd state the facts as they were. I would give the statement as you have it without the cussedness. Let me try my hand at it. —*Lamon Papers, Drafts and Anecdotes, folder 1 (c. 1887). An edited version is in Lamon-2, 147.*

When he had finished writing a statement to be signed by Lamon, Lincoln said: You know, Hill, that this is the truth and the whole truth about that affair, but I dislike to appear as an apologist for an act of my own which I know was right. Keep this paper and we will see about it.[289] —*Lamon-2, 149. {C}*

30. *During the bitter controversy that raged in 1891 between John G. Nicolay and Alexander K. McClure (q.v.) over whether Lincoln had secretly maneuvered to secure the vice-presidential nomination for Andrew Johnson in 1864, Lamon wrote a letter parroting McClure and at the same time injecting himself into the story. He declared that the President, after talking with McClure, sent for Leonard Swett and enlisted him too in the movement to nominate John-*

son. Swett asked whether Lincoln's name could be used in the enterprise and received this reply:

No, I will address a letter to Lamon here embodying my views, which you, McClure, and other friends may use if it be found absolutely necessary. Otherwise, it may be better that I should not appear actively on the stage of this theater. —*Lamon to McClure, August 16, 1891, in McClure-1, 478.* {E}

No such letter, nor any contemporary reference to it, has ever been found. Neither is there any corroborating testimony from Swett, who died in 1889 and who was reliably reported on the eve of the Baltimore convention to be thinking of Joseph Holt for the vice-presidential nomination.[290] On June 5, 1864, the day before Lamon left for Baltimore, John Hay had a conversation with him and then wrote in his diary: "Says he feels inclined to go for Cameron for Vice Prest on personal grounds. Says he thinks Lincoln rather prefers Johnson or some War Democrat as calculated to give more strength to the ticket."[291] During Johnson's presidency, however, Lamon wrote to him asking for appointment as territorial governor of Colorado and declaring: "Lincoln . . . authorized me long before the Baltimore Convention to use at my own discretion my knowledge of his preference for you to be second on the ticket."[292]

31. *Speaking, apparently, of the Ashley bill, a reconstruction measure that included black suffrage when it was introduced in December 1864, Lincoln said:*

While I am in favor of freedom to all of God's human creatures, with equal political rights under prudential restrictions, I am not in favor of unlimited social equality. There are questions arising out of our complications that trouble me greatly. The question of universal suffrage to the freedman in his unprepared state is one of doubtful propriety. I do not oppose the justice of the measure; but I do think it is of doubtful political policy and may rebound like a boomerang not only on the Republican party, but upon the freedman himself and our common country. —*Lamon-2, 242.* {C}

According to John Hay's diary, Lincoln expressed similar concern to Nathaniel P. Banks and Montgomery Blair.[293]

32. *According to Lamon, Lincoln "more than once" said with respect to Count Adam Gurowski, one of his most splenetic critics from the radical side:*

So far as my personal safety is concerned, Gurowski is the only man who has given me a serious thought of a personal nature. From the known disposition of the man, he is dangerous wherever he may be. I have sometimes thought that he might try to take my life. It would be just like him to do such a thing. —*Lamon-2, 274.* {C}

Although this passage is suspect as a direct quotation supposedly uttered several times, it is not beyond belief that Lincoln more than once expressed some kind of concern about Gurowski.

33. *A short time before his death, Lincoln said:*

If I had done as my Washington friends, who fight battles with their tongues instead of swords far from the enemy, demanded of me, Grant, who has proved himself so great a military captain, would never have been heard of again. —*Lamon Papers: Memorandum on Lincoln and Grant, pp. 6-7. A revised version is in Lamon-2, 186. {C}*

34. *"Only a few days before his assassination," according to Lamon, Lincoln had a startling dream, and, "after worrying over it for some days," he spoke as follows to a small group that included his wife ("I give it," wrote Lamon, "as nearly in his own words as I can, from notes which I made immediately after its recital"):*

It seems strange how much there is in the Bible about dreams. There are, I think, some sixteen chapters in the Old Testament and four or five in the New in which dreams are mentioned, and there are many other passages scattered throughout the book which refer to visions. If we believe the Bible, we must accept the fact that in the old days, God and His angels came to men in their sleep and made themselves known in dreams. Nowadays, dreams are regarded as very foolish and are seldom told, except by old women and by young men and maidens in love.

Asked by Mrs. Lincoln whether he believed in dreams, he responded: I can't say that I do, but I had one the other night which has haunted me ever since. After it occurred, the first time I opened the Bible, strange as it may appear, it was at the twenty-eighth chapter of Genesis, which relates the wonderful dream Jacob had. I turned to other passages and seemed to encounter a dream or a vision wherever I looked. I kept on turning the leaves of the old book, and everywhere my eye fell upon passages recording matters strangely in keeping with my own thoughts—supernatural visitations, dreams, visions, and so forth.

About ten days ago, I retired very late. I had been up waiting for important dispatches from the front. I could not have been long in bed when I fell into a slumber; for I was weary. I soon began to dream. There seemed to be a death-like stillness about me. Then I heard subdued sobs, as if a number of people were weeping. I thought I left my bed and wandered downstairs. There the silence was broken by the same pitiful sobbing, but the mourners were invisible. I went from room to room; no living person was in sight, but the same mournful sounds of distress met me as I passed along. It was light in all the rooms; every object was familiar to me, but where were all the people who were grieving as if their hearts would break? I was puzzled and alarmed. What could be the meaning of all this? Determined to find the cause of a state of things so mysterious and so shocking, I kept on until I arrived at the East Room, which I entered. There I met with a sickening surprise. Before me was a catafalque, on which rested a corpse wrapped in funeral vestments. Around it were stationed soldiers who were acting as guards, and there was a throng of people, some gazing mournfully upon the corpse, whose face was covered, others weeping pitifully. "Who is dead in the White House?" I demanded of one of the soldiers. "The President," was his answer. "He was killed by an assassin." Then came a loud burst of grief from the crowd, which awoke me from my dream. I slept no more that night, and although it was only a dream, I have been strangely annoyed by it ever since.

Alluding to the dream again at some later time, the President said: Hill, your apprehension of harm to me from some hidden enemy is downright foolishness. For a long time you have been trying to keep somebody—the Lord knows who—from killing me. Don't you see how it will turn out? In this dream, it was not me but some other fellow that was killed. It seems that this ghostly assassin tried his hand on someone else. . . . Well, let it go. I think the Lord in His own good time and way will work this out all right. God knows what is best. —*Lamon-2, 114-18.* {E}

Lamon's confused chronology well suits the fantastic quality of the whole story, which has nevertheless been accepted by a number of biographers and other writers.[294]

35. *On April 11, 1865, as he prepared to leave on a trip to Richmond, Lamon visited Lincoln in the company of John P. Usher and urged him not to go out at night, especially to the theater. Lincoln responded:*

Usher, this boy is a monomaniac on the subject of my safety. I can hear him or hear of his being around at all times of the night to prevent somebody from murdering me. He thinks I shall be killed, and we think he is going crazy. What does anyone want to assassinate me for? If anyone wants to do so, he can do it any day or night, if he is ready to give his life for mine. It is nonsense. —*Lamon-2, 280-81.* {C}

Lamon's warning about the theater seems incredibly prophetic, but there is considerable evidence of his worry about the danger of assassination.

MELVILLE D. LANDON   *A New York* Tribune *correspondent.*

1. *On July 12, 1863, Lincoln remarked that:*

Meade's force was concentrated for battle and was only one and three-quarters of a mile long.

He acknowledged that: Meade was a little slow in getting after Lee after Gettysburg.

He said, however, that: Lee's Pennsylvania campaign was a providential thing for us. At one time he thought it would be Antietam over again, but now it was all right.

Landon added that Lincoln talked of "dispatch," "reinforcing," and "pushing Lee." — Landon to Sydney Howard Gay, July 12, 1863, Gay Papers. {B}

JOHN M. LANSDEN   *A student at Illinois College, Jacksonville, in 1861; later a resident of Cairo, Illinois.*

1. *On a train headed east from Springfield on January 30, 1861, Lansden heard Lincoln comment on the report that a hundred guns had been fired in Memphis to celebrate the secession of Texas:*

Yes, yes, she came in afiring and she goes out afiring.[295]

Then he recalled that: when Texas was admitted into the Union, December 29, 1845, such guns were fired in many parts of the country. — *Lansden, 57 (1914). {D}*

Lincoln did indeed travel on an eastbound train that day, but the assertion that he was accompanied by David Davis and Edward Bates casts doubt on Lansden's story.

AUGUSTE LAUGEL (1830–1914)   *French writer, a friend of Charles Sumner, who visited the United States during the Civil War and wrote a book about it.[296]*

1. *On January 7, 1865, while waiting with other people to see the President, Laugel heard him respond to a distressed woman who wanted her husband released from service so that he could rescue his family from poverty:*

I cannot grant your request. I can disband all the Union armies, but I cannot send a single soldier home. Only the colonel of his regiment can do that for your husband. . . . I sympathize in your disappointment, but consider that all of us in every part of the country are today suffering what we have never suffered. *As the interview ended, Lincoln wrote a few words on a piece of paper and handed it to the woman. — Laugel diary, 88. {B}*

2. *On January 13, Laugel went to Ford's Theatre with the Lincolns and Sumner to see Edwin Forrest in* King Lear. *Whenever Tad asked for an explanation, his father's answer was:*

My child, it is in the play.

Near the end, as the villainous Edmund was thrust through with a sword, Lincoln said: I have only one reproach to make of Shakespeare's heroes—that they make long speeches when they are killed. —89. {B}

JOHN LELLYET   *A resident of Davidson County, Tennessee, one of the state's leading supporters of the Democratic nominee for the presidency in 1864.*

1. *On October 15, 1864, Lellyet called at the White House to present a protest from himself and certain other Tennesseans against the election rules and procedures laid down by Andrew Johnson as military governor. According to his obviously hostile account, Lincoln said:*

May I inquire how long it took you and the New York politicians to concoct this paper? . . . I will answer that I expect to let the friends of George B. McClellan manage their side of this contest in their own way, and I will manage my side of it in my way. *— Lellyet's letter the same day to the New York* World, *published October 18 and reprinted in* Collected Works, *VIII, 58-61n.* {A}

CHARLES EDWARDS LESTER (1815-1890) *Clergyman turned author, one of whose many publications was an early biography of Charles Sumner. During the Civil War, Lester worked in Washington hospitals.*

   1. *In September 1861, at the time of the furor over Frémont's proclamation of emancipation in Missouri, the President said to Lester:*

It would do no good to go ahead any faster than the country would follow. . . . I think Sumner and the rest of you would upset our applecart altogether if you had your way. We'll fetch 'em; just give us a little time. We didn't go into the war to put down slavery, but to put the flag back, and to act differently at this moment, would, I have no doubt, not only weaken our cause but smack of bad faith; for I never should have had votes enough to send me here if the people had supposed I should try to use my power to upset slavery. Why, the first thing you'd see, would be a mutiny in the army. No, we must wait until every other means has been exhausted. This thunderbolt will keep.

After some argument from Lester, Lincoln reiterated: The powder in this bombshell will keep dry, and when the fuse is lit, I intend to have them touch it off themselves. *— Lester, 359-60 (1874).* {C}

   2. *When Lincoln, on April 16, 1862, signed the bill abolishing slavery in the District of Columbia, he expressed gratification that it included the two principles of compensation and colonization. He is quoted as saying:*

I am so far behind the Sumner lighthouse that I will stick to my old colonization hobby. *— 386.* {D}

It is not clear that Lester was an auditor of this remark.

N. LEVERING *An Illinoisan who studied law with Lincoln's friend Leonard Swett in Bloomington and then moved to Iowa in the 1850s.*

   1. *Lincoln arrived for the circuit court term in September 1854, and Levering heard him say facetiously to a group of men with whom he was talking on the street:*

Well, I am the handsomest man in Bloomington.
Asked whether he would leave that to the ladies, he replied: Yes, to one down in Springfield. *— Levering, 505 (1896).* {C}

   2. *Seeing the antislavery radical Ichabod Codding get off a train, Lincoln said:*

Look, why there is Codding. Just look at him. He has preached abolition so long that he is now turning black. —*506.* *{C}*

THOMAS LEWIS   *Springfield lawyer, businessman, and a lay leader of the First Presbyterian Church.*

1. *Lincoln, according to Lewis, "used to say":*

When I came to Springfield, I brought my entire estate, real and personal, in a carpetbag. —*Lewis, 134 (1899).* *{C}*

2. *Soon after the Reverend James Smith (q.v.) arrived in Springfield and near the time of his son Eddie's death in February 1850, Lincoln told Lewis:*

that when on a visit somewhere, he had seen and partially read a work of Dr. Smith on the evidences of Christianity which had led him to change his views about the Christian religion; that he would like to get that work to finish the reading of it, and also to make the acquaintance of Dr. Smith. —*Lewis to James A. Reed, January 6, 1873, in Reed, 339.*[297] *{C}*

FRANCIS LIEBER (1798–1872)   *German-American political philosopher who taught for many years at South Carolina College and then at Columbia College and the Columbia Law School.*

1. *Speaking of his recent message to Congress and Lieber's writings on the Constitution, Lincoln said in August 1861:*

They will say that I borrowed two or three expressions from you and put them into my message, but I assure you I did not do it; they are really my own. —*Lieber to Henry Boynton Smith, August 15, 1861, Lieber Papers.* *{A}*

GEORGE B. LINCOLN   *A New York businessman who visited Springfield in January 1861.*

1. *As he tried on a stovepipe hat that had been sent to him as a gift by a New York hatmaker, the President-elect said:*

It fits me perfectly. Wife, if nothing else comes of this scrape, we are going to have some new clothes, are we not? —*George B. Lincoln to the editor of the St. Johnsbury (Vt.)* Caledonian, *November 13, 1890, typescript copy in the Tarbell Papers.* *{C}*

MARY TODD LINCOLN (1818–1882)   *Lincoln's wife for twenty-two years and his widow for seventeen. Her few recollective quotations of him come to us through intermediaries.*

1. *Mrs. Lincoln confirmed the general impression that her husband was an indulgent father, one who often said:*

It is my pleasure that my children are free, happy, and unrestrained by paternal tyranny. Love is the chain whereby to lock a child to its parent. —*Notes of William H. Herndon, presumably made at the time of his only interview with Mary Lincoln in September 1866 (9:1568-69), Herndon-Weik Collection.*[298] *{C}*

2. *Concerning talk in some quarters that Seward intended to rule him, he said:*

I shall rule myself, shall obey my own conscience and follow God in it. — *Notes by Herndon on the interview of September 1866, an expanded version (9:1559-63) apparently written at least two months later.*[299] *{D}*

3. *Of newspaper attacks upon him:*

I care nothing for them. If I'm right, I'll live, and if wrong, I'll die anyhow; so let them pass unnoticed. —*Ibid.* *{D}*

4. *On Chase and others conspiring against him:*

Do good to those who hate you and turn their ill-will into friendship. — *Ibid.* *{D}*

5. *When Vice President Andrew Johnson turned up at City Point in early April 1865, Lincoln said to his wife:*

For God's sake, don't ask Johnson to dine with us. —*Ibid.* *{C}*

David Dixon Porter and William H. Crook (qq.v.) likewise recalled that Lincoln expressed an unwillingness to see Johnson on this occasion.

6. *According to Noyes W. Miner, pastor of the First Baptist Church in Springfield, Mary Lincoln told him that on April 14, 1865, she tried to persuade her husband not to go to the theater, but he replied:*

A large number of overjoyed and excited people will visit me tonight. I must have a little rest. My hands are swollen and my arms are lame by shaking hands with the multitude, and the people will pull me to pieces. —*Miner, 52-53 (1882). {D}*

7. *Miner also recalled Mrs. Lincoln's telling him that at Ford's Theatre, Lincoln resumed talk begun earlier in the day about what they should do after his term expired. He said:*

We will not return immediately to Springfield. We will go abroad among strangers where I can rest. . . . We will visit the Holy Land and see those places hallowed by the footsteps of the Savior.

In his last words before the fatal bullet was fired, he added that: there was no city on earth he so much desired to see as Jerusalem. —*Miner, 54. {D}*

One may doubt that Lincoln would have expressed such reverent aspirations while watching the comedy "Our American Cousin."

ROBERT TODD LINCOLN (1843-1926)   *Lincoln's oldest son, a student at Harvard during most of the Civil War and then briefly a member of Ulysses S. Grant's staff. He was later secretary of war, minister to Great Britain, and president of the Pullman Company.*

1. *On July 15, the day after Lee crossed the Potomac back into Virginia, Robert Lincoln told John Hay that his father was deeply grieved and had said:*

If I had gone up there, I could have whipped them myself. — Hay-1, 67. {B}

2. *In a later account, he recalled having found his father in tears and quoted him as saying:*

My boy, when I heard that the bridge at Williamsport had been swept away, I sent for General Haupt and asked him how soon he could replace the same. He replied, "If I were uninterrupted I could build a bridge with the material there within twenty-four hours and, Mr. President, General Lee has engineers as skillful as I am." Upon hearing this I at once wrote Meade to attack without delay, and if successful to destroy my letter, but in case of failure to preserve it for his vindication. I have just learned that at a council of war of Meade and his generals, it had been determined not to pursue Lee, and now the opportune chance of ending this bitter struggle is lost. — *As related to and remembered by a golfing partner, Thacher, 282–83 (1927).* {D}

This secondhand quotation, recalled and recorded some sixty years after the fact, is itself dubious material, but the letter to Meade may be more credible. Robert Lincoln told the story a number of times, beginning as early as 1872, and he apparently remained convinced of its truth, while acknowledging that it had been denied by some persons and was supported by no existing evidence except his own memory.[300]

3. *Testifying in 1878 before an army board reviewing the dismissal of General Fitz-John Porter, Robert Lincoln recalled his father's saying in January 1863 that:*

the case would have justified, in his opinion, a sentence of death. — Senate Document 37, p. 855. {C}

4. *After graduating from Harvard in 1864, Robert declared that if he could not join the army he would go back to Harvard and study law. His father replied:*

If you do, you should learn more than I ever did, but you will never have so good a time. — *Robert Lincoln as quoted shortly after his death by a reporter from Manchester, Vermont, in the New York* Herald Tribune, *July 27, 1926.* {D}

There is no assurance that the reporter heard this anecdote directly from Robert Lincoln.

THOMAS LINCOLN (1778–1851)   *Father of Abraham Lincoln.*

1. *Thomas Lincoln's step-granddaughter recalled his telling of a time in Indiana when the family had only roast potatoes for dinner. After he returned thanks, his son Abraham said with a long face:*

I call these very poor blessings. —*Harriet Hanks Chapman to Herndon, December 10, 1866 (8:1270–71), Herndon-Weik Collection.* {D}

USHER F. LINDER (1809–1876)   *An Illinois lawyer and politician with whom Lincoln was long acquainted.*

1. *Of his father's older brother Mordecai, Lincoln once remarked:*

I have often said that Uncle Mord had run off with all the talents of the family. —*Linder, 38 (1879).* {C}

2. *Several weeks after his aborted duel with James Shields in September 1842, Lincoln said:*

To tell you the truth, Linder, I did not want to kill Shields and felt sure that I could disarm him, having had about a month to learn the broadsword exercise; and furthermore, I didn't want the damned fellow to kill me, which I rather think he would have done if we had selected pistols. —*66–67.* {C}

JOHN H. LITTLEFIELD   *A law student in the Lincoln and Herndon office, 1859–60. He soon abandoned law to become a painter.*

1. *According to Littlefield, Lincoln once reacted sharply to a visitor's obscene joke, saying:*

Young man, never come here with such a story. If there had been any real wit in it you might have been pardoned. —*Littlefield, 447 (1895).* {C}

2. *At another time, Lincoln remarked:*

John, it depends a great deal on how you state a case. When Daniel Webster stated a case, it was half argument. Now, you take the subject of predestination; you state it one way, and you cannot make much of it; you state it another, and it seems quite reasonable. —*Littlefield, 447.* {C}

3. *Speaking of the Yazoo River expedition, launched in December 1862, Lincoln said to Littlefield and several other visitors by way of preamble:*

that he found it necessary to yield here a little and there a little in order to keep peace in the family and that if he interfered in a plan that was not essential, vital, the West Pointers who had the execution of all plans would in some way or other obstruct or defeat the execution of his scheme. Therefore, inasmuch as they had to be depended upon at **last**, he found it best to trust them at **first** and rely on events and the power of persuasion to rectify errors.

Then, pointing to the map on the wall, he continued: How can a force go down a river that is only a few rods wide when it cannot get down a river that is a mile wide? And if it could, it would only wind about and come out into the same river that it is contended by the military officers you cannot pursue — the Mississippi — and for this reason you wish to leave the Mississippi above Vicksburg. This expedition proposes to follow the Yazoo and come out in the Mississippi. What have you accomplished? You have gained nothing. I can't better make this clear than by relating an incident that came under my own observation. There was a man in Illinois a good many years since that was troubled with an old sow and her pigs. Again and again, the old man and his sons drove her out and repeatedly found her in the lot. One day, he and his boys searched about and found that she got into the lot through a certain hollow log that had been placed in the fence. They took out this log and built up the fence by placing the log a little differently than before, and the next day, what was the astonishment of the old lady to find that she and her litter came out of the log **outside** of the field instead of **inside**. It is just so with the Yazoo River expedition. It comes out of the same side of the log. — *Littlefield to Herndon, December 11, 1866 (8:1282–85), Herndon-Weik Collection.* {C}

A Boston merchant recalled hearing Lincoln tell the same story in connection with the Vicksburg campaign.[301]

MARY A. LIVERMORE (1820–1905)   *Reformer, editor, author, and lecturer; active during the Civil War in the work of the Sanitary Commission.*

   1. *In November 1862, Mrs. Livermore and a number of other women associated with the Sanitary Commission called on Lincoln, hoping for a word of good cheer. Instead, he said:*

I have no word of encouragement to give. The military situation is far from bright, and the country knows it as well as I do. The fact is, the people haven't yet made up their minds that we are at war with the South. They haven't buckled down to the determination to fight this war through; for they have got the idea into their heads that we are going to get out of this fix, somehow, by strategy. That's the word — **strategy**! General McClellan thinks he is going to whip the rebels by strategy, and the army has got the same notion. They have no idea that the war is to be carried on and put through by hard, tough fighting that will hurt somebody, and no headway is going to be made while this delusion lasts. . . .

   When you came to Washington, ladies, some two weeks ago, but very few soldiers came on the trains with you — that you will all remember. But when you go back you will find the trains and every conveyance crowded with them. You won't find a city on the route, a town or a village, where soldiers and officers on furlough are not plenty as blackberries. There are whole regiments that have two-thirds of their men absent — a great many by desertion, and a great many on leave granted by company officers, which is almost as bad. General McClellan is all the time calling for more troops, more troops, and they are sent to him, but the deserters and furloughed men outnumber the recruits. To fill up the army is like undertaking to shovel fleas. You take up a shovelful, but before you can dump them anywhere they are gone. It is like trying to ride a balky horse. You coax and cheer and spur and lay on the whip, but you don't get ahead an inch; there you stick. . . .

And the desertion of the army is just now the most serious evil we have to encounter. At the battle of Antietam, General McClellan had the names of about 180,000 men on the army rolls. Of these, 70,000 were absent on leave granted by company officers, which, as I said before, is almost as bad as desertion. For the men ought not to ask for furloughs with the enemy drawn up before them, nor ought the officers to grant them. About 20,000 more were in hospital or were detailed to other duties, leaving only some 90,000 to give battle to the enemy. General McClellan went into the fight with this number. But in two hours after the battle commenced, 30,000 had straggled or deserted, and so the battle was fought with 60,000, and as the enemy had about the same number, it proved a drawn game. The rebel army had coiled itself up in such a position that if McClellan had only had the 70,000 absentees and the 30,000 deserters, he could have surrounded Lee, captured the whole rebel army, and ended the war at a stroke without a battle.

We have a stragglers' camp out here in Alexandria, in connection with the convalescent camp, and from that camp, in three months, General Butler has returned to their regiments 75,000 deserters and stragglers who have been arrested and sent there. Don't you see that the country and the army fail to realize that we are engaged in one of the greatest wars the world has ever seen and which can only be ended by hard fighting? General McClellan is responsible for the delusion that is untoning the whole army—that the South is to be conquered by strategy.

Asked whether it might not therefore be more humane in the end to enforce the death penalty against deserters, he said: It might seem so. But if I should go to shooting men by scores for desertion, I should soon have such a hullabaloo about my ears as I haven't had yet, and I should deserve it. You çan't order men shot by dozens or twenties. People won't stand it, and they ought not to stand it. No, we must change the condition of things in some other way. The army must be officered by fighting men. Misery loves company, you know, and it may give you some consolation to know that it is even worse with the rebel army than it is with ours. I receive their papers daily, and they are running over with complaints of the desertion of their soldiers. We are no worse off than they are, but better, and that is some comfort. — *Livermore, 556-59 (1890). {D}*

This would appear to be recollection supplemented with a good deal of literary invention. Lincoln's comparing an army to a shovelful of fleas was also recalled by John Hay and Richard Cunningham McCormick (qq.v.).

2. In another interview the next day, one of the women asked Lincoln whether he thought the country's cause was lost, and he replied:

Oh, no, our affairs are by no means hopeless, for we have the right on our side. We did not want this war, and we tried to avoid it. We were forced into it. Our cause is a just one, and now it has become the cause of freedom. And let us also hope it is the cause of God, and then we may be sure it must ultimately triumph. But between that time and now, there is an amount of agony and suffering and trial for the people that they do not look for, and are not prepared for. —561. {C}

3. At one time, according to Livermore, she heard the President's response to a plea for the pardon of a man convicted as a Confederate spy and sentenced to a long term in prison:

There is not a word of this true, and you know it as well as I do. He **was** a spy, he has been a spy, he ought to have been hanged as a spy. From the fuss you folks are making about him, who are none too loyal, I am convinced he was more valuable to the cause of the enemy than we have yet suspected. You are the third set of persons that has been to me to get him pardoned. Now I'll tell you what, if any of you come bothering me any more about his being set at liberty, that will decide his fate. I will have him hanged, as he deserves to be. —568. {D}

Needless to say, if Lincoln ever made such a threat, he had no legal power to carry it out.

4. To several members of Congress present when he was appealed to by a woman whose husband had been sentenced to death for killing his superior officer:

Oh, dear, dear! These cases kill me! I wish I didn't have to hear about them! What shall I do? You make the laws, and then you come with heartbroken women and ask me to set them aside. You have decided that if a soldier raises his hand against his superior officer, as this man has done, he shall die! Then if I leave the laws to be executed, one of these distressing scenes occurs, which almost kills me. —572–73. *According to Livermore, Lincoln, as he began to read the record of the case, soon realized and announced that he had already commuted the man's sentence to a prison term. {C}*

5. At a reception, upon being introduced to Elizabeth Peabody, sister-in-law of Horace Mann and Nathaniel Hawthorne, Lincoln said:

When I first came to Washington, Horace Mann was in the zenith of his power, and I was nobody. But he was very kind to me, and I shall never forget it. —575. {C}

B. B. LLOYD   *A Springfield dentist.*

1. *Just before Lincoln left for Washington in February 1861, Lloyd warned him to be on guard against the threat of assassination. Lincoln responded:*

I will be cautious, but God's will be done. I am in his hands and will be during my administration, and what he does, I must bow to. —*Lloyd's statement taken down by Herndon, November 29, 1866 (8:1152), Herndon-Weik Collection. {C}*

DAVID ROSS LOCKE (1833–1888)   *Ohio journalist and one of the most popular satirists of the Civil War era, better known by his pseudonym, Petroleum V. Nasby.*

1. *At Quincy, Illinois, in October 1858, speaking of an inordinately vain politician, recently deceased:*

If General —— had known how big a funeral he would have had, he would have died years ago. —*Rice AT, 442 (1886). {C}*

2. *Of the contest with Douglas:*

You can't overturn a pyramid, but you can undermine it; that's what I have been trying to do. —443. {C}

3. *In a speech at Columbus, Ohio, on September 16, 1859, Lincoln reiterated his opposition to social equality between the races and reaffirmed his perfunctory endorsement of the Illinois law against interracial marriage. When Locke asked whether such a prohibition was worthwhile, he said:*

The law means nothing. I shall never marry a Negress, but I have no objection to anyone else doing so. If a white man wants to marry a Negro woman, let him do it—if the Negro woman can stand it. —446-47. {C}

4. *During the same interview:*

Slavery is doomed, and that within a few years. Even Judge Douglas admits it to be an evil, and an evil can't stand discussion. In discussing it, we have taught a great many thousands of people to hate it who had never given it a thought before. What kills the skunk is the publicity it gives itself. What a skunk wants to do is to keep snug under the barn in the daytime, when men are around with shotguns. —447. {C}

5. *Locke visited the White House in 1864 seeking pardon for a soldier who had deserted to go home and marry his fiancée, having learned that she was being courted with some success by a rival. Lincoln signed the necessary paper, saying:*

I want to punish the young man—probably in less than a year he will wish I had withheld the pardon. We can't tell, though. I suppose when I was a young man, I should have done the same fool thing. —450. {D}

All pardoning stories should be read with some skepticism, and this one seems more unlikely than the average.

6. *After asking whether the people of Ohio held him personally responsible for the loss of friends in the war, Lincoln added:*

It's a good thing for individuals that there's a government to shove over their acts upon. No man's shoulders are broad enough to bear what must be. —451. {C}

7. *Asked why he did not take some kind of stand on a quarrel between two prominent Republicans, he said:*

I learned a great many years ago, that in a fight between man and wife, a third party should never get between the woman's skillet and the man's ax-helve. —451. {C}

8. *Speaking of a brilliant but dishonest official:*

It's a big thing for B—— that there is such a thing as a deathbed repentance. —451. {C}

9. *In discussion of a senator accused of corruption, the President said that:*

he could not understand why men should be so eager after wealth.[302] Wealth [he added] is simply a superfluity of what we don't need. —452. {C}

JOHN A. LOGAN (1826–1886) *Illinois Democratic politician who became a distinguished Civil War general and then a Republican congressman and senator.*

1. *On February 24, 1861, when Logan urged him to take a strong stand against secession, Lincoln said:*

As the country has placed me at the helm of the ship, I'll try to steer her through. —*Logan, 142 (1886). {C}*

STEPHEN T. LOGAN (1800–1880) *Springfield lawyer and politician, Lincoln's second law partner, 1841–44.*

1. *Shortly before his inauguration in 1861, Lincoln read his inaugural address to Logan, who urged him to modify one sentence that the South would take as a threat.[303] Lincoln replied:*

It is not necessary for me to say to you that I have great respect for your opinion, but the statements you think should be modified were carefully considered by me—and the probable consequences, as far as I can anticipate them. The statements express the convictions of duty that the great office I shall endeavor to fill will impose upon me, and if there is patriotism enough in the American people, the Union will be saved; if not, it will go down, and I will go with it. —*Logan's remarks at a meeting of the Springfield bar on the day of Lincoln's death, as later reported in Zane, 434-35 (1912).* {D}

JAMES J. LORD   *Lord was listed in a Springfield directory for 1860–61 as "Proprietor of Dr. Topping's Alterative Sirup."*

1. *Lord declared that he heard Lincoln say to a prospective client one morning in about 1859:*

Yes, there is no reasonable doubt but that I can gain your case for you. I can set a whole neighborhood at loggerheads. I can distress a widowed mother and her six fatherless children and thereby get for you $600 which you seem to have a legal claim to, but which rightfully belongs, it appears to me, as much to the woman and her children as it does to you. You must remember that some things that are legally right are not morally right. I shall not take your case, but I will give you a little advice, for which I will charge you nothing. You seem to be a sprightly, energetic man. I would advise you to try your hand at making $600 in some other way. *— Lord's statement, undated but c. 1866 (11:3157–58), Herndon-Weik Collection. {D}*

This intrinsically hard-to-believe recollection from an auditor whose identity is not entirely clear was published with some variations in Herndon, II, 345–46n, and thereby contributed to the legend of Lincoln as a lawyer who never accepted a case that did not square with his principles.[304]

GEORGE B. LORING (1817–1891)   *Massachusetts physician and Democratic politician who became a Republican during the Civil War and was later elected to Congress.*

1. *In a discussion shortly after he arrived in Washington as president-elect, Lincoln said to Loring:*

I like your man Banks and have tried to find a place for him in my cabinet, but I am afraid I shall not quite fetch it. *— Loring's recollections in the New York* Tribune, *August 9, 1885. {C}*

BENSON J. LOSSING (1813–1891)   *Wood-engraver, editor, and historian, employed for a time in the War Department during the Lincoln presidency.*

1. *In December 1864, Lincoln gave Lossing and Isaac N. Arnold an account of his clandestine journey between Philadelphia and Washington in February 1861:*

I arrived at Philadelphia on the 21st. I agreed to stop overnight, and on the following morning hoist the flag over Independence Hall. In the evening there was a great crowd where I received my friends at the Continental Hotel. Mr. Judd, a warm personal friend from Chicago, sent for me to come to his room. I went and found there Mr. Pinkerton, a skillful police detective, also from Chicago, who had been employed for some days in Baltimore, watching or searching for suspicious persons there. Pinkerton informed me that a plan had been laid for my assassination, the exact time when I expected to go through Baltimore being publicly known. He was well informed as to the plan, but did not know that the conspirators would have pluck enough to execute it. He urged me to go right through with him to Washington that night. I didn't like that. I had made engagements to visit Harrisburg and go from there to Baltimore, and I resolved to do so. I could not believe that there was a plot to murder me. I made arrangements, however, with Mr. Judd for my return to Philadelphia the next night if I should be convinced that there was danger in going through Baltimore. I told him that if I should meet at Harrisburg, as I had at other places, a delegation to go with me to the next place (then Baltimore), I should feel safe and go on.

When I was making my way back to my room through crowds of people, I met Frederick Seward. We went together to my room, when he told me that he had been sent, at the instance of his father and General Scott, to inform me that their detectives in Baltimore had discovered a plot there to assassinate me. They knew nothing of Pinkerton's movements. I now believed such a plot to be in existence.

The next morning I raised the flag over Independence Hall and then went on to Harrisburg with Mr. Sumner, Major (now General) Hunter, Mr. Judd, Mr. Lamon, and others. There I met the legislature and people, dined, and waited until the time appointed for me to leave. In the meantime, Mr. Judd had so secured the telegraph that no communication could pass to Baltimore and give the conspirators knowledge of a change in my plans.

In New York, some friend had given me a new beaver hat in a box, and in it had placed a soft wool hat. I had never worn one of the latter in my life. I had this box in my room. Having informed a very few friends of the secret of my new movements, and the cause, I put on an old overcoat that I had with me, and putting the soft hat in my pocket, I walked out of the house at a back door, bareheaded, without exciting any special curiosity. Then I put on the soft hat and joined my friends without being recognized by strangers; for I was not the same man. Sumner and Hunter wished to accompany me. I said no; you are known, and your presence might betray me. I will only take Lamon (now marshal of this district), whom nobody knew, and Mr. Judd. Sumner and Hunter felt hurt.

We went back to Philadelphia and found a message there from Pinkerton (who had returned to Baltimore), that the conspirators had held their final meeting that evening, and it was doubtful whether they had the nerve to attempt the execution of their purpose. I went on, however, as the arrangement had been made, in a special train. We were a long time in the station at Baltimore. I heard people talking around, but no one particularly observed me. At an early hour on Saturday morning, at about the time I was expected to leave Harrisburg, I arrived in Washington. —*Lossing, I, 279-80 (1866). {D}*

The length of this narrative, together with the absence of any indication of its being based upon notes taken at the time, raises doubts about Lossing's assertion that it was reproduced substantially in Lincoln's own words.

2. According to Lossing, on the day in mid-November 1861 when the news reached Washington of the seizure of two Confederate agents traveling on the British ship Trent, *he had a brief interview with the President, who said:*

I fear the traitors will prove to be white elephants. We must stick to American principles concerning the rights of neutrals. We fought Great Britain for insisting, by theory and practice, on the right to do precisely what Captain Wilkes has done. If Great Britain shall now protest against the act and demands their release, we must give them up, apologize for the act as a violation of our doctrines, and thus forever bind her over to keep the peace in relation to neutrals, and so acknowledge that she has been wrong for sixty years. —II, 156-57 (1868). {D}

There is good reason to doubt that Lincoln was immediately so certain of the right course to follow in the Trent *affair.*[305]

SAMUEL K. LOTHROP   *A Boston clergyman.*

1. In his sermon after the assassination, Lothrop recalled hearing Lincoln say in the fall of 1861 to a woman seeking the release of her brother from detention on charges of disloyalty:

Madam, I desire to say that there is no man who feels a deeper or more tender sympathy than I do with all cases of individual sorrow, anxiety, and grief like yours, which these unhappy troubles occasion, but I see not how I can prevent or relieve them. I am here to administer this government, to uphold the Constitution, to maintain the Union of the United States. That is my oath. Before God and man, I must, I mean to the best of my ability to keep that oath, and however much my personal feelings may sympathize with individual sorrows and anxieties, I must not yield to them. They must all give way before the great public exigencies of the country.

According to Lothrop, Lincoln wrote on the petition that he had no objection to the man's release if the general in charge thought it compatible with the public safety. —Sermons, 258-59 (1865). {C}

Lothrop's assertion that he was repeating "very nearly" Lincoln's exact words cannot be taken very seriously.

THOMAS LOWRY   *In the 1850s, a youthful resident of Pleasantview, Illinois, about fifty miles northwest of Springfield.*

1. In about 1857, Lincoln told of having visited Lowry's uncle in Pekin while on the judicial circuit:

As I was going up the path from the street to the house, some boys were playing marbles near the walk. I stopped and put my hand on the head of

Mr. Lowry's boy and said, "My boy, you're playing marbles!" The urchin looked up and replied: "Any damn fool ought to see that." —*Lowry, 12 (1910).* {C}

AGNES HARRISON MACDONELL *English girl who attended a White House reception in February 1863 and wrote home about it to her parents.*[306]

1. *Responding to her statement that the people in her family were with him "in heart and soul, especially since the 1st of January":*

I am very glad to hear it, very glad, though I may not know them personally. That is one of the evils of being so far apart. We have a good deal of salt water between us. When you feel kindly towards us we cannot, unfortunately, be always aware of it. But it cuts both ways. When you, in England, are cross with us, we don't feel it quite so badly. —*Macdonell, 568.* {A}

2. *Lincoln also said to her that:*

he thought there were three parties in England: an aristocratic party, which will not be sorry to see the Republic break up; a class allied to the South through trade relations; and a third, larger, or if not larger, of more import, which sympathizes warmly with the cause of the North. —*568.* {B}

ALLAN B. MAGRUDER *A Virginian who, on the eve of the Civil War, was practicing law in Washington, D.C.*

1. *In early April 1861, Magruder was enlisted by the President and the Secretary of State as a messenger to George W. Summers, a leading Virginia unionist. Lincoln said of Summers:*

that he thought very highly of him as a prudent and wise man; that he had great confidence in him; that indeed he had confidence in all those Virginians; that although they might differ from him about secession, he believed they were men who could be depended on in any matter in which they pledged their honor; and that when they gave their word, they would always keep it.

He then continued: Tell Mr. Summers I want to see him at once; for there is no time to be lost. What is to be done must be done quickly. . . . This is Tuesday; I will give him three days. Let him come by Friday next. . . . If Mr. Summers cannot come himself, let him send some friend of his, some Union man in the convention in whom he has confidence and who can confer freely with me. —*Magruder, 439 (1875).* {C}

Instead of Summers, it was John B. Baldwin (q.v.) who went to confer with Lincoln.

WILLIAM WYNDHAM MALET (1804-1885)   *An English clergyman who visited the United States on family business in 1862.*

1. *Lincoln talked with Malet for about twenty minutes on May 31 and, among other things, told him that:*

they used hard, unbituminous coal in the United States navy, giving great force of fire without the slightest smoke, so that the approach of their men-of-war is not seen over the horizon or in rivers. —*Malet, 17 (1863).* {C}

2. *In the same conversation, Lincoln lamented the war and said that:*

if he could have foreseen it, he would not have accepted the office of president. —*17.* {C}

ROBERT MALLORY (1815-1885)   *Unionist congressman from Kentucky throughout the Civil War. He opposed emancipation and Lincoln's re-election.*

1. *Mallory, together with Senator Lazarus W. Powell and another member of Congress, called at the White House to protest the arrest of a fellow Kentuckian named Frank Wolford. In the course of the conversation, Lincoln said:*

Well, I don't exactly know what he was arrested for, but I reckon he was arrested for making speeches calculated to prevent men from enlisting in the army.

In response to a remark by Mallory, the President declared: that the supposition that he wanted to destroy the Constitution was utterly impossible and that his whole aim was to preserve it.

After further discussion, he said: I don't want to argue with you, Mallory. You will beat me in the argument, but I have established my rule in this matter and intend to stand by it.

Asked what that rule was, he replied: to arrest anybody who says or does anything calculated to prevent any person from enlisting in the army or discouraging enlistments, either white or black.

After some threatening talk from Powell, he said: That's the way you all talk, and now if I release Wolford, you will say that I did it because I was afraid to hold him. —*Extract from a recent speech by Mallory,* The Crisis *(Columbus, Ohio), October 12, 1864.* {C}

The account of the interview is part of a sweeping attack on the Lincoln administration. Lincoln did eventually order Wolford's release.

ABSALOM H. MARKLAND (1825-1888)   *A lawyer and bureaucrat in Washington during the 1850s, Markland became the officer in charge of mail for Grant's command.*

1. *Soon after his inauguration, Lincoln said to a group of friends:*

The disunionists did not want me to take the oath of office. I have taken it, and I intend to administer the office for the benefit of the people, in accordance with the Constitution and the law. — *Rice AT, 317 (1886). {C}*

2. *On Grant's proclamation after occupying Paducah in September 1861:*

The modesty and brevity of that address to the citizens of Paducah show that the officer issuing it understands the situation and is a proper man to command there at this time. — *322. {C}*

3. *In the summer of 1864, Postmaster General Blair wanted certain orders issued concerning postal service within army lines. Grant, when approached, said that they should come from Stanton, but the latter refused to comply. Markland was then sent to explain the problem to Lincoln, who responded:*

If I understand the case, General Grant wants the orders issued, and Blair wants them issued, and you want them issued, and Stanton won't issue them. Now, don't you see what kind of a fix I will be in if I interfere? I'll tell you what to do: If you and General Grant understand one another, suppose you try to get along without the orders, and if Blair or Stanton make[s] a fuss, I may be called in as a referee, and I may decide in your favor. — *328-29. {C}*

JAMES H. MATHENY (1818-1890) *Springfield lawyer and court clerk, later a county judge. Matheny, a Whig who somewhat belatedly became a Republican, may have been best man at Lincoln's wedding.*

1. *According to Matheny as recorded by William H. Herndon, Lincoln often told him:*

that he was driven into the marriage.

Matheny added (but there is no indication whether he claimed to be still repeating what Lincoln had told him): that it was concocted and planned by the Edwards family—that Miss Todd, afterwards Mrs. Lincoln, told Lincoln that he was in honor bound to marry her. — Matheny statement, May 3, 1866 (8:733-35), Herndon-Weik Collection. {D}

THOMAS S. MATHER (?-1890) *Springfield businessman and local Republican leader who was the Illinois adjutant-general at the beginning of the Civil War and later became a colonel of artillery.*

1. *In late January 1861, according to Mather, the President-elect sent him to Washington to talk with Winfield Scott about the safety of Washington and at the same time assess the General's loyalty to the Union. His instructions were explicit:*

Senator Seward, Mr. Washburne, and other good friends have certified to General Scott's loyalty, high character, and personal integrity, and he himself has written to me offering his services without reserve; but he is a Virginian, you know, and while I have no reason or evidence to warrant me in questioning him or his motives, still, I shall feel better satisfied if you will visit him in my behalf. When you call, insist on a personal interview, and do not leave till you have seen and sounded him. Listen to the old man and look him in the face, note carefully what he says and how he says it, and then, when you return with your report, I shall probably be well enough informed to determine with some degree of accuracy where he stands and what to expect of him. — *Mather's account as given to Jesse W. Weik, in Weik-1, 594 (1911).*[307] {D}

Contemporary evidence indicates that Mather was sent to Washington by Governor Richard Yates.[308]

NETTIE COLBURN MAYNARD (1841–1892) *A spiritualist and practicing medium who allegedly held a number of séances attended by Lincoln.*

1. *At a sitting in Georgetown on the night of February 5, 1863, a spirit controlling Nettie advised Lincoln to raise the morale of the army by visiting the front. He said:*

If that will do any good, it is easily done. . . . Matters are pretty serious down there, and perhaps the simplest remedy is the best. I have often noticed in life that little things have sometimes greater weight than larger ones. — *Maynard, 87, 88 (1891).* {E}

Evidence that Lincoln attended séances is weak, depending almost entirely on the statements of spiritualists. In this instance, there is stronger evidence that the Lincolns entertained at home during the evening of February 5.[309]

2. *At the same meeting, which one scholar has called Lincoln's "best authenticated experience with spiritualism,"*[310] *another medium present caused a grand piano to move up and down while she played it. Lincoln and several other men climbed upon the piano in an effort to hold it down, but the movement continued. Lincoln concluded that the phenomenon was caused by some "invisible power" and suggested the following response to any scoffer:*

You should bring such person here, and when the piano seems to rise, have him slip his foot under the leg and be convinced (doubtless) by the weight of **evidence** resting upon his **understanding**. —*90–91.* {E}

GEORGE B. MCCLELLAN (1826–1885) *Commander of the Army of the Potomac from the summer of 1861 until November 1862 and for approximately four months during that time, commander in chief of all Union armies. McClellan's renditions of Lincoln's words were undoubtedly affected by his own vanity and his abiding contempt for the President, whom he referred to privately as an "idiot" a "well-meaning baboon," and "the original gorilla." For example, after the two successful Union engagements immediately preceding the battle of Antietam, Lincoln telegraphed: "Your despatches of to-day received. God bless you, and all with you. Destroy the rebel army, if possible." McClellan, writing to his wife just two weeks* *later, complained that he had heard nothing from Washington about his recent victories "except from the President in the following **beautiful** language. 'Your dispatch received. God bless you and all with you. Can't you beat them some more before they get off?'!!!"*[311]

1. *In August 1861, without consulting McClellan, Lincoln appointed Illinoisan David Hunter a major general of volunteers, explaining that:*

the people of Illinois seemed to want somebody to be a sort of father to them, and he thought Hunter would answer that purpose. —*McClellan-2, 160 (1887). {C}*

2. *As they left Seward's house one evening in November 1861, Lincoln remarked:*

that it had been suggested to him that it was no more safe for me than for him to walk out at night without some attendants . . . that they would probably give more for my scalp at Richmond than for his. —*McClellan to his wife, November 17, 1861, in McClellan-1, 136. {B}*

3. *When a magician giving a private performance asked Lincoln for his handkerchief, he replied:*

You've got me now, I ain't got any! —*November 21, 1861, McClellan-1, 137. {B}*

4. *The day after the appointment of Stanton, Lincoln went to McClellan's house to apologize for not consulting him on the subject. He said:*

that he knew Stanton to be a friend of mine and assumed that I would be glad to have him secretary of war, and that he feared that if he told me beforehand "some of those fellows" would say that I had dragooned him into it. —*McClellan-2, 161. {C}*

5. *Even McClellan acknowledged Lincoln's skill as a storyteller. One night, the General read a dispatch from a regimental commander that obviously overstated the fierceness of a recent engagement. Lincoln said that:*

it reminded him of a notorious liar, who attained such a reputation as an exaggerator that he finally instructed his servant to stop him, when his tongue was running too rapidly, by pulling his coat or touching his feet. One day the master was relating wonders he had seen in Europe and described a building which was about a mile long and a half-mile high. Just then the servant's heel came down on the narrator's toes, and he stopped abruptly. One of the listeners asked how broad this remarkable building might be; the narrator modestly replied, "About a foot!" —*McClellan-2, 162.*[312] *{C}*

6. *Concerning the order of March 31, 1862, transferring a division from the Army of the Potomac to the newly created Mountain Department in western Virginia, which he had justified as a necessary response to pressure, Lincoln said:*

that he knew this thing to be wrong and . . . that the pressure was only a political one to swell Frémont's command.

He promised that: he would allow no other troops to be withdrawn from my command. —*McClellan-2, 165. {C}*

7. *Early in the morning of March 8, 1862, at a time when he was perfecting his plan for a flanking movement toward Richmond by way of Urbanna, near the mouth of the Rappahannock, McClellan (according to his memoirs) was called to the White House for discussion of what Lincoln called "a very ugly matter." The President said that:*

it had been represented to him . . . that my plan of campaign . . . was conceived with the traitorous intent of removing its defenders from Washington and thus giving over to the enemy the capital and the government thus left defenseless.

To McClellan's indignant demand for a retraction, he replied: that he merely repeated what others had said and that he did not believe a word of it. —*McClellan-2, 195–96. {D}*

This recollection is questionable because there is no evidence that anyone who then knew about the Urbanna plan suspected McClellan of treasonable purposes.[313]

8. *After Pope's defeat in the second battle of Bull Run, Lincoln said that:*

he regarded Washington as lost.

He asked if McClellan: would, under the circumstances, as a favor to him, resume command and do the best that could be done. —*McClellan-2, 535. {D}*

Whatever Lincoln may have feared, he is not likely to have declared that he "regarded" the capital as lost.

9. *In early October, after the battle of Antietam, Lincoln visited the Army of the Potomac and, as McClellan remembered it, declared:*

that he was fully satisfied with my whole course from the beginning; that the only fault he could possibly find was that I was perhaps too prone to be sure that everything was ready before acting, but that my actions were all right when I started; . . . that he regarded me as the only general in the service capable of organizing and commanding a large army, and that he would stand by me; . . . that he wished me to continue my preparations for a new campaign, not to stir an inch until fully ready, and when ready, to do what I thought best. —*McClellan-2, 627–28. {D}*

The final part of this passage is scarcely credible in view of considerable evidence that Lincoln was prodding McClellan to move immediately against Lee's army.[314] *Allen Thorndike Rice recalled that McClellan, shortly before his death, quoted Lincoln as having said to him:* General, you have saved the country. You must remain in command and carry us through to the end.

And when McClellan expressed the fear that he would not be allowed enough time for preparation: General, I pledge myself to stand between you and harm. —*Rice AT, xxxix–xl (1886). {D}*

JOHN MCCLINTOCK (1814–1870) *Methodist clergyman and editor who during the Civil War held pastorates in New York City and Paris. He was later the first president of Drew Theological Seminary.*

1. *Talking with McClintock, probably in 1864, about the effects of the Emancipation Proclamation in Europe, Lincoln said:*

Ah, Providence is stronger than either you or I. When I issued that proclamation, I was in great doubt about it myself. I did not think that the people had been quite educated up to it, and I feared its effects upon the border states. Yet I think it was right. I knew it would help our cause in Europe, and I trusted in God and did it. —*Sermon preached April 16, 1865, in* Voices, *136. {C}*

ALEXANDER K. MCCLURE (1828–1909) *A Republican editor and legislator who was one of the powers in Pennsylvania politics and an ally of the state's wartime governor, Andrew G. Curtin. McClure talked with Lincoln now and then but probably exaggerated the amount of time he spent in his company, and it was surely an overstatement to say: "In all of the many grave political emergencies arising from the new and often appalling duties imposed by internecine war, I was one of those called to the inner councils of Abraham Lincoln."*[315] *Some of McClure's recollections are so dubious as to cast a certain amount of doubt on everything he wrote about Lincoln.*

1. *At Harrisburg, Pennsylvania, on February 22, 1861, Lincoln listened to proposals for a secret passage through Baltimore and asked his advisers:*

What would the nation think of its president stealing into the capital like a thief in the night? —*McClure-1, 52 (1892). {C}*

2. *On the problem of office-seekers at the beginning of his presidency, Lincoln remarked:*

I seem like one sitting in a palace, assigning apartments to importunate applicants while the structure is on fire and likely soon to perish in ashes. —*McClure-1, 63–64. {D}*

This is a variation on a Lincoln quotation published many years earlier by Henry J. Raymond (q.v.) and no doubt familiar to McClure. In a later version, McClure changed the metaphor, saying that he once heard Lincoln define his position as: one who was sitting in a vast temple hearing the clamor of those who wanted to enter and enjoy it, when its consuming flames were kissing the heavens. —*McClure-4, 204 (1902). {D}*

3. *In spite of reassurances from General Scott during a conference at the White House on April 15, 1861, Lincoln said with reference to the Confederate commander at Charleston:*

It does seem to me, General, that if I were Beauregard, I would take Washington. —*McClure-1, 69.* {D}

4. *After the battle of Shiloh in April 1862, McClure urged that Grant be removed from command. Lincoln replied:*

I can't spare this man; he fights. —*McClure-1, 196.* {D}

Accompanying misstatements of fact by McClure raise doubts about the authenticity of this famous quotation.[316]

5. *In a discussion soon after the battle of Gettysburg, Lincoln said:*

Now don't misunderstand me about General Meade. I am profoundly grateful down to the bottom of my boots for what he did at Gettysburg, but I think that if I had been General Meade I would have fought another battle. —*McClure-1, 360.* {C}

6. *In 1863, when McClure and other Pennsylvanians sought a diplomatic appointment for Governor Andrew G. Curtin, the President acknowledged that Curtin was entitled to the honor, but then he added:*

I'm in the position of young Sheridan when old Sheridan called him to task for his rakish conduct and said to him that he must take a wife; to which young Sheridan replied: "Very well, father, but whose wife shall I take?" It's all very well to say that I will give Curtin a mission, but whose mission am I to take? —*McClure-1, 263.* {C}

It is not unlikely that Lincoln was familiar with this old wheeze. According to George W. Julian (q.v.), he also used it with respect to the problem of finding a command for Frémont.[317]

7. *Conferring with a group of Pennsylvanians about an approaching political contest in their state, he said:*

You know I never was a contriver. I don't know much about how things are done in politics, but I think you gentlemen understand the situation in your state, and I want to learn what may be done to ensure the success we all desire. —*McClure-1, 87.* {C}[318]

8. *As the Chase presidential boom got under way in 1863, Lincoln remarked:*

McClure, how would it do if I were to decline Chase? . . . I don't know exactly how it might be done, but that reminds me of a story of two Democratic candidates for senator in Egypt, Illinois, in its early political times. That section of Illinois was almost solidly Democratic, as you know, and nobody but Democrats were candidates for office. Two Democratic candidates for senator met each other in joint debate from day to day and gradually became more and more exasperated at each other, until their discussions were simply disgraceful wrangles, and they both became ashamed of them. They finally agreed that either should say anything he pleased about the other and it should not be resented as an offense, and from that time on, the campaign progressed without any special display of ill temper. On election night, the two candidates, who lived in the same town, were receiving their returns together, and the contest was uncomfortably close. A distant precinct, in which one of the candidates confidently expected a large majority, was finally reported with a majority against him. The disappointed candidate expressed great surprise, to which the other candidate answered that he should not be surprised, as he had taken the liberty of declining him in that district the evening before the election. He reminded the defeated candidate that he had agreed that either was free to say anything about the other without offense and added that under that authority, he had gone up into that district and taken the liberty of saying that his opponent had retired from the contest, and therefore the vote of the district was changed, and the declined candidate was thus defeated.

With a hearty laugh, Lincoln added: I think I had better decline Chase. — *McClure-1, 135–36. {D}*

   9. *In May 1864, when McClure assured him that his renomination was a foregone conclusion, Lincoln said:*

Well, McClure, what you say seems to be unanswerable, but I don't quite forget that I was nominated for president in a convention that was two-thirds for the other fellow. —*McClure-1, 137. {C}*

In an interview in 1890, McClure quoted Lincoln somewhat differently: Yes, McClure, you are probably right, but I cannot forget that the convention which nominated me for president, until near its close, was considered to be safe for another man. — *Wilson RR-2, 538. {D}*

If Lincoln really made such a statement, he was inaccurate. Even before the balloting began at Chicago in 1860, it was plain that Seward, the front-runner, had a hard fight on his hands.

   10. *According to McClure, just before the Republican national convention of 1864, to which he was a delegate, Lincoln summoned him to Washington and requested him to support Andrew Johnson for vice president instead of the incumbent Hannibal Hamlin. Lincoln explained that:*

he based his preference for Johnson not on personal grounds, but on the fact that the nomination of a southern man like Johnson, would tend to desectionalize the South. — *Wilson RR-2, 536. {D}*

In McClure-1, 128–29, there is a more extended and considerably different summary of Lincoln's stated reasons for preferring Johnson: First, he was the most conspicuous, most aggressive, and the most able of all the War Democrats of that time and was just in the position to command the largest measure of sympathy and support from that very important political element. Dix, Dickinson, Butler, and Holt had made no such impressive exhibition of their loyalty as had Johnson in Tennessee. He was then just in the midst of his great work of rehabilitating his rebellious state and restoring it to the Union, and his loyal achievements were therefore fresh before the people and certain to continue so during the campaign. . . . Second, the stronger and more imperative reason . . . the great peril of the Union at that day was the recognition of the Confederacy by England and France, and every month's delay of the overthrow of the rebellious armies increased the danger. Extraordinary efforts had been made . . . to stimulate the Union sentiment, especially in England, but with only moderate success, and there was no safety from one day to another against a war with England and France that would have been fatal to the success of the Union cause. The only possible way to hinder recognition was to show successful results of the war in restoring the dissevered states to their old allegiance . . . By no other method could the Union sentiment abroad be so greatly inspired and strengthened as by the nomination and election of a representative southern man to the vice presidency from one of the rebellious states in the very heart of the Confederacy. {E}

It is difficult to credit Lincoln's advancing the absurd argument that nomination of a southerner for vice president was the best way to prevent British and French recognition of the Confederacy (a danger that had, in any case, virtually disappeared by June of 1864). McClure is the leading authority for the view that Lincoln, while pretending to be neutral, secretly maneuvered to secure Johnson's nomination. In 1891, he and John G. Nicolay engaged in an acrimonious public controversy on the subject. Ward Hill Lamon was one of a number of men who corroborated McClure; John Hay and Noah Brooks were among those siding with Nicolay. The latter was probably wrong in his insistence that Lincoln favored the renomination of Hamlin, and modern historians, with some exceptions, have been disposed to believe McClure. Nevertheless, his testimony should be viewed with skepticism, and not only because it was challenged by several persons closer to the President than he was. For one thing, in Lincoln's only contemporary written statement on the subject, he expressed a determination not to interfere with the vice-presidential nomination.[319] Furthermore, there appears to be no reliable evidence that Lincoln actively intervened to influence the vote of any other delegate to the convention. And one should also note that the Pennsylvania delegates at Baltimore, including McClure, did not play a crucial role in the nomination of Johnson. It was their chairman, Simon Cameron, who placed Hamlin's name in nomination, and they gave the Vice President their unanimous support until the balloting made it clear that he could not win, at which point they joined a number of other delegations in switching to Johnson.[320]

11. *On about August 13, 1864, a dejected Lincoln told McClure that:*

of all the Republican members of the House, he could name but one in whose personal and political friendship he could absolutely confide. That one man was Isaac N. Arnold of Illinois. —*McClure-1, 125-26. {C}*

12. *During the same discussion, according to McClure, Lincoln read a paper he had written proposing to pay the southern states $400 million as compensation for their slaves, on condition that they should resume their allegiance to the United States and accept emancipation. He then said:*

If I could only get this proposition before the southern people, I believe they would accept it, and I have faith that the northern people, however startled at first, would soon appreciate the wisdom of such a settlement of the war. One hundred days of war would cost us the $400 million I would propose to give for emancipation and a restored republic, not to speak of the priceless sacrifice of life and the additional sacrifice of property; but were I to make this offer now, it would defeat me inevitably and probably defeat emancipation. —*McClure-1, 126-27, substantially repeated, 241. {D}*

On February 5, 1865, Lincoln submitted such a plan to the cabinet in the form of a proposed message to Congress.[321] *Members voiced their unanimous disapproval, and he put it aside. There appears to be no corroboration for McClure's assertion that Lincoln not only drafted the proposal and revealed its content to him some six months earlier, but discussed it "repeatedly" in subsequent conversations between them.*

13. *When McClure sought to learn his intentions with respect to the chief justiceship, Lincoln replied:*

Well, McClure, the fact is I'm "shut pan" on that question. —*McClure-1, 78. {D}*

John Hay (q.v.) made note of Lincoln's using the same expression on the same subject, and McClure could have read about it in Nicolay and Hay, IX, 391-92.

14. *Shortly before the election of 1864, Lincoln indicated a reluctance to approach Grant about furloughing some Pennsylvania troops so that they could vote. He said to McClure:*

I have no reason to believe that Grant prefers my election to that of McClellan. —*McClure-1, 203. {D}*

Contemporary documents indicate that Grant emphatically favored Lincoln's re-election and that Lincoln knew it.[322]

15. *At about the same time, Lincoln told McClure that:*

his name would go into history darkly shadowed by a fraternal war that he would be held responsible for inaugurating if he were unable to continue in office to conquer the rebellion and restore the Union. — *McClure-2, 711 (1900). {C}*

16. *More than a decade after he published his recollections without mention of it, McClure recalled having heard Lincoln say:*

I have always felt that God must love common people, or he wouldn't have made so many of them. — *McClure-5, 91 (1904). {C}*

John Hay's diary (Hay-1, 143), which provides the earliest version of this remark, had not yet been published in 1903 and thus presumably constitutes independent corroboration. The New York Tribune *of December 20, 1903, printed McClure's story with modifications that gave the quotation its classic form: "Well, God must love the common people, He's made so many of 'em."*

JOHN MCCONNELL (1824–1898) *Illinois farmer and Civil War officer, whom Lincoln labeled "a sterling man."* [323]

1. *After his election to the legislature in 1854, Lincoln resigned in order to be a candidate for the United States Senate, and a Democrat was elected in his place. When McConnell spoke to him about this setback, he replied that:*

it reminded him of the big lubberly boy who stubbed his toe while running and sat down on a stump and was holding his foot in his hand. A man came along and asked him how he felt, and he said he was too big to cry, and it hurt too bad to laugh.[324] — *McConnell's statement in the Chicago* Times-Herald, *August 25, 1895. {D}*

Other versions of this story were published as early as 1859. Charles S. Zane (q.v.) recalled that Lincoln made such a remark after his defeat in 1858.

2. *In 1860, McConnell saw the President-elect being attacked by a goat that some youngsters had been teasing. Lincoln held the animal by his horns and tried to reason with him, thus:*

I didn't bother you. It was the boys. Why don't you go and butt the boys? I wouldn't trouble you. — *Ibid. {C}*

RICHARD CUNNINGHAM MCCORMICK (1832–1901) *New York journalist and Republican leader, appointed secretary of Arizona Territory in 1863, later governor and territorial delegate in Congress.*

1. *In New York City on February 27, 1860, the day of his Cooper Union address, discussing personal finances with an Illinois acquaintance of former years:*

I have the cottage at Springfield and about $8,000 in money. If they make me vice president with Seward, as some say they will, I hope I shall be able to increase it to $20,000, and that is as much as any man ought to want. — *McCormick's recollection in the New York* Post, *May 3, 1865. {D}*

Such unrestrained talk about his private affairs and political hopes would have been uncharacteristic.[325]

2. *The same day, upon being introduced to George Bancroft:*

I am on my way to Massachusetts, where I have a son at school, who, if report be true, already knows much more than his father. —*Ibid.* {D}

Robert Lincoln was then at school in New Hampshire.

3. *In 1862, on the problem of accounting for all the men on the army rolls:*

They are like fleas; the more you shovel them up in the corner the more they get away from you. —*Ibid.* {C}

John Hay and Mary A. Livermore (qq.v.) noted similar expressions.

4. *In 1863, to John A. Gurley, the newly appointed governor of Arizona Territory:*

Tell the miners I hope to visit them and dig some gold and silver after the war. —*Ibid.* {C}

5. *Later in 1863, when suddenly faced with the need to name a chief justice for Arizona Territory, Lincoln said that he had already made his choice:*

It is Grimes's man, and I must do something for Grimes. I have tried hard to please him from the start, but he complains, and I must satisfy him if possible. —*Ibid.* {C}

In Hay-1, 235, Lincoln likewise expresses concern about his relations with Iowa's Senator James W. Grimes.

HUGH McCULLOCH (1808–1895)   *Indiana banker appointed controller of the currency in 1863 and secretary of the treasury in 1865.*

1. *Soon after March 4, 1865, McCulloch expressed concern about Andrew Johnson's behavior at the inaugural ceremony. Lincoln replied:*

I have known Andy Johnson for many years. He made a bad slip the other day, but you need not be scared; Andy ain't a drunkard. —*McCulloch, 373 (1889).* {C}

2. *In one of his last conversations with McCulloch, Lincoln said:*

I am here by the blunders of the Democrats. If, instead of resolving that the war was a failure, they had resolved that I was a failure and denounced me for not more vigorously prosecuting it, I should not have been re-elected, and I reckon that you would not have been secretary of the treasury. — *McCulloch, 162.* {C}

3. *On the day of his assassination, looking "cheerful and happy," Lincoln said to McCulloch:*

We must look to you, Mr. Secretary, for the money to pay off the soldiers. —222. {C}

JOSEPH E. MCDONALD (1819–1891)   *Indiana lawyer and politician who was the state's attorney general in the 1850s and the Democratic candidate for governor in 1864. He later served a term in the United States Senate.*

1. *In 1857, speaking of a murder case he had recently prosecuted, Lincoln told McDonald that his sleep had been disturbed by worry over the harshness of his attack on the defendant, Isaac Wyant:*

I acted on the theory that he was "possuming" insanity, and now I fear I have been too severe and that the poor fellow may be insane after all. If he cannot realize the wrong of his crime, then I was wrong in aiding to punish him. —*Statement of McDonald to Jesse W. Weik, August 28, 1888, in Herndon, II, 344n.*[326] {D}

McDonald's recollection is unreliable. He mistakenly placed the trial in 1858 and seems to have forgotten that Wyant was, in fact, acquitted by the jury. Thus, there was little reason for Lincoln to lose sleep about "aiding to punish" him.

2. *Early in 1865, McDonald and a colleague, accompanied by Senator Thomas A. Hendricks of Indiana, consulted the President about their clients, Lambden Milligan and others, who had been sentenced to death by a military tribunal. During the interview, McDonald maintained that members of the organization called the "Sons of Liberty" were not a disloyal element. Lincoln responded:*

I think your view the right one. I do not believe that 100,000 Democrats in Indiana are disloyal, and my friend General Singleton has told me substantially what you have. He and I have been friends for years—were Whigs together, and when the party went to pieces, he went to the Democrats and I to the Republicans, and though we have drifted apart politically, we are nonetheless friends, and I know that he won't lie. He told me that he was a member of the organization and gave me an outline of its principles. — *Interview in the Pittsburgh* Commercial, *reprinted in the New York* Times, *December 28, 1882.* {D}

Either Lincoln was dissembling or McDonald exaggerated his forbearance toward Peace Democrats.

3. *In the discussion of Milligan's sentence, Lincoln said:*

If I was the butcher, there wouldn't be much meat eaten in this world. The death penalty is one of the most difficult questions with which I have to deal. When a soldier deserts to go over to the enemy and is captured, I let the law take its course, but when a man has been a long time in the service and has not had a furlough, and who, when on picket, gets to thinking of his wife and children and breaks for tall timber, I never let them hurt a hair of his head. And now, don't give yourself any concern about this case. The papers have not reached me yet, and I don't intend to be in a hurry about getting hold of them when they do come. I hope, before very long, that things over the way [pointing across the Potomac] will be in such shape that we can all join in a grand jubilee. —*Ibid.*[327] {C}

According to David Davis, who perhaps heard it from McDonald, Lincoln told the latter that he would not hang the men, but added: "I guess I'll keep them in prison awhile to keep them from killing the government."[328]

4. *During a discussion of Horace Greeley's peace negotiation at Niagara Falls in July 1864, Lincoln said:*

In some respects Mr. Greeley is a great man, but in many others he is wanting in common sense. I am well satisfied with his good faith. And gentlemen, I tell you, there has never been a time since the war began when I was not willing to stop it if I could do so and preserve the Union, and earlier in the war I would have omitted some of the conditions of my note to the rebel commissioners, but I had become satisfied that no lasting peace could be built up between the states in some of which there were free and in others, slave institutions, and, therefore, I made the recognition of the abolition of slavery a *sine qua non.* —*Ibid.* {C}

IRVIN MCDOWELL (1818–85)   *Union general in command at the first battle of Bull Run, later a corps commander.*

1. *At a conference on January 10, 1862, that included Seward, Chase, McDowell, and General William B. Franklin, but not General McClellan, who had been ill with typhoid fever, Lincoln began by speaking:*

of the exhausted condition of the Treasury; of the loss of public credit; of the Jacobinism in Congress; of the delicate condition of our foreign relations; of the bad news he had received from the West, particularly as contained in a letter from General Halleck on the state of affairs in Missouri; of the want of cooperation between General Halleck and General Buell; but more than all, the sickness of General McClellan.

He was [he said] in great distress, and as he had been to General McClellan's house and the General did not ask to see him, and as he must talk to somebody, he had sent for General Franklin and myself to obtain our opinion as to the possibility of soon commencing active operations with the Army of the Potomac.

If something was not soon done, the bottom would be out of the whole affair, and if General McClellan did not want to use the army, he would like to borrow it, provided he could see how it could be made to do something. —*McDowell memorandum in Raymond-1, 773 (1865).* {B}

According to Raymond, Lincoln later endorsed the accuracy of the memorandum, "except the phrase attributed to me 'of the Jacobinism of Congress,' which phrase I do not remember using literally or in substance, and which I wish not to be published in any event."[329]

2. *At another meeting two days later, Lincoln was urged to cancel Burnside's expedition to North Carolina and add that force to McClellan's. He replied that:*

he disliked exceedingly to stop a thing long since planned, just as it was ready to strike. —776. {B}

JOHN J. MCGILVRA (1827–1903)   *Chicago lawyer whom Lincoln appointed United States attorney for Washington Territory. His assertion that during a visit to Washington, D.C., in the winter of 1863–64, he called "frequently" upon Lincoln is probably an exaggeration.*

1. *In McGilvra's presence, Lincoln became impatient with the inventor of a sighting device for rifles that had already been rejected by the War Department. He asked permission to have it tested by men in the ranks. Said the President:*

Ah, what you want, then, is a license to go down to the army and peddle your looking-glass machine among the soldiers, is it? Good day, sir. — *McGilvra speech, 1896, in Doig, 310.* {C}

2. *Told by his son Robert on one occasion that the family carriage was out of repair and could not be driven to the theater that evening, Lincoln said:*

Well, then, Bob, we will just take our feet in our hands and paddle over there. —*311.* {C}

HENRY MCHENRY   *An acquaintance and onetime client of Lincoln who lived in Petersburg, Illinois, the town closest to New Salem.*

1. *In contrast with Abner Y. Ellis's recollection (q.v.), McHenry remembered the following words from Lincoln's first political speech after his discharge from service in the Black Hawk War:*

Gentlemen, I have just returned from the campaign. My personal appearance is rather shabby and dark. I am almost as red as those men I have been chasing through the prairies and forests on the rivers of Illinois. — *McHenry to Herndon, May 29, 1865 (7:105–11), Herndon-Weik Collection.* {C}

JAMES M. MCKAYE (1805–1888)   *An antislavery New Yorker who in 1863 was a member of a commission investigating the condition of freedmen in coastal South Carolina.*

1. *Told of the blacks' worshipful attitude toward him, Lincoln said:*

It is a momentous thing to be the instrument, under Providence, of the liberation of a race. —*McKaye's account retold in Carpenter-1, 733–34 (1865).* {D}

WILLIAM MCNEELY   *A New Salem acquaintance for whom Lincoln once surveyed a parcel of land.*

    1. *McNeely remembered Lincoln's saying on one occasion that:*

a fool could learn about as well as a wise man, but after he had learned, it did not do him any good. —*Oldroyd, 393 (1882).* {C}

GEORGE GORDON MEADE (1815–1872)   *Union general, commander of the Army of the Potomac at Gettysburg and thereafter until the end of the war.*

    1. *During Lincoln's visit to the army at Fredericksburg on May 23, 1862, Meade praised his recent revocation of General David Hunter's order liberating slaves in the South Atlantic states. Lincoln said:*

I am trying to do my duty, but no one can imagine what influences are brought to bear on me. —*Meade to his wife, May 23, 1862, in Meade, I, 267.* {A}

    2. *Visiting the army several days after the battle of Chancellorsville, the President remarked:*

that the result was in his judgment most unfortunate; that he did not blame anyone—he believed everyone had done all in his power; and that the disaster was one that could not be helped. Nevertheless, he thought its effect, both at home and abroad, would be more serious and injurious than any previous act of the war. —*Meade to his wife, May 8, 1863, in I, 372.* {B}

JOSEPH MEDILL (1823–1899)   *Longtime editor of the Chicago* Tribune, *whose recollections contributed more to the Lincoln myth than to Lincoln biography. Medill, for instance, lent credence to the notorious "reconstruction" by Henry C. Whitney (q.v.) of Lincoln's famous "lost speech" of 1856, pronouncing it a work of "remarkable accuracy."* [330]

    1. *In 1855, Lincoln said to Medill, who had only recently assumed control of the* Tribune *in partnership with Charles H. Ray:*

I like your paper; I didn't like it before you boys took hold of it; it was too much of a Know-Nothing sheet. —*Medill in interview by Newton Macmillan, Chicago* Tribune, *April 14, 1895.* [331] {C}

    2. *Replying on August 27, 1858, to Medill's warning that it would be unwise to ask Douglas the second on his list of questions prepared for the debate that day at Freeport:*

Well, I do not agree with you. Judge Douglas is more anxious to be elected president two years from now than he is to be re-elected to the Senate for the third time this fall. Can't you see that if he answers my question as you seem to think he will, he will exasperate every slaveholder in the South, because they all hold to the doctrine that the people of the South have an equal constitutional right to take every species of their property into the territories as freely as the citizens of the North may carry all kinds of their property into any territory? Every slaveholder believes that under the compromises of the Constitution a southern slaveholder can take his bondsmen into Kansas and keep and work them there during the period that Kansas has a territorial government only, with just as much right to protection from the federal law as a Massachusetts abolitionist would have if he went into the territory with a span of horses to farm, or if some of our Illinois people should go over there with mules for the same purpose. Now, that being so, don't you see that if Douglas replies in the way you imagine he will he would lose every supporter he expects to get in the South, and under the Democratic rule of requiring a two-thirds majority to nominate, it would be impossible for him to be a successful candidate of the Democratic party in 1860? Now, on the other hand, if he should reply in the negative and declare that a majority of the people of the territory cannot drive out any slaves that may be brought in or exclude slaves from being brought in, and thus deny the power of the squatters to protect themselves from slavery, he would stand a mighty slim chance of being elected to the Senate, and he would probably render it impossible, if he were nominated, to carry any northern state. And if he answers as you believe he will, it will cost him a good many votes down in Egypt, where the old settlers come mostly from the slave states and feel about the same as the people of the South. — *Medill reminiscence, Chicago* Tribune, *May 19, 1895.* {E}

This effusion is not merely an example of inflated recollection. It is false testimony, whether from bad memory or deliberate choice. Contemporary evidence shows that Medill actually urged Lincoln to ask just such a question.[332]

3. *Medill recalled that in the early part of 1860, Lincoln repeatedly said to him:*

See here, you boys have got me up a peg too high. How about the vice presidency—won't that do? — *Macmillan interview as continued in the Chicago* Tribune, *April 21, 1895.* {D}

There appears to be no reliable evidence that Lincoln talked this way to anybody.

4. *According to Medill, Lincoln said to him a few days after the presidential election:*

Do you recollect the argument we had on the way up to Freeport two years ago over my question that I was going to ask Judge Douglas about the power of squatters to exclude slavery from territories? . . . Now don't you think I was right in putting that question to him?

After Medill responded that they had both been right because Douglas's reply, while severely damaging his chances for the presidency, secured his re-election to the Senate, Lincoln continued: And I have won the place that he was playing for. —*Chicago* Tribune, *May 19, 1895.* {E}

5. *On a visit to the White House during the war, Medill allegedly asked Lincoln why he delivered that "radical speech" in 1858 (meaning the House-Divided speech) and allegedly received this reply:*

Well, after you fellows had got me into that position of standard-bearer, I concluded to take a stand that reflected the real heartfelt thoughts of our party on that terrible slavery question. It was ground we could afford to be beaten on in the preliminary battle with slavery. So I concluded to say something that would make everybody think. —*Chicago* Tribune, *April 14, 1895.* {D}

Another contribution to the myth that Lincoln in 1858 was thinking primarily of the coming contest for the presidency, rather than the immediate race for the Senate.[333]

6. *Medill recalled that when he urged emancipation, Lincoln responded:*

I dare not issue this thunderbolt until the Union armies shall have won some decisive victory. The effect of a proclamation now would be to alienate the Union Democrats in the North and in the army, without whose aid we must fail; for the zeal of the abolitionists has been well-nigh exhausted by the sacrifice of its eldest born these two years past. —*Medill interview in the* Washington Post, *April 28, 1895.* {D}

By the summer of 1862, when Lincoln resolved to issue an emancipation proclamation, only one year had passed since the first major battle of the war, and abolitionist zeal, far from being exhausted, was stronger than ever.

7. *In 1864, when Medill and two other spokesmen for Chicago asked that the city be excused from furnishing any more men in the draft:*

Gentlemen, after Boston, Chicago has been the chief instrument in bringing this war on the country. It is you who are largely responsible for making blood flow as it has. You called for war until we had it. You called for emancipation, and I have given it to you. Whatever you have asked, you have had. The Northwest has opposed the South as New England has opposed the South. Now you come here begging to be let off from the call for men which I have made to carry out the war you have demanded. You ought to be ashamed of yourselves. I have a right to expect better things of you. Go home, and raise your 6,000 extra men. And you, Medill, you are acting like a coward. You and your *Tribune* have had more influence than any paper in the Northwest in making this war. You can influence great masses, and yet you cry to be spared at a moment when your cause is suffering. Go home and send us those men. —*Ida M. Tarbell's interview with Medill, June 25, 1895, Tarbell Papers; printed with a minor revision in Tarbell, III, 149.* {C}

8. *On December 21, 1864, Lincoln told Medill that things were "looking better than at any time since the war began" and that there was strong reason to hope for a "speedy and successful termination." Referring to the recent collapse of John B. Hood's counteroffensive in Tennessee, he said:*

The present condition of Hood's army reminds me of the story of Bill Sykes's dog. Did you ever hear it?

Well, the thing happened down below Beardstown on the Illinois River a good many years ago. Sykes owned a long-legged, wolfish "yaller" dog that was in the habit of prowling about and breaking into the neighbors' meat houses, killing sheep, and committing other depredations. People had tried to shoot and poison him, but somehow they failed to dispatch the brute. At last a neighbor named John Henderson concluded he would try an experiment on him. The dog had plundered his milk house, eaten his cream, and upset the crocks of milk. So he took a coon's bladder, which one of his boys had dried, filled it with powder, scooped out the soft part of a biscuit, slipped in the bag of powder, and when the dog next came in sight, he stuck a piece of punk in the mouth of the bladder, set fire to it, closed up the biscuit with butter, and laid it down. In a minute, the dog came along, smelled the bread, and gobbled it down of a single gulp. "All right," says Henderson, "we shall soon see how things will work." In a minute or two, there was a tremendous explosion, as if a torpedo had gone off under one of our gunboats. The head of the yaller dog rolled down the hill; the hind legs flew some distance, catching on a fence stake; the forequarters fell on the porch; and the intestines scattered around on the ground for a couple of rods.

"Well," says a neighbor who happened to come along, "I guess you have got rid of that cussed dog at last." "Yes," says Henderson, "I reckon that **that** dog, **as a dog**, won't be of much account hereafter." So with Hood's army; I reckon that **that** army, **as an army**, won't be of much account hereafter. — *Medill's correspondence of December 22 in the Chicago* Tribune, *December 25, 1864. {B}*

Zall, 63, gives a different Medill version and notes other versions of this oft-repeated story. It will also be found in Chandler-1, 449.

9. *Speaking of Sherman's whereabouts during the final days of the war, Lincoln said:*

that reminds me of the horse-jockey in Kentucky who got baptized in the river. He asked to be immersed the second time. The preacher demurred, but the horse-jockey insisting, prevailed. When he came up from the second ducking he gasped: "There! Now the devil may go to hell." — *Washington* Post, *April 28, 1895. {D}*

The relevance of the story to the subject is far from clear.

MONTGOMERY C. MEIGS (1816–1892)   *Army engineer who in the 1850s super-vised construction of the Washington Aqueduct and the wings and dome of the Capitol. He was the army's quartermaster-general throughout the Civil War.*

1. *Near the end of March 1861, Meigs learned directly from the President:*

that he had verbally directed General Scott to hold all these forts and make arrangements to reinforce them on the 5th of March. That about the 10th, finding nothing done, he had thought it best to put himself on record and had repeated the order in writing. That he learned that the *Brooklyn* had gone to Key West, and as she had the troops for Pickens on board, he supposed that his orders had fizzled out. That General Scott had told him he did not think that Pickens ought to be held, and this had given him a cold shock. . . .

After further consultation, Lincoln ordered Meigs and Erasmus D. Keyes: to see General Scott, tell him [the] instructions of the President and that he wished this thing done and not to let it fail unless he can show why the refusing him something he asked is necessary. I depend [he said] upon you gentlemen to push this thing through. —*Diary entry, March 31, 1861, in Meigs, 300. {B}*

2. *On January 10, 1862, Lincoln said to Meigs in great distress:*

General, what shall I do? The people are impatient; Chase has no money, and he tells me he can raise no more; the General of the Army has typhoid fever. The bottom is out of the tub. What shall I do? —*Recollection (1888) in Meigs, 292. {C}*

SAMUEL H. MELVIN   *Springfield druggist, later president of the California state board of pharmacy.*

1. *In a contribution to the Nicolay-McClure controversy over the vice-presidential nomination in 1864, Melvin recalled that at the White House a few days before the Baltimore convention, Lincoln said that:*

all things considered, . . . he would prefer to have Hamlin again associated with him on the ticket. —*Melvin to John G. Nicolay, July 25, 1891, Nicolay Papers. {C}*

BENJAMIN F. MILLARD   *A clergyman who called at the White House in March 1861.*

1. *Millard heard Lincoln's response to a Maryland woman whose brother, a naval officer, had been arrested after resigning his commission, presumably with intent to support the Confederacy. Lincoln said:*

Do you really think, now, that it was quite loyal in him to send in his resignation in such a crisis?

Indicating, nevertheless, a willingness to do what he could for her brother, he added: But the fact is, there are some of us here who have taken an oath to support this old government. — *Millard's letter in the New York* Times, *November 6, 1864.*[334] {C}

ANSON S. MILLER (1810–1891)   *Lawyer-politician, state legislator, and probate judge in Rockford, Illinois. Miller was for some twenty years acquainted with Lincoln, who in 1864 offered him an appointment as a territorial judge.*[335]

1. *After the Republican state convention at Decatur in May 1860, Miller asked Lincoln whether he was going to the national convention in Chicago. He replied:*

No. You fellows have talked of me for the presidency, and I think I would look better at home. . . . I have never asked a man to help me in this matter; neither shall I. But, when you and the other friends go to the convention, if you can use my name to carry out our principles, do so, whatever position you may assign me. But, if you choose to give me no place, **you** know that I am used to working in the ranks. But, Judge, if I had the making of the president, I would make William H. Seward president. — *Miller to an interviewer in 1867, Tyler, 255–56.* {D}

Certain factual inaccuracies in Miller's statements to Tyler reinforce one's general doubt about the credibility of this recollection.

2. *Talking with Miller in 1863 about his house in Springfield, Lincoln said:*

Well, Judge, I don't know when I shall ever see that home again. I certainly shan't before we get through this scrape. — *257.* {C}

JAMES MILLIKIN   *A Pennsylvania judge, spokesman for the state's iron and coal industry.*

1. *In Philadelphia on February 21, 1861, Millikin informed Lincoln that the opposition of certain Pennsylvania Republicans to the appointment of Simon Cameron to the cabinet had been withdrawn. The President-elect replied:*

that it relieved him greatly. . . . he was not, however, prepared to decide the matter and would not until he should reach Washington; that it had been suggested it would perhaps be proper and desirable to retain some of the present cabinet officers, for a short time, at least, if they would consent to remain. — *Millikin to Cameron, February 22, 1861, in Pratt-2, 59.* {B}

Lincoln spoke in similar fashion to Titian J. Coffey (q.v.). Among possible holdovers, he named Joseph Holt, secretary of war, but on March 5, he nominated Cameron for that position.

JACOB M. MILSLAGLE (1839–?)   *In his boyhood, a resident of Sangamon County.*

1. *Milslagle recalled Lincoln's saying at dinner when he asked for corn bread:*

That is my kind of bread. —*Signed statement in the Lincoln Reminiscences File, ISHL. {C}*

NOYES W. MINER   *Springfield minister, neighbor of the Lincolns from the mid-1850s to 1861. The religiosity expressed in some of the passages that follow may reflect Miner's capacity for invention or Lincoln's capacity for taking on the coloration of his audience.*

   1. On the subject of poverty and hard work, Lincoln once said to Miner:

I have seen a good deal of the backside of this world. —*Miner, 12 (1882). {C}*

   2. Lincoln on one occasion told Miner:

that he would never take a case unless he thought there was merit in it. —*Miner, 21-22. {C}*

   3. Miner visited the White House in April 1862, just after the battle of Shiloh, and told a downhearted president that the Christians of the country were praying mightily for him. Lincoln said:

I believe that, and this is an encouraging thought to me. If I were not sustained by the prayers of God's people, I could not endure the constant pressure. I should give up hoping for success. —*Miner to J. Young Scammon and others, August 1, 1871, published in the New York Times, March 23, 1872. Of this interview Miner later wrote, "I afterwards took full notes."*[336] *{C}*

   4. During the same conversation, Miner asked whether he believed that the rebellion could be put down, and Lincoln replied:

You know I am not of a very hopeful temperament. I can take hold of a thing and hold on a good while. But trusting in God for help, and believing that our cause is just and right, I firmly believe we shall conquer in the end. But the struggle will be protracted and severe, involving a fearful loss of property and life. What strange scenes are these through which we are passing. I am sometimes astonished at the part I am acting in this terrible drama. I can hardly believe that I am the same man I was a few years ago when I was living in my humble way with you in Springfield. I often ask myself the question, "When shall I awake and find it all a dream?" —*Ibid. {C}*

   5. Lincoln went on to say:

This getting the nomination for president and being elected is all very pleasant to a man's ambition, but to **be** the president and to meet the responsibilities and discharge the duties of the office in times like these is anything but pleasant. I would gladly, if I could, take my neck from under the yoke and go home with you to Springfield and live, as I used, in peace with my friends, than to endure this harassing kind of life. But it has pleased

Almighty God to place me in my present position, and, looking up to Him for wisdom and divine guidance, I must work out my destiny as best I can. —*Ibid.* {C}

6. *According to a letter said to have been written by Miner to one of his daughters on April 12, 1862, Lincoln fed a cat at the dinner table, saying:*

If the gold fork was good enough for Buchanan, I think it is good enough for Tabby. —*Hill MM, 9 (1923).* {D}

GEORGE W. MINIER   *Illinois resident.*

1. *In* Case v. Snow Brothers, *which, according to Minier, was argued in the county court at Tremont, Illinois, in 1847, Lincoln represented the plaintiff, suing to collect a note received in payment for a plow and oxen. The Snows pleaded that the note had no legal force because they had been minors at the time they signed it. Lincoln said in his brief closing argument:*

Gentlemen of the jury, are you willing to allow these boys to begin life with this shame and disgrace attached to their character? If you are, I am not. The best judge of human character that ever wrote has left these immortal words for all of us to ponder.

Here, he quoted the passage from Othello *that begins: "Good name in man and woman, dear my lord, / Is the immediate jewel of their souls." Then he continued:* Gentlemen of the jury, these poor, innocent boys would never have attempted this low villainy, had it not been for the advice of these lawyers. . . . And now, gentlemen, you have it in your power to set these boys right before the world. —*Minier statement, April 10, 1882, in Herndon, III, 619-20; also in Oldroyd, 187-89.* {D}

No trace of this case has been found in the court records or in the Herndon-Weik Collection.[337]

2. *Minier once heard Lincoln speak on the tariff in this fashion:*

I confess that I have not any very decided views on the question. A revenue we must have. In order to keep house, we must have breakfast, dinner, and supper, and this tariff business seems to be necessary to bring them. But yet, there is something obscure about it. It reminds me of the fellow that came into a grocery down here in Menard County at Salem, where I once lived, and called for a picayune's worth of crackers; so the clerk laid them out on the counter. After sitting awhile, he said to the clerk, "I don't want these crackers. Take them, and give me a glass of cider." So the clerk put the crackers back into the box and handed the fellow the cider. After drinking, he started for the door. "Here, Bill," called out the clerk, "pay me for your cider." "Why," said Bill, "I gave you the crackers for it." "Well, then, pay me for the crackers." "But I haint had any," responded Bill. "That's so," said the clerk. "Well, clear out! It seems to me that I've lost a picayune somehow, but I can't make it out exactly." So [Lincoln continued after the laughter had subsided] it is with the tariff; somebody gets the picayune, but I don't exactly understand how. — *Oldroyd, 189-90. {D}*

Ezra M. Prince recalled hearing Lincoln use the same old story at Blooming-ton on September 16, 1856, to illustrate the fraudulence of Douglas's popular sovereignty.[338]

ORMSBY M. MITCHEL (1809–1862)   *Astronomer and Union general who died of yellow fever while commanding forces in South Carolina.*

    1. Reportedly, Lincoln said on one occasion when General McClellan failed to show up for a meeting at the White House:

Never mind; I will hold McClellan's horse if he will only bring us success. — *Mitchel's account to his son, F. A. Mitchel, whose letter is cited in Nicolay and Hay, IV, 469n (1890). {E}*

This familiar quotation is suspect, not only because of its weak provenance but because the alleged meeting is unsubstantiated by any contemporary evidence and seems unlikely to have taken place.[339]

    2. On July 25, 1862, Mitchel told Salmon P. Chase that the President had asked him earlier that day:

with what force he could take Vicksburg and clear the river, and, with the black population on its banks, hold it open below Memphis. — *Chase, 352. {B}*

GEORGE H. MONROE (1826–1903)   *A young Massachusetts Whig, later a well-known Boston journalist, who heard Congressman Lincoln speak at Dedham on the afternoon of September 20, 1848.*

    1. After he had talked for only a half-hour, Lincoln heard the bell sum-moning passengers to the train and announced that he must leave immediately. Voices from the audience urged him to continue, but he said:

I can't take any risks. I have engaged to go to Cambridge, and I must be there. I came here as I agreed, and I am going there in the same way. — *Monroe's letter (signed "Templeton") to the Boston* Herald, *April 26, 1885. {C}*

RISDON M. MOORE   *A college professor who became a colonel commanding an Illinois regiment of volunteers. During the Black Hawk War, his father had ar-ranged the wrestling match between Lincoln and Lorenzo Dow Thompson that is also described by William G. Greene (q.v.)*

    1. On August 8, 1860, according to Moore, he called on Lincoln with a delegation of McKendree College students to express their support for his presi-dential candidacy. He was introduced in the presence of other political leaders, and Lincoln said:

I want to know which of the Moore families you belong to, before we go further, as I have a grudge against one of them.

After Moore identified himself more precisely, Lincoln explained how the wrestling match had come about and then continued: Gentlemen, I felt of Mr. Thompson, the St. Clair champion, and told my boys I could throw him, and they could bet what they pleased. You see, I had never been thrown, or dusted, as the phrase then was, and, I believe, Thompson said the same to the St. Clair boys, that they might bet their bottom dollar that he could down me. You may think a wrestle, or "wrastle," as we called such contests of skill and strength, was a small matter, but I tell you the whole army was out to see it. We took our holds, his choice first, a side hold. I then realized from his grip for the first time that he was a powerful man and that I would have no easy job. The struggle was a severe one, but after many passes and efforts he threw me. My boys yelled out "a dog fall," which meant then a drawn battle, but I told my boys it was fair, and then said to Thompson, "now it's your turn to go down," as it was my hold then, Indian hug. We took our holds again and after the fiercest struggle of the kind that I ever had, he threw me again, almost as easily at my hold as at his own. My men raised another protest, but I again told them it was a fair down. Why, gentlemen, that man could throw a grizzly bear. —*Moore RM, 434 (1904).* {D}

Moore's father had already told him the story of the match, and one suspects that this rather lengthy passage is a blend of what he remembered hearing from both men.

JAMES K. MOORHEAD (1806–1884) *Pennsylvania businessman and Republican congressman.*

1. *In January 1861, Moorhead and another Pennsylvania politician, Alexander Cummings, visited Springfield to urge the appointment of Simon Cameron to a cabinet position. They found Lincoln unreceptive. He said:*

All through the campaign my friends have been calling me "Honest Old Abe," and I have been elected mainly on that cry. What will be thought now if the first thing I do is to appoint Cameron, whose very name stinks in the nostrils of the people for his corruption? —*Moorhead statement, May 12 and 13, 1880, Nicolay Papers.* {C}

CHARLES S. MOREHEAD (1802–1868) *Antebellum governor of Kentucky, who owned plantation properties in Mississippi. He had served in Congress when Lincoln was there and claimed to have been "upon very intimate terms" with him. He was a member of the Washington peace convention in February 1861. Morehead's hostility to the Lincoln administration was intensified by his arrest and imprisonment for approximately four months beginning in September 1861. After his release, he left the country and went to Canada, Europe, and Mexico, returning after the war to Mississippi.*

1. *On February 26 or 27, 1861,*[340] *soon after his arrival in Washington, Lincoln had an interview with a number of men from the upper South, including Morehead and several other members of the peace convention. To this group he said:*

that he was accidentally elected president of the United States; that he had never aspired to a position of that kind; that it had never entered into his head; but that from the fact of his having made a race for the Senate of the United States with Judge Douglas in the state of Illinois, his name became prominent, and he was accidentally selected and elected afterwards as president of the United States; that running that race in a local election, his speeches had been published; and that anyone might examine his speeches, and they would find that he had said nothing against the interests of the South. He defied them to point out any one sentence in all the various addresses that he had made in that canvass that could be tortured into enmity against the South, except . . . one expression, namely, that "a house divided against itself must fall; they must either be all slave or all free states," and . . . he explained afterwards that that was an abstract opinion and never intended to be made the basis of his political action.

He remarked at the same time: that the clause in the Constitution of the United States requiring fugitive slaves to be delivered up was a constitutional provision, was a part of the organic law of the land, and that he would execute that with more fidelity than any southern man they could possibly find, and he could not imagine what was the cause of the deep and apparently settled enmity that existed towards him throughout the entire South.

Asked for guarantees to the South, he said: that he was willing to give a constitutional guarantee that slavery should not be molested in any way directly or indirectly in the states; that he was willing to go further and give a guarantee that it should not be molested in the District of Columbia; that he would go still further and say that it should not be disturbed in the docks, arsenals, forts, and other places within the slaveholding states; but as for slavery in the territories, that his whole life was dedicated in opposition to its extension there; that he was elected by a party which had made that a portion of its platform, and he should consider that he was betraying that party if he ever agreed, under any state of the case, to allow slavery to be extended in the territories.

Reminded that a majority had voted against him in the recent election, he replied: that if he was a minority president, he was not the first, and that at all events, he had obtained more votes than we could muster for any other man.

Urged to withdraw federal troops from forts within the seceded states and to avoid taking any kind of coercive action, he responded with one of Aesop's fables: Aesop, you know, illustrates great principles often by making mute animals speak and act, and according to him there was a lion once that was desperately in love with a beautiful lady, and he courted the lady, and the lady became enamored of him and agreed to marry him, and the old people were asked for their consent. They were afraid of the power of the lion with his long and sharp claws and his tusks, and they said to him, "We can have no objection to so respectable a personage as you, but our daughter is frail and delicate, and we hope that you will submit to have your claws cut off and your tusks drawn, because they might do very serious injury to her." The lion submitted, being very much in love. His claws were cut off and his tusks drawn, and they took clubs, then, and knocked him on the head.

After an emotional appeal from the elderly Virginia statesman, William Cabell Rives, Lincoln exclaimed: Mr. Rives! Mr. Rives! if Virginia will stay in, I will withdraw the troops from Fort Sumter.[341]

As the meeting ended, Lincoln said: Well, gentlemen, I have been wondering very much whether, if Mr. Douglas or Mr. Bell had been elected president, you would have dared talk to him as freely as you have to me. — *Morehead, 67-72 (1862). {D}*

This is the account of a bitter critic, who followed it by accusing Lincoln of a "duplicity unparalleled" in history.[342] With respect to evacuation of the forts, in particular, it differs from Lincoln's own version of what he said and how the southerners responded, as recorded in Hay-1, 30. The same sort of Sumter-for-Virginia bargain may have been offered to John B. Baldwin (q.v.) about five weeks later.

EDWIN D. MORGAN (1811–1883)   *Civil War governor of New York, elected to the United States Senate in 1863.*

1. *Soon after issuance of the Emancipation Proclamation, Lincoln said to Morgan:*

We are a good deal like whalers who have been long on a chase. At last we have got our harpoon fairly into the monster, but we must now look how we steer, or with one flop of his tail, he will yet send us all into eternity. — *Morgan's statement to Francis B. Carpenter in 1864, quoted in Carpenter-2, 75 (1866). {D}*

RICHARD PRICE MORGAN (1819–1910)   *Civil engineer, superintendent of the Chicago and Alton Railroad at Bloomington in the 1850s.*

1. *According to Morgan, he stood next to Lincoln in Bloomington in the summer of 1856 and heard him say in a speech:*

You can fool some of the people all of the time and all of the people some of the time, but you can't fool all of the people all of the time. —*Phillips-2, 102 (1910)*. {D}

There is good reason to doubt that Lincoln ever uttered these words, even though Morgan's account is partly corroborated by that of William Pitt Kellogg (q.v.).[343]

2. *On May 9, 1860, at the Republican state convention in Decatur, John Hanks caused a sensation when he and a companion brought in two rails, together with a banner proclaiming Lincoln to be "the Rail Candidate for President." After inspecting them, Lincoln said:*

Well, that was a long time ago. However, it is possible I may have split these rails, but I cannot identify them . . . I can only say I have split a great many better-looking ones. —*91-92*. {C}

3. *After the state convention had instructed national delegates to support him for the presidency, Lincoln replied to a question about his chances:*

I reckon I'll get about a hundred votes at Chicago, and I have a notion that will be the high mark for me. —*94*. {C}

DANIEL J. MORRELL (1821–1885)   *Iron manufacturer in Johnstown, Pennsylvania, later a member of Congress.*

1. *Concerning a soldier charged with desertion, who had gone home during an inactive military period to earn money for support of his mother, Lincoln said:*

Well, he is a good son. He went to save his mother. I do not think it would do him any good to shoot him, do you? —*Morrell's account given to Andrew Carnegie some days after the incident, as related by Carnegie in the New York Sun, February 12, 1911*. {D}

LOT M. MORRILL (1813–1883)   *Senator from Maine during the Civil War and Reconstruction era.*

1. *Morrill recalled Lincoln's saying on one occasion:*

I don't know but that God has created some one man great enough to comprehend the whole of this stupendous crisis and transaction from beginning to end and endowed him with sufficient wisdom to manage and direct it. I confess I do not fully understand and foresee it all. But I am placed here where I am obliged to the best of my poor ability to deal with it. And that being the case, I can only go just as fast as I can see how to go. —*Interview, September 20, 1878, Nicolay Papers*. {C}

2. *A tearful Baltimore woman seeking release of her son, a prisoner of war, recited proudly his Confederate military record. Lincoln said:*

And now that he is taken prisoner, it is the first time, probably, that you have ever shed tears over what your boy has done. Good morning, Madam,

I can do nothing for your boy today. — *Interview, undated but probably 1878, Nicolay Papers.* {C}

JOHN LOTHROP MOTLEY (1814–1877)   *Historian, author of* The Rise of the Dutch Republic, *whom Lincoln appointed minister to Austria.*

1. *On June 17, 1861, Lincoln said concerning military operations and his general in chief:*

Scott will not let us outsiders know anything of his plans. — *Motley to his wife, June 20, 1861, in Motley, II, 143.* {A}

2. *In another conversation four days later, Motley spoke eloquently in defense of England, this at a time when Americans were angry about the Queen's recent proclamation of neutrality, which recognized the Confederacy as a belligerent in international law. Lincoln replied that he thought Motley was right, adding, however:*

But it does not so much signify what I think; you must persuade Seward to think as you do. — *Motley to his wife, June 23, 1861, in II, 159.* {A}

JAMES E. MURDOCH (1811–1893)   *Actor and elocutionist who visited the White House more than once and whose dramatic readings Lincoln heard a number of times.*

1. *Murdoch was in Springfield on business late in 1860 and met Lincoln at the studio of the sculptor Thomas D. Jones (q.v.). In a literary discussion, Lincoln compared the personalities of Falstaff and Sam Weller and said of Dickens that:*

his works of fiction were so near the reality that the author seemed to him to have picked up his materials from actual life as he elbowed his way through its crowded thoroughfares, after the manner, in a certain sense, of Shakespeare himself. — *Oldroyd, 347 (1882).* {D}

The weight of the slender evidence is on the side of Lincoln's being little acquainted with the work of novelists.[344]

2. *During the same discussion, Lincoln expressed his belief that Hamlet's speech beginning "To be, or not to be" was less impressive than Claudius's speech beginning "Oh, my offence is rank":*[345]

The former is merely a philosophical reflection on the question of life and death, without actual reference to a future judgment, while the latter is a solemn acknowledgment of inevitable punishment hereafter for the infraction of divine law. Let anyone reflect on the moral tone of the two soliloquies, and there can be no mistaking the force and grandeur of the lesson taught by one and the merely speculative consideration in the other of an alternative for the ills that flesh is heir to. — *348.* {C}

GUSTAVUS A. MYERS   *A Richmond attorney.*

1. *On April 5, 1865, John A. Campbell (q.v.) took Myers with him when he visited Lincoln aboard a gunboat in the James River. General Godfrey Weitzel, commander of the Union force that had just occupied Richmond, also attended the meeting. The President read a prepared statement of basic peace terms,*[346] *adding comments as he went along. He declared that:*

he could not retract from anything he had heretofore announced as his opinion in his public message to Congress, and independently of his own opinions about the question of property in slaves, he could not without a violation of good faith change any of his sentiments in that behalf. In reference to confiscation of property, **that** was in his power, and he should be disposed to exercise that power in the spirit of sincere liberality. It had not gone to any great extent, and, except in the cases of the rights of third persons intervening by purchase, a question he must of course leave to the courts to decide, he did not think there would [be] any insurmountable obstacle in adjusting the matter.

Professing himself really desirous to see an end to the struggle, he said: he hoped in the providence of God that there never would be another.

He also told them that: he was thinking over a plan by which the Virginia legislature might be brought to hold their meeting in the Capitol in Richmond, for the purpose of seeing whether they desired to take any action on behalf of the states in view of the existing state of affairs . . . the outline of his plan being, that safe conduct should be given to the members to come hither, and that after a reasonable time were allowed them to deliberate, should they arrive at no conclusion, they would have safe conduct afforded them to leave Richmond.

In response to remarks by Campbell and Myers, he said that: he had never attached much importance to the oath of allegiance being required, but that General Weitzel was present and that it depended on his view. —*Myers, 321–22 (1865). {B}*

━━━

EDWARD D. NEILL (1823–1893)   *Army and hospital chaplain who in 1864 became an assistant secretary in the White House.*

1. *The morning after his re-election, Lincoln spoke in kindly fashion of his defeated opponent. He told Neill:*

that General Scott had recommended McClellan as an officer who had studied the science of war and had been in the Crimea during the war against Russia; and that he told Scott that he knew nothing about the science of war, and it was very important to have just such a person to organize the raw recruits of the Republic around Washington. —*Neill, 28 (1885).* *{C}*

2. *Asked whether his visit on June 16, 1864, to the Sanitary Fair in Philadelphia had been pleasant, he replied that:*

it was, and the ladies, he believed, had made several thousand dollars by placing him on exhibition. —*29. {C}*

3. *In response to an inquiry from the Assistant Adjutant General about certain papers that he had under review:*

Tell him they are still in soak. —*29. {C}*

4. *When Stanton refused Lincoln's request that he see a man proposing to provide a home for soldiers' orphans:*

Well! well! The requests of the commander in chief don't amount to much. —*32-33. {C}*

5. *To his doorkeeper when the war was over:* This talk about Mr. Davis tires me. I hope he will mount a fleet horse, reach the shores of the Gulf of Mexico, and drive so far into its waters that we shall never see him again. —*40. {D}*

It is not clear that Neill heard Lincoln make this remark.

WILLIAM A. NEWELL (1817–1901) *A former Know-Nothing governor of New Jersey who was elected to Congress as a Republican in 1864.*

1. *According to Newell's testimony in 1878 before an army board reviewing the dismissal of General Fitz-John Porter, Lincoln had told him in 1864:*

that he had not been able to give that personal attention to the case which its merits required; that he had accepted the opinion of the Judge Advocate General and of the War Department as the basis of his action; that if any new evidence exculpatory of General Porter could be introduced, he would be very glad to give him an opportunity to have it presented; that he had had a high regard for General Porter personally and as a soldier, and that he hoped that he would be able to vindicate himself in that way. —Senate Document 37, p. 320. *{C}*

JOHN W. NICHOLS *Union soldier whose company of Pennsylvania volunteers was for a time detailed to serve as a presidential bodyguard.*

1. *One mid-August night, probably in 1864, when Nichols was on sentry duty at the Soldiers' Home, there was the sound of a rifle shot. Then a bareheaded figure came riding at high speed up to the gate. It was the President, who said while dismounting:*

He came pretty near getting away with me, didn't he? He got the bit in his teeth before I could draw the rein.

Lincoln went on to explain: that somebody had fired a gun off at the foot of the hill, and that his horse had become scared and jerked his hat off.

The next day, Nichols and another soldier found the hat with a bullet hole in the crown. When it was shown to him, Lincoln said that: it was put there by some foolish gunner and was not intended for him.

He added that: he wanted the matter kept quiet. — *Interview in the Wheeling* Register, *reprinted in the New York* Times, *April 6, 1887. {C}*

Ward Hill Lamon (q.v.) provided an account of this incident as supposedly given to him by Lincoln.[347]

JOHN G. NICOLAY (1832–1901) *Lincoln's private secretary throughout his presidency and afterward coauthor with John Hay of the ten-volume "official" biography,* Abraham Lincoln: A History *(1890). When Nicolay was a small child, his family emigrated from Bavaria and settled eventually in Pike County, Illinois. At the age of sixteen, he went to work for the Pittsfield* Free Press, *rising in half a dozen years from printer's devil to editor and proprietor. It was during this period that he began his lifelong friendship with John Hay, who for a time attended an academy in Pittsfield. Nicolay sold his newspaper in 1856 and accepted appointment as clerk for the Illinois secretary of state in Springfield. There he became well acquainted with Lincoln, who, after his nomination for the presidency, chose the young German-American to be his private secretary. Later, as president-elect, Lincoln acceded to Nicolay's proposal that Hay be taken along to Washington as a second member of the secretarial staff. After the Civil War, Nicolay served a term as consul at Paris and was for fifteen years marshal of the United States Supreme Court. His principal contribution to Lincoln source material is in the form of memoranda that he sometimes made of presidential remarks and conversations.*[348] *In the 1870s, he also interviewed and took statements from a number of men who had been associated with Lincoln. Like Hay, he never himself provided much in the way of reminiscence about life with the "Tycoon," and the two men were disposed to exclude such material from their biography, considering it to be generally unreliable.*

1. *Nicolay heard Lincoln's lecture on "Discoveries and Inventions" in Springfield on April 26, 1860, and later recalled that he characterized laughter as:*

the joyous, beautiful, universal evergreen of life. — *Nicolay, 832 (1894). {C}*

2. *Shortly before the presidential election, Lincoln said to a visitor from New York:*

I declare to you this morning, General, that for personal considerations, I would rather have a full term in the Senate—a place in which I would feel more consciously able to discharge the duties required and where there was more chance to make reputation and less danger of losing it—than four years of the presidency. — *Nicolay memorandum, October 25, 1860, Nicolay Papers.* {A}

3. *A visitor on November 5, 1860, urged that Lincoln offer some reassurance to southern men who were honestly alarmed. He said:*

There are no such men. [I] have thought much about it. It is the trick by which the South breaks down every northern man. I would go to Washington without the support of the men who supported me and were my friends before election. I would be as powerless as a block of buckeye wood. The honest man (you are talking of honest men) will look at our platform and what I have said. There they will find everything I could now say or which they would ask me to say. All I could say would be but repetition. Having told them all these things ten times already, would they believe the eleventh declaration? Let us be practical. There are many general terms afloat, such as "conservatism," "enforcement of the irrepressible conflict at the point of the bayonet," "hostility to the South," and so forth — all of which mean nothing without definition. What then could I say to allay their fears, if they will not define what particular act or acts they fear from me or my friends? . . .

To the assertion that the South was arming itself, he replied: The North does not fear invasion from the slave states, and we of the North certainly have no desire and never had to invade the South. . . . If I shall begin to yield to these threats, if I begin dallying with them, the men who have elected me, if I shall be elected, would give me up before my inauguration, and the South, seeing it, would deliberately kick me out. . . . If I should be elected the first duty to the country would be to stand by the men who elected me. — *Memorandum, November 5, 1860.*[349] {A}

4. *On November 15, 1860, with the secession movement under way in the South, Lincoln remarked:*

My own impression is at present (leaving myself room to modify the opinion if, upon a further investigation, I should see fit to do so) that this government possesses both the authority and the power to maintain its own integrity. That, however, is not the ugly point of this matter. The ugly point is the necessity of keeping the government together by force, as ours should be a government of fraternity. — *Memorandum, November 15, 1860.*[350] {A}

5. *Ten days after the election, Judge Daniel Breck of Kentucky called to urge the formation of a conservative cabinet, excluding obnoxious men like William H. Seward in order to save the country. Lincoln replied:*

that so far as he knew, not one single prominent public Republican had justly made himself obnoxious to the South by anything he had said or done, and that they had only become so because the southern politicians had so persistently bespotted and bespattered every northern man by their misrepresentations to rob them of what strength they might otherwise have.

He told Breck: that the substance of his plan was that the Republicans should now again surrender the government into the hands of the men they had just conquered and that the cause should take to its bosom the enemy who had always fought it and who would still continue to fight and oppose it.

He ended by saying that: he should, however, give his views a serious and respectful consideration. —*Memorandum, November 16, 1861. {B}*

6. *To two men from Indiana pressing the claims of Caleb B. Smith to a place in the cabinet, Lincoln said that:*

being determined to act with caution and not embarrass himself with promises, he could only say that he saw no insuperable objections to Indiana's having a man, nor to Smith's being the man. —*Memorandum, December 11, 1860. {B}*

7. *On December 13, Lincoln declared:*

The very existence of a general and national government implies the legal power, right, and duty of maintaining its own integrity. This, if not expressed, is at least implied in the Constitution. The right of a state to secede is not an open or debatable question. It was fully discussed in Jackson's time and denied not only by him, but by the vote of Congress. It is the duty of a president to execute the laws and maintain the existing government. He cannot entertain any proposition for dissolution or dismemberment. He was not elected for any such purpose. As a matter of theoretical speculation it is probably true that if the people, with whom the whole question rests, should become tired of the present government, they might change it in the manner prescribed by the Constitution. —*Nicolay and Hay, III, 248, citing a Nicolay memorandum. {A, B}*

8. *In an interview with Edward Bates on December 15, Lincoln made his first offer of a place in the cabinet. He explained that:*

in doing this, he did not desire to burden him with one of the drudgery offices. Some of his friends have asked for him the State Department. He could not now offer him this, which was usually considered the first place in the cabinet, for the reason that he should offer that place to Mr. Seward, in view of his ability, his integrity, and his commanding influence and fitness for the place. He did this as a matter of duty to the party and to Mr. Seward's many and strong friends, while at the same time it accorded perfectly with his own personal inclinations, notwithstanding some opposition on the part of sincere and warm friends. He had not yet communicated with Mr. Seward, and did not know whether he would accept the appointment, as there had been some doubts expressed about his doing so. He would probably know in a few days. He therefore could not now offer him the State Department, but would offer him what he supposed would be most congenial and for which he was certainly in every way qualified, namely: the attorney generalship.

Lincoln expressed gratification when Bates accepted; then he said that: by way of preparing himself for the questions which the new administration were likely to encounter, he desired him between this time and the inauguration, to examine very thoroughly and make himself familiar with the Constitution and the laws relating to the question of secession, so as to be prepared to give a definite opinion upon the various aspects of the question. On one other point he desired him also to make some examination. Under the present administration the mails in the South had been violated with impunity and with the sanction of the government. Under the new government, he feared some trouble from this question. It was well understood by intelligent men that the perfect and unrestrained freedom of speech and the press which exists at the North was practically incompatible with the existing institutions at the South, and he feared that radical Republicans at the North might claim at the hands of the new administration the enforcement of the right and endeavor to make the mail the means of thrusting upon the South matter which even their conservative and well-meaning men might deem inimical and dangerous. *—Memorandum, December 15, 1860. {B}*

Bates (q.v.) left his own briefer record of the interview.

9. *Told by Nicolay of a rumor that President Buchanan had ordered Major Anderson to surrender Fort Moultrie if attacked, Lincoln exclaimed:*

If that is true, they ought to hang him. *—Memorandum, December 22, 1860. {A}*

10. *During the same discussion, he said:*

Among the letters you saw me mail yesterday was one to Washburne, who had written me that he had just had a long conversation with General Scott and that the General felt considerably outraged that the President would not act as he wished him to in reinforcing the forts. I wrote to Washburne to tell General Scott confidentially that I wished him to be prepared, immediately after my inauguration, to make arrangements at once to hold the forts, or if they have been taken, to take them back again.[351]

Later, in a conversation with his partner, William H. Herndon, he repeated the substance of his message to Scott and then added: There can be no doubt that in any event, that is good ground to live and to die by. *—Ibid. {A}*

11. *On March 2, 1861, Seward withdrew his acceptance of appointment as secretary of state. Lincoln replied two days later, asking him to reconsider and remarking, as he handed Nicolay the letter to copy:*

I can't afford to let Seward take the first trick. —*Nicolay and Hay, III, 371.* {C}

12. *On April 20, 1861, the day after federal troops were attacked in Baltimore, Lincoln received messengers from Mayor George W. Brown bearing a request that no more troops try to pass through the city. He said to them half playfully:*

If I grant you this, you will come tomorrow demanding that no troops shall pass around. — *Undated Nicolay memorandum.*[352] {C}

13. *During a meeting with Brown and several other persons the next day, Lincoln said that:*

the capital being in the center of Maryland and being in danger, the troops must come to defend it and must of necessity come through Maryland, there being no other route. — *Ibid.* {C}

14. *Concerning the crisis of the Union, the President declared that:*

the real question involved in it (as he had about made up his mind, though he should still think further about it while writing his message) was whether a free and representative government had the right and power to protect and maintain itself. Admit the right of a minority to secede at will, and the occasion for such secession would almost as likely be any other as the slavery question. — *Memorandum, May 7, 1861.* {B}

15. *In conversation with Orville H. Browning (q.v.), Lincoln remarked:*

Browning, of all the trials I have had since I came here, none begin to compare with those I had between the inauguration and the fall of Fort Sumter. They were so great that could I have anticipated them, I would not have believed it possible to survive them. The first thing that was handed to me after I entered this room, when I came from the inauguration, was the letter from Major Anderson saying that their provisions would be exhausted before an expedition could be sent to their relief. — *Memorandum, July 3, 1861.* {A}

16. *In July 1861, it became public knowledge that during the Fort Sumter crisis three months earlier, James E. Harvey, a journalist recently named minister to Portugal, had sent telegrams to a South Carolinian, Andrew G. McGrath, giving him inside information on the administration's intentions with respect to the fort. Discussing the affair with Senator Browning on July 13, Lincoln and Seward undertook to explain Harvey's conduct and its relation to the presence of Confederate "commissioners" in Washington. The President said:*

He had been for many years one of those newsmongers connected with newspapers whose constant passion is to obtain "items" and as such was still here. He was a South Carolinian, had been a classmate and intimate friend of Judge McGrath, who had been corresponding with him to keep himself posted about the probable action of the government. Harvey, being of the compromising and conciliating class of politicians, had constantly hoped for a peaceable arrangement and had frequently advised McGrath. The commissioners had come here, and though they never presented themselves either in person or by letter to me, yet they had informally left, so that it fell in Mr. Seward's hands, a paper setting for[th] their mission, and so on. He in reply had informally written an answer (without signature) which was permitted again to fall into their hands, and which informed them substantially that they could not be received. Justice Campbell of the Supreme Court was also here and exerting himself constantly to effect some understanding or agreement. In this way, he became a sort of medium of communication between Governor Seward and the commissioners, talking frequently with each.

During the time when we were all debating what was to be done with Fort Sumter, it seemed that all our secrets got out, and the impression gradually gained ground outside that it was to be evacuated. Though that was never determined, some members of the cabinet being for it and others against it, yet the idea got out and gained credence until even the commissioners and Judge Campbell believed it. I think that perhaps during the time I told Mr. Seward he might say to Judge Campbell that I should not attempt to provision the fort without giving them notice. That was after I had duly weighed the matter and come to the deliberate conclusion that that would be the best policy. If there was nothing before to bind us in honor to give such notice, I felt so bound after this word was out, and accordingly the notice was given. Harvey, who was laboring in the same way, had been writing to McGrath that he believed the fort would be evacuated, and when he accidentally discovered the expedition was going to provision it, he believed his honor involved and felt it his duty to give McGrath notice, which he did. — *Memorandum, July 13, 1861.*[353] *{A}*

17. *At about 5:00 P.M. on February 20, 1862, Lincoln came into the secretarial office and said:*

Well, Nicolay, my boy is gone—he is actually gone. *Then he burst into tears and left.* — *Nicolay memorandum in notebook for February–March 1862, Nicolay Papers. {A}*

18. *Concerning the fiasco of the canal boats that were inches too wide to pass through a lock, Lincoln said to Randolph B. Marcy, McClellan's father-in-law and chief of staff:*

Why in the [tar]nation, General Marcy, couldn't the General have known whether a boat would go through that lock before he spent a million dollars getting them there? I am no engineer, but it seems to me that if I wished to know whether a boat would go through a hole, or a lock, common sense would teach me to go and measure it. I am almost despairing at these results. Everything seems to fail. The general impression is daily growing that the General does not intend to do anything. By a failure like this we lose all the prestige we gained by the capture of Fort Donelson. I am grievously disappointed and almost in despair. —*Memorandum, February 27, 1862.* {A}

At about the same time, Lincoln complained to Charles Sumner (q.v.) on the subject.

19. *In a message to Congress on March 6, 1862, Lincoln proposed a program of federal compensation to any state that would adopt gradual abolition of slavery.*[354] *Three days later, he talked about it with Frank Blair:*

Since I sent in my message, about the usual amount of calling by the border-state congressmen has taken place; and although they have all been very friendly, not one of them has yet said a word to me about it. Garrett Davis has been here three times since, but although he has been very cordial, he has never opened his mouth on the subject. Now I should like very much sometime soon to get them all together here and have a frank talk about it. I desired to ask you whether you were aware of any reason why I should not do so.

Blair suggested that it might be better to wait until the army did something further. Lincoln replied: That is just the reason why I do not wish to wait. If we should have successes, they may feel and say: The rebellion is crushed and it matters not whether we do anything about this matter. I want them to consider it and interest themselves in it as an auxiliary means for putting down the rebels. I want to tell them that if they will take hold and do this, the war will cease—there will be no further need of keeping standing armies among them—and that they will get rid of all the troubles incident thereto. If they do not, the armies must stay in their midst. It is impossible to prevent Negroes from coming into our lines. When they do, they press me on the one hand to have them returned, while another class of our friends will on the other, press me not to do so. —*Memorandum, March 9, 1862, in notebook for February-March 1862.* {A}

20. *When a worried Salmon P. Chase one day asked what should be done about the dreadful rate of government expenditure, Lincoln is said to have replied:*

Well, Mr. Secretary, I don't know, unless you give your paper mill another turn. —*Nicolay's undated recollection as told to his daughter Helen, Nicolay Papers.* {D}

21. *In December 1863, with the 38th Congress about to convene, Lincoln*

was still worried about rumors that Emerson Etheridge, the retiring clerk of the House of Representatives, intended to interpret a new law in such a way as to exclude some Republican members and thereby turn control of that body over to the Democrats.[355] He said to Schuyler Colfax:

The main thing, Colfax, is to be sure to have all our men there. Then if Mr. Etheridge undertakes revolutionary proceedings, let him be carried out on a chip and let our men organize the House. If the worst comes to the worst, a file of "invalids" may be held convenient to take care of him. — *Memorandum, December 6, 1863. {A}*

The final sentence, perhaps because of its unclarity, is omitted from the quotation as printed in Nicolay and Hay, VII, 391.

22. *Upon receiving the good news that Longstreet had failed in his siege of Knoxville and was in retreat toward Virginia with Burnside in pursuit, Lincoln said to Nicolay:*

This is one of the most important gains of the war. The difference between Burnside saved and Burnside lost is one of the greatest advantages of the war. It secures us East Tennessee.

During the same conversation he also remarked: Now, if this Army of the Potomac was good for anything, if the officers had anything in them, if the army had any legs, they could move 30,000 men down to Lynchburg and catch Longstreet. Can anybody doubt if Grant were here in command that he would catch him? There is not a man in the whole Union who would for a moment doubt it. But I do not think it would do to bring Grant away from the West. I talked with General Halleck this morning about the matter, and his opinion was the same. — *Memorandum, December 7, 1863. {A}*

23. *Concerning the letter of October 5, 1863, in which he had responded to the complaints of Kansas and Missouri Radicals, Lincoln remarked some two months later:*

When the Missouri delegation was appointed and it was known they were coming to see me, Seward asked that until I should hear and decide their case in my own mind, I would not say a word to him on the subject or in any way ask his opinion concerning the controversy, so that hereafter we might both say that he had taken no part whatever in the matter, to which I agreed. Yet Wendell Phillips said in a late speech that Seward had written the whole of that letter. — *Memorandum, December 8, 1863. {A}*

24. *When it was announced that Fernando Wood, a Democratic congressman and former mayor of New York, had called to see him, Lincoln said:*

I would rather he should not come about here so much. Tell Mr. Wood that I have nothing as yet to tell him on the subject we conversed about when he was last here. . . . I can tell you what Wood wants. He came here one day last week to urge me to publish some sort of amnesty for the northern sympathizers and abettors of the rebellion, which would include Vallandigham and permit him to return, and promised that if I would do so, they would have two Democratic candidates in the field at the next presidential election. —*Memorandum, December 14, 1863.* {A}

25. *On March 8, 1864, when Lincoln received Grant at the White House, he said to him:*

Tomorrow, at such time as you may arrange with the Secretary of War, I desire to make you a formal presentation of your commission as lieutenant general. I shall then make a very short speech to you, to which I desire you to reply for an object, and that you may be properly prepared to do so, I have written what I shall say (only four sentences in all), which I will read from my manuscript as an example which you may follow and also read your reply, as you are perhaps not as accustomed to speaking as I myself; and I therefore give you what I shall say that you may consider it and form your reply. There are two points that I would like to have you make in your answer: First, to say something which shall prevent or obviate any jealousy of you from any of the other generals in the service, and secondly, something which shall put you on as good terms as possible with the Army of the Potomac. Now consider whether this may not be said to make it of some advantage; and if you see any objection whatever to doing it, be under no restraint whatever in expressing that objection to the Secretary of War, who will talk further with you about it. —*Memorandum, March 8, 1864, printed with a few minor verbal changes in Nicolay and Hay, VIII, 340-41.* {A}

26. *According to Nicolay's later recollection, before leaving for Baltimore in early June 1864 to attend the national convention of the Republican or Union party, he asked Lincoln about his wishes with respect to the vice-presidential nomination. The President answered:*

that all the various candidates and their several supporters being his friends, he deemed it unbecoming in him to advocate the nomination of any one of them; but that privately and personally he would be best pleased if the convention would renominate the old ticket that had been so triumphantly elected in 1860 and which would show an unbroken faith and leadership in the Republican party and an unbroken and undivided support of that party to the administration and in the prosecution of the war. —*Undated Nicolay manuscript, perhaps written in 1891 at the time of his controversy with Alexander K. McClure (q.v.) on the subject.* {C}

27. *Commenting on Henry J. Raymond's proposal to send a peace mission to Richmond, Lincoln said that:*

it would be utter ruination. —*Nicolay to John Hay, August 25, 1864, Nicolay Papers.* {B}

28. *During the period when he was thinking about the appointment of a successor to Chief Justice Taney, who died in October 1864, Lincoln received what Nicolay described as a "kind and friendly letter" from Chase in Ohio. Smiling, he said:*

File it with his other recommendations. —*Nicolay and Hay, IX, 391-92.* {C}

29. *In January 1865, Lincoln was urged to recruit Charles Sumner's acquiescence in a political deal intended to facilitate passage of the Thirteenth Amendment in the House of Representatives. He replied:*

I can do nothing with Mr. Sumner in these matters. While Mr. Sumner is very cordial with me, he is making his history in an issue with me on this very point. He hopes to succeed in beating the president so as to change this government from its original form and making it a strong centralized power. . . . I think I understand Mr. Sumner, and I think he would be all the more resolute in his persistence on the points which Mr. Nicolay has mentioned to me if he supposed I were at all watching his course on this matter. —*Memorandum, January 18, 1865.* {A}

30. *To warnings that his life was in danger, Nicolay recalled, Lincoln would always answer as follows:*

I will be careful. But I cannot discharge my duties and withdraw myself entirely from danger of an assault. I see hundreds of strangers every day, and if anybody has the disposition to kill me he will find opportunity. To be absolutely safe I should lock myself up in a box. —*Nicolay interview in the Chicago* Herald, *December 4, 1887.* {C}

MOSES F. ODELL (1818-1866) *Democratic congressman from New York during the Civil War.*

1. *Odell once asked Lincoln whether he had really made the joke about sending some of Grant's brand of whiskey to every other general in the army. He replied:*

No, that is too good for me. —*As related by Odell in Nadal, 371 (1906).* {D}

A secondhand recollection, but it accords with one by Albert B. Chandler (q.v.).

RICHARD J. OGLESBY (1824-1899) *Illinois lawyer, soldier, and Whig-Republican politician, elected governor in 1864 and later a United States senator.*

1. *Oglesby recalled "distinctly" Lincoln's once saying to him:*

Dick, remember to keep close to the people; they are always right and will never mislead anyone. — *Interview in the Chicago* Tribune, *February 16, 1884.* {C}

GODLOVE S. ORTH (1817–1882)   *Indiana politician elected to Congress seven times, beginning in 1862.*

1. *Talking with Nicolay in 1873, Orth remembered that "J. K. Dubois of Illinois came to Springfield determined to get a place in Lincoln's Cabinet." Orth spoke to the President about it and received this reply:*

Well you see, I like Uncle Jesse very much, but I must do something for this great Methodist Church. There's Seward is an Episcopalian, Chase is an Episcopalian, Bates is an Episcopalian, and Stanton swears enough to be one. Of course until the matter was brought to my attention I didn't know anything about the churches to which my cabinet belonged. But in this way I have without any intention whatever in the matter selected them all from a single church. — *Interview February 20, 1873, Nicolay Papers.* {D}

This recollection remains less than credible even if one assumes that Orth mistakenly said (or Nicolay mistakenly wrote) "Springfield" when he meant "Washington."

ROBERT DALE OWEN (1801–1877)   *Scottish-born social reformer who represented an Indiana district in Congress during the 1840s and by the eve of the Civil War had become a leading advocate of emancipation.*

1. *In November 1863, as Owen told the story to Francis B. Carpenter, he called on the President and read to him a lengthy historical paper on amnesty in relation to treason and rebellion. When he had finished and handed over the document, Lincoln said:*

Mr. Owen, it is due to you that I should say that you have conferred a very essential service, both upon me and the country, by the preparation of this paper. It contains that which it was exceedingly important that I should know, but which, if left to myself, I never should have known, because I have not the time necessary for such an examination of authorities as a review of this kind involves. And I want to say, secondly, if I had had the time, I could not have done the work so well as you have done it. — *Carpenter-2, 100–101 (1866).* {D}

There appears to be only a flimsy basis for the tradition that Lincoln on this occasion remarked: "Well, for those who like that sort of thing, I should think it is just about the sort of thing they would like."[356]

JOHN M. PALMER (1817–1900)   *Illinois politician and Civil War general, later governor, senator, and presidential candidate.*

1. *During a trial at Chicago in the late 1850s, Robert S. Blackwell was delivering an elaborate address to the jury and at one point described in great detail the habits of storks in Holland. Lincoln remarked to a fellow lawyer:*

That beats me! Blackwell can concentrate more words into the fewest ideas of any man I ever knew. The storks of Holland! Why, they would eat him up before he began to get half through telling that story about them. — *Palmer-1, II, 642–43 (1899). {C}*

2. *Speaking to Palmer as a member of the Washington peace conference in February 1861, Lincoln said:*

There is now going to be a long war, and what we now want is time. Promise them anything. — *Clipping, Lincoln reminiscences file, ISHL, of an interview in the Chicago* Post, *marked "1892 (?)." {D}*

3. *In February 1863, Lincoln asked about soldiers' attitudes towards the Emancipation Proclamation, and Palmer said there were some who thought that it should have been accompanied by a call for slave uprisings. Lincoln replied:*

You were all opposed to the proclamation when it was first issued, were you not? . . . Well, don't you see that on an average, I am about right? — *Palmer-2 (1901), 153. {C}*

4. *During the war, Lincoln once said to Palmer:*

I have no policy; my hope is to save the Union. I do the best I can today, with the hope that when tomorrow comes I am ready for its duty. — *Palmer-1, II, 759. {C}*

An interviewer quoted Palmer as dating this remark in February 1865 and phrasing it as follows: It was a time when a man with a policy would have been fatal to the country. I have never had a policy. I have simply tried to do what seemed best each day, as each day came. — *Clipping labeled "St. Paul* Dispatch, *2-15-1896," Tarbell Papers. {C}*

The Prince de Joinville (q.v.) likewise quoted Lincoln to the effect that he had no policy.

SAMUEL C. PARKS (1820–1917)   *A lawyer and local Republican leader in Logan County, Illinois, Parks was acquainted with Lincoln both in politics and in legal practice. Lincoln appointed him associate justice of the supreme court of Idaho Territory.*

1. *Speaking of Lincoln in court, Parks declared: "When he thought he was wrong he was the weakest lawyer I ever saw." As an illustration, Parks recalled*

Lincoln's telling him and another attorney with whom he was associated in defending a client accused of larceny:

If you can say anything for the man, do it. I can't. If I attempt it, the jury will see that I think he is guilty and convict him. —*Parks to Herndon, March 25, 1866 (8:688–91), Herndon-Weik Collection. {C}*

2. *On another occasion, Lincoln became disillusioned with his client's character and slipped away to the hotel. When sent for, he said:*

Tell the judge that I can't come. My hands are dirty, and I came over to clean them. —*Ibid. {D}*

It is not clear that Parks was the auditor of this remark.

3. *Responding to a request that he join Parks and Herndon in arguing a certain case, Lincoln said:*

Tell Harris it's no use to waste money on me in that case; he'll get beat. —*Ibid. {C}*

4. *After Lincoln's defeat as a senatorial candidate in 1855, Parks assured him that next time he would be elected. Lincoln replied that:*

he thought before that time the taste for the senatorship would get out of his mouth.

On a later occasion, he told Parks that: his defeat was the best thing that ever happened him. —*Parks, 11 (1909).*[357] *{C}*

5. *After he had delivered his House-Divided speech on June 16, 1858, Lincoln was urged by Parks to modify one passage before the text was published. He responded:*

I think that the time has come to say it, and I will let it go as it is. —*Parks, 12. {C}*

RICHARD C. PARSONS (1826–1899) *Ohio lawyer and legislator who was appointed a collector of internal revenue in 1862 and later served a term in Congress.*

1. *As an emissary from Governor William Dennison and Senator Salmon P. Chase, Parsons visited the President-elect in December 1860, assuring him that office-seeking formed no part of his mission. Lincoln replied that:*

as most of his visitors wanted something and generally wanted it pretty bad, he was glad to find nobody in Ohio had any such itching. —*Parsons in the Cleveland* Leader, *reprinted in the New York* Times, *August 9, 1887. {C}*

2. *When Lincoln asked whether Chase wanted anything, Parsons answered, "Yes, Mr. President, he wants something very much, but nothing you can give him." Lincoln responded:*

Oh, well, he will have to wait a little for that. —*Ibid. {C}*

3. *Going through his mail, Lincoln found a handbill with a sketch of him hanging on a gallows, together with a verse that read:*

> Two posts upright,
> One beam crossed tight,
> One rope pendant,
> Abe on the end on't.

He commented: Bad as the poetry is, the likeness is worse, but the man who sent it did his best, both in literature and art. —*Ibid.* {C}

4. *When Parsons, as he said good-bye, pressed for some kind of statement about the secession crisis, Lincoln replied:*

Chase and Dennison know as much about the situation as I do. One thing, however, you can say, if my opinion is of any value, and that is the Union must be preserved. Yes, the Union must be preserved at all hazards. —*Ibid.* {C}

WILLIAM AGNEW PATON *Nephew of Dr. Cornelius R. Agnew, who was surgeon general of the state of New York and a member of the Sanitary Commission. Young Paton secured an interview with the President in October 1862 simply to tell him: "All the boys in my school are for you."*

1. *After some conversation, Lincoln put his hand on the boy's head and said:*

You come of good people, you will soon be a grown man. Be a good man. Be a good American. Our country may have need of your services some day. —*Paton, 709 (1913).* {C}

ROBERT PATTERSON (1792–1881) *Union general whose much-criticized role in the first Bull Run campaign put an end to his military career.*

1. *In an interview sometime after the battle, Lincoln said:*

General Patterson, I have never found fault with you or censured you; I have never been able to see that you could have done anything else than you did do. Your hands were tied; you obeyed orders and did your duty, and I am satisfied with your conduct.

Commenting on Patterson's request for an investigation, Lincoln said: that he would cheerfully accede to any practicable measure to do me justice, but that I need not expect to escape abuse as long as I was of any importance or value to the community; that he received infinitely more abuse than I did, but that he had ceased to regard it, and I must learn to do the same. — *Patterson, 18–19 (1865).* {C}

WILLIAM W. PATTON (1821–1889) *Congregational minister and, from 1877 until his death, president of Howard University.*

1. *In a paper read in 1887, Patton presented a report of Lincoln's meeting*

with a delegation of Chicago clergymen on September 13, 1862. The text (written down soon after the interview, according to Patton) is quite similar to the one published in Collected Works, *V, 419–25 (based upon two contemporary newspaper accounts), except that it includes the following additional passage:*

I have been much gratified with this interview. You have done your duty; I will try to do mine. In addition to what I have already said, there is a question of expediency as to time, should such a proclamation be issued. Matters look dark just now. I fear that a proclamation on the heels of defeat would be interpreted as a cry of despair. It would come better, if at all, immediately after a victory. I wish I could say something to you more entirely satisfactory. —*Patton, 32.* {C}

HENRY A. PEARSON   *An Illinois cavalry officer in the Civil War.*

1. *In a speech in 1906, Pearson recalled that Lincoln, during his visit to Evanston on April 3, 1860, praised the performance of a quartet, saying to its leader:*

Young man, I wish I could sing as well as you. Unfortunately I know only two tunes, one is "Old Hundred," and the other isn't. —*Currey, 5.* {D}

In another version of this old quip, which Lincoln possibly used more than once, the song is "Hail Columbia."[358] *More commonly, the remark is attributed to Ulysses S. Grant, and the tune is "Yankee Doodle."*

EBENEZER PECK (1805–1881)   *A Chicagoan associated with Lincoln in early Republican politics. For many years reporter of the Illinois supreme court, he was appointed a judge of the United States Court of Claims in 1863.*

1. *Several weeks before the presidential election of 1864, Peck asked Lincoln if it might not be well to state publicly that if any state in rebellion should cease hostilities, he would favor recognizing that state and restoring its people to all their previous rights within the Union, slavery notwithstanding. The President replied that:*

although there would be no hesitation on his part so to say and act, if the fact should so be, and the event should occur, yet he did not feel justified so to avow in advance, especially where so many imputations would rest upon a declaration having the appearance of propitiating [soliciting?] votes from men who are not cordial in support of his general administration. —*Peck to James W. Singleton, October 14, 1864, in Pratt-2, 113.* {B}

About six weeks later, Singleton (q.v.) told Orville H. Browning that Lincoln, in a conversation with him before the election, had indicated a willingness to restore southern states to the Union without settling the question of slavery.

THOMAS F. PENDEL   *A longtime White House employee who, according to his own statement, began work there as a guard in November 1864.*

1. *The Lincoln remembered by Pendel was ambivalent about the problem of his personal security. He said on one occasion:*

Pendel, I do not like to be guarded, but I have received a number of threatening letters lately. I have no fears, however. That fellow we saw over at the War Department crouching at the foot of the stairs, and who eyed me suspiciously, answers perfectly the description of a man I was warned to look out for in a letter I received the other day. — *Pendel as quoted in the New York* Tribune, *November 16, 1902. {D}*

2. *To two southern women, Lincoln first said no, then:*

Yes, I will give you a pass to Richmond. I would rather have you there, because if you stay here you'll just inform the Confederacy of what we are doing. — *Interview with Pendel in 1886, typewritten copy, Sandburg Collection, folder 193. {C}*

3. *To a young officer seeking a transfer to Winfield Scott Hancock's corps:*

Hancock says you are a gallant officer, sir, but you are not a sober officer. — *Ibid. {C}*

SOLOMON NEWTON PETTIS (1827–1900) *Pennsylvania lawyer whom Lincoln appointed a territorial judge, later a member of Congress.*

1. *As Democrats were gathering for their national convention in August 1864, Lincoln remarked that:*

if the convention at Chicago nominated General McClellan and put him upon a platform pledging the party to a vigorous prosecution of the war, as indicated by Dean Richmond of New York, the result in November would not only be doubtful, but the chances were in favor of the Democracy.

Upon reading the Chicago platform, which decried "four years of failure" and called for an immediate effort to end hostilities, he said that:

the danger was past . . . after the expenditure of blood and treasure that had been poured out for the maintenance of the government and the preservation of the Union, the American people were not prepared to vote the war a failure. — *Pettis interview, Washington* Post, *August 16, 1891. {C}*

CHARLES H. PHILBRICK

1. *In October 1864, apparently referring to the recent vote abolishing slavery in Maryland, Lincoln said that:*

it was a victory worth double the number of electoral votes of the state because of its moral influence. — *Philbrick to John G. Nicolay, October 28, 1864, Nicolay Papers. {B}*

WENDELL PHILLIPS (1811–1884) *Noted abolitionist orator and social reformer who in 1860 called Lincoln the "Slave-Hound of Illinois."*

1. *In an interview with Phillips on March 18, 1862, Lincoln said:*

The Negro who has once touched the hem of the government's garment shall never again be a slave. —*Phillips's speech in Chicago, March 28, 1862, as reported the next day in the Chicago* Tribune. *{D}*

The phrasing sounds more like Phillips on the platform than Lincoln in conversation.

2. *Lincoln's last words in the interview were about the presidency:*

It is a big job; the country little knows how big. —*Speech in Boston, April 17, published in the* Liberator, *April 25, 1862. {C}*

3. *According to Phillips in a general attack on the administration, Lincoln failed to keep this promise, made to him and a group of antislavery leaders on January 25, 1863:*

Gentlemen, I know that I am to lose 200,000 men before the first day of July. I know that when they go out of the ranks, the Confederate will time his deadliest effort at that moment, and I mean before that time comes to put the 200,000 muskets which they drop into the hands of the Negroes of the southern states. —*Speech July 4 in the* Liberator, *July 10, 1863. {D}*

4. *During the same meeting in January 1863, according to Phillips, Lincoln said of the Emancipation Proclamation that:*

he believed . . . that it was a great mistake. —*Excerpt from a recent Phillips lecture,* Liberator, *November 20, 1863.*

In a later speech, Phillips quoted Lincoln as saying that: he doubted whether the proclamation had not done more harm than good. —*Liberator, January 1, 1864. {C}*

DONN PIATT (1819–1891) *Talented, opinionated, and somewhat erratic Ohio journalist and politician. He was a Civil War officer, rising to the rank of lieutenant colonel and serving for a time as chief of staff to General Robert C. Schenck. Lincoln, according to Piatt, never forgave him for one act of insubordination and blocked his promotion to brigadier general. There is a good deal of factual inaccuracy in Piatt's recollections.*

1. *In Springfield, immediately after his election to the presidency, Lincoln expressed an opinion that southern secessionists were bluffing:*

They won't give up the offices. Were it believed that vacant places could be had at the North Pole, the road there would be lined with dead Virginians. —*Rice AT, 481 (1886).*[359] *{C}*

2. *Some two weeks later, Piatt predicted war, and Lincoln said laughingly that the fall of pork at Cincinnati had affected him. When Piatt insisted that the land would soon be whitened with military tents, Lincoln replied:*

Well, we won't jump that ditch until we come to it. I must run the machine as I find it. —*Rice AT, 484.* *{C}*

3. *Presumably at about the same time, Lincoln said with respect to secession:*

If our southern friends are right in their claim, the framers of the government carefully planned the rot that now threatens their work with destruction. If one state has the right, at will, to withdraw, certainly a majority have the right, and we have the result given us of the states being able to force out one state. That is logical. —*Rice AT, 485.* *{D}*

Piatt claimed to have written this statement down at the time. It was an argument that Lincoln developed in his message to Congress of July 4, 1861.

4. *Piatt remembered Lincoln as a man who carried his responsibilities lightly. He recalled hearing him say to General Schenck at the darkest period of the war:*

I enjoy my rations and sleep the sleep of the innocent. —*Rice AT, 484.* *{D}*

This is contrary to much other testimony about the effect of mental strain on Lincoln's sleep and other personal habits.

5. *General Daniel Tyler reproached Lincoln for interfering with army discipline by pardoning deserters. Congress, he added, had taken the responsibility for their punishment. Lincoln replied impatiently:*

Yes, Congress has taken the responsibility, and left the women to howl about me. —*Rice AT, 489.* *{C}*

6. *Lincoln, according to Piatt, had no hold on the affections of the people. He once said to Piatt and others that:*

he felt like a surveyor in the wild woods of the West, who, while looking for a corner, kept an eye over his shoulder for an Indian. —*Piatt, 73 (1887).* *{C}*

THOMAS J. PICKETT (1821–1891)   *An Illinois editor whose friendship with Lincoln dated from the 1840s. A state senator at the beginning of the war, he received a minor appointment from Lincoln as army quartermaster's agent at Rock Island but eventually entered military service and rose to the rank of colonel.*

1. *During the presidential campaign of 1844, Lincoln engaged in debate at Peoria with William L. May, a former congressman who had changed parties several times. In his opening speech, May ridiculed the Whig pole in the town square, saying that like the Whig party, it was hollow and without a heart. Lincoln responded that:*

the Whigs of Peoria had no cause to be especially proud of their pole; it was not made of the best timber and was not straight, but there was one thing about it he could explain, account for, and admire. The hollow place at the butt of the pole was where Colonel May had crawled out of the Whig party, and his party friends now propose to close it up so that the colonel could never return. —*Pickett, 5 (1881). {D}*

It is not clear that Pickett was himself an auditor of this exchange.[360]

2. *When asked to name his favorite Lincoln speech in the debates with Douglas, Pickett chose the one delivered at Freeport. Lincoln replied:*

It is very singular; I have asked many friends that question but none agree with me. I was better pleased with myself at Ottawa than at any other place. —8-9. {C}

EDWARD L. PIERCE (1829–1897)   *Massachusetts lawyer and public official, who was in his younger years a protégé of Salmon P. Chase and at a later time, the biographer of Charles Sumner. He did not admire Lincoln.*

1. *On February 15, 1862, Salmon P. Chase, who had made Pierce a special Treasury agent dealing with the problem of freedmen at Port Royal, South Carolina, sent him to talk with the President about it. Pierce remembered the interview as an unpleasant one in which Lincoln said impatiently:*

that he ought not to be troubled with such details, that there seemed to be a great itching to get Negroes within our lines, and that the Senate the other day hesitated to confirm General Halleck [as a major general] because he had excluded them.

Lincoln did, however, provide Pierce with a note in effect approving of his mission.[361] *—Pierce to Herndon, September 15, 1889 (10:2545-57), Herndon-Weik Collection. {C}*

FRANCIS H. PIERPONT (1814–1899)   *Lawyer and businessman who headed the rump government organized by Virginians loyal to the Union. Thus in the official view of the United States he was the governor of Virginia from 1861 to 1868, and, in popular parlance, he was the "father" of West Virginia.*

1. *On April 10, 1865, the day after his return from Richmond and City Point, Lincoln summoned Pierpont to a conference during which he talked about his recent discussions with John A. Campbell (q.v.) and his plan for calling the Confederate legislature of Virginia into session. According to Pierpont's account written perhaps in 1879, the President said:*

But your government at Alexandria was fully in my mind, and I intended to recognize the restored government, of which you were head, as the rightful government of Virginia. My plan then was to authorize in my proclamation the assembling of those men to do a single act—that was to withdraw the army of Virginia, then cooperating with the Confederate army, from the field; and with this act I expected their powers as legislators to cease. They had put the army in the field, why not take it out and quit?

The drafting of that order, though so short, gave me more perplexity than any other paper I ever drew up. I went to the boat at seven o'clock and worked at that proclamation until one before I got it to suit me. My object was so to draw the paper as to give no authority to do anything except to take the rebel soldiers out of the field, and at the same time, in no way compromise your position as governor of the restored government of Virginia.

I issued that proclamation, which you have seen, authorizing the assembling of the so-called Confederate legislature of Virginia.[362] Then I gave it to the general commanding the post and gave him full oversight of the legislature when it assembled, with general power to disperse it, if it manifested a refractory spirit. But if I had known that General Lee would surrender so soon I would not have issued the proclamation.

There is one question on which I should like to have information. I tried to get some in Richmond, but it was all a sealed book. I could get no information as to the feeling of the people. How will they receive you, who have antagonized them from the beginning of the war? Will they rush forward and try to seize all the offices? Will they sulk and do nothing? *—Pierpont manuscript quoted in Ambler, 256–57. {D}*

Factual inaccuracies and the length of this recollective quotation make it dubious as anything more than a rough approximation of what Lincoln said.

2. *During the same interview, Lincoln talked extensively about reconstruction, saying that:*

All the intercourse for four years had been cut off. No information had been received, except distorted accounts given by army raiders or persons who had occasionally come through the lines. Soldiers who had come through knew nothing about the feeling of the people.

In addition to other misfortunes to the southern people, in their own estimation, four million slaves had been made freemen. Most of these were in their old quarters on their late masters' farms. The very sight of these was a source of irritation. What was to be the future status of the white man who had been in rebellion as to voting, holding office, making state and national laws? If allowed to make state laws, what would be the fate of the freedmen? Were they to be allowed to make their own laws or should the military rule? Were there any friends left in the southern states of the old Union? Was there any Union sentiment among the southern people that had sufficient force to develop itself, now that the war was over? If so, what were to be the measures adopted in order to give that sentiment an opportunity to develop? . . .

There had been two political parties in the South, and would they continue to act separately? He thought they would, and one party would affiliate with the Republican party, and the other with the northern Democracy. But the great fact forced itself on him that on his part, he had been struggling for years to maintain a union of the states, and there never could be any union until all the southern states were represented in Congress; and that a free people who paid taxes must in some way be represented; that to prohibit them from participating in the government would soon create sympathy and clamor in their behalf at the North. . . .

The idea that had most favor in his mind was to place a military commander in each state and let him suggest to leading men favorable to the old Union, if he could find them, that it would be to their interest to call conventions which should be the spontaneous action of the people. Let the conventions adopt a constitution recognizing the Constitution of the United States as the supreme law of the land, and, with other usual provisions, make their laws accordingly by their legislatures. Then they would, under this action, elect their members to both houses of Congress. That military rule should be relaxed as they progressed in each state, and when their members of Congress presented themselves on the floor of each house for admission, Congress would decide if they had a republican form of government and admit or reject them. That the President would issue no proclamation in the case; that he would encourage such action through discreet commanders of the army in each state. —*257-58*. {D}

The final paragraph was, of course, a summary of the reconstruction program that Lincoln had already initiated in several states.

3. *Concerning his own trials and troubles in office, Lincoln said:*

Amid them all I have been angry but once since I came to the White House. Then, if I had encountered the man who caused my anger, I certainly would have hurt him.

In a reference to the days of his youth, he added: When I had to measure my strength with that of other reputed strong men, I found I had great power in my arms. —*259*. {C}

EDWARDS PIERREPONT (1817–1892)   *New York lawyer and judge, later attorney general of the United States.*

1. *Shortly before issuing the Emancipation Proclamation, Lincoln said to Pierrepont and General James S. Wadsworth:*

It is my last card, and I will play it and may win the trick. —*Pierrepont's account as recorded by Robert C. Winthrop on July 31, 1863, Winthrop, 229.* {D}

FREDERICK A. PIKE (1816–1886)   *Congressman from Maine for eight years beginning in 1861.*

1. *Speaking of his troubles with McClellan, Lincoln said that:*

he was a minority president; how could he remove a majority general? — *recounted in Adams S. Hill to Sydney Howard Gay, undated but probably October 1862, Gay Papers. {D}*

It is possible that Congressman-elect James G. Blaine, who accompanied Pike to the White House, was Hill's informant.

ALLAN PINKERTON (1819–1884) *Famous detective, founder of Pinkerton's National Police Agency in Chicago. His operatives reported a plot to assassinate Lincoln when he passed through Baltimore in 1861.*

1. *On February 21 in Philadelphia, Lincoln rejected advice that he elude the conspirators by taking the next train to Washington. He said:*

that he had an engagement for the next morning to raise a flag on Independence Hall in Philadelphia, and that he had also promised the citizens of Pennsylvania to meet them at Harrisburg on the following day; that he had positively engaged this to Governor Curtin, and that he would fulfill those engagements under any and all circumstances, even if he met with death in doing so. *Thereafter, he added, he would place himself entirely in Pinkerton's hands. — Pinkerton to Herndon, August 23, 1866 (8:813-28), Herndon-Weik Collection. {C}*

JAMES PIPER *An Illinois farmer.*

1. *Piper shot several of his neighbor's hogs, part of a herd that had invaded his cornfield. The neighbor, when he saw the damage done by the animals, acknowledged that he would have acted in the same way. Piper, who had consulted Lincoln about the problem, told him what had happened. Lincoln said:*

You civilized the man and the hogs both. *— Piper's dictated recollections, Metamora (Illinois)* Herald, *August 21, 1921, clipping in the Lincoln reminiscences file, ISHL. {C}*

JOHN PITCHER *A lawyer and friend of Lincoln's youth in Indiana.*

1. *Pitcher recalled Lincoln's account of how he had pulled corn to pay Josiah Crawford for Weems's* Life of Washington, *which had been damaged by rain while in his possession:*

You see, I am tall and long-armed, and I went to work in earnest. At the end of the two days, there was not a corn-blade left on a stalk in the field. I wanted to pay full damage for all the wetting the book got, and I made a clean sweep. *— Pitcher's undated statement in Herndon, I, 61n. {C}*

The incident is corroborated by other testimony.[363]

JAMES POLLOCK (1810–1890) *Pennsylvania Whig congressman during the 1840s, governor in the late 1850s, and a member of the Washington peace convention in February 1861. Lincoln appointed him director of the United States Mint in Philadelphia.*

1. According to Pollock, he was present when Stephen A. Douglas called on the President-elect a few days before the inauguration and pledged his support against the "treasonable designs" of the secessionists. Lincoln replied:

God bless you, Douglas! With such pledges and such assurances from my political opponents, and with God's help, we must succeed. Oh, how you have cheered and warmed my heart! The danger is great, but with such words from such friends, why should we fear. Our Union cannot be destroyed. With all my heart, I thank you. The people with us and God helping us, all will yet be well.

After Douglas's departure, Lincoln exclaimed: Oh, Pollock, what a noble man Douglas is! We have always been opposed politically, but now when the country needs the help of every true patriot, he forgets party and pledges his aid to me and the Union. How such words of his encourage me! I hardly know how to express my feeling for him. I did not expect such pledge—such promise of cooperation. —*Pollock, 169.* {E}

This is a fair sample of the rubbish sometimes offered, even by persons of considerable standing, as recollected words of Lincoln. Douglas did indeed meet with Lincoln more than once in late February 1861, but his principal purpose in doing so was to urge support for compromise measures. It was on April 14, after the attack on Fort Sumter, that he visited the President and pledged his help in preserving the Union. There appears to be no corroborating evidence of Pollock's presence at any of their conversations.

REBECCA R. POMROY (1817–1884) *Civil War nurse from Massachusetts who, after Willie's death, stayed in the White House for extended periods, taking care of Tad Lincoln and his mother. Lincoln called her "one of the best women I ever knew."*[364] *Her reminiscences stress and probably exaggerate his displays of religiosity.*

1. Concerning Tad, Lincoln said:

I hope you will pray for him and, if it is God's will, that he may be spared—and also for me; for I need the prayers of many. —*Pomroy, 47.* {C}

2. On the subject of favorite books of the Bible, Lincoln agreed with Mrs. Pomroy in liking the Psalms:

Yes, they are the best, for I find in them something for every day of the week. —*47.* {C}

3. Mrs. Pomroy's proposal to hold a prayer meeting in the hospital where she nursed wounded soldiers met with Lincoln's approval. He said:

If there were more praying and less swearing, it would be better for our country; and we all need to be prayed for, officers as well as privates; and if I were near death, I think I should like to hear prayer. —*48.* {C}

BENJAMIN PERLEY POORE (1820–1887) *Journalist, editor, and author, who lived for most of his career in Washington, D.C. The factual inaccuracy of what Poore wrote about Lincoln does not inspire confidence in his recollection of the man's words.*[365]

1. *Poore remembered Congressman Lincoln's telling in the House post-office room how, as a captain in the Black Hawk War, he had marched his men, twenty abreast, toward a narrow gate:*

I could not for the life of me remember the proper word of command for getting my company endwise so that it could get through the gate, so as we came near the gate I shouted: "This company is dismissed for two minutes, when it will fall in again on the other side of the gate!". . . I sometimes think here, that gentlemen in yonder who get into a tight place in debate, would like to dismiss the House until the next day and then take a fair start. —*Rice AT, 218–19 (1886). {D}*

This same story was told by Herndon, who implied that he had heard it directly from Lincoln, but it was a story making the rounds in 1860 without any reference to Lincoln.[366]

2. *Narration of a wrestling match during the Black Hawk campaign:*

He was at least two inches taller than I was, and somewhat heavier, but I reckoned that I was the most wiry, and soon after I had tackled him, I gave him a hug, lifted him off the ground, and threw him flat on his back. That settled his hash. —*219. {D}*

Such boasting was not Lincoln's style. Compare this account of a contest won with the accounts by William G. Greene and Risdon M. Moore of a contest lost.

3. *According to Poore, he visited the President-elect after his arrival at Willard's Hotel in February 1861 and was given an account of the misplaced inaugural address:*

When we reached Harrisburg and had washed up, I asked Bob where the message was, and was taken aback by his confession that in the excitement caused by the enthusiastic reception, he believed he had let a waiter take the gripsack. My heart went up into my mouth, and I started downstairs, where I was told that if a waiter had taken the gripsack, I would probably find it in the baggage room. Going there, I saw a large pile of gripsacks and other baggage and thought that I discovered mine. My key fitted it, but on opening, there was nothing inside but a few paper collars and a flask of whiskey. A few moments afterward I came across my gripsack, with the document in it all right, and now I will show it to you—on your honor, mind! —*224. {D}*

It is unlikely that Lincoln would have referred to the address as a "message" or permitted a newspaper correspondent to read it. In an account published some years later, Ward H. Lamon (q.v.) claimed to have participated in the search for the lost satchel. Another version associates the incident with Cleveland, but Robert Lincoln himself later stated that it took place in Indianapolis.[367]

DAVID DIXON PORTER (1813–1891)   *One of the major naval figures of the Civil War. Porter commanded the* Powhatan *when it was sent by Seward to the relief of Fort Pickens in April 1861. He participated in the successful assault on New Orleans and, as commander of the Mississippi squadron, in the capture of Vicksburg. In later life, Porter wrote some amateurish fiction and some undistinguished history. His Civil War memoirs are generally regarded as more entertaining than reliable. What follows is a selection from his profuse quotation of Lincoln.*

1. *According to Porter, Lincoln readily approved placing the* Powhatan *under Porter's command and transferring it from the Fort Sumter expedition to the Fort Pickens expedition. As he signed the necessary orders on April 1, he said:*

Seward, see that I don't burn my fingers.

Seward's vigorous intervention into naval affairs at this time reminded him of a story: This looks to me very much like the case of two fellows I once knew; one was a gambler, the other a preacher. They met in a stage, and the gambler induced the preacher to play poker, and the latter won all the gambler's money. "It's all because we have mistaken our trades," said the gambler; "you ought to have been a gambler and I a preacher, and, by ginger, I intend to turn the tables on you next Sunday and preach in your church," which he did. —*Porter DD, 15–16 (1885).* {C}

Lincoln's role in the assignment of the Powhatan *to Porter has been a matter of historical controversy. Gideon Welles understood from him that he had signed the orders without reading them, but that is not easy to believe.*[368]

2. *Welles complained about the transfer of the* Powhatan, *and Lincoln directed Seward to recall the vessel from the Fort Pickens expedition. Porter ignored Seward's message, however, insisting that it did not take precedence over a presidential order. In a conversation eighteen months later, when Seward spoke of how Porter's action had "saved" Fort Pickens, Lincoln said:*

Yes, and got me into hot water with Mr. Welles, for which I think he has never forgiven me. I believe he would forget it, but, Seward, you won't let him. You are always flaunting your claimed success in his face and deprecating the Fort Sumter expedition. It's like shaking a red rag at a bull. If it hadn't been for Seward, Captain, Mr. Welles would have tried you by court-martial for disobeying Seward's telegram, although you were simply carrying out my written orders—a fact which none of us remembered until you were beyond our reach. —*120.* {D}

3. *In November 1861, according to Porter, he went to see Lincoln, accom-*

panied by Welles, and laid out a proposal for the capture of New Orleans, whereupon Lincoln launched into a story:

There was an old woman in Illinois who missed some of her chickens and couldn't imagine what had become of them. Someone suggested that they had been carried off by a skunk; so she told her husband he must sit up that night and shoot the critter. The old man sat up all night and next morning came in with two pet rabbits. "Thar," he said, "your chickens are all safe; thar's two of them skunks I killed." "Them ain't skunks," said the old woman, "them's my pet rabbits; you allers was a fool!" "Well, then," returned the old man, "if them ain't skunks I don't know a skunk when I sees it." Now, Mr. Secretary [Lincoln continued] the navy has been hunting pet rabbits long enough; suppose you send them after skunks. It seems to me that what the lieutenant proposes is feasible. He says a dozen ships will take the forts and city, and there should be twenty thousand soldiers sent along to hold it. After New Orleans is taken, and while we are about it, we can push on to Vicksburg and open the river all the way along. We will go and see General McClellan and find out if he can't manage to get the troops. —64-65. {D}

Porter's recollection of the origins of the attack on New Orleans differs from that of other witnesses, and he certainly inflated his own role in the inception of the project.[369]

4. *At City Point, Virginia, in late March 1865, Lincoln said to Porter regarding surrender terms for the Confederates:*

Get them to plowing once and gathering in their own little crops, eating popcorn at their own firesides, and you can't get them to shoulder a musket again for half a century. —285. {C}

5. *At a conference with Grant, Sherman, and Porter on March 28, 1865, Lincoln remarked:*

Let them once surrender and reach their homes, they won't take up arms again. Let them all go, officers and all. I want submission and no more bloodshed. Let them have their horses to plow with, and, if you like, their guns to shoot crows with. I want no one punished; treat them liberally all round. We want those people to return to their allegiance to the Union and submit to the laws. Again I say, give them the most liberal and honorable terms. —314. {C}

Porter claimed that his account of this meeting was based upon notes made the same evening.

6. *Asked how he had slept one night on the* Malvern *at City Point, Lincoln said:*

I slept well, but you can't put a long blade into a short scabbard. I was too long for that berth. — 285. {C}

7. *Informed that Vice President Johnson and a companion had arrived at City Point and wanted to call on him, Lincoln exclaimed:*

Don't let those men come into my presence. I won't see either of them; send them away. They have no business here, anyway, no right to come down here without my permission. I won't see them now and never want to lay eyes on them. I don't care what you do with them, nor where you send them, but don't let them come near me. — 287. {D}

One may doubt that Lincoln expressed himself so intemperately, but Mary Lincoln and William H. Crook (qq.v.) likewise recalled that he was unwilling to see Johnson.

8. *Upon receiving news that Union forces were entering Richmond:*

Thank God that I have lived to see this! It seems to me that I have been dreaming a horrid dream for four years, and now the nightmare is gone. I want to see Richmond. — 294. {C}

9. *On April 4, Lincoln started for Richmond on the* Malvern, *but circumstances compelled him and his party to finish the journey on an oar-driven barge. Lincoln said:*

Admiral, this brings to my mind a fellow who once came to me to ask for an appointment as minister abroad. Finding he could not get that, he came down to some more modest position. Finally, he asked to be made a tidewaiter. When he saw he could not get that, he asked me for an old pair of trousers. But it is well to be humble. — 294-95. {D}

10. *When liberated slaves fell to their knees before him during his visit to Richmond on April 4, Porter's idealized Lincoln is quoted as saying:*

Don't kneel to me. That is not right. You must kneel to God only and thank him for the liberty you will hereafter enjoy. I am but God's humble instrument, but you may rest assured that as long as I live, no one shall put a shackle on your limbs, and you shall have all the rights which God has given to every other free citizen of this republic.

Later, he made another little speech to the throng of blacks: My poor friends, you are free — free as air. You can cast off the name of slave and trample upon it; it will come to you no more. Liberty is your birthright. God gave it to you as he gave it to others, and it is a sin that you have been deprived of it for so many years. But you must try to deserve this priceless boon. Let the world see that you merit it and are able to maintain it by your good works. Don't let your joy carry you into excesses. Learn the laws and obey them; obey God's commandments and thank him for giving you liberty, for to Him you owe all things. — *Porter 295, 297-98.* {D}

11. *Lincoln stopped to look at Libby Prison, and when there was talk of tearing it down, he said:*

No, leave it as a monument. —299. {C}

12. *At Richmond, the President received a visit from the southerner Duff Green, who proceeded to denounce him at some length. After listening patiently for a while, Porter's Lincoln finally interrupted the tirade, saying:*

Stop, you political tramp, you, the aider and abettor of those who have brought all this ruin upon your country, without the courage to risk your person in defense of the principles you profess to espouse! A fellow who stood by to gather up the loaves and fishes, if any should fall to you! A man who had no principles in the North and took none South with him! A political hyena who robbed the graves of the dead and adopted their language as his own! You talk of the North cutting the throats of the southern people. You have all cut your own throats and, unfortunately, have cut many of those of the North. Miserable impostor, vile intruder! Go, before I forget myself and the high position I hold! Go, I tell you, and don't desecrate this national vessel another minute! —308. {E}

This purple patch, a reminder of Porter's dubious merit as a novelist, may by itself be ample reason for doubting all the words he attributed to Lincoln.[370]

13. *Back at City Point, when he saw some Confederate prisoners who seemed happy that the war was over:*

They will never shoulder a musket again in anger, and if Grant is wise, he will leave them their guns to shoot crows with and their horses to plow with. It would do no harm. —312. {C}

14. *On April 5, Seward sent a telegram asking whether he might join Lincoln at City Point. According to Dixon, the President said:*

No, I don't want him. Telegraph him that the berths are too small, and there's not room for another passenger. . . . he'd talk to me all day about Vattel and Puffendorf. The war will be over in a week, and I don't want to hear any more of that. —285.[371] {E}

Actually, Lincoln telegraphed to Seward: "I think there is no probability of my remaining here more than two days longer. If that is too long come down."[372]

ELBERT S. PORTER (1820–1888) *Clergyman and for many years editor of the* Christian Intelligencer, *a publication of the Dutch Reformed Church.*

1. *One evening in July 1862 at the Soldiers' Home, Lincoln spoke of slavery as a thing that had grown up with the nation and grown into it. He said:*

that one section was no more responsible than another for its original existence here, and that the whole nation having suffered from it, ought to share in efforts for its gradual removal. —*Sermon preached April 16, 1865, in* Voices, *237.* {C}

2. In an article about the same visit published many years later, Porter expanded his recollection of Lincoln's words:

Gentlemen, this American slavery is no small affair, and it cannot be done away with at once. It is a part of our national life. It is not of yesterday. It began in colonial times. In one way or another it has shaped nearly every-thing that enters into what we call government. It is as much northern as it is southern. It is not merely a local or geographical institution. It belongs to our politics, to our industries, to our commerce, and to our religion. Every portion of our territory in some form or another has contributed to the growth and the increase of slavery. It has been nearly two hundred years coming up to its present proportions. It is wrong, a great evil indeed, but the South is no more responsible for the wrong done to the African race than is the North.

At this point, Lincoln walked over to Porter and placed a hand on the back of his head. Then he continued: Here is a tumor, drawing upon the vitality of your body. You must be rid of it or it will destroy your life. Now we bring in three physicians to have a consultation over this tumor. All agree at once that it must be removed, but each one has his own opinion of the proper course to be pursued. One wants to poultice it and sweat it and so evaporate it. Another is positive that it should be taken out at once, that it should be cut around and pulled out, even at the risk of the patient's life. But the third doctor says, "Gentlemen, I differ from you both as to the treatment proposed. My advice is to prepare the patient for the opera-tion before venturing upon it. He must be depleted and the amount of his blood diminished." Now, my opinion is that the third doctor is about right. —*Undated clipping of Porter's article, "An Evening with Mr. Lincoln," in a Porter family scrapbook.*[373] {C}

HORACE PORTER (1837–1921) *West Point graduate who distinguished himself as an ordnance officer and in April 1864 became aide-de-camp to General Grant. In later years, he was a railroad executive and served as ambassador to France. He was also a celebrated raconteur, and it seems likely that some of the stories he attributed to Lincoln were drawn from sources other than his own memory of presidential utterances.*

1. Arriving at City Point by river-steamer on June 21, 1864, for his first visit to the army under Grant's command, Lincoln confessed:

I don't feel very comfortable after my trip last night on the bay. It was rough, and I was considerably shaken up. My stomach has not yet entirely recovered from the effects.

An officer recommended a glass of champagne as a sure cure for seasickness, and the President replied: No, my friend; I have seen too many fellows seasick ashore from drinking that very stuff. —*Porter H-1, 217 (1897).* {C}

2. *Later that same day, Grant suggested visiting some black troops who had recently fought well in an attack on the works at Petersburg. Lincoln said:*

Oh, yes, I want to take a look at those boys. I read with the greatest delight the account given in Mr. Dana's dispatch to the Secretary of War of how gallantly they behaved. He said they took six out of the sixteen guns captured that day. I was opposed on nearly every side when I first favored the raising of colored regiments, but they have proved their efficiency, and I am glad they have kept pace with the white troops in the recent assaults. When we wanted every able-bodied man who could be spared to go to the front, and my opposers kept objecting to the Negroes, I used to tell them that at such times it was just as well to be a little color-blind. I think, General, we can say of the black boys what a country fellow who was an old-time abolitionist in Illinois said when he went to a theater in Chicago and saw Forrest playing *Othello*. He was not very well up in Shakespeare and didn't know that the tragedian was a white man who had blacked up for the purpose. After the play was over, the folks who had invited him to go to the show wanted to know what he thought of the actors, and he said: "Waal, layin' aside all sectional prejudices and any partiality I may have for the race, derned if I don't think the nigger held his own with any of 'em." —*Porter H-1, 218-19.* {D}

The story is more credible than some of the remarks preceding it. Many northerners were ahead of Lincoln in favoring the enlistment of blacks, and it would have been absurd to claim otherwise.

3. *On a trip up the James the next day, some strong positions that had been seized and fortified by Union troops were pointed out to Lincoln. He said:*

When Grant once gets possession of a place, he holds on to it as if he had inherited it. —*Porter H-1, 223.* {C}

4. *In a discussion of the approaching presidential election:*

Among all our colleges, the Electoral College is the only one where they choose their own masters. —*Porter H-1, 223.* {C}

5. *When talk turned to the battles still lying ahead:*

I cannot pretend to advise, but I do sincerely hope that all may be accomplished with as little bloodshed as possible. —*Porter H-1, 223.* {C}

6. *It was during that same first visit to Grant's headquarters, according to Porter, that Lincoln declared:*

The other day, I had a little fever and a rash on the skin and I sent for the doctor. He said, "I think this is a case of the measles," and I cried, "Good, at last I have got something I can give to people." —*Porter H-2, 12 (1909).* {E}

A more believable version of this story made the rounds after Lincoln came down with a case of varioloid in late November 1863.[374]

7. During Lincoln's visit to City Point in March 1865, he spoke of wartime relations with Britain, saying:

England will live to regret her inimical attitude toward us. After the collapse of the rebellion, John Bull will find that he has injured himself much more seriously than us.[375]

And more specifically of the Trent *affair:* Seward studied up all the works ever written on international law and came to cabinet meetings loaded to the muzzle with the subject. We gave due consideration to the case, but at that critical period of the war it was soon decided to deliver up the prisoners. It was a pretty bitter pill to swallow, but I contented myself with believing that England's triumph in the matter would be short-lived, and that after ending our war successfully, we would be so powerful that we could call her to account for all the embarrassments she had inflicted upon us. —*Porter H-1, 407-8.*[376] {C}

EMIL PREETORIUS (1827-1905) *Editor of a German-language newspaper in St. Louis, Preetorius was the secretary of a large delegation of Missouri and Kansas Radicals who presented an "address" to the President on September 30, 1863.*

1. In a preliminary meeting with Preetorius, Lincoln declared that:

he would rather be a follower than a leader of public opinion.

He defended his cautious policy respecting slavery in Missouri and the other southern states not covered by the Emancipation Proclamation, saying: We need the border states. Public opinion in them has not matured. We must patiently educate them up to the right opinion. —*Statement of Preetorius to J. McCan Davis, December 2, 1898, Tarbell Papers.*[377] {C}

EZRA M. PRINCE (1831-1908) *In 1856, Prince arrived from Harvard to settle in Bloomington, Illinois, and become one of its leading lawyers.*

1. After stopping together at a wayside tavern between Bloomington and Tremont, where the food was bad and the total charge was seventy-five cents, Lincoln said:

Pretty cheap for supper, breakfast, and lodging and horse-keep, but perhaps considering what we got, it was enough. —*Prince, 7.* {C}

2. On the same journey, Lincoln recalled that:

at schooling, he had almost nothing. When quite a lad, a private school was started in their neighborhood. There were then no public schools in the state. His father sent him to this school with the avowed determination of giving him a thorough education. And what [*Lincoln asked*] do you think my father's idea of a thorough education was? . . . It was to have me cipher through the rule of three. —7. {C}

Leonard Swett (q.v.) recalled a similar comment.

3. *Asked for his opinion of Douglas's ability, Lincoln replied:*

that he was a very strong logician; that he had very little humor or imagination, but where he had right on his side very few could make a stronger argument; that he was an exceedingly good judge of human nature, knew the people of the state thoroughly and just how to appeal to the[ir] prejudices and was a very powerful opponent, both on and off the stump. —10. {C}

ADDISON G. PROCTOR (1838–1925) *New Englander who moved to Kansas as a young man. He was a delegate to the Republican national convention that nominated Lincoln in 1860.*

1. *In 1863, Proctor accompanied Congressman Abel C. Wilder when he visited the White House with a bundle of petitions calling for the reinstatement of General James G. Blunt, who had been removed from his command in Kansas following an investigation of corruption therein. Lincoln said:*

Never mind opening the papers, Wilder. I will not look at them. I don't doubt that they represent all you claim, that they represent the Republican party of Kansas, but I will not consider them. Wilder, you tell the Republican party of Kansas for me that they cannot afford to have Mr. Lincoln grant this request. This is all I care to say at this time. —*Proctor, 619 (1905)*.

In a later version, Proctor quoted Lincoln as saying: I have looked into that matter pretty thoroughly. I am satisfied that Blunt is dishonest. Now, that is the long and short of it. There is a divide going on down there somewheres. He knew about it, and I believe he is guilty and has guilty knowledge of where that divide comes in. Now, I am not going to let any man rest in authority where I have any doubt about his integrity, if I can help it. I will not do it, Wilder; I will not do it. —*Manuscript of a public address, undated but apparently delivered in the 1920s, Proctor Papers. {D}*

Factual errors tend to discredit these recollections.[378]

D. V. PURINGTON *Junior member of the staff of General Godfrey Weitzel when Lincoln visited the Army of the Potomac in 1865.*

1. *At a lunch, when Weitzel asked how many of the stories attributed to him were really his, Lincoln replied:*

I do not know, but of those I have seen, I should say about one-half. —*Purington (1907). {C}*

ALEXANDER RAMSEY (1815–1903) *During the Civil War, Ramsey was the governor of Minnesota, then United States senator.*

    1. *Calling on the President in March 1863 to urge a military appointment, Ramsey also asked his intentions regarding those Sioux Indians who had been spared from execution for their part in the Minnesota uprising of 1862. Lincoln said that:*

it was a disagreeable subject, but he would take it up and dispose of it.

After the election of 1864, Ramsey remarked "jocularly" to Lincoln that if he had hung all the condemned Indians, Minnesota would have given him a larger majority. The President replied: I could not afford to hang men for votes. — *Ramsey Diary, March 25, 1863; November 23, 1864, Ramsey Papers.* {B, A}

AMINDA ROGERS RANKIN   *Mother of Henry B. Rankin (q.v.).*

    1. *In 1846, Lincoln campaigned successfully for a seat in Congress against the noted Methodist circuit rider, Peter Cartwright, some of whose supporters accused his opponent of being an infidel. That same summer, according to Rankin, his mother and Lincoln held a conversation about religion, the substance of which she dictated to him in 1889. Lincoln began by praising the value of religious education and went on to say:*

that he was nine years old when his mother died; that his instruction by her in letters and morals, and especially the Bible stories, and the interest and love he acquired in reading the Bible through this teaching of his mother, had been the strongest and most influential experience in his life. . . . that the Bible she had read, and had taught him to read, was the greatest comfort he and his sister had after their mother was gone. . . . that for years afterwards, and even yet, when he read certain verses which he had in early boyhood committed to memory by hearing her repeat them as she went about her household tasks, the tones of his mother's voice would come to him and he would seem to hear her speak those verses again.

    Queried about the charges of infidelity, Lincoln said: Mrs. Rankin, you have asked me a question opening up a subject that is being thrust into this congressional campaign and which I have resolved to ignore. It is one having no proper place, or call for an answer by me, in the political present or future before us. I will not discuss the character and religion of Jesus Christ on the stump. That is no place for it, though my opponent, a minister of His gospel, thinks it is. But in this private circle of friends, with the inquiry coming from you, Mrs. Rankin, who have known me as long as any of my Salem friends and in some respects more intimately than any of them, I will frankly answer your question. I do not wish what I may say here now to be quoted in this congressional canvass to anyone, and I am sure that I can depend that every one of you will respect my wishes.

At the time you refer to, I was having serious questionings about some portions of my former implicit faith in the Bible. The influences that drew me into such doubts were strong ones, men having the widest culture and strongest minds of any I had known up to that time. In the midst of those shadows and questionings, before I could see my way clear to decide on them, there came into my life sad events and a loss that you were close to and you knew a great deal about how hard they were for me; for you were, at the time, a mutual friend. Those days of trouble found me tossed amidst a sea of questionings. They piled big upon me, experiences that brought with them great strains upon my emotional and mental life. Through all, I groped my way until I found a stronger and higher grasp of thought, one that reached beyond this life with a clearness and satisfaction I had never known before. The Scriptures unfolded before me with a deeper and more logical appeal, through these new experiences, than anything else I could find to turn to, or ever before had found in them.

I do not claim that all my doubts were removed then, or since that time have been swept away. They are not. Probably it is to be my lot to go on in a twilight, feeling and reasoning my way through life, as questioning, doubting Thomas did. But in my poor maimed, withered way, I bear with me, as I go on, a seeking spirit of desire for a faith that was with him of the olden time, who, in his need, as I in mine, exclaimed: "Help thou my unbelief."

I do not see that I am more astray—though perhaps in a different direction—than many others whose points of view differ widely from each other in the sectarian denominations. They all claim to be Christian and interpret their several creeds as infallible ones. Yet they differ and discuss these questionable subjects without settling them with any mutual satisfaction among themselves.

I doubt the possibility or propriety of settling the religion of Jesus Christ in the models of man-made creeds and dogmas. It was a spirit in the life that He laid stress on and taught, if I read aright. I know I see it to be so with me.

The fundamental truths reported in the four gospels as from the lips of Jesus Christ, and that I first heard from the lips of my mother, are settled and fixed moral precepts with me. I have concluded to dismiss from my mind the debatable wrangles that once perplexed me with distractions that stirred up, but never absolutely settled anything. I have tossed them aside with the doubtful differences which divide denominations—sweeping them all out of my mind among the nonessentials. I have ceased to follow such discussions or be interested in them.

I cannot without mental reservations assent to long and complicated creeds and catechisms. If the church would ask simply for assent to the Savior's statement of the substance of the law: "Thou shalt love the Lord thy God with all thy heart, and with all thy soul, and with all thy mind, and thy neighbour as thyself,"—that church would I gladly unite with. — *Rankin-1, 320-26 (1916). {D}*

This outpouring from Mrs. Rankin's "very tenacious verbal memory" has been quoted extensively by leading students of Lincoln's religion.[379]

HENRY B. RANKIN (1837–1927)   *Illinois businessman, born at Petersburg near New Salem, who in later life claimed to have studied law in the Lincoln-Herndon office from 1856 to 1861.*[380] *His two books about Lincoln have been accepted at face value by some biographers, but a majority of scholars consider them unreliable.*

1. *In a speech at Petersburg during the campaign of 1856, according to Rankin, Lincoln said:*

When I see strong hands sowing and reaping and threshing wheat, and those same hands grinding and making that wheat into bread, I cannot refrain from wishing and believing that those hands some way, in God's good time, shall own the mouth they feed. —*Rankin-1, 211 (1916). {D}*

2. *To Whig friends who, in the presidential election of 1856, supported Millard Fillmore because he was "the good man," Lincoln suggested:*

that they vote for God—the best being—who had as good a chance for being elected president as Fillmore in that campaign. —*Rankin-2, 136-37 (1924). {D}*

Rankin does not say that he himself heard Lincoln make this remark.

ROBERT S. RANTOUL (1832–1922)   *Massachusetts lawyer and public official, son of a well-known political leader and reformer, Robert Rantoul, Jr.*

1. *When the two were introduced at a White House reception in 1863, the President asked:*

I wonder if you are connected with a lawyer of that name who came to Illinois about 1850 to secure from our legislature the charter of the Illinois Central Railroad?

Told that the man was Rantoul's father, Lincoln let loose "a great roar of laughter" and said that: he did all he could to stop it but was not successful. . . . he was retained by local capitalists who, although they could not then build the road as they had already been intending, were very unwilling that eastern capitalists should step in and secure a grant which would make it forever impossible for them to build a road. But they were defeated. — *Rantoul, 84 (1908). {D}*

There appears to be no contemporary evidence to support this recollection. It seems unlikely that Lincoln, who had always strongly favored such a railroad, would have put himself in the position of delaying its construction. The bill awarding the charter to the Rantoul group was approved almost unanimously by the legislature.[381]

CHARLES H. RAY (1821-1870)   *Editor of the Chicago* Tribune *throughout the Civil War.*

1. *At the time of Salmon P. Chase's visit to Springfield in early January 1861, Lincoln said:*

Take him all in all, he is the foremost man in the party. *—Charles H. Ray to Elihu B. Washburne, January 7, 1861, Washburne Papers. {A}*

HENRY J. RAYMOND (1820-1869)   *Journalist, politician, and bitter rival of Horace Greeley, Raymond was the founding editor of the New York* Times *and a fairly consistent supporter of the Lincoln administration throughout the Civil War.*

1. *Within a month after his inauguration in 1861, Lincoln told Raymond that:*

he wished he could get time to attend to the southern question; he thought he knew what was wanted and believed he could do something towards quieting the rising discontent, but the office-seekers demanded all his time. I am [he said] like a man so busy in letting rooms in one end of his house, that he can't stop to put out the fire that is burning the other. *— Raymond-1, 720 (1865). {C}*

Alexander K. McClure (q.v.) recalled Lincoln's using a similar analogy.

2. *At a White House reception, January 24, 1863, Raymond spoke to Lincoln about Hooker's open abuse of Burnside and other senior officers. The President whispered in his ear:*

That is all true. Hooker does talk badly, but the trouble is, he is stronger with the country today than any other man.

Asked how revelation of the man's conduct and true character would affect his standing, Lincoln replied: The country would not believe it; they would say it is all a lie. *—Journal entry the same day in Raymond-2, 705. {A}*

3. *In 1864, on the subject of Chase's presidential aspirations, Lincoln said that it was important to have the Treasury vigorously administered, and then he continued:*

R[aymond], you were brought up on a farm, were you not? Then you know what a chin-fly is. My brother and I were once plowing corn on a Kentucky farm, I driving the horse and he holding the plow. The horse was lazy, but on one occasion rushed across the field so that I, with my long legs, could scarcely keep pace with him. On reaching the end of the furrow, I found an enormous chin-fly fastened upon him, and knocked him off. My brother asked me what I did that for. I told him I didn't want the old horse bitten in that way. "Why," said my brother, "that's all that made him go." Now, if Mr. [Chase] has a presidential chin-fly biting him, I'm not going to knock him off, if it will only make his department **go.** —*Raymond-1, 720. {D}*

Lincoln, whose only brother died in infancy, probably did little plowing in Kentucky, which he left at the age of eight. It is possible that Raymond just got a few details wrong and that Lincoln actually spoke of plowing corn with his stepbrother, John D. Johnston, in Indiana. It is also possible that Lincoln or Raymond invented the story.

OWEN T. REEVES (1829–1913?)   *Lawyer and judge in Bloomington, Illinois.*

1. *Talking with Reeves about the new house of a prominent local lawyer and businessman, Lincoln said:*

I was thinking it isn't the best thing for a man in a town like Bloomington to build a house so much better than his neighbors. —*Statement of Reeves in Steevens, 40 (1916). {C}*

JOHN F. REYNOLDS (1820–1863)   *Union general from Pennsylvania, a corps commander killed in the first day of fighting at Gettysburg.*

1. *In early June 1863, when Reynolds criticized Hooker's performance as army commander during the Chancellorsville campaign, Lincoln said:*

that he was not disposed to throw away a gun because it missed fire once; that he would pick the lock and try it again. —*Reynolds's account as told to George Gordon Meade and reported in Meade to his wife, June 13, 1863, Meade, I, 385. {D}*

ALBERT RHODES (1840–?)   *A writer and United States consul in Jerusalem and several European cities.*

1. *On March 27, 1863, Lincoln addressed a group of more than a dozen Indian chiefs who were visiting Washington. Rhodes recalled being present on the occasion and hearing the President say:*

My red brethren are anxious to be prosperous and have horses and carriages like the palefaces. I propose to tell them how they may get them. The plan is a simple one. You all have land. We will furnish you with agricultural implements, with which you will turn up the soil, by hand if you have not the means to buy an ox, but I think with the aid which you receive from the government, you might at least purchase one ox to do the plowing for several. You will plant corn, wheat, and potatoes, and with the money for which you will sell these you will be able each to buy an ox for himself at the end of the first year. At the end of the second year, you will each be able to buy perhaps two oxen and some sheep and pigs. At the end of the third, you will probably be in a condition to buy a horse, and in the course of a few years, you will thus be the possessor of horses and carriages like ourselves. I do not know any other way to get these things. It is the plan we have pursued, at least those of us who have them. You cannot pick them off the trees, and they do not fall from the clouds. —*Rhodes, 9-10 (1876). {C}*

This account is different in detail but similar in its general theme to the contemporary newspaper report of Lincoln's remarks.[382]

ALEXANDER H. RICE (1818-1895)   *Civil War congressman, later governor of Massachusetts.*

   1. *In 1864, sometime after Rice had been re-elected with a large majority, rather than by the narrow margin expected, Lincoln said to him:*

Well, your district proved to be a good deal like a jug after all, with the handle all on one side. —*Rice's reminiscence in the Boston* Journal, *reprinted in the Washington* Post, *September 24, 1889. {C}*

   2. *Rice sought pardon for a youth convicted of stealing from his employer's mail while carrying it to and from the post office. Lincoln spoke of his preceding visitor and indulged in some playful irony:*

Yes, he was the last person in this room before you came, and his errand was to get a man pardoned out of the penitentiary, and now you have come to get a boy out of jail. I'll tell you what it is, we must abolish those courts, or they will be the death of us. I thought it bad enough that they put so many men in the penitentiaries for me to get out, but if they have now begun on the boys and the jails and have roped you into the delivery, let's after them! And they deserve the worst fate because, according to the evidence that comes to me, they pick out the very best men and send them to the penitentiary; and this present petition shows they are playing the same game on the good boys and sending them all to jail. The man you met on the stairs affirmed that his friend in the penitentiary is a most exemplary citizen, and Massachusetts must be a happy state if her boys out of jail are as virtuous as this one appears to be who is in. Yes, down with the courts and deliverance to their victims, and then we can have some peace!

   Continuing in a more sober mood, the President said that: he could quite understand how a boy from simple country life might be overcome by the sight of universal abundance in a large city and by a full supply of money in the pockets of almost everybody, and be led to commit even such an offense as this one had done, and yet not be justly put into the class of hopeless criminals; and if he could be satisfied that this was a case of that kind and that the boy would be placed under proper influences and probably saved from a bad career, he would be glad to extend the clemency asked for. — *Oldroyd, 383-84 (1882). {C}*

In a later version, Rice quoted Lincoln thus: I am bothered to death about these pardon cases, but I am a little encouraged by your visit. They are after me on the **men**, but appear to be roping you in on the **boys**. What shall we do? The trouble appears to come from the courts. Let's abolish the courts, and I think that will end the difficulty. — *Rice AH, 434 (1895)*. {C}

MARIA HALL RICHARDS (?–1913)   *A young woman who spent two weeks as a nurse at the White House in February 1862, preceding Rebecca Pomroy in that role.*

    1. At the dinner table, talk once turned to the early days of the war when many army and navy officers were resigning their commissions to support the Confederacy. Lincoln remarked:

If they had only known it, they could have come up the river to take possession, and we could not have prevented it. . . . We did not know which way to look or who could be trusted.

Referring to the newspaper clamor for punishment of the defectors, he said:
True, they ought to be hung, but then, well, you see, we couldn't hang everybody. — *Richards, 52 (1921)*. {D}

Posthumously published recollections, with no dating or other description of the original manuscript.

ALBERT D. RICHARDSON (1833–1869)   *Adventurous journalist and author, born in Massachusetts. A war correspondent for the New York* Tribune, *he was captured in May 1863 and spent the next year and a half in various Confederate prisons before making his escape.*

    1. Richardson heard Lincoln address a small audience at Troy, Kansas, on a bitterly cold day in December 1859. At one point in the speech, he told a story to illustrate the windings of the Democratic party on the slavery question:

A lad, plowing upon the prairie, asked his father in what direction he should strike a new furrow. The parent replied, "Steer for that yoke of oxen standing at the further end of the field." The father went away, and the lad obeyed. But just as he started, the oxen started also. He kept steering for them, and they continued to walk. He followed them entirely around the field and came back to the starting-point, having furrowed a circle instead of a line. — *Richardson, 314-15 (1865)*. {C}

    2. Richardson, who was in the South at the time of the attack on Fort Sumter, arrived in Washington on April 19 and, presumably that same day, was taken to the White House for a talk with the President. Among other things, Lincoln said:

Mr. Douglas spent three hours with me this afternoon. For several days he has been too unwell for business and has devoted his time to studying war matters until he understands the military position better, perhaps, than any one of the cabinet. By the way, the conversation turned upon the rendition of slaves. "You know," said Douglas, "that I am entirely sound on the Fugitive Slave Law. I am for enforcing it in all cases within its true intent and meaning, but, after examining it carefully, I have concluded that a Negro insurrection is a case to which it does not apply." — *Richardson, 116-17.* {D}

*A newspaper version in 1865, said to be drawn from advance sheets of Richardson's book, is different in phrasing and in one important fact. It quotes Lincoln as beginning: "Douglas spent three hours with me this **morning**."* [383] *The last meeting between Lincoln and Douglas for which there is reliable evidence took place on April 14 and lasted two hours. It seems unlikely that they held another, even longer conference just five days later, although there is partial corroboration from a somewhat untrustworthy source — namely, Henry C. Whitney (q.v.).*

3. In March 1863, Richardson and James M. Winchell of the New York Times *visited the President with a memorial asking him to set aside the conviction of Thomas W. Knox, a journalist banished by court-martial from the military department under Grant's command. Lincoln said to Richardson:*

Oh, yes I remember you perfectly well. You were out on the prairies with me on that winter day when we almost froze to death. You were then correspondent of the Boston *Journal*. That German from Leavenworth was also with us — what was his name? . . . Yes, Hatterscheit! By the way, that reminds me of a little story which Hatterscheit told me during the trip. He bought a pony of an Indian, who could not speak much English, but who, when the bargain was completed, said: "Oats — no! Hay — no! Corn — no! Cottonwood — yes! Very much!" Hatterscheit thought this was mere drunken maundering, but a few nights after, he tied his horse in a stable built of cottonwood logs, fed him with hay and corn, and went quietly to bed. The next morning he found the grain and fodder untouched, but the barn was quite empty, with a great hole on one side, which the pony had gnawed his way through. Then he comprehended the old Indian's fragmentary English.

Lincoln was then reminded of having remarked, after crossing a little stream, the Indian name of which meant weeping water: that, as laughing water, according to Longfellow, was "Minnehaha," the name of this rivulet should evidently be "Minne-boohoo." — *Richardson, 319-20.* {C}

The latter story about Lincoln had been in circulation since 1860. Richardson could have been the source. [384]

4. When presented with the memorial, Lincoln declared that he would intervene only if Grant acquiesced. He added:

I should be glad to serve you or Mr. Knox or any other loyal journalist. But just at present, our generals in the field are more important to the country than any of the rest of us or all the rest of us. It is my fixed determination to do nothing whatever which can possibly embarrass any one of them. Therefore, I will do cheerfully what I have said, but it is all I can do. . . . God knows that I want to do what is wise and right, but sometimes it is very difficult to determine —*Richardson, 320, 323.*[385] {C}

Winchell's account (q.v.) quotes Lincoln in different language but to the same effect.

5. *During that same conversation, according to Richardson, Lincoln talked candidly about military affairs, but with the stipulation that his remarks must not be put into print. Of Rear Admiral Samuel F. Du Pont and the pending attack on Charleston, he said that:*

Du Pont had promised some weeks before, if certain supplies were furnished, to make the assault upon a given day. The supplies were promptly forwarded; the day came and went without any intelligence. Some time after, he sent an officer to Washington, asking for three more ironclads and a large quantity of deck-plating as indispensable to the preparations.

Lincoln continued: I told the officer to say to Commodore Du Pont that I fear he does not appreciate at all the value of time. —*Richardson, 323.* {C}

The substance of this passage had been summarized by Richardson in a letter written the day of the interview, with Lincoln's message to Du Pont quoted as follows:

I fear neither you nor your officers appreciate the supreme importance to us of **time**. The more you prepare, the more the enemy will be prepared. —*Richardson to Sydney Howard Gay, March 20, 1863, Gay Papers.* {A}

6. *Turning his attention to the failures of the Army of the Potomac, Lincoln said:*

I do not, as some do, regard McClellan either as a traitor or an officer without capacity. He sometimes has bad counselors, but he is loyal, and he has some fine military qualities. I adhered to him after nearly all my constitutional advisers lost faith in him. But do you want to know when I gave him up? It was after the battle of Antietam. The Blue Ridge was then between our army and Lee's. We enjoyed the great advantage over them which they usually had over us: we had the short line, and they the long one, to the rebel capital. I directed McClellan peremptorily to move on Richmond. It was eleven days before he crossed his first man over the Potomac; it was eleven days after that before he crossed the last man. Thus he was twenty-two days in passing the river at a much easier and more practicable ford than that where Lee crossed his entire army between dark one night and daylight the next morning. That was the last grain of sand which broke the camel's back. I relieved McClellan at once. As for Hooker, I have told **him** forty times that I fear he may err just as much one way as McClellan does the other—may be as overdaring as McClellan is overcautious. — *Richardson, 323-24. {D}*

The credibility of this passage is affected by the fact that after Antietam, Lincoln wanted and repeatedly urged McClellan to attack Lee's army, not Richmond.

7. *During the same interview, Lincoln also commented on Grant's river strategy in the ongoing Vicksburg campaign:*

Of course, men who are in command and on the spot know a great deal more than I do. But immediately in front of Vicksburg, where the river is a mile wide, the rebels plant batteries which absolutely stop our entire fleets. Therefore, it does seem to me that upon narrow streams like the Yazoo, Yalobusha, and Tallahatchie, not wide enough for a long boat to turn around in, if any of our steamers which go there ever come back, there must be some mistake about it. If the enemy permits them to survive, it must be either through lack of enterprise or lack of sense. —*Richardson, 324-25. {C}*

This passage likewise echoed part of Richardson's letter to Gay, March 20, 1863, which summarized Lincoln's remarks as follows: He is not sanguine about Vicksburg. He thinks all these side expeditions through the country dangerous. . . . If the rebels can blockade us on the Mississippi, which is a mile wide, they can certainly stop us on the little streams not much wider than our gunboats and shut us up so we can't get back again. He thinks this is specially true in a case like this, where the project has been so long mooted that news of it has gone to Europe and come back. . . . His only hope about the matter is that the military commanders on the ground know prospects and possibilities better than he can. *{B}*

WILLIAM A. RICHARDSON (1811-1875) *Illinois congressman closely associated in politics with Stephen A. Douglas, to whose senatorial seat he succeeded in 1863.*

1. *On July 23, 1861, in the presence of Richardson and three other members of Congress, General Winfield Scott declared that he had allowed the battle of Bull Run to be fought against his judgment. Lincoln responded:*

Your conversation seems to imply that I forced you to fight this battle. — *Richardson's remarks the next day in the House of Representatives,* Congressional Globe, *37* Congress, *1 session, 246. {A}*

Scott appears to have denied having any such intention, but there was some controversy about it on the House floor.[386]

ALBERT G. RIDDLE (1816–1902) *Congressman from Ohio for a single term beginning in 1861.*

1. *In April 1864, just before returning to army service, Francis P. Blair, Jr., for the second time denounced Salmon P. Chase in the House of Representatives, charging that he was using Treasury patronage to advance his presidential aspirations. Chase threatened to resign unless Lincoln disavowed Blair's attack, and Riddle, together with another Ohioan, visited the White House to query the President on the subject. Lincoln said:*

The Blairs are, as you know, strong, tenacious men, having some peculiarities, among them the energy with which their feuds are carried on. . . . As you know, they labored for ten years to build up an antislavery party in Missouri, and in an action of ejectment to recover that party in the state, they could prove title in any common-law court. Frank has in some way permitted himself to be put in a false position. He is in danger of being kicked out of the house built by himself, and by a set of men rather new to it. You know that they [the Blairs] contributed more than any twenty men to bring forward Frémont in 1855. I know that they mainly induced me to make him a major general and send him to Missouri.

Lincoln explained how he had enabled Blair to resume his military career and then added: Within three hours I heard that this speech had been made, when I knew that another beehive was kicked over. My first thought was to have canceled the orders restoring him to the army and assigning him to command. Perhaps this would have been best. On such reflection as I was able to give to the matter, however, I concluded to let them stand. If I was wrong in this, the injury to the service can be set right. — *Riddle, 273, 275 (1895). {C}*

According to Riddle, this recollection was based upon a report of the interview drafted at Chase's request some two or three weeks after it took place.

2. *Turning his attention to Maryland politics, Lincoln said:*

that in the formation of his cabinet, he was for some days balancing between Montgomery Blair and Henry Winter Davis, and finally settled on Mr. Blair. . . . that in the disposition of the Maryland patronage, he had, as far as possible, met the wishes of Mr. Davis. Subsequently, he regarded Mr. Davis as holding ground not the most favorable to the best interests of the country. Still later, that gentleman made a speech in the House which wholly disabused his mind, and he was greatly rejoiced to find his first opinion of him correct. In Mr. Davis's contest for Congress, he had rendered him all the aid he consistently could. He also understood that Mr. Chase favored Mr. Davis's Union opponent. Since that election, Mr. Davis had desired some aid in the Maryland constitutional election, which he could not see his way to afford him, and Mr. Davis had become very cool towards him. —275-76. {C}

3. *Asked whether his letter of February 29, 1864, still expressed his views on Chase's continuation in the cabinet:*

It does most fully. I cannot see now, as I could not then, how the public service could be advanced by his retirement. —276. {C}

EDWARD HASTINGS RIPLEY (1839–1915) *Union officer from Vermont, a brigade commander whose troops were among the first to enter Richmond in April 1865.*

1. *The day after Lincoln visited the Confederate capital, Ripley spoke to him about a reported plot against his life. The President replied:*

No, General Ripley, it is impossible for me to adopt and follow your suggestions. I deeply appreciate the feeling which has led you to urge them on me, but I must go on as I have begun in the course marked out for me; for I cannot bring myself to believe that any human being lives who would do me any harm. —*Ripley, 307-8 (1865).* {C}

JOHN E. ROLL (1814–1901) *Springfield carpenter and brick mason, who did some work on the Lincoln house in 1849 and 1850; later a building contractor, real estate agent, and shoe merchant.*

1. *During discussion one day on the train to Alton, someone asked Lincoln if he was an abolitionist, and he replied:*

I am mighty near one. —*Roll as quoted by his son in Roll, 159 (1927).* {D}

2. *Roll recalled hearing Lincoln say in a speech:*

that we were all slaves one time or another, but that white men could make themselves free and the Negroes could not.

Then he added: There is my old friend John Roll. He used to be a slave, but he has made himself free, and I used to be a slave, and now I am so free that they let me practice law. —*Roll's statement in the Chicago* Times-Herald, *August 25, 1895.* {D}

Roll associated these remarks with "that time he said the country could not live half slave and half free"—that is, with the House-Divided speech.

JAMES S. ROLLINS (1812–1888) *Civil War congressman from Missouri.*

1. *According to Rollins, during a visit to the White House in August 1863, he proposed that an effort be made to get General Sterling Price to defect from the Confederacy. Lincoln laughed at the idea, but arranged with General Ethan Allen Hitchcock to provide Rollins with the needed military pass for a messenger, saying as he did so:*

Now, Rollins, this is a very delicate business, and I don't want you to get me into any scrape about it. This is your project and not mine. If Sterling Price will come back, all I have to say [is], I will do the fair thing by him, and if you can get him to come back and disband his men, it will be equal to a half-dozen victories to the Union side. But this thing must not go into the papers or be spoken of outside of you, Hitchcock and myself. — *Oldroyd, 497 (1882).* {E}

It seems very unlikely that this conversation ever took place. Rollins in fact made the proposal by mail, writing from Columbia, Missouri, on July 26 and giving no indication of any intention to go to Washington in the weeks ahead. Lincoln replied favorably in a letter dated "August, 1863."[387]

2. In December 1864, Lincoln talked with Rollins about the proposed constitutional amendment abolishing slavery, which earlier that year had passed the Senate but failed in the House:

You and I were old Whigs, both of us followers of that great statesman, Henry Clay, and I tell you I never had an opinion upon the subject of slavery in my life that I did not get from him. I am very anxious that the war should be brought to a close at the earliest possible date, and I don't believe this can be accomplished as long as those fellows down South can rely upon the border states to help them. But if the members from the border states would unite, at least enough of them to pass the thirteenth amendment to the Constitution, they would soon see they could not expect much help from that quarter and be willing to give up their opposition and quit their war upon the government. This is my chief hope and main reliance, to bring the war to a speedy close, and I have sent for you as an old Whig friend to come and see me, that I might make an appeal to you to vote for this amendment. It is going to be very close; a few votes one way or the other will decide it.

Assured of Rollins's support, Lincoln then said: I would like you to talk to all the border-state men whom you can approach properly and tell them of my anxiety to have the measure pass, and let me know the prospect of the border-state vote . . . The passage of this amendment will clinch the whole subject; it will bring the war, I have no doubt, rapidly to a close. —*492–93.* {C}

3. Rollins recalled that sometime during the winter of 1864–65, he transmitted to Lincoln a warning that a box containing explosive material would be sent to him at the White House. Lincoln thanked him and said:

I have received quite a number of threatening letters since I have been president, and nobody has killed me yet, and the truth is, I give very little consideration to such things. . . . I promise you if I find any boxes on my table directed to me, I won't open them. . . . Rollins, I don't see what on

God's earth any man would wish to kill me for, for there is not a human being living to whom I would not extend a favor and make them happy if it was in my power to do so. —*501-2.* {D}

There appears to be no corroboration of this incident.

MATIAS ROMERO (1837–1898) *Diplomatic representative of the Mexican Republic who visited the President-elect in January 1861 by instruction from his government.*

1. *During their conversation, Lincoln asked about the situation of the peons working on the haciendas, adding:*

It is said that they are in a condition of slavery more abominable than that of blacks on the plantations in the South of this country, and it is believed that the abuses that unfortunately happen in some places are widespread in the republic and that they are authorized by law. — *Romero to Mexico's minister of foreign relations, January 23, 1861, Reservado, Numero 2, Archivo de Relationes Esteriores, Mexico, D.F., copy provided by the Manuscript Division, Library of Congress.*[388] {A}

JOHN ROMINE (born c. 1805) *Farmer in Spencer County, Indiana, for whom Lincoln worked in 1829.*

1. *Lincoln said to Romine one day that:*

his father taught him to work but never learned him to love it. — *Herndon's memorandum of Romine's statement, September 14, 1865 (7:378), Herndon-Weik Collection.* {C}

ALEXANDER MILTON ROSS (1832–1897) *Canadian physician, naturalist, and reformer, whose account of being enlisted as a Union agent by Lincoln lacks corroboration. There are grounds for the suspicion that his autobiographical record, although accepted by many historians, is partly imaginative literature.*[389]

1. *At a White House dinner in 1861, Lincoln introduced Ross as "a red-hot abolitionist from Canada." A member of Congress from Indiana (Ross apparently meant Schuyler Colfax) remarked somewhat offensively that he wished American Negroes would emigrate to Canada. Said Lincoln:*

It would be all the better for the Negroes, that's certain.

And then in jocular fashion to the Congressman: If you are not careful, you will bring on a war with Canada. I think we have got a big enough job on hand now. — *Ross, 134-35 (1875).* {D}

2. *After dinner, according to Ross, Lincoln took him aside and said:*

Mr. S[umner] sent for you at my request; we need a confidential person in Canada to look after the rebel emissaries there and keep us posted as to their schemes and objects. You have been strongly recommended to me for the position. Your mission shall be as confidential as you please. No one here but your friend Mr. S[umner] and myself shall have any knowledge of your position. Your communications may be sent direct to me under cover to Major ——. Think it over tonight, and if you can accept the mission, come up and see me at nine o'clock tomorrow morning. —Ross, 136. {E}

Ross provided another version with slightly different wording in Oldroyd, 419-20 (1882), where he identified his friend as Sumner. He quoted Lincoln as saying when they parted the next day, "Let me hear from you once a week at least," but there is no evidence of any correspondence between the two men, or between Ross and Sumner, throughout the Civil War.

3. *Ross agreed to serve, but said that he would do so more enthusiastically if the war were being fought to free the slaves. Lincoln replied:*

I sincerely wish that all men were free, and I especially wish for the complete abolition of slavery in this country; but my private wishes and feelings must yield to the necessities of my position. My first duty is to maintain the integrity of the Union. With that object in view, I shall endeavor to save it, either with or without slavery. . . . If the destruction of the institution of slavery should be one of the results of this conflict which the slaveholders have forced upon us, I shall rejoice as hearty as you. In the meantime, help us to circumvent the machinations of the rebel agents in Canada. There is no doubt they will use your country as a communicating link with Europe and also with their friends in New York. It is quite possible also that they may make Canada a base to annoy our people along the frontier. Keep us well posted of what they say and do. —Ross, 137-38. {E}

Compare with Oldroyd, 420-21.

4. *Walking with Ross toward the Capitol, Lincoln was accosted by a man applying for an office. He exclaimed:*

No, sir! I am not going to open shop here.

Then, as they continued their walk: These office-seekers are a curse to this country. No sooner was my election certain than I became the prey of hundreds of hungry, persistent applicants for office, whose highest ambition is to feed at the government crib. —Ross, 138-39. {C}

Herndon, III, 507n, gives Lincoln's own account of such an incident.

5. *Soon thereafter, an army officer approached and made some kind of request, to which the President replied good-humoredly:*

No, I can't do that; I must not interfere; they would scratch my eyes out, if I did. You must go to the proper department. —Ross, 139. {C}

6. *At a later time, either in September 1862 or January 1863, Ross allegedly visited Lincoln again, getting him out of bed at midnight to deliver some "rebel mail" from Canada. Lincoln waved aside his apologies, saying:*

No, no, you may rout me up whenever you please. I have slept with one eye open since I came to Washington; I never close both, except when an office-seeker is looking for me. I am glad you are pleased with the Emancipation Proclamation, but there is work before us yet; we must make that proclamation effective by victories over our enemies. It's a paper bullet, after all, and of no account, except we can sustain it. —*Ross, 146-47.* {D}

F. A. ROWE   *A Union naval officer.*

1. *During preparations for the attack on Norfolk in May 1862, Lincoln asked numerous questions, such as:*

How are we to find a good landing point where the depth of the water is sufficient for our boats to land?

He went along on a sounding expedition, which came under fire from enemy pickets. Urged to move to a less exposed part of the boat, he acquiesced, saying: Although I have no feeling of danger myself, perhaps for the benefit of our country, it would be well to step aside. —*Rowe's Reminiscences (1905).* {C}

2. *After asking for and receiving a demonstration of the Sawyer gun:*

Why, that is perfectly magnificent to fire such a distance with such accuracy. —*Ibid.* {C}

JULIUS HEATH ROYCE   *New York businessman who owned property in Bloomington, Illinois.*

1. *At a Bloomington hotel in 1859 or 1860, when asked about the book in which he was absorbed:*

I am reading Homer, the *Iliad* and *Odyssey*. You ought to read him. He has a grip and he knows how to tell a story. —*Williams T, 196 (1920).* {D}

This is Royce's recollection as told to his son-in-law.

SAMUEL B. RUGGLES (1800–1881)   *New York lawyer, civic leader, canal commissioner, and railroad promoter.*

1. *On November 25, 1862, Lincoln complained to Ruggles about increased freight charges, adverting with special displeasure to the fact that New York canal rates had been raised immediately after Confederate forces seized a portion of the Baltimore and Ohio Railroad. He went on to say emphatically that:*

until he could be satisfactorily assured that adequate measures would be adopted to terminate this abuse, he should feel but little inclined to exert his influence or authority to secure the enlargement of the New York Canal locks.[390] —*Ruggles to Edwin Morgan, November 28, 1862, ISHL.* {B}

JAMES F. RUSLING (1834–1918)   *Union army officer from New Jersey, a quartermaster who served for a time on the staff of General Daniel E. Sickles.*

1. *On July 5, 1863, Lincoln visited Sickles, who, at Gettysburg three days*

earlier, had suffered a leg wound that necessitated amputation. Responding to a question from Sickles, the President explained why he had not been fearful during the battle:

In the pinch of your campaign up there, when everybody seemed panic-stricken, and nobody could tell what was going to happen, oppressed by the gravity of our affairs, I went into my room one day and locked the door and got down on my knees before Almighty God and prayed to him mightily for victory at Gettysburg. I told him this was his war and our cause, his cause, but that we couldn't stand another Fredericksburg or Chancellorsville. And I then and there made a solemn vow to Almighty God that if he would stand by our boys at Gettysburg, I would stand by him. And he **did**, and I **will**. And after that, I don't know how it was and I can't explain it, but soon a sweet comfort crept into my soul that things would go all right at Gettysburg, and that is why I had no fears about you. —*Rusling, 431 (1895). {D}*

Independently or not, Sickles (q.v.) and Rusling both recalled Lincoln's telling them that he had prayed for a victory at Gettysburg, but there is little resemblance between their respective recollections of the words he used in doing so. The Washington Chronicle, July 6, 1863, listed five officers accompanying Sickles, and Rusling's name was not among them.

2. *Asked about Vicksburg during the same conversation, he said that:*

Grant was still pegging away down there, and he thought a good deal of him as a general and wasn't going to remove him, though urged to do so.

Then he added: Besides, I have been praying over Vicksburg also and believe our Heavenly Father is going to give us victory there too, because we need it in order to bisect the Confederacy and have the Mississippi flow unvexed to the sea. —*431. {D}*

The final clause contributes to one's doubt about the credibility of this recollection, though it is not impossible that Lincoln was trying out phrasing that he would use in a public letter some two months later.[391]

WILLIAM H. RUSSELL (1820–1907)   *Noted English journalist who served the London* Times *as its Civil War correspondent from 1861 to 1863. Russell's My Diary North and South, published in 1863, was not really a diary, but rather a reconstruction based upon his notebooks and dispatches.*[392]

1. *When the two men were introduced on March 27, 1861, Lincoln said:*

Mr. Russell, I am very glad to make your acquaintance, and to see you in this country. The London *Times* is one of the greatest powers in the world—in fact, I don't know anything which has much more power, except perhaps the Mississippi. I am glad to know you as its minister. —*Russell WH-2, I, 56–57 (1863). {C}*

The only thing he wrote in his private diary about this conversation with Lincoln was: "Power of The Times."[393]

2. *During a state dinner at the White House the following evening, Attorney General Edward Bates was complaining about the appointment of a mediocre lawyer to a certain judicial position, and the President responded:*

Come now, Bates, he's not half as bad as you think. Besides that, I must tell you, he did me a good turn long ago. When I took to the law, I was going to court one morning with some ten or twelve miles of bad road before me, and I had no horse. The judge overtook me in his wagon. "Hollo, Lincoln! Are you not going to the courthouse? Come in and I'll give you a seat." Well, I got in, and the judge went on reading his papers. Presently the wagon struck a stump on one side of the road; then it hopped off to the other. I looked out, and I saw the driver was jerking from side to side in his seat; so says I, "Judge, I think your coachman has been taking a little drop too much this morning." "Well I declare, Lincoln," said he, "I should not much wonder if you are right, for he has nearly upset me half a dozen of times since starting." So, putting his head out of the window, he shouted, "Why, you infernal scoundrel, you are drunk!" Upon which, pulling up his horses, and turning round with great gravity, the coachman said, "By gorra! that's the first rightful decision you have give for the last twelvemonth." — *Russell WH-2, I, 63–64.*[394] *{C}*

It has been suggested that the judge in question was David Davis, appointed to the Supreme Court in 1862.[395] *More probably, Lincoln was just telling a joke, not recounting an actual experience.*

3. *Visiting Seward in his home on November 14, 1861, Lincoln found Russell there, along with Henry J. Raymond, editor of the New York* Times. *"Here," Seward remarked, "are the two* Times — *if we only get them to do what we want all would go well." Lincoln replied:*

Oh, if the *Times* go for us, the other *Times* will follow. — *Russell WH-1, 174. {A}*

The version that Russell published in 1863 illustrates the constructive element in reminiscence: Yes, if the bad Times would go where we want them, good Times would be sure to follow. — *Russell WH-2, II, 402. {C}*

HENRY SAMUEL (Born c. 1839)   *Secretary of a committee concerned with the recruitment of black troops.*

1. *In 1864, members of the committee visited the White House to urge that*

blacks employed by the army receive wages equal to those of white laborers. Lincoln said in a jocular tone:

Well, gentlemen, you wish the pay of Cuffie raised.

When Samuel expressed displeasure at his use of the word "Cuffie," the President replied: I stand corrected, young man, but you know I am by birth a southerner and in our section that term is applied without any idea of an offensive nature. I will, however, at the earliest possible moment, do all in my power to accede to your request. —*Samuel (1889). {D}*

John G. Nicolay subsequently labeled the account "utterly untrustworthy." [396]

ROBERT C. SCHENCK (1809–1890)   *Ohio Whig and Republican congressman who became a Civil War general.*

   1. *Once, after receiving some bad news from the army, Lincoln said:*

You have little idea of the terrible weight of care and sense of responsibility of this office of mine. Schenck, if to be at the head of Hell is as hard as what I have to undergo here, I could find it in my heart to pity Satan himself. — *As told to Allen Thorndike Rice in Rice AT, xxix (1886). {D}*

RUDOLPH SCHLEIDEN (1815–1895)   *Minister from Bremen.*

   1. *Schleiden reported to his government that at a dinner given by him on March 1, 1861, Lincoln said:*

I don't know anything about diplomacy. I will be very apt to make blunders. —*Lutz, 210. {A}*

Schleiden also reported home that Lincoln, when asked by members of the Washington peace convention to remove federal troops from Fort Sumter, had replied: "Why not? If you will guarantee to me the State of Virginia I shall remove the troops. A state for a fort is no bad business." —211. It seems clear, however, that Schleiden did not himself hear Lincoln speak these words.

JOHN M. SCHOFIELD (1831–1906)   *This West Point graduate and Union general held several commands in Missouri during the Civil War. Many years later, he served briefly as secretary of war and eventually became the army's commander in chief.*

   1. *In December 1863, when Schofield told his side of his difficulties with the Radical Republican faction in Missouri, Lincoln said:*

I believe you, Schofield; those fellows have been lying to me again. — *Schofield, 108 (1897). {C}*

   2. *A year later, Schofield paid a second visit to the White House, having long since been transferred out of Missouri to other assignments. Lincoln said:*

Well, Schofield, I haven't heard anything against you for a year. —*110. {C}*

CARL SCHURZ (1829-1906) *A German-American leader whom Lincoln appointed minister to Spain, then successively brigadier general and major general of volunteers. Schurz served as a division commander in several of the biggest battles of the war. He was later a senator and cabinet member and also distinguished himself as editor, author, and civil-service reformer.*

1. *Schurz delivered a campaign speech at a Republican rally in Springfield on July 24, 1860, and during a long conversation earlier in the day, Lincoln talked about the pressure for patronage, which he had already begun to feel:*

Men like you, who have real merit and do the work, are always too proud to ask for anything. Those who do nothing are always the most clamorous for office and very often get it, because it is the only way to get rid of them. But if I am elected, they will find a tough customer to deal with, and you may depend upon it that I shall know how to distinguish deserving men from the drones. *—Schurz to his wife, July 25, 1860, in Schurz-1, I, 120. {A}*

2. *On February 9, 1861, at a time when Seward in Washington seemed to be nudging the Republican party toward some kind of sectional compromise, Schurz visited Springfield again and found the President-elect "firm as a stone wall and clear as crystal." Lincoln said that:*

Seward made all his speeches without consulting him. *—Schurz to his wife the same day, Schurz-2, 247. {B}*

3. *On February 10, which was the eve of his departure for Washington, Lincoln read Schurz the draft of his inaugural address and then said:*

Now you know better than any man in this country how I stand, and you may be sure that I shall never betray my principles and my friends. *—Schurz to his wife the same day, Schurz-1, I, 179. {A}*

4. *In April 1861, after the firing on Fort Sumter and before northern troops arrived in Washington, Lincoln related an incident characteristic of the situation:*

One afternoon after he had issued his call for troops, he sat alone in this room, and a feeling came over him as if he were utterly deserted and helpless. He thought any moderately strong body of secessionist troops, if there were any in the neighborhood, might come over the "long bridge" across the Potomac and just take him and the members of the cabinet—the whole lot of them. Then he suddenly heard a sound like the boom of a cannon. "There they are!" he said to himself. He expected every moment somebody would rush in with the report of an attack. The White House attendants, whom he interrogated, had heard nothing. But nobody came, and all remained still. Then he thought he would look after the thing himself. So he walked out and walked and walked until he got to the Arsenal. There he found the doors all open and not a soul to guard them. Anybody might have gone in and helped himself to the arms. There was perfect solitude and stillness all around. Then he walked back to the White House without noticing the slightest sign of disturbance. He met a few persons on the way, some of whom he asked whether they had not heard something like the boom of a cannon. Nobody had heard anything, and so he supposed it must have been a freak of his imagination. —*Schurz-3, II, 227-28. {C}*

5. *During the same conversation, Schurz expressed doubt about going to Spain, now that civil war had begun. After a moment of thought, Lincoln said:*

that he fully understood and appreciated my feelings, but that he would not advise me to give up the Spanish mission. He thought that this diplomatic position might eventually offer me a greater field of usefulness. The war might be over very soon. Many people whose opinions were entitled to respect thought so. Mr. Seward was speaking of sixty or ninety days. He himself was not at all as sanguine as that, but he might be wrong. However, in a few weeks we would, as to that point, see more clearly. —*Schurz-3, II, 228-29. {C}*

6. *Before Schurz's departure for Spain in the late spring of 1861, Lincoln said:*

that he deplored having given so little attention to foreign affairs and being so dependent upon other people's judgment, and that he felt the necessity of "studying up" on the subject as much as his opportunities permitted him. —*Schurz-3, II, 242-43. {C}*

7. *In March 1862, after listening to Schurz's report of a recent emancipation meeting in New York, Lincoln:*

expressed his satisfaction with what had been done and trusted that the public discussion of the subject would go on so as to familiarize the public mind with what would inevitably come if the war continued. He was not altogether without hope that the proposition he had presented to the southern states in his message of March 6th would find favorable consideration, at least in some of the border states. He had made the proposition in perfect good faith; it was, perhaps, the last of the kind; and if they repelled it, theirs was the responsibility. —*Schurz-3, II, 328-29. {C}*

8. *Schurz introduced a German count who wanted an army appointment and proceeded to give the President a detailed description of his distinguished ancestry. Lincoln interrupted, saying:*

Well, that need not trouble you. That will not be in your way, if you behave yourself as a soldier. —*Schurz-3, II, 340. {C}*

9. *Concerning General David Hunter's proclamation in May 1862 emancipating slaves in the South Atlantic states, Lincoln said:*

I wanted him to **do** it, not say it. —*Schurz's account to George W. Smalley in Smalley to Sydney Howard Gay, June 21, 1862, Gay Papers. {D}*

10. *Warned by Schurz that the Maryland delegation in Congress would expect an answer from him about the problem of slaves escaping from their state into the District of Columbia, the President replied:*

Well, I shall say to them, "I am engaged in putting down a great rebellion in which I can only succeed by the help of the North, which will not tolerate my returning your slaves, and I cannot try experiments. You cannot have them." —*Ibid. {D}*

11. *Schurz wrote two letters to the President in November 1862, placing the blame for military failures and recent electoral setbacks on the administration's policy of assigning command to men who were hostile to the Republican cause and resistant to vigorous prosecution of the war. Lincoln responded sharply both times, but then, according to Schurz, sent a note inviting him to call at the White House. In the resulting interview, Lincoln explained that Schurz had provided him a welcome opportunity to answer his critics. Slapping Schurz's knee and laughing, he exclaimed:*

Didn't I give it to you hard in my letter? Didn't I? But it didn't hurt, did it? I did not mean to, and therefore I wanted you to come so quickly. Well, I guess we understand one another now, and it's all right. —*Schurz-3, II, 396. {D}*

Actually, it was Schurz, rather than Lincoln, who asked for an interview after their second exchange of letters, and there appears to be no evidence, aside from Schurz's statement, that such a meeting ever took place.[397]

12. *One summer evening in 1864 at the Soldiers' Home,[398] Lincoln spoke of the continued opposition to him within the Republican party:*

They urge me with almost violent language to withdraw from the contest, although I have been unanimously nominated, in order to make room for a better man. I wish I could. Perhaps some other man might do this business better than I. That is possible. I do not deny it. But I am here, and that better man is not here. And if I should step aside to make room for him, it is not at all sure—perhaps not even probable—that he would get here. It is much more likely that the factions opposed to me would fall to fighting among themselves and that those who want me to make room for a better man would get a man whom most of them would not want in at all. My withdrawal, therefore, might and probably would bring on a confusion worse confounded. God knows, I have at least tried very hard to do my duty—to do right to everybody and wrong to nobody. And now to have it said by men who have been my friends and who ought to know me better that I have been seduced by what they call the lust of power, and that I have been doing this and that unscrupulous thing hurtful to the common cause, only to keep myself in office! Have they thought of that common cause when trying to break me down? I hope they have. —*Schurz-3, III, 103-4.* {C}

13. *Speaking in the same conversation of his differences with Congress on reconstruction, he emphasized that:*

looked at from a constitutional standpoint, the executive could do many things by virtue of the war power which Congress could not do in the way of ordinary legislation. —*Schurz-3, III, 104.* {C}

14. *On April 1, 1865, after visiting the presidential party at City Point, Schurz prepared to depart via government tug, but Lincoln said:*

Oh, you can do better than that. Mrs. Lincoln is here and will start back for Washington in an hour or two. She has a comfortable steamboat to carry her, on which there will be plenty of room for both of you, if you keep the peace. You can accompany her, if you like. —*Schurz-3, III, 110.* {C}

GLENNI W. SCOFIELD (1817-1891) *Congressman from Pennsylvania.*

1. *Scofield sought clemency for a private convicted of knocking down his captain. Lincoln wearily suggested that Congress handle the problem. When asked how, he said:*

Pass a law that a private shall have a right to knock down his captain. — *Oldroyd, 369 (1882).* {C}

JAMES M. SCOVEL (1833-1904) *A Douglas Democrat of Camden, New Jersey, who became a strong supporter of the Lincoln administration and was elected to the state legislature in 1863 on the Union-Republican ticket. A few samples of Scovel's various recollections of Lincoln will suffice. They are often so wildly inaccurate and improbable as to cast doubt on everything he wrote.*[399]

1. *At the time of the* Trent *crisis, we are told, Lincoln sent "more than one" personal letter to Queen Victoria and in each instance received an answer.*[400] *He read her first reply aloud to Seward and Scovel, then remarked:*

I think the friendship of Queen Victoria will carry America safely across the dangerous quicksands of diplomacy threatening to involve the United States in war with England in regard to the capture of Slidell and Mason. —*Scovel-3, 269 (1901).* {E}

No such letters were written.

2. *After retailing a story that McClellan's Harrison Landing letter of July 7, 1862, was viewed by Lincoln as a bid for the presidency and prompted him to issue the Emancipation Proclamation as a countermeasure, Scovel recalled the President's saying soon afterward:*

I told you a year ago that Henry Ward Beecher and Horace Greeley gave me

no rest because I would not free the Negroes. The time had not come. . . .
I was tired that day. But you will see no trace of doubt or hesitation in my
signature to my greatest and most enduring contribution to the history of
the war. —*Scovel-1, 506 (1891). {D}*

3. *To an army officer who had been dismissed from the service for drunken-
ness and whose features showed clear signs of his dissipation, Lincoln said sadly:*

Colonel, I know your story. But you carry your own condemnation in
your face.

Then to Scovel when the officer had left: I dare not restore this man to his
rank and give him charge of a thousand men, when he "puts an enemy into
his mouth to steal away his brains." —*Scovel-1, 500. {D}*

4. *One Sunday after the surrender of Vicksburg, says Scovel, the President
remarked:*

I fully appreciated the real strength of Grant's character when he spent a
whole day with me in Washington and asked that eight major generals and
thirteen brigadier generals should be retired, solely to make room for the
soldiers who had won and worn their "wounds and honors a' front." In vain,
I told General Grant that many of these officers were my personal friends,
but he insisted. At last I yielded, and by doing so greatly strengthened the
army. —*Scovel-2, 204 (1901). {E}*

*Lincoln and Grant did not meet for the first time until March 1864, some eight
months after the fall of Vicksburg, and there was never any such wholesale
purge of Union generals.*

5. *According to Scovel, Lincoln said to him just a few days before the assassination:*

Young man, if I am permitted to rule this nation for four years more, this
government will become what it ought to be, what its Divine Author intended it to be, no longer a vast plantation for breeding human beings for
purposes of lust and bondage, but it will become a new Valley of Jehosaphat,
where all the glad nations of the earth will assemble together worshiping
a common God and celebrating the resurrection of human freedom. —
Scovel-3, 271. {D}

JOHN LOCKE SCRIPPS (1818–1866) *Chicago editor who wrote a campaign
biography of Lincoln in 1860 and was appointed the city's postmaster in 1861.*

1. *When Scripps visited Springfield to discuss the biography with him, Lincoln said:*

Why, Scripps, it is a great piece of folly to attempt to make anything out
of my early life. It can all be condensed into a single sentence, and that
sentence you will find in Gray's Elegy: "The short and simple annals of the

poor." That's my life, and that's all you or anyone else can make of it. — *Scripps to Herndon, June 24, 1865 (7:196–98), Herndon-Weik Collection.* {C}

WILLIAM J. SEAVER *A young man from Boston who worked as a store clerk and bank clerk in Springfield during the late 1850s.*

1. *One day, some of the clerks were criticizing a lady patron as unsophisticated and deficient in tact, though possessing many good qualities. Lincoln said:*

That reminds me of a girl who wasn't much of a dancer. Her friends said that what she lacked in dancing she made up in turning round. —*Seaver, 244 (1911).* {C}

2. *Seaver recalled Lincoln's once answering some remark of his with a common expression of the day:*

You'll know more when the steamer gets in. —*244.* {C}

PAUL SELBY (1825–1913) *Illinois journalist, editor of the* Morgan Journal *in Jacksonville during the 1850s.*

1. *During a speech at the Decatur convention of anti-Nebraska editors, February 22, 1856, after there had been some talk of making him the gubernatorial candidate of the emerging Republican movement:*

I wish to say why I should not be a candidate. If I should be chosen, the Democrats would say it was nothing more than an attempt to resurrect the dead body of the old Whig party. I would secure the vote of that party and no more, and our defeat will follow as a matter of course. But I can suggest a name that will secure not only the old Whig vote, but enough anti-Nebraska Democrats to give us the victory. That man is Colonel William H. Bissell. —*Selby's statement in Tarbell, II, 85.* {C}

FRANCES ADELINE (FANNY) SEWARD (1844–1866) *Daughter of William H. Seward.*

1. *On April 9, 1865, Lincoln returned from the Virginia military front and went immediately to the home of William H. Seward, who had been seriously injured in a fall from a carriage. Lying across the foot of Seward's bed in what proved to be their last hour together, he told of his visit to Richmond and said that:*

one of his latter acts was going through a hospital of seven thousand men and shaking hands with each one. He . . . worked as hard at it as sawing wood. —*Fanny Seward's diary, entry dated April 9 but written after Lincoln's death, Seward Papers.* {C}

Lincoln visited hospital camps at City Point on April 8. After meeting the President at a White House reception in 1861, Herman Melville noted in his journal: "He shook hands like a good fellow — working hard at it like a man sawing wood at so much a cord."[401]

FREDERICK W. SEWARD (1830–1915)   *Son of William H. Seward and assistant secretary of state throughout the Civil War.*

1. *On February 21, 1861, Seward arrived in Philadelphia with a warning from his father and General Scott concerning an assassination plot. Lincoln queried him about the source of the information and said:*

There were stories or rumors some time ago, before I left home, about people who were intending to do me a mischief. I never attached much importance to them—never wanted to believe any such thing. So I never would do anything about them in the way of taking precautions and the like. Some of my friends, though, thought differently—Judd and others—and without my knowledge, they employed a detective to look into the matter. It seems he has occasionally reported what he found, and only today, since we arrived at this house, he brought this story, or something similar to it, about an attempt on my life in the confusion and hurly-burly of the reception at Baltimore. . . . If different persons, not knowing of each other's work, have been pursuing separate clues that led to the same result, why then it shows there may be something in it. But if this is only the same story filtered through two channels and reaching me in two ways, then that don't make it any stronger. . . . You need not think I will not consider it well. I shall think it over carefully and try to decide it right, and I will let you know in the morning. —*Seward FW-1, 510 (1891).*[402] {C}

2. *After submitting his resignation as secretary of state on December 17, 1862, William H. Seward expressed relief at the prospect of being freed from official cares. Lincoln responded:*

Ah, yes, Governor, that will do very well for you, but I am like the starling in Sterne's story, "I can't get out." —*Seward FW-2, 147 (1891).* {D}

This exchange, according to Frederick Seward, took place in the Seward home. Whether he heard it himself or was told about it by his father, is not made clear.

3. *Frederick Seward was present with his father on January 1, 1863, when Lincoln, preparing to sign the Emancipation Proclamation, declared:*

I never in my life felt more certain that I was doing right than I do in signing this paper. But I have been receiving calls and shaking hands since nine o'clock this morning till my arm is stiff and numb. Now, this signature is one that will be closely examined, and if they find my hand trembled, they will say "he had some compunctions." But, anyway, it is going to be done. —*Seward FW-2, 151.* {C}

Somewhat different is an earlier version by Schuyler Colfax (q.v.), as told to Francis B. Carpenter.[403]

4. *At the cabinet meeting on April 14, 1865, after some talk about the possible escape of Confederate leaders:*

I should not be sorry to have them out of the country, but I should be for following them up pretty close to make sure of their going. —*Seward FW-2, 274. {C}*

5. *During the same meeting, Lincoln remarked that:*

a peculiar dream of the previous night was one that had recurred several times in his life: a vague sense of floating—floating away on some vast and indistinct expanse toward an unknown shore. The dream itself was not so strange as the coincidence that each of its previous recurrences had been followed by some important event or disaster. —*Seward FW-2, 274. {C}*

Welles (q.v.), in his diary, wrote more fully about this revelation and the discussion that it inspired.

6. *When discussion turned to problems of reconstruction, he said:*

We can't undertake to run state governments in all these southern states. Their people must do that, though I reckon that at first, they may do it badly. —*Seward FW-2, 275. {C}*

WILLIAM H. SEWARD (1801–1872)   *New York governor and senator, secretary of state throughout the Lincoln and Johnson administrations.*

1. *After hearing Seward speak at a Whig meeting in Boston on September 22, 1848, Lincoln said to him:*

Governor Seward, I have been thinking about what you said in your speech. I reckon you are right. We have got to deal with this slavery question and got to give much more attention to it hereafter than we have been doing. —*Seward FW-1, 80 (1891). {D}*

It is not clear whether Seward wrote out this recollection or merely told it to his son Frederick.

2. *Probably on the morning of February 23, 1861, Lincoln said:*

One part of the business, Governor Seward, I think I shall leave almost entirely in your hands; that is, the dealing with those foreign nations and their governments. —*Seward FW-1, 511. {D}*

Presumably, Lincoln's words as Seward recounted them to his son Frederick.[404]

3. *Seward recalled being present one day when Lincoln, besieged by a large number of office-seekers, told them a long story about a king who discovered a weather-wise jackass and appointed him as his minister. The President ended by remarking:*

And here is where the king made a great mistake.

Asked how so, he said: Why, ever since that time, every jackass wants an office. Gentlemen, leave your credentials, and when the war is over, you'll hear from me. —*Seward as quoted in* Leslie's Illustrated Newspaper, *October 31, 1863, p. 87. {D}*

4. *In December 1861, after a cabinet discussion of the seizure of Mason and Slidell from the British ship* Trent, *Lincoln said to his secretary of state:*

Governor Seward, you will go on, of course, preparing your answer, which, as I understand, will state the reasons why they ought to be given up. Now I have a mind to try my hand at stating the reasons why they ought not to be given up. We will compare the points on each side.

The next day, however, Lincoln confessed: I found I could not make an argument that would satisfy my own mind, and that proved to me your ground was the right one. —*Seward FW-3, 189–90 (1916). {D}*

Here, Frederick Seward may have been himself an auditor, but it seems more likely that Lincoln's words were repeated to him by his father.

5. *In 1863, during one of their evening talks, Lincoln told Seward:*

that he now hoped to see him his successor . . . that the friends who had been so disappointed at Chicago in 1860 would thus find all made right at last. —*Seward FW-2, 196 (1891). {D}*

Again, Frederick Seward may have heard Lincoln make this remark but more probably was told about it by his father.

6. *After one of the cabinet meetings in 1865, Postmaster General William Dennison looked at the old chair in which Lincoln did some of his writing and remarked that the presidency deserved a better piece of furniture. Lincoln replied:*

You think that's not a good chair, Governor? There are a great many people that want to sit in it, though. I'm sure I've often wished some of them had it instead of me. —*Seward FW-2, 265. {D}*

Presumably related by Seward to his son.

WILLIAM H. SEWARD, JR (1839–1920). *Son of Lincoln's secretary of state. He interrupted his incipient career as a banker to serve with distinction in the Army of the Potomac and rose to the rank of brigadier general.*

1. *Lincoln visited Seward's regiment at a fort on the Potomac and, after the usual dress parade, made a thorough inspection of the soldiers' quarters, cook tent, hospital tent, and other facilities. Then he said:*

Colonel, you seem to have a fine body of well-drilled soldiers, so far as I understand it, but I am especially pleased to see that they are well taken care of. —*Seward WHJr, 105 (1909). {C}*

2. *Early in 1863, Seward was summoned to the White House, where the President said to him:*

We wish to communicate with General Banks, now in New Orleans, just about to start on his campaign through the Teche country. All communication by land being cut off, our messenger must go by sea, and as this takes

a long time, it is probable that his army will be well advanced in Louisiana before you can reach him. Most of this country is hostile, but General
Banks must be found wherever he may be. You will therefore have to take
the chances of riding alone, as no guard which you could take would be
of sufficient protection. Our dispatch, which is now being prepared in the
War Department, is of great importance and must not fall into the enemy's
hands. Commit your dispatch to memory; conceal it, and, in case of possible capture, destroy it. Start tonight if possible. And now good-bye, my
boy. God bless you! — *106. {C}*

*The dispatch presumably had to do with the Red River campaign of March and
April 1863, but there is also evidence that it related to a peacemaking scheme in
which the central figure was an adventurous chiropodist, Dr. Isachar Zacharie
(q.v.).*[405]

JOHN F. SEYMOUR   *Brother of Horatio Seymour, the New York Democratic
leader who was elected governor in 1862.*

   1. *After his inauguration in January 1863, Horatio Seymour sent his brother
to Washington to assure the President of his support in the war effort. During
one of their discussions, Lincoln said:*

that if he could see you, he would say to you that his desire was to maintain
this government; that he had the same stake in the country with you; that
he had two children and he presumed you had as many; that there could
be no next presidency if the country was broken up, no next president
if there was no presidency; that he was a party man and did not believe
in any man who was not; that a party man was generally selfish, yet he
had appointed most of the officers of the army from among Democrats
because most of the West Point men were Democrats, and he believed a
man educated in military affairs was better fitted for military office than
an uneducated man, and because antislavery men, being generally much
akin to peace, had never interested themselves in military matters and in
getting up companies, as Democrats had. That when the army was unsuccessful, everyone was dissatisfied and criticized the administration; that if
a cartman's horse ran away, all the men and women in the streets thought
they could do better than the driver, and so it was with the management
of the army; that the complaints of his own party gave the Democrats the
weapons of their success. That in this contest he saw but three courses to
take: one was to fight until the leaders were overthrown; one was to give up
the contest altogether; and the other was to negotiate and compromise with
the leaders of the rebellion. This he thought impossible so long as Davis
had the power. . . . their lives were in the rebellion; they therefore would
never consent to anything but separation and acknowledgment. If he was
mistaken in this opinion, he would be very glad to know of any fact we

might have or hear to the contrary. —*Seymour to his brother, January 19, 1863, in Wall, 30.* {B}

Part of Lincoln's statement was quoted in the press as follows: "Tell your brother that he cannot be next president of the United States unless there shall be a United States to preside over."[406] *From such talk, it appears, sprang the preposterous story of Thurlow Weed (q.v.) that Lincoln expressly offered to support Horatio Seymour for the presidency if he would give full support to the war.*

MAHLON SHAABER   *A seventeen-year-old Pennsylvania volunteer in 1861, later chief of police in Reading.*

1. *Lincoln called Shaaber out of the ranks one day, having noticed him because he was 6 feet, 6½ inches tall, but weighed only about 140 pounds. During their conversation, the youth received some advice on his habits in camp:*

I should eat no pies or pastry in any form . . . advised against the use of intoxicating beverages . . . when lying down to sleep, I should always rest the head lower than the chest and should expand my lungs.

The President added worriedly: I am afraid you will not stand the service. —*Interview, Reading* Eagle, *February 7, 1909.* {D}

JOHN P. C. SHANKS (1826–1901)   *Union colonel who served with Frémont in Missouri and Virginia.*

1. *In mid-June 1862, after Stonewall Jackson's campaign in the Shenandoah Valley and before the Seven Days' battles near Richmond, Lincoln said with respect to Frémont that:*

he must hold the valley, using his judgment as to whether to stay at Mount Jackson or at Strasburg, while Banks must hold the pass with Sigel. . . . If either was attacked, the other must march to his assistance. He did not believe the enemy could muster enough to whip both. The great struggle would be at Richmond. —*Shanks's account as told to the New York* Tribune *correspondent Adams S. Hill and reported in Hill to Sydney Howard Gay, June 18, 1862, Gay Papers.*

In another letter to Gay, undated but written at about the same time, Hill said that Lincoln told Shanks: that each major general in the valley needed troops and that none could have them. {D}

BENJAMIN F. SHAW   *Editor of the Dixon (Ill.) Telegraph.*

1. *Lincoln was in Decatur on February 22, 1856, as a convention of editors began the statewide organization of the Republican party. He spoke at a dinner that evening and, according to Shaw, said that:*

he felt like the ugly man riding through a wood who met a woman, also on horseback, who stopped and said: "Well, for land sake, you are the homeliest man I ever saw." "Yes, madam, but I can't help it," he replied. "No, I suppose not," she observed, "but you might stay at home." —*Shaw manuscript quoted in Kyle, 37. Ezra M. Prince is also said to have heard Lincoln tell this story.*[407] {C}

GEORGE W. SHAW *Springfield attorney.*

1. *Shaw was in the audience when Lincoln spoke at Tremont, Illinois, during the presidential campaign of 1856. There was no newspaper report of his remarks, but Shaw recalled hearing him say:*

They tell me that if the Republicans prevail, slavery will be abolished and whites and blacks will intermarry and form a mongrel race. Now, I have a sister-in-law down in Kentucky, and if any one can show me that if Frémont is elected she will have to marry a Negro, I will vote against Frémont, and if that isn't *argumentum ad hominem* it is *argumentum ad womanum.* —*Shaw, 18 (1924).* {C}

2. *In the same speech:*

The Constitution requires us to submit to an election of president in a lawful manner, and if Frémont is lawfully elected by a majority of the American people, and a minority won't submit to the election, we'll make 'em. —*18.* {C}

3. *At some time or other on the subject of law:*

It is horse sense refined. —*22.* {C}

4. *Once, after the conclusion of an expensive suit, Shaw remarked that the proceedings had cost the county $300. Lincoln replied:*

Yes, they do things quicker in Turkey, but perhaps our way is as good. —22. {C}

PHILIP H. SHERIDAN (1831–1888) *Irish-American graduate of West Point who became one of the most successful Union generals.*

1. *In April 1864, after having been chosen to head the cavalry corps of the Army of the Potomac, Sheridan paid his respects to Lincoln, who said that:*

he hoped I would fulfill the expectations of General Grant in the new command I was about to undertake.

He added that: thus far the cavalry of the Army of the Potomac had not done all it might have done. —*Sheridan, I, 347 (1888).* {C}

Lincoln concluded the conversation, says Sheridan, by quoting in jest "that stale interrogation so prevalent during the early years of the war, 'Who ever saw a dead cavalryman?'"

2. *In August 1864, Sheridan was appointed to command the Army of the Shenandoah. During a short conversation, Lincoln said frankly:*

that Mr. Stanton had objected to my assignment to General Hunter's command because he thought me too young, and that he himself had concurred with the Secretary; but now, since General Grant had plowed round the difficulties of the situation by picking me out to command the boys in the field, he felt satisfied with what had been done and hoped for the best. — 463-64. {C}

JOHN SHERMAN (1823-1900)   *Ohio senator, brother of General William T. Sherman. He was later secretary of the treasury and secretary of state.*

1. *In December 1864, when Sherman asked about his brother's situation in Georgia, Lincoln said:*

I know what hole he went in at, but I can't tell what hole he will come out of. —*Sherman letter to Alexander K. McClure, January 29, 1892, in McClure-1,* 238. {C}

Lincoln said approximately the same thing in responding to a serenade on December 6.[408]

2. *In their last conversation, which was about reconstruction, Lincoln declared:*

that he could not say whether Louisiana was out or in the Union, but that it was easier to get her in than to decide that question. —*Sherman's eulogy of Lincoln, May 6, 1865, copy in Hay Papers-LC.* {C}

WILLIAM T. SHERMAN (1820-1891)   *Civil War general, brother of Senator John Sherman. The reliability of his* Memoirs, *especially with respect to details, has been persuasively challenged.*[409]

1. *Soon after Lincoln's inauguration, Sherman arrived in Washington from Louisiana, where he had been the superintendent of a military academy. In answer to a question from the President, he said that the people down there were preparing for war. Lincoln responded:*

Oh, well, I guess we'll manage to keep house. —*Sherman, I, 168 (1875).* {C}

2. *Following the first Battle of Bull Run in July 1861, Lincoln visited troops under Sherman's command. He made a little speech, having first been asked by Sherman to discourage hurrahs and other such displays from his audience. When the cheering began, he said:*

Don't cheer, boys. I confess I rather like it myself, but Colonel Sherman here says it is not military, and I guess we had better defer to his opinion.

He reasserted himself in his closing remarks, however, declaring: that as president, he was commander in chief; that he was resolved that the soldiers should have everything that the law allowed; and he called on one and all to appeal to him personally in case they were wronged. —*Sherman, I, 189-90.* {C}

3. *Later in the day, Lincoln made approximately the same speech to another group of soldiers, and at its close, an officer came forward with a grievance. In a dispute over his term of service, Sherman had threatened to treat him as a mutineer and shoot him. Lincoln's response was given in a stage whisper:*

Well, if I were you, and he threatened to shoot, I would not trust him, for I believe he would do it.

When Sherman later explained the circumstances to Lincoln, he said: Of course I didn't know anything about it, but I thought you knew your own business best. —*Sherman, I, 190-91.* {C}

4. *During conferences at City Point, March 27-28, 1865, the President, responding to questions from Sherman about the approaching end of the war, said that:*

he was all ready; all he wanted of us was to defeat the opposing armies and to get the men composing the Confederate armies back to their homes, at work on their farms and in their shops. As to Jefferson Davis, he was hardly at liberty to speak his mind fully, but . . . he ought to clear out, escape the country; only it would not do for him to say so openly.

At this point, according to Sherman, Lincoln told the story, reported in different contexts by Grant (q.v.) and others, about the man who wanted a bit of brandy put into his drink "unbeknownst" to him.[410] *Lincoln authorized Sherman:* to assure Governor Vance and the people of North Carolina that, as soon as the rebel armies laid down their arms and resumed their civil pursuits, they would at once be guaranteed all their rights as citizens of a common country; and that to avoid anarchy the state governments then in existence, with their civil functionaries, would be recognized by him as the government *de facto* till Congress could provide others. —*Sherman, II, 326-27.* {C}

5. *Told by Grant and Sherman that further fighting was to be expected, Lincoln asked:*

Must more blood be shed? Cannot this last bloody battle be avoided?

Speaking of the Confederate soldiers, he said in substance: that he contemplated no revenge, no harsh measures, but quite the contrary; and that their suffering and hardships during the war would make them the more submissive to law. —*Sherman to Isaac N. Arnold, November 28, 1872, in Arnold-3, 422.* {C}

6. *Presumably at about the same time, Lincoln is said to have told Sherman why he had come to have an especially friendly feeling toward him and Grant:*

It was because you never found fault with me from the days of Vicksburg down. —*Sherman as quoted by Allen Thorndike Rice in Rice AT, xxviii (1886).* {D}

JAMES SHORT   *A New Salem friend whom Lincoln called "as honorable a man as there is in the world." He received a minor federal appointment in 1861.*[411]

    1. *Lincoln told Short that once, during his surveying career:*

he was put to bed in the same room with two girls, the head of his bed being next to the foot of the girls' bed. In the night he commenced tickling the feet of one of the girls with his fingers. As she seemed to enjoy it as much as he did, he then tickled a little higher up, and as he would tickle higher the girl would shove down lower, and the higher he tickled the lower she moved.

Short added: "He never told how the thing ended." —Short's recollection as reported in N. W. Branson to William H. Herndon, August 3, 1865 (7:288-91), Herndon-Weik Collection. {D}

Herndon later fashioned a different and much more elaborate version of this story, dating the incident in the early 1850s, instead of in the 1830s, and making it a very humiliating experience for Lincoln.[412]

JAMES SHRIGLEY   *A clergyman whom Lincoln appointed hospital chaplain.*

    1. *Shrigley recalled that he visited the White House "a few days" before the issuance of the preliminary Emancipation Proclamation and heard Lincoln say to Congressman John Covode:*

I have studied that matter well; my mind is made up—it **must be done**. I am driven to it. There is to me no other way out of our troubles. But although my duty is plain, it is in some respects painful, and I trust the people will understand that I act not in anger, but in expectation of a greater good. — *Oldroyd, 335 (1882). {D}*

It seems unlikely that Lincoln would have spoken thus to a congressman before revealing his intention to the cabinet on September 22, 1862 (the very date of the proclamation), and there is no evidence of any contact with Covode in the intervening hours before the document was made public.

DANIEL E. SICKLES (1825-1914)   *New York congressman, a Democrat who became a major general and commanded an army corps at the battles of Chancellorsville and Gettysburg.*

    1. *Arriving at army headquarters one day in the summer of 1861, Lincoln said:*

Gentlemen, I am sure you must have been listening to a good story from the laughter I heard in the hall. Can't we have it repeated? I always enjoy a good laugh. — *Sickles interview in the New York Sun, February 12, 1911. {C}*

    2. *Told on the same occasion that General McClellan, who was resting after having been at the front all night, would join them soon, Lincoln replied:*

Oh, don't hurry. Cameron and I haven't much to do. Tell George we will wait here and enjoy ourselves while he finishes his nap. —*Ibid.* {C}

3. *While visiting the Army of the Potomac in April 1863, Lincoln was kissed in Sickles's presence by Princess Salm-Salm, the wife of a German officer serving in the Union army.*[413] *At a White House dinner soon afterward, Mrs. Lincoln treated Sickles very coldly, but Lincoln found a way to make her laugh and restore a friendly atmosphere. He said to Sickles:*

I am told, General, that you are an extremely religious man.

When Sickles denied it, he continued: I believe that you are not only a great Psalmist, but a Salm-Salmist. —*New York* Tribune, *May 21, 1899.* {D}

A later version from Sickles locates the placating of Mary Lincoln on a steamer; a still later one puts it in a carriage and omits all mention of the pun.[414]

4. *During a visit to the wounded Sickles on July 5, 1863, Lincoln explained why he had been so confident of Union success at Gettysburg:*

When Lee crossed the Potomac and entered Pennsylvania, followed by our army, I felt that the great crisis had come. I knew that defeat in a great battle on northern soil involved the loss of Washington, to be followed perhaps by the intervention of England and France in favor of the Southern Confederacy. I went to my room and got down on my knees in prayer. Never before had I prayed with so much earnestness. I wish I could repeat my prayer. I felt I must put all my trust in Almighty God. He gave our people the best country ever given to man. He alone could save it from destruction. I had tried my best to do my duty and had found myself unequal to the task. The burden was more than I could bear. I asked Him to help us and give us victory now. I was sure my prayer was answered. I had no misgivings about the result at Gettysburg.

When he arose to go, Lincoln said: Sickles, I have been told, as you have been told perhaps, your condition is serious. I am in a prophetic mood today. You will get well. —*New York* Sun, *February 12, 1911.* {D}

James F. Rusling (q.v.) likewise recalled Lincoln's telling him and Sickles how he had prayed for a victory at Gettysburg, but there is little resemblance between the Rusling and Sickles versions of the words he used.

5. *In the spring of 1864, Lincoln explained why he shrank from openly seeking re-election:*

Sickles, I must not do it. To avow oneself a candidate for the presidency at this time—to step forward and avow oneself ready to assume the heavy burdens which must come to the president for four years—is something that no man should do. And the people might rightly look with disfavor and suspicion upon one who openly declared that he was ready for the next four years to assume these burdens. —*Sickles interview, New York* Times, *July 10, 1891. {D}*

JULES SIEGFRIED (1836–1922)   *A French businessman who visited Lincoln in the late summer or fall of 1861.*

   1. *Pressed for time, Lincoln said:*

I cannot detain you because I must go at once to review the army of General McClellan. But, in fact, why not come with me? You can be given a horse, be provided with some kind of uniform, and follow me with the staff officer. —*Translated from Siegfried, 15.*[415] *{C}*

POLLARD SIMMONS   *A New Salem acquaintance of Lincoln.*

   1. *At the age of twenty-four, upon receiving word from Simmons of his appointment as deputy county surveyor by Democrat John Calhoun, Lincoln asked whether he would have to make any sacrifice of principle, adding:*

If I can be perfectly free in my political action, I will take the office, but if my sentiments or even expression of them is to be abridged in any way, I would not have it or any other office. —*Herndon, I, 120. {D}*

This is dubious material. In his book, Herndon asserted that he heard the story directly from Simmons, but in a letter to Weik he said that it had been told to him by a man named Fisk, who had heard it from Simmons.[416]

JAMES W. SINGLETON (1811–1892)   *Illinois antiwar Democrat of southern antecedents, later a member of Congress.*

   1. *Sometime before the presidential election of 1864, according to Singleton, Lincoln showed him his correspondence with Horace Greeley regarding the latter's peace negotiations at Niagara Falls. Then he said that his letter beginning:*

"To whom it may concern" put him in a false position—that he did not mean to make the abolition of slavery a condition, and that after the election he would be willing to grant peace with an amnesty and restoration of the Union, leaving slavery to abide the decisions of judicial tribunals.[417] — *As told to Orville H. Browning in Browning, I, 694. {D}*

Curiously, Browning (q.v.) recorded hearing the same thing directly from Lincoln some two months later.

   2. *Not long after the assassination, Singleton recalled having told Lincoln late in 1864 that he would like to visit Richmond and do something to help achieve peace. Lincoln replied:*

that he would be glad if he would do so; that he did not desire to subjugate the South; that he wanted that they should come back feeling that they had done so of their own accord; that he anticipated much trouble from the subject of reorganization, unless he could bring the states back in some sort

of freedom; that he disliked the idea of governing the South by military sat-
raps; that it would cost an already burdened country too much, and would
not pay expenses.

*According to Singleton, he went to Richmond carrying a Lincoln memorandum
on peace policy, held talks with Confederate leaders, and arranged a meeting between General Grant and General Lee that was forestalled, presumably by the
secretary of war, Edwin M. Stanton. —Singleton's statement to a correspondent of the Chicago Republican, reprinted in the New York Times, June 25,
1865. {D}*

*Singleton's purpose in visiting Richmond was to launch a speculative trade in
cotton and tobacco. It is doubtful that he had any authority from Lincoln to
engage in peace negotiations.[418]*

*3. In their last conversation, Lincoln spoke of the Confederate general
Richard S. Ewell, saying:*

I have pardoned his wife, and, Singleton, I did it for Montgomery Blair. He
brought the paper here to me, all tied up in white ribbon, and I signed it.
Blair is a good fellow. I like him. They have not treated him as well as he
deserves, and I am sorry for it. I would like to do more for him than I can.
—*Ibid.*[419] {C}

BENJAMIN H. SMITH (1828–1900)   *Disciples of Christ clergyman in Illinois
and Missouri.*

*1. According to Smith, Lincoln once asked him to preach a sermon in private
and afterwards told two stories, the second being about a black preacher whose
effort to elucidate certain church doctrine left his listener totally confused. Then
Lincoln continued:*

Elder Smith, I understand your explanation of foreordination, election, and
predestination; I understand your plea for a return to the apostolic order
of things religious; but the way preachers have generally explained these
things, the more they explained, the less I understood them, and my mind
got more and more muddled. And I must confess that the latter story sometimes expresses a state of my mind that to me is dangerous. The preachers
have preached and talked this "miraculous conversion" and such other (to
me) very absurd theories of religion and given such contradictory explana-
tions of the Bible, that I have honestly at times doubted the whole thing. —
Smith's statement c. 1890, reprinted in Jones ED, 75. {C}

DEWITT C. SMITH   *In 1908, a resident of Normal, Illinois.*

*1. At Shelbyville on August 9, 1856, Lincoln engaged in debate with
Anthony Thornton, a Whig lawyer who was in the process of becoming a
Democrat. Smith recalled that Lincoln began by saying:*

It is a matter of great regret to me that I have so learned, so able, and so eloquent a man as my friend Anthony here to reply to what I shall say. On the other hand, I take some comfort from the fact that there are but sixteen Republicans in Shelby County, and therefore, however poorly I may defend my cause, I can hardly harm it, if I do it no good. Anthony and I were always old-line Whigs, and we stumped parts of Illinois and Indiana together in 1844 in advocacy of the election of Henry Clay, the Whig candidate for president. We have always been in substantial agreement on all public questions up to this time, but we have sometimes crossed swords in court, and you know Anthony, that whenever we have, you have always cut me as a file cuts soft soap. —*Smith's reminiscences, dated July 22, 1908, ISHL. {C}*

EDWARD DELAFIELD SMITH (1826–1878) *The United States district attorney in New York who prosecuted and won conviction of a New England sea captain, Nathaniel Gordon, on the capital charge of engaging in the African slave trade.*

    1. *Urged by Smith to resist pressure for clemency, Lincoln said:*

Mr. Smith, you do not know how hard it is to have a human being die when you know that a stroke of your pen may save him. —*Smith's account soon afterwards to his chief deputy, in Allen, 444 (1895). {D}*

Secondhand testimony, but not otherwise lacking in credibility. Lincoln granted Gordon only a two-week reprieve. Executed on February 21, 1862, he was the only American slave-trader ever to suffer such punishment.

GABRIEL LEWIS SMITH (1829–1906). *A lawyer who lived and practiced most of his life in Elmira, New York.*

    1. *On March 12, 1860, Smith traveled a hundred miles or so on an Erie train with Lincoln, who was headed home after his speaking tour of New England, following delivery of his Cooper Institute address. Asked about the Democratic party and its leader, Lincoln said:*

Judge Douglas, with great ability and great ambition, has no superior in making the worse appear the better reason, but he is without moral sense so far as concerns the slavery question, and he has split his party wide open by the repeal of the Missouri Compromise and his nostrum of squatter sovereignty. The southern Democrats will refuse to support him for president this year, and he cannot hope to win without them. Four years ago, I could see no prospect of the Republican party winning before 1864 at the earliest; now I believe that with the right candidate on the right platform we shall win an easy victory in November. —*Related by Smith in old age to Rufus Rockwell Wilson and published many years thereafter in Wilson RR-2, 214–15 (1945). {D}*

GEORGE PLUMER SMITH   *A resident of Philadelphia.*

1. *Soon after the fall of Fort Sumter, certain pro-Union men from the Wheeling area sought to obtain some federal weapons for defense against Virginia troops. Smith introduced them to the President, who said:*

I don't know about that—why, don't you see that you ask of me about the greatest stretch of power I could exercise—ordering **arms** out of the arsenals into the hands of men not enlisted in the services of the government! Why, that might result like your putting an axe in the hands of a fellow you did not know, to cut down a tree, which he might do—but, afterwards, would turn round and brain you with it. —*Smith interview, March 5, 1878, Nicolay Papers.* {C}

2. *During the same discussion , Lincoln said of his interview with John B. Baldwin on April 4, 1861:*

I talked to him till late, gave him a bed, and nearly all next day we were at it, I using all the representations in my power to have him urge his fellow members to stand by me and save the Union. But I found him "very fishy" on the matter and finally told him to say from me to the Union men in the convention that if they would forthwith adjourn *sine die*, without any further action, I pledged myself, as soon thereafter as I could arrange, to order the troops (or Major Anderson) from Fort Sumter back to Fort Moultrie, trusting then to the better feeling in the cotton states, aided by Virginia and other border states, to soothe the angry passions and save us from the last dread catastrophe, fratricidal war, now upon us. —*Ibid.* {D}

There appears to be no other evidence that the Lincoln-Baldwin discussion extended to a second day. Baldwin himself said that it lasted about an hour. In an earlier and probably more accurate account, Smith reported Lincoln as saying that: among other influences, he had sent for Mr. Baldwin of Augusta County, a member of the convention, and had him in the White House with him alone and told him if they would pass resolutions of adherence to the Union, then adjourn and go home, he . . . would take the responsibility, at the earliest proper time, to withdraw the troops from Fort Sumter and do all within the line of his duty to ward off collision. —*Smith to John Hay, January 9, 1863, Lincoln Papers.*[420] {C}

Baldwin (q.v.) later denied that such an offer was made, whereas John M. Botts (q.v.) testified that in conversations with him, Lincoln asserted, and Baldwin admitted, that it had been made.

GOLDWIN SMITH (1823–1910)   *English historian and journalist. A professor at Oxford during the Civil War years, he later moved to the United States and then to Canada.*

1. *Soon after his re-election in 1864, Lincoln received a visit from Smith and at one point in their conversation, remarked that:*

in reckoning the number of those who had perished in the war, a fair percentage must be deducted for ordinary mortality, which would have carried off under any circumstances a certain proportion of the men, all of whom were generally set down as victims of the sword. . . . Very exaggerated accounts of the carnage had been produced by including among the killed large numbers of men whose term of enlistment had expired and who had been on that account replaced by others or had re-enlisted themselves.

To illustrate his point, he told a story: A Negro had been learning arithmetic. Another Negro asked him, if he shot at three pigeons sitting on a fence and killed one, how many would remain. "One," replied the arithmetician. "No," said the other Negro, "the other two would fly away." — *Smith G, 301 (1865). {C}*

Smith (or Lincoln) muddled the story a bit.

JAMES SMITH   *In the 1850s, pastor of Springfield's First Presbyterian Church, which Mary and the children attended regularly and in which Lincoln rented a pew. Smith was appointed consul at Dundee, Scotland, in 1863. Later, he became one of the first persons to engage William H. Herndon in controversy over Lincoln's religion.*

1. *Lincoln, according to Smith, examined his book* The Christian's Defense *(1843) and concluded that:*

the argument in favor of the divine authority and inspiration of the Scriptures was unanswerable.

Smith also recalled that Lincoln spoke to the Bible Society of Springfield, closing with some such statement as this: It seems to me that nothing short of infinite wisdom could by any possibility have devised and given to man this excellent and perfect moral code. It is suited to men in all conditions of life and includes all the duties they owe to their Creator, to themselves, and to their fellow men. — *Smith to Herndon, January 24, 1867 (9:1409–20), Herndon-Weik Collection;* Illinois State Journal *(Springfield), March 12, 1867.*[421] *{C}*

There appears to be no other evidence of Lincoln's having delivered such an address, and all testimony regarding Lincoln's religion should probably be regarded with skepticism. Nevertheless, Ninian W. Edwards and Thomas Lewis (qq.v.) confirmed his expression of such sentiments in the early 1850s.

JAMES SPEED (1812–1887)   *Kentucky lawyer, brother of Joshua F. Speed, and attorney general in the final months of the Lincoln administration.*

1. *In a conversation about the Gettysburg Address, Lincoln told Speed that:*

he had never received a compliment he prized more highly than that contained in a letter from Edward Everett, written to him a few days after that speech was delivered and commenting upon it.[422]

He went on to relate that: When requested to deliver an address on the occasion of the dedication of the national cemetery at Gettysburg, he was very uncertain whether his duties would not detain him at Washington but was anxious to go and desired to be prepared to say some appropriate thing. The day before he left Washington, he found time to write about half of a speech. He took what he had written with him to Gettysburg; then he was put in an upper room in a house, and he asked to be left alone for a time. He then prepared a speech but concluded it so shortly before it was to be delivered he had not time to memorize it. After the speech was delivered and taken down by the reporters, he compared what he had actually said with what he had written, and the difference was so slight he allowed what he had said to remain unchanged. *—Speed's statement to a reporter in the* Louisville *Commercial, November 12, 1879.*[423] {C}

2. *On the day of Lincoln's death, Speed told Salmon P. Chase that at the cabinet meeting on April 14, the President had said that:*

he thought [he] had made a mistake at Richmond in sanctioning the assembling of the Virginia legislature and had perhaps been too fast in his desires for early reconstruction. *—Chase, 530.* {B}

Secondhand testimony, but recorded contemporaneously and in accord with other evidence.

JOSHUA F. SPEED (1814–1882)   *Kentuckian who lived in Springfield from 1835 to 1841 and became Lincoln's closest friend.*

1. *Speaking as a candidate for re-election to the legislature in the summer of 1836, Lincoln locked horns with George Forquer, one of Springfield's leading political figures:*

The gentleman commenced his speech by saying that this young man will have to be taken down, and he was sorry that the task devolved upon him. I am not so young in years as I am in the tricks and trades of a politician, but, live long or die young, I would rather die now than, like the gentleman, change my politics and simultaneous with the change, receive an office worth $3,000 per year, and then have to erect a lightning rod over my house to protect a guilty conscience from an offended God. *—Speed, 18 (1884).*[424] {C}

2. *Riding along a country road with five other men, Lincoln stopped to put some baby birds back in their nest. His companions were much amused, and he responded:*

Gentlemen, you may laugh, but I could not have slept well tonight, if I had not saved those birds. Their cries would have rung in my ears. *—Speed, 26.* {C}

3. *Lincoln on how his mind worked:*

I am slow to learn and slow to forget that which I have learned. My mind is like a piece of steel, very hard to scratch anything on it and almost impossible after you get it there to rub it out. — *Speed to William H. Herndon, December 6, 1866, copy in the Beveridge Papers; printed in Herndon, III, 522.*[425] *{C}*

4. *According to Speed, Lincoln in 1840 asked him to deliver a letter to Mary Todd breaking off their engagement. Speed refused and persuaded him to speak to her in person. Asked afterwards whether he had followed instructions, Lincoln said:*

Yes, I did, and when I told Mary I did not love her, she burst into tears and almost springing from her chair and wringing her hands as if in agony, said something about the deceiver being himself deceived. . . . To tell the truth, Speed, it was too much for me. I found the tears trickling down my own cheeks. I caught her in my arms and kissed her.

Speed remarked in disgust that his friend had more or less renewed the engagement instead of terminating it. Lincoln said: Well, if I am in again, so be it. It's done, and I shall abide by it. — *Herndon, II, 213. {D}*

This account was apparently synthesized from the following passage in Herndon's undated notes on an interview with Speed (11:3169–74), Herndon-Weik Collection: "Went to see 'Mary'—told her that he did not love her. She rose and said 'The deceiver shall be decieved, wo is me,' alluding to a young man she fooled. Lincoln drew her down on his knee—kissed her—& parted."

5. *On election day, August 3, 1840, Lincoln quarreled with a Democrat, Reuben Radford, about the polls. He said:*

Radford, you will spoil and blow if you live much longer.

Later, he admitted having been tempted to strike the man: I intended to knock him down and go away and leave him a-kicking. — *Herndon's undated interview (11:3169–74). {D}*

6. *During his period of depression in early 1841, Lincoln said to Speed:*

that he had done nothing to make any human being remember that he had lived; and that to connect his name with the events transpiring in his day and generation and so impress himself upon them as to link his name with something that would redound to the interest of his fellow man was what he desired to live for.

After issuing the Emancipation Proclamation more than twenty years later, Lincoln reminded Speed of that conversation and said: I believe that in this measure my fondest hopes will be realized. — *Speed to Herndon, February 9, 1866 (8:590–92). {C}*

A different version of his 1841 remark is in Speed, 39.

7. Speed recalled being present when a delegation from the Ohio Valley states called at the White House with complaints and demands. Lincoln responded with a story about a family that never stayed very long in one place:

The chickens of the family got so used to being moved that whenever they saw the wagon sheets brought out, they laid themselves on their backs and crossed their legs, ready to be tied. Now, gentlemen, if I were to listen to every committee that comes in that door, I had just as well cross my hands and let you tie me. Nevertheless, I am glad to see you. —*Speed, 30. {C}*

8. Asked when he slept, Lincoln replied:

Just when everybody else is tired out. —*Speed to Herndon, May 8, 1866, Herndon-Springer, II, 324. {C}*

9. At the Soldiers' Home in the summer of 1864, Speed found Lincoln reading the Bible and said that he himself was still a religious skeptic. Lincoln replied:

You are wrong, Speed. Take all of this book upon reason that you can and the balance on faith, and you will live and die a happier and better man. —*Speed, 32-33. {C}*

10. Echoing the words of a Kentucky politician who had been queried in public about his faith, Lincoln said:

Speed, you had better be without money than without religion. —*Herndon's undated interview (11:3169-74). {C}*

11. Concerning a number of men in prison for resisting military conscription in western Pennsylvania, Lincoln said one day in late February 1865:

Well, these fellows have suffered long enough, and I have thought so for some time, and now that my mind is on it, I believe I will turn out the flock. —*Speed to Herndon, January 12, 1866 (8:499-504).*

In Speed, 27, Lincoln is quoted as saying more expansively: I have been thinking so for some time and have so said to Stanton, and he always threatened to resign if they were released. But he has said so about other matters and never did. So now, while I have the paper in my hand, I will turn out the flock. *{D}*

Lincoln was not ordinarily sympathetic to draft-dodgers.

12. On the same day, a woman whose son he had ordered released from prison thanked Lincoln and spoke of meeting him again in heaven. He said:

I am afraid with all my troubles I shall never get there, but if I do, I will find you. That you wish me to get there is the best wish you could make for me.

After the woman's departure, Speed expressed concern about the effect of such interviews on Lincoln's health. He replied: I am very unwell. My feet and hands are always cold. I suppose I ought to be in bed. But things of that sort don't hurt me; for, to tell you the truth, that scene which you witnessed is the only thing I have done today which has given me any pleasure. I have in that made two people happy. That old lady was no counterfeit. The mother spoke out in all the features of her face. It is more than we can often say that in doing right, we have made two people happy in one day. Speed, die when I may, I want it said of me by those who know me best . . . that I always plucked a thistle and planted a flower where I thought a flower would grow. —*Speed to Herndon, January 12, 1866 (8:499–504). {C}*

An edited version is in Herndon, III, 527–28, misdated December 6, 1866. Another version with different details and different phrasing is in Speed, 27–28.

THOMAS STACKPOLE   *A White House guard whom Lincoln once recommended as someone he had come to know "rather intimately."*[426]

1. *Tad's mother threatened to whip him after he defaced his copper-toed shoes as a gesture against Copperheads. He ran to Lincoln, who said:*

I guess I must exercise my executive clemency a little and pardon you, my patriotic boy. You shall not be whipped for this offense. Go and explain your case to your mother as it now stands. —*Interview, Washington Chronicle, June 18, 1865. {C}*

2. *When Stackpole complained that a pet goat was troublesome, the President replied:*

It interests the boys and does them good; let the goat be. —*Ibid. {C}*

3. *Hearing the doorkeeper try to dissuade some children who wanted to see him, Lincoln said:*

Let the little codgers take their turn. —*Ibid. {C}*

EDWARD STANLY (1810–1872)   *Former Whig congressman from North Carolina, a Unionist whom Lincoln appointed military governor of that state in 1862.*

1. *Five days after the issuance of the preliminary Emancipation Proclamation on September 22, 1862, James C. Welling, associate editor of the* National Intelligencer, *assertedly recorded in his diary that Stanly had told him the substance of an interview with Lincoln in which the latter stated:*

that the proclamation had become a civil necessity to prevent the Radicals from openly embarrassing the government in the conduct of the war. . . . that without the proclamation for which they had been clamoring, the Radicals would take the extreme step in Congress of withholding supplies for carrying on the war, leaving the whole land in anarchy. . . . that he had prayed to the Almighty to save him from this necessity, adopting the very language of our Savior—"If it be possible, let this cup pass from me"—but the prayer had not been answered. —*Rice AT, 533 (1886). {D}*

If Welling's excerpt from his diary is accepted as authentic, the fact that this quotation was both recalled and recorded contemporaneously makes it somewhat more credible than the average secondhand recollection.

EDWIN M. STANTON (1814–1869)   *Ohio Democrat, briefly a member of Buchanan's cabinet, whom Lincoln appointed secretary of war in 1862. He held that position until 1868.*

   1. *Stanton transmitted Lincoln's views concerning fugitive slaves who sought refuge within Union lines:*

He is of opinion that, under the law of Congress, they cannot be sent back to their masters; that in common humanity they must not be permitted to suffer for want of food, shelter, or other necessaries of life; that to this end, they should be provided for by the Quartermaster's and Commissary's departments; and that those who are capable of labor should be set to work and paid reasonable wages. In directing this to be done, the President does not mean, at present, to settle any general rule in respect to slaves or slavery, but simply to provide for the particular case under the circumstances in which it is now presented. —*Stanton to Benjamin F. Butler, July 3, 1862, Butler-1, II, 41–42. {D}*

There is no way of knowing Lincoln's share in the wording of this statement.

   2. *At some time after Lincoln's death, Stanton talked about him to a group that included James R. Young, a Pennsylvania journalist who near the end of the century became a member of Congress. Looking back thirty years to that interview, Congressman Young recalled especially Stanton's account of how Lincoln reacted to the battle of Chancellorsville. Upon receiving news of the defeat, the President said:*

My God, Stanton, our cause is lost! We are ruined; we are ruined; and such a fearful loss of life! My God! This is more than I can endure.

Then, after some minutes of silence: If I am not about early tomorrow, do not send for me, nor allow anyone to disturb me. Defeated again, and so many of our noble countrymen killed! What will the people say?

A few days later, Lincoln told Stanton: that when he started to leave the War Department on that evening, he had fully made up his mind to go immediately to the Potomac River and there end his life, as many a poor creature (but none half so miserable as he was at that time) had done before him. —*Young's statement in the Philadelphia* Times, *reprinted in the New York* Tribune, *August 13, 1899.*[427] *{D}*

Although Lincoln's momentary despair after Chancellorsville is otherwise documented, this recollection is doubly suspect because of weak provenance and factual error.[428]

3. *A certain Judge Hamilton Ward recalled Stanton's telling him how Lincoln on September 22, 1862, read from Artemas Ward and then said:*

Gentlemen, why don't you laugh? With the fearful strain that is upon me night and day, if I did not laugh I should die, and you need this medicine as much as I do. . . . Gentlemen, I have called you here upon very important business. I have prepared a little paper of much significance. I have made up my mind that this paper is to issue; that the time is come when it should issue; that the people are ready for it to issue. It is due to my cabinet that you should be the first to hear and know of it, and if any of you have any suggestions to make as to the form of this paper or its composition, I shall be glad to hear them. But the paper is to issue.

Whereupon he read his draft of the preliminary Emancipation Proclamation. Later, when Stanton had expressed his pleasure and was leaving, Lincoln said: Stanton, it would have been too early last spring. —*Interview with Ward in the Lockport (N.Y.) Journal, May 21, 1893, as reprinted in Whipple W, 482, 483. {D}*

4. *According to Stanton, just a few days before Lee's surrender at Appomattox, he tendered his resignation and the President responded:*

Stanton, you cannot go. Reconstruction is more difficult and dangerous than construction or destruction. You have been our main reliance; you must help us through the final act. The bag is filled. It must be tied and tied securely. Some knots slip; yours do not. You understand the situation better than anybody else, and it is my wish and the country's that you remain.

As Stanton proceeded to explain the arrangements he had made for the conduct of the department after he had left, Lincoln said triumphantly: Stanton, you give the very reason why you should not resign. You admit that you have looked into the future, foreseen troubles there, and tried to prepare in advance for my relief and the benefit of the nation. Your recitation sustains me exactly. You must stay. —*Stanton to James M. Ashley, September 14, 1866, in Flower, 311.*[429] *{D}*

This recollection was self-serving, politically motivated, and chronologically erroneous,[430] *but there seems to be no evidence controverting the central assertion that at some point during those final days, Stanton sought to resign and was persuaded otherwise by Lincoln.*

ROBERT LIVINGSTON STANTON (1810–1885) *Presbyterian minister, college president, and author. Stanton was an abolitionist who lived many years in the South.*

1. *It was probably on May 17, 1864, that Lincoln, while writing a note in Stanton's behalf, said to him:*

When I write an official letter, I want to be sure it is correct, and I find I am sometimes puzzled to know how to spell the most common word. I found about twenty years ago that I had been spelling one word wrong all my life up to that time. It is *very*. I used always to spell it with two r's—v-e-r-r-y. And then there was another word which I found I had been spelling wrong until I came here to the White House. It is *opportunity*. I had always spelled it op-per-tunity. —*Stanton RL, 6 (c. 1883); also in Stanton RB, 38 (1920), an article by his son.*[431] {C}

2. *In early June, Lincoln said with respect to the approaching National Union convention at Baltimore:*

that he was not at all anxious about the result; that he wanted the people to be satisfied, but as he now had his hand in, he should like to keep his place and finish up the war; and yet, if the people wished a change in the presidency, he had no complaint to make. —*Stanton RL, 8; also in Stanton RB, 39.* {C}

3. *During the same conversation, it was suggested that the President's letter of January 2, 1863, to General Samuel R. Curtis seemed to take both sides in the controversy over the proposed expulsion of the Reverend Samuel B. McPheeters from the state of Missouri.*[432] *Lincoln responded:*

That forcibly reminds me of what occurred many years ago in Illinois. A farmer and his son were out in the woods one day, hunting a sow and pigs. At length, after a long and fruitless search for them, they came to what they call "a branch" out there, where they saw tracks and rootings on each side. "Now, John," said the old man, "you take up on this side of the branch and I'll go up t'other, for we'll be sure to find the old critter on both sides." — *Stanton RL, 10-11; also in Stanton RB, 40, with some minor changes.* {C}

In his memoirs, Henry B. Stanton recorded the same story, presumably as related to him by his brother, but he set the telling of it at a different time and in different circumstances, and he added these further words attributed to Lincoln: Gentlemen, that is just where I stand in regard to your controversies in St. Louis. I am on both sides. I can't allow my generals to run the churches, and I can't allow your ministers to preach rebellion. Go home, preach the Gospel, stand by the Union, and don't disturb the government with any more of your petty quarrels. —*Stanton HB, 234-35.* {D}

John J. Janney (q.v.) recalled hearing Lincoln tell the hog story at about the same time in discussing a Democratic congressman, Samuel S. Cox.

4. *During discussion of a petition for pardon, Lincoln was asked whether he would receive a delegation of leading men from Baltimore to speak in its behalf. He replied:*

No, I will not receive a delegation from Baltimore for any purpose. I have received many delegations from Baltimore since I came into office, composed of its most prominent citizens. They have always come to gain some advantage for themselves or for their city. They have always had some end of their own to reach, without regard to the interests of the government. But no delegation of the leading citizens of Baltimore has ever come to me to express sympathy or give me any aid in upholding the government and putting down the rebellion. No, I will receive no delegation from Baltimore. —*Stanton RL, 25.* {C}

JAMES B. STEEDMAN (1817–1883) *Ohio newspaperman and Democratic politician who became a Union general. His greatest distinction was achieved as a division commander at the battle of Chickamauga.*

  1. *Summoned to Washington in the fall of 1863, several weeks after the defeat at Chickamauga, Steedman displayed a reluctance to answer the President's request for his estimate of General Rosecrans. Lincoln said:*

It is the man who does not want to express an opinion whose opinion I want. I am besieged on all sides with advice. Every day I get letters from army officers asking me to allow them to come to Washington to impart some valuable knowledge in their possession.

After finally extracting from Steedman a statement that General George H. Thomas would probably be a better commander in the circumstances, Lincoln replied: I am glad to hear you say so. That is my own opinion exactly, but Mr. Stanton is against him, and it was only yesterday that a powerful New York delegation was here to protest against his appointment because he is from a rebel state and cannot be trusted. —*Steedman as quoted in the Toledo (Ohio)* Journal, *reprinted in the New York* Times, *March 7, 1879.* {C}

Thomas was appointed commander of the Army of the Cumberland on October 20, 1863.

ALEXANDER H. STEPHENS (1812–1883) *Antebellum congressman from Georgia, vice president of the Confederacy. Lincoln met Stephens and two other Confederate commissioners (Robert M. T. Hunter and John A. Campbell) at Hampton Roads, Virginia, on February 3, 1865, to discuss terms of peace. The conference grew out of the private diplomacy of Francis P. Blair, who had approached Jefferson Davis with a proposal to stop the fighting and turn American military power against the French armies supporting Maximilian's regime in Mexico. In his recollective summary of the four-hour meeting published five years afterward, Stephens wrote, "I have not undertaken to do more than to present substantially, what verbally passed between all the parties therein mentioned." There is no other detailed report of the conference with which to check the accuracy of an account that runs to twenty pages in print. Much of it seems credible, but some passages are less so.*

  1. *When Stephens asked how peace could be restored, Lincoln replied that:*

there was but one way that he knew of, and that was for those who were resisting the laws of the Union to cease that resistance. All the trouble came from an armed resistance against the national authority.

Stephens then brought up the possibility of diverting attention from the war to some other problem so that passions on both sides could be allowed to cool, and Lincoln said in substance: I suppose you refer to something that Mr. Blair has said. Now it is proper to state at the beginning, that whatever he said was of his own accord and without the least authority from me. When he applied for a passport to go to Richmond, with certain ideas which he wished to make known to me, I told him flatly that I did not want to hear them. If he desired to go to Richmond of his own accord, I would give him a passport; but he had no authority to speak for me in any way whatever. When he returned and brought me Mr. Davis's letter, I gave him the one to which you alluded in your application for leave to cross the lines.[433] I was always willing to hear propositions for peace on the conditions of this letter and on no other. The restoration of the Union is a *sine qua non* with me, and hence my instructions that no conference was to be held except upon that basis.

Stephens persisted in urging a cessation of hostilities while the Mexican problem was being dealt with, but Lincoln answered emphatically that: he could entertain no proposition for ceasing active military operations which was not based upon a pledge first given for the ultimate restoration of the Union. He had considered the question of an armistice fully, and he could not give his consent to any proposition of that sort on the basis suggested. The settlement of our existing difficulties was a question now of supreme importance, and the only basis on which he would entertain a proposition for a settlement was the recognition and reestablishment of the national authority throughout the land.

As the discussion continued, Lincoln found it necessary to repeat that: he could not entertain a proposition for an armistice on any terms while the great and vital question of reunion was undisposed of. That was the first question to be settled. He could enter into no treaty, convention, or stipulation, or agreement with the Confederate states, jointly or separately, upon that or any other subject, but upon the basis first settled, that the Union was to be restored. Any such agreement or stipulation would be a quasi recognition of the states then in arms against the national government as a separate power. That he never could do. —*Stephens, II, 600–602, 608 (1870).* {C}

2. *Hunter argued that executives had been known to enter into agreements with parties in arms against public authority, and he pointed to the example of Charles I. Lincoln, who knew a straight line when he heard it, replied:*

I do not profess to be posted in history. On all such matters I will turn you over to Seward. All I distinctly recollect about the case of Charles I is that he lost his head in the end.[434] —*Stephens, II, 613.* {C}

3. *Stephens asked what position the Confederate states would occupy if the war were to cease. Would they, for instance, be admitted to representation in Congress? Lincoln said that:*

his own individual opinion was, they ought to be. He also thought they would be, but he could not enter into any stipulation upon the subject. His own opinion was that when the resistance ceased and the national authority was recognized, the states would be immediately restored to their practical relations to the Union. —*Stephens, II, 612.* {C}

4. *Stephens also asked whether the entire slave population would be regarded as free by virtue of the Emancipation Proclamation. Lincoln said:*

that was a judicial question. How the courts would decide it, he did not know and could give no answer. His own opinion was that as the proclamation was a war measure and would have effect only from its being an exercise of the war power, as soon as the war ceased, it would be inoperative for the future. It would be held to apply only to such slaves as had come under its operation while it was in active exercise. This was his individual opinion, but the courts might decide the other way and hold that it effectually emancipated all the slaves in the states to which it applied at the time. So far as he was concerned, he should leave it to the courts to decide. He never would change or modify the terms of the proclamation in the slightest particular.

Speaking at some length on the subject, he said: that it was not his intention in the beginning to interfere with slavery in the states; that he never would have done it if he had not been compelled by necessity to do it to maintain the Union; that the subject presented many difficult and perplexing questions to him; that he had hesitated for some time and had resorted to this measure only when driven to it by public necessity; that he had been in favor of the general government prohibiting the extension of slavery into the territories but did not think that that government possessed power over the subject in the states, except as a war measure; and that he had always himself been in favor of emancipation, but not immediate emancipation, even by the states. Many evils attending this appeared to him.

Rising up, he continued: Stephens, if I were in Georgia and entertained the sentiments I do—though, I suppose, I should not be permitted to stay there long with them—but if I resided in Georgia with my present sentiments, I'll tell you what I would do if I were in your place. I would go home and get the governor of the state to call the legislature together and get them to recall all the state troops from the war, elect senators and members to

Congress, and ratify this constitutional amendment **prospectively**, so as to take effect, say, in five years. Such a ratification would be valid in my opinion. I have looked into the subject and think such a prospective ratification would be valid. Whatever may have been the views of your people before the war, they must be convinced now that slavery is doomed. It cannot last long in any event, and the best course, it seems to me, for your public men to pursue would be to adopt such a policy as will avoid, as far as possible, the evils of immediate emancipation. This would be my course, if I were in your place. —*Stephens, II, 610-11, 613-14. {D}*

It seems unlikely that Lincoln would have recommended "prospective" ratification of the Thirteenth Amendment or expressed a view that such bizarre action would be constitutional.

5. In answer to the question whether Virginia would be restored to her prewar boundaries, he replied that:

he could only give an individual opinion, which was that Western Virginia would be continued to be recognized as a separate state in the Union. —*Stephens, II, 616. {C}*

6. Near the end of the meeting, Lincoln declared that:

so far as the confiscation acts and other penal acts were concerned, their enforcement was left entirely with him, and on that point he was perfectly willing to be full and explicit, and on his assurance perfect reliance might be placed. He should exercise the power of the executive with the utmost liberality.

He went on to say that: he would be willing to be taxed to remunerate the southern people for their slaves. He believed the people of the North were as responsible for slavery as the people of the South, and if the war should then cease, with the voluntary abolition of slavery by the states, he should be in favor, individually, of the government paying a fair indemnity for the loss to the owners. He believed this feeling had an extensive existence at the North. He knew some who were in favor of an appropriation as high as $400 million for this purpose. I could mention persons [said he] whose names would astonish you who are willing to do this, if the war shall now cease without further expense and with the abolition of slavery as stated. But on this subject, he could give no assurance, enter into no stipulation. He barely expressed his own feelings and views and what he believed to be the views of others upon the subject. —*Stephens, II, 617. {C}*

7. According to the later account of Evan P. Howell, a journalist associated with the Atlanta Constitution, *Stephens recalled during a conversation in 1882 that at the Hampton Roads conference, Lincoln took him aside and said:*

I believe you and I can settle this matter. I know you, and you know me.

I have confidence in your integrity and believe you have in mine. I do not think you would ask me to do anything improper, and I would not require your consent to anything which I believed unjust. I will write one word at the top of this sheet of paper, and that word will be "Union," and with that as a basis, you may write out the terms of settlement, and on that I will use all my influence to have Congress settle as we agree.

Told that the Confederate commissioners were empowered to negotiate only on the basis of southern independence, Lincoln replied: Then, I am not responsible for any further bloodshed. I had hoped the war would end with this conference, but it is impossible to make any settlement with the instructions by which you are bound. I trust you will consider confidential what has occurred between us. — *Howell's statement in the Washington* Post, *May 8, 1895.* {D}

A secondhand quotation that is questionable in any case. At a time when the Thirteenth Amendment had just passed Congress, it would have been absurd for Lincoln to offer restoration of the Union without reference to the status of slavery.

THADDEUS STEVENS (1792–1868) *Lawyer and congressman from Pennsylvania, controversial leader of Radical Reconstruction.*

1. *After Lincoln proclaimed a blockade of southern ports in April 1861, Stevens complained that the ports should simply have been closed. A formal blockade, he pointed out, had the effect of recognizing the insurgent states as an independent belligerent under international law. Lincoln replied:*

Well, that's a fact. I see the point now, but I don't know anything about the law of nations, and I thought it was all right. . . . I'm a good enough lawyer in a western law court, I suppose, but we don't practice the law of nations up there, and I supposed Seward knew all about it, and I left it to him. But it's done now and can't be helped, so we must get along as well as we can. — *Interview in New York* Herald, *July 8, 1867.* {D}

Seward understood and undoubtedly discussed with Lincoln the choice between proclaiming a blockade under international law and closing southern ports under municipal law. The latter policy was unacceptable to Britain and would have plunged the United States into a quarrel with that nation.

WILLIAM M. STEWART (1827–1909) *A New Yorker who joined the gold rush to California and became a prominent lawyer there, then moved to Nevada and was elected to the United States Senate in 1864. He later played a leading role in the framing of the Fifteenth Amendment.*

1. *Soon after taking his seat in the Senate, Stewart visited Lincoln, who said:*

I am glad to see you here. We need as many loyal states as we can get, and, in addition to that, the gold and silver in the region you represent has made it possible for the government to maintain sufficient credit to continue this terrible war for the Union. I have observed such manifestations of the patriotism of your people as assure me that the government can rely on your state for such support as is in your power. —*Stewart, 168 (1908).* {C}

The substance of this passage may well be Lincoln's, but not the stilted language.

2. *One morning, Stewart handed the President a petition from the other Nevada senator, James W. Nye, asking the restoration of a certain sutler to his previous position. Lincoln said:*

This is a case of a rich Israelite. He has been removed at the request of Mr. Stanton. Mr. Stanton says he is dishonest and cannot be trusted. If I should interfere in the matter it would cause a heated controversy with Mr. Stanton. You tell Brother Nye what I have said, and if he thinks the matter of sufficient importance to require me to quarrel with Mr. Stanton, to come and see me and give me his reasons. —*170.* {C}

Nye did not follow up on the invitation because, Stewart thought, "he did not want to hear an anecdote."

3. *At City Point about ten days before Lee's surrender, Stewart was given a captured Confederate horse to ride, and it bolted with him toward enemy lines. Lincoln, who had watched the adventure, said afterwards:*

I'm glad that horse did not make it necessary for me to make an application to the General of the Confederate army for an exchange of prisoners for a United States senator, as we have never captured any Confederate senators. —*186.* {C}

4. *Indicating a belief that there was just one more battle to fight, Lincoln added:*

And after that battle, this will be one country. —*186.* {C}

SMITH STIMMEL *Ohio youth who in 1863 became a member of Lincoln's mounted escort.*

1. *Early in the summer of 1864, some members of the mounted troop became impatient with their routine duty, and one complained to Lincoln that he would rather be at the front. Lincoln replied:*

Well, my boy, that reminds me of an old farmer friend of mine in Illinois, who used to say he never could understand why the Lord put a curl in a pig's tail. It did not seem to him to be either useful or ornamental, but he guessed the Lord knew what he was doing when he put it there. I do not myself see the necessity of having soldiers traipsing around after me wherever I go, but Stanton, who knows a great deal more about such things than I do, seems to think it is necessary, and he may be right; and if it is necessary to have soldiers here, it might as well be you as someone else. If you were sent to the front, someone would have to come from the front to take your place. It is a soldier's duty to obey orders without question, and in doing that you can serve your country as faithfully here as at the front, and I reckon it is not quite as dangerous here as it is there. —*Stimmel, 26-27 (1928).* {D}

It is not entirely clear that Stimmel heard Lincoln make these remarks. His account corroborates (or perhaps merely echoes) a similar story told by Robert W. McBride, who was likewise a member of the bodyguard.[435]

WILLIAM O. STODDARD (1835-1925)   *An Illinois journalist who was appointed to a clerkship in the Department of the Interior and then seconded to the White House for secretarial work. In later life a prolific writer, Stoddard probably overstated the extent of his intimacy with the President. (An additional Stoddard item is associated with John Hay.)*[436]

1. *To a job-hunter at a White House reception, the President said:*

Want to be paymaster, eh? Well, some people would rather take money in than pay it out. It would about kill some men I know to make paymasters of them. —*Stoddard-1, 90 (1890).* {D}

This quotation is part of an unbelievably detailed account of the reception line.

2. *On the quality of preachers seeking and obtaining military appointments:*

I do believe that our army chaplains, take them as a class, are the very worst men we have in the service. —*Stoddard letter in the New York* Citizen, *October 6, 1866.*[437] {D}

3. *In response to some remarks about McClellan:*

Well, gentlemen, for the organization of an army—to prepare it for the field—and for some other things, I will back General McClellan against any general of modern times—I don't know but of ancient times either—but I begin to believe that he will never get ready to fight. —*Stoddard letter in the New York* Citizen, *September 22, 1866.* {C}

4. *Asking that Stoddard listen to the draft of an important document, Lincoln remarked:*

I can always tell more about a thing after I've heard it read aloud and know how it sounds. Just the reading of it to myself doesn't answer as well either. . . . What I want is an audience. Nothing sounds the same when there isn't anybody to hear it and find fault with it. —*Stoddard-1, 227-28.* {C}

5. *On one occasion, Lincoln talked playfully of moving his office to a small-pox hospital in the hope that the location would reduce the stream of visitors, but then he added:*

Well, no, it wouldn't. They'd all go and get vaccinated, and they'd come

buzzing back, just the same as they do now, or worse. —*Stoddard-1, 192.*
{C}

6. *On the way to test-fire some new rifles, Lincoln said:*

Our folks are not getting near enough to the enemy to do any good with them just now. We've got to get guns that'll carry further. —*Stoddard-1, 42.* *{C}*

7. *When a clergyman called to complain that too many battles were being fought on Sunday, Lincoln replied:*

I think you had better consult the Confederate commanders a little. — *Stoddard-1, 164. {C}*

8. *Stoddard recalled Lincoln's saying after the battle of Fredericksburg in December 1862 that:*

if the same battle were to be fought over again, every day, through a week of days, with the same relative results, the army under Lee would be wiped out to its last man, the Army of the Potomac would still be a mighty host, the war would be over, the Confederacy gone, and peace would be won at a smaller cost of life than it will be if the week of lost battles must be dragged out through yet another year of camps and marches and of deaths in hospitals, rather than upon the field. No general yet found can face the arithmetic, but the end of the war will be at hand when he shall be discovered. —*Stoddard-1, 179. {D}*

One could wish that this remarkable quotation came from a more reliable source.

9. *Responding to a question from Stoddard about Grant:*

Well, I hardly know what to think of him altogether. I never saw him myself till he came here to take the command. He's the quietest little fellow you ever saw. . . . Why, he makes the least fuss of any man you ever knew. I believe two or three times he has been in this room a minute or so before I knew he was here. It's about so all around. The only evidence you have that he's in any place is that he makes things git! Wherever he is, things move! . . .

Grant is the first general I've had. He's a general! . . . You know how it's been with all the rest. As soon as I put a man in command of the army, he'd come to me with a plan of campaign and about as much as say, "Now, I don't believe I can do it, but if you say so, I'll try it on," and so put the responsibility of success or failure on me. They all wanted me to be the general. Now, it isn't so with Grant. He hasn't told me what his plans are. I don't know, and I don't want to know. I'm glad to find a man who can go ahead without me. . . . You see, when any of the rest set out on a campaign, they'd look over matters and pick out some one thing they were short of and they knew I couldn't give them and tell me they couldn't hope to win unless they had it; and it was most generally cavalry. . . . Now, when Grant took hold, I was waiting to see what his pet impossibility would be, and I reckoned it would be cavalry, as a matter of course, for we hadn't horses enough to mount even what men we had. There were 15,000 or thereabouts up near Harper's Ferry and no horses to put them on. Well, the other day, just as I expected, Grant sent to me about those very men; but what he wanted to know was whether he should disband them or turn them into infantry. He doesn't ask me to do impossibilities for him, and he's the first general I've had that didn't! —*Stoddard-1, 220-22. {D}*

10. *Stoddard was appointed United States marshal for the eastern district of Arkansas in September 1864. Lincoln, he says, spoke to him as follows before he left:*

The war is nearly over. Just when it will end I can't say, but it won't be a great while. Then the government forces must be withdrawn from all the southern states. Sooner or later, we must take them all away. Now, what I want you to do is this: do all you can, in any and every way you can, to get the ballot into the hands of the freedmen. We must make voters of them before we take away the troops. The ballot will be their only protection after the bayonet is gone, and they will be sure to need all they can get. I can see just how it will be. —*Stoddard-1, 244.*

In Stoddard-2, 217, another sentence was added: The time is not ripe for saying all this publicly, but that time will come. *{E}*

This quotation is inconsistent, not only with the powers and duties of a federal marshal, but also with the military situation in September 1864 and with Lincoln's racial policy at that time.[438]

WILLIAM M. STONE (1827–1893) *Iowa lawyer and newspaper publisher who commanded an infantry regiment during the Civil War and was elected governor in 1863.*

1. *At the time of the Baltimore convention in June 1864, Lincoln said to Stone concerning the vice presidency that:*

it might be deemed advisable to select some prominent Union Democrat in order to encourage that sentiment throughout the country and satisfy southern men that the Republican party was not acting altogether upon strict party lines, but was willing to cooperate with any set of men who desired to assist in saving the Union.

The President added that: the loyal element in the Democratic party had rendered us great assistance in their unselfish devotion to the Union, and it was but just that they should be recognized. — *Washington* Post, *July 20, 1891. {C}*

Stone's recollection, which may have been self-serving,[439] *only partly corrobo-*

rated the testimony of Alexander K. McClure (q.v.) that Lincoln secretly intervened to secure the nomination of Andrew Johnson; for Stone went on to say that the President named a half-dozen Democrats worthy of consideration (including Johnson) but "shrewdly avoided expressing any preference."

GEORGE STONEMAN (1822–1894) *Union general, a professional soldier who was later governor of California.*

    1. *At McClellan's headquarters one night early in the war, Lincoln said as he arose to leave:*

Tomorrow night I shall have a terrible headache. Tomorrow is hangman's day and I shall have to act upon death sentences. —*Oldroyd, 221 (1882). {C}*

To Benjamin F. Butler and Leonard Swett (qq.v.), Lincoln spoke of "butcher day."

HARRIET BEECHER STOWE (1811–1896) *Mrs. Stowe had been famous for a decade as the author of* Uncle Tom's Cabin *when she visited Lincoln in late November 1862. She wrote no account of their interview. It is unverified family tradition that he greeted her with the remark: "Is this the little woman who made this great war?"*[440]

    1. *In an article on Lincoln published about a year later, Stowe mentioned in passing that he had said to her:*

Whichever way it ends, I have the impression that I shan't last long after it's over. —*Stowe, 284. {C}*

JAMES M. STRADLING *A cavalry sergeant on furlough who visited the White House in early March 1863, seeking riverboat transportation back to his unit.*

    1. *According to Stradling's supposedly contemporary account, he was ushered into Lincoln's office at a time when Senator Benjamin F. Wade was present and just as General Joseph Hooker was leaving. The problem of transportation having been resolved, Lincoln said:*

Senator, we have had the head of the army here a few minutes ago, and learned from him all he cared to tell. Now we have here the tail of the army, so let us get from him how the rank and file feel about matters. I mean no reflection on you, Sergeant, when I say the tail of the army.

He went on to remark that: a great many men had deserted in the last few months, and he was endeavoring to learn the cause. . . . there must be some good reason for it. Either the army was opposed to him, to their generals, or the Emancipation Proclamation, and he was very desirous of learning from the rank and file about the conditions in the army.

He then added: None of the generals desert or resign, and we could spare a number of them better than we can spare so many privates. —*Letter to John W. Gilbert of Greenville, Pennsylvania, March 6, 1863, in Stradling, 17–18. {D}*

There appears to be no corroborating evidence of Stradling's visit or of visits by Hooker and Wade at this time. Wade had an appointment to see Lincoln on March 7.[441]

2. *Drawn into a discussion of the disaster at Fredericksburg, Stradling asserted that Burnside should have flanked Lee's army instead of making a frontal attack upon it. Lincoln replied:*

What you have stated, Sergeant, seems very plausible to me. When General Hooker left us but a few minutes ago, he said, "Mr. President, I have the finest army that was ever assembled together, and I hope to send you good news very soon." That is just the language General Burnside used when he left me shortly before the battle of Fredericksburg. And such a disaster that followed still makes my heart sick. —23. {D}

3. *In response to a direct question, Stradling said that some desertions had undoubtedly been caused by the Emancipation Proclamation, which disgruntled many soldiers. Lincoln responded with a little speech:*

The proclamation was, as you state, very near to my heart. I thought about it and studied it in all its phases long before I began to put it on paper. I expected many soldiers would desert when the proclamation was issued, and I expected many who care nothing for the colored man would seize upon the proclamation as an excuse for deserting. I did not believe the number of deserters would materially affect the army. On the other hand, the issuing of the proclamation would probably bring into the ranks many who otherwise would not volunteer.

After I had made up my mind to issue it, I commenced to put my thoughts on paper, and it took me many days before I succeeded in getting it into shape so that it suited me. Please explain to your comrades that the proclamation was issued for two reasons. The first and chief reason was this, I felt a great impulse moving me to do justice to five or six millions of people. The second reason was that I believed it would be a club in our hands with which we could whack the rebels. In other words, it would shorten the war. I believed that under the Constitution I had a right to issue the proclamation as a "military necessity." —28–30. {D}

One would like to see the original letter before swallowing the patness of this passage.

MRS. J. W. STREVELL   *A resident of Pontiac, Illinois.*

1. *Mrs. Strevell recalled that Lincoln, after delivering a lecture in Pontiac in the fall of 1859, was invited by her husband to have a dish of raw oysters. He said:*

Mr. Strevell, if I should eat a raw oyster with you, it would be the first time I had ever eaten one. I like them cooked. — *Undated statement, Tarbell Papers.* {D}

There appears to be no record of such a lecture.

2. *Asked by Strevell whether he had any hope of receiving the Republican presidential nomination, he replied:*

No, I have thought I might possibly get the second place. — *Ibid.* {D}

GEORGE TEMPLETON STRONG (1820-1875) *Patrician New York lawyer, treasurer of the Sanitary Commission, and one of the most notable diarists in American history. His diary contains several striking descriptions of Lincoln, along with a few quotations in which he tried to recapture some of the pronunciation.*

1. *On October 17, 1861, regarding policy for exchange of prisoners, Lincoln said that:*

such exchange implied recognition of the rebel government as a legitimate belligerent power.

He spoke: of the flag of truce sent out to recover Colonel Cameron's body after the battle of Bull Run, and of General Scott's reluctance to send it. — *Strong, III, 188.* {B}

The reference is to Simon Cameron's brother, James.

2. *On January 28, 1862, Strong and the president of the Sanitary Commission asked Lincoln to consult them before making any medical appointments. After some thought, he replied:*

Well, gentlemen, I guess there's nothing wrong in promising that anybody shall be heered before anything's done. — *III, 204.* {A}

3. *When something was said about Radical pressure for a change in the status of slaves:*

Wa-al, that reminds me of a party of Methodist parsons that was traveling in Illinois when I was a boy thar, and had a branch to cross that was pretty bad—ugly to cross, ye know, because the waters was up. And they got considerin' and discussin' how they should git across it, and they talked about it for two hours, and one on 'em thought they had ought to cross one way when they got there, and another another way, and they got quarrelin' about it, till at last an old brother put in, and he says, says he, "Brethren, this here talk ain't no use. I never cross a river until I come to it." — *III, 204-5.* {A}

4. *During the same interview, Strong presented a formal request for pardon of a mariner imprisoned for manslaughter. Lincoln said:*

It must be referred to the Attorney General, but I guess it will be all right, for me and the Attorney General's very chickenhearted! — *III, 205.* {A}

WILLIAM K. STRONG (1805–1867)   *New York merchant and War Democrat whom Lincoln appointed a brigadier general in 1861.*

   1. In a letter written on December 23, 1862, to General Samuel R. Curtis, commander of the Department of Missouri, Strong reported a conversation with Lincoln two days earlier. The President, speaking of the recent Union defeat at Fredericksburg, said that:

we were not as bad off as he apprehended. The army is not demoralized, but no onward movement can take place very soon where they now are. The Banks diversion south has disappointed the country, and upon the whole, we are not at a winning point just now, except in your department. The aspect about Nashville is not altogether cheering, and the cavalry raids upon the Mobile and Ohio Railroad in Grant's department will require prompt attention on his part before they make too wide openings. — *Curtis Papers.* {B}

In what may or may not have been part of this summary of Lincoln's remarks, Strong added: "If Vicksburg can be taken and the Mississippi successfully kept open it seems to me [they] will be about the most important fruits of the campaigns yet set in motion."

JOHN T. STUART (1807–1885)   *A cousin of Mary Lincoln and Lincoln's first law partner. Stuart was a leading Whig politician, serving several terms in the state legislature and in Congress.*

   1. In 1850, Stuart predicted that one day the political choice would lie between abolitionists and Democrats. Lincoln answered:

When that time comes, my mind is made up. The slavery question can't be compromised. — *Stuart statement, undated but c. July 21, 1865 (7:254–55), Herndon-Weik Collection.*[442] {C}

   2. In the spring of 1865, Stuart asked whether he intended to return eventually to Springfield, and Lincoln replied:

Mary does not expect ever to go back there and don't want to go, but I do. I expect to go back and make my home in Springfield for the rest of my life. — *John G. Nicolay interview with Stuart, June 24, 1865, in Hay Collection-Brown.* {C}

Lincoln expressed himself similarly to the Marquis de Chambrun (q.v.) at about the same time.

SAMUEL D. STURGIS (1822–1889)   *Civil War general, a career officer who in the summer of 1862 commanded the defenses of Washington.*

   1. While riding back toward Washington after a review of troops, Lincoln said:

Sturgis, I cannot call to mind now any single event of my administration that gave me so much pain or wounded me so deeply as the singular behavior of Colonel Magruder on the very night before he abandoned us. . . . he came to see me the very evening before he left and voluntarily said, while expressing his abhorrence of secession, "Sir, I was brought up and educated under the glorious old flag. I have lived under it and have fought under it, and sir, with the help of God, I shall fight under it again and, if need be, shall die under it." The very next day, Magruder abandoned us, so that at the very moment he was making to me these protestations of loyalty and devotion, he must have had his mind fully made up to leave; and it seemed the more wanton and cruel in him because he knew that I had implicit confidence in his integrity. The fact is, when I learned that he had gone over to the enemy and I had been so completely deceived in him, my confidence was shaken in everybody, and I hardly knew who to trust any more. —*Sturgis to the editor of the Philadelphia* Evening Telegraph, *June 12, 1870, autograph draft, Sturgis Papers. {C}*

The essence of this quotation is corroborated in the diary of John Hay (q.v.).

JULIAN M. STURTEVANT (1805–1886)   *Congregational clergyman and for many years president of Illinois College at Jacksonville. Lincoln once referred to him as "one of my most highly valued personal friends."*[443]

1. *Sturtevant recalled Lincoln's saying in a speech at Jacksonville (probably either on September 2, 1854, or September 6, 1856):*

My friends, we know that slavery is not right. If it were right, some men would have been born with no hands and two mouths, for it was designed that they should not work, but only eat. Other men would have been born with no mouth and four hands, because it was the design of the Creator that they should work that other men might eat. We are all born with a mouth to eat and hands to work, that every man may eat the products of his own labor and be satisfied. —*Sturtevant, 287–88 (1896). {C}*

2. *In late September, during the senatorial contest of 1858, Lincoln confessed to Sturtevant that he was weary, adding:*

If it were not for one thing, I would retire from the contest. I know that if Mr. Douglas's doctrine prevails, it will not be fifteen years before Illinois itself will be a slave state. —*Sturtevant, 292. {C}*

3. *In a conversation sometime in the late 1850s, Sturtevant remarked that recent antislavery excitement in St. Louis sprang entirely from concern for the white man. Lincoln replied:*

I must take into account the rights of the poor Negro. —*Oldroyd, 274 (1882). {C}*

CHARLES SUMNER (1811–1874)   *Antislavery senator from Massachusetts, chairman of the Senate committee on foreign relations, 1861–71.*

1. *In 1861, after nominating Charles Francis Adams and John Lothrop Motley as ministers to Great Britain and Austria respectively, Lincoln said:*

Now, Mr. Sumner, I hope you will give me a little time before I hear from Massachusetts again. —*As later recounted to Edward Everett Hale, in Hale, II, 78 (1904). {D}*

2. *At a dinner for the diplomatic corps on June 4, 1861, Lincoln said:*

that he had no complaints to make of any power; that in the delay attending a new organization here, it is very natural they could not see their way clearly as to its footing, but that time would make all things right. —*Sumner to James A. Hamilton, June 8, 1861, in Hamilton, 483. {B}*

3. *On November 30, 1861, Lincoln and Sumner discussed a plan for gradual emancipation subsequently set forth in the presidential message of March 6, 1862. As Sumner reported the conversation to Edward Everett Hale, Lincoln said:*

Well, Mr. Sumner, the only difference between you and me on this subject is a difference of a month or six weeks in time. —*Hale memorandum, April 26, 1862, in Lincoln Collection-Brown, subsequently published in Hale, II, 189-97. {C}*

This secondhand recollection is supported by Sumner, writing to John A. Andrew on December 27, 1861: "He tells me that I am ahead of him only a month or six weeks." —Sumner Papers.

4. *In late December 1861, on the same subject:*

I know very well that the name which is connected with this act will never be forgotten. —*Hale memorandum, April 26, 1862. {C}*

5. *On December 22, with respect to the* Trent *affair, Lincoln told Sumner:*

There will be no war unless England is bent upon having one. —*Sumner to John Bright, December 23, 1861, Sumner Letters, II, 87. {A}*

6. *Also during the* Trent *crisis, Lincoln said, referring to the British minister:*

I never see Lord Lyons. If it were proper, I should like to talk with him that he might hear from my lips how much I desire peace. If we could talk together he would believe me. —*Sumner to Richard Cobden, December 31, 1861, Sumner Letters, II, 94. {A}*

7. *On March 1, 1862, Lincoln told Sumner of an incident that had caused him to express himself angrily:*

General McClellan announced to him an expedition, which was to cross the river in force and to occupy Winchester in Virginia. The first crossing was to be by a pontoon, which was to be thrown over the river, where the canal boats were to be taken from the neighboring canal, and turned into a bridge, which would be necessary for the large number of forces required. The expedition failed, as on crossing the river it was discovered that the canal boats could not be got into the river. General McClellan should have ascertained this in advance, before he promised success. —*Sumner to John A. Andrew, March 2, 1862, Sumner Letters, II, 103. {B}*

John G. Nicolay (q.v.) heard Lincoln complain to McClellan's father-in-law, Randolph B. Marcy, about the canal-boats fiasco.

8. *Speaking of the Peninsular campaign, Lincoln said to Sumner on April 26, 1862:*

that McClellan had gone to Yorktown very much against his [Lincoln's] judgment, but that he did not feel disposed to take the responsibility of overruling him. —*Sumner to John A. Andrew, April 27, 1862, Sumner Letters, II, 112. {B}*

9. *Describing the retreat by forces under Nathaniel P. Banks after the battle of Winchester on May 25, 1862, Lincoln said that:*

Banks's men were running and flinging away their arms, routed and demoralized.

Sumner commented, "Another Bull Run." —Sumner to Richard Henry Dana, Jr., June 1, 1862, Sumner Letters, II, 116. {B}

10. *Disappointed with Frémont's performance as commander of the Mountain Department in the spring of 1862, Lincoln said nevertheless:*

We can't do with Frémont as we should with another general. He has the people behind him. —*Sumner's account to George W. Smalley in Smalley to Sydney Howard Gay, June 27, 1862, Gay Papers. {D}*

11. *On July 4, 1862, Sumner urged Lincoln to celebrate the day by issuing a proclamation of emancipation. He replied:*

I would do it if I were not afraid that half the officers would fling down their arms and three more states would rise. —*Sumner to John Bright, August 5, 1862, Sumner Letters, II, 121. {C}*

Several days after the conversation, Sumner told the New York Tribune correspondent Adams S. Hill that Lincoln had objected to a general proclamation, saying that it would be "too big a lick" and adding that: there were two objections: first, that half the army would lay down its arms if emancipation were declared; second, that three more states would rise—Kentucky, Maryland, Missouri.

He also suggested that: a decree would be a *brutum fulmen*, ignoring the slave telegraph and not realizing the distinction between a blast of John Brown's pennywhistle and one from the government war trumpet. —*Hill to Gay, undated but probably July 9, 1862, Gay Papers. {D}*

12. *Sumner quoted Lincoln as saying with respect to emancipation:*

Wait—time is essential. —*Sumner to Elizabeth, Duchess of Argyll, August 11, 1862, Sumner Papers.* {C}

13. *Christmas eve, 1862, Lincoln assures Sumner, not for the first time, that emancipation will indeed be proclaimed on January 1. He says of himself that:*

he is hard to be moved from any position which he has taken.

He also informs Sumner of his plan: to employ African troops to hold the Mississippi River and also other posts in the warm climates, so that our white soldiers may be employed elsewhere. —*Sumner to John Murray Forbes, December 25, 1862, Sumner Papers.* {B}

14. *A few days later, the President said:*

that he could not stop the proclamation if he would, and would not if he could. —*Sumner to Forbes, December 28, 1862,* Sumner Letters, *II, 136.* {B}

15. *Writing to General Benjamin F. Butler on January 8, 1863, Sumner quoted Lincoln as saying:*

that he hoped very soon to return you to New Orleans. He was anxious to keep you in the public service and to gratify you, as you had deserved well of the country. —Sumner Letters, *II, 139.* {B}

16. *In a private conversation with Sumner aboard the* River Queen *on April 9, 1865, Lincoln remarked:*

They say I have been under Seward's influence; I have counseled with you twice as much as I ever did with him. —*Sumner to Francis W. Bird, April 16, 1871,* Sumner Letters, *II, 549.* {C}

This would seem to have been hyperbole, either on Lincoln's part or on Sumner's.

17. *During the same visit to City Point, one member of the party insisted that Jefferson Davis should be punished. Lincoln said that:*

he must repeat the words quoted in his late address, "Judge not that ye be not judged." —*Sumner to the Duchess of Argyll, April 24, 1865,* Sumner Letters, *II, 295.* {C}

GEORGE SUMNER (1817–1863) *European traveler and author, younger brother of Charles Sumner. He visited Springfield in January 1861 to deliver a public lecture on Spain and had a long interview with Lincoln, whom he found "firm as a rock."*

1. *Responding to Sumner's plea that the Republican party be kept above suspicion:*

We will try not to begin with a cloud upon it. —*Sumner to John A. Andrew, January 21, 1861, in Pratt-2, 40.* {A}

2. *On compromise with the South:*

Give them personal liberty bills, and they will pull in the slack, hold on, and insist on the border-state compromises. Give them that, they'll again pull in the slack and demand Crittenden's compromise. That pulled in, they will want all that South Carolina asks.

Lincoln told Sumner that to a Missouri Republican who wanted him to issue a back-down declaration he had replied that: he would sooner go out into his backyard and hang himself.

Sumner also quoted Lincoln as saying to him: By no act or complicity of mine shall the Republican party become a mere sucked egg, all shell and no principle in it. —41-42. {A}

BYRON SUNDERLAND (1819-1901)   *Pastor of the First Presbyterian Church in Washington for forty-five years, Senate chaplain during part of the Lincoln administration and again in the 1870s.*

1. *At the time of the* Trent *crisis, Lincoln responded to a speaker's praise of Great Britain by telling a story:*

It makes me think of an Indian chief that we had out West. He was visited by an Englishman once who tried to impress him with the greatness of England. "Why," said he to the chief, "the sun never sets on England." "Humph!" said the Indian. "I suppose it's because God wouldn't trust them in the dark." —*Ida M. Tarbell's notes of an undated interview with Sunderland, Tarbell Papers.* {C}

2. *It was near the end of 1862, according to Sunderland, that Lincoln talked with a group of friends for half an hour about God and the war. He began by saying:*

The ways of God are mysterious and profound beyond all comprehension— "who by searching can find Him out?" Now, judging after the manner of men, taking counsel of our sympathies and feelings, if it had been left to us to determine it, we would have had no war. And going further back to the occasion of it, we would have had no slavery. And tracing it still further back, we would have had no evil. There is the mystery of the universe which no man can solve, and it is at that point that the human understanding utterly backs down. And then there is nothing left but for the heart of man to take up faith and believe and trust where it cannot reason. Now, I believe we are all agents and instruments of Divine providence. On both sides we are working out the will of God; yet how strange the spectacle! Here is one half the nation prostrated in prayer that God will help them to destroy the Union and build up a government upon the cornerstone of human bondage. And here is the other half equally earnest in their prayers and efforts to defeat a purpose which they regard as so repugnant to their ideas of human nature and the rights of society, as well as liberty and independence. They want slavery; we want freedom. They want a servile class; we want to make equality practical as far as possible. And they are Christians, and we are Christians. They and we are praying and fighting for results exactly the opposite. What must God think of such a posture of affairs? There is but one solution—self-deception. Somewhere there is a fearful heresy in our religion, and I cannot think it lies in the love of liberty and in the aspirations of the human soul.

What I am to do in the present emergency time will determine. I hold myself in my present position and with the authority vested in me as an instrument of Providence. I have my own views and purposes. I have my convictions of duty and my notions of what is right to be done. But I am conscious every moment that all I am and all I have is subject to the control of a higher power, and that power can use me or not use me in any manner and at any time, as in His wisdom and might may be pleasing to Him.

Nevertheless, I am no fatalist. I believe in the supremacy of the human conscience and that men are responsible beings; that God has a right to hold them, and will hold them, to a strict personal account for the deeds done in the body. But, sirs, I do not mean to give you a lecture upon the doctrines of the Christian religion. These are simply with me the convictions and realities of great and vital truths, the power and demonstration of which I see now in the light of this, our national struggle, as I have never seen before. God only knows the issue of this business. He has destroyed nations from the map of history for their sins. Nevertheless, my hopes prevail generally above my fears for our own republic. The times are dark, the spirits of ruin are abroad in all their power, and the mercy of God alone can save us. —*Sunderland to James A. Reed, November 15, 1872, in Reed,* 342-43. {D}

The length of this recollection alone makes it dubious as anything more than a Sunderland sermon based on a certain amount of Lincoln text.

ALONZO M. SWAN *A newspaperman in Canton, Illinois, who later moved to Albuquerque, New Mexico, where he reportedly served a term in prison.*

1. *Once when Swan and Colonel John M. Farnsworth visited the White House, they found the President watching some soldiers perform as minstrels for Tad. He said that:*

he had rather see a good Negro show than a French opera at any time.

Then he continued: Farnsworth, some of my friends are much shocked at what I suppose they consider my low tastes in indulging in stories some of which, I suppose, are not just as nice as they might be, but I tell you the truth when I say that a real smutty story, if it has the element of genuine wit in its composition, as most of such stories have, has the same effect on me that I think a good square drink of whiskey has to an old toper. It puts new life into me. The fact is, I have always believed that a good laugh was good for both the mental and physical digestion. —*Undated statement by Swan, Tarbell Papers.* {D}

This is not in itself an unbelievable statement, but with respect to truthfulness, Swan's reputation was said to be "decidedly bad."[444]

DAVID M. SWARR   *In the 1880s, a resident of Lancaster, Pennsylvania.*

   1. *Swarr paid a visit to President-elect Lincoln in December 1860 and asked him whether he thought southerners would carry out their threats to secede. Lincoln replied:*

I do not think they will. A number from different sections of the South pass through here daily, and all that call appear pleasant and seem to go away apparently satisfied, and if they only give me an opportunity, I will convince them that I do not wish to interfere with them in any way, but protect them in everything that they are entitled to. But if they do, the question will be and it must be settled, come what may. —*Swarr to John G. Nicolay and John Hay, January 1, 1886, Nicolay Papers.* {C}

LEONARD SWETT (1825–1889)   *Bloomington attorney, friend of David Davis, closely associated with Lincoln in Illinois law and politics. After the war, he moved his practice to Chicago.*

   1. *In the fall of 1853, while traveling on the judicial circuit, Lincoln responded to Swett's inquiry about his childhood:*

I can remember our life in Kentucky: the cabin, the stinted living, the sale of our possessions, and the journey with my father and mother to southern Indiana [where his mother soon died]. It was pretty pinching times at first in Indiana, getting the cabin built and the clearing for the crops, but presently we got reasonably comfortable, and my father married again. . . . My father had suffered greatly for the want of an education, and he determined at an early day that I should be well educated. And what do you think he said his ideas of a good education were? We had an old dog-eared arithmetic in our house, and father determined that somehow, or somehow else, I should cipher through that book. —*Rice AT, 457–58 (1886).* {C}

A similar comment about his education was recalled by Ezra M. Prince (q.v.). There is reason to doubt that Thomas Lincoln took such a strong interest in his son's education, but the evidence is conflicting.[445]

   2. *During the same conversation, Lincoln told of earning his first half dollar and then losing it in the river. He said:*

I can see the quivering and shining of that half dollar yet, as in the quick current it went down the stream and sunk from my sight forever. —*Rice AT, 458.* {D}

This story had already been told in Carpenter-1, 754 (1865). Egbert L. Viele (q.v.) provided a longer and much different version.

3. Looking back on the indebtedness resulting from his disastrous venture into storekeeping in the 1830s, Lincoln remarked:

That debt was the greatest obstacle I have ever met in life. I had no way of speculating and could not earn money except by labor, and to earn by labor eleven hundred dollars, besides my living, seemed the work of a lifetime. There was, however, but one way. I went to the creditors and told them that if they would let me alone, I would give them all I could earn over my living, as fast as I could earn it. *—Rice AT, 465-66. {C}*

4. Lincoln also recalled one of the things that helped him pay off his debts:

At that time, members of the legislature got four dollars a day, and four dollars a day was more than I had ever earned in my life. *—Rice AT, 466. {C}*

5. Between the second and third debate with Douglas in 1858, Lincoln called some lawyers together at the home of David Davis and said:

Gentlemen, I am going to put to Douglas the following questions, and the object of this meeting is to have each of you assume you are Douglas and answer them from his standpoint.[446] *— 8 (1887). {C}*

6. Discussing the House-Divided speech with Swett and others in the summer of 1859, Lincoln said:

Well, gentlemen, you may think that speech was a mistake, but I never have believed it was, and you will see the day when you will consider it was the wisest thing I ever said. *—Swett to Herndon, January 17, 1866, Herndon-Springer, II, 92. The original letter has not been found. A variant version containing both more and less than the Springer copy is in Herndon III, 528-38. {C}*

7. One day in the late 1850s when Lincoln was sitting as judge pro tem in Clinton, Illinois, Swett heard him decide the case of a merchant seeking payment for a suit sold to a minor without authority from his father. Judge Lincoln held that the bill was too high, adding:

I have very rarely in my life worn a suit of clothes costing twenty-eight dollars. *—Swett to Herndon, January 15, 1866 (8:510-15), Herndon-Weik Collection. {C}*

8. Swett recalled that Lincoln once said to a man who was about to compliment him on a speech that he had just made:

Tell me quick. I am like the Indiana boy with his gingerbread. Nobody who likes it as well gets so little of it. *—Swett to Mrs. David Davis, July 9, 1886, Orme Papers. {D}*

It is not clear that Swett heard this remark directly from Lincoln.

9. *Shortly before the Republican national convention at Chicago in 1860, Lincoln said to Swett that:*

he was almost too much of a candidate to go, and not quite enough to stay home. —*Swett to Josiah H. Drummond, May 27, 1860, reprinted in Wilson RR-2, 293-98, from a July 1891 issue of the Portland* Express.[447] {C}

10. *On about August 20, 1862, after reading aloud a statement of Robert Dale Owen favoring emancipation:*

That is a very able paper indeed. He makes a very strong argument. I have written something on this subject myself, but it is not so able an argument as this. —*Swett's statement to John G. Nicolay, March 14, 1878, Nicolay Papers.* {C}

Lincoln had read to the cabinet on July 22 his draft of a proclamation of emancipation.

11. *Swett returned to Washington in mid-September 1862, and Lincoln asked him:*

How long have you been in the city?

Told just since the day before, the President said: Sit down; I want to consult you. If you had been here a week, I would not give a cent for your opinion.

According to Swett, they then talked for the rest of the morning about the forthcoming Emancipation Proclamation. — 8. {C}

12. *In the summer of 1863, responding to the plea that he take more care about his personal safety:*

I cannot be shut up in an iron cage and guarded. If I have business at the War Office, I must take my hat and go there, and if to kill me is within the purposes of this rebellion, no precaution can prevent it. You may guard me at a single point, but I will necessarily be exposed at others. People come to see me every day and I receive them, and I do not know but that some of them are secessionists or engaged in plots to kill me. The truth is, if any man has made up his mind that he will give his life for mine, he can take mine. —*Swett-1, 187-88 (1887).* {C}

13. *In October 1863, Swett urged Lincoln to strengthen himself against Chase and other political rivals by recommending in his annual message that Congress pass a constitutional amendment abolishing slavery. He responded:*

Is not that question doing well enough now? . . . I have never done an official act with a view to promote my own personal aggrandizement, and I don't like to begin now. I can see that time coming. Whoever can wait for it will see it; whoever stands in its way will be run over by it. —*Swett to*

Herndon, January 17, 1866, Herndon-Springer, II, 94–95; variant version in Herndon, III, 531. {C}

14. *One day after a pleasant talk, Lincoln pointed to some court-martial papers on his table and said abruptly:*

Get out of the way, Swett; tomorrow is butcher day, and I must go through these papers and see if I cannot find some excuse to let these poor fellows off. *—Swett to Herndon, January 17, 1866, Herndon-Springer, II, 100; variant version in Herndon, III, 535. {C}*

Lincoln spoke similarly to George Stoneman (q.v.), and Benjamin F. Butler (q.v.) also recalled his using the phrase "butcher's day." The work of reviewing military sentences was often heavy. On one Saturday, John Hay noted, "I ran the Tycoon through one hundred court martials! A steady sitting of six hours."[448]

15. *Swett was present when a prominent New York Republican urged the removal of a certain officeholder. Lincoln said:*

You cannot think —— to be half as mean to me as I know him to be, but I cannot run this thing upon the theory that every officeholder must think I am the greatest man in the nation, and I will not. —Swett-2, 7. *{C}*

16. *One night in the middle of the war, after discussion of discord in the country and especially problems in Missouri and Kentucky, Lincoln remarked:*

I may not have made as great a president as some other men, but I believe I have kept these discordant elements together as well as anyone could. *— Swett to Herndon, January 17, 1866, as printed in Herndon, III, 533. {D}*

The passage of which the quotation is a part does not appear in the Herndon-Springer copy of the letter and may be extraneous matter accidentally introduced.

17. *After General Benjamin F. Butler's defeat at Drewry's Bluff near Richmond in May 1864, Lincoln says that:*

Butler with 10,000 men can hold out indefinitely. He is on the defensive but he [Lincoln] thinks him safe. *—Swett to William W. Orme, May 27, 1864, Orme Papers. {B}*

18. *During the campaign of 1864, replying to Swett's question whether he expected to be re-elected:*

Well, I don't think I ever heard of any man being elected to an office unless someone was for him. *—Statement March 14, 1878, Nicolay Papers. {C}*

WAIT TALCOTT (1807–1890)   *Rockford industrialist and briefly a state legis-*
lator. Lincoln described Talcott as "one of the best men there is" and in 1862
appointed him collector of internal revenue for northern Illinois.[449]

1. *Shortly before the election of 1860, Lincoln said:*

I know you Talcotts are all strong abolitionists, and while I had to be very
careful in what I have said, I want you to understand that your opinions
and wishes have produced a much stronger impression on my mind than
you may think. —*Emerson R, 13 (1909). {D}*

A secondary recollection, recorded by Talcott's daughter and son-in-law.

JAMES TAUSSIG (1821–1916)   *A lawyer and one of the leaders of the Radical
Republican faction in Missouri.*

1. *In the late spring of 1863, Taussig visited the White House to present
a copy of resolutions adopted at a mass meeting of German-Americans in St.
Louis on May 10. They were severely critical of the President and the General
in Chief, Henry W. Halleck.*[450] *During the course of a long conversation that
followed, Lincoln said in substance that:*

it may be a misfortune for the nation that he was elected president. But,
having been elected by the people, he meant to be president, and to perform
his duty according to his best understanding, if he had to die for it. No
general will be removed, nor will any change in the cabinet be made, to suit
the views or wishes of any particular party, faction, or set of men. General
Halleck is not guilty of the charges made against him, most of which arise
from misapprehension or ignorance of those who prefer them.

The President went on to say: that it was a mistake to suppose that Generals John C. Frémont, Benjamin F. Butler, and Franz Sigel are "systematically kept out of command," as stated in the fourth resolution; that, on the
contrary, he fully appreciated the merits of the gentlemen named; that by
their own action they had placed themselves in the positions which they
occupied; that he was not only willing but anxious to place them again
in command as soon as he could find spheres of action for them, without
doing injustice to others, but that at present he had more pegs than holes
to put them in.

*With respect to the recent transfer of military command in Missouri from
Samuel R. Curtis to John M. Schofield, he explained:* that General Curtis was
not relieved on account of any wrong act or great mistake committed by
him. The system of provost marshals established by him throughout the
state gave rise to violent complaint. That [he] had thought at one time to
appoint General Frémont in his place; that at another time, he had thought
of appointing General McDowell, . . . a good and loyal, though very un-

fortunate soldier; and that at last General Schofield was appointed, with a view, if possible, to reconcile and satisfy the two factions in Missouri. He has instructions not to interfere with either party, but to confine himself to his military duties. — *Taussig's letter to committee members,* Missouri Democrat *(St. Louis), June 9, 1863.* {C}

2. *Concerning complaints of a want of unity in the cabinet, Lincoln intimated:*

that each member of the cabinet was responsible mainly for the manner of conducting the affairs of his particular department; that there was no centralization of responsibility for the action of the cabinet anywhere, except in the president himself. — *Ibid.* {C}

3. *As for the problem of disunity in Missouri:*

The dissensions between Union men in Missouri are due solely to a factious spirit which is exceedingly reprehensible. The two parties ought to have their heads knocked together. Either would rather see the defeat of their adversary than that of Jefferson Davis. To this spirit of faction is to be ascribed the failure of the legislature to elect senators and the defeat of the Missouri Aid bill in Congress, the passage of which [he] strongly desired. — *Ibid.*[451] {C}

4. *The President also declared that:*

the Union men in Missouri who are in favor of gradual emancipation represented his views better than those who are in favor of immediate emancipation. In his speeches, he had frequently used as an illustration the case of a man who had an excrescence on the back of his neck, the removal of which, in one operation, would result in the death of the patient, while tinkering it off by degrees would preserve life. . . . the Radicals in Missouri had no right to consider themselves the exponents of his views on the subject of emancipation in that state. — *Ibid.* {C}

5. *At the close of the conversation, Lincoln remarked that:*

there was evidently a serious misunderstanding springing up between him and the Germans of St. Louis, which he would like to see removed. — *Ibid.* {C}

THOMAS C. TEASDALE (1808–1891) *Baptist minister in Columbus, Mississippi, who led a campaign to establish a home for children orphaned by the war.*

1. *In March 1865, Teasdale visited Washington and presented a petition for the government's cooperation with the orphanage project. The President declared:*

You ask me to give you relief in a case of distress, just such as we have been striving to produce. We want to bring you rebels into such straits that you will be willing to give up this wicked rebellion.

Acknowledging, however, that the project deserved special sympathy, he went on to say: Well, I will **authorize** General Canby to grant the petition of your board, provided it does not interfere with any of his military movements. I will not **order** it to be done.[452] — *Teasdale, 199-200 (1887). {C}*

JOHN M. THAYER (1820-1906)   *Lawyer and Union general, later a United States senator and governor of Nebraska.*

1. *At one point in a discussion that lasted more than an hour, Thayer asked Lincoln how he felt about the French occupation of Mexico and received this reply:*

I'm not exactly scared but don't like the looks of the thing. Napoleon has taken advantage of our weakness in our time of trouble and has attempted to found a monarchy on the soil of Mexico in utter disregard of the Monroe Doctrine. My policy is, attend to only one trouble at a time. If we get well out of our present difficulties and restore the Union, I propose to notify Louis Napoleon that it is about time to take his army out of Mexico. When that army is gone, the Mexicans will take care of Maximilian. — *Thayer's reminiscence in the* New York Sun, *reprinted in Nichols, 317 (1896). {D}*

2. *During the same interview, according to Thayer, Lincoln gave a rather verbose account of how he had responded to criticism of Grant's fondness for whiskey by proposing to send some of the same brand to his other generals. He then went on to say:*

What I want and what the people want is generals who will fight battles and win victories. Grant has done this, and I propose to stand by him. — *313. {D}*

Chronology casts doubt on this quotation and the one above. Even before Maximilian arrived in Mexico, Grant had been installed as commander in chief.

NELSON THOMASSON   *The son of a Chicago lawyer and former congressman with whom Lincoln was acquainted.*[453]

1. *Lincoln came into the War Department one day when Thomasson, John Hay, and Henry Villard were present. He began writing a communication and at one point asked:*

Young gentlemen, when do you use a semicolon?

After receiving several replies, he said: I never use it much, but when I am in doubt what to use, I generally employ the little fellow. — *Thomasson, [3]. {C}*

GEORGE THOMPSON   *A member of the mayor's staff in New York City.*

1. *On February 20, 1860, Lincoln attended a performance of Verdi's "Un Ballo in Maschera," and Thompson suggested that during the ball scene, he might like to go up on the stage in mask. Lincoln replied:*

No, I thank you, one is enough. The papers say I wear a mask already. — *Thompson's account, reported in the New York* Herald, *February 21, 1861.* {A}

JARED D. THOMPSON   *A resident of New Haven, Connecticut.*

1. *According to Thompson, he and another man called at the White House during the week of February 14-20, 1864. After they had discussed the case of a certain colonel held on charges by authority of General Benjamin F. Butler, the President said:*

Well then, from what you say, gentlemen, I think you agree with me that General Butler is not fit to have a command. . . . I did not give General Butler a command until the people at the North held public meetings asking me to do so. — *Sworn statement by Thompson, February 23, 1864, Butler-1, III, 465-66.* {C}

Lincoln, it appears, responded promptly to the statement with an endorsement of Butler's "ability and fidelity."[454]

JOSEPH P. THOMPSON (1819-1879)   *Congregational clergyman in New York City, prominent also as an editor and a prolific author. His published accounts of a conversation with Lincoln on September 6, 1864, were based, he said, on "memoranda made at the time."*

1. *Lincoln had recently proclaimed Sunday, September 11, a day of thanksgiving for Union victories in Mobile Bay and Georgia. When Thompson commended the action, he replied:*

I would be glad to give you such a proclamation every Sunday for a few weeks to come. — *Thompson, 50 (1866).* {C}

2. *In discussing whether the recent rise in Union sentiment had been caused by the capture of Atlanta or the Democratic platform, Lincoln said:*

I guess it was the victory; at any rate I'd rather have that repeated. — *Sermon preached April 30, 1865, in* Voices, *191 (1865). The sentence is phrased somewhat differently in Thompson, 50.* {C}

3. *Of the recent death of the noted Confederate raider, John Hunt Morgan, he remarked:*

Well, I wouldn't crow over anybody's death, but I can take this as resignedly as any dispensation of Providence. Morgan was a coward, a nigger-driver, a low creature, such as you northern men know nothing about. — *Voices, 191.* {D}

The second sentence does not sound like Lincoln and may be more reflective of Thompson's own intense antislavery feeling. A variant version contains the added statement (referring to slave-traders): Southern slaveholders despise them. — *Thompson, 50.*

4. *With respect to the approaching presidential election, Lincoln said:*

I rely upon the religious sentiment of the country, which I am told is very largely for me. —Voices, *191. {C}*

5. *Thompson remarked that the Democratic nominee, George B. McClellan, seemed to be as slow in getting on his party's platform as he had been in taking Richmond. Lincoln responded:*

I think he must be entrenching.

Thompson spoke of rumors that McClellan would decline the nomination because of the Chicago platform. Lincoln said: Well, he doesn't know yet whether he will accept or decline. And he never will know. Somebody must do it for him. For, of all the men I have had to do with in my life, indecision is most strongly marked in General McClellan—if that can be said to be strong which is the essence of weakness. —*Thompson, 50. {C}*

6. *Concerning a volume of antislavery essays by the New Haven clergyman Leonard Bacon, he said:*

I read that book some years ago and at first did not exactly know what to make of it, but afterwards, I read it over more carefully and got hold of Dr. Bacon's distinctions, and it had much to do in shaping my own thinking on the subject of slavery. He is quite a man. —*Thompson, 51. {D}*

There appears to be no other indication of this influence.

7. *During further discussion of slavery, Thompson drew a distinction between the subjection of captives and paupers, allowed by Mosaic law, and chattel slavery. Lincoln acknowledged that this would relieve the question of Hebrew servitude, but then he added:*

However, I have sometimes thought that Moses didn't quite understand the Lord along there. —*Thompson, 51. {C}*

THEODORE TILTON (1835–1907) *New York journalist who in 1863 became editor of the* Independent, *a Congregationalist weekly.*

1. *In early June 1864, Tilton and William Lloyd Garrison attended the Union (Republican) convention at Baltimore. Hoping that Garrison, as a kind of commemoration, might return to the jail cell he had occupied thirty-four years earlier, the two men were disappointed to find that the building had been torn down and replaced. They told Lincoln about it when they visited him right after the convention, and he remarked:*

Well, Mr. Garrison, when you first went to Baltimore, you couldn't get **out**; but the second time, you couldn't get **in**. —Independent, *June 16, 1864. {A}*

Garrison himself, writing to his wife on June 9, quoted Lincoln as saying: "Then, you could not get out of prison; now you cannot get in."[455]

2. *During the same interview, Lincoln was told of the convention's enthusiastic response to Senator Edwin D. Morgan's call for a constitutional amendment abolishing slavery. He said:*

It was I who suggested to Mr. Morgan that he should put that idea into his opening speech. —*Ibid. {A}*

CHARLES A. TINKER (1838–1917) *Cipher clerk in the War Department, later a Western Union superintendent.*

1. *On September 23, 1863, after composing a telegraphic response to a crank, Lincoln said:*

I guess on the whole, Mr. Tinker, you need not send that. I will pay no attention to the crazy fellow. —*Tinker to General George H. Thomas, May 27, 1867, ISHL; printed in* Collected Works, *VI, 475-76n. {C}*

2. *After someone's performance of a task had proved to be not entirely satisfactory, Lincoln declared:*

When you want a thing done right, go do it yourself. —*Tinker, 443 (1895). {C}*

Another War Department telegrapher, Albert B. Chandler, quoted substantially the same remark.[456]

3. *On one occasion, Secretary Seward spoke of having heard that the President had stepped aside for a colored woman at a muddy crossing. Lincoln replied:*

Well, I don't remember it, but I always make it a rule, if people don't turn out for me, I will for them. If I didn't, there would be a collision. —*Tinker, 443-44. {C}*

4. *After receiving the message that Andrew Johnson had been nominated as his running mate:*

Well, I thought possibly he might be the man. Perhaps he is the best man, but . . . *At which point, says Tinker, Lincoln rose and left the telegraph office.* —*Tinker, 444. {C}*

SAMUEL H. TREAT (1811–1887) *Illinois supreme court justice for fourteen years and then, beginning in 1855, a federal district judge for the southern part of the state.*

1. *Treat recalled that Lincoln made the following statement in his first appearance before the supreme court:*

This is the first case I have ever had in this court, and I have therefore examined it with great care. As the court will perceive by looking at the abstract of the record, the only question in the case is one of authority. I have not been able to find any authority sustaining my side of the case, but I have found several cases directly in point on the other side. I will now give these cases to the court and then submit the case. — *Treat's undated statement (11:3183), Herndon-Weik Collection.* {E}

This portrayal of Lincoln as an absurdly over-honest lawyer, which was given status by its publication in Herndon, II, 323, has been exposed as not in accord with the facts.[457]

LAMBERT TREE　*A Chicago lawyer.*

　1. *One day in the late 1850s, Lincoln entered Tree's office with a lawbook in his hand and said:*

Tree, I have come to return you the book I borrowed, and I hope you don't mind my having had a new cover put on it. It is too good a book for the disreputable-looking one it had. — *Tree, 591 (1911).* {C}

BENJAMIN C. TRUMAN (1835–1916)　*Journalist who served during much of the Civil War as an aide to Andrew Johnson, military governor of Tennessee.*

　1. *In the company of John W. Forney, by whom he was employed as a war correspondent, Truman visited the White House in November 1862 to deliver messages from Johnson. Lincoln remarked:*

As I have often heard my friend Forney here say, Andrew Johnson is the Andrew Jackson of the war.

Then he told Truman to say to Johnson: that he had the greatest confidence in him; and that he trusted that, with Rosecrans at the head of the army in Tennessee, the state would once more be rid of its enemies in arms; and that our plans for the reconstruction of Tennessee would rapidly follow.

At another meeting in the summer of 1863, Lincoln again praised Johnson's performance as military governor but added: I hope Mr. Johnson won't be too severe. — *Truman's letter in the New York* Times, *July 13, 1891.* {C}

SOJOURNER TRUTH (1797–1883)　*Former slave who in the 1840s began to travel about the country preaching abolition.*

　1. *Visiting Lincoln on October 29, 1864, Sojourner told him that he was the best president yet. He replied:*

I expect you have reference to my having emancipated the slaves in my proclamation. But [mentioning Washington and several other presidents] they were all just as good, and would have done just as he had done if the time had come. If the people over the river [pointing across the Potomac] had behaved themselves, I could not have done what I have, but they did not, and I was compelled to do these things. — *Sojourner Truth to Oliver Johnson, November 17, 1864, in* National Anti-Slavery Standard *(New York), December 17, 1864.* {C}

Truth, who was illiterate, dictated the letter to a friend. The wording is some-

what different in her later recollection of the meeting and also in the contemporary account provided by Lucy Colman (q.v.), the woman who accompanied her to the White House.[458]

CHARLES K. TUCKERMAN (1821–1896) *A New York man who was involved in the plan, approved by Lincoln, to colonize blacks on Cow Island off Haiti. He was later minister to Greece.*

   1. Meeting Tuckerman while strolling out of doors early one morning, Lincoln said that:

it was the first time that he had been able to look about the grounds or to enter the conservatory since he had taken possession of the White House.

He then went on to point out certain architectural changes "since Madison's day." — Tuckerman, 412 (1888). {C}

   2. Once, when Tuckerman suggested that Lincoln's signature on a document would easily settle the matter in hand, he replied irritably:

Oh, I know that, and so it would be very easy for me to open that window and shout down Pennsylvania Avenue, only I don't mean to do it just now. —412. {C}

JOHN P. USHER (1816–1889) *Indiana lawyer and politician who served as assistant secretary and then secretary of the interior in the Lincoln administration.*

   1. At a cabinet meeting in December 1862, when Chase predicted that the House of Representatives would not seat two recently elected Louisiana Unionists, Lincoln exclaimed:

Then, I am to be bullied by Congress am I? I'll be damned if I will. — *Usher interview, October 8, 1878, Nicolay Papers. {C}*

A milder version is in Rice AT, 93 (1886).

   2. After receiving a gloomy letter from Governor Oliver P. Morton of Indiana, Lincoln said:

Don't you know, Usher, that Morton is one of the very best governors we've got? Well, it's so, but he's the easiest stampeded of any man you ever saw. — *Usher as quoted by a correspondent of the Chicago Tribune, May 2, 1882. {C}*

   3. In 1864:

General Grant is the most extraordinary man in command that I know of. I heard nothing direct from him and wrote to him to know why and whether I could do anything to promote his success, and Grant replied that he had tried to do the best he could with what he had; that he believed if he had more men and arms he could use them to good advantage and do more than he had done, but he supposed I had done and was doing all I could; that if I could do more he felt that I would do it. —*Usher, 33–34 (1887). {C}*

4. *On issuing permits to pass through army lines into enemy territory:*

I cannot always know whether a permit ought to be granted, and I want to oblige everybody when I can, and Stanton and I have an understanding that if I send an order to him that cannot be consistently granted, he is to refuse it, which he sometimes does; and that led to a remark which I made the other day to a man who complained of Stanton, that I hadn't much influence with this administration, but expected to have more with the next. —*Rice AT, 100. {C}*

A slightly different version, told in 1887 to a Kansas audience, is in Usher, 24. Thurlow Weed (q.v.) and others recalled the remark about influence with the administration.

5. *At a cabinet meeting on February 5, 1865, Lincoln read a proposed message to Congress recommending payment of $400 million (Usher mistakenly remembered it as $300 million) to the slaveholding states, once all resistance to national authority had been abandoned and the amendment abolishing slavery had been ratified by the requisite number of states. The cabinet expressed unanimous disapproval, and he responded:*

You are all against me. How long has this war lasted, and how long do you suppose it will still last? We cannot hope that it will end in less than a hundred days. We are now spending three millions a day, and that will equal the full amount I propose to pay, to say nothing of the lives lost and property destroyed. I look upon it as a measure of strict and simple economy. —*Usher interview, October 11, 1877, Nicolay Papers. {C}*

Another version is in the New York Times, *November 1, 1885, and in Rice AT, 98.*

PETER VAN BERGEN   *Landowner in the Springfield area who sued Lincoln for an unpaid debt in 1834, but later became his client in a number of lawsuits.*

1. *Presumably in 1863, Lincoln showed Van Bergen the relevant war maps and said:*

Grant here displayed about Vicksburg more generalship than ever was shown by any general in America. —*Undated Van Bergen statement (11: 3187), Herndon-Weik Collection. {C}*

CLARISSA (MRS. NORMAN) VANNATTAN.[459]   *A neighbor of William H. Herndon in his later years.*

1. *To a thirteen-year-old girl (Mrs. Vannattan's sister) whom he caught as she was about to take a bad fall backward on a Springfield street, Lincoln remarked:*

Now you can say you have been in Abraham's bosom. —*As told to Herndon and recalled by him for Weik, August 8, 1890 (10:2700-2703), Herndon-Weik Collection. Also, with slight variation, in an undated note to Weik (11:2879-80). {D}*

CORNELIUS VAN SANTVOORD (1816–1901)   *An army chaplain who watched and listened as Lincoln received a series of visitors one day in the winter of 1862-63. His account published twenty years later was based, he said, on notes jotted down soon after the interviews.*

1. *To a lieutenant who wanted to be appointed colonel of a black regiment, Lincoln said:*

The whole thing amounts only to a colonelcy for the applicant, as, should a regiment be raised, in six months there would be a colonel without a Negro left in the command.

When the man protested that his purpose was to serve the cause, not himself: That may be your purpose, but the certain effect nonetheless will be what I have described. —*Van Santvoord, 612 (1883). {C}*

2. *To a disabled soldier who wanted a job in Washington but had no documents to offer:*

What, no papers, no credentials, nothing to show how you lost your leg? How am I to know that you lost it in battle, or did not lose it by a trap after getting into somebody's orchard? ... Well, well, it is dangerous for an army man to be wandering around without papers to show where he belongs and what he is, but I will see what can be done for you. —*612-13. {C}*

3. *To a man who pleaded for the use of Lincoln's name in a commercial venture:*

No! I'll have nothing to do with this business, nor with any man who comes to me with such degrading propositions. What! Do you take the president of the United States to be a commission broker? You have come to the wrong place, and for you and everyone who comes for such purposes, there is the door! —*613. {C}*

4. *To a Scotsman who brought praise for the Emancipation Proclamation from some of his countrymen:*

Well, I am inclined to remain firm but do not say I will, certainly, though all others should fail, as Peter once said and repeated with so much confidence, and only saw his folly and weakness as the cock crew. Yet, God helping me, I trust to prove true to a principle which I feel to be right, of which the public sentiment approves, and which the country is prepared to support and maintain. Tell this to your friends at home with my acknowledgments for their sympathy and good wishes. —*613*. *{C}*

5. *After measuring a man whom he had pronounced taller than himself:*

There, it is as I told you. I knew I couldn't be mistaken. I rarely fail in taking a man's true altitude by the eye.

When the man pointed out that Lincoln was wearing slippers instead of boots: Not enough to amount to anything in this reckoning. You ought at least to be satisfied, my honest friend, with the proof given that you actually stand higher today than your president. —*614*. *{C}*

EGBERT L. VIELE (1825–1902)　*Engineer, Civil War general, and in later life, briefly a New York congressman. Viele accompanied Lincoln, Stanton, and Chase on the revenue cutter* Miami *when they visited Fortress Monroe in May 1862. He became military governor of Norfolk after its capture.*

1. *When Chase remarked that he had forgotten to write an important letter before leaving Washington, Lincoln said that:*

a man was sometimes lucky in forgetting to write a letter, for he seldom knew what it contained until it appeared again some day to confront him with an indiscreet word or expression. —*Viele-1, 814 (1878).*⁴⁶⁰ *{C}*

In a later version, Viele quoted Lincoln as saying: Chase, never regret what you don't write; it is what you do write that you are often called upon to feel sorry for. —*Viele-2, 440 (1895). {C}*

2. *Stanton then told how, just before his departure, he had received from a general an unclear telegram requiring an immediate answer and had taken the chance of replying: "All right; go ahead." Lincoln observed:*

I suppose you meant that it was all right if it was good for him, and all wrong if it was not. That reminds me of a story about a horse that was sold at the crossroads near where I once lived. The horse was supposed to be fast, and quite a number of people were present at the time appointed for the sale. A small boy was employed to ride the horse backward and forward to exhibit his points. One of the would-be buyers followed the boy down the road and asked him confidentially if the horse had a splint. "Well, mister," said the boy, "if it's good for him he has got it, but if it isn't good for him he hasn't." —*Viele-2, 440. {C}*

3. *Lincoln recounted how, having resolved to discourage military commanders from issuing grandiloquent proclamations, he had broached the subject to General Burnside and Commodore Goldsborough before they set out on their expedition to the North Carolina coast:*

Would you believe it? When I spoke of proclamations, each pulled one out of his pocket that had been prepared in advance without consultation. I had no idea of catching them in the very act! — *Viele-1, 815.* {C}

4. *One morning on deck, according to Viele, Lincoln picked up an ax and held it at arm's length for several minutes with just his thumb and forefinger. He said that:*

he could do this when he was eighteen years of age and had never seen a day since that time when he could not. — *Viele-1, 815.* {C}

A similar story was told by Henry W. Knight (q.v.).

5. *To Viele on another morning:*

If I have one vice, and I can call it nothing else, it is not to be able to say no! Thank God for not making me a woman, but if He had, I suppose He would have made me just as ugly as He did, and no one would ever have tempted me. It was only the other day, a poor parson whom I knew some years ago in Joliet came to the White House with a sad story of his poverty and his large family—poor parsons seem always to have large families—and he wanted me to do something for him. I knew very well that I could do nothing for him, and yet I couldn't bear to tell him so, and so I said I would see what I could do. The very next day the man came back for the office which he said that I had promised him—which was not true, but he seemed really to believe it. Of course there was nothing left for me to do except to get him a place through one of the secretaries. But if I had done my duty, I should have said "no" in the beginning. — *Viele-1, 818.* {C}

The remark about being fortunate in not having been born a woman also appears in Herndon, II, 325n, 374.

6. *After the captain of the cutter had inflicted some boring personal reminiscences on the assembled company, Lincoln announced that he, too, had once been something of a sailor, and then he continued:*

When I was a young man about eighteen years of age, I was living in Kentucky, and, like everybody else in that part of the country at that time, I was obliged to struggle pretty hard for a living. I had been at work all winter helping a man distill a quantity of whiskey, and as there was little or no money in the country, I was obliged to take the pay for my winter's services in whiskey. You were not around in those days, Chase, with your greenback-printing machine. Whiskey was more plentiful than almost anything else, and I determined, if possible, to find a market for my share in some other locality, so as to get the largest amount possible for my winter's work. Hearing that a man living a short distance up the Ohio River was building a flatboat to send to New Orleans as soon as the water in the river was at a proper stage, I paid him a visit and made an agreement with him that if he would take my whiskey to that city, I would go with him and work my passage. Before the boat was completed and ready to start, I made up my mind that I should find a good deal of whiskey in New Orleans when I arrived there, and having found a man who had a lot of tobacco that he was sending to market, I made a trade with him for half of my whiskey, so that if whiskey should be down when I got there, tobacco might be up, or vice versa; at any rate, I should not have all my eggs in the same basket. The boat was ready at the proper time and stopped at our landing for me and my whiskey and tobacco. My short experience as a sailor began from that moment. Our voyage down the river was not attended by much excitement or any catastrophe. Floating with the current during the day, we always tied up to a tree on the bank of the river at night. One evening, just after we had tied up the flatboat, two men came down to the shore and asked me what I would charge them to row them out in the small boat that we had with us into the middle of the river to meet a steamboat that was coming up the river and on which they wanted to take passage. I told them I thought it would be worth a shilling apiece, and the bargain was made. I pulled out into the stream and delivered them safe on board the steamer and, to my astonishment, received for my services a dollar. It was the first money I had had for some time. On my way back to the flatboat, I made a calculation to myself that I had been gone about an hour, and that if I could earn a dollar every hour and live long enough, I would be a rich man before I died.

The captain inquired how the whiskey and tobacco sold in New Orleans, and Lincoln, with a twinkle in his eye, replied: Captain, I was only relating to you my experience as a marine, not as a merchant. —*Viele-1, 816-17.* {D}

The length and inaccuracy of this recollection make it suspect.[461] *A different version of the story, supposedly told to Seward and others gathered at the White House, was published thirteen years earlier in Carpenter-1, 754, without identification of the source.*[462] *Partial versions were provided by Alban Jasper Conant and Leonard Swett (qq.v.).*

7. *Once, says Viele, he went to see the President and found him being shaved. Lincoln remarked:*

I hope I don't scare you; I look frightful enough by nature without the addition of this lather. —*Viele-2, 441.* {C}

8. *At another time, Lincoln said:*

I wish George Washington or some of those old patriots were here in my place so that I could have a little rest. —*Viele-2, 441.* {C}

9. *In Norfolk on January 1, 1863, thousands of blacks celebrated the Emancipation Proclamation, apparently without realizing that it did not apply to them. Viele went to see Lincoln, who explained:*

This is the difficulty: we want to keep all that we have of the border states, those that have not seceded and the portions of those which we have occupied; and in order to do that, it is necessary to omit those areas I have mentioned from the effect of this proclamation. — *Viele-2, 440.* {C}

But Lincoln also had compelling constitutional reasons for excluding the border states from his edict.

10. *Subsequently, as an administrator of conscription in Ohio, Viele had occasion to complain about the conduct of Governor David Tod. Lincoln said:*

Well, now, you remember what I told you about the border states. The same thing applies to the governors of the loyal states. We cannot afford to quarrel with them about collateral issues. We want their soldiers. — *Viele-2, 440–41.* {C}

HENRY VILLARD (1835–1900) *German-born journalist, later one of the country's leading financiers and railroad promoters.*

1. *During the contest with Douglas in 1858, Lincoln told Villard that:*

when he was clerking in a country store, his highest political ambition was to be a member of the state legislature. Since then [he continued], I have grown some, but my friends got me into **this** business. I did not consider myself qualified for the United States Senate, and it took me a long time to persuade myself that I was. Now, to be sure, I am convinced that I am good enough for it; but, in spite of it all, I am saying to myself every day: "It is too big a thing for you; you will never get it." Mary insists, however, that I am going to be senator and president of the United States, too. Just think of such a sucker as me as president! — *Villard, I, 96 (1904).* {D}

Much of this recollection lacks credibility. Lincoln had tried very hard to win a Senate seat four years earlier, without displaying any doubts about his qualifications, and he was certainly not a diffident entrant into the contest with Douglas.

2. *On November 27, 1860, one man among a group of visitors expressed regret that the new administration must deal first with the vexatious slavery question. Lincoln was reminded of a story:*

Many years ago an unsophisticated farmer—more honest than learned— commonly known as "Old Zach ———," undertook to run for the office of justice of the peace in Kentucky. Being successful, the first case he was called upon to adjudicate was a criminal prosecution for the abuse of Negro slaves. Its merits being somewhat beyond his comprehension, he sought enlightenment (after hearing the evidence) in the statutes of the commonwealth and various handbooks for justices of the peace he had provided himself with on assuming the ermine. But his search for precedents proved in vain, and growing still more puzzled, he exclaimed at last, angrily, "I will be damned if I don't feel almost sorry for being elected, when the niggers is the first thing I have to attend to." — *Villard's dispatch of November 28 in the New York* Herald, *December 2, 1860. {A}*

3. *On December 19, 1860, a Mississippi secessionist joined the conversation in Lincoln's reception room at the state Capitol and heard Lincoln say:*

that the main differences between northerners and southerners were that the former held slavery to be wrong and opposed its further extension, while the latter thought it right and endeavored to spread it; that, although the Republicans were anti-extensionists; they would not interfere with slavery where it existed, and that as to his own intentions, the slave states would find that their slave property would be as secure from encroachments as it had been under Mr. Buchanan.

At the southerner's request, Lincoln furnished him an inscribed copy of the debates with Douglas, remarking that: he hoped its possession would not give him any trouble on his return to Mississippi. — *Villard's dispatch of December 19 in the New York* Herald, *December 24, 1860. {B}*

Another account of this incident, though substantially similar, included the additional statement by Lincoln that: if the southern states concluded upon a contingent secession, that is, upon awaiting aggressive acts on the part of his administration, they would never go out of the Union. — *Correspondence of the Cincinnati* Commercial *as reprinted in the New York* Times, *December 27, 1860.*[463] *{B}*

4. *At one of the station stops on his way to Washington in February 1861, Lincoln told the crowd a story:*

There was a man who was to be nominated at a political convention and hired a horse of a livery keeper to journey there. The horse was so confoundedly slow, however, that the man arrived too late, and found his opponent nominated and the convention adjourned. When he arrived home he said to the stableman, "This is a fine animal of yours—a fine animal." "Do you think so?" "Certainly, but never sell him to an undertaker." "Undertaker! Why not?" "Because if the horse were hitched to a hearse, resurrection day would come before he reached the cemetery." So if my journey goes on at this slow rate it will be resurrection day before I reach the capital. — *Villard's dispatch of February 18 in the* Herald, *February 20, 1861. {A}*

The artist Alban Jasper Conant claimed that he told Lincoln this story in Springfield in September 1860. — Conant, 515 (1909).

5. *Another story recounted in the same dispatch was probably told in private:*

I once knew a good, sound churchman, whom we'll call Brown, who was on a committee to erect a bridge over a very dangerous and rapid river. Architect after architect failed, and at last Brown said he had a friend named Jones who had built several bridges and could build this. "Let's have him in," said the committee. In came Jones. "Can you build this bridge, sir?" "Yes," replied Jones; "I could build a bridge to the infernal regions, if necessary." The sober committee were horrified, but when Jones retired, Brown thought it but fair to defend his friend. "I know Jones so well," said he, "and he is so honest a man and so good an architect that, if he states soberly and positively that he can build a bridge to Hades, why, I believe it. But I have my doubts about the abutment on the infernal side." So, when politicians said they could harmonize the northern and southern wings of the Democracy, why, I believed them. But I had my doubts about the abutment on the southern side.[464] {A}

6. *Shortly before his inauguration, on the subject of patronage problems:*

Yes, it was bad enough in Springfield, but it was child's play compared with this tussle here. I hardly have a chance to eat or sleep. I am fair game for everybody of that hungry lot. — *Villard, I, 156.* {C}

LEONARD W. VOLK (1828–1895) *Sculptor who in March 1860 made a life mask of Lincoln that subsequently served as a model for many statues. Volk's assertion in an article published twenty-one years later that he measured Lincoln at six feet and one inch, if it was not merely a typographical error, casts some doubt upon the accuracy of his memory with respect to the following quotations.*

1. I don't like to hear cut-and-dried sermons. No—when I hear a man preach, I like to see him act as if he were fighting bees! — *Volk, 226 (1881).* {C}

2. The truth is I don't know much of history, and all I do know of it I have learned from law books. —*226.* {C}

3. I am bored nearly every time I sit down to a public dining-table by some one pitching into me on politics. —*226.* {C}

4. It is true that I did split rails, and one day while I was sharpening a wedge on a log, the ax glanced and nearly took my thumb off, and there is the scar, you see. —*228.* {C}

DANIEL W. VOORHEES (1827–1897) *Democratic congressman and later senator from Indiana.*

1. *Voorhees recalled Lincoln's saying to him on one occasion:*

No one need ever expect me to sanction the shooting of a man for running away in a battle. I won't do it. A man can't help being a coward any more than he could help a humpback, if he were born with one. . . . In any contest or controversy which arises between the head and the heels, I never knew the heels to get anything but the best of it. No, sir, they needn't send any leg cases to me at all. I'll never order a man shot for any such offense. —

Interview of Voorhees by Dan Quinn (Alfred Henry Lewis) in the Kansas City Times, *undated transcript, Sandburg Collection, folder 209. {D}*

Lincoln was also quoted by Joseph Holt (q.v.) on "leg cases."

2. *At another time, Lincoln said with a "pathetic look":*

Voorhees, doesn't it seem strange that I should be here—I, a man who couldn't cut a chicken's head off—with blood running all around me? — *Ibid. {D}*

JAMES S. WADSWORTH (1807–1864) *Union general of strong antislavery sentiments and the unsuccessful Republican nominee for governor of New York in 1862. He was killed at the battle of the Wilderness.*

1. *According to New York* Tribune *correspondent Adams S. Hill, Lincoln told Wadsworth in October 1862 of his doubts about McClellan. He said that:*

he'd got tired of his excuses; he'd remove him but for the election; thought it not best to do it till after November's voting. —*Hill to Sydney Howard Gay, October 13, 1862, Gay Papers. {D}*

LEWIS WALLACE (1827–1905) *Indiana lawyer and politician who became a Civil War general; later the author of* Ben Hur *and many other books.*

1. *One day in early July 1862, soon after the Seven Days' battles, Wallace escorted two women to the White House and found the President preparing to leave for the James River. Lincoln whispered to him:*

I must go to Harrison's Landing to keep McClellan from surrendering the army. —*Wallace speech on February 12, as reported in the Indianapolis* Journal, *February 14, 1898; also in Wallace, II, 669 (1906). {D}*

This quotation, which seems dubious on its face, provoked some angry protests. An Indianapolis man reportedly challenged Wallace to a duel.[465]

2. *In March 1864, when he became commander of the Middle Department with headquarters in Baltimore, Wallace called on the President, who remarked at the close of their interview:*

I came near forgetting that there is an election nearly due over in Maryland, but don't **you** forget it.

On March 31, Lincoln summoned Wallace and told him: I sent for you to say that I watched the boiling of the kettle over in Maryland, and I think you managed it beautifully. It was a good thing, that getting Governor Bradford between you and the enemy here in Congress. Winter Davis is happy over it. Keep right along now, and get Davis and the Governor together. And— yes, yes—be fair, but whenever there is a doubt with a benefit in it, don't fail to give the benefit where it will do the most good.[466] — *Wallace, II, 670, 684. {D}*

Wallace's chronology is confused. He seems to have mistakenly recalled that the March 31 conversation with Lincoln came after Maryland voters had elected a constitutional convention favoring emancipation. In fact, that election did not take place until April 6.

JOHN B. WEBER (Born 1810)   *As sheriff of Sangamon County in the mid-1850s, Weber was a Democrat turning Republican who, according to Lincoln, worked "furiously" for him in the campaign of 1858.*

    1. *Sometime around 1843, Lincoln entertained Weber with this gross anecdote:*

A toper named Bill got brutally drunk and staggered down a narrow alley, where he laid himself down in the mud and remained there until the dusk of the evening, at which time he recovered from his stupor. Finding himself very muddy, he immediately started for a pump (a public watering place on the street) to wash himself. On his way to the pump, another drunken man was leaning over a horse post. This, Bill mistook for the pump and at once took hold of the arm of the man for the handle, the use of which set the occupant of the post to throwing up. Bill, believing all was right, put both hands under and gave himself a thorough washing. He then made his way to the grocery for something to drink. On entering the door, one of his comrades exclaimed in a tone of surprise, "Why, Bill, what in the world is the matter?" Bill said in reply, [My] God, you ought to have seen me before I was washed. — *Weber to Herndon, November 5, 1866 (8:1020-23), Herndon-Weik Collection. {C}*

The fact that this story dates back to the eighteenth century does not rule out the possibility that Lincoln made use of it.[467]

THOMAS WEBSTER, JR. (1818–1894)   *Businessman and Republican politician who tried unsuccessfully to obtain appointment as collector of the port of Philadelphia.*

    1. *In mid-November 1860, when Webster mentioned that he had come to Springfield from Mansfield, Ohio:*

Mansfield is a great place. It was that town that first saw my fitness for the presidency. — *Webster to John Sherman, November 15, 1860, in McCorison, 300. {A}*

    2. *Talking with several Kentuckians, Lincoln remarked that:*

in 1832 the South made a special complaint against a law of recent origin. Now they had no new law, or new interpretation of old law, to complain of—no specialty whatever, nothing but the naked desire to go out of the Union. — *Ibid., 301. {B}*

SAMUEL R. WEED (1837–1918)   *Reporter for a St. Louis newspaper who spent November 6, 1860, in Springfield. His account of that election day, written in 1882, was not published until half a century later. There appears to be no corroboration of his assertion that he was one of the small group that waited with Lincoln in the local telegraph office for the election results.*

1. *At one point, Lincoln said that:*

elections in this country were like big boils—they caused a great deal of pain before they came to a head, but after the trouble was over, the body was in better health than before. He hoped that the bitterness of the canvass would pass away as easily as the core of a boil. — *Weed SR, 8. {C}*

2. *In a lighter vein, he remarked that:*

it was lucky for him that the women couldn't vote; otherwise, the monstrous portraits of him which had been circulated during the canvass by friends as well as by foes would surely defeat him. —*8. {C}*

3. *At 10 P.M., with no returns yet received from New York, he said that:*

the news would come quick enough if it was good, and if bad, he was not in any hurry to hear it.

As more and more favorable reports arrived: Well, the agony is most over, and you will soon be able to go to bed.

At midnight, a telegram from New York announced that he had won that state by a margin of 50,000 votes. He put it in his pocket and said that: it was about time he went home and told the news to a tired woman who was sitting up for him.

Before he could leave, however, the crowd hustled him to a neighboring restaurant where refreshments were prepared. He submitted good-naturedly, saying that: as he had been in the hands of his friends for the past five months, he might as well make it one night more. —*9. {C}*

4. *The next day, he said repeatedly to callers:*

Well, boys, your troubles are over now, but mine have just commenced. — *21. {C}*

5. *One old farmer said to Lincoln that he had not voted for him but was glad that he had been elected. Lincoln replied:*

Well, my old friend, when a man has been tried and pronounced not guilty he hasn't any right to find fault with the jury. —*21. {C}*

THURLOW WEED (1797–1882)   *Editor of the Albany* Evening Journal *and longtime associate of William H. Seward in New York politics. As an Anti-Mason, then a Whig, and finally a Republican, Weed was widely regarded as the very model of a wily and unscrupulous political manager.*

1. *Weed, who had called on Lincoln after his nomination in May 1860, paid*

another visit to Springfield on December 20 for discussion of cabinet appointments and the secession crisis. Joining in the conference were Lincoln's friends David Davis and Leonard Swett. Editorially, Weed had spoken out for a policy of moderation, denouncing radical abolitionists as well as southern disunionists. Lincoln commented:

This is a heavy broadside. You have opened your fire at a critical moment, aiming at friends and foes alike. It will do some good or much mischief.

He added that: while there were some loud threats and much muttering in the cotton states, he hoped that by wisdom and forbearance the danger of serious trouble might be averted, as such dangers had been in former times. *— Weed T-3, 603-5 (1883). {C}*

2. *At another point in the conference, Lincoln remarked:*

that he did not quite like to hear southern journals and southern speakers insisting that there must be no "coercion"; that while he had no disposition to coerce anybody, yet, after he had taken an oath to execute the laws, he should not care to see them violated. *— Weed T-2, 251 (1871). {C}*

3. *When their discussion turned to the makeup of his administration, Lincoln said:*

that the making of a cabinet, now that he had it to do, was by no means as easy as he had supposed; that he had, even before the result of the election was known, assuming the probability of success, fixed upon the two leading members of his cabinet, but that in looking about for suitable men to fill the other departments, he had been much embarrassed, partly from his want of acquaintance with the prominent men of the day and partly, he believed, that while the population of the country had immensely increased, really great men were scarcer than they used to be. *— Weed T-2, 250. {C}*

4. *Lincoln said it gave him satisfaction to reflect that:*

he was coming into office unembarrassed by promises. He owed, he supposed, his exemption from importunities to the circumstance that his name as a candidate was but a short time before the people and that only a few sanguine friends anticipated the possibility of his nomination. I have not [he continued] promised an office to any man, nor have I, but in a single instance, mentally committed myself to an appointment; and as that relates to an important office in your state, I have concluded to mention it to you, under strict injunctions of secrecy, however. If I am not induced by public considerations to change my purpose, Hiram Barney will be collector of the port of New York— *Weed T-2, 255. {C}*

This would appear to be a contradiction (whether in what Lincoln said or in what Weed remembered) of the above-quoted statement that he had "fixed upon the two leading members of his cabinet" at the time of the election.

5. *Weed protested that four cabinet seats out of seven were too many to give to former Democrats. Lincoln replied that:*

as a Whig, he thought he could afford to be liberal to a section of the Republican party without whose votes he could not have been elected.

He added: You seem to forget that I expect to be there; and counting me as one, you see how nicely the cabinet would be balanced and ballasted. Besides, in talking of General Cameron, you admitted that his political status was unexceptionable. I suppose we could say of General Cameron, without offense, that he is not Democrat enough to hurt him. I remember that people used to say without disturbing my self-respect that I was not lawyer enough to hurt me. — *Weed T-2, 253–54. {C}*

6. *When Weed expressed misgivings about the appointment of Cameron, Lincoln said:*

Pennsylvania, any more than New York or Ohio, cannot be overlooked. Her strong Republican vote, not less than her numerical importance, entitles her to a representative in the cabinet. — *Weed T-3, 608. {C}*

7. *When Weed proposed Henry Winter Davis instead of Montgomery Blair, Lincoln laughingly replied:*

Davis has been posting you up on this question.[468] He came from Maryland and has got Davis on the brain. Maryland must, I think, be like New Hampshire, a good state to move from. — *Weed T-3, 607. {C}*

8. *According to Weed, his recommendation that someone from North Carolina or Tennessee be named to the cabinet met with "strong counter views" from Lincoln, who asked:*

If, contrary to our hopes, North Carolina and Tennessee should secede, could their men remain in the cabinet? Or, if they remained, of what use would they be to the government?

After further urging, Lincoln "yielded" so far as to say that: he would write a letter to the Honorable John A. Gilmer . . . briefly stating his views of the duty of the government in reference to important questions then pending, and inviting him, if those views met his approval, to accept a seat in the cabinet.

Then he added: Now, if Mr. Gilmer should come in, somebody must stay out, and that other somebody must be either Judge Blair or Mr. Bates. — *Weed T-3, 611. {D}*

Although Weed's account has generally been accepted at face value, there is reason to doubt that Lincoln was so reluctant to make such an appointment.[469]

9. *As Weed was about to take his leave, Lincoln said:*

You have not asked for any offices. . . . You have the reputation of taking time by the forelock. I was warned to be on my guard against you, and the joke of the matter is, that those who gave the warning are after offices themselves, while you have avoided the subject. — *Weed T-1, 437 (1870).*

A year later, Weed provided another version that was quite similar in its substance but very different in its wording: Some gentlemen who have been quite nervous about the object of your visit here would be surprised, if not incredulous, were I to tell them that during the two days we have passed together, you have made no application, suggestion, or allusion to appointments. . . . So much were you misunderstood that I have received telegrams from prominent Republicans warning me against your efforts to forestall important appointments in your state. Other gentlemen who have visited me since the election have expressed similar apprehensions, but I have remarked that while our friends were extremely sensitive in relation to **your** designs, they brought along an ax or two of their own to be ground. — *Weed T-2, 255. {D}*

There is bound to be some skepticism about such a self-serving recollection from the likes of Thurlow Weed.

10. *Sometime later, Lincoln told Weed that:*

immediately after his election, thinking that the Vice President, from his high character and long experience, was entitled to a voice in the cabinet, the selection of the New England man was conceded to him, and that Mr. Hamlin named "Father Welles." — *Weed T-3, 614. {C}*

11. *Soon after the outbreak of the Civil War, Lincoln spoke to Weed of his "considerable experience in belling cats" and then declared that:*

in view especially of the influence the *Herald* was exerting in Europe, he deemed it of the greatest importance that Mr. Bennett should be satisfied that the course of the *Herald* was endangering the government and Union.

He added his belief that: if Mr. Bennett could be brought to see things in that light he would change his course. — *Weed T-3, 616. {C}*

12. *A Democratic resurgence in 1862 included the election of Horatio Seymour as governor of New York. In April 1864, Weed wrote a letter to the Albany Evening Journal (with which he was no longer associated), declaring that soon after the 1862 elections, Lincoln had said to him:*

that, as the governor of the empire state and the representative man of the Democratic party, Governor Seymour had the power to render great public service; and that if he exerted that power against the rebellion and for his country, he would be our next president. — *Albany Atlas and Argus, April 16, 1864. {C}*

Weed added: "I think Mr. Lincoln authorized me to say so, from him, to Governor Seymour. At any rate, I did repeat the conversation to him." Lincoln appears to have spoken in somewhat similar terms to the Governor's brother, John F. Seymour (q.v.).

By the 1880s, when Weed was past eighty years of age, Lincoln's merely predictive and perhaps casual remark had been expanded into a definite offer. What the President had said in December 1862, as Weed now reported it to his grandson, was this: Governor Seymour has greater power just now for good than any other man in the country. He can wheel the Democratic party into line, put down rebellion, and preserve the government. Tell him for me, that if he will render this service to his country, I shall cheerfully make way for him as my successor. *—Barnes TW, 428 (1884).*[470] {D}

In the story as Weed also told it around 1880 to journalist William A. Croffut, Lincoln's language became even more emphatic: Governor Seymour could do more for our cause than any other man living. He has been elected governor of our largest state. If he would come to the front, he could control his partisans and give a new impetus to the war. I have sent for you, Mr. Weed, to ask you to go to Governor Seymour and tell him what I say. Tell him, now is his time. Tell him I do not wish to be president again, and that the leader of the other party, provided it is in favor of a vigorous war against the rebellion, should have my place. Entreat him to give the true ring to his annual message, and if he will, as he easily can, place himself at the head of a great Union party, I will gladly stand aside and help to put him in the executive chair. All we want is to have the rebellion put down. *—Rice AT, xxxi (1886).*[471] {E}

In all its mutations, this remarkable tale is incompatible with Weed's own contemporary account of the interview that he had with Seymour in December 1862.[472] *The story is rendered all the more dubious by Weed's astonishing sequel, wherein Lincoln, after being disappointed by Seymour, makes the same offer to McClellan in June 1863. Weed, of course, is his intermediary:* Tell the General that we have no wish to injure or humiliate him; that we wish only for the success of our armies; that if he will come forward and put himself at the head of a Union-Democratic party, and, through that means, push forward the Union cause, I will gladly step aside and do all I can to secure his election in 1864. *—Rice AT, xxxii. See also Barnes TW, 428-29.* {E}

McClellan, when asked by Croffut, said flatly: "Mr. Lincoln never offered me the presidency in any contingencies."[473]

13. *Lincoln summoned Weed to Washington in February 1863 and said to him:*

We are in a tight place. Some money for a legitimate war purpose is needed immediately. There is no appropriation from which it can be lawfully taken. In this perplexity the Secretary of War suggested that you should be sent for. Can you help us to $15,000? — *Weed statement in the New York* Times, *February 18, 1870. {C}*

It appears that the money was raised; for pledges of $1,000 apiece were obtained from fifteen New York businessmen. But the precise purpose of the fund has never been determined.[474]

14. *One evening in December 1863, with Weed present, Leonard Swett asked Lincoln whether he was thinking about re-election. The President replied:*

Swett, how did you know that the bee was buzzing about my ears?[475] Until very recently I expected to see the Union safe and the authority of the government restored before my term of service expired. But as the war has been prolonged, I confess that I should like to see it out in this chair. I suppose that everybody in my position finds some reason, good or bad, to gratify or excuse their ambition. — *Weed's statement in the New York* Commercial, *probably in 1867, undated clipping in the Nicolay Papers. {D}*

With a strong Chase-for-president movement being organized in December 1863, there would have been little reason for anyone to ask Lincoln such a question.

15. *Sometime after his re-election, Lincoln said to Weed:*

I expect to have more influence with this administration than I had with the last one. You thought that Mr. Seward's friends did not get their share of the patronage, and I admit that in officering the ship, the Chase men had the advantage, but hereafter I shall try to make things more even. — *Weed in the New York* Tribune, *July 5, 1878. {C}*

John P. Usher (q.v.) and others recalled the remark about influence with the administration.

16. *In February 1865, Lincoln asked Weed who should replace William P. Fessenden as secretary of the treasury. Weed suggested Senator Edwin D. Morgan of New York. Lincoln replied:*

I anticipated this name, and even if I had not intended to consult your wishes, I should have felt quite safe in trusting the matter to your judgment. I can afford to give Governor Morgan the Treasury, even though Mr. Seward has the State Department, because the Governor can be confirmed and the people will sustain the appointment. But this could not be done if a word or a whisper of it gets out. Can you and I keep the secret?

Morgan declined to serve, however, and at another conference, Weed suggested calling Charles Francis Adams home from London to take the position. Lincoln said: I have thought of that too, but will it do to have so long an interregnum? . . . will it do to let the financial department, on which so much depends, be run by deputy?

When Weed then named Senator Lafayette S. Foster, the response was: An excellent man and one whom I would readily appoint, if Connecticut were large enough to be entitled to two members of the cabinet.

As a last resort, Weed suggested Hannibal Hamlin, who was about to relinquish the office of vice president, but Lincoln dismissed that idea, saying: Hamlin has the Senate on the brain, and nothing more or less will cure him.

After that, Weed gave up, and Lincoln said: Let us fall back on Mr. McCulloch, who now seems most available.

But if we can believe Weed in this instance, Lincoln did not settle finally on Hugh McCulloch until he, Weed, had interviewed the man and found him acceptable. — Weed T-1, 437. {D}

GRENVILLE M. WEEKS (1837–1919)   *Physician and Union military surgeon who served first in the navy and then in the army.*

1. *Seeking an appointment on the medical staff of the army after having been wounded in the* Monitor's *battle with the* Merrimac, *Weeks went to the White House during a presidential reception. An officer blocked his entry and ordered him to go to the end of the line, but Lincoln intervened, saying:*

Hereafter, whether the caller is an officer or private, Major, be a gentleman.

Then to Weeks: You are wounded, sir. There's a place for you, however, if you can use your head. — *Weeks interview in the New York* Times, *June 16, 1916. {C}*

GODFREY WEITZEL (1835–1884)   *Union general who commanded the troops that entered Richmond after its evacuation by Confederate forces in early April 1865.*

1. *A controversy arose over certain formalities with respect to the reopening of churches in occupied Richmond. Replying to a telegram from Lincoln (Collected Works, VIII, 405–6), Weitzel reminded him of his advice not to insist on "little points" and of his saying that:*

you would not order me, but if you were in my place you would not press them. — *Weitzel to Lincoln, April 12, 1865, OR, Series I, Volume 46, Part III, 724. {B}*

LAWRENCE WELDON (1829–1905)   *Lawyer in Clinton, Illinois, who rode the circuit with Lincoln during the 1850s and was appointed a United States district attorney in 1861. He later served on the United States Court of Claims.*

1. *At Bloomington in 1854, Lincoln refused the offer of a drink from Douglas and said in response to his question:*

I do not in theory, but I do in fact, belong to the temperance society, in this, to wit, that I do not drink anything and have not done so for a very many years. — *Rice AT, 198 (1886). {C}*

In a more familiar but later and secondhand version, Weldon quotes Lincoln as saying:

I'm not a temperance man, but I'm temperate in this, to wit: I don't drink. —*Hill FT, 36* (1906).

2. *In* Dungey v. Spencer *at Clinton, Illinois, in September 1855, Lincoln represented the plaintiff, a dark-skinned Portuguese suing for damages because the defendant, his brother-in-law, had repeatedly called him a "nigger." Weldon, one of the defense attorneys, recalled some of Lincoln's opening argument:*

I do not believe that the best way to build up and maintain a good reputation is to go to law about it, and during my practice at the bar it has been my uniform policy to discourage slander suits. But, gentlemen, in this case, forbearance had ceased to be a virtue, and this courtroom, dedicated to the sacred cause of justice, is the only place where my client can seek protection and vindication. If the malice of the defendant had rested satisfied with speaking the words once or twice, or even thrice, my client would have borne it in silence. But when he went from house to house, gabbling, yes **gabbling** about it, then it was that my client determined to bring this suit. Gentlemen of the jury, my client is not a Negro, though it is no crime to be a Negro, no crime to be born with a black skin. But my client is not a Negro. His skin may not be as white as ours, but I say he is not a Negro, though he may be a Moor.

Dungey won his suit, whereupon defense counsel, acknowledging that Spencer had been foolish, urged Lincoln to secure partial remission of the $600 judgment. Lincoln said: Well, I will cheerfully advise my client to remit on the most favorable terms. The defendant is a fool. But he has one virtue. He is industrious and has worked hard for what he has, so I am not disposed to hold him responsible. If every fool was to be dealt with by being held responsible in money for his folly, the poorhouses of the country would have to be enlarged very much beyond their present capacity. — *Weldon, 451 (1895). {C}*

Dungey remitted two-thirds of the judgment, not all of it as Weldon recalled.[476]

3. *In the procession preceding his speech at Clinton during the campaign of 1858, someone in the crowd referred to him as "old Mr. Lincoln," and when asked how he felt about it, he replied:*

Oh, they have been at that trick many years. They commenced it when I was scarcely thirty. — *Rice AT, 198 (1886). {C}*

4. *When Weldon asked him for help with a legal paper he did not understand, Lincoln said:*

Wait until I fix this plug for my gallus [suspender], and I will pitch into that like a dog at a root. — *Rice AT, 201. {C}*

GIDEON WELLES (1802–1878)   *Connecticut editor and politician of Jacksonian background who helped found the Republican party in his state and became secretary of the navy in 1861. His diary is one of the best sources of inside information on the Lincoln administration.*[477]

1. *On March 29, 1861, after having been informed that the troops defending Fort Sumter could not hold out beyond the middle of April, Lincoln declared in cabinet meeting that:*

he would send supplies to the garrison, and if the secessionists forcibly resisted, on them would be the responsibility of initiating hostilities. This conclusion, though it conflicted in some degree with the views of the military gentlemen, he felt to be a political necessity. He could not, consistently with his convictions of his duty and with the policy which he had enunciated in his inaugural, order the evacuation of Sumter; and it would be inhuman on his part to permit the heroic garrison to be starved into a surrender without an attempt to relieve it. — *Welles-2, 47 (1870). {C}*

2. *On April 1, 1861, Welles received a letter signed by the President issuing several important orders with respect to naval organization and the disposition of naval forces. One of the orders would have placed Captain Samuel Barron, a Virginian with secessionist leanings, in a key position as head of the navy's bureau of detail.*[478] *When Welles asked Lincoln for an explanation, he expressed surprise at having sent such a document and explained:*

that Mr. Seward, with two or three young men, had been there through the day on a subject which he had in hand and had been some time maturing; that it was Seward's specialty, to which he had yielded, but as it involved considerable details, and he had his hands full and more too, he had left Mr. Seward to prepare the necessary papers, which he had signed without reading—for he had not time, and if he could not trust Seward, he knew not whom he could trust.

After further discussion, Lincoln reiterated: that they were not his instructions, that the paper was an improper one; that he wished me to give it no more attention than I thought proper—treat it as canceled or as if it had never been written. . . . He remembered that both Seward and Porter had something to say about Barron, as if he was a superior officer, perhaps, without any superior in the navy. — *Welles-1, I, 17-18. {C}*

The first chapter of the Welles diary in its published form, which covers the period of the Fort Sumter crisis, is a narrative written several years after the events described.[479]

3. *At about midnight on April 5, when Lincoln learned that conflicting*

orders had been issued assigning the warship Powhatan *both to the Fort Pickens expedition and to Captain Samuel Mercer for use in the relief of Fort Sumter, he told Seward:*

that the *Powhatan* must be restored to Mercer, that on no account must the Sumter expedition fail.

He explained to Welles: that Mr. Seward had his heart set on reinforcing Fort Pickens, and that between them, they had arranged for supplies and re-inforcements to be sent out at the same time we were fitting out for Sumter, but with no intention whatever of interfering with the latter. — *Welles-1, I, 24-25. {C}*

4. *On the question whether to appoint Edward C. Carrington (favored by Bates) or Edwin M. Stanton (favored by Seward and Chase) as United States attorney for the District of Columbia, the President said that:*

he thought it judicious to draw in as much of the Democratic element as possible, and he was willing to try Stanton, but the office came more im-mediately under the Attorney General, and he would turn the question over to him. — *Welles-1, I, 57. {C}*

Carrington was appointed.

5. *On Sunday, July 13, 1862, Welles and Seward accompanied Lincoln to the funeral of Stanton's infant child. During the carriage ride, he broached the subject of emancipation by presidential proclamation. Dwelling earnestly, says Welles, on "the gravity, importance, and delicacy of the movement," he said that:*

he had given it much thought and he had about come to the conclusion that we must free the slaves or be ourselves subdued. — *Welles-1, I, 70. {C}*

From the language, it seems clear that this entry was written anywhere from several days to several weeks after the event.

In an article published in 1872, Welles provided a far more extensive re-port of what Lincoln said on this occasion: He was convinced that we could not carry on a successful war by longer pursuing a temporizing and for-bearing policy toward those who disregarded law and Constitution and were striving by every means to break up the Union. Decisive and extreme measures must be adopted. His reluctance to meddle with this question, around which there were thrown constitutional safeguards, and on which the whole southern mind was sensitive, was great. He had tried various expedients to escape issuing an executive order emancipating the slaves, the last and only alternative, but it was forced upon him by the rebels themselves. He saw no escape. Turn which way he would, this disturbing element which caused the war rose up against us, and it was an insuperable obstacle to peace. He had entertained hopes that the border states, in view of what appeared to him inevitable if the war continued, would consent to some plan of prospective and compensated emancipation; but all his suggestions, some made as early as March, met with disfavor, although actual hostilities had then existed for a year. Congress was now about adjourning and had done nothing final and conclusive—perhaps could do nothing on this question. He had, since his return from the army the last week, called the members of Congress from the border states together and presented to them the difficulties which he encountered, in hopes they would be persuaded, in the gloomy condition of affairs, to take the initiative step toward emancipation; but they hesitated, and he apprehended would do nothing. Attached as most of them and a large majority of their constituents were to what they called their labor system, they felt it would be unjust for the government which they supported to compel them to abandon that system, while the states in flagrant rebellion retained their slaves and were spared the sacrifice. A movement toward emancipation in the border states while slavery was recognized and permitted in the rebel states would, they believed, detach many from the Union cause and strengthen the insurrection. There was, he presumed, some foundation for their apprehension. What had been done and what he had heard satisfied him that a change of policy in the conduct of the war was necessary and that emancipation of the slaves in the rebel states must precede that in the border states. The blow must fall first and foremost on them. Slavery was doomed. This war, brought upon the country by the slave-owners, would extinguish slavery, but the border states could not be induced to lead in that measure. They would not consent to be convinced or persuaded to take the first step. Forced emancipation in the states which continued to resist the government would of course be followed by voluntary emancipation in the loyal states with the aid we might give them. Further efforts with the border states would, he thought, be useless. That was not the road to lead us out of this difficulty. We must take a different path. We wanted the army to strike more vigorous blows. The administration must set the army an example and strike at the heart of the rebellion. The country, he thought, was prepared for it. The army would be with us. War had removed constitutional obligations and restrictions with the declared rebel communities. The law required us to return the fugitives who escaped to us. This we could and must do with friends, but not with enemies. We invited all, bond and free, to desert those who were in flagrant war upon the Union and come to us; and uniting with us, they must be made free from rebel authorities and rebel masters.

If there was no constitutional authority in the government to emancipate the slaves, neither was there any authority, specified or reserved, for the slaveholders to resist the government or secede from it. They could not at the same time throw off the Constitution and invoke its aid. Having made war upon the government, they were subject to the incidents and calamities of war, and it was our duty to avail ourselves of every necessary measure to maintain the Union. If the rebels did not cease their war, they must take the consequences of war. . . . He had given the subject much thought and had about come to the conclusion that it was a military necessity, absolutely essential to the preservation of the Union. We must free the slaves or be ourselves subdued. The slaves were undeniably an element of strength to those who had their service, and we must decide whether that element should be with us or against us. For a long time, the subject had lain heavy on his mind. His interview with the representatives of the border states had forced him slowly, but he believed correctly, to this conclusion. — *Welles-2, 237–39 (1872). {D}*

It would probably be wise to regard this lengthy passage as a combination of Lincoln core and Welles elaboration.

6. *In a discussion at the White House on August 15, 1862, it was said that Mark Howard of Connecticut claimed to have secured Welles's appointment. Lincoln said that:*

he had a slight acquaintance with Mr. Howard himself. Had met him in Illinois and knew [him] as a friend of mine. Had received letters from him expressing regard for me, and one signed jointly by Howard and Senator Dixon. But these gentlemen did not originate his action in relation to me. The truth is [he continued] — and I may as well state the facts to you; for others know them — on the day of the presidential election, the operator of the telegraph in Springfield placed his instrument at my disposal. I was there without leaving, after the returns began to come in until we had enough to satisfy us how the election had gone. This was about two in the morning of Wednesday. I went home, but not to get much sleep, for I then felt, as I never had before, the responsibility that was upon me. I began at once to feel that I needed support — others to share with me the burden. This was on Wednesday morning, and before the sun went down, I had made up my cabinet. It was almost the same as I finally selected. One or two changes were made, and the particular position of one or two was unsettled. My mind was fixed on Mr. Welles as the member from New England on that Wednesday. Some other names passed through my mind, and some persons were pressed upon me, but the man and the place were fixed in my mind then, as it now is. My choice was confirmed by Mr. Howard, by Senator Dixon, Preston King, Vice President Hamlin, Governor Morgan, and others, but the selection was my own and not theirs, and Mr. Howard is under a mistake in what he says. — *Welles-1, I, 81–82. {B, A}*

Other evidence suggests that Lincoln was not so firmly committed to the appointment of Welles at such an early date.[480]

7. *After the second battle of Bull Run in late August 1862, Lincoln asked Welles which general should replace Pope, and he suggested Hooker. Lincoln replied:*

I think as much as you or any other man of Hooker, but I fear he gets excited. — *Welles-1, I, 229. {C}*

Written retrospectively on January 24, 1863.

8. *At a cabinet meeting on September 2, the President confirmed that he had placed McClellan in command of the defense of Washington. He said that:*

he had done what seemed to him best. Halleck had proposed it.[481] McClellan knows this whole ground; his specialty is to defend; he is a good engineer, all admit; there is no better organizer; he can be trusted to act on the defensive; but having the slows, he is good for nothing for an onward movement.[482] — *Welles-1, I, 105. {B, A}*

Francis P. Blair, Sr. (q.v.), also recorded Lincoln's use of the word "slows" with respect to McClellan.

9. *In a talk with Welles on September 5, recorded two days later, Lincoln declared:*

I must have McClellan to reorganize the army and bring it out of chaos. But there has been a design, a purpose in breaking down Pope without regard of consequences to the country. It is shocking to see and know this, but there is no remedy at present. McClellan has the army with him. — *Welles-1, I, 113. {A}*

In a later version of the same discussion, the above quotation is preceded by Lincoln's assertion that: most of our troubles grew out of military jealousies. Whether changing the plan of operations [discarding McClellan and placing Pope in command] was wise or not, was not now the matter in hand. These things, right or wrong, had been done. If the administration had erred, the country should not have been made to suffer nor our brave men been cut down and butchered. Pope should have been sustained, but he was not. These personal and professional quarrels came in. Whatever may have been said to the contrary, it could not be denied that the army was with McClellan. He had so skillfully handled his troops in not getting to Richmond as to retain their confidence. The soldiers certainly had not transferred their confidence to Pope. He could, however, do no more good in this quarter. It was humiliating, after what had transpired and all we knew, to reward McClellan and those who failed to do their whole duty in the hour of trial, but so it was. Personal considerations must be sacrificed for the public good. He had kept aloof from the dissensions that prevailed and intended to. — *Welles-3, 197 (1874). {C}*

10. *On September 8, 1862, speaking of the two-day battle at Bull Run:*

We had the enemy in the hollow of our hands on Friday, if our generals, who are vexed with Pope, had done their duty. All of our present difficulties and reverses have been brought upon us by these quarrels of the generals. . . . Pope did well, but there was an army prejudice against him, and it was necessary he should leave. He had gone off very angry, and not without cause, but circumstances controlled us. — *Welles-1, I, 116.* {A}

11. *During the same conversation, Lincoln said that:*

Halleck selected McClellan to command the troops against the Maryland invasion.

He added: I could not have done it, for I can never feel confident that he will do anything. — *Welles-1, I, 116.* {B, A}

Despite Lincoln's assertion, it seems very unlikely that he played such a passive role in this crucial decision. Halleck (q.v.) maintained that it was Lincoln's decision to restore McClellan to field command.[483]

12. *The same day, speaking in Welles's presence to Hiram Barney, who thought the troops were becoming demoralized, Lincoln said:*

he was shocked to find that of 140,000 whom we were paying for in Pope's army, only 60,000 could be found. McClellan brought away 93,000 from the Peninsula but could not today count on over 45,000, and as regarded demoralization, there was no doubt that some of our men permitted themselves to be captured in order that they might leave on parole, get discharged, and go home. Where there is such rottenness, is there not reason to fear for the country? — *Welles-1, I, 117.* {B}

It is not clear whether the final sentence is quotation of Lincoln or comment by Welles.

13. *At a cabinet meeting on September 12, the President repeated what he had said to Welles four days earlier:*

that the selection of McClellan to command active operations was not made by him but by Halleck; and . . . that the latter was driven to it by necessity. He had arranged his army corps and designated the generals to lead each column and called on Burnside to take chief command. But Burnside declined and declared himself unequal to the position. Halleck said he consequently had no alternative but McClellan.

The officers and soldiers [Lincoln continued] were pleased with the selection, but I wish you to understand it was not made by me. McClellan has great powers of organization and discipline; he comprehends and can arrange combinations better than any of our generals, and there his usefulness ends. He can't go ahead; he can't strike a blow. He got to Rockville, for instance, on Sunday night, and in four days he advanced to Middlebrook, ten miles, in pursuit of an invading enemy. This was rapid movement for him. When he went up the Peninsula there was no reason why he should have been detained a single day at Yorktown, but he waited and gave the enemy time to gather his forces and strengthen his position. — *Welles-1, I, 124. {B, A}*

14. *At the same meeting, when Blair denounced Pope as a liar, Lincoln acknowledged the General's infirmity, but added that:*

a liar might be brave and have skill as an officer. Pope had great cunning. He had published his report, for instance, which was wrong—an offense for which, if it can be traced to him, Pope must be amenable, but it can never, by any skill, be traced to him. — *Welles-1, I, 126. {B}*

15. *On September 22, 1862, in a special cabinet meeting concerned with the Emancipation Proclamation, Lincoln stated:*

that the question was finally decided, the act and the consequences were his; but that he felt it due to us to make us acquainted with the fact and to invite criticism on the paper which he had prepared. There were, he had found, some differences in the cabinet, but he had, after consulting each and all, individually and collectively, formed his own conclusions and made his own decision.

In the course of the discussion that followed, he said that: he had made a vow, a covenant, that if God gave us the victory in the approaching battle, he would consider it an indication of divine will and that it was his duty to move forward in the cause of emancipation. It might be thought strange that he had in this way submitted the disposal of matters when the way was not clear to his mind what he should do. God had decided this question in favor of the slaves. He was satisfied it was right, was confirmed and strengthened in his action by the vow and the results. His mind was fixed, his decision made, but he wished his paper announcing his course as correct in terms as it could be made without any change in his determination.

Blair questioned the wisdom of the proclamation because of the disturbing effect it would have in the border states and because of the encouragement it would give to political enemies in the North. Lincoln replied that: he had considered the danger to be apprehended from the first objection, which was undoubtedly serious, but the objection was certainly as great not to act; as regarded the last, it had not much weight with him. — *Welles-1, I, 142–44.*[484] *{B}*

16. *Lincoln introduced the subject of colonization at a cabinet meeting on September 24:*

He thought a treaty could be made to advantage [for territory] to which the Negroes could be sent.[485] Several governments had signified their willingness to receive them.

When Bates expressed himself in favor of compulsory deportation, Lincoln objected emphatically: Their emigration must be voluntary and without expense to themselves.[486] — *Welles-1, I, 152. {B}*

17. *On November 4, 1862, when it was suggested that General Halleck should take command of the army in person, Lincoln said and the cabinet agreed:*

that Halleck would be an indifferent general in the field; that he shrank from responsibility in his present position; that he is a moral coward, worth but little except as a critic, though intelligent and educated. — *Welles-1, I, 180. {D}*

It is not clear how much of this passage is a Lincoln statement and how much is cabinet and especially Welles concurrence.

18. *At a cabinet meeting on December 19, Lincoln gave an account of his meeting the night before with a committee of the Republican senatorial caucus. He said that:*

the evening was spent in a pretty free discussion and animated conversation. No opposition was manifested towards any other member of the cabinet than Mr. Seward. Some not very friendly feelings were shown towards one or two others, but no wish that anyone should leave but the Secretary of State. Him they charged, if not with infidelity, with indifference, with want of earnestness in the war, with want of sympathy with the country in this great struggle, and with many things objectionable, and especially with a too-great ascendancy and control of the President. This was the point and pith of their complaint.

Continuing with his report, Lincoln said that: in reply to the committee, [he] stated how this movement shocked and grieved him; that the cabinet he had selected in view of impending difficulties and of all the responsibilities upon him; that the members and himself had gone on harmoniously; that there had never been serious disagreement, though there had been differences; that in the overwhelming troubles of the country which had borne heavily upon him he had been sustained and consoled by the good feeling and the mutual and unselfish confidence and zeal that pervaded the cabinet.

To the cabinet he then declared: that the movement was uncalled for, that there was no such charge, admitting all that was said, as should break up or overthrow a cabinet, nor was it possible for him to go on with a total abandonment of old friends. — *Welles-1, I, 194-95. {B}*

19. *During a combined meeting of the cabinet and the senatorial committee in the evening of the same day, Lincoln declared that all members of the cabinet, though not thinking alike on all subjects, had acquiesced in measures when once decided. He added that:*

the necessities of the times had prevented frequent and long sessions of the cabinet and the submission of every question at the meetings. — *Welles-1, I, 196.* {B}

20. *On December 20, Welles urged the President not to accept Seward's resignation, which had been offered in response to the pressure from Republican senators. Lincoln, much gratified, said that:*

if carried out as the senators prescribed, the whole government must cave in. It could not stand, could not hold water. The bottom would be out.

Later that same morning, when Chase handed his resignation to Lincoln, the latter said with a triumphant laugh: This cuts the Gordian knot. I can dispose of this subject now. I see my way clear. — *Welles-1, I, 200, 202.* {B, A}

21. *In the spring of 1863, Admiral Samuel F. Du Pont was preparing to launch an attack on Fort Sumter. Lincoln said to Welles on April 2 that:*

the long delay of Du Pont, his constant call for more ships, more ironclads, was like McClellan calling for more regiments. Thought the two men were alike, and . . . he was prepared for a repulse at Charleston. — *Welles-1, I, 259.* {B}

Eleven years later, Welles expanded this diary entry into the following quotation: He, as well as McClellan hesitates — has the slows. McClellan always wanted more regiments; Du Pont is everlastingly asking for more gunboats, more ironclads. He will do nothing with any. He has intelligence and system and will maintain a good blockade. You did well in selecting him for that command, but he will never take Sumter or get to Charleston. He is no Farragut, though unquestionably a good routine officer, who obeys orders and in a general way carries out his instructions. — *Welles-3, 200.* {C}

22. *On the same day, Welles explained his opposition to Seward's proposal for issuing letters of marque. Lincoln, he recorded in his diary, listened carefully, agreed with most of what he said, and controverted nothing (Welles-1, I, 256–59). Writing about the conversation a decade later, however, Welles recalled that Lincoln had thought privateering should be given a trial:*

Let us see who the men are that are ready and anxious to aid the government in this way; perhaps you are mistaken and Seward right. Chase, who knows or ought to know the commercial sentiment, has come into Seward's views. It may be well to make the experiment.

When Welles added a further protest, Lincoln said that: he had confidence in my judgment and my opinions, but I might be mistaken. The State and the Treasury took a different view, and if I was right in my belief that the merchants would not engage in privateering, no harm could come from the trial. If Seward was mistaken and the substantial men of the country held off, the credit would be mine, and all would then be satisfied. — *Welles-3, 162.* {D}

23. *Commenting on a disagreement between Welles and Seward over seizure of British mail from a blockade runner, the* Peterhoff, *Lincoln said on April 18:*

that the subject involved questions which he did not understand; that his object was to keep the peace; for we could not afford to take upon ourselves a war with England and France, which was threatened if we stopped their mails. — *Welles-1, I, 275–76. In the end, Lincoln sided with Seward, and the* Peterhoff's *mails were surrendered to British authorities.*[487] {B}

24. *On May 4, 1863, with the battle of Chancellorsville in progress, Lincoln met Welles at the War Department and said that:*

he had a feverish anxiety to get facts — was constantly up and down; for nothing reliable came from the front. — *Welles-1, I, 291.* {B}

25. *Shown two dispatches of Seward to the British minister regarding prize captures, Welles urged that the executive branch not intervene in such matters but leave them rather to the courts. Lincoln replied that:*

he could see I was right, but that in this instance, perhaps it would be best if I did not seriously object, that these dispatches should go on. — *Welles-1, I, 297.* {B}

26. *There was a sharp exchange between Chase and Blair on May 26, 1863, regarding enforcement of the Fugitive Slave Act in a specific case arising in the District of Columbia. The President said that:*

this was one of those questions that always embarrassed him. It reminded him of a man in Illinois who was in debt and terribly annoyed by a pressing creditor, until finally the debtor assumed to be crazy whenever the creditor broached the subject.

He continued: I have on more than one occasion, in this room, when beset by extremists on this question, been compelled to appear to be very mad. I think none of you will ever dispose of this subject without getting mad. — *Welles-1, I, 313.* {B, A}

27. *On June 14, with Lee's army on the move, Welles suggested that Hooker had an opportunity to cut it in two and perhaps capture part of it. Lincoln replied gloomily:*

that it would seem so, but that our folks appeared to know but little how things are and showed no evidence that they availed themselves of any advantage. — *Welles-1, I, 328.* {B}

28. *Concerning the recent rout of General Robert H. Milroy's division at Winchester by part of Lee's army as it advanced toward Pennsylvania, Lincoln said on June 17 that:*

this would be a capital joke [for] Orpheus C. Kerr to get hold of. He could give scope to his imagination over the terror of broken squads of panic-stricken teamsters, frightened at each other and alarming all Pennsylvania.

When someone asked who this person Kerr was, he exclaimed: Why, have you not read those papers? They are in two volumes; anyone who has not read them must be a heathen.

He added that: he had enjoyed them greatly, except when they attempted to play their wit on him, which did not strike him as very successful, but rather disgusted him. Now [said he], the hits that are given to you, Mr. Welles, I can enjoy, but I dare say they may have disgusted you while I was laughing at them. So vice versa as regards myself.

He then spoke of a poem by Kerr: that mythologically described McClellan as a monkey fighting a serpent representing the rebellion, but the joke was the monkey continually called for "more tail," "more tail," which Jupiter gave him. — *Welles-1, I, 333.* {B, A}

Ulysses S. Grant (q.v.) provided a more elaborate version of the monkey fable as told to him by Lincoln a year later.

29. *Speaking of the battle of Chancellorsville, fought in early May 1863, Lincoln said on June 20 that:*

if Hooker had been killed by the shot which knocked over the pillar that stunned him, we should have been successful. — *Welles-1, I, 336.* {B}

30. *On June 26, with Lee's army across the Potomac and advancing into Pennsylvania, Lincoln said:*

We cannot help beating them, if we have the man. How much depends in military matters on one mastermind! Hooker may commit the same fault as McClellan and lose his chance. We shall soon see, but it appears to me he can't help but win. — *Welles-1, I, 344.* {A}

31. *At a cabinet meeting on June 28, Lincoln read a telegram from Hooker asking to be relieved of command. He then said that:*

he had for several days, as the conflict became imminent, observed in Hooker the same failings that were witnessed in McClellan after the battle of Antietam—a want of alacrity to obey and a greedy call for more troops which could not and ought not to be taken from other points. He would strip Washington bare, had demanded the force at Harper's Ferry, which Halleck said could not be complied with . . . Hooker had taken umbrage at the refusal, or at all events had thought it best to give up the command. — *Welles-1, I, 348.* {B}

32. *Asked at the same meeting about General John A. Dix, a former Democratic senator now commanding the Department of Virginia, Lincoln said that:*

a blow might at this time be struck at Richmond, but [he] had not faith much could be accomplished by Dix. But, though not much of a general, there were reasons why he did not like to supersede him. — *Welles-1, I, 350.* {B}

33. *During a cabinet discussion on July 5 of the proposed visit to Washington by Alexander H. Stephens, ostensibly to discuss prisoner exchanges, but actually as a step toward negotiating peace, Lincoln said that:*

he was at first disposed to put this matter aside without many words or much thought, but a night's reflection and some remarks yesterday had modified his views. While he was opposed to having Stephens and his vessel come here, he thought it would be well to send someone, perhaps go himself, to Fortress Monroe. — *Welles-1, I, 359.* {B}

The cabinet opposed any such action, and Stephens was neither received in Washington nor parleyed with elsewhere at this time.

34. *The President said despondently on July 7 that:*

Meade still lingered at Gettysburg, when he should have been at Hagerstown or near the Potomac to cut off the retreating army of Lee. While unwilling to complain, and willing and anxious to give all praise to the General and army for the great battle and victory, he feared the old idea of driving the rebels out of Pennsylvania and Maryland, instead of capturing them, was still prevalent among the officers. He hoped this was not so, had spoken to Halleck and urged that the right tone and spirit should be infused into officers and men, and General Meade specially reminded of his wishes and expectations. But General Halleck gave him a short and curt reply, showing that he did not participate and sympathize in this feeling, and [said Lincoln] I drop the subject. . . . It being strictly a military question, it is proper I should defer to Halleck, whom I have called here to counsel, advise, and direct me in these matters, where he is an expert. — *Welles-1, I, 363–64.* {B, A}

35. *Later that same day, Welles returned to the White House with the news that Vicksburg had fallen. Lincoln threw his arm around him and exclaimed:*

What can we do for the Secretary of the Navy for this glorious intelligence? He is always giving us good news. I cannot, in words, tell you my joy over this result. It is great, Mr. Welles, it is great! — *Welles-1, I, 364.* {A}

36. *By July 14, it had become plain that Lee's army was crossing the Potomac back into Virginia without serious hindrance. Lincoln said to Welles:*

that he had dreaded, yet expected this; that there has seemed to him for a full week a determination that Lee should escape with his force and plunder. And that, my God [he continued], is the last of this Army of the Potomac! There is bad faith somewhere. Meade has been pressed and urged, but only one of his generals was for an immediate attack, was ready to pounce on

Lee; the rest held back. What does it mean, Mr. Welles? Great God! what does it mean?

But when Welles suggested that he should have issued peremptory orders, Lincoln softened his tone and said that: Halleck knew better than he what to do. He was a military man, had a military education. He had brought him here to give him [the President] military advice. His views and mine [Lincoln continued] are widely different. It is better that I, who am not a military man, should defer to him, rather than he to me. — *Welles-1, I, 370–71. {B, A}*

37. *Declaring at a cabinet meeting on July 17 that he was not yet ready to give up on Meade, Lincoln added:*

He has committed a terrible mistake, but we will try him farther. — *Welles-1, I, 374. {A}*

38. *In response to a question from Welles on July 26, 1863:*

Well, to be candid, I have no faith that Meade will attack Lee; nothing looks like it to me. I believe he can never have another as good opportunity as that which he trifled away. Everything since has dragged with him. No, I don't believe he is going to fight. — *Welles-1, I, 383. {A}*

Many years later, the journalist William A. Croffut quoted the journalist A. Homer Byington as having been told by Welles that he heard Lincoln say directly to Meade at a cabinet meeting: Do you know, General, what your attitude towards Lee for a week after the battle of Gettysburg reminded me of? . . . I'll be hanged if I could think of anything else than an old woman trying to shoo her geese across a creek. — *Croffut's correspondence in the St. Paul and Minneapolis* Pioneer Press, *December 7, 1884. {D}*

This familiar Lincoln quotation is very dubious stuff, not only because of its totem-pole provenance, but also because it seems unlikely that Lincoln would have spoken so demeaningly to his commanding general or that Welles would have failed to record such a remark in his diary along with his account of Meade's visit (Welles-1, I, 404).

39. *When Welles protested that the administration was yielding too much to Britain on naval matters, Lincoln replied that:*

he thought it for our interest to strengthen the present ministry and would therefore strain a point in that direction. — *Welles-1, I, 409. {B}*

40. *Lincoln was disturbed about interference with the draft by certain state judges, including Walter H. Lowrie, chief justice of the Pennsylvania supreme court. At a cabinet meeting on September 14, 1863, he intimated that:*

he would not only enforce the law, but if Judge Lowrie and others continued to interfere, he would send them after Vallandigham. As considerable discussion had taken place, he was prepared to act, though willing to listen to and, if mistaken, to defer to others. —*Welles-1, I, 432. {B}*

41. *On the afternoon immediately following the battle of Chickamauga (September 19-20, 1863), Lincoln told Welles that:*

a dispatch was sent to him at the Soldiers' Home shortly after he got asleep and so disturbed him that he had no more rest, but arose and came to the city and passed the remainder of the night awake and watchful. —*Welles-1, I, 438. {B}*

42. *The same day, responding to a question from Welles, Lincoln said that he could not learn that Meade was doing anything or wanted to do anything. He then continued:*

It is the same old story of this Army of the Potomac. Imbecility, inefficiency—don't want to **do**—is defending the Capital. . . . Oh, it is terrible, terrible, this weakness, this indifference of our Potomac generals, with such armies of good and brave men. . . . What can I do, with such generals as we have? Who among them is any better than Meade? To sweep away the whole of them from the chief command would cause a shock and be likely to lead to combinations and troubles greater than we now have. I see all the difficulties as you do. They oppress me. —*Welles-1, I, 439-40. {A}*

43. *The autumn elections of 1863 included an Ohio gubernatorial contest in which the notorious Clement L. Vallandigham was the nominee of the antiwar Democrats. Lincoln was greatly cheered by the returns and on October 14 told Welles that:*

he had more anxiety in regard to the election results of yesterday than he had in 1860 when he was chosen. He could not have believed four years ago that one genuine American would or could be induced to vote for such a man as Vallandigham; yet he has been made the candidate of a large party, their representative man, and has received a vote that is a discredit to the country. —*Welles-1, I, 470. {B}*

44. *Speaking of an article on administration policy in the* North American Review, *Lincoln said that he thought it:*

very excellent, except that it gave him overmuch credit.[488] —*Welles-1, I, 504. {B}*

45. *A conversation at the White House on January 8, 1864, became anecdotal, and Lincoln mentioned that:*

he was selected by the people of Springfield to deliver a eulogy on the death of Mr. Clay, of whom he had been a warm admirer. This he found to be difficult writing so as to make an address of fifty minutes. In casting about for the material, he had directed his attention to what Mr. Clay had himself done in the line of eulogy and was struck with the fact that, though renowned as an orator and speaker, he had never made any effort of the sort, and the only specimen he could find was a few lines on the death of Mr. Calhoun. Referring to the subject and this fact on one occasion when Seward was present, that gentleman remarked that the failure was characteristic and easily accounted for. Mr. Clay's self-esteem was so great that he could tolerate no commendation of others, eulogized none but the dead, and would not himself speak in laudatory terms of a contemporary. — *Welles-1, I, 506–7.* {B}

46. *The Spanish reannexation of Santo Domingo in 1861 remained an embarrassing diplomatic problem for the United States throughout the war. To resist it or to recognize it would cause trouble, either with Spain or with American blacks and their abolitionist supporters. During a discussion of the subject at a cabinet meeting on February 2, 1864, Lincoln remarked that:*

the dilemma reminded him of the interview between two Negroes, one of whom was a preacher endeavoring to admonish and enlighten the other. "There are," said Josh, the preacher, "two roads for you, Joe. Be careful which you take. One ob dem leads straight to hell; de odder go right to damnation." Joe opened his eyes under the impressive eloquence and awful future and exclaimed, "Josh, take which road you please; I go troo de wood." I am not disposed [continued the President] to take any new trouble just at this time and shall neither go for Spain nor the Negro in this matter, but shall take to the woods. — *Welles-1, I, 519–20.* {B, A}

When Welles later recorded this story in slightly different language, he added a concluding line from Lincoln: We will maintain an honest and strict neutrality. — *Welles-3, 184.* {C}

47. *As the cabinet was about to meet on February 19, a plump lady from Dubuque, Iowa, pressed forward, saying that she had come to have a look at President Lincoln. He responded with a laugh:*

Well, in the matter of looking at one another, I have altogether the advantage. — *Welles-1, I, 528.* {A}

48. *After listening to a denunciation of General Nathaniel P. Banks, whose Red River campaign had ended disastrously, Lincoln said that:*

he had rather cousined up to Banks, but for some time past had begun to think he was erring.

He then recited some lines from Thomas Moore's Lalla Rookh *beginning:* "Oh, ever thus, from childhood's hour, I've seen my fondest hopes decay." — *Welles-1, II, 26.* {B}

49. *Having talked with a certain Charles Atkinson about trade with the Confederacy, Lincoln said during a cabinet meeting on July 5, 1864, that:*

Mr. Atkinson had impressed him with some very striking facts. The most prominent was that although the rebels sold less cotton, they received about as much for it in consequence of [the] high price as when they had more. . . . [He] thought it might be well to take measures to secure the cotton, but was opposed to letting the rebels have gold. — *Welles-1, II, 66.* {B}

50. *On August 8, Lincoln had a conversation with Welles and Blair about the Wade-Davis manifesto, which denounced his pocket veto of the Wade-Davis reconstruction bill. He said that:*

he had not and probably should not read it. From what was said of it, he had no desire to, could himself take no part in, such a controversy as they seemed to wish to provoke. — *Welles-1, II, 98.* {B}

51. *After a quarrel with Horace Greeley over publication of their correspondence respecting the Niagara Falls peace conference,*[489] *Lincoln said at the cabinet meeting on August 19, 1864:*

In early life, and with few mechanics and but little means in the West, we used to make our shoes last a great while with much mending, and sometimes, when far gone, we found the leather so rotten the stitches would not hold. Greeley is so rotten that nothing can be done with him. He is not truthful; the stitches all tear out. — *Welles-1, II, 112.* {A}

52. *Going to the White House on August 25, Welles found the President making a statement to several men about some document of his. He said that:*

he supposed his style was peculiar and had its earmarks, so that it could not be mistaken. — *Welles-1, II, 119.* {B}

53. *Trade with the South was again a subject of cabinet discussion on September 5. The President said that:*

extensive regions lay open where neither party was in possession, where there was an abundance of cotton which the parties or owners would bring forward, but the moment the cotton appeared, approaching a market, it was immediately seized and appropriated by our own soldiers and others. It was plunder. He desired to correct this and wished Mr. Fessenden to so modify and so shape his regulations as to effect this. — *Welles-1, II, 139.* {B}

54. *At a special cabinet meeting on September 17 devoted to the subject of abandoned plantations, Lincoln said that:*

he wished some means devised to relieve him from these questions. He could not undertake to investigate them. — *Welles-1, II, 150.* {B}

55. *In a discussion with Welles on November 23 about the appointment of a chief justice, Lincoln said that:*

there was a great pressure and a good many talked of, but that he had not prepared his message [to Congress] and did not intend to take up the subject of judge before the session commenced.

He added: There is a tremendous pressure just now for Evarts of New York, who I suppose is a good lawyer. — *Welles-1, II, 181.* {B, A}

56. *At a cabinet meeting on November 25, Usher alluded to the gold forthcoming from certain western territories. Lincoln said that:*

he had been giving that subject a good deal of attention, and he was opposed to any excitement on the subject. He proposed that the gold should remain in the mountains until the war was over; for it would now only add to the currency and we had already too much currency. It would be better to stop than to increase it. — *Welles-1, II, 180.* {B}

57. *Concerning a young woman of Confederate sympathies who wanted to rejoin her fiancé in Richmond after a separation of three years, the President said that:*

he would give her a pass. . . . The war had depopulated the country and prevented marriages enough, and if he could do a kindness of this sort, he was disposed to, unless I advised otherwise. — *Welles-1, II, 208.* {B}

58. *Attorney General James Speed suggested on January 6, 1865, that the Confederates would soon begin to enlist their slaves and even make officers of them. Lincoln replied that:*

when they had reached that stage the cause of war would cease and hostilities with it. The evil would cure itself. — *Welles-1, II, 222.* {B}

59. *At the cabinet meeting on January 17, 1865, Lincoln says that:*

he is amused with the manners and views of some who address him, who tell him that he is now re-elected and can do just as he is a mind to, which means that he can do some unworthy thing which the person who addresses him has a mind to. — *Welles-1, II, 227.* {B}

60. *As the war neared its end, Lincoln expected Confederate leaders to flee the country, and, says Welles, he often expressed a wish that:*

they might be facilitated in their escape and no strenuous efforts made to prevent their egress. — *Welles-2, 184 (1872).* {C}

61. *On March 3, the day before his second inauguration, Lincoln gave notice that he intended to appoint Hugh McCulloch as secretary of the treasury. He added:*

that doing this rendered a change necessary or essential in the Interior, concerning which he already had had conversation with Mr. Usher and should have more to say; that in regard to the other gentlemen of the cabinet, he wished none of them to resign, at least for the present; for he contemplated no resignation. — *Welles-1, II, 251.* {B}

McCulloch and Usher were both Indianians. The tradition against having more than one cabinet member from a single state gave Lincoln a good excuse for removing the mediocre Usher.

62. *On April 12 and 13, Lincoln talked with Welles about the strategy of calling the Virginia legislature together. Welles opposed it, believing that such a hostile assemblage might conspire against federal authority. Lincoln said he had no fear of that:*

They were too badly beaten, too much exhausted. His idea was that the members of the legislature, being the prominent and influential men of their respective counties, had better come together and undo their own work. He felt assured they would do this, and the movement he believed a good one. Civil government must be reestablished as soon as possible. There must be courts and law and order, or society would be broken up, the disbanded armies would turn into robber bands and guerrillas, which we must strive to prevent. These were the reasons why he wished them to come together and turn themselves and their neighbors into good Union men. But as we all took a different view, he had perhaps made a mistake, and was ready to correct it if he had.[490] — *Welles-1, II, 279–80. {B}*

63. *At the cabinet meeting on April 14, 1865, Stanton announced that he had drafted a plan for reconstruction and submitted it to the President. Lincoln said that:*

he proposed to bring forward that subject, although he had not had time as yet to give much attention to the details of the paper which the Secretary of War had given him only the day before; but that it was substantially, in its general scope, the plan which we had sometimes talked over in cabinet meetings. We should probably make some modifications, prescribe further details. There were some suggestions which he should wish to make, and he desired all to bring their minds to the question; for no greater or more important one could come before us or any future cabinet. He thought it providential that this great rebellion was crushed just as Congress had adjourned and there were none of the disturbing elements of that body to hinder and embarrass us. If we were wise and discreet, we should reanimate the states and get their governments in successful operation, with order prevailing and the Union reestablished, before Congress came together in December. This he thought important. We could do better, accomplish more without than with them. There were men in Congress who, if their motives were good, were nevertheless impracticable and who possess feelings of hate and vindictiveness in which he did not sympathize and could not participate. He hoped there would be no persecution, no bloody work, after the war was over. None need expect he would take any part in hanging or killing those men, even the worst of them. Frighten them out of the

country, open the gates, let down the bars, scare them off. . . . Enough lives
have been sacrificed. We must extinguish our resentments if we expect harmony and union. There was too much of a desire on the part of some of our
very good friends to be masters, to interfere with and dictate to those states,
to treat the people not as fellow citizens. There was too little respect for
their rights. He did not sympathize in these feelings. Louisiana had framed
and presented one of the best constitutions that had ever been formed. He
wished they had permitted Negroes who had property, or could read, to
vote; but this was a question which they must decide for themselves. Yet
some, a very few of our friends, were not willing to let the people of the
states determine these questions, but, in violation of first and fundamental
principles, would exercise arbitrary power over them. These humanitarians
break down all state rights and constitutional rights. Had the Louisianians
inserted the Negro in their constitution, and had that instrument been in
all other respects the same, Mr. Sumner would never have excepted to that
constitution. The delegation would have been admitted, and the state all
right. Each house of Congress had the undoubted right to receive or reject
members; the executive had no control in this matter. But Congress had
nothing to do with the state governments, which the President could recognize and under existing laws, treat as other states, give them the same
mail facilities, collect taxes, appoint judges, marshals, collectors, and so
forth, subject, of course, to confirmation. There were men who objected
to these views, but they were not here, and we must make haste to do our
duty before they came here. — Welles-2, 190–92 (1872). {D}

*There is only slight basis in the Welles diary for this long passage recollected
seven years later. It may well be a blend of Lincoln's last remarks on restoration
of the Union and Welles's increasingly sour view of Radical Reconstruction.*[491]

64. *At that same cabinet meeting, it was noted that there had been no recent word from Sherman in North Carolina, where his army faced the most
important Confederate force still in the field. The President remarked that:*

it would, he had no doubt, come soon, and come favorable, for he had
last night the usual dream which he had preceding nearly every great and
important event of the war. Generally, the news had been favorable which
succeeded this dream, and the dream itself was always the same.

Asked for details, he said: that he seemed to be in some singular, indescrib-
able vessel, and that he was moving with great rapidity.[492] That he had this
dream preceding Sumter, Bull Run, Antietam, Gettysburg, Stone[s] River,
Vicksburg, Wilmington, etc.

After some discussion, he continued: I had this strange dream again last night,
and we shall, judging from the past, have great news very soon. I think it

must be from Sherman. My thoughts are in that direction, as are most of yours. — *Welles-1, II, 282–83. {B, A}*

Welles wrote this entry three days later, after the assassination. Frederick W. Seward (q.v.), who attended the cabinet meeting, later recalled the President's telling about the dream.

M. WENTWORTH   *A contributor to* Putnam's Magazine *whose good faith, according to an editorial footnote, was "well endorsed." She claimed that for a number of days, with Lincoln's permission, she listened and took notes as he received a great variety of importunate persons in the executive chamber. Here are two selections from what is, for the most part, dubious material.*

   1. *To one petitioner:*

No, no, I cannot! I cannot, good woman—I cannot! I might grant such requests a thousand a day. I can't turn the government inside out and upside over. I can't please everybody. I must do my duty, stern duty, as I see it. Nobody wants their friends drafted. Nobody wants them taken as deserters. He should not have been absent so long. He should not have taken upon himself the appearance of a deserter. — *Wentworth, 529 (1870). {D}*

   2. *To a visitor who spoke of the danger of assassination:*

I do not consider that I have ever accomplished anything without God; and if it is His will that I must die by the hand of an assassin, I must be resigned. I must do my duty as I see it and leave the rest with God. I go to amusements very much against my inclinations. I go simply because I must have change. I laugh because I must not weep; that's all—that's all. —*533. {D}*

WILLIAM A. WHEELER (1819–1887)   *New York Republican, a member of Congress during the first half of the Civil War and later vice president in the administration of Rutherford B. Hayes.*

   1. *Having been awakened by Wheeler and a companion to suspend the execution of a soldier, Lincoln went impatiently to the War Department to await the acknowledgment of his order. When it came, he said:*

Now you just telegraph that mother that her boy is safe, and I will go home and go to bed. I guess we shall all sleep better for this night's work. — *Wheeler's communication to the Malone (N.Y.)* Palladium, *reprinted in the New York* Times, *May 10, 1885. {D}*

Another folkloric story of a sleeping sentinel not yet out of his teens and his widowed mother's only son.

   2. *Wheeler, after a frustrating argument with Edwin M. Stanton over an appointment approved by Lincoln, asked the President which was the paramount power in the government, he or the Secretary of War. Lincoln replied:*

Well, it is generally **supposed** I am. —*Ibid. {D}*

Wheeler dated the incident late November 1861, but Stanton did not become secretary of war until the following January.[493]

HENRY B. WHIPPLE (1822–1901) *Protestant Episcopal Bishop in Minnesota, a leading crusader for reform of the Indian system.*

　　1. After Whipple described the mistreatment of the Indians in some detail, Lincoln said:

Did you ever hear of the southern man who bought monkeys to pick cotton? They were quick; their long, slim fingers would pull out the cotton faster than Negroes; but he found it took two overseers to watch one monkey. This Indian business needs ten honest men to watch one Indian agent. —*Whipple HB, 438 (1890). {C}*

HORACE WHITE (1834–1916) *Journalist who covered the Lincoln-Douglas debates for the Chicago* Press and Tribune; *later associated with Edwin L. Godkin in the management of the New York* Post *and the* Nation.

　　1. At the office of the Illinois State Journal, *where White was reading proof of the House-Divided speech after its delivery on June 16, 1858, Lincoln said:*

that he had taken a great deal of pains with this speech and that he wanted it to go before the people just as he had prepared it. —*White's essay in Herndon-2nd, II, 92 (1913). {C}*

Nevertheless, the Journal's *printing of the speech contained a major error of transposition that found its way even into the* Collected Works.[494]

　　2. On the same occasion, Lincoln told White:

that some of his friends had scolded him a good deal about the opening paragraph and the "house divided against itself" and wanted him to change it or leave it out altogether, but that he believed he had studied this subject more deeply than they had and that he was going to stick to that text whatever happened. —*Herndon-2nd, II, 92. {C}*

In a later version, White quoted Lincoln as saying: that he had been urged by his friends in Springfield not to use the words, "this government cannot endure permanently half slave and half free" because the phrase would be misinterpreted and misrepresented and would probably cause his defeat in the election, but that his mind was made up and he was determined to use those very words, because they were true and because the time had come to say so. He would rather be defeated in the election than keep silent or half silent any longer. —*White, 16 (1914). {D}*

This recollection may be regarded as corroborating, or as merely echoing, the earlier testimony of William H. Herndon, with which White was familiar. The quixotism of the final sentence is not in accord with Lincoln's intense desire to capture Douglas's seat in the Senate.

3. *Lincoln spoke at Beardstown on August 12, 1858, and the next day White asked him to write out his concluding apostrophe to the Declaration of Independence. Lincoln replied:*

that he had but a faint recollection of any portion of the speech; that, like all his campaign speeches, it was necessarily extemporaneous; and that its good or bad effect depended upon the inspiration of the moment.

He added: that I had probably overestimated the value of the remarks referred to.

White thereupon wrote out the peroration from memory with, he thought, "absolute fidelity as to ideas and commendable fidelity as to language." He read it to Lincoln, who said: Well, those are my views, and if I said anything on the subject I must have said substantially that, but not nearly so well as that is said. — *White to Herndon, May 17, 1865 (7:52-55), Herndon-Weik Collection.[495] {D}*

A cloud of doubt hangs over White's story because the passage as presented in the Press and Tribune *was associated with Lincoln's speech at Lewistown on August 17, rather than the speech at Beardstown on the 12th, and the correspondent providing it signed himself "G.P." Both in 1858 and in 1860, the passage was widely quoted in the Republican press.[496]*

4. *Presumably at some time during the campaign of 1858, Lincoln remarked to White that:*

he had never taken a drink of any alcoholic beverage in the past twenty years. — *White to Jesse W. Weik, December 14, 1913 (13:1056-58), Herndon-Weik Collection. {C}*

5. *One day, White asked Lincoln how he managed to make his speeches more varied than those of Douglas. He said that:*

for his own part, he could not repeat a speech the second time, although he might make one bearing some similarity to a former one. The subject with which he was charged was crowding for utterance all the time; it was always enlarging as he went on from place to place.

He added: that Douglas was not lacking in versatility, but that he had formed a theory that the speech which he was delivering at his small meetings was the one best adapted to secure votes, and since the voters at one meeting would not be likely to hear him at any other, they would never know that he was repeating himself, or if they did know, they would probably think that it was the proper thing to do. — *White, 29. {C}*

6. *At another time, White noted the scarcity of humor in Lincoln's speeches and asked why he did not oftener "turn the laugh" on Douglas. He replied:*

that he was too much in earnest and that it was doubtful whether turning the laugh on anybody really gained any votes. — *Herndon-2nd, 101-2. {C}*

HENRY C. WHITNEY (1831–1905) *Lawyer of New England background who settled in Urbana, Illinois, in 1854 and for several years rode the judicial circuit with Lincoln. Decades later, after his somewhat checkered legal career was interrupted in a Chicago courtroom by gunfire that left him seriously wounded, Whitney took up Lincoln biography, resolved to "work the business part of it for all it is worth." Before long, he had produced a rambling, inflated book that nevertheless came to be widely regarded as the best account by a contemporary of Lincoln's life on the circuit. Like many other recollective writers, Whitney tended to exaggerate the degree of his intimacy with Lincoln and to remember past events with mingled accuracy and inaccuracy. His credibility is also impaired by considerable evidence of a readiness at times to supplement memory with deliberate invention.[497] Furthermore, some of Whitney's letters reveal an animosity toward Lincoln that is suppressed in his published writings.[498]*

1. *In court at Bloomington in 1854 or 1855, Judge David Davis expressed surprise at the length of a document that had been drafted by a somewhat indolent lawyer. Lincoln said:*

It's like the lazy preacher that used to write long sermons, and the explanation was, he got to writing and was too lazy to stop. — *Whitney-1, 44 (1892); also told in Whitney to Jesse W. Weik, September 17, 1887 (12:385–88), Herndon-Weik Collection. {C}*

2. *During a discussion one night of possible flaws in America's greatest hero:*

Let us believe, as in the days of our youth, that Washington was spotless; it makes human nature better to believe that one human being was perfect: that human perfection is possible. — *Whitney-1, 45–46. {C}*

3. *Whitney once heard Lincoln say:*

that all other pleasures had a utility, but that music was simply a pleasure and nothing more, and that he fancied that the Creator, after providing all the mechanism for carrying on the world, made music as a simple, unalloyed pleasure, merely as such. — *Whitney-1, 156. {C}*

4. *Writing to Herndon in 1866, Whitney recalled being told by Lincoln:*

that he had taken you in as a partner, supposing that you had system and would keep things in order, but that you would not make much of a lawyer; but that he found that you had no more system than he had, but that you were a fine lawyer, so that he was doubly disappointed. — *Whitney's undated statement probably written in November 1866, Herndon-Springer, II, 426–33; published with some changes in Herndon, II, 313. {C}*

5. *On his financial arrangements with Herndon:*

Billy and I never had the scratch of a pen between us; we just divide as we go along. — *Whitney-1, 460. {C}*

6. *After his visit to Cincinnati in September 1855 for the McCormick reaper trial, Lincoln said of the presiding judge, Justice John McLean:*

He has considerable vigor of mind, but not the least discrimination. If you were to point your finger at him and also a needle, he wouldn't know which was the sharper. — *Whitney-1, 185; also in Whitney to Weik, September 17, 1887 (12:385–88), Herndon-Weik Collection. {C}*

In Herndon, II, 356, Herndon quotes similar words, implying that they were said to him.

7. *As an example of Lincoln's tendency sometimes to indulge in "flimsy reasoning," Whitney recalled hearing him tell this prosaic story:*

I went out to the commons [outskirts] to drive up my cow. She was a new cow and I didn't know her thoroughly, but I did know her calf. I could not pick out my cow from other cows who resembled each other, but I knew my calf, and so I waited a little while, and my calf went to a cow and sucked her, and in that way I knew it was my cow. — *Whitney to Herndon, June 23, 1887 (10:2151–56), Herndon-Weik Collection. {C}*

8. *Among a group of lawyers, Lincoln raised a question about court procedure addressed to no one in particular. It was Judge David Davis who replied, and Lincoln said with a laugh:*

I asked that question hoping that you would answer. I have that very question to present to the court in the morning, and I am glad to find out that the court is on my side. — *Whitney-2, 180 (1907). {C}*

9. *Of lawyer and judge T. Lyle Dickey, Lincoln remarked:*

He can draw such fine distinctions where I can't see any distinction; yet I have no doubt a distinction does exist. — *Whitney-2, 183. {C}*

10. *At Bloomington on May 28, 1856, the eve of the state Republican convention, Lincoln watched the arrival of delegates from Chicago and remarked:*

That's the best sign yet. Judd is there, and he's a trimmer. — *Whitney-1, 75. {D}*

Norman B. Judd had not been a "trimmer" in Illinois antislavery politics, and there was no reason to doubt that he would attend the convention, which, in fact, elected him chairman of the state central committee.

11. *At the Republican national convention in June 1856, Lincoln received 110 votes on an informal first ballot for the vice-presidential nomination. When the news reached him, he said:*

I reckon that ain't me; there's another great man in Massachusetts named Lincoln, and I reckon it's him. — *Whitney-1, 80, elaborated from Whitney's undated statement, Herndon-Springer, II, 426–33. {D}*

*If Lincoln made this remark, he was probably joking. Levi Lincoln of Massa-
chusetts was 73 years old at the time.*

　12. *On the way to deliver a political address in 1856, Lincoln said:*

I do wish it was through. When I have to speak, I always feel nervous till
I get well into it. . . . I hide it as well as I can, but it's just as I tell you. —
Whitney-1, 37. {C}

*Whitney, perhaps mistakenly, placed the speech at a church in Champaign
(West Urbana).*[499] *In another version, he gave the date as 1857:* I wish it was
over. . . . When I have to make a speech, I always want it over. — *Whitney's
undated statement, Herndon-Springer, II, 426–33.*

　13. *Avoiding a seat at the head of a dinner table, Lincoln said with a chuckle:*

Let Whitney run the carving. — *Whitney-2, 168.* {C}

　14. *During a procession into Monticello in 1858, Lincoln pulled Whitney
into his carriage and exclaimed:*

I'm mighty glad you are here. I hate to be stared at, all by myself; I've been a
great man such a mighty little time that I'm not used to it yet. — *Whitney-1,
37.* {C}

　15. *Introduced at the Centralia railroad station to a woman who professed
to be a great admirer of Henry Clay, Lincoln said:*

Howdo! Howdo! I don't know how to talk to ladies. — *Whitney-1, 37.* {C}

　16. *At some time or other, Whitney declared that he did not like Judd because of the latter's opposition to Lincoln in the senatorial contest of 1855.
Lincoln replied:*

I can't harbor enmity to any one; it's not my nature. — *Whitney-1, 143.* {C}

　17. *At another time, Lincoln said of Judd and Charles H. Ray (editor of
the Chicago* Press and Tribune*):*

Judd and Ray and those fellows think I don't see anything, but I see all
around them; I see better what they want to do with me than they do
themselves. — *Whitney-1, 147.* {C}

　18. *On January 5, 1859, the day that the Illinois legislature re-elected
Douglas to the Senate, Whitney visited Lincoln's office and found him, he says,
"steeped in the bitter waters of hopeless despair." During the many hours they
sat together in gloomy companionship, Lincoln said:*

I expect everyone to desert me except Billy. — *Whitney to Herndon, July 18,
1887 (10:2163–64), Herndon-Weik Collection.* {D}

*Whitney provided several other accounts of this session with a man allegedly
sunk in despondency, and his description has served more than one writer as an
illustration of Lincoln's depressive tendencies.*[500] *But the accounts are far from*

consistent, and there is a wealth of contemporary evidence indicating that the story is questionable.[501] *Far from remaining downcast after his defeat in the November election, Lincoln was soon urging his political associates to cheer up and gird themselves for the next battle two years ahead. Furthermore, his own future looked bright in January 1859; for he had established a national reputation in the contest with Douglas and was already being talked of as a presidential candidate. Whitney himself recalled that at a meeting of Republican strategists the very next evening (January 6, 1859), Lincoln's presidential prospects were discussed.*[502] *Herndon, it is true, likewise recalled a remark from Lincoln about being deserted by everyone "except Billy," but he placed it some two months earlier, and he also wrote that Lincoln came out of the 1858 campaign "a new man, vigorous, healthy, fresh as a young man, better colored, more elastic, more cheerful, less sad, stronger and improved every way."*[503]

19. *At Chicago in April 1860, after a ten-minute conversation with Mayor John Wentworth, Lincoln reported to Whitney:*

He had a long story to tell me about Judd and others designing to spring Trumbull on the convention for president and dropping me. Finally I asked him what I could do about it — I saw that he expected me to do something — and he said *sotto voce*: "Do like Seward does, get some one to **run** you." . . . I gave him no encouragement at all. I merely told him that events, and not a man's own exertions in his behalf, made presidents.

When Whitney remarked on the skill with which Wentworth had organized his mayoral campaign, Lincoln said: Yes, on a small field, which he can reach and superintend in person, he is a great organizer. — *Whitney-1, 146–47. {C}*

On October 17, 1861, according to Hay-1, 29, Lincoln himself told Seward and others of having such a conversation with Wentworth, but he placed it in Springfield, rather than in Chicago.

20. *One morning in February 1861, we are told, Whitney called on the President-elect, learned that he was at a local hotel talking with Edward Bates, waited until he returned home, and was then asked to accompany him on his trip that very day over to Charleston in Coles County for a farewell visit with his stepmother. Whitney agreed to go part of the way, and as they walked to the station, Lincoln said:*

I'm worrying some to know what to do with my house. I don't want to sell myself out of a home, and if I rent it, it will be pretty well used up before I get back.

While waiting for the train, he remarked to the railroad superintendent: You are a heap better off running a good road than I am playing president. When I first knew Whitney, I was getting on well. I was clean out of politics and contented to stay so; I had a good business and my children were coming up, and were interesting to me; but now, here I am . . .

And, says Whitney, "he broke off abruptly, as if his feelings overpowered him."
— Whitney-1, 495–96. {E}

The factual errors and improbabilities in this bit of reminiscence nourish the suspicion that it is outright invention.[504]

21. *After his secret passage through Baltimore in February 1861, Lincoln told Whitney:*

I do not think I should have been killed, or even that a serious attempt would have been made to kill me unless some excitement had arisen; but Judd and other cool heads thought I had better take the course I did, and I reckon they were right. It ain't best to run a risk of any consequence for looks' sake. — *Whitney-2, 306. {C}*

22. *On March 5, 1861, Whitney recalled, he heard Lincoln complain of the patronage pressure being applied by David Davis:*

There's Davis, with that way of making a man do a thing whether he wants to or not, has forced me to appoint Archy Williams judge in Kansas right off and John Jones to a place in the State Department, and I have got a bushel of dispatches from Kansas wanting to know if I'm going to fill up **all** the offices from Illinois. — *Whitney to Herndon, June 23, 1887 (10:2151–56), Herdon-Weik Collection.*[505]

Whitney-1, 582–83, contains another version, with the date changed to March 8 and the following sentence added: It's an awful thing to say, but I wish I was back home and somebody else was here in my place. {D}

This passage reflects an anti-Davis bias sometimes visible in Whitney's writing, although in 1861, he himself tried assiduously to obtain a federal appointment through Davis's influence. Lincoln eventually made him an army paymaster.[506]

23. *Besides receiving several delegations and other visitors on July 26, 1861, Lincoln presided over a cabinet meeting that lasted more than four hours. Yet, according to Whitney, he called at the White House on no particular business and spent the entire afternoon alone with the President, except for a brief inter-ruption by Seward.*[507] *Concerning the recent disaster at Bull Run, Lincoln is said to have declared:*

Here is the topographical engineers' map that we planned the battle by. I gave Scott my views. I showed him the enemies' forces, their positions and entrenchments, their railway facilities, capacities for reinforcing, and what Johns[t]on might do. I particularly tried to impress on him the disadvan-tage Patterson's forces labored under of having no communication but by a common road; but to all I could urge or suggest or doubt, Scott would not reply in detail or specifically, but would scout the idea that we could be defeated; and I really could not get him down to a consideration of the subject in a practical way. He would insist that we couldn't be beat nohow, and that was all there was of it. *— Whitney-1, 502, an elaboration of an account in Whitney's undated statement, Herndon-Springer, II, 426–33, where Lincoln is also quoted as saying:* You see, I was right and Scott now knows it, I reckon. My plan was and still is to make a strong feint against Richmond and distract their forces before attacking Manassas. *{D}*

It seems unlikely that Lincoln would have so misrepresented his and Scott's respective attitudes toward giving battle at Bull Run.[508]

24. *As for future military operations:*

We must drive them away from here [Manassas] and clean them out of this part of the state so as they can't threaten us here and get into Maryland. Then we must keep up as good a blockade as we can of their ports. Then we must march an army into east Tennessee and liberate the Union sentiment there and let the thing work. We must then rely upon the people getting tired and saying to their leaders, "We have had enough of this thing." Of course we can't conquer them if they are determined to hold out against us. . . . The great trouble about this whole thing is that Union men at the South won't fight for their rights. *— Whitney's undated statement, Herndon-Springer, II, 426–33.*

A revised version is in Whitney-1, 502–3, where Lincoln is quoted as saying: It is plain to me that it's no use of trying to subdue those people if they remain united and bound they won't be subdued.[509]

To which Whitney appended this unconvincing warranty: "As I have never heard of these sentiments being expressed to any one else, I have endeavored to be very accurate about my statements, as I am very positive about my recollection. I have given the substance, certainly, and almost the very language used." *{D}*

25. *At one point in their discussion, Whitney said, "I expect McClellan will be your successor." Lincoln answered:*

I am perfectly willing, if he can only put an end to this war. *— Whitney's statement, probably November 1866. {D}*

At this time, thirty-four-year-old George B. McClellan, after distinguishing himself in some minor engagements, was just taking command of troops in the Washington area. He did not become commander in chief until November 1861. It was therefore a little early for talk of his being the next president.

26. *During this same interview, Lincoln described his last meeting with Stephen A. Douglas:*

He came rushing in one day and said he had just got a telegraph dispatch from some friends in Illinois urging him to come out and help get things right in Egypt, and that he would go or stay in Washington, just where I thought he could do the most good. I told him to do as he chose, but that he could probably do best in Illinois. Upon that he just shook hands with me and hurried away to catch the next train. — *Whitney's statement, probably November 1866.* {D}

The version in Whitney-1, 501, has somewhat different wording. Douglas's last visit to the White House of which there is any reliable record took place on April 14, 1861, some five or six days before his departure for Illinois. It lasted about two hours and was made in the company of George Ashmun, a Massachusetts Republican. But according to the not entirely credible recollection of Albert D. Richardson (q.v.), the two men had another even longer interview on April 19.[510]

27. *According to Whitney, during the same discussion he received this reply when he spoke of Sam Houston's brother William:*

Don't bother me about Bill Houston. He has been here sitting on his ass all summer waiting for me to give him the best office I've got. — *Whitney's undated statement, Herndon-Springer, II, 426–33.* {D}

JOHN H. WICKIZER *Bloomington attorney, for a time a member of the Illinois legislature, who rode the law circuit with Lincoln in the 1850s. He was appointed an assistant quartermaster in 1862.*

1. *On the road between Bloomington and Metamora in 1855, after clubbing an old sow until she stopped trying to eat one of her offspring, Lincoln exclaimed:*

By jings, the unnatural old brute shall not devour her own progeny. — *Wickizer to Herndon, November 25, 1866 (8:1136–38), Herndon-Weik Collection.*[511] {C}

2. *At Bloomington in 1858, a young lawyer was asked about a case he had just lost, and he replied: "It's gone to hell." Said Lincoln:*

Oh, well, then you'll see it again. — *Ibid.* {C}

SAMUEL WILKESON (1817–1889) *Correspondent for the New York* Tribune, *later a newspaper editor and secretary of the Northern Pacific Railroad.*

1. *Speaking of the cabinet crisis precipitated by the proffered resignation of Seward, Lincoln said that:*

if there was any worse hell than he had been in for two days, he would like to know it. — *Wilkeson to Sydney Howard Gay, December 19, 1862, Gay Papers.* {B}

MORTON SMITH WILKINSON (1819-1894) *Senator from Minnesota during the Civil War.*

1. *In 1862, after listening for a while to a man who boasted that, if made a brigadier general, he would quickly suppress the Indian uprising in Minnesota, Lincoln said:*

Sir, since the war began I have received a great deal of advice from all classes of men, and in the army great promises have been made, and my experience and observation has been that those who promise the most do the least. — *Wilkinson's reminiscences in the New York* Tribune, *July 12, 1885. {C}*

2. *Once in the summer of 1863, Lincoln said to Wilkinson:*

I have here some papers which I started in this morning to carefully examine. They contain the entire proceedings of a military court for the trial of a young soldier for desertion. And they contain minutes of the testimony taken on the trial, together with the conviction and sentence to death of the boy. I have read just three pages of the testimony, and have found this: "The boy said when first arrested that he was going home to see his mother." I don't think that I can allow a boy to be shot who tried to go home to see his mother. I guess I don't want to read any more of this. —*Ibid. {D}*

3. *In December 1863, discussing promotion of John M. Schofield to major general, Lincoln said "in substance" to Wilkinson and Senator Zachariah Chandler:*

I suppose you gentlemen are opposed to the confirmation of General Schofield in consequence of your dislike of his civil administration in Missouri. If so, that is what I want to talk with you about. Sherman says that Schofield will fight and that he is a good soldier. Sherman says he would like to have him and that he will give him a corps and put him at active duty in the field. Now if you will confirm Schofield, I will send him down there to Sherman, and I will send Rosecrans up to take his place. And I think that this will so harmonize matters that the whole thing will hang together. —*Wilkinson's statement, May 22, 1876, in Nicolay Papers. {C}*

In a later account of the interview, Wilkinson also quoted Lincoln as remarking about Rosecrans: that both Grant and Sherman appeared to dislike him, though he did not know the reason why; and that this attitude placed Rosecrans in a very unpleasant position.

He continued: Rosecrans has a great many friends; he fought the battle of Stone[s] River and won a brilliant victory, and his advocates begin to grumble about his treatment. —*New York* Times, *July 12, 1885. {C}*

4. *On one occasion, when several congressional leaders were urging Lincoln to remove a certain official, he said:*

Well, gentlemen, it does seem to me that wherever I have a particular friend in office, everybody is down on him. —*Ibid.* {C}

[GEORGE] FORRESTER WILLIAMS (1837–1920)   *A war correspondent for the* New York *Times.*

   1. *After reporting the early stages of General Philip H. Sheridan's Shenandoah Valley campaign in August 1864, Williams visited the White House by presidential invitation. Lincoln said to him:*

You perhaps wonder what interest I can find in talking to a newspaper correspondent. But I am always seeking information, and you newspapermen are so often behind the scenes at the front I am frequently able to get ideas from you which no one else can give me. — *Williams F, 2400 (1901).* {C}

   2. *Later in the same conversation, Lincoln asked if Williams regarded Sheridan as a great commander and received a favorable answer. He then said:*

General Grant does seem to be able to pick out the right man for the right place and at the right time. He is like that trip-hammer I saw the other day. He is always certain in his movements and always the same. —*2400.* {C}

HENRY WILSON (1812–1875)   *Antislavery senator from Massachusetts who was later vice president and the author of a three-volume history of the slavery conflict.*

   1. *In reply to Wilson's warning that he would wear himself out trying to see all the people waiting in his anteroom:*

They don't want much, and they don't get but little, and I must see them. —*Wilson to Herndon, May 30, 1867 (9:1468–75), Herndon-Weik Collection.* {C}

   2. *Responding to Wilson's request that a soldier be pardoned:*

My officers tell me the good of the service demands the enforcement of the law, but it makes my heart ache to have the poor boys shot. I will pardon him, and then you will all join in blaming me for it. You all censure me for granting pardons, and yet you all ask me to do so. —*Ibid.* {C}

   3. *Presumably on Wilson's authority, it was reported that Lincoln, in talking with him about certain generals, had remarked:*

They remind me of a little joke. A sarcastic Athenian gravely proposed in the public assembly that a decree should be passed that asses were horses. The motion was voted down as ridiculous, when the proposer retorted, "But this is the way you make your generals, dubbing with the title men who have learned nothing of war." —Frank Leslie's Illustrated Newspaper, *April 25, 1863.* {D}

   4. *Speaking of his call for 100,000 militia dated June 15, 1863, Lincoln tells Wilson that:*

the proclamation for six-months men was issued without his knowledge and when he was sick in bed, Seward, Stanton, and Halleck agreeing to the forgery. . . . he shall stand by the proclamation now, however. — *Wilson's statement to New York* Tribune *correspondent Adams S. Hill, reported in Hill to Sydney Howard Gay, undated but near the end of June 1863, Gay Papers.*[512] {D}

Lincoln may have been somewhat indisposed on June 15, but he wrote several letters and transacted other business that day.[513] *The quality of Lincoln's signature, insofar as it is revealed in a photocopy, does not lend positive support to the story of a forgery.*[514]

5. *In the same conversation, which was held soon after the removal of Joseph Hooker from command of the Army of the Potomac, Lincoln told Wilson that:*

Hooker had a stronger force than [the] enemy, after leaving a sufficient garrison for Washington. But a few cavalry dashes scared him. — *Ibid.* {D}

6. *In August 1864, Lincoln spoke of the coming presidential campaign and the pressure upon him to modify his recent letter in effect refusing to consider any peace proposal that did not include "the integrity of the whole Union and the abandonment of slavery":*

I do not know what the result may be. We may be defeated; we may fail, but we will go down with our principles. I will not modify, qualify, nor retract my proclamation, nor my letter.[515] — *Wilson to Herndon, May 30, 1867 (9:1468–75).* {C}

7. *Wilson urged the appointment of Chase as chief justice in spite of his unseemly conduct toward Lincoln. The President replied:*

Oh, as to that, I care nothing. Of Mr. Chase's ability and of his soundness on the general issues of the war there is, of course, no question. I have only one doubt about his appointment. He is a man of unbounded ambition and has been working all his life to become president. That he can never be, and I fear that if I make him chief justice, he will simply become more restless and uneasy and neglect the place in his strife and intrigue to make himself president. If I were sure that he would go on the bench and give up his aspirations and do nothing but make himself a great judge, I would not hesitate a moment. — *Nicolay and Hay, IX, 394, citing a Nicolay memorandum of an interview with Wilson in April 1874.* {C}

JAMES F. WILSON (1828–1895) *Civil War congressman from Iowa, later a senator, whose recollective quotations of Lincoln do not inspire confidence in their reliability.*

1. *According to Wilson, he and several other men called at the White House in June 1862, and during an extensive discussion of public affairs, Lincoln re-*

sponded to one man's assertion that God would lead them to victory if they did right by striking down slavery:

My faith is greater than yours. I not only believe that Providence is not un-mindful of the struggle in which this nation is engaged; that if we do not do right, God will let us go our own way to our ruin; and that if we do right, He will lead us safely out of this wilderness, crown our arms with victory, and restore our dissevered union, as you have expressed your belief; but I also believe that He will compel us to do right in order that He may do these things, not so much because we desire them as that they accord with His plans of dealing with this nation, in the midst of which He means to establish justice. I think He means that we shall do more than we have yet done in furtherance of His plans, and He will open the way for our doing it. I have felt His hand upon me in great trials and submitted to His guidance, and I trust that as He shall further open the way I will be ready to walk therein, relying on His help and trusting in His goodness and wisdom. — *Wilson JF, 668-69 (1896). {E}*

Lincoln spoke these words, we are told, standing with his right arm outstretched and "his face aglow like the face of a prophet." Wilson's inaccurate background details further deplete his credibility.[516] A much shorter version of this story placed in a different setting is offered by Oliver O. Howard (q.v.).

2. Wilson claimed to have had "numerous conversations" with Lincoln about suspension of the writ of habeas corpus. On one occasion, he praised the letter of June 12, 1863, to Erastus Corning and others. Possibly, there is a kernel of verity in this long-winded reconstruction of Lincoln's reply:

When it became necessary for me to write that letter, I had it nearly all in there [pointing to a drawer in his desk], but it was in disconnected thoughts, which I had jotted down from time to time on separate scraps of paper. I had been worried a good deal by what had been said in the newspapers and in Congress about my suspension of the writ of habeas corpus and the so-called arbitrary arrests that had followed. I did not doubt my power to suspend the writ, nor the necessity which demanded its exercise. But I was criticized harshly, and sometimes by men from whom I expected more generous treatment and who ought to have known more and better than the character of their expressions indicated. This caused me to examine and reexamine the subject. I gave it a great deal of thought; I examined and studied it from every side; indeed, it was seemingly present with me continually. Often an idea about it would occur to me which seemed to have force and make perfect answer to some of the things that were said and written about my actions. I never let one of those ideas escape me, but wrote it on a scrap of paper and put it in that drawer. In that way I saved my best thoughts on the subject, and, you know, such things often come in a kind of intuitive way more clearly than if one were to sit down and deliberately reason them out.

To save the results of such mental action is true intellectual economy. It not only saves time and labor, but also the very best material the mind can supply for unexpected emergencies. Of course, in this instance, I had to arrange the material at hand and adapt it to the particular case presented. But that was an easy task compared with what immediate original composition of such a paper would have been. I am satisfied with the result and am content to abide the judgment of the future on that paper and of my action on the great subject and grave question to which it relates. Many persons have expressed to me the opinion you have of that paper, and I am pleased to know that the present judgment of thoughtful men about it is so generally in accord with what I believe the future will, without serious division, pronounce concerning it. I know that I acted with great deliberation and on my conscience when I suspended the writ of habeas corpus. It was with great reluctance that I came to recognize the necessity which demanded it. But when that became plain to my mind, I did not hesitate to do my duty. I have had to do many unpleasant things since the country imposed on me the task of administering the government, and I will continue to do them when they come in the line of my official duty, always with prayerful care, and without stopping to consider what personal result may come to me. — 670-71. {D}

3. *After agreeing to intervene in the case of an Iowa soldier wrongly accused of desertion, Lincoln added:*

I know it is a small thing, as some would look at it, as it only relates to a private soldier, and we have hundreds of thousands of them. But the way to have good soldiers is to treat them rightly. At all events, that is my order in this case.

Later, he said to Wilson: I am glad you stuck to it and that it ended as it did; for I meant it should so end, if I had to give it personal attention. A private soldier has as much right to justice as a major general. —674-75. {C}

JAMES GRANT WILSON (1832-1914) *Union officer, brother-in-law of Senator James Dixon of Connecticut, and for more than half a century an amazingly prolific editor and author. There may be as much invention as remembrance in his recollected words of Lincoln.*

1. *Responding in the autumn of 1858 to Judge Samuel Treat's remark that George Washington had been a champion wrestler in his youth:*

It is rather a curious thing, my young friend, but that is exactly my record. I could outlift any man in southern Illinois when I was young, and I never was thrown. There was a big fellow named Jack Armstrong, strong as a Russian bear, that I could not put down; nor could he get me on the ground.

If George was loafing around here now, I should be glad to have a tussle with him, and I rather believe that one of the plain people of Illinois would be able to manage the aristocrat of old Virginia. — *Wilson JG-1, 516 (1909).* {D}

2. *Wilson recalled that Lincoln had frequently used the expression "plain people" and on one occasion had said:*

I think the Lord must love the plain people, he has made so many of them. — *Wilson JG-1, 516.* {D}

Other versions of this quotation provided by John Hay (q.v.), and Alexander K. McClure (q.v.) had already appeared in print.

3. *In the spring of 1860, Lincoln visited the office of Wilson's literary journal, the* Chicago Record, *and noted with pleasure the busts of Shakespeare and Burns:*

They are my two favorite authors, and I must manage to see their birthplaces some day, if I can contrive to cross the Atlantic. — *Wilson JG-1, 517.* {D}

4. *One day in the winter of 1862–63, after hearing Lincoln turn aside an importunate congressman with a droll remark, Wilson asked whether that was his way of managing politicians. Lincoln replied:*

Well, Colonel, you must not think you have got all the strategy in the army; we have to have a little bit for Washington. — *Wilson JG-2, 396 (1913).* {C}

5. *On February 12, 1865, to a man considerably taller than he:*

My friend, will you kindly permit me to inquire if you know when your feet get cold? — *Wilson JG-1, 672.* {C}

6. *At a performance of "The Magic Flute" on March 15, 1865, Mrs. Lincoln suggested leaving before the end, but Lincoln said:*

Oh, no, I want to see it out. It's best when you undertake a job, to finish it. — *Wilson JG-1, 673.* {C}

According to Wilson, this remark and the following story were recorded in his diary.

7. *During that same evening, the President told of:*

a southern Illinois preacher who, in the course of his sermon, asserted that the Savior was the only perfect man who had ever appeared in this world; also, that there was no record in the Bible, or elsewhere, of any perfect woman having lived on the earth. Whereupon there arose in the rear of the church a persecuted-looking personage who, the parson having stopped speaking, said, "I know a perfect woman, and I've heard of her about every day for the last six years." "Who was she?" asked the minister.

"My husband's first wife," replied the afflicted female. — *Wilson JG-1, 673.* {C}

8. *At about the end of March 1865, says Wilson, he attended the theater with Lincoln, who, after the first act, confessed a lack of interest in the play:*

I have not come for the play, but for the rest. I am being hounded to death by office-seekers, who pursue me early and late, and it is simply to get two or three hours' relief that I am here. I wonder if we shall be tormented in heaven with them, as well as with bores and fools? — *Wilson JG-1, 529.* {D}

Lincoln was away from Washington from March 23 until April 9. Wilson may have been thinking of the March 15 performance of "The Magic Flute."

MATTHEW WILSON (1814–1892) *The artist who painted the last Lincoln portrait from life.*

1. *Wilson told Forney that during work on the painting, Lincoln opened a piece of mail and then pointed to a pigeonhole, saying:*

Here is another of these letters. In that place I have filed eighty just such things as these. I know I am in danger, but I am not going to worry over threats like these. — *Forney, II, 425 (1881).* {D}

Either Wilson or Forney dated this incident two weeks before the assassination, perhaps meaning to say two months. The portrait was completed in February 1865, and from March 23 to April 9, Lincoln was away on his trip to the military front in Virginia.

ROBERT L. WILSON (1805–1880) *A political associate of Lincoln in the Illinois legislature, one of the "long nine." In later life, he was a probate judge and a leading citizen of Sterling, Illinois.*

1. *Once during his New Salem days, Lincoln said to Wilson that:*

although he appeared to enjoy life rapturously, still he was the victim of terrible melancholy. He sought company and indulged in fun and hilarity without restraint or stint as to time. Still, when by himself, he was so overcome with mental depression that he never dare[d] carry a knife in his pocket. — *Wilson to Herndon, February 10, 1866 (8:602-17), Herndon-Weik Collection.* {C}

2. *According to Wilson, Lincoln often told him that:*

he never drank, had no desire for the drink, nor the companionship of drinking men. — *Ibid.* {C}

3. *Following an unpleasant conversation with Congressman Galusha A. Grow about a patronage matter, Lincoln said to Wilson that:*

he had then been president five months and was surprised anybody would want the office.

He went on to state: that [before] he was inaugurated, he supposed that although he realized that the labor of administering the affairs of the nation would be arduous and severe, and that he had made up his mind that he could and would do it, all the duties were rather pleasant and agreeable except making the appointments. He had started out with the determination to make no improper appointments, and to accomplish that result, he imposed upon himself the labor of an examination into the qualifications of each applicant. He found to his surprise that members of his cabinet, who were equally interested with himself in the success of his administration, had been recommending parties to be appointed to responsible positions who were often physically, morally, and intellectually unfit for the place. It did appear that most of the cabinet officers and members of Congress had a list of appointments to be made, and many of them were such as ought not to be made, and they knew, and their importunities were urgent in proportion to the unfitness [of] the appointee. He was so badgered with applications for appointments that he thought sometimes that the only way that he [could] escape from them would be to take a rope and hang himself on one of the trees in the lawn south of the president's house. *—Ibid.* {C}

4. *Wilson one day remarked that the president's office business was rather like that of justice of the peace. Lincoln replied:*

Yes, but it is hardly as respectable.

Then he added that: when he first commenced doing the duties, he was entirely ignorant, not only of the duties, but of the manner of doing the business. He was like the justice of the peace who would often speak of the first case he had ever tried and called it his "great first case least understood." *—Ibid.* {C}

5. *The night after the battle of Bull Run in July 1861, Wilson and two congressmen tried in vain to obtain information about it from Lincoln, who said that:*

it was contrary to army regulations to give military information to parties not in military service.

Pressed by Wilson to say at least whether the news was good or bad, he replied: Damned bad. *—Ibid. Herndon, III, 542, gives a corrupt version of this exchange.*[517] {C}

WILLIAM BENDER WILSON (1839–1919) *Manager of the War Department's telegraph office in 1861–62.*

1. *At the request of Congress, Lincoln proclaimed September 26, 1861, as "a day of public humiliation, prayer and fasting."*[518] *Finding the telegraph operators very busy on that date, he remarked:*

Gentlemen, this is fast day, and I am pleased to observe that you are working as fast as you can; the proclamation was mine, and that is my interpretation of its bearing upon you. — *Wilson WB, III (1892). {C}*

2. *Then, changing the subject to the Confederate threat in Kentucky, he said:*

Now, we will have a little talk with Governor Morton, at Indianapolis. I want to give him a lesson in geography. [The] Bowling Green affair I set him all right upon; now I will tell him something about Muldraugh Hill. Morton is a good fellow, but at times he is the skeeredest man I know of.[519] —*III. {C}*

3. *On another day in September 1861, Wilson responded to the President's request for news with the pronouncement: "Good news, because none." Lincoln replied:*

Ah! my young friend, that rule don't always hold good; for a fisherman don't consider it good luck when he can't get a bite. —*III. {C}*

4. *When Seward frowned on his use of the expression "by jings," Lincoln said to the telegraphers:*

Young gentlemen, excuse me for swearing before you; **by jings** is swearing, for my good old mother taught me that anything that had a **by** before it is swearing. I won't do so any more. —*112. {C}*

JAMES M. WINCHELL *A Washington correspondent of the New York* Times, *Winchell in January 1864 drafted the letter known as the "Pomeroy Circular," which attacked Lincoln and urged the elevation of Chase to the presidency in his place.*

1. *In March 1863, Winchell, together with Albert D. Richardson and one other man, sought revocation of a court-martial decision banishing Thomas W. Knox, a New York* Herald *correspondent, from the area of Grant's command. Lincoln said:*

Well, you want me to make an order setting aside the action of the court. I wish to do what is right and what you ask; for it seems to me, from all the evidence, that our newspaper friend has been a little too severely dealt with. Still, I am not on the spot to judge of all the circumstances, and General Grant is; and I do not see how I can properly grant your request without being sustained by his consent. But let us see what we can do. I will write something to put our ideas into shape, but I had better make this conditional on the approval of General Grant. You see, it would not seem right for me to send back a correspondent to the General's headquarters in case he knew of any reason why the man should not be there.[520] — *Winchell, 36 (1873). {C}*

In Richardson's account of this meeting (q.v.), the words attributed to Lincoln are quite different, although their effect is about the same.

2. At the same meeting, Lincoln expressed pessimism about current operations in the field and spoke of his own limited control over them:

I am as powerless as any private citizen to shape the military plans of the government. I have my generals and my War Department, and my subordinates are supposed to be more capable than I am to decide what movements shall or shall not be undertaken. I have once or twice attempted to act on my own convictions and found that it was impracticable to do so. I see campaigns undertaken in which I have no faith and have no power to prevent them, and I tell you that sometimes when I reflect on the management of our forces, I am tempted to despair; my heart goes clear down into my boots. —*37-38.* {C}

3. In the spring of 1864, after the collapse of the Chase boom, Winchell sounded out Lincoln's intentions respecting a second term and listened, he says, to an hour-long monologue in reply. In essence, the President said:

that, as yet, he was not a candidate for renomination . . . that with one or two exceptions, he had scarcely conversed on the subject with his most intimate friends. He was not quite sure whether he desired a renomination. Such had been the responsibility of the office—so oppressive had he found its cares, so terrible its perplexities—that he felt as though the moment when he could relinquish the burden and retire to private life would be the sweetest he could possibly experience. But . . . he would not deny that a re-election would also have its gratification to his feelings. He did not seek it, nor would he do so. He did not desire it for any ambitious or selfish purpose, but after the crisis the country was passing through under his presidency and the efforts he had made conscientiously to discharge the duties imposed upon him, it would be a very sweet satisfaction to him to know that he had secured the approval of his fellow citizens and earned the highest testimonial of confidence they could bestow. . . . He should make no promises of office to anyone as an inducement for support. If nominated and elected, he should be grateful to his friends and consider that they had claims on him, but the interest of the country must always be first. Meantime, he supposed he should be a candidate; things seemed to be working in that direction. —*40-41.* {C}

ROBERT C. WINTHROP (1809–1894)   *Conservative Whig congressional leader during the 1840s. He supported the Bell-Everett ticket in 1860 and McClellan in 1864.*

1. When Winthrop expressed approval of his revocation of Frémont's emancipation edict in Missouri, Lincoln replied:

There is a good deal of old Whig left in me yet. —*Winthrop, 222 (1897).* {B}

Apparently taken from notes made by Winthrop at the time.

2. *On April 25, 1863, Lincoln told Winthrop:*

that his anxieties of mind had not affected his health and that he weighed 180 pounds. —228. {B}

From a diary entry of that date.

ANNIE WITTENMYER (1827–1900) *An Iowan who worked to improve conditions in military hospitals and provide aid for widows and orphans of Union soldiers. She was later the first president of the Woman's Christian Temperance Union.*

1. *One day Mrs. Wittenmyer was discussing her work with Lincoln when a telegram arrived. After reading it, he said:*

This is good news indeed. This Sheridan is a little Irishman, but he is a big fighter. — *Wittenmyer, 240 (1895). {C}*

SIMON WOLF (1836–1923) *Lawyer, civic leader, and author, Wolf lived most of his life in Washington, D.C., and was one of the leading American Jews of his time.*

1. *When Wolf congratulated him on the issuance of the Emancipation Proclamation, Lincoln said:*

It was not only the Negro that I freed, but the white man no less. — *Wolf S, 8 (1918). {C}*

2. *Responding to a plea from Wolf and Thomas Corwin in behalf of a Jewish soldier condemned to death for desertion, the President said:*

Impossible to do anything. I have no influence with this administration. Stanton has put his foot down and insists upon one of two things, either that I must quit or he will quit.

After Wolf explained, however, that the soldier had been summoned to the bedside of his dying mother, Lincoln sent a telegram stopping the execution. Told later that the man had been killed at Cold Harbor, he said: I thank God for having done what I did. —6-7. {D}

This is too perfectly in tune with the Lincoln myth not to arouse some doubt.

3. *Told of a coming local production of* Hamlet, *Lincoln remarked:*

Why would I not make a splendid grave digger, for am I not quoted as a fellow of infinite jest and humor, and is not my present life typical of that vocation? —7. {C}

KATE TANNATT WOODS (1838–1910) *A volunteer nurse in Washington during the Civil War.*

1. *Asked why he allowed himself to be maligned by certain newspapers, Lincoln replied:*

Child, if you will take care of my Republican friends, I will look after my Democratic enemies. — *Woods, 86 (c. 1862). {A}*

J. J. WRIGHT   *An Indiana physician who later moved to Emporia, Kansas.*
  1. *On June 5, 1864, when asked whether he would like to visit his old home in Kentucky after the war, Lincoln replied:*

I would like it very much. I remember that old home very well. Our farm was composed of three fields. It lay in the valley surrounded by high hills and deep gorges. Sometimes when there came a big rain in the hills, the water would come down through the gorges and spread all over the farm. The last thing that I remember of doing there was one Saturday afternoon. The other boys planted the corn in what we called the big field—it contained seven acres—and I dropped the pumpkin seeds. I dropped two seeds every other hill and every other row. The next Sunday morning there came a big rain in the hills. It did not rain a drop in the valley, but the water coming down through the gorges washed ground, corn, pumpkin seeds and all clear off the field. — *Memorandum of a statement by Wright, dated April 18, 1896, Tarbell Papers. {C}*

RICHARD YATES (1815–1873)   *Whig congressman in the 1850s and Civil War governor of Illinois.*
  1. *Once, when Yates urged more radical policies, Lincoln replied:*

Dick, hold fast and see the salvation of God. — *Speech of October 20, 1863, in Washington, reported the next day in the Washington* Chronicle; *repeated October 29 in New York, reported in the New York* Herald, *October 30. {C}*

Lincoln was quoting from Exodus, 14:13, where Moses told frightened Israelites beside the Red Sea: "Stand still, and see the salvation of the Lord."

  2. *After a visit to the White House in April 1864, Yates reported having heard this remark from the President:*

Dick, I'll tell you the difference between the concrete and the abstract. When the Senate passed a resolution requesting me not to appoint any more brigadiers, as the vacancies were all full, that's the concrete. But when a senator comes up here with a long petition and a longer face requesting me to make a brigadier out of some scallawag of a friend of his, as it happens every day, I call that the abstract. — *Yates's account in the* Bureau County Patriot *(Princeton, Illinois), May 10, 1864, transcript in the Sandburg Papers, folder 249. {C}*

Either Lincoln or Yates or the Patriot *got it backward.*

3. *According to Yates, in an account provided by his son, he visited the White House with William Pitt Kellogg on April 14, 1865, at which time Lincoln said to the latter:*

I am going to send you to New Orleans to be collector of the port—you will have 2,000 employees under you, all northerners, because substantially all southerners are disfranchised; but I want you to make love to those people down there. —*Speech in Congress of Richard Yates, Jr., February 12, 1921,* Congressional Record, *66th Congress, 3rd session, 3077.* {D}

This, being secondhand reminiscence, is questionable material. Nevertheless, the meeting did take place, although the date, according to Kellogg himself, was April 12, rather than April 14.[521]

GEORGE H. YEAMAN (1829–1908) *Kentucky Unionist who served in Congress during the latter part of the Civil War.*

1. *Asking Yeaman to come back at another time, Lincoln said:*

I am just going to hear a pullet crow. I am going to hear Miss —— lecture. —*Yeaman's recollections in the New York* Tribune, *April 9, 1899.* {C}

Very likely, the unnamed person was Anna Elizabeth Dickinson (q.v.), the young abolitionist orator whose lecture Lincoln attended on January 16, 1864.

2. *Yeaman pleaded for mercy in the case of some Kentucky boys who had seized a mail bag and scattered its contents. Lincoln, after resisting for a time, finally said:*

I will turn these boys out on one condition, . . . that you pledge your personal honor that they will behave themselves in the future. . . . We'll try this once, but if these boys cut up any more shines, you must not come back to me again in their behalf. —*Ibid.* {C}

JOHN RUSSELL YOUNG (1840–1899) *Journalist associated during the Civil War with the Philadelphia* Press.

1. *After the delivery of the Gettysburg Address, Young, who had been taking it down for the* Press, *leaned across the aisle and asked if that was all. Lincoln replied:*

Yes, for the present. —*Young, I, 69 (1901).* {D}

A good story, but it seems unlikely that Young was sitting that close to the President.

ISACHAR ZACHARIE *New York chiropodist who operated successfully on Lincoln's feet and received a testimonial from him.*[522] *Zacharie's activities in Louisi-*

ana as a putative observer for Lincoln and as an agent of the commanding general, Nathaniel Banks, are shrouded in mystery. There is reason to doubt the reliability of his self-promotional letters, which are the principal source of information on the subject, but he did, apparently, have ready access to the President.

1. During 1863, Zacharie became involved with Banks in a vague scheme for securing a negotiated peace. In July, he failed to obtain a pass to Richmond from the Lincoln administration, but after another visit to the White House in September, he reported to Banks that the President had told him:

Mr. Chase and others was too much opposed to me, from letters that had been received from my enemies at New Orleans, that at that time he could not entertain any proposition from me. But now he was satisfied and was able to satisfy all who was opposed to me that I was all right, and was now willing to afford me every facility to carry out my plans and felt sure that I would be successful.

According to Zacharie's account, he proceeded to Richmond, where he conferred with Judah P. Benjamin and other members of the Confederate cabinet, but nothing came of his peace negotiations because Lincoln and Seward were afraid of opposition within their party. Lincoln, he said, told him: had he the least idea that I would have been received that he would have never permitted me to have gone. —*Zacharie to Banks, September 8, December 28, 1863, in Harrington, 81, 86.*[523] {D}

CHARLES S. ZANE (1831–1915) *Springfield lawyer, partner of William H. Herndon for approximately seven years after Lincoln became president. Zane was later an Illinois circuit judge and chief justice of Utah Territory.*

1. When Zane once asked whether he was worn out after having spoken to a political meeting, Lincoln replied:

No, I can speak three or four hours at a time without feeling weary. —*Zane, 435 (1912).* {C}

2. Lincoln was "a great eater of apples," Zane recalled:

Apples agree with me; a large percent of professional men abuse their stomachs by imprudence in drinking and eating, and in that way health is injured and ruined and life is shortened. —*435.* {C}

3. Zane heard Lincoln say in about 1858:

that the Know-Nothings—their ideas and platform—wanted to circumscribe the election franchise, universal suffrage; that he was opposed to it; that he wanted to lift men up and give them a chance. —*Undated statement taken down by Herndon (11:3226), Herndon-Weik Collection.* {C}

4. After his defeat in the senatorial contest of 1858:

It hurts too much to laugh and I am too big to cry. Well, I shall now have to get down to the practice. It is an easy matter to adjust a harvester to tall or short grain by raising or lowering the sickle, but it is not so easy to change our feelings and modes of expression to suit the stump or the bar. —*Zane, 432. {D}*

The first sentence is traditional. Earlier versions, none coming directly from an auditor, date back to 1859 and 1862.[524] *John McConnell (q.v.) told an interviewer in 1895 that Lincoln made such a remark to him in 1854.*

5. *May 18, 1860, upon receiving word of his nomination:*
When the second ballot came, I knew this must come.

Responding to the remark that no doubt he would soon be the subject of a book: There is not much in my past life about which to write a book, as it seems to me.

Jestingly, to the friends gathered outside: Gentlemen, you had better come up and shake my hand while you can. Honors elevate some men.

And then, after a few minutes of receiving congratulations: Well, gentlemen, there is a little woman at our house who is probably more interested in this dispatch than I am; if you will excuse me, I will take the dispatch up and let her see it. —*Undated statement to Herndon (11:3229-32). {C}*

Variant versions are in another undated statement (11:3222-23) and in Zane, 437-38.

REFERENCE MATTER

NOTES

1. *Collected Works*, V, 542–43, 550–51; VI, 6–7.

2. Whether it was in reference to McClellan's appointment in July 1861 as commander of what came to be called the Army of the Potomac, or to his appointment as general in chief several months later, the statement was untrue. See Charles Winslow Elliott, *Winfield Scott: The Soldier and the Man* (New York: Macmillan Co., 1937), 733–39; Sears, 96, 122–23.

3. In May 1863, Lincoln pardoned on grounds of ill health Albert Horn, owner of the slaver *City of Norfolk*, who had served just seven months of a five-year sentence. Warren S. Howard, *American Slavers and the Federal Law, 1837–1862* (Berkeley: University of California Press, 1963), 189, 233–34. It appears from the records that Lincoln received petitions for clemency from seven persons convicted under the slave-trade laws and that he pardoned four of them. J. T. Dorris, "President Lincoln's Clemency," *ISHSJ*, 20 (1927–28): 547–68.

4. The correspondent has been identified as probably Ellis Henry Roberts (1827–1918), editor of the *Herald* and later a member of Congress and treasurer of the United States. See *Lincoln Herald*, 46 (Feb. 1944): 26–28, where the article is reproduced. The case referred to was presumably *Dawson v. Ennis and Ennis* in the U.S. Circuit Court.

5. *Collected Works*, IV, 149–54, 183.

6. Sandburg, *War Years*, III, 343–45, reproduces the entire Boston *Gazette* article. See also Richard N. Current, *The Lincoln Nobody Knows* (New York: McGraw-Hill Book Co., 1958), 55–57, 66–68; Russell M. and Clare R. Goldfarb, *Spiritualism and Nineteenth-Century Letters* (Rutherford, N.J.: Fairleigh Dickinson University Press, 1978), 42–44. Harriet M. Shelton, *Abraham Lincoln Returns* (New York: Evans Publishing Co., 1957), uses the Shockle story to support the argument that Lincoln was a spiritualist. According to *Lincoln Day by Day*, III, 181, it was on April 23, 1863, that Lincoln "allegedly" attended the Shockle performance, but the *Gazette* correspondent wrote his article on that date and placed the séance "a few evenings since." Other known activities of the President make April 18 and 19 out of the question, leaving the 20th or 21st as the likely date of this unlikely event. It is perhaps not without significance that Welles should have said nothing in his diary about having any such remarkable experience.

7. Writing on Monday, May 25, the correspondent said that Lincoln's remarks were made "last Sunday night," which could have meant either May 17 or May 24.

8. See Lincoln to Stanton, Dec. 21, 1863, *Collected Works*, VII, 84.

9. Fessenden's version was: "He said he had one thing that nobody wanted." Fessenden, I, 267. Clark E. Carr, in his *My Day and Generation* (Chicago: A. C. McClurg & Co., 1908), 252–53, wrote that Lincoln in the winter of 1862 showed him and Owen Lovejoy the pustules of varioloid on his wrists and declared that he

now had something he "could give to everybody." But that would have been nearly a year before Lincoln actually contracted the disease. Horace Porter (q.v.) mistakenly associated the wisecrack with an attack of measles.

10. Correspondence of Dec. 3, Chicago *Tribune*, Dec. 6, 1863.

11. See Zall, 153.

12. This interview has commonly been misdated March 12, the day before Lincoln wrote his significant letter on the subject to Michael Hahn, *Collected Works*, VII, 243.

13. The petition itself may be read in Aptheker, I, 494–95.

14. See *Collected Works*, VIII, 20–22, 267–68. On March 20, 1865, Grant wrote to James W. Singleton: "I now have made up my mind to give no sanction whatever to trade of any kind beyond the limits of our picket lines. I am satisfied that to do so would benefit the enemy and prove proportionally injurious to the country." John Y. Simon, ed., *The Papers of Ulysses S. Grant*, XIV (Carbondale, Ill.: Southern Illinois University Press, 1985), 188.

15. For the practical political reasons behind the House-Divided speech, see Fehrenbacher-1, 70–95.

16. See *Collected Works*, V, 388–89, for Lincoln's famous reply to Horace Greeley's editorial, "The Prayer of Twenty Millions."

17. The Baldwin interview has been a subject of much historical analysis and controversy. See, for example, Nicolay and Hay, III, 423–28; Wilmer L. Hall, "Lincoln's Interview with John B. Baldwin," *South Atlantic Quarterly*, 13 (1914): 260–69; Potter, 356–58; Richard N. Current, *Lincoln and the First Shot* (Philadelphia: J. B. Lippincott Co., 1963), 94–96; Crofts, 301–6. According to Charles S. Morehead (q.v.) and Lincoln himself as quoted in Hay-1, 30, he had made the same offer to a group of southerners shortly before his inauguration.

18. Howard to William H. Herndon, Nov. 18, 1866 (8:1045–48), Herndon-Weik Collection.

19. See Holzer et al., 50–56.

20. *Collected Works*, VIII, 307–8. See also Douglas Fermer, *James Gordon Bennett and the 'New York Herald'* (Woodbridge, Eng.: Boydell Press, 1986), 285–96.

21. See *Collected Works*, IV, 52.

22. Bateman wrote to Isaac N. Arnold that Holland's rendering of the statement was "substantially correct." Arnold-3 (1885), 179n.

23. For Herndon's denunciation of the Bateman story as "false," see his undated memorandum (11:3527–39), Herndon-Weik Collection. According to Herndon in other statements, he forced Bateman to retract at least part of what he had told Holland. See William E. Barton, *The Soul of Abraham Lincoln* (New York: George H. Doran Co., 1920), 114–27.

24. See *Collected Works*, III, 360–61. Perhaps on this occasion his presence in the telegraph office rekindled Lincoln's interest in the origins of human communication, but it is also possible that the lecture on "Discoveries and Inventions," first published in 1894, inspired Bates to some inventive recollection.

25. In a footnote, Bates added that according to another telegrapher, Albert B. Chandler, Lincoln made exactly the same remark on the night of his re-election.

26. An undated memorandum in the Nicolay Papers attributes this story to Robert Todd Lincoln as follows: "It reminded him of a little Frenchman out west who was so short that the seat of his trousers rubbed out his footprints as he walked

in the snow." For still another version, one without an identified auditor, see Zall, 112.

27. Bibb was introduced to Lincoln by Orville H. Browning, who noted it in his diary, II, 17.

28. See *Collected Works*, IV, 323–24.

29. For Halleck's order, dated December 12, 1861, see *OR*, Ser. II, Vol. 1, pp. 150–51.

30. In the text of the Lamon book, the story is related without identification of the intermediary source, but a note on p. 289 presents a confirmatory letter from Pleasonton stating: "Mr. F. P. Blair, Senior, told me the incident of conveying in person President Lincoln's letter to McClellan."

31. See Sears, 364–66. According to the Lamon memorandum, Lincoln made a definite offer to McClellan in a letter that was received favorably by the General but was rejected by his political friends. There appears to be no evidence supporting this statement.

32. The letter, written August 24, 1861, to John C. Frémont, was published in the New York *Tribune*, Mar. 4, 1862.

33. *Congressional Globe*, 36 Cong., 2 sess., 1335–36. For the text of the bill, see p. 1001. See also Potter, 275–77.

34. For Lewis's testimony and other statements on the subject, see Botts, 197–98, 201–2.

35. Without citation of his source, Albert Bushnell Hart, *Salmon Portland Chase* (Boston: Houghton, Mifflin & Co., 1899), 435, quotes Lincoln as saying: "Chase is about one and a half times bigger than any other man that I ever knew."

36. Slightly different versions of this and the preceding quotation as recalled by Boutwell had appeared two years earlier in James G. Blaine's *Twenty Years of Congress from Lincoln to Garfield* (2 vols.; Norwich, Conn.: Henry Bill, 1884), I, 439.

37. The Lincolns began to use the Soldiers' Home as a summer retreat in 1862.

38. Endorsing Briggs's application in July 1862 for the position of arbitrator under the new slave-trade treaty with England. The appointment went to another man, however. See *Collected Works*, III, 494; V, 339, 366–67, 403.

39. A shorter and perhaps more believable version from an interview in an unidentified paper is in *Memoirs of Abraham Lincoln in Edgar County, Illinois* (Edgar County Historical Society, 1925), 27: "Tell him I can't see him any more about that matter. I've seen him as many times as I can. I wish that man would let me alone. I've seen him again and again. I've done everything for him that I can do, and he knows it just as well as I do; and I've told him over and over, and he ought to let me alone, but he won't stop following me up. He knows I can't do anything more for him. I declare, if he don't let me alone, I'll tell him what I did a fellow the other day, that I'll undo what I have done for him."

40. In 1888, John Hay expressed the private opinion that Brooks was inventing "rubbish" about Lincoln "by the ream." Hay to Nicolay, July 14, Hay Collection-Brown. That the relations between Brooks and the two secretaries were less than cordial is indicated by his dispatch of November 7 in the Sacramento *Union*, Dec. 4, 1863, wherein he described them as "snobby and unpopular."

41. There are no communications of any kind to Brooks in the *Collected Works*. There is only one letter from Brooks to Lincoln in the Lincoln Papers at the Library

of Congress, and it begins: "Not being able to see you when I have called." Brooks's name does not appear at all in the Welles, Chase, or Browning diaries. He is mentioned once in the diary of Edward Bates and twice (without reference to Lincoln) in the diary of John Hay. Francis B. Carpenter, in recalling his six months in the White House, said nothing of any visit by Brooks. But for testimony to Brooks's intimacy with Lincoln, see Wayne C. Temple and Justin G. Turner, "Lincoln's 'Castine': Noah Brooks," *Lincoln Herald*, 72 (1970): 113–14. (This full-length biography, published serially in volumes 72–74, is based on Temple's 1956 doctoral dissertation.) It appears to have been Mary Lincoln who most energetically sought to have Brooks installed in Nicolay's place. See Anson G. Henry to his wife, Mar. 13, 1865, Henry Papers (the letter is published in Pratt-2, 117). On March 11, Nicolay was appointed consul in Paris, but the evidence that Lincoln actually offered the secretarial position to Brooks is primarily in the recollective statements to that effect by Brooks himself. For one of the earliest, see *The Character and Religion of President Lincoln: A Letter of Noah Brooks, May 10, 1865* (Champlain, N.Y., 1919), 9.

42. Brooks mistakenly dated the speech late September 1856.

43. Lincoln addressed Republican rallies at Oregon on July 25 and August 16, 1856. Brooks mistakenly placed the meeting in October.

44. For other narrators of this story, see Zall, 128–29.

45. Washington *Chronicle*, Feb. 27, 1864. The mistake was not just a slip of the pen. In Brooks-5, 71–72, there is a rather long story about how Lincoln obtained use of the box at Ford's Theatre that night only because a group of army officers agreed to vacate it. Brooks's claim to have frequently attended the theater with Lincoln is uncorroborated.

46. For the case of the so-called "*Chapman* pirates," see *U.S. v. Greathouse et al.*, 26 Federal Cases 18 (1863); Robert J. Chandler, "The Release of the *Chapman* Pirates: A California Sidelight on Lincoln's Amnesty Policy," *Civil War History*, 23 (1977): 129–43.

47. In his dispatch, Brooks introduced the quotation thus: "The President said the other day . . ."

48. According to the Brooks dispatch, this visitation took place on October 18. *Lincoln Day by Day*, III, 291, apparently without good reason, dates it October 23.

49. For Lincoln's interesting exchange of letters with Hackett, see *Collected Works*, VI, 392–93, 558–59.

50. The October 25 New York *Times* version of Lincoln's remarks is printed in *Collected Works*, VIII, 75. Brooks's dispatch was apparently written on the 26th and misdated the 24th; for he said that the little speech had been given the "day before yesterday." The *Times* dispatch indicates that the event took place on the 24th.

51. The Washington *Morning Chronicle*, Nov. 2, 1864, confirms the "jubilation" held by "colored citizens" at a church on 15th Street between I and K streets, but the reporter left as the procession was being organized and said nothing about the visit to the White House.

52. A strong indication that the conversation took place in November, rather than in the following April, is provided by Brooks's dispatch of November 11, in the Sacramento *Union*, Dec. 10, 1864. There he declared: "The President had written out his speech, being well aware that the importance of the occasion would give it significance, and he was not willing to run the risk of being betrayed by the excitement of the occasion into saying anything which would make him sorry when

he saw it in print." No such comment appears in the report of the April 11 speech, dispatch of April 12 in the *Union*, May 8, 1865.

53. Brooks-5, 199–200. For a summary of discrepancies in the various versions, see Fehrenbacher-2, 273.

54. See *Collected Works*, VIII, 236, for a brief speech on January 24, 1864, in which Lincoln said of Everett: "His life was a truly great one."

55. *Collected Works*, I, 378.

56. Although Brooks gave only the man's initial, he was probably referring to Morton S. Wilkinson of Minnesota, the only senator who fits his description. Dole was commissioner of Indian affairs.

57. See *Collected Works*, VIII, 393.

58. In this letter, Brooks was doubly mistaken when he dated the response April 9 and described it as a celebration of the fall of Richmond.

59. See Colfax-2 and Brooks-5, 229–30. Since Brooks, in writing the latter recollective work, made extensive use of his wartime dispatches to the *Union*, it seems not unlikely that he deliberately chose to abandon his earlier falsehood.

60. See *Collected Works*, VII, 413–14.

61. In the preceding session, the House and Senate had passed different versions of a bill to subsidize emancipation in Missouri, but they had been unable to reach agreement on a compromise. *Congressional Globe*, 37 Cong., 1 sess., 208–9, 903, 1056. The measure was not revived by the 38th Congress.

62. The same story, with variant wording, is in a statement by Brown, Chicago *Times-Herald*, Aug. 25, 1895.

63. According to a report later circulated, one of the visitors declared that 75,000 Marylanders would contest the passage of troops over their state's soil, and Lincoln replied that he presumed there was room enough on her soil to bury 75,000 men. Orville J. Victor, ed., *Incidents and Anecdotes of the War* (New York: James D. Torrey, 1862), 79.

64. Although issued over Brown's signature, the statement was actually written by S. T. Wallis, one of the men accompanying him to the interview with Lincoln. Brown, 73.

65. Hay-1, 6, 7.

66. *Collected Works*, V, 98–99.

67. See *Collected Works*, V, 192.

68. Compare with Lincoln's letter to Reverdy Johnson, July 26, 1862, *Collected Works*, V, 342–43.

69. See *Collected Works*, VII, 63–64; 484–85.

70. See Lincoln to Hurlbut, Nov. 14, 1864, *Collected Works*, VIII, 106–8.

71. *Collected Works*, VII, 435, 451; VIII, 152.

72. Bundy repeated the story, identifying Wilson as the paymaster, in a letter to James R. B. Van Cleave, July 20, 1908, Centennial Reminiscences.

73. See *Collected Works*, II, 243–44.

74. Weik names the case as *Hildreth v. Turner*, but those two men were on the same side in the case that at the appellate level was designated *Edmunds v. Hildreth et al.*, 16 Illinois 214. A companion case involving the cradle was *Edmunds v. Myers et al.*, 16 Illinois 207. In both instances, Lincoln represented the defendants in error and was defeated.

75. Mark E. Neely, Jr., "Abraham Lincoln and Black Colonization: Benjamin

Butler's Spurious Testimony," *Civil War History*, 25 (1979): 76–83. If Butler's self-serving memoirs are to be believed, Lincoln offered to give him Grant's command in January 1863, sought him as a running mate in 1864, and later sounded him out about replacing Stanton as secretary of war. Contemporary evidence supporting these claims is lacking, although Simon Cameron, not the most reliable of witnesses, later attested that he had carried the vice-presidency offer to Butler and Butler's refusal back to Lincoln. His story is supported by the not always reliable Alexander K. McClure. See Butler-2, 550, 633–35, 769; Benjamin F. Butler, "Vice-Presidential Politics in '64," *North American Review*, 141 (Oct. 1885): 331–34; McClure-1, 118–19.

76. For still another version of this traditional family story, see the account of William J. Butler, *Illinois State Journal* (Springfield), Feb. 28, 1937.

77. Howard JQ, 396–97, wherein it is Lincoln, rather than Butler, who brings up the study of law. In the later, more detailed version reproduced here, Butler mistakenly remembered the conversation as having taken place after Lincoln's last winter at Vandalia, that is, in 1839, but it was in 1835 that Peter Van Bergen levied on Lincoln's personal property to collect a debt growing out of the failure of the Lincoln-Berry store. By that time, according to Lincoln's own testimony (*Collected Works*, IV, 65), he had already begun to study law. William H. Herndon, writing to Jesse W. Weik, Jan. 15, 16, 1886 (9:1936–39, 1946–47), Herndon-Weik Collection, declared that Butler boarded Lincoln without charge for five years. The statement was echoed more cautiously in Herndon, I, 185–86. But on November 10, 1888 (10:2381–84), Herndon expressed to Weik the opinion that the story of such charity was untrue.

78. In the source, Gillmore's name is misspelled "Gilmore."

79. The interviewer, misunderstanding Cameron, wrote "Weed" instead of "Wade."

80. *Collected Works*, VIII, 386–87.

81. See also John A. Campbell to Benjamin R. Curtis, July 20, 1865, *Century Magazine*, 38 (Oct. 1889): 950–54.

82. See *Collected Works*, III, 182; Holzer, 229–30.

83. The incident was related (with Cannon identified only as an army colonel) in the sermon delivered by John McClintock on April 16, 1865; also by Joseph P. Thompson (with Cannon identified) in his sermon of April 30, 1865, *Voices*, 135, 194–95. Carpenter-2, 115–16 (1866), repeats Thompson's version. Cannon himself described the incident to Herndon, Oct. 7, c. 1889 (10:2342–52), Herndon-Weik Collection.

84. See Mary Lincoln to Henry C. Deming, Dec. 16, 1867, in Justin G. Turner and Linda Levitt Turner, *Mary Todd Lincoln: Her Life and Letters* (New York: Alfred A. Knopf, 1972), 463–64. Carpenter himself wrote: "I *loved* him heart and soul, but he cared little for *me*, perhaps would never have thought of me a half dozen times had he lived." To Herndon, Jan. 16, 1867 (9:1377–90), Herndon-Weik Collection.

85. In Carpenter-2, 21, these two words are replaced with: "He said in substance."

86. The verse Lincoln referred to was:

> "The mossy marbles rest
> On the lips that he has pressed
> In their bloom,

> And the names he loved to hear
> Have been carved for many a year
> On the tomb."

87. For earlier versions, indicating that this was a well-worn joke, see Zall, 67–68.

88. Zall, 69, points out that a lawyer is similarly characterized in Joseph G. Baldwin's *Flush Times of Alabama and Mississippi* (1853).

89. See Zall, 47–48; Cullom-2, 99.

90. Augusta (Ga.) *Chronicle and Sentinel*, quoted in Barrett, 827. Stephens insisted in 1865 that the newspaper report was more accurate and that Lincoln's punch line was simply: "Let 'em root." See Zall, 49.

91. According to Locke, he first met Lincoln in 1858, met him again in 1859, received a letter from him in 1863, and called on him at the White House that same year and again in 1864. Rice AT, 439–50. Furthermore, such ignorance of Nasby among knowledgeable politicians in 1865 is hard to believe. The pieces had been appearing in newspapers since the beginning of the war and had been published as a book in 1864.

92. The *Post* described its informant as "an eminent portrait painter" who was well acquainted with Mr. Lincoln and often admitted to "intimate and unreserved conversation with him." Johnson's "error" was, of course, his unseemly harangue at the inauguration ceremony.

93. *Collected Works*, IV, 114–15; Holzer et al., 21–25.

94. Chandler or his interviewer mistakenly dated this meeting September 1864. Chief Justice Taney died on October 12, and Chase was nominated on December 6.

95. See *Collected Works*, VI, 439.

96. See *Collected Works*, VI, 428–29.

97. See Joseph George, Jr., "The Lincoln Writings of Charles P. T. Chiniquy," *ISHSJ*, 69 (1976): 17–25.

98. A comparison of two passages on this critical subject in Chittenden's *Recollections* serves to illustrate his general unreliability. The book begins with these words: "When the notes were made which are now expanded into a volume, I had no purpose beyond that of recording, so far as I had time and opportunity, my personal knowledge of current events, which might afterwards possess some interest for my family and my immediate personal friends. Neither then nor for a quarter of a century afterwards had any thought of their publication occurred to me." But later, as he prepares to describe Chase's resignation and its aftermath, we are told: "I have written the following account largely from personal knowledge, from what I myself saw and heard. The principal incidents were written in my journal about the time they occurred. It has been the regret of my subsequent life that I did not at the time know how great a man Mr. Lincoln was; that I did not at the time write out and preserve an account of many other things said and done by him. *This occurrence was an exception*. I felt at the time that Mr. Lincoln was revealing himself to me in a new and elevated character, and I undertook to record the words in which that revelation was made." Chittenden, 1, 369. Italics added.

99. William E. Barton, *The Life of Abraham Lincoln* (2 vols.; Indianapolis: Bobbs-Merrill Co., 1925), II, 250–51. In 1899, Charles Francis Adams, Jr., demonstrated the unreliability of Chittenden's account of how the issuance of $10 million in govern-

ment bonds helped prevent delivery of the Laird rams to the Confederacy. "Where his story was not a pure figment of the imagination," Adams wrote, "his memory deceived him at almost every point." Chittenden, 194-211; Adams paper on the Laird rams in *MHSP*, n.s., 13 (Oct. 1899): 196.

100. New York *Herald*, Feb. 24, 1861.

101. New York *Herald*, Feb. 24, 1861. According to the reporter, Lincoln received the peace conference delegates at 9:00 P.M., then a large group of ladies, each introduced by her male escort, and then the members of the Buchanan cabinet at 10:00 P.M.

102. Chittenden devoted a whole chapter to the incident in his *Recollections*, and it was later published as a separate book, *Lincoln and the Sleeping Sentinel: The True Story* (New York: Harper & Brothers, 1909).

103. New York *Tribune*, Sept. 9, 10, 1861. Sandburg, III, 528-33, credits the Chittenden account but is otherwise a perceptive discussion of the Scott affair and the Lincoln legend that grew out of it.

104. Bray Hammond, *Sovereignty and an Empty Purse: Banks and Politics in the Civil War* (Princeton, N.J.: Princeton University Press, 1970), 196-202, 229-35.

105. Walter B. Stevens, *Missouri: The Center State, 1821-1915* (2 vols.; Chicago: S. J. Clarke Publishing Co., 1915), I, 329.

106. See Lincoln's letter to Clay, Aug. 12, 1862, *Collected Works*, V, 368.

107. James B. Fry, who accompanied Lincoln to Gettysburg, had "no recollection of seeing him writing or even reading his speech during the journey." Rice AT, 403.

108. Coffey was also the retailer of a notable Lincoln witticism from a source that he identified only as "a friend." A delegation seeking to influence the appointment of a commissioner to the Sandwich Islands, argued that their candidate was in bad health and would benefit from residence in that balmy climate. Lincoln replied: "Gentlemen, I am sorry to say that there are eight other applicants for that place, and they are all sicker than your man." Rice AT, 239-40.

109. William H. Herndon wrote "This is true" after Cogdal's assertion that he had often talked with Lincoln about religion in the Lincoln-Herndon office. Herndon's undated memorandum of an interview (11:3006-7), Herndon-Weik Collection. There is no correspondence between Lincoln and Cogdal in the *Collected Works* or in the Lincoln Papers.

110. For an attack on Cogdal's credibility, see Randall-1, II, 333-35; for defenses, see John Y. Simon, "Abraham Lincoln and Ann Rutledge," *Journal of the Abraham Lincoln Association*, 11 (1990): 24-26; Douglas L. Wilson, "Abraham Lincoln, Ann Rutledge, and the Evidence of Herndon's Informants," *Civil War History*, 36 (1990): 315-17. The fullest treatment, John Evangelist Walsh, *The Shadows Rise: Abraham Lincoln and the Ann Rutledge Legend* (Urbana: University of Illinois Press, 1993), 79-85, is likewise favorable but in some degree circular in that it adduces as evidence of credibility certain statements of fact in the very document whose credibility is supposedly under examination. Benjamin F. Irwin informed Herndon that Cogdal had quoted Lincoln as saying in 1860 that Ann Rutledge was then living in Iowa and that "he really did love the woman in 1834 and loved her still in 1860." Irwin to Herndon, Sept. 22, 1866 (8:924-25), Herndon-Weik Collection.

111. Another version, with the third sentence omitted, is in Rankin-2, 290.

112. See *Collected Works*, VIII, 405-6. The question at issue was whether it was

enough for Richmond clergy to refrain from praying for Jefferson Davis or whether they must also include prayers for Abraham Lincoln in their services.

113. Forney's speech at Weldon, Pennsylvania, printed in the Rochester (N.Y.) *Express* and quoted in Carpenter-2, 269–70. The trembling hand is attested to in Charles Sumner to George Livermore, Jan. 9, 1863, *Sumner Letters*, II, 139–40.

114. For a similar recollective quotation, see Edna Dean Procter, "At a Lincoln Reception," *National Magazine*, 29 (Apr. 1909): 519.

115. It was on May 11, 1864, in a letter to General Halleck that Grant declared his intention "to fight it out on this line if it takes all summer." *OR*, Ser. I, Vol. 36, Pt. II, 627.

116. William Lloyd Garrison described Conway in 1864 as "impulsive, eccentric, reckless, highly imaginative, and ambitious at this time for 'radical' distinction." Garrison, V, 220.

117. See *Collected Works*, III, 438–62.

118. According to Conwell, Lincoln greeted him by saying, "I am a very busy man and have no time to spare; so tell me in the fewest words what it is you want." But then the President supposedly spent several hours with the 21-year-old youth, talking of many things, reading selections from Artemus Ward and telling a number of stories. Conwell also claimed to have heard the Cooper Institute address in 1860, and, if we are to believe him, Lincoln stumbled embarrassingly through the early part of his manuscript, then put it aside and for the rest of the time spoke extemporaneously, with dazzling success. See Conwell, 13–22, 32–63, 68–74. Conwell, 5–8, says that he visited Lincoln in order to plead for the life of a condemned soldier, but according to a later writer, he, Conwell, had been court-martialed for being AWOL and was seeking to have the verdict expunged from his record. See W.C. Crosby, "Acres of Diamonds," *American Mercury*, 14 (May 1928): 110.

119. Dispatch of January 23, Chicago *Tribune*, Jan. 28, 1862.

120. New York *Tribune*, Jan. 24, 1862. See also Croffut's letter appearing the same day in the Washington *National Republican*.

121. Crook, although he was on duty at the White House for only three months, declared that Lincoln often talked with him about the possibility of an attempt being made on his life. Crook, 74.

122. The letter, though unsigned, is written on the superintendent's letterhead stationery.

123. See John G. Nicolay, "Lincoln's Gettysburg Address," *Century Magazine*, 47 (Feb. 1894): 601–2; Louis A. Warren, *Lincoln's Gettysburg Declaration* (Fort Wayne, Ind.: Lincoln National Life Foundation, 1964), 69–70, 72.

124. Published posthumously from one of Curtis's letters, date not given.

125. See *Collected Works*, VI, 173–74.

126. Ida M. Tarbell, *All in the Day's Work: An Autobiography* (New York: Macmillan Co., 1939), 174–77.

127. For demolition of Dana's story, see Earl S. Pomeroy, "Lincoln, the Thirteenth Amendment, and the Admission of Nevada," *Pacific Historical Review*, 12 (1943): 362–68.

128. The interviewer was Ferdinand C. Iglehart, a Methodist minister who was on the editorial staff of the *Christian Herald*.

129. Wood had been in charge of the special train carrying Lincoln from Springfield to Washington in February 1861.

130. Orme wanted leave in order to deal with the estate of his father-in-law, William McCullough, who had been killed in battle on December 5. It was at Davis's urging that Lincoln wrote his famous letter of condolence to young Fanny McCullough. See *Collected Works*, VI, 16–17; King, 205.

131. Misdated Sept. 10, 1866, in Herndon, III, 556n.

132. The offending critic was Charles C. Fulton, editor of the Baltimore *American*, generally regarded as an ally of Montgomery Blair and therefore of his brother-in-law, Assistant Secretary of the Navy Gustavus V. Fox.

133. See *Collected Works*, VI, 170, 173–74.

134. The letter, though undated, was written on the same day as the interview, which took place on Saturday, May 2. See Davis to Lincoln, May 4, 1863, Lincoln Papers.

135. Another version, traced no further than Ralph Y. McGinnis, *Quotations from Abraham Lincoln* (Chicago: Nelson-Hall, 1979), 14: "Stanton reminds me of an old Methodist preacher out West who became so energetic in the pulpit that his parishioners talked of putting rocks in his pockets to hold him down. Now we may be obliged to serve Stanton in the same way, but I guess we'll let him jump a while first."

136. See Matthew, 22: 37–39.

137. The reference here is to the peace mission of James F. Jaquess and James R. Gilmore (q.v.) in July 1864, but the results of that enterprise were not yet known to Lincoln when he defined his position with respect to Greeley and the Niagara Falls negotiations.

138. Compare Lincoln's supposed summary of the opening exchange of correspondence between him and Greeley with the actual text of the letters in *Collected Works*, VII, 435. Lincoln would have known, for example, that only one of the Confederate agents, Clement C. Clay, was a former senator and that he was a Democrat, rather than a Whig.

139. See *Collected Works*, V, 484–85.

140. Herndon to Jesse W. Weik, Jan. 8, 1886 (9:1906–9), Herndon-Weik Collection; Henderson, 198; Bateman, 9–11. The story was also published, without identification of an auditor, by the New York *Post*, Feb. 17, 1864.

141. Dicey repeated this story with somewhat different wording in "Lincolniana," *Macmillan's Magazine*, 12 (June 1865): 191.

142. See *Collected Works*, II, 375.

143. For the legend of the "Peoria truce," supposedly honored by the two men at Lacon, but violated by Douglas at Princeton the very next day, see Herndon, II, 373–74; Paul M. Angle, "The Peoria Truce," *ISHSJ*, 21 (1928–29): 500–505; Ernest E. East, "The 'Peoria Truce': Did Douglas Ask for Quarter?" *ibid.*, 29 (1936–37): 70–75.

144. In January 1865, Lincoln received from the presidential electors of New York a recommendation endorsing Dittenhoefer's application for appointment as federal district judge in South Carolina. *Collected Works*, VIII, 212. There is no correspondence between the two men in the *Collected Works* or in the Lincoln Papers.

145. Port Hudson (May 27), Millikens Bend (June 7), and Fort Wagner (July 18) were engagements in which black troops fought and distinguished themselves. The

"proclamation" referred to was Lincoln's order of July 30, 1863, cited in the following note.

146. See *Collected Works*, VI, 357; VII, 345–46; J. G. Randall, *Constitutional Problems under Lincoln* (rev. ed.; Urbana: University of Illinois Press, 1951), xvi-xvii.

147. See Herndon, II, 399–400; Jesse W. Weik memorandum, Aug. 3, 1887 (12:486), Herndon-Weik Collection.

148. Zall, 40–41.

149. Pratt-1, 59. The charges against Edwards in 1833 were rape and riot.

150. The reporter mistakenly wrote "Howard" here. There is no Howard County in Illinois, and elsewhere in the interview, Edwards spoke of "old Menard," his home county.

151. See her statement to William H. Herndon in 1865 (11:2963–67), Herndon-Weik Collection.

152. The final sentence, written on the reverse side of the page, does not appear in the microfilm edition, but is to be found in the Herndon-Springer copy of the statement, I, 403.

153. James Herndon to Herndon, May 29, 1865 (7:87–89), Herndon-Weik Collection. In the biography, Herndon declared: "I obtained this speech from A. Y. Ellis who in 1865 wrote it out," but Ellis had written only: "I have a coppy of his first speach hear it is." In a letter to James H. Wilson, Nov. 22, 1890 (10:2747), Herndon said of the speech "I got it from two intelligent men who heard it shot off in a hurry."

154. Misdated July 16, 1866, in Herndon, II, 269.

155. The salutation is simply "Dear Friend," but that the letter was addressed to Mrs. Spafford is clear from Ellsworth's subsequent letter to Carrie Spafford, Mar. 24, 1861.

156. Fell remembered the date of the speech as September 19, but it was actually delivered on September 26.

157. Fessenden remembered having this conversation with Lincoln on July 2, the morning after the Senate received and confirmed his nomination, but according to Hay-1, 201–3, it took place on July 1.

158. See *Collected Works*, VII, 412–14, 419.

159. See Charles H. Coleman, "Lincoln's 'Rum Sweat' Facts or Fiction?" *Lincoln Herald*, 56 (Spring-Summer, 1954): 28–30. Uncritical use of the Floyd story was made by Milton H. Shutes in *Lincoln and the Doctors: A Medical Narrative of the Life of Abraham Lincoln* (New York: Pioneer Press, 1933), 59–61. Floyd's assertion that Lincoln did some legal work for him is ostensibly confirmed in a letter that appears in *Collected Works*, II, 332–33, but this document proves to have no corroborative value. The source given by the editors is Gilbert A. Tracy, ed., *Uncollected Letters of Abraham Lincoln* (Boston: Houghton Mifflin Co., 1917), 66; and Tracy, one discovers, took it directly from Floyd's "rum-sweat" article.

160. New York *Post*, Aug. 4, 1862; New York *Tribune*, Aug. 5, 1862.

161. See Lincoln's General War Order No. 3, dated March 8, 1862, *Collected Works*, V, 151.

162. James Harrison Wilson, "Reminiscences of General Grant," *Century Magazine*, 30 (Oct. 1885): 954.

163. A slightly variant version, quoted from a Gardner speech of February 8,

1890, is in Edward L. Pierce to William H. Herndon, Feb. 12, 1890 (13:501–3), Herndon-Weik Collection. Pierce stated in the letter that he had asked Gardner to write out his recollections for Herndon.

164. Hertz, 288–92, 321–30, mixes the January 31 and December 8 letters.

165. See also Gillespie to Herndon, Sept. 19, 1866 (8:905–8), Herndon-Weik Collection.

166. For Lincoln's intervention in the case of a civilian sentenced to death by a military commission for parole violation, see *Collected Works*, V, 170; and for a discussion of the rarity of such punishment by the judge advocate reviewing the case, see *OR*, Ser. II, Vol. 1, pp. 372–73.

167. Gilmore-3, vii-viii. Although Gilmore claimed to have had interviews with Lincoln beginning as early as April 1861, it was probably not until near the end of May 1863 that the two men met for the first time. See in the Lincoln Papers his letter of May 27, requesting an interview, and his letter of July 27, which he began by explaining again who he was and reminding the President of their previous meeting. Likewise heavily discountable is Gilmore's assertion that Jaquess had long been "on terms of considerable intimacy" with Lincoln; for Lincoln himself wrote in 1863: "I have but a slight personal acquaintance with Col. Jaquess." Gilmore-2, 435; *Collected Works*, VI, 236.

168. Even Carl Sandburg, although he made credulous use of Gilmore's reminiscences, acknowledged: "We are constantly suspicious of his quoted utterances." Sandburg, I, xiii, 401–3.

169. Gilmore to Lincoln, July 17, 24; Sydney Howard Gay to Lincoln, July 26, enclosing letter of Edmonds to Gilmore, July 21, 1864, Lincoln Papers. Gay, editor of the New York *Tribune*, corroborated Gilmore's assertion that the proposal had Greeley's endorsement.

170. The story is likewise accepted in Sandburg, II, 548.

171. For the texts of the real order (never actually issued) and the spurious proclamation published in the New York *World*, see *Collected Works*, VII, 344, 347–50. See also note 256 below.

172. According to Gilmore, he also consulted Congressman James A. Garfield, who approved of the project but could not attend the evening conference because of another engagement. Garfield and Chase, as well as Lincoln, were conveniently dead when Gilmore published his account.

173. Among historians accepting Gilmore's account are Edward Chase Kirkland, *The Peacemakers of 1864* (New York: Macmillan Co., 1927), 91–92; Randall and Current, 165–66. Chase's diary entry for July 6, 1864, runs to several pages of detail about meetings with a number of persons (Chase, 477–79). Yet there is no mention in it of his conferring with Gilmore, dining with him, and then accompanying him to the White House for a conference of several hours with the President. Furthermore, the spuriousness of the seven-point peace program attributed to Lincoln seems plain from the testimony of Confederate officials and Gilmore himself. There is no indication that Gilmore and Jaquess submitted that program to Jefferson Davis, no evidence that they said anything to him about the future basis of southern representation or about payment for emancipated slaves or about calling a national convention. Instead, they proposed something not in the program—namely, that the disposition of slavery and other issues outstanding between North and South

be settled by popular vote. In a public letter written several weeks after his return from Richmond, Gilmore denied a Confederate assertion that he and Jaquess had represented themselves as authorized presidential messengers. Lincoln, he said, had provided them with a pass to Grant's headquarters and a note to Grant asking that they be passed through the lines into Confederate territory. "And that," he added, "is all that the President did, or wrote, or said, or caused to be done, or written, or said in relation to this whole matter." It seems likely that in this instance, he was telling the truth. See the New York *Tribune*, Sept. 5, 1864; *OR, Navies*, Ser. II, Vol. 3, pp. 1190-94; Jefferson Davis, *The Rise and Fall of the Confederate Government* (2 vols.; New York: D. Appleton Co., 1881), II, 610. For an interview in which Jaquess likewise denied that he and Gilmore had any authority to speak for Lincoln, see the New York *Times*, July 21, 1864.

174. Gilmore's earliest published account of the mission, which appeared as Edmund Kirke, "Our Visit to Richmond," *Atlantic Monthly*, 14 (Sept. 1864): 372-83, carried no mention of any authorization or participation by Lincoln, but it served Lincoln's purpose of dramatizing the unwillingness of Jefferson Davis to negotiate on any basis except southern independence.

175. Herndon, II, 306-7.

176. This anecdote and the one about the Dutch Gap Canal (Item 6) were among several written by Grant for his *Memoirs*, but omitted from the published version.

177. Porter H-1, 415 (1897); Porter DD, 309-11 (1885).

178. See *Harper's New Monthly Magazine*, 31 (Sept. 1865): 539; Sherman, II, 326-27.

179. See McCulloch, 408; Rice AT, 97. Alexander K. McClure asserted in McClure-3, xiii, that Lincoln told the story to him and two other men in the spring of 1865. Carpenter-1, 757, reported it in 1865 as told in connection with letting Jacob Thompson escape through Portland, Maine. Conway-2, I, 345-46, claimed unconvincingly to have heard the story from Lincoln's lips in 1862.

180. See *Collected Works*, II, 96.

181. This story has the smell of myth, but Lincoln did not contradict or revise it when he corrected a number of errors in a campaign biography. See the facsimile edition, with Lincoln's annotations, of Howells, 38-39. Greene told the story again in a letter to Herndon, May 30, 1865 (7:91-103), Herndon-Weik Collection.

182. Grinnell, 86-87. His biographer says that Grinnell was "constitutionally inaccurate" but accepts the Greeley story and quotes uncritically from Grinnell's recollected words of Lincoln. See Charles E. Payne, *Josiah Bushnell Grinnell* (Iowa City: State Historical Society of Iowa, 1938), 26-27, 144-45, 302.

183. The holograph note has never been produced. The text appears in *Collected Works*, VII, 379, citing *Complete Works* (1905), XI, 133, where it is described only as "Card to Secretary of War." This item did not appear in Nicolay and Hay's *Complete Works* (1894), and one suspects that Francis D. Tandy, publisher and probably the real editor of the 1905 edition, simply took it from Grinnell's book.

184. See Lincoln to Grover, Jan. 15, 1860, *Collected Works*, III, 514.

185. Some and perhaps many of Lincoln's visits to the theater went unrecorded in newspapers and other contemporary records. Nevertheless, for what it is worth, *Lincoln Day by Day* notes his attendance 10 times at Ford's Theatre and 21 times at Grover's. For information on Grover and the text of a preposterous statement

made by him in the year of his death about Lincoln at Gettysburg, see the *Lincoln Newsletter* of Lincoln College, 12 (Fall 1993): 4–6.

186. See Bates DH-1, 267–68; Carpenter-2, 166.

187. Undated Herndon ms. (11:3527–32), Herndon-Weik Collection.

188. David Rankin Barbee, "President Lincoln and Doctor Gurley," *ALQ*, 5 (1948–49): 23.

189. The text of the order, as provided by Hagner, is in *Collected Works*, VI, 378.

190. Hamlin's speech against certain features of the Clayton compromise was delivered on July 22, 1848. *Congressional Globe*, 30 Cong., 1 sess., App., 1145–48.

191. William H. Herndon, not wholly unbiased on the subject, to be sure, said that "Dennis Hanks would go a mile out of his way to lie." Herndon to Ward H. Lamon, Feb. 25, 1870, Lamon Papers. Henry C. Whitney called him a "common liar." Whitney to Jesse W. Weik, Sept. 7, 1893, Weik Papers, ISHL.

192. *Collected Works*, IV, 63–64.

193. The letter was written by Herndon and signed by Hanks with an "X."

194. Hanks to Herndon, June 13, 1865 (7:156–60); and undated Hanks statement taken down by Herndon (11:3064–77), Herndon-Weik Collection. In his autobiography written for John L. Scripps in 1860, Lincoln stated: "Hanks had not gone to New-Orleans, but having a family, and being likely to be detained from home longer than at first expected, had turned back from St. Louis." Hanks himself asserted, however, that he went all the way to New Orleans and also made the return trip with Lincoln. To a newspaper interviewer in 1881, he boasted that he had made *two* flatboat trips with Lincoln from Illinois to New Orleans. Correspondence of the Philadelphia *Times*, June 2, 1881, reprinted in the New York *Times*, June 7, 1881.

195. In Herndon, III, 441, the word used at this point is "immortalist," Herndon apparently having misread his own handwriting. The Universalist church, which arose near the end of the 18th century, rejected the doctrine of eternal damnation.

196. A variant version, Harlan's statement in an interview shortly before his death, is in Tarbell, III, 103–4. Lincoln's offer to resign was not mentioned in the account of the meeting that appeared in the New York *Tribune*, Aug. 5, 1862 (reproduced in *Collected Works*, V, 356–57); but it was reported in the Cincinnati *Gazette*, Aug. 6, 1862, with the additional assertion that one of the senators present exclaimed: "I hope, in God's name, Mr. President, you will." See also the issues of August 11 and 14.

197. Cordelia A. P. Harvey, "A Wisconsin Woman's Picture of President Lincoln," *Wisconsin Magazine of History*, 1 (1917–18): 233–55. This slightly revised version of the original letter was apparently used by Mrs. Harvey as a lecture after the war.

198. See, for example, Cullom-2, 91.

199. *Collected Works*, V, 59.

200. The Hawkins manuscript was published in *Bookmen's Holiday: Notes and Studies Written in Tribute to Harry Miller Lydenberg* (New York: New York Public Library, 1943). The quotations from Lincoln are on pp. 11, 19, and 23.

201. Haworth, who was interviewed by Stevens in 1908, claimed to have a gavel and a cane presented to him by Lincoln, made from the famous rails displayed by John Hanks in 1860. That his main interest was in selling those "relics" is apparent from his letters of June 25 and December 29, 1908, to James R. B. Van Cleave, Centennial Reminiscences.

202. Hawthorne's article, "Chiefly About War-Matters," appeared in the *Atlantic Monthly* for July 1862, but the account of his visit to the White House was excised because the editor, James T. Fields, thought it lacking in taste. Fields published the stricken passage in 1871.

203. A variant version, with a summary of Lincoln's other remarks to the soldiers, is in Nicolay and Hay, IV, 152-53.

204. The *Times* editorial, Apr. 25, 1861, was headed: "Wanted—A Leader!"

205. For Lincoln's trenchant reply to Harris, see *Collected Works*, IV, 351-52.

206. See *Collected Works*, IV, 357-58.

207. See *Collected Works*, VIII, 200-201, 267, 343-44, 410.

208. See *Collected Works*, IV, 557.

209. *Collected Works*, V, 155.

210. McClellan's actual phrasing was: "To leave Pope to get out of his scrape & at once use all our means to make the Capital perfectly safe." McClellan-1, 416.

211. *Collected Works*, V, 442-43, 508-9.

212. The word "live" appears in the manuscript diary but is omitted in the Dennett edition.

213. For Lincoln's letter of reprimand, see *Collected Works*, VI, 538-39.

214. Meade's general order of July 4, 1863, in Meade, II, 122-23.

215. Here are Lincoln's further remarks as reconstructed from notes by Stoddard and included in Hay's memorandum. Concerning the Republican schism in Missouri he said:

"These so-called Conservatives will avoid, as a general thing, votes or any actions which will in any way interfere with or imperil the success of their party. For instance, they will vote for supplies and such other measures as are absolutely necessary to sustain this government. They will do this selfishly. They do not wish that the government should fall; for they expect to obtain possession of it. At the same time, their support will not be hearty; their votes are not equal to those of the real friends of the administration. They do not give as much strength. They are not worth so much. My Radical friends will therefore see that I understand and appreciate their position. Still, you appear to come before me as my friends, *if I agree with you, but not otherwise*. I do not here speak of mere personal friendship as between man and man. When I speak of my friends, I mean those who are friendly to my measures, to the policy of the government. I am well aware that by many—by some even among this delegation (I shall not name them)—I have been in public speeches and in printed documents charged with tyranny and willfulness, with a disposition to make my own personal will supreme. I do not intend to be a tyrant. At all events, I shall take care that in my own eyes, I do not become one. I shall always try and preserve one friend within me, whoever else fails me, to tell me that I have not been a tyrant and that I have acted right. I have no right to act the tyrant to mere political opponents. If a man votes for supplies of men and money, encourages enlistments, discourages desertions, does all in his power to carry the war on to a successful issue, I have no right to question him for his abstract political opinions. I must make a dividing-line somewhere between those who are the opponents of the government and those who only oppose peculiar features of my administration while they sustain the government.

"In the Vallandigham case, a commander in the field decided that a certain political enemy of the government had become dangerous in a military point of view and that he must be removed. I believe that he was justifiable in coming to such a decision. In cases where political opponents do not in any way interfere with or hinder military operations, I have judged it best to let them alone.

"My friends in Missouri last winter did me a great unkindness. I had relied upon my Radical friends as my mainstay in the management of affairs in that state, and they disappointed me. I had recommended gradual emancipation, and Congress had endorsed that course. The Radicals in Congress voted for it. The Missouri delegation in Congress went for it—went, as I thought, right. I had the highest hope that at last Missouri was on the right track. But I was disappointed by the immediate emancipation movement. It endangers the success of the whole advance towards freedom. But you say that the gradual emancipation men were insincere, that they intended soon to repeal their action, that their course and their professions are purely fraudulent. Now, I do not think that a majority of the gradual emancipationists are insincere. Large bodies of men cannot play the hypocrite. I announced my own opinion freely at the time. I was in favor of gradual emancipation. I still am so. You must not call yourselves my friends if you are only so while I agree with you. According to that, if you differ with me you are not my friends. But the mode of emancipation in Missouri is not my business. That is a matter which belongs exclusively to the citizens of that state. I do not wish to interfere. I desire, if it pleases the people of Missouri, that they should adopt gradual emancipation. I think that your division upon this subject jeopardizes the grand result. I think that a union of all antislavery men upon this point would have made emancipation a fixed fact forever. Still, I do not assume any control. I am sorry to see antislavery men opposing such a movement, but I will take up the subjects you have laid before me without prejudice, without pique, without resentment, and will try and do what is best for all, as affecting the grand result to which we all are looking."

216. Carpenter's six-month stay in the White House, it should be noted, came to an end at least two weeks before publication of the Wade-Davis manifesto. Zall, 32, shows that the story did not originate with Lincoln.

217. Horace White, a journalist associated with the Chicago *Tribune* during the Civil War, later wrote that Lincoln's "moral obtuseness" in retaining Ward H. Lamon as United States marshal for the District of Columbia was what alienated Grimes. White to Jesse K. Weik, Aug. 12, 1914 (13:1123-27), Herndon-Weik Collection. See Grimes's attack on Lamon in *Congressional Globe*, 37 Cong., 2 sess., 310-11 (Jan. 14, 1862).

218. For details of the Ashley bill and what happened to it, see Belz, 251-67.

219. *Collected Works*, IV, 130n.

220. In an interview some years earlier (Tarbell Papers and Tarbell, IV, 19-21), Henderson had provided a slightly different version.

221. Thomas J. Henderson, "Recollections of Lincoln: Characteristic Incidents in the Early Life of the Great President," typescript, ISHL.

222. Paul M. Angle in his introduction to *Herndon's Lincoln* (New York: De Capo Press, 1983; originally published in 1930), xl. Donald, 351, declares that "Herndon's own recollections, though occasionally biased, are on the whole remarkably accurate."

223. Compare the quotation in Herndon, II, 366, beginning "It is the most glittering, ostentatious, and displaying property in the world" with the same quotation

in Gillespie to Herndon, Jan. 31, 1866 (8:536–55), Herndon-Weik Collection, published in Hertz, 291.

224. Herndon to Weik, Dec. 1, 1888 (10:2410–17), Herndon-Weik Collection.

225. Matheny associated the exchange on Negro suffrage with a debate at the Market House in Jacksonville on March 17. It is known that Lincoln made use of the charge against Van Buren, though perhaps not for the first time, in a debate with Douglas and others at Tremont on May 2. See *Collected Works*, I, 209–10.

226. The case may have been *Rebecca Thomas v. Erastus Wright*, an appeal in the Sangamon County Circuit Court in 1846. According to William D. Beard of the Lincoln Legal Papers staff, the record shows a judgment in favor of the plaintiff, but with only $35 awarded, instead of the $200 recalled by Herndon. The case file is missing.

227. Writing to Weik, Oct. 10, 1888 (10:2353–56), Herndon-Weik Collection, Herndon said Lincoln told him that "his mother was a kind of genius—a great hearted and big headed woman." See also Herndon's statement written at Greencastle, Indiana, and dated August 20, 1887, in Hertz, 410–12.

228. Herndon to James H. Wilson, Oct. 1, 15, 1889 (10:2575, 2578–80), Herndon-Weik Collection. Herndon came to believe that his partner was ashamed of his mother and the whole "lecherous" Hanks family. He considered it highly significant that Lincoln never visited his mother's grave and never had any kind of marker put on it, as he did on his father's grave. Herndon, it should be noted, also cherished and disseminated the notion that Lincoln himself had been fathered by someone other than Thomas Lincoln. See the letters to Lamon cited in the text; the letters to Weik of January 19, 1886 (9:1952–55) and December 1, 1888 (10:2410–17); and Donald, 307–9.

229. The words "patiently" and "ages" are questionable.

230. For Lincoln's one passing remark about woman suffrage, see *Collected Works*, I, 48.

231. See also Herndon to James H. Wilson, Sept. 23, 1889 (10:2564); and Herndon to Weik, July 23, 1890 (10:2688–91), Herndon-Weik Collection.

232. See *Collected Works*, I, 382.

233. See Herndon, II, 367–69; *Collected Works*, II, 240–47.

234. Herndon to Weik, Jan. 6, 1887 (2054–55); Jan. 23, 28, 1889 (10:2468–71, 2472–73), Herndon-Weik Collection.

235. The letter itself is undated, but Herndon dated it in his next letter.

236. Weik-2, 239, quotes a different version by Herndon in which Lincoln says: "The evidence of defeat, the recital of what was not as well as what cannot be done, serves to put the scientist or philosopher on his guard—sets him to thinking on the right line."

237. According to both the *Illinois State Journal* and the *Illinois State Register* of June 11, 1856, the meeting held the night before to ratify the nominations of the Bloomington convention was well attended.

238. "Stool pigeon" at this time meant a decoy, not a police informer.

239. See Lincoln's eloquent fragment on Niagara Falls in *Collected Works*, II, 10–11; also Donald, 128.

240. Lincoln to Robert Moseley, July 2, 1858, *Collected Works*, II, 483. Harding to Herndon, Jan. 7, 1867 (9:1364), Herndon-Weik Collection, confirms the incident without dating it.

241. See *Collected Works*, II, 430, 456–57; Herndon, II, 391.

242. Compare the sources cited with Herndon to Weik, Oct. 29, 1885 (9:1805–6), Herndon-Weik Collection.

243. In Herndon, III, 436, the word used is "repeatedly." To Henry C. Whitney, Herndon wrote on April 16, 1887, "Lincoln once said to me: 'I fear that I shall meet with some terrible end.'" Bound with Herndon's letters to and from Charles H. Hart, Huntington Library.

244. See also Herndon to Weik, Jan. 22, 1887 (10:2070–77), Herndon Weik Collection; and Herndon, II, 325.

245. Herndon to Weik, Nov. 17, 1885 (9:1819–20), Herndon-Weik Collection.

246. Herndon to Wendell Phillips, Dec. 28, 1860, Bartlett, 160.

247. Herndon himself mistakenly wrote that this, his one and only visit to Washington during Lincoln's presidency, took place in late summer 1861. Herndon, III, 506.

248. For the portrait, see Holzer et al., 44.

249. This letter is not now in the Gay Papers, but presumably it was when Starr, the first scholar to use the papers, wrote *Bohemian Brigade* in the early 1950s.

250. *Congressional Globe*, 37 Cong., 2 sess., 2041.

251. See *Collected Works*, VI, 241.

252. For Lincoln's own challenge to Hill's veracity, see *Collected Works*, IV, 104–8.

253. Another version of the Hillis story as told to Anderson is in Rankin-2, 72–80. See also Whitney-1, 51, where Lincoln is quoted as saying of Mrs. Hillis: "She is the only woman that ever appreciated me enough to pay me a compliment."

254. Cramer, 101–24. Laski had earlier repeated Holmes's story to Alexander Woollcott, who published "Get Down, You Fool," in the *Atlantic Monthly*, 161 (Feb. 1938): 169–73.

255. Speech on the Sub-Treasury, Dec. 26, 1839, *Collected Works*, I, 178.

256. For the story of the spurious proclamation and the Lincoln administration's excessive reaction to it, see Harper, 289–303; *Collected Works*, VII, 347–50. Howard has also been identified as the author of the false report that Lincoln slipped through Baltimore in February 1861 wearing "a Scotch plaid cap and a very long military cloak." Harper, 89.

257. Howard identified the man only as "Senator D." It might have been James R. Doolittle of Wisconsin, who was given to lecturing on the Bible and its prophecies, or perhaps James Dixon of Connecticut.

258. See *Collected Works*, VII, 530–31; VIII, 17.

259. See *Collected Works*, VI, 310–11.

260. Lincoln (and Hutchins, too, for that matter) would have said "minister," instead of "ambassador," a diplomatic rank not created by Congress until 1893.

261. See Welles-1, II, 112; *Collected Works*, VIII, 307–8.

262. See Harper, 314–15; Sandburg, III, 249; Don C. Seitz, *Horace Greeley, Founder of the New York Tribune* (Indianapolis: Bobbs-Merrill Co., 1926), 267–70; James H. Trietsch, *The Printer and the Prince* (New York: Exposition Press, 1955), 278–81, 321.

263. As it stands, the sentence is a non sequitur. Jayne may have intended to write "agree" instead of "disagree"; for Lincoln was supposedly explaining why he

intended to propound the house-divided doctrine *in spite of* opposition from most of his advisers.

264. Information on Johns and the assault cases was provided by Dennis E. Suttles of the Lincoln Legal Papers project.

265. *Collected Works*, VIII, 337.

266. Mrs. Judd remembered the year as 1856, but she said that Lincoln had come to Chicago as a counsel in the Rock Island bridge suit. That would set the date in early July 1857. However, she also recalled Lincoln's mentioning his lecture on discoveries and inventions at Bloomington (delivered in April 1858), which would fix the time as no earlier than the summer of 1858.

267. According to Judd, he and Ebenezer Peck went to Mendota and routed Lincoln out of bed for a conference at 2:00 A.M. on August 27, the day of the Freeport debate. But it has always been understood that Lincoln stayed the night of the 26th at Amboy, and in any case, Judd was that same night on his way from Chicago to Springfield for a meeting of the state central committee. It is not impossible, to be sure, that he managed to go by way of Amboy and was later mistaken only with respect to the place where they held their conference. See Joseph Medill to Lincoln, [Aug. 27], 1858, Lincoln Papers.

268. John Locke Scripps, *Life of Abraham Lincoln*, ed. by M. L. Houser (Peoria, Ill., 1931), 64, where the first sentence of the quotation is: "I am killing larger game." See also Fehrenbacher-1, 122–26. In the same letter to Weik, Herndon named Charles H. Ray and Ebenezer Peck as corroborators of Judd's story, but he added: "I do not think that Mr. Lincoln ever uttered the words as stated, though he looked at the time for the office. I think at most that the words as above are inferences, legitimate ones. Lincoln never told mortal man his purposes and plans—never." More than half a century later, a certain Murray Nelson asserted that he had been present when Lincoln told Judd and others that he was "killing bigger game." New York *Times*, Feb. 8, 1914.

269. See Jean H. Baker, *Mary Todd Lincoln* (New York: W. W. Norton & Co., 1987), 212–13.

270. It is barely possible that some such conversation might have occurred earlier in the Lincoln administration, but Mrs. Keckley indicated that it took place sometime after Kate Chase became Mrs. William Sprague—that is, after November 1863. By then, Chase was emerging as a rival for the presidency, and his relations with Lincoln were severely strained.

271. Kellogg said that Lincoln used the epigram to emphasize the sophistry of "Douglas's position upon the question of unfriendly legislation." But it was not until after the Dred Scott decision in 1857 that Douglas took up the idea of "unfriendly legislation" in an effort to salvage the principle of popular sovereignty. The quotation with slightly different wording had already appeared in a collection of Lincoln stories, McClure-3, 124. Efforts to trace its origins resulted in some recollections that Lincoln had made the statement during a speech at Clinton, Illinois, in 1858. See *Complete Works* (1905), III, 349n. The epigram did not appear in the ninth edition of John Bartlett's *Familiar Quotations* (1903), but it was included in the tenth (1914).

272. Kent also told this story to Jesse W. Weik, Nov. 21, 1916 (14:1286), Herndon-Weik Collection.

273. The clipping is identified as being from the Milwaukee *Free Press*, Feb. 11, 1907, but the quotation was not found in that issue.

274. Quoted in Herndon, III, 441, where the ascription is to "I. W. Keyes."

275. The entire passage, with some variations in phrasing, is quoted in Carpenter-2, 264, and attributed to a "correspondent of the Boston 'Journal.'"

276. The article, though unsigned, is convincingly identified as the work of Kirkland. Mabbott, 163.

277. Lamar's story was first transmitted to Herndon by J. W. Wartman, July 21, 1865 (7:262–66), Herndon-Weik Collection.

278. Lamon to President Andrew Johnson, undated draft, Lamon Papers.

279. *Collected Works*, VII, 414–15; Lamon to Richard Yates, July 3, 1864, Lamon Papers. For Lamon's involvement with Swett in the New Almaden quicksilver mine and in cotton trading, see Swett to Lamon, June 24, 1863; Jan. 1, Feb. 8, 21, Mar. 30, 1865; Swett to George F. Harding, Jan. 15, 1864; James H. Patterson to Lamon, Dec. 30, 1864; Jan. 3, 11, 1865, Lamon Papers.

280. The parasitic quality of Lamon's reminiscences can be seen, for instance, in connection with the incident of the double image, recalled by Lincoln in 1864 and narrated by Noah Brooks (q.v.) as early as 1865. The 1872 Lamon biography quoted the Brooks account in full, mistakenly attributing it to John Hay, but in the *Recollections*, Lamon assimilated the story to his own experience, presenting it as though told to him directly by Lincoln. Lamon-1, 476–77; Lamon-2, 112–13.

281. For example, Lamon did not name the town where the exchange with Ficklin took place, but he said that it was down in "Egypt" and that on this occasion, Lincoln spoke first. Thus he mistakenly associated the incident with the third debate at Jonesboro, instead of the fourth debate at Charleston. His account of what happened conflicts in several ways with contemporary newspaper reports. See the Chicago *Press and Tribune* account in *Collected Works*, III, 182–83, and the Chicago *Times* account in Holzer, 229–30.

282. Sterling, 24–25; Helen Nicolay, *Personal Traits of Abraham Lincoln* (New York: Century Co., 1912), 163–65; Robert Todd Lincoln to Judd Stewart, Jan. 8, 1920, Stewart Papers. In his earlier book, Lamon devoted two pages to Lincoln's visit to Harrisburg but did not mention the incident of the lost inaugural address. Lamon-1, 522–23.

283. Francis E. Spinner was treasurer of the United States.

284. Lamon enclosed all of this narrative in quotation marks, after having declared: "At this distance of time I will not pretend to give the exact words of this interview, but will state it according to my best recollection."

285. See *Collected Works*, VI, 2. One of the two brothers, John C. Black, survived to become an Illinois congressman, a United States attorney, and a civil service commissioner.

286. It is not unlikely that Lamon had read a story in the Washington *Post* second-handedly quoting the Methodist bishop Edward R. Ames as recalling that Lincoln had said to him in June 1863 that Grant had promised to capture Vicksburg by July 4. Undated clipping in the Tarbell Papers.

287. Lamon-2, 174, 175–76. See Frank L. Klement, "Ward H. Lamon and the Dedication of the Soldiers' Cemetery at Gettysburg," *Civil War History*, 31 (1985): 308, where it is said that "Lamon's position on the speaker's platform would have put him out of hearing of comments made by Everett and Seward to each other."

288. *Collected Works*, VII, 514.

289. For the text of Lincoln's statement, which was not made public, see Lamon-2, 147–49, or *Collected Works*, VII, 548–49.

290. See *Collected Works*, VII, 376–78.

291. Hay-1, 185. In the same entry, Hay wrote: "Talking with Swett tonight, found he was talking Holt for Vice Prest."

292. Lamon to Johnson, undated draft, Lamon Papers. This letter may never have been sent; it is not in the Andrew Johnson Papers, Manuscript Division, Library of Congress. The several letters from Lamon to Johnson in the collection contain no mention of the vice-presidential nomination.

293. Hay-1, 244–46. On Lincoln and the Ashley bill generally, see Belz, 251–67; LaWanda Cox, *Lincoln and Black Freedom: A Study in Presidential Leadership* (Columbia: University of South Carolina Press, 1981), 119–21.

294. See, for example, Sandburg, IV, 243–45; Wolf WJ, 28–29; Stephen B. Oates, *With Malice Toward None: The Life of Abraham Lincoln* (New York: Harper & Row, 1977), 425–26; Jim Bishop, *The Day Lincoln Was Shot* (New York: Harper & Brothers, 1955), 54–56. According to Lamon, Lincoln experienced this strikingly premonitory dream just a few days before his death, but he is quoted as describing it some ten days afterwards and as discussing it again at an even later time. There was no contemporary mention of the dream, not even after the assassination, by Lamon himself or by Mary Lincoln or anyone else who supposedly heard Lincoln's account of it. Furthermore, in fashioning the story, Lamon seems to have forgotten that Lincoln, who is quoted as saying that on the night of the dream he had been "waiting for important dispatches from the front," was actually *at the front* from March 24 to April 9, the day of Lee's surrender.

295. The Texas convention did not pass an ordinance of secession until February 1, but by a vote of 152 to 6 on January 29 it adopted a resolution indicating its intention to do so.

296. Auguste Laugel, *The United States During the War* (New York: Ballière Brothers, 1866).

297. In a later version (*Leslie's Weekly*, Feb. 16, 1899, p. 134), Lincoln said that he got hold of the book while visiting his wife's family in Kentucky. That would have been, presumably, in November 1847, though Lewis mistakenly placed the visit in the 1850s.

298. For discussion of the controversy growing out of this interview, see Donald, 280–81; Ruth Painter Randall, *Mary Lincoln: Biography of a Marriage* (Boston: Little, Brown, & Co., 1953), 395–96, 426–28.

299. There are three different sets of Herndon notes on the interview. Expert guidance respecting them has been provided by Douglas L. Wilson, coeditor with Rodney O. Davis of a forthcoming edition of the letters and statements of Herndon's informants. Herndon, III, 511–14, is a synthesis drawing on all three sets.

300. See Paul M. Angle, ed., *A Portrait of Abraham Lincoln in Letters by His Oldest Son* (Chicago: Chicago Historical Society, 1968), 60. James Harlan, wartime senator from Iowa, attested to the truth of the story but did not say whether his information had come from Abraham Lincoln or from Robert Lincoln, his son-in-law. Harlan to Isaac N. Phillips, Apr. 17, 1897, in Phillips-1, 47n. For a comprehensive discussion, see Gabor S. Boritt, " 'Unfinished Work': Lincoln, Meade, and Gettys-

burg," in Boritt, ed., *Lincoln's Generals* (New York: Oxford University Press, 1994), 98–101, 212–14.

301. Endicott, 226.

302. The senator was probably John P. Hale of New Hampshire, who was no doubt guilty of impropriety but not demonstrably of dishonesty. In 1865, Lincoln appointed him minister to Spain. See Richard H. Sewell, *John P. Hale and the Politics of Abolition* (Cambridge, Mass.: Harvard University Press, 1965), 214–22.

303. The sentence in question was: "The power confided to me will be used to hold, occupy and possess the property, and places belonging to the government, and to collect the duties and imposts." This was itself a substitution for an earlier, even more forceful sentence. See *Collected Works*, IV, 254, 266.

304. The book gives only the last name, "Lord," whereas the name "A. F. Lord" is written on the manuscript version. However, Mrs. James Judson Lord in an undated letter to James R. Van Cleave, Centennial Reminiscences, identified her husband as the Lord in question.

305. According to the diary of Edward Bates, for instance, Lincoln as late as December 25 evinced some reluctance to release the two men in compliance with British demands. Bates E, 216.

306. Internal evidence indicates that Macdonell's letter, though dated "Feb., 1864," was written a year earlier. The phrase "1st of January" obviously refers to the Emancipation Proclamation as a recent event. In addition, she mentioned hearing Clement L. Vallandigham speak in the House of Representatives, and his term as an Ohio congressman ended March 3, 1863.

307. A later version in Weik-2, 304–5 (1922), has somewhat different wording.

308. Writing to Yates from Washington on January 29, 1861, Mather reported on his conference with Scott but made no mention of Lincoln. Yates Papers, ISHL.

309. See *Lincoln Day by Day*, III, 167.

310. Jay Monaghan, "Was Abraham Lincoln Really a Spiritualist?" *ISHSJ*, 34 (1941): 222.

311. *Collected Works*, V, 426; McClellan-1, 486.

312. For the possible source of this story in the *Family Joe Miller* (1848), see Zall, 97.

313. See Sears, 159.

314. Sears, 332.

315. McClure-1, 461. On the same page, McClure declared: "I saw Abraham Lincoln at all hours of the day and night during his Presidential service." For other such extravagant claims, see pp. 111, 134. It should be noted, however, that Lincoln's friend Leonard Swett quoted him as saying that McClure "had more brain power than any man he had ever known." Swett-1, 185.

316. For a severe critique of McClure's recollection, see Simpson, 83–85.

317. See Zall, 127, for an 1822 version of this "jestbook favorite."

318. The phrasing was considerably different in a later version that began: "You know that I never was much of a conniver." McClure-3, xvi.

319. *Collected Works*, VII, 376–78; Hay-1, 186. On a letter sent by Nicolay from Baltimore, Lincoln wrote: "Wish not to interfere about V.P. Can not interfere about platform. Convention must judge for itself." Hay then implemented the endorsement in a letter to Nicolay declaring: "The President wishes not to interfere in the

nomination even by a confidential suggestion." Some historians have brushed aside this communication as merely a statement of Lincoln's official public attitude masking his true intent. Yet Nicolay's letter was, in effect, an inquiry from the chairman of the Illinois delegation, Burton C. Cook, who wanted to know and follow the President's wishes. If Lincoln was indeed trying to control the action of the convention, why should he have revealed his inner purposes to McClure while misleadingly concealing them from Cook?

320. The McClure-Nicolay debate, which appeared in the Philadelphia *Times* and various other newspapers during July 1891, is reprinted in McClure-1, 457–70. For Hay's agreement with Nicolay, see the interview reported in the New York *Times*, July 10, 1891.

321. *Collected Works*, VIII, 260–61; Welles-1, II, 237.

322. Simpson, 85.

323. *Collected Works*, VI, 490.

324. In what was probably a typographical error, the newspaper text misquoted McConnell as dating the incident in 1836. He accurately named Jonathan McDaniel as the Democrat who was victorious in 1854.

325. An article in the Chicago *Tribune*, Feb. 7, 1909, attributed approximately the same story to New York lawyer Cephas Brainerd, one of the two men who annotated Lincoln's Cooper Institute address for publication as a Republican pamphlet.

326. Apparently a later expansion of the following notes taken by Weik during the interview: "Next day L. asked MD on way to Court House if 'Wyant was possuming' L. said 'I wasnt certain W. was possuming—said if he thought he was W was insane he didnt want to push him—if he didnt realize crime he didn't want to punish him." Memorandum Book II, Weik Papers, transcript provided by Douglas L. Wilson.

327. The story is told somewhat differently in McDonald's 1888 interview with Weik, as presented in Herndon, III, 556–57n. Weik's memorandum of the interview (see the preceding note) contains only the following reference to this discussion: "Int as Consp trials—McD & H. spent an entire evening till 11 PM. with L." See also McDonald's account given the journalist W. H. Smith, who retold it at the age of 92 in the New York *Herald Tribune*, Feb. 7, 1932.

328. Davis statement, Sept. 19–20, 1866 (8:885–904), Herndon-Weik Collection. The passage appears in Herndon, III, 556n, but is misdated Sept. 10, 1866.

329. Raymond-1, 772; *Collected Works*, VIII, 39. The memorandum was also published in William Swinton, *Campaigns of the Army of the Potomac* (New York: Charles B. Richardson, 1866), 79–85.

330. Medill to the editor, May 15, 1896, *McClure's Magazine*, 7 (Sept. 1896): 320.

331. This interview, a copyrighted news release from the publisher of *McClure's Magazine*, was later reproduced, with many changes of wording, in an article for the *Saturday Evening Post* by H. I. Cleveland, who did not make it clear that the interviewer was someone other than himself.

332. See Fehrenbacher-1, 122–26.

333. In Cleveland, 85, the phrasing was changed to read: "Well, after you fellows had got me into that mess and began tempting me with offers of the presidency, I began to think, and I made up my mind that the next president of the United States

would need to have a stronger antislavery platform than mine. So I concluded to say something." This adulterated version of what was in any case a very dubious quotation received wide circulation in Richard Hofstadter, *The American Political Tradition and the Men Who Made It* (New York: Alfred A. Knopf, 1948), 114n.

334. The name is actually spelled "Millerd" here, but in a later, variant account by the same writer (New York *Times*, Mar. 15, 1885), the spelling is more credibly "Millard."

335. *Collected Works*, VII, 483.

336. Miner, 48.

337. So says William D. Beard of the Lincoln Legal Papers project.

338. Prince, 3–4; and see Zall, 83–84.

339. The meeting supposedly included Mitchel and Governor William Dennison of Ohio. A date when those two men and McClellan were all in Washington has not been discovered. F. A. Mitchel made no mention of the incident in his book, *Ormsby Macknight Mitchel: Astronomer and General* (Boston: Houghton, Mifflin & Co., 1887).

340. Morehead said only that the meeting took place several days after Lincoln's arrival in Washington on February 23. Baringer-2, 314–18, fixes the date as February 27 but gives no reason for doing so. *Lincoln Day by Day* simply follows Baringer. However, an Associated Press story filed on February 27 and published the next day in the New York *Tribune* and New York *Times* began with these words: "Last night, ex-Senator Bell of Tennessee, Judge Douglas, Mr. Guthrie, Mr. Rives, Gov. Hicks, and others urgently appealed to Mr. Lincoln to interpose for a settlement. Their interview continued several hours." Although Rives and Guthrie were the only men named as participants by both Morehead and the Associated Press correspondent, it seems likely that this was the meeting Morehead attended. There were no newspaper reports of such a meeting on the 27th.

341. The name is spelled "Reeves" in the document because that is how it was pronounced.

342. According to Morehead, he wrote down the entire conversation soon after it occurred, but that document has never been found. In a letter written some ten months before his Liverpool speech, he spoke of Lincoln's offer to withdraw the troops from Fort Sumter if Virginia would stay in the Union, and he said the "impression" left on his mind was that the administration would not resort to coercion. He seemed, however, to place the blame for the government's alleged duplicity (and for his own arrest) almost entirely on Seward. Morehead to Crittenden, Feb. 23, 1862, in Mrs. Chapman Coleman, ed., *The Life of John J. Crittenden, with Selections from His Correspondence and Speeches* (2 vols.; Philadelphia: J.B. Lippincott & Co., 1871), II, 338.

343. Morgan's recollection differed from Kellogg's, not only in the phrasing of the aphorism, but also in the exact time of its use. He associated it with the impromptu speech delivered by Lincoln in Bloomington on the evening of May 28, 1856, rather than with the famous "lost speech" delivered at the Republican state convention the next day. In a letter to Richard W. Gilder, Mar. 8, 1909, Gilder Papers, New York Public Library, Morgan declared that he had been talking about Lincoln's epigram "for more than fifty years."

344. See Mearns, 76–78.

345. See Lincoln's letter to James H. Hackett, Aug. 17, 1863, *Collected Works*, VI, 392–93.

346. *Collected Works*, VIII, 386–87.

347. Lamon dated the incident 1862. The Nichols interview seems to place it in 1864, but the text is not entirely clear on that point. The year 1864 is specified in another Nichols statement, the text of which appears in Logan, 646–47n, citing a St. Paul *Pioneer Press* article reprinted in the New York *Tribune*, Aug. 16, 1885. Upon examination, however, that issue of the *Tribune* proves to contain no such article, and there is no reference to it in the *Tribune* index for 1885 or other nearby years.

348. From their form, as well as the circumstances, it would appear that Nicolay usually wrote these memoranda, not as the words were spoken, but soon thereafter.

349. An edited but substantially accurate version is in Nicolay and Hay, III, 279–82.

350. A slightly modified version is in Nicolay and Hay, III, 247–48.

351. The letter is in *Collected Works*, IV, 159.

352. A modified version is in Nicolay and Hay, IV, 127. For Lincoln's written reply, see *Collected Works*, IV, 340.

353. Browning, I, 480–81, mentions the discussion and provides information on action taken by the Republican senatorial caucus with respect to the Harvey affair.

354. *Collected Works*, V, 144–46.

355. See his letters on the subject to the Vice President and several members of Congress, *Collected Works*, VI, 546–47, 549–50.

356. But see Richard Hanser, "Old Abe *v.* Incomparable Max," *Lincoln Herald*, 70 (Fall 1968): 137–41. As David C. Mearns demonstrated in *Lincoln Herald*, 67 (Summer 1965): 102, the quip may have originated in a facetious testimonial published by Artemus Ward.

357. Parks had previously provided the latter quotation in a statement given William H. Herndon, printed in Horace White, *The Life of Lyman Trumbull* (Boston: Houghton Mifflin Co., 1913), 46–47n.

358. Zall, 146.

359. This essay was republished a year later in Piatt, 27–49.

360. It seems even more doubtful that Pickett heard the response that Lincoln supposedly made to May's subsequent complaint that he had indulged in personalities: "Colonel, I was like the little boy who kissed the girl at school. When the teacher asked him why he had acted so rudely, [he] replied, 'She stood so fair I couldn't help it!' " Pickett, 6.

361. *Collected Works*, V, 132. In another part of the letter, Pierce quoted Lincoln as saying "niggers," instead of "Negroes." As he noted, Lincoln's temper was probably affected by the serious illness of his son Willie, who died just five days later. Pierce had reported this conversation with the President (omitting any reference to Halleck), in "The Freedmen at Port Royal," *Atlantic Monthly*, 12 (Sept. 1863): 296–97.

362. See *Collected Works*, VIII, 389, 406–7. The document in question was not actually a proclamation, but rather a letter to Godfrey Weitzel, the Union general in command at Richmond. Weitzel was directed not to make it public.

363. See August H. Chapman to Herndon, Sept. 8, 1865 (7:301–24); Elizabeth Crawford's statement, Sept.16, 1865 (7:365–71), Herndon-Weik Collection.

364. *Collected Works*, V, 326–27.

365. See Ben: Perley Poore, *Perley's Reminiscences of Sixty Years in the National Metropolis* (2 vols.; Philadelphia: Hubbard Brothers, 1886), I, 341–42.

366. Herndon, I, 93; Zall, 88.

367. Sterling, 24–25; Robert Todd Lincoln to Judd Stewart, Jan. 8, 1920, Stewart Papers.

368. See Welles-1, I, 25, 27; Niven, 613, n. 10, and the works cited there.

369. See Niven, 379–82.

370. See Crook, 56–57, for a more credible account of the confrontation with Green. William H. Herndon rejected Porter's account as contrary to Lincoln's nature and style. Herndon to Weik, Oct. 5, 1890 (10:2725-28); Feb. 26, 1891 (10:2797-2800), Herndon-Weik Collection.

371. See Welles-1, II, 275, for a comment on Seward's proposed visit to City Point, which became impossible in any case when he was severely injured in a carriage accident.

372. *Collected Works*, VIII, 387.

373. The copy provided by *American Heritage* was received by that magazine in 1980 from Porter's great-grandson, Richard W. Sackett of Bethesda, Md.

374. See pp. 12–13 above.

375. At this point, says Porter, Lincoln regaled his audience with an anecdote about a barber who cut through a customer's cheek into his own finger, which he was holding inside the man's mouth. An earlier source places the telling of the story in different circumstances, and it is a joke that goes back at least to 1818. See Zall, 34.

376. Here, says Porter (408-9), Lincoln had another illustrative anecdote to offer—about a man on his deathbed who made peace with his worst enemy, but added: "If I should happen to get well, mind, that old grudge stands." The story had appeared a decade earlier, with a different context, in Browne FF, 459-60.

377. The statement was quoted at length in Tarbell, III, 174.

378. For one thing, Governor Thomas Carney of Kansas was said to be among the petitioners, whereas, in fact, he had called for the dismissal of Blunt, who in turn denounced him as a liar and thief. Furthermore, Lincoln's one stated complaint against Blunt was that he had lent army support to some lynchings within his command. See *Collected Works*, VI, 395-97.

379. See William J. Wolf, *The Almost Chosen People: A Study of the Religion of Abraham Lincoln* (Garden City, N.Y.: Doubleday & Co., 1959), 50-51; Elton Trueblood, *Abraham Lincoln, Theologian of American Anguish* (New York: Harper & Row, 1973), 21-22, 99-100.

380. For a discussion of this claim, see John J. Duff, *A. Lincoln, Prairie Lawyer* (New York: Rinehart & Co., 1960), 290-92.

381. See Paul W. Gates, "The Struggle for the Charter of the Illinois Central Railroad," *Transactions of the Illinois State Historical Society*, 1933, pp. 55-66, which does not mention Lincoln. Mark E. Steiner, an expert on Lincoln and the Illinois Central, is of the opinion that Lincoln lobbied *for* the charter in 1851, but he acknowledges that the evidence is not conclusive.

382. See *Collected Works*, VI, 151-53.

383. Sacramento *Union*, May 22, 1865.

384. *Harper's Weekly*, Apr. 28, 1860; *Godey's Lady's Book and Magazine*, 68 (June 1864): 583.

385. See *Collected Works*, VI, 142–43.

386. *Congressional Globe*, 37 Cong., 1 sess., 387–88 (Aug. 1, 1861).

387. *Collected Works*, VI, 360. The letter reads: "Yours in reference to General Sterling Price is received. If he voluntarily returns and takes the oath of allegiance to the United States, before the next meeting of Congress, I will pardon him, if you shall then wish me to do so." Rollins asserted that Lincoln wrote this note and handed it to him when he asked for something in writing on the subject. The very wording of the first sentence indicates otherwise, however.

388. Translated by Liliana Suarez Navaz and Alvaro Del Val.

389. Compare Fred Landon, "A Daring Canadian Abolitionist," *Michigan History Magazine*, 5 (1921): 364–73; Sandburg, II, 34; III, 433–34; Robin W. Winks, *Canada and the United States: The Civil War Years* (Baltimore: Johns Hopkins Press, 1960), 232–33; Winks, *The Blacks in Canada* (New Haven, Conn.: Yale University Press, 1971), 260; Carl Ballstadt, "Alexander Milton Ross," *Dictionary of Canadian Biography*, Vol. XII (Toronto: University of Toronto Press, 1990), 924–28. Winks acknowledges in his later book that Ross "portrayed himself larger than life." Ballstadt concludes that the achievements claimed by Ross "are not, at this time, borne out by enough authenticating, objective evidence."

390. See *Collected Works*, V, 270, 526, and G.S. Boritt, *Lincoln and the Economics of the American Dream* (Memphis: Memphis State University Press, 1978), 212–13, 224.

391. See *Collected Works*, VI, 409. An earlier version, with wordier quotation of Lincoln, appeared in the New York *Tribune*, Nov. 29, 1891. Rusling asserted unconvincingly that it was based on "full notes" made shortly after the conversation and that much of his account was consequently "ipsissima verba."

392. Russell WH-1, vii.

393. Russell WH-1, 26.

394. At the time, Russell noted only: "Dined with President & his Cabinet ministers. Fish dinner." Russell WH-1, 27.

395. Zall, 37.

396. Nicolay to Arthur J. McElhone, June 22, 1899, Nicolay Papers.

397. See *Collected Works*, V, 493–95, 509–11.

398. Schurz dated this meeting "late in July," but from the available evidence it appears more likely to have taken place in the middle of August. See *Collected Works*, VII, 466; VIII, 550.

399. Lincoln did know Scovel and undoubtedly talked with him several times at the White House. There are 26 letters from Scovel to Lincoln in the Lincoln Papers, but none from Lincoln to Scovel in the *Collected Works*.

400. In an earlier version, Lincoln wrote just one letter to the Queen. Scovel, "Personal Recollections of Abraham Lincoln," *Lippincott's Magazine*, 44 (Aug. 1889): 244–45.

401. Jay Leyda, ed., *The Melville Log* (2 vols.; New York: Harcourt Brace & Co., 1951), II, 637.

402. This account, according to Frederick Seward, was "written afterward," but remained unpublished until 1891. He subsequently incorporated it in his own remi-

niscences, Seward FW-3, 137–38. According to William H. Seward, Jr., Lincoln also said to his brother at this time: "Mr. Seward, I would almost rather be assassinated than to have the Union fall."—Seward WHJr, 107.

403. A contemporary mention of the incident of the trembling hand is in a letter from Charles Sumner to George Livermore, Jan. 9, 1863, *Sumner Letters*, II, 139–40.

404. In a differently worded version, Frederick Seward later wrote that Lincoln made the remark to his father while they were returning from church on Sunday, February 24. Seward FW-3, 147.

405. See Harrington, 76–86; Glyndon G. Van Deusen, *William Henry Seward* (New York: Oxford University Press, 1967), 379–80.

406. New York *Tribune*, Mar. 25, 1863.

407. Phillips-2, 65–66. For a contemporary newspaper report of another story that Lincoln told on this occasion, see *Collected Works*, II, 333.

408. *Collected Works*, VIII, 154.

409. Albert Castel, "Prevaricating Through Georgia: Sherman's *Memoirs* as a Source on the Atlanta Campaign," *Civil War History*, 40 (1994): 48–71; but see also in the same issue, 72–78: John F. Marszalek, "Sherman Called It the Way He Saw It."

410. Sherman recounted the story to a correspondent of the Cincinnati *Gazette* in 1865. See *Harper's New Monthly Magazine*, 31 (Sept. 1865): 539; also Sherman, II, 326–27.

411. See *Collected Works*, I, 321; IV, 326.

412. Herndon to Jesse K. Weik, Jan. 5, 1889 (10:2448–51), Herndon-Weik Collection. Herndon said that Lincoln had told it to him, Milton Hay, and James Matheny, all three of them "recollecting the story alike."

413. Felix, Prince Salm-Salm, a colonel in the 68th New York Infantry, is usually referred to in the OR simply as "Prince Salm." On his wife, see the essay, "The President and the Princess," in David Chambers Mearns, *Largely Lincoln* (New York: St. Martin's Press, 1961), 96–113.

414. New York *Times*, Feb. 13, 1910; New York *Sun*, Feb. 12, 1911. In the latter version, the Princess was just the first of about thirty women who, at Sickles's suggestion, lined up to kiss the President.

415. This memoir by his son was said to be based largely on Jules Siegfried's journal.

416. Herndon to Weik, Feb. 18, 1887 (10:2110–13), Herndon-Weik Collection.

417. See *Collected Works*, VII, 451.

418. Randall and Current, 330–31, presents Singleton's visit to Richmond as a peace mission, but the contemporary evidence supporting such a view appears to be largely newspaper gossip. Browning, who was associated with Singleton in the trading scheme and discussed it several times with Lincoln, said nothing in his diary about the visit's having any other purpose. In correspondence, Lincoln likewise treated the visit solely as a trading venture and one that could proceed only with Grant's approval. See Browning, I, 699; II, 1–2, 4, 5, 6, 7, 10–11, 12, 17, 26; *Collected Works*, VIII, 200–201, 267, 343–44, 353.

419. See *Collected Works*, VIII, 372.

420. At the time, Lincoln "imposed strict silence" with respect to what he had said. Smith asked in his letter to Hay whether that restriction still applied, and Hay

answered for the President: "He directs me to state in reply that your statement is substantially correct, but that, for the present, he prefers that you would still withhold it from the public." Hay to Smith, Jan. 10, 1863, Lincoln Papers.

421. The latter part of the quotation was included only in the letter as Smith released it for newspaper publication. It may be found also in Reed, 338.

422. See *Collected Works*, VII, 24–25n.

423. In a letter to Dr. John R. Sutherland, Apr. 13, 1887 (newspaper clipping, Nicolay Papers), Speed reiterated that Lincoln had told him he wrote part of the speech before leaving Washington and finished it after arriving at Gettysburg.

424. A slightly different version is in an undated statement by Speed, taken down by Herndon (11:3174–77), Herndon-Weik Collection. Still another variant version, apparently making use of both Speed accounts, is in Herndon, I, 172.

425. The original of the letter is missing. The text, derived from both photostatic and transcribed copies made for Albert J. Beveridge, was supplied by Douglas L. Wilson. Herndon, III, 521–28, prints most of this letter, together with two other letters from Speed (Jan. 12, Feb. 9, 1866), as though all three were a single communication dated December 6, 1866.

426. *Collected Works*, V, 447.

427. Sandburg, II, 97, associates this narrative with another journalist, John Russell Young, who was certainly a close friend of Stanton in the latter's last years. However, John Russell Young was never a member of Congress, and the article, attributed to "Congressman Young," appeared eight months after his death. James R. Young served in the House of Representatives from 1897 to 1903.

428. In the article, Stanton is quoted as saying, contrary to fact, that he accompanied Lincoln on a visit to Hooker's defeated army soon after the battle. It was supposedly on their return trip that the President spoke of having considered suicide.

429. A typescript copy of the letter, with a few verbal variations, is in the Tarbell Papers.

430. Lincoln was at City Point from March 24 to April 8 and did not see Stanton during that time.

431. See *Collected Works*, VII, 345, for a note from Lincoln to Edwin M. Stanton asking that Robert L. Stanton (no relation) be appointed a visitor to West Point.

432. *Collected Works*, VI, 33–34.

433. See *Collected Works*, VIII, 220–21, 274–76.

434. A slightly variant version, attributed to Stephens, appeared in a Georgia newspaper in 1865, quoted in Barrett, 826.

435. Robert W. McBride, *Personal Recollections of Abraham Lincoln, by a Member of His Bodyguard* (Indianapolis: Bobbs-Merrill Co., 1926), 55.

436. For Stoddard's reconstruction from notes of part of Lincoln's response to the Kansas-Missouri delegation on September 30, 1863, see note 215 above. For an account of how Stoddard misrepresented himself as the first editor to propose nomination of Lincoln for the presidency, see Baringer-1, 80–83.

437. Transcriptions of this and the following quotation from the New York *Citizen* were provided by Michael Burlingame.

438. Although he favored limited black suffrage in Louisiana, Lincoln, as late as December 1864, expressed disapproval of proposed legislation enfranchising

all southern Negroes. He raised no objection to the reconstruction constitution drafted for Arkansas in 1864, even though it excluded blacks from suffrage and officeholding. See Hay-1, 244–45; Fehrenbacher-2, 154–55.

439. For Stone's bizarre behavior during the vice-presidential balloting, see William Frank Zornow, *Lincoln and the Party Divided* (Norman: University of Oklahoma Press, 1954), 102; H. Draper Hunt, *Hannibal Hamlin of Maine, Lincoln's First Vice-President* (Syracuse, N.Y.: Syracuse University Press, 1969), 186–87.

440. See Fields A, 268–69.

441. *Collected Works*, VI, 128. Hooker's correspondence inspires doubt that he was in Washington at this time. See *OR*, Ser. I, Vol. 25, pt. II, 119, 123, 127–128, 129.

442. Reproduced with slightly different wording in Herndon, II, 362.

443. *Collected Works*, VI, 160.

444. J. McCan Davis (a onetime resident of Canton) to Ida M. Tarbell, Mar. 17, 1899, Tarbell Papers.

445. See John Y. Simon, *House Divided: Lincoln and His Father* (Fort Wayne, Ind.: Louis A. Warren Lincoln Library and Museum, 1987), 6–7; Mearns, 51–52.

446. According to Swett, this practice session took place about ten days before the debate at Charleston (September 18), but he probably meant Jonesboro (September 15), where Lincoln put a fifth question to Douglas after commenting on the latter's answers to the four previously asked at Freeport. Lincoln was Davis's guest in Bloomington the night of September 3.

447. The quotation is on p. 294. There is also a typewritten copy in the Herndon-Weik Collection (12:79–86). For other persons supposedly hearing this remark, see Whitney-1, 86–87; Stevens, 41; and Charles A. Burley to William E. Barton, Mar. 27, 1923, Barton Papers. Joseph Cannon (q.v.) recalled that Lincoln made such a remark about attending the *state* Republican convention at Springfield.

448. Hay to John G. Nicolay, July 19, 1863, Hay Collection-Brown.

449. *Collected Works*, V, 379, 397.

450. The resolutions appeared in the *Missouri Democrat* (St. Louis), May 11, 1863.

451. For the failure of Congress to pass the bill subsidizing emancipation in Missouri, see *Congressional Globe*, 37 Cong., 1 sess., 1056.

452. At that time, General Edward R. S. Canby was commander of the Military Division of Western Mississippi.

453. See *Collected Works*, VI, 83.

454. *Collected Works*, VII, 207.

455. Garrison, V, 209–10.

456. Chandler interview with Ida M. Tarbell, Sept. 16, 1898, Tarbell Papers.

457. John T. Richards, *Abraham Lincoln: The Lawyer-Statesman* (Boston: Houghton Mifflin Co., 1916), 56–58.

458. *Narrative of Sojourner Truth* (Battle Creek, Mich., 1875), 178; Lucy N. Colman, letter in Rochester (N.Y.) *Express*, Nov. 10, as reprinted in Sacramento *Union*, Dec. 14, 1864. Most notably, the *Narrative* quoted Lincoln as saying "which gave me the opportunity to do these things," instead of "and I was compelled to do these things." The visit has become encrusted with legend. See Carleton Mabee, "Sojourner Truth and President Lincoln," *New England Quarterly*, 61 (1988): 519–29.

459. The name has variant spellings, including Vannatten and Vannattin, but it is Vannattan in the Sangamon County directory for 1866.

460. According to Chester D. Bradley, "President Lincoln's Campaign Against the Merrimac," *ISHSJ*, 51 (1958): 77n, this article "contains many serious errors."

461. Lincoln, who lived in Indiana at the time of this trip, not Kentucky, wrote in his autobiographical sketch (June 1860) that he went as "a hired hand merely." *Collected Works*, IV, 62.

462. The Carpenter version was repeated almost word for word without attribution by William D. Kelley in Rice AT, 279–80 (1886).

463. It is possible that Villard was also the man who supplied the story to the Cincinnati *Commercial*; for he had recently been one of that paper's correspondents. John G. Nicolay described the incident in a letter written the same day to his future wife, Therena Bates (Nicolay Papers). Several weeks earlier, there circulated a curiously similar story of an anxious Mississippian who visited Lincoln and was given similar assurances, including expression of the opinion that in twelve months, slave property would be worth more than ever before. Chattanooga *Gazette*, reprinted in New York *Herald*, Nov. 30, 1860.

464. According to Benjamin Perley Poore, Lincoln told this story in the winter of 1863–64 to a man offering a plan for the capture of Richmond. Chicago *Tribune*, Jan. 9, 1864.

465. New York *Times*, Feb. 20, 1898.

466. Cf. Lincoln to Edwin M. Stanton, Mar. 31, 1864, *Collected Works*, VII, 276–77.

467. See Zall, 58–59.

468. That is, David Davis, Lincoln's friend and political adviser. He and Henry Winter Davis were cousins.

469. See *Collected Works*, IV, 151–53; Randall-1, I, 267–68. Historians using the Weed account include Baringer-2, 121; Potter, 152; Crofts, 221–22.

470. In an anonymous version of the story that had circulated several years earlier, there was no mention of Weed as an intermediary; instead, Lincoln was said to have made his remarkable offer directly to Seymour in an "urgent letter." New York *Times*, Sept. 18, 1877.

471. Croffut's account also appears in his posthumously published memoirs: *An American Procession, 1855–1914: A Personal Chronicle of Famous Men* (Boston: Little, Brown & Co., 1931), 226–33. In the summer of 1882, just a few months before his death, Weed told the story again to a correspondent of the Utica *Observer*, and by then it had been embellished further with the assertion that Lincoln made his approach to Seymour after "long and anxious consideration and discussion," and with the agreement of "many of his most powerful friends." See the Washington *Post*, Feb. 4, 1883.

472. See Weed to Seward, Jan. 1, 1863, Seward Papers, describing a two-hour discussion with Seymour, who proved to be so long-windedly "morbid" on the subject of arbitrary arrests that Weed told him he was talking like the New England Federalists of 1814. One sentence in the letter may reveal the seed from which sprouted Weed's later fantasy: "After he had spoken for half-an-hour, I asked him to consider the question from a different stand-point, to suppose himself at the head of the Government, with a third of the states in open Rebellion, and secret

treason all round him." No letter from Weed to Seward in this period contains any hint of Lincoln's offering to support Seymour as his successor. The central weakness of Weed's story is the very absurdity of the strategy ascribed to Lincoln, who never in his darkest hours was foolish enough to believe that Republicans would acquiesce in such an abdication of power or that the war could be more vigorously prosecuted under Democratic leadership. Nevertheless, it should be noted that the respected Lincoln biographer James G. Randall took the story seriously, and so did historian William B. Hesseltine. It has been given renewed life by novelists Gore Vidal and William Safire. Randall-2, 312–14; William B. Hesseltine, *Lincoln and the War Governors* (New York: Alfred A. Knopf, 1948), 282. Vidal, *Lincoln: A Novel* (New York: Random House, 1984), 401; Safire, 923–25, 1100–1102. Safire quotes Lamon-2, 215–17, as corroboration, but Lamon is chronically untrustworthy, and in this instance, he placed the offer to Seymour in July 1863, some seven months after the date given by Weed. For the statement of Croffut that John Hay had said he was "acquainted with Lincoln's effort to stir up McClellan and Seymour," see Rice AT, xxxvii–xxxviii. For slender evidence that Edwin M. Stanton may have flirted with the idea of supporting Seymour in 1864, see Edwards Pierrepont to Seymour, Feb. 22, 1863, in Otto Eisenschiml, "An Intriguing Letter," *Autograph Collector's Journal,* 1 (Oct. 1948): 13–14.

473. Rice AT, xxxiv. To be sure, McClellan's memory was demonstrably fallible, but it is not likely that he would have forgotten such a flattering offer or denied that it had been tendered. According to another account by Croffut, Weed told him that the offer to McClellan was made in the winter of 1862, thus apparently confusing it with the alleged offer to Seymour. See Croffut to John Hay, Nov. 16, no year given, Hay Collection-Brown. In this communication, Croffut claimed (in contrast with his statement to Rice) that he had obtained "partial confirmation" of Weed's story from McClellan and from McClellan's close friend Samuel L. M. Barlow.

474. See *Collected Works,* VI, 112–13, where evidence is offered that the money was needed for use in the approaching New Hampshire and Connecticut elections. That explanation does not seem exactly to fit Lincoln's words as Weed remembered them, but then Weed was never a reliable source of exact quotation. Safire, 1031–33, discusses the problem at some length, speculating wildly that Lincoln may have been "on the take," needing the money to pay his wife's bills or to cover up discrepancies in the White House accounts.

475. In his letter published in the New York *Tribune,* July 5, 1878, Weed quoted Lincoln as saying: "Swett, do *you* know, that that bee has been buzzing in my bonnet for several days?"

476. Information supplied by Mark E. Steiner of the Lincoln Legal Papers staff indicates that aside from this mistake, Weldon was substantially accurate in his recollection of the facts of the case. It is perhaps worth noting also that a son born to Mrs. Dungey in 1855 was named Abraham.

477. The diary is a contemporary source, although Welles later made numerous changes in the manuscript. The resulting textual complexities are not reproduced in this book, which presents his words as he originally wrote them.

478. *Collected Works,* IV, 318–19.

479. For a still later account of this incident published in 1870, see Welles-2, 55–61.

480. See Niven, 314–22.

481. In revising the diary later, Welles changed "proposed" to "agreed to."

482. A later version with verbal differences is in Welles-3, 195–96. In his diary on September 8, Welles repeated Lincoln's assertion that McClellan had the "slows." Welles-1, I, 118.

483. See Sears, 263–64, where it is suggested that the President was trying to distance himself from the political consequences of the move. In his diary for September 10, Welles reiterated that Lincoln had told him that the appointment of McClellan was "Halleck's doings." Welles-1, I, 122.

484. In an article published in 1872, Welles provided a fuller account of the cabinet meeting with somewhat different phrasing of Lincoln's words. Curiously, he misread his diary and dated the meeting Saturday, September 20, instead of Monday the 22nd. See Welles-2, 245–48.

485. At this point, Welles later added: "Thought it essential to provide an asylum for a race which we had emancipated, but which could never be recognized or admitted to be our equals." Of course, the proclamation issued in September 1862 was prospective and conditional and had emancipated nobody.

486. Welles, writing on Friday, September 26, said that the meeting had been held on "Tuesday last," but Chase's diary clearly indicates that it took place on Wednesday, the 24th.

487. For a brief summary of the case, see Niven, 455–58.

488. The author of the article, published in the January 1864 issue, was James Russell Lowell. See Lincoln's letter to the publishers of the magazine in *Collected Works*, VII, 132.

489. For the substance of the disagreement, see *Collected Works*, VII, 482–83, 489–90, 494.

490. In an article published in 1872, Welles presented a slightly variant version of what Lincoln said on this occasion. See Welles-2, 187–88.

491. In his diary, Welles recorded Lincoln's response to Stanton as follows: ". . . we were requested by the President to deliberate and carefully consider the proposition. He remarked that this was the great question now before us, and we must soon begin to act. Was glad Congress was not in session." Welles-1, II, 281.

492. Here, Welles later added the phrase, "towards an indefinite shore," which, in an article published in 1872, became: "towards a dark and indefinite shore." Welles-2, 188–89.

493. Ward Hill Lamon promptly called this mistake to Wheeler's attention. Wheeler replied that he was clearly mistaken about the date but that the incident itself was "vividly impressed" on his memory. See Lamon-2, 231–35n.

494. See Fehrenbacher-2, 275–77.

495. The peroration, together with White's account of how it came to be written, was published in Herndon, II, 417–18.

496. See *Collected Works*, II, 544–47.

497. Whitney was publicly accused of having manufactured salacious evidence against the woman who shot him in 1888. Two Lincoln speeches that he published in the 1890s are probably spurious, one of them being his alleged reconstruction from notes of the famous "lost speech" of 1856. In 1896, he offered to provide four other Lincoln speeches for *Century Magazine*. See Paul M. Angle's introduction to Henry Clay Whitney, *Life on the Circuit with Lincoln* (Caldwell, Idaho: Caxton Printers, 1940), 19–30; Benjamin P. Thomas, *Portrait for Posterity: Lincoln and His Biogra-*

phers (New Brunswick, N.J.: Rutgers University Press, 1947), 165–76; Phillips-1, 59–62; John G. Nicolay to R. U. Johnson, Jan. 6, 1897, in *ALQ*, I (1940–41): 161–62.

498. See, for example, Whitney to Herndon, June 23, 1887 (10:2151–56), Herndon-Weik Collection, which is generally hostile to Lincoln. To Jesse W. Weik on September 17, 1887 (12:385–88), he confided that "the great majority of Lincoln's stories were very nasty." Writing to Weik some ten years later, he labeled the Gettysburg Address "a fraud—an abortion" and "hogwash." In the same letter, dated only "March 6" (14:1496–97), he hinted at an abnormal relationship between Lincoln and Horace White, writing: "He liked White (altho no one else did) and I could narrate (if I dared) one of the strangest incidents of a minor sort in the career of A. Lincoln, anent this association."

499. *Lincoln Day by Day* indicates three speeches at Urbana in 1856, but none at Champaign.

500. See, for example, Charles B. Strozier, *Lincoln's Quest for Union: Public and Private Meanings* (New York: Basic Books, 1982), 209. Gore Vidal in "Lincoln Up Close," *New York Review of Books*, Aug. 15, 1991, p. 21, cited Whitney's statement as proof that "after Lincoln's defeat by Douglas for the US Senate, he was pretty loonlike for a time; and he thought that the gates of political opportunity had slammed shut for him." Donald, 126, accepts the Whitney story.

501. In one of his accounts, Whitney said that he tried to rally Lincoln's spirits; in another, he said that his mood was the same as Lincoln's and their conversation "cheerless and lugubrious"; in the third, he said that he upbraided Lincoln for courting defeat by his adherence to Owen Lovejoy and the abolitionists. Only in writing to Herndon, from whom he was seeking information for his book, did Whitney quote Lincoln as paying special tribute to Herndon's loyalty. Elsewhere, we are told merely that Lincoln several times remarked: "I expect everybody to desert me." There are other discrepancies among the various accounts, and Whitney's assertion that he was alone with Lincoln from 2:00 P.M. until bedtime is open to question because Lincoln had several cases in court that day, including one in the Illinois supreme court. *Lincoln Day by Day*, II, 239.

502. Lincoln's letters to Anson S. Miller, Eleazar A. Paine, M. M. Inman, Charles H. Ray, B. Clarke Lundy, and Alexander Sympson in *Collected Works*, III, 340, 341, 342, 346; Baringer-1, 48–64; Whitney-1, 83–84; 467–68.

503. Herndon to Weik, Oct. 29, 1885 (9:1805–6); Jan. 23, 1889 (10:2468–71), Herndon-Weik Collection.

504. Lincoln's two meetings with Bates in Springfield took place in December, not in February. He traveled to Charleston on January 30, not in February, and there is no corroborating evidence that he invited Whitney to go along. It seems unlikely that so shortly before his departure for Washington he was still undecided about what to do with his house. According to Pratt-1, 88, Lincoln rented it in February to Lucian A. Tilton, president of the Great Western Railroad and presumably a reliable tenant.

505. See also an undated Whitney statement (11:3212–16), Herndon-Weik Collection.

506. See King, 310. Writing to Herndon Aug. 23, 1887 (10:2179–82), Herndon-Weik Collection, Whitney said of Davis: "I can never forget his kindness to me in

the first years of my acquaintance"; but writing again four days later (10:2183–92), he said: "Davis was always rich and always a hog."

507. Whitney wrote that Lincoln on this occasion "was apparently devoid of care for the time being," but a few paragraphs later, he described him as "tired, jaded and wretched." Whitney-1, 500, 503.

508. For an assertion that Lincoln did, at the last moment, recommend on strategic grounds a delay in the attack at Manassas, see the remarks of Francis Preston Blair, Jr., *Congressional Globe*, 37 Cong., 1 sess., 387.

509. In a letter to Herndon Nov. 13, 1866 (8:1037–40), Herndon-Weik Collection, Whitney likewise asserted that on this occasion, Lincoln expressed the "gravest doubts" that the rebellion could be suppressed. See also his letter of August 27, 1887 (10:2183–92), quoting Lincoln as follows: "There is no use, Whitney, in trying to conquer so many people so long as they are united on the proposition that they won't be conquered."

510. Ashmun's recollection, New York *Tribune*, Oct. 31, 1864; Nicolay and Hay, IV, 80; Robert W. Johannsen, *Stephen A. Douglas* (New York: Oxford University Press, 1973), 859–60, 863.

511. According to Wickizer, the incident occurred while they were traveling from Metamora to Bloomington, but Lincoln's itinerary was the reverse of that. *Lincoln Day by Day*, II, 142.

512. Hill referred to his informant merely as "Wilson," but presumably it was Henry Wilson, who was chairman of the Senate committee on military affairs.

513. On June 11, 1863, Lincoln sent a telegram to Mrs. Lincoln in Philadelphia saying: "I am very well." On June 15, he telegraphed: "Tolerably well. Have not rode out much yet . . . perhaps, shall ride out soon." *Collected Works*, VI, 260, 277.

514. This statement is made after consultation with James Gilreath, Rare Books and Special Collections Division, Library of Congress. For the text of the proclamation, see *Collected Works*, VI, 277–78. The document itself is in the National Archives.

515. For the letter, written in connection with Horace Greeley's Niagara Falls negotiation and addressed, "To Whom it may concern," see *Collected Works*, VII, 451. Wilson mistakenly referred to it as having been addressed to one of the Confederate agents in Canada, Clement C. Clay.

516. Wilson declared inaccurately, for instance, that J. E. B. Stuart's ride around the Army of the Potomac (June 12–15) had cut off communication with McClellan and left Lincoln fearing a major disaster. Wilson also recalled that the group "heartily commended" the Emancipation Proclamation—this at a time when Lincoln had not yet even discussed the idea of issuing such a document with members of his cabinet.

517. In addition to a number of changes in phrasing, the biography quoted Wilson as attributing to Lincoln one sentence that does not appear in Wilson's letter: "These war fellows are very strict with me, and I regret that I am prevented from telling you anything; but I must obey them, I suppose, until I get the hang of things."

518. *Collected Works*, IV, 482–83. Wilson mistakenly remembered the date as September 27.

519. See Lincoln's telegram to Oliver P. Morton, Sept. 26, 1861, *Collected Works*, IV, 537.

520. See *Collected Works*, VI, 142–43.

521. Kellogg, 333. Kellogg was commissioned on April 13. *Collected Works*, VIII, 410.

522. *Collected Works*, V, 436.

523. See also Fred Harvey Harrington, *Fighting Politician: Major General N. P. Banks* (Philadelphia: University of Pennsylvania Press, 1948), 125–27; Bertram W. Korn, *American Jewry and the Civil War* (Cleveland: World Publishing Co., 1961), 194–202. Harrington reveals that Zacharie was, among other things, a plagiarist.

524. Without naming a source, the Cincinnati *Enquirer*, Sept. 16, 1859, quoted Lincoln as saying: "Well, I feel just like the boy who stubbed his toe—too damned badly hurt to laugh and too damned proud to cry." According to *Leslie's Magazine*, Nov. 22, 1862, John Forney asked how he felt about the recent Democratic victories in the New York election, and Lincoln replied: "Somewhat like that boy in Kentucky who stubbed his toe while running to see his sweetheart. The boy said he was too big to cry and far too badly hurt to laugh."

BIBLIOGRAPHICAL
ABBREVIATIONS

Allen: Ethan Allen, "Lincoln and the Slave Trader Gordon," *Independent*, 47 (Apr. 4, 1895): 444.

ALQ: Abraham Lincoln Quarterly.

Ambler: Charles H. Ambler, *Francis H. Pierpont, Union War Governor of Virginia and Father of West Virginia* (Chapel Hill: University of North Carolina Press, 1937).

Aptheker: Herbert Aptheker, ed., *A Documentary History of the Negro People in the United States* (2 vols.; New York: Citadel Press, 1965).

Arnold-1: Isaac N. Arnold, *The History of Abraham Lincoln and the Overthrow of Slavery* (Chicago: Clarke & Co., 1866).

Arnold-2: Isaac N. Arnold, *Abraham Lincoln: A Paper Read Before the Royal Historical Society, London, June 16, 1881* (Chicago: Fergus Printing Co., 1881).

Arnold-3: Isaac N. Arnold, *The Life of Abraham Lincoln* (Chicago: Jansen, McClurg & Co., 1885).

Ashley-1: James M. Ashley, *Reminiscences of the Great Rebellion: Calhoun, Seward and Lincoln* (n.p., 1890).

Ashley-2: James M. Ashley, *Address at the Fourth Annual Banquet of the Ohio Republican League* (New York, 1891).

Atkinson: Eleanor Atkinson, "Lincoln's Boyhood: Reminiscences of His Cousin and Play-Mate, Dennis Hanks," *American Magazine*, 65 (Feb. 1908): 360-69.

Aubere: Jewell H. Aubere, "A Reminiscence of Abraham Lincoln: A Conversation with Speaker Cannon," *World's Work*, 13 (1907): 8528-30.

Bancroft: T. B. Bancroft, "An Audience with Abraham Lincoln," *McClure's Magazine*, 32 (Feb. 1909): 447-50.

Baringer-1: William E. Baringer, *Lincoln's Rise to Power* (Boston: Little, Brown & Co., 1937).

Baringer-2: William E. Baringer, *A House Dividing: Lincoln as President Elect* (Springfield, Ill.: Abraham Lincoln Association, 1945).

Barlow Papers: Samuel S. L. Barlow Papers, Huntington Library.

Barnes JS: John S. Barnes, "With Lincoln from Washington to Richmond in 1865," *Appleton's Magazine*, 9 (May, June 1907): 515-24, 742-51.

Barnes TW: Thurlow Weed Barnes, *Memoir of Thurlow Weed* (Boston: Houghton, Mifflin & Co., 1884).

Barrett: Joseph H. Barrett, *Life of Abraham Lincoln* (Cincinnati: Moore, Wilstach & Baldwin, 1865).

Bartlett: Irving H. Bartlett, *Wendell and Ann Phillips: The Community of Reform, 1840-1880* (New York: W. W. Norton & Co., 1981).

Barton Papers: William E. Barton Papers, University of Chicago Library.

Bateman: Newton Bateman, *Abraham Lincoln: An Address* (Galesburg, Ill.: Cadmus Club, 1899).

Bates DH-1: David Homer Bates, *Lincoln in the Telegraph Office: Recollections of the United States Military Telegraph Corps During the Civil War* (New York: Century Co., 1907).

Bates DH-2: David Homer Bates, *Lincoln Stories, Told by Him in the War Department During the Civil War* (New York: William Edwin Rudge, 1926).

Bates E: Howard K. Beale, ed., *The Diary of Edward Bates*, Volume IV of the *Annual Report of the American Historical Association for the Year 1930* (Washington, D.C.: Government Printing Office, 1933).

Battles and Leaders: Robert Underwood Johnson and Clarence Clough Buel, eds., *Battles and Leaders of the Civil War* (4 vols.; New York: Century Co., 1887–88).

Belz: Herman Belz, *Reconstructing the Union: Theory and Policy During the Civil War* (Ithaca, N.Y.: Cornell University Press, 1969).

Beveridge Papers: Albert J. Beveridge Papers, Manuscript Division, Library of Congress.

Bingham: John A. Bingham, "Abraham Lincoln," *The Current*, 5 (Apr. 24, 1866): 281–83.

Blakeslee: Francis D. Blakeslee, "The Lincoln That I Knew," *Zion's Herald*, Feb. 5, 1936, pp. 128–29.

Blodgett: *Autobiography of Henry W. Blodgett* (Waukegan, Ill., 1906).

Bonham: Jeriah Bonham, *Fifty Years' Recollections* (Peoria, Ill.: J. W. Franks & Sons, 1883).

Boteler: Alexander R. Boteler, "Mr. Lincoln and the Force Bill," in *The Annals of the War, Written by Leading Participants, North and South* (Philadelphia: Times Publishing Co., 1879), 220–27.

Botts: John Minor Botts, *The Great Rebellion: Its Secret History, Rise, Progress, and Disastrous Failure* (New York: Harper & Brothers, 1866).

Boutwell-1: George S. Boutwell, "The Career of Abraham Lincoln," *Independent*, 47 (Apr. 4, 1895): 435–36.

Boutwell-2: George S. Boutwell, *Reminiscences of Sixty Years in Public Affairs* (2 vols.; New York: McClure, Phillips & Co., 1902).

Bowen: Henry C. Bowen, "Recollections of Abraham Lincoln," *Independent*, 47 (Apr. 4, 1895): 431–32.

Brooks-1: [Noah Brooks], "Some Reminiscences of Abraham Lincoln," Marysville (Calif.) *Appeal*, Nov. 4, 1860.

Brooks-2: Noah Brooks, "Personal Recollections of Abraham Lincoln," *Harper's New Monthly Magazine*, 31 (July 1865): 222–30.

Brooks-3: Noah Brooks, "Personal Reminiscences of Lincoln," *Scribner's Monthly*, 15 (Feb., Mar. 1878): 561–69, 673–81.

Brooks-4: Noah Brooks, "Lincoln's Imagination," *Scribner's Monthly*, 18 (Aug. 1879): 584–87.

Brooks-5: Noah Brooks, *Washington in Lincoln's Time*, edited by Herbert Mitgang (New York: Rinehart & Co., 1958; originally published in 1895).

Brooks-6: Noah Brooks, "Lincoln Reminiscences," *Magazine of History*, 9 (Feb. 1909): 107–8.

Brooks-7: Noah Brooks, *Abraham Lincoln: The Nation's Leader in the Great Struggle Through Which Was Maintained the Existence of the United States* (Washington, D.C.: National Tribune, 1888, 1909).

Brown: George William Brown, *Baltimore and the Nineteenth of April, 1861: A Study of the War* (Baltimore: N. Murray, 1887).

Browne FF: Francis Fisher Browne, *The Every-Day Life of Abraham Lincoln* (New York: N. D. Thompson, 1886).

Browne RH: Robert H. Browne, *Abraham Lincoln and the Men of His Time* (2 vols.; Cincinnati: Jennings and Pye, 1901).

Browning: Theodore Calvin Pease and James G. Randall, eds., *The Diary of Orville Hickman Browning* (2 vols.; Springfield: Illinois State Historical Library, 1925-33).

Burt: Silas W. Burt, "Lincoln on His Own Story-Telling," *Century Magazine*, 73 (Feb. 1907): 499-502.

Butler-1: *Private and Official Correspondence of Gen. Benjamin F. Butler During the Period of the Civil War* (5 vols.; Norwood, Mass.: Plimpton Press, 1917).

Butler-2: Benjamin F. Butler, *Butler's Book* (Boston: A. M. Thayer & Co., 1892).

Butterfield: Julia Lorrilard Butterfield, *A Biographical Memorial of General Daniel Butterfield* (New York: Grafton Press, 1904).

Cadwallader: Benjamin P. Thomas, ed., *Three Years with Grant, as Recalled by War Correspondent Sylvanus Cadwallader* (New York: Alfred A. Knopf, 1955).

Cannon: Le Grand B. Cannon, *Personal Reminiscences of the Rebellion, 1861-1866* (New York, 1895).

Carlson: Oliver Carlson, *The Man Who Made News: James Gordon Bennett* (New York: Duell, Sloan & Pearce, 1942).

Carpenter-1: Frank [Francis] B. Carpenter, "Anecdotes and Reminiscences," in Henry J. Raymond, *The Life and Public Services of Abraham Lincoln* (New York: Derby & Miller, 1865), Appendix, 725-66.

Carpenter-2: F[rancis] B. Carpenter, *Six Months at the White House with Abraham Lincoln: The Story of a Picture* (New York: Hurd & Houghton, 1866).

Caton: John Dean Caton, *Early Bench and Bar of Illinois* (Chicago: Chicago Legal News Co., 1893).

Centennial Reminiscences: Lincoln Centennial Association Reminiscences File, Illinois State Historical Library.

Chambrun: Marquis de Chambrun, "Personal Recollections of Mr. Lincoln," *Scribner's Magazine*, 13 (Jan. 1893): 26-38.

Chandler-1: Albert B. Chandler, "As Lincoln Appeared in the War Department," *Independent*, 47 (Apr. 4, 1895): 448-49.

Chandler-2: Albert B. Chandler's article from *Sunday Magazine*, reprinted as "Lincoln and the Telegrapher," *American Heritage*, 12 (Apr. 1961): 32-34.

Chapman: Ervin Chapman, *Latest Light on Abraham Lincoln and War-Time Memories* (2 vols.; New York: Fleming H. Revell Co., 1917).

Chase: John Niven et al., eds., *The Salmon P. Chase Papers*, Volume I, *Journals, 1829-1872* (Kent, Ohio: Kent State University Press, 1993).

Chiniquy: Charles P. T. Chiniquy, *Fifty Years in the Church of Rome* (labeled 42nd ed.; Chicago: Craig Press, 1892; first published in 1885).

Chittenden: L[ucius] E. Chittenden, *Recollections of President Lincoln and His Administration* (New York: Harper & Brothers, 1891).

Clark: Thomas M. Clark, *Reminiscences* (New York: Thomas Whittaker, 1895).

Clay: *The Life of Cassius Marcellus Clay: Memoirs, Writings, and Speeches . . . ,* Volume I (Cincinnati: J. Fletcher Brennan & Co., 1886).

Cleveland: H. I. Cleveland, "Booming the First Republican President: A Talk with Abraham Lincoln's Friend, the Late Joseph Medill," *Saturday Evening Post,* 172 (Aug. 5, 1899): 84–85.

Cochrane: Henry Clay Cochrane, "With Lincoln to Gettysburg, 1863," in *Abraham Lincoln: Military Order of the Loyal Legion of the United States, Commandery of the State of Pennsylvania, Memorial Meeting, February 13, 1907* (n.p., 1907), 9–12.

Coffin: Charles Carleton Coffin, *Abraham Lincoln* (New York: Harper & Brothers, 1893).

Colby Memorandum: James F. Colby's Memorandum of a statement by William E. Chandler made Nov. 6, 1911, and recalled "shortly after it took place," Chandler Collection, New Hampshire Historical Society.

Cole-1: *Memoirs of Cornelius Cole, Ex-Senator of the United States from California* (New York: McLoughlin Brothers, 1908).

Cole-2: Cornelius Cole, "The Lincoln I Knew," as told to Maybel Sherman, *Colliers,* 71 (Feb. 10, 1923): 29.

Colfax-1: Schuyler Colfax, *Life and Principles of Abraham Lincoln* (Philadelphia: James B. Rodgers, 1865).

Colfax-2: Speech of Schuyler Colfax at Central City, Colorado Territory, May 29, 1865, in Sacramento *Union,* June 20, 1865.

Collected Works: Roy P. Basler, Marion Dolores Pratt, and Lloyd A. Dunlap, eds., *The Collected Works of Abraham Lincoln* (9 vols.; New Brunswick, N.J.: Rutgers University Press, 1953–55).

Collis: Septima M. Collis, *A Woman's War Record, 1861–1865* (New York: G. P. Putnam's Sons, 1889).

Colman: Lucy N. Colman, *Reminiscences* (Buffalo, N.Y.: H. L. Green, 1891).

Complete Works: John G. Nicolay and John Hay, *Complete Works of Abraham Lincoln* (enlarged ed., 12 vols.; New York: Francis D. Tandy Co., 1905).

Conant: Alban Jasper Conant, "A Portrait Painter's Reminiscences of Lincoln," *McClure's Magazine,* 32 (Mar. 1909): 512–16.

Conway-1: Moncure D. Conway, "Personal Recollections of President Lincoln," *Fortnightly Review,* 1 (May 1865): 56–65.

Conway-2: Moncure D. Conway, *Autobiography: Memories and Experiences* (2 vols.; Boston: Houghton, Mifflin & Co., 1904).

Conwell: Russell H. Conwell, *Why Lincoln Laughed* (New York: Harper & Brothers, 1922).

Cooke: Jay Cooke, "Interview with Lincoln" (excerpt from an unpublished memoir written in 1890), *American History Illustrated,* 7 (Nov. 1972): 10–11.

Cramer: John H. Cramer, *Lincoln Under Enemy Fire* (Baton Rouge: Louisiana State University Press, 1948).

Croffut: William A. Croffut, "Lincoln's Washington: Recollections of a Journalist Who Knew Everybody," *Atlantic Monthly,* 145 (Jan. 1930): 55–65.

Croffut and Morris: W[illiam] A. Croffut and John M. Morris, *The Military and Civil History of Connecticut During the War of 1861–65* (New York: Ledyard Bill, 1868).

Crofts: Daniel W. Crofts, *Reluctant Confederates: Upper South Unionists in the Secession Crisis* (Chapel Hill: University of North Carolina Press, 1989).

Crook: Margarita Spalding Gerry, comp. and ed., *Through Five Administrations: Reminiscences of Colonel William H. Crook, Body-Guard to President Lincoln.* (New York: Harper & Brothers, 1910).

Cullom-1: Shelby M. Cullom, "Lincoln and His Relations with Congress," in Nathaniel William MacChesney, ed., *Abraham Lincoln: The Tribute of a Century, 1809-1909* (Chicago: A. C. McClurg & Co., 1910), 500-503.

Cullom-2: Shelby M. Cullom, *Fifty Years of Public Service* (Chicago: A. C. McClurg & Co., 1911).

Cunningham JL: John L. Cunningham, *Three Years with the Adirondack Regiment, 118th New York Volunteers Infantry* (privately printed, 1920).

Cunningham JO: J[oseph] O. Cunningham, "The Bloomington Convention of 1856 and Those Who Participated in It," *Transactions of the Illinois State Historical Society for the Year 1905*, 101-10.

Currey: J. Seymour Currey, *Abraham Lincoln's Visit to Evanston in 1860* (Evanston: City National Bank, 1914).

Curtis GW: George William Curtis, "Four Glimpses of President Lincoln," *Independent*, 47 (Apr. 4, 1895): 429.

Curtis Papers: Samuel R. Curtis Papers, Western Americana Collection, Beinecke Rare Book and Manuscript Library, Yale University.

Dahlgren: Madeleine Vinton Dahlgren, *Memoir of John A. Dahlgren, Rear-Admiral United States Navy* (Boston: James R. Osgood & Co., 1882).

Dall: Mrs. C. H. [Caroline W. H.] Dall, "Pioneering," *Atlantic Monthly*, 19 (Apr. 1867): 403-16.

Dana: Charles A. Dana, *Recollections of the Civil War: With the Leaders at Washington and in the Field in the Sixties* (New York: D. Appleton & Co., 1898).

Davis Papers: David Davis Papers, Illinois State Historical Library.

Dawes: H[enry] L. Dawes, "Recollections of Stanton Under Lincoln," *Atlantic Monthly*, 73 (Feb. 1894): 162-69.

Deming: Henry C. Deming, *Eulogy of Abraham Lincoln* (Hartford: A. N. Clark & Co., 1865).

Depew: Chauncey M. Depew, *My Memories of Eighty Years* (New York: Charles Scribner's Sons, 1924).

Dicey: [Edward Dicey], "Washington During the War," *Macmillan's Magazine*, 6 (May 1862): 16-29.

Dickson: William M. Dickson, "Abraham Lincoln at Cincinnati," *Harper's New Monthly Magazine*, 69 (June 1884): 62-66.

Dittenhoefer: Abram J. Dittenhoefer, *How We Elected Lincoln: Personal Recollections of Lincoln and Men of His Time* (New York and London: Harper & Brothers, 1916).

Dodge: Grenville M. Dodge, *Personal Recollections of President Abraham Lincoln, General Ulysses S. Grant and General William T. Sherman* (Council Bluffs, Ia., 1914).

Doig: Ivan Doig, "The Genial White House Host and Raconteur," *Journal of the Illinois State Historical Society*, 62 (1969): 307-11.

Donald: David Donald, *Lincoln's Herndon* (New York: Alfred A. Knopf, 1948).

Du Pont: John D. Hayes, ed., *Samuel Francis Du Pont: A Selection from His Civil War Letters* (3 vols.; Ithaca, N.Y.: Cornell University Press, 1969).

Duvergier: Ernest Duvergier de Hauranne, *A Frenchman in Lincoln's America*, translated and edited by Ralph H. Bowen, Volume II (Chicago: R. R. Donnelley & Sons, 1975).

Eaton: John Eaton, *Grant, Lincoln and the Freedmen: Reminiscences of the Civil War* (New York: Negro Universities Press, 1969; originally published in 1907).

Ellsworth Papers: Elmer E. Ellsworth Papers, Illinois State Historical Library.

Emerson R: *Mr. and Mrs. Ralph Emerson's Personal Recollections of Abraham Lincoln* (Rockford, Ill., 1909).

Emerson RW: Linda Allardt and David W. Hill, eds., *The Journals and Miscellaneous Notebooks of Ralph Waldo Emerson*, Volume XV (Cambridge: Belknap Press of Harvard University Press, 1982).

Endicott: William Endicott, "Reminiscences of Seventy-Five Years," *Proceedings of the Massachusetts Historical Society*, 46 (1912–13): 208–33.

Eytinge: *The Memories of Rose Eytinge: Being Recollections and Observations of Men, Women, and Events During Half a Century* (New York: Frederick A. Stokes Co., 1905).

Fehrenbacher-1: Don E. Fehrenbacher, *Prelude to Greatness: Lincoln in the 1850's* (Stanford, Calif.: Stanford University Press, 1962).

Fehrenbacher-2: Don E. Fehrenbacher, *Lincoln in Text and Context: Collected Essays* (Stanford, Calif.: Stanford University Press, 1987).

Fessenden: Francis Fessenden, *Life and Public Services of William Pitt Fessenden* (2 vols.; Boston: Houghton, Mifflin & Co., 1907).

Field: Maunsell B. Field, *Memories of Many Men and of Some Women* (New York: Harper & Brothers, 1874).

Fields A: Annie Fields, ed., *Life and Letters of Harriet Beecher Stowe* (Boston: Houghton Mifflin & Co., 1897).

Fields JT: James T. Fields, "Our Whispering Gallery," *Atlantic Monthly*, 27 (Apr. 1871): 510–12.

Fiske AL: A. Longfellow Fiske, "A Neighbor of Lincoln," *Commonweal*, 15 (Mar. 2, 1932): 494.

Fiske S: Stephen Fiske, "When Lincoln Was Inaugurated," *Ladies' Home Journal*, Mar. 1897, pp. 7–8.

Flower: Frank Abial Flower, *Edwin McMasters Stanton: The Autocrat of Rebellion, Emancipation, and Reconstruction* (Akron, Ohio: Saalfield Publishing Co., 1905).

Floyd: George P. Floyd, "Abraham Lincoln's Rum Sweat: A Vigorous Remedy That Helped Him During His Presidential Campaign," *McClure's Magazine*, 30 (Jan. 1908): 303–8.

Forbes: Sarah Forbes Hughes, ed., *Letters and Recollections of John Murray Forbes* (2 vols.; Boston: Houghton, Mifflin & Co., 1899).

Forney: John W. Forney, *Anecdotes of Public Men* (2 vols.; New York: Harper & Brothers, 1874–81).

Fox: Robert Means Thompson and Richard Wainwright, eds., *Confidential Correspondence of Gustavus Vasa Fox, Assistant Secretary of the Navy, 1861–1865* (2 vols.; New York: Naval History Society, 1918).

Fox Diary: Diary of Virginia Woodbury Fox, Microfilm edition of the Papers of Levi Woodbury, Manuscript Division, Library of Congress.

Frémont: Pamela Herr and Mary Lee Spence, eds., *The Letters of Jessie Benton Frémont* (Urbana: University of Illinois Press, 1993).

French: Benjamin Brown French (Donald B. Cole and John J. McDonough, eds.), *Witness to the Young Republic: A Yankee's Journal, 1828–1870* (Hanover, N.H.: University Press of New England, 1989).

French Papers: Benjamin Brown French Papers, Manuscript Division, Library of Congress.

Fuller: Frank Fuller, *A Day with the Lincoln Family* (3-page pamphlet; New York, n.d.), copy in Illinois State Historical Library.

Garrison: Walter M. Merrill, ed., *The Letters of William Lloyd Garrison* (6 vols.; Cambridge, Mass.: Harvard University Press, 1971–81).

Gay Papers: Sydney Howard Gay Papers, Rare Book and Manuscript Library, Columbia University.

Gibbon: John Gibbon, *Personal Recollections of the Civil War* (New York: G. P. Putnam's Sons, 1928).

Gilmore-1: Edmund Kirke [James R. Gilmore], *Down in Tennessee and Back by Way of Richmond* (New York: Carleton, 1864).

Gilmore-2: Edmund Kirke [James R. Gilmore], "A Suppressed Chapter of History," *Atlantic Monthly*, 59 (Apr. 1887): 435–48.

Gilmore-3: James R. Gilmore, *Personal Recollections of Abraham Lincoln and the Civil War* (Boston: L. C. Page & Co., 1898).

Gobright: Lawrence A. Gobright, *Recollection of Men and Things at Washington During the Third of a Century* (Philadelphia: Claxton, Remsen & Haffelfinger, 1869).

Grant: *Personal Memoirs of U. S. Grant* (2 vols.; New York: Charles L. Webster & Co., 1885–86).

Greeley: "Greeley's Estimate of Lincoln: An Unpublished Address by Horace Greeley," *Century Magazine*, 42 (July 1891): 371–82.

Green: Duff Green, *Facts and Suggestions, Biographical, Historical, Financial and Political, Addressed to the People of the United States* (New York: Richardson & Co., 1866).

Greene: Gilbert J. Greene, "Lincoln the Comforter" (recorded by Charles T. White), *McClure's Magazine*, 54 (Dec. 1922): 11–13, 88.

Grimsley: Elizabeth Todd Grimsley, "Six Months in the White House" (a memoir written in 1895), *Journal of the Illinois State Historical Society*, 19 (Oct.–Jan. 1926–27): 43–73.

Grinnell: Josiah Bus[h]nell Grinnell, *Men and Events of Forty Years* (Boston: D. Lothrop Co., 1891).

Grover: Leonard Grover, "Lincoln's Interest in the Theater," *Century Magazine*, 77 (Apr. 1909): 943–50.

Gulliver: John P. Gulliver, "A Talk with Abraham Lincoln," *Independent*, 16 (Sept. 1, 1864): 1.

Hagner: Alexander B. Hagner, *A Personal Narrative of the Acquaintance of My Father and Myself with Each of the Presidents of the United States* (Washington, D.C., 1915).

Hale: Edward Everett Hale, *Memories of a Hundred Years* (rev. ed., 2 vols. in 1; New York: Macmillan Co., 1904).

Halpine: Charles G. Halpine, *Baked Meats of the Funeral: Collection of Essays, Poems, Speeches, Histories and Banquets* (New York: Carleton, 1866).

Halpine Papers: Charles G. Halpine Papers, Huntington Library.

Hamilton: James A. Hamilton, *Reminiscences* (New York: Charles Scribner & Co., 1869).

Hamlin: Charles Hamlin, "A Side-Light and an Incident," *Independent*, 47 (Apr. 4, 1895): 450.

Harlan: James Harlan, *Recollections of Abraham Lincoln* (n.p., n.d.) An address at Iowa Wesleyan College, April 28, 1898.

Harper: Robert S. Harper, *Lincoln and the Press* (New York: McGraw-Hill Book Co., 1951).

Harrington: Fred Harvey Harrington, ed., "A Peace Mission of 1863," *American Historical Review*, 46 (1940-41): 76-86.

Haupt: Herman Haupt, *Reminiscences of General Herman Haupt* (Milwaukee: Wright and Joys Co., 1901).

Hawkins manuscript: Rush C. Hawkins, "A Mission to President Lincoln," manuscript dated 1893, Lincoln Collection-Brown.

Hay-1: Tyler Dennett, ed., *Lincoln and the Civil War in the Diaries and Letters of John Hay* (New York: Dodd, Mead & Co., 1939).

Hay-2: John Hay, "The Heroic Age in Washington," lecture (1871), John Hay Collection, John Hay Library, Brown University.

Hay-3: John Hay, "Life in the White House in the Time of Lincoln," *Century Magazine*, 41 (Nov. 1890): 33-37.

Hay-4: John Hay, *Addresses of John Hay* (New York: Century Co., 1906).

Hay Collection-Brown: John Hay Collection, John Hay Library, Brown University.

Hay Papers-LC: John Hay Papers, Manuscript Division, Library of Congress.

Healy: George P. A. Healy, *Reminiscences of a Portrait Painter* (Chicago: A. C. McClurg & Co., 1894).

Hein: O. L. Hein, *Memories of Long Ago* (New York: G. P. Putnam's Sons, 1925).

Helm: Katherine Helm, *The True Story of Mary, Wife of Lincoln, Containing the Recollections of Mary Lincoln's Sister Emilie (Mrs. Ben Hardin Helm), Extracts from Her War-Time Diary, Numerous Letters and Other Documents Now First Published* (New York: Harper & Brothers, 1928).

Henderson JB: John B. Henderson, "Emancipation and Impeachment," *Century Magazine*, 85 (Dec. 1912): 196-209.

Henry Papers: Anson G. Henry Papers, Illinois State Historical Library.

Herndon: William H. Herndon and Jesse K. Weik, *Herndon's Lincoln: The True Story of a Great Life* (3 vols.; Chicago: Belford-Clarke Co., 1889).

Herndon-2nd: William H. Herndon and Jesse K. Weik, *Abraham Lincoln: The True Story of a Great Life* (2 vols.; New York: D. Appleton & Co., 1913).

Herndon-Springer: Copies of William H. Herndon's Lincoln material transcribed in 1866 by John G. Springer, 3 vols., Huntington Library.

Herndon-Weik Collection: Microfilm edition of the Papers of William H. Herndon and Jesse W. Weik, Manuscript Division, Library of Congress.

Herndon-2L: William H. Herndon, "An Analysis of the Character of Abraham Lincoln," *Abraham Lincoln Quarterly*, 1 (1940-41): 403-41. Herndon's second lecture on Lincoln, delivered Dec. 26, 1865.

Herndon-3L: William H. Herndon, "Facts Illustrative of Mr. Lincoln's Patriotism and Statesmanship," *Abraham Lincoln Quarterly*, 3 (1944–45): 178–203. Herndon's third lecture on Lincoln, delivered Jan. 24, 1866.

Hertz: Emanuel Hertz, *The Hidden Lincoln, from the Letters and Papers of William H. Herndon* (New York: Viking Press, 1938).

Hill FT: Frederick Trevor Hill, *Lincoln the Lawyer* (New York: Century Co., 1906).

Hill MM: Reminiscences of Mary Miner Hill, Mar. 21, 1923, typescript, Illinois State Historical Library.

Hitchcock: W. A. Croffut, ed., *Fifty Years in Camp and Field: Diary of Major-General Ethan Allen Hitchcock, U.S.A.* (Freeport, N.Y.: Books for Libraries Press, 1971; originally published in 1909).

Holland: J[osiah] G. Holland, *The Life of Abraham Lincoln* (Springfield, Mass.: Gurdon Bill, 1866).

Holzer: Harold Holzer, ed., *The Lincoln-Douglas Debates* (New York: Harper Collins, 1993).

Holzer et al.: Harold Holzer, Gabor S. Boritt, and Mark E. Neely, Jr., *The Lincoln Image: Abraham Lincoln and the Popular Print* (New York: Charles Scribner's Sons, 1984).

House Document 1056: "Homestead of Abraham Lincoln: Speeches in the House of Representatives, April 5, 12, 1916, on a Bill to Accept a Deed of Conveyance from the Lincoln Farm Association to the United States of the Homestead of Abraham Lincoln, near the Town of Hodgenville, State of Kentucky," *House Document*, 64 Congress, 1 session, Number 1056 (Serial 7099).

House Report 30: "Report of the Joint Committee on Reconstruction," *House Report*, 39 Congress, 1 session, Number 30, Part II (Serial 1273).

Howard JJr: Joseph Howard, Jr., "Reminiscences of Stephen A. Douglas," *Atlantic Monthly*, 8 (Aug. 1861): 205–13.

Howard JQ: Roy P. Basler, ed., "James Quay Howard's Notes on Lincoln," *Abraham Lincoln Quarterly*, 4 (1946–47): 386–400.

Howard OO: Oliver O. Howard, "Personal Recollections of Abraham Lincoln," *Century Magazine*, 75 (Apr. 1908): 873–77.

Howe: M. A. DeWolfe Howe, *The Life and Letters of George Bancroft* (2 vols.; New York: Charles Scribner's Sons, 1908).

Howells: W[illiam] D[ean] Howells, *Life of Abraham Lincoln* (Bloomington: Indiana University Press, 1960). A facsimile of the 1860 edition, with Lincoln's annotations.

Hoyt: John W. Hoyt, "Some Personal Recollections of Abraham Lincoln," *Transactions of the Wisconsin Academy of Sciences, Arts, and Letters*, 16, part 2 (1910): 1305–9.

Huidekoper: H. S. Huidekoper, *Personal Notes and Reminiscences of Lincoln* (Philadelphia: Bicking Print, 1896).

Hunt: Eugenia Jones Hunt, "My Personal Recollections of Abraham Lincoln and Mary Todd Lincoln," *Abraham Lincoln Quarterly*, 3 (1944–45): 235–52.

ISHL: Illinois State Historical Library, Springfield.

ISHSJ: *Journal of the Illinois State Historical Society*.

Jacobs: Hannah Slater Jacobs, "Lincoln Listened to a Little Girl Whose Father Needed a Good Turn," as told to her daughter, Frances J. Nickels, *Good Housekeeping*, 94 (Feb. 1932): 42–43, 119.

Janney: John J. Janney memoir in Ellen B. Fredericks, ed., "Talking with the President: Four Interviews with Abraham Lincoln," *Civil War Times Illustrated*, 26 (Sept. 1987): 33–36.

Jayne: William Jayne, *Personal Reminiscences of the Martyred President Abraham Lincoln* (Chicago, 1908). An address delivered in 1900.

Johns: Jane Martin Johns, *Personal Recollections of Early Decatur, Abraham Lincoln, Richard J. Oglesby, and the Civil War* (Decatur, Ill.: Decatur Chapter Daughters of the American Revolution, 1912).

Johnson Papers, X: Paul Bergeron, ed., *The Papers of Andrew Johnson*, Volume X (Knoxville: University of Tennessee Press, 1992).

Johnson BB: Byron Berkeley Johnson, *Abraham Lincoln and Boston Corbett, with Personal Recollections of Each* (Waltham, Mass., 1914).

Johnson RW: Richard W. Johnson, *Memoir of Maj.-Gen. George H. Thomas* (Philadelphia: J. B. Lippincott & Co., 1881).

Jones ED: Edgar DeWitt Jones, *Lincoln and the Preachers* (New York: Harper & Brothers, 1948).

Jones TD: Thomas D. Jones, *Memories of Lincoln* (New York: Press of the Pioneers, 1934), reprinted from Sacramento *Weekly Union*, Nov. 4, 1871.

Julian: George W. Julian, *Political Recollections, 1840-1872* (Chicago: Jansen, McClurg & Co., 1884).

Kaine: John Langdon Kaine, "Lincoln as a Boy Knew Him," *Century Magazine*, 85 (Feb. 1913): 555–59.

Keckley: Elizabeth Keckley, *Behind the Scenes, or, Thirty Years a Slave, and Four Years in the White House* (New York: G. W. Carleton & Co., 1868).

Kelley: William D. Kelley, *Lincoln and Stanton: A Study of the War Administration of 1861 and 1862, with Special Consideration of Some Recent Statements of Gen. Geo. B. McClellan* (New York: G. P. Putnam's Sons, 1885).

Kellogg: Paul M. Angle, ed., "The Recollections of William Pitt Kellogg," *Abraham Lincoln Quarterly*, 3 (Sept. 1945): 319–39.

Keyes: E. D. Keyes, *Fifty Years' Observation of Men and Events, Civil and Military* (New York: Charles Scribner's Sons, 1884).

King: Willard L. King, *Lincoln's Manager: David Davis* (Cambridge, Mass.: Harvard University Press, 1960).

Kinkaid: Robert L. Kinkaid, *The Wilderness Road* (Middleboro, Ky., 1966).

Knight: Henry W. Knight, "Personal Recollections of Abraham Lincoln," *Independent*, 47 (Apr. 4, 1895): 446.

Koerner: Thomas J. McCormack, ed., *Memoirs of Gustave Koerner, 1809-1896* (2 vols.; Cedar Rapids, Iowa: Torch Press, 1909).

Kune: Julian Kune, *Reminiscences of an Octogenarian Hungarian Exile* (Chicago, 1911).

Kyle: Otto R. Kyle, "Mr. Lincoln Steps Out: The Anti-Nebraska Editors' Convention," *Abraham Lincoln Quarterly*, 5 (1948-49): 25–37.

Lamon Papers: Ward Hill Lamon Papers, Huntington Library.

Lamon-1: Ward H[ill] Lamon, *The Life of Abraham Lincoln from His Birth to His Inauguration as President* (Boston: James R. Osgood & Co., 1872).

Lamon-2: Ward Hill Lamon, *Recollections of Abraham Lincoln, 1847-1865*, edited by Dorothy Lamon Teillard (2nd ed.; Washington, D.C., 1911).

Lansden: John M. Lansden, "Abraham Lincoln, Judge David Davis and Judge Edward Bates," *Journal of the Illinois State Historical Society*, 7 (1914): 56–58.

Laugel diary: A portion of the diary of Auguste Laugel, as translated and published in *The Nation*, 75 (July 31, 1902): 88–89.

Lee: Virginia Jeans Laas, ed., *Wartime Washington: The Civil War Letters of Elizabeth Blair Lee* (Urbana: University of Illinois Press, 1991).

Lester: C[harles] Edwards Lester, *Life and Public Services of Charles Sumner* (New York: United States Publishing Co., 1874).

Levering: N. Levering, "Recollections of Abraham Lincoln," *Iowa Historical Record*, 12 (1896): 492–507.

Lewis: Thomas Lewis, "New Light on Lincoln's Life," *Leslie's Weekly*, Feb. 16, 1899, pp. 134–35.

Lieber Papers: Francis Lieber Papers, Huntington Library.

Lincoln Collection-Brown: Abraham Lincoln Collection, John Hay Library, Brown University.

Lincoln Day by Day: Earl Schenck Miers, William E. Baringer, and C. Percy Powell, eds., *Lincoln Day by Day: A Chronology* (3 vols.; Washington, D.C.: Lincoln Centennial Commission, 1960).

Lincoln Papers: Microfilm edition of the Robert Todd Lincoln Collection of the Papers of Abraham Lincoln, Manuscript Division, Library of Congress.

Linder: Usher F. Linder, *Reminiscences of the Early Bench and Bar of Illinois* (Chicago: Chicago Legal News Co., 1879).

Littlefield: John H. Littlefield, "Recollections of One Who Studied Law with Lincoln," *Independent*, 47 (Apr. 4, 1895): 447.

Livermore: Mary A. Livermore, *My Story of the War* (Hartford, Conn.: A. D. Worthington & Co., 1890).

Logan: John A. Logan, *The Great Conspiracy: Its Origin and History* (New York: A. R. Hart & Co., 1886).

Lossing: Benson J. Lossing, *Pictorial History of the Civil War in the United States of America*, Volume I (Philadelphia: George W. Childs, 1866); Volume II (Hartford, Conn.: T. Belknap, 1868).

Lowry: Thomas Lowry, *Personal Reminiscences of Abraham Lincoln* (Minneapolis, 1910).

Lutz: Ralph Haswell Lutz, "Rudolph Schleiden and the Visit to Richmond, April 25, 1861," *Annual Report of the American Historical Association for the Year 1915* (Washington, D.C.: Government Printing Office, 1917), 209–16.

Mabbott: Thomas O. Mabbott and Philip D. Jordan, "The Prairie Chicken: Notes on Lincoln and Mrs. Kirkland," *Journal of the Illinois State Historical Society*, 25 (1932–33): 154–66.

Macdonell: Agnes Macdonell, "America Then and Now: Recollections of Lincoln," *Contemporary Review*, 111 (May 1917): 562–69.

Magruder: Allan B. Magruder, "A Piece of Secret History: President Lincoln and the Virginia Convention of 1861," *Atlantic Monthly*, 35 (Apr. 1875): 438–45.

Malet: William Wyndham Malet, *An Errand to the South in the Summer of 1862* (London: Richard Bentley, 1863).

Marten: James Marten, " 'Dancing attendance in the antichambers of the great': A Texas Unionist Goes to Washington, 1863," *Lincoln Herald*, 90 (1988): 84–86.

Maynard: Nettie Colburn Maynard, *Was Abraham Lincoln a Spiritualist? Or, Curious Revelations from the Life of a Trance Medium* (Philadelphia: Rufus C. Hartranft, 1891).

McClellan-1: Stephen W. Sears, ed., *The Civil War Papers of George B. McClellan: Selected Correspondence, 1860–1865* (New York: Ticknor & Fields, 1989).

McClellan-2: George B. McClellan, *McClellan's Own Story* (New York: Charles I. Webster & Co., 1887).

McClure-1: A[lexander] K. McClure, *Abraham Lincoln and Men of War-Times* (4th ed.; Philadelphia: Times Publishing Co., 1892).

McClure-2: A[lexander] K. McClure, "How We Make Presidents: Recollections of Lincoln's Two Campaigns," *Saturday Evening Post*, 172 (Feb. 10, 1900): 710–12.

McClure-3: Alexander K. McClure, ed., *Abe Lincoln's Yarns and Stories* (Chicago: Educational Company, 1901).

McClure-4: *Alexander K. McClure's Recollections of Half a Century* (Salem, Mass.: Salem Press Co., 1902).

McClure-5: Alexander K. McClure, "His Career Was a Climax of Ceaseless Self-Culture," *Success*, Feb. 1904, pp. 91–94.

McCorison: J. L. McCorison, Jr., ed., "Impressions of the President-Elect, 1860: A Letter of Thomas Webster, Jr.," *Abraham Lincoln Quarterly*, 3 (1944–45): 291–301.

McCulloch: Hugh McCulloch, *Men and Measures of Half a Century* (New York: Charles Scribner's Sons, 1889).

McPherson: Edward McPherson, *The Political History of the United States of America, During the Great Rebellion* (Washington, D.C.: Philp & Solomons, 1864).

Meade: George Meade, *The Life and Letters of George Gordon Meade* (2 vols.; New York: Charles Scribner's Sons, 1913).

Mearns: David C. Mearns, "Mr. Lincoln and the Books He Read," in *Three Presidents and Their Books* (Urbana: University of Illinois Press, 1955).

Meigs: "General M. C. Meigs on the Conduct of the Civil War," *American Historical Review*, 26 (1920–21): 285–303.

MHSP: *Proceedings of the Massachusetts Historical Society.*

Miner: Noyes W. Miner, "Personal Reminiscences of Abraham Lincoln," manuscript dated 1882, Illinois State Historical Library.

Moore F: Frank Moore, ed., *The Rebellion Record: A Diary of American Events, with Documents, Narratives, Illustrative Incidents, Poetry, etc.* (12 vols.; New York: G. P. Putnam and D. Van Nostrand, 1861–69).

Moore RM: Risdon M. Moore, "Mr. Lincoln as a Wrestler," *Transactions of the Illinois State Historical Society for the Year 1904*, 433–34.

Morehead: Speech of Charles S. Morehead delivered at Liverpool, England, Oct. 9, 1862, printed in the Liverpool *Mercury*, Oct. 13, 1862, and partly reproduced in David Rankin Barbee and Milledge L. Bonham, Jr., eds., "Fort Sumter Again," *Mississippi Valley Historical Review*, 28 (1941–42): 63–73.

Motley: George William Curtis, ed., *The Correspondence of John Lothrop Motley* (3 vols.; New York: Harper & Brothers, 1900).

Mowry: William A. Mowry, "Reminiscences of Lincoln Told by the Late Ex-Governor Curtin of Pennsylvania," *Independent*, 49 (Aug. 1897): 1068–69.

Myers: Gustavus Myers, "Memoranda" (Apr. 1865), in *Virginia Magazine of History and Biography*, 41 (Oct. 1933): 318–22.

Nadal: E. S. Nadal, "Some Impressions of Lincoln," *Scribner's Magazine*, 39 (Mar. 1906): 368–77.

Neill: Theodore C. Blegen, ed., *Abraham Lincoln and His Mailbag: Two Documents by Edward D. Neill, One of Lincoln's Secretaries* (St. Paul: Minnesota Historical Society, 1964).

Nichols: Clifton M. Nichols, *Life of Abraham Lincoln* (New York: Mast, Crowell & Kirkpatrick, 1896).

Nicolay: John G. Nicolay, "Lincoln's Literary Experiments," *Century Magazine*, 47 (Apr. 1894): 823-32.

Nicolay and Hay: John G. Nicolay and John Hay, *Abraham Lincoln: A History* (10 vols.; New York: Century Co., 1890).

Nicolay-Hay Papers: Papers of John G. Nicolay and John Hay, Illinois State Historical Library.

Nicolay Papers: John G. Nicolay Papers, Manuscript Division, Library of Congress.

Niven: John Niven, *Gideon Welles: Lincoln's Secretary of the Navy* (New York: Oxford University Press, 1973).

Oldroyd: Osborn H. Oldroyd, ed., *The Lincoln Memorial: Album-Immortelles* (New York: G. W. Carleton & Co., 1882).

OR: *The War of the Rebellion: A Compilation of the Official Records of the Union and Confederate Armies* (128 vols.; Washington, D.C.: Government Printing Office, 1880-1901).

OR, Navies: *Official Records of the Union and Confederate Navies in the War of the Rebellion* (30 vols.; Washington, D.C.: Government Printing Office, 1892-1922).

Orme Papers: William W. Orme Papers, Illinois State Historical Library.

Palmer-1: John M. Palmer, ed., *The Bench and Bar of Illinois* (2 vols.; Chicago: Lewis Publishing Co., 1899).

Palmer-2: *Personal Recollections of John M. Palmer: The Story of an Earnest Life* (Cincinnati: R. Clarke Co., 1901).

Parks: LeRoy H. Fischer, ed., "Samuel C. Parks's Reminiscences of Abraham Lincoln," *Lincoln Herald*, 68 (Spring 1966): 11-19 (a speech delivered in 1909).

Paton: William Agnew Paton, "A Schoolboy's Interview with Abraham Lincoln," *Scribner's Magazine*, 54 (Dec. 1913): 709-10.

Patterson: Robert Patterson, *A Narrative of the Campaign in the Valley of the Shenandoah in 1861* (Philadelphia: Sherman & Co., 1865).

Patton: William W. Patton, *President Lincoln and the Chicago Memorial on Emancipation* (Baltimore, 1888).

Peskin: Alan Peskin, ed., "Two White House Visits: Congressman James H. Campbell Prods President Lincoln and Shares 'A Dish of Gossip with the First Lady,'" *Lincoln Herald*, 94 (Winter 1992): 157-58.

Phillips-1: Isaac N. Phillips, *Abraham Lincoln: A Short Study of a Great Man and His Work* (Bloomington, Ill., 1901).

Phillips-2: Isaac N. Phillips, ed., *Abraham Lincoln, by Some Men Who Knew Him* (Bloomington, Ill.: Pantagraph Printing & Stationery Co., 1910).

Piatt: Donn Piatt, *Memories of the Men Who Saved the Union* (New York: Belford, Clarke & Co., 1887).

Pickett: Thomas J. Pickett, "Reminiscences of Abraham Lincoln," *Lincoln Herald*, 45 (Dec. 1943): 3-10, a reprint of Pickett's article in the Lincoln, Nebraska, *State Journal*, Apr. 12, 1881.

Pinkerton: [Allan Pinkerton], *History and Evidence of the Passage of Abraham Lincoln from Harrisburg, Pa., to Washington, D.C., on the Twenty-second and Twenty-third of February, Eighteen Hundred and Sixty-one* (Chicago, 1868).

Pollock: Esther Cowles Cushman, ed., "Douglas the Loyal: A Hitherto Unpublished Manuscript by James Pollock, Previously Governor of Pennsylvania," *Journal of the Illinois State Historical Society*, 23 (Apr. 1930): 163–70.

Pomroy: Rebecca R. Pomroy, "What His Nurse Knew," *Magazine of History*, 32 (No. 1, Extra Number 125, 1926): 46–49.

Porter DD: [David Dixon] Porter, *Incidents and Anecdotes of the Civil War* (New York: Appleton & Co., 1885).

Porter H-1: Horace Porter, *Campaigning with Grant* (New York: Century Co., 1897).

Porter H-2: Porter's speech in *Addresses Delivered Before the Commandery of the State of New York, Military Order of the Loyal Legion of the United States, at the Regular Meeting Held February 3, 1909, at Delmonico's in Observance of the One Hundredth Anniversary of the Birth of President Abraham Lincoln* (n.p., 1909), 10–15.

Potter: David M. Potter, *Lincoln and His Party in the Secession Crisis* (New Haven, Conn.: Yale University Press, 1942).

Pratt-1: Harry E. Pratt, *The Personal Finances of Abraham Lincoln* (Springfield, Ill.: Abraham Lincoln Association, 1943).

Pratt-2: Harry E. Pratt, ed., *Concerning Mr. Lincoln* (Springfield, Ill.: Abraham Lincoln Association, 1944).

Prince: Ezra M. Prince, "A Day with Abraham Lincoln," manuscript, Tarbell Papers.

Proctor: Addison G. Proctor, "Lincoln's Honesty," *Harper's Weekly*, 49 (Apr. 29, 1905): 619.

Proctor Papers: A. G. Proctor Papers, Chicago Historical Society.

Purington: D. V. Purington, letter in *Century Magazine*, 74 (Sept. 1907): 809.

Ramsey Papers: Alexander Ramsey Papers, Minnesota Historical Society.

Randall-1: J. G. Randall, *Lincoln the President: Springfield to Gettysburg* (2 vols.; New York: Dodd, Mead & Co., 1946).

Randall-2: J. G. Randall, *Lincoln the President: Midstream* (New York: Dodd, Mead & Co., 1953).

Randall and Current: J. G. Randall and Richard N. Current, *Lincoln the President: Last Full Measure* (New York: Dodd, Mead & Co., 1955).

Rankin-1: Henry B. Rankin, *Personal Recollections of Abraham Lincoln* (New York: Knickerbocker Press, 1916).

Rankin-2: Henry B. Rankin, *Intimate Character Sketches of Abraham Lincoln* (Philadelphia: J. B. Lippincott Co., 1924).

Rantoul: Robert S. Rantoul, "Reminiscences of Abraham Lincoln," *Proceedings of the Massachusetts Historical Society*, 1908, pp. 84–87.

Raymond-1: Henry J. Raymond, *The Life and Public Services of Abraham Lincoln* (New York: Derby & Miller, 1865).

Raymond-2: "Extracts from the Journal of Henry J. Raymond," *Scribner's Magazine*, 19 (Jan., Mar. 1880): 419–24, 703–10.

Reed: James A. Reed, "The Later Life and Religious Sentiments of Abraham Lincoln," *Scribner's Monthly*, 6 (July 1873): 333–43.

Reep: Thomas P. Reep, *Lincoln at New Salem* (Petersburg, Ill.: Old Salem Lincoln League, 1927).

Rhodes: Albert Rhodes, "A Reminiscence of Abraham Lincoln," *St. Nicholas*, 4 (Nov. 1876): 8–10.

Rice AH: Alexander H. Rice, "Incidents of President Lincoln's Sympathy," *Independent*, 47 (Apr. 4, 1895): 434.

Rice AT: Allen Thorndike Rice, ed., *Reminiscences of Abraham Lincoln by Distinguished Men of His Time* (New York: North American Publishing Co., 1886).

Richards: Maria Hall (Mrs. Lucas) Richards, "Lincoln Cheers His Sick Boy," *Delineator*, Feb. 1921, pp. 11, 52.

Richardson: Albert D. Richardson, *The Secret Service, the Field, the Dungeon, and the Escape* (Hartford, Conn.: American Publishing Co., 1865).

Riddle: Albert G. Riddle, *Recollections of War Times: Reminiscences of Men and Events in Washington, 1860–1865* (New York: G. P. Putnam's Sons, 1895).

Ripley: Otto Eisenschiml, ed., *Vermont General: The Unusual War Experiences of Edward Hastings Ripley, 1862–1865* (New York: Devin-Adair Co., 1960).

Roberts: Octavia Roberts, "We All Knew Abr'ham," *Abraham Lincoln Quarterly*, 4 (1946–47): 17–29.

Roll: John Linden Roll, "Sangamo Town," *Journal of the Illinois State Historical Society*, 19 (1927): 153–60.

Ross: Alexander Milton Ross, *Recollections and Experiences of an Abolitionist from 1855 to 1865* (Toronto: Rowsell and Hutchinson, 1875).

Rowe's Reminiscences: "Captain F.A. Rowe's Reminiscences," 8 unnumbered pages in Philip Corell, ed., *History of the Naval Brigade, 99th N.Y. Volunteers, Union Coast Guard, 1861–65* (New York, 1905).

Rusling: James F. Rusling, "Lincoln's Faith in Prayer," *Independent*, 47 (Apr. 4, 1895): 431.

Russell AP: A. P. Russell, "Abraham Lincoln," typescript copy, Barton Papers.

Russell WH-1: Martin Crawford, ed., *William Howard Russell's Civil War: Private Diary and Letters, 1861–1862* (Athens: University of Georgia Press, 1992).

Russell WH-2: William Howard Russell, *My Diary North and South* (2 vols.; London: Bradbury and Evans, 1863).

Safire: William Safire, *Freedom: A Novel of Abraham Lincoln and the Civil War* (Garden City, N.Y.: Doubleday & Co., 1987).

Samuel: Henry Samuel, "My Interview with Lincoln," typescript dated Mar. 8, 1889, Illinois State Historical Library.

Sandburg: Carl Sandburg, *Abraham Lincoln: The War Years* (4 vols.; New York: Harcourt, Brace & World, 1939).

Sandburg Collection: Carl Sandburg Civil War Collection, Illinois Historical Survey, University of Illinois, Urbana-Champaign.

Schofield: John M. Schofield, *Forty-Six Years in the Army* (New York: Century Co., 1897).

Schurz-1: Frederic Bancroft, ed., *Speeches, Correspondence and Political Papers of Carl Schurz* (6 vols.; New York: G. P. Putnam's Sons, 1913).

Schurz-2: Joseph Schafer, trans. and ed., *Intimate Letters of Carl Schurz, 1841–1869* (Madison: State Historical Society of Wisconsin, 1926).

Schurz-3: Frederic Bancroft and William A. Dunning, eds., *The Reminiscences of Carl Schurz* (3 vols.; New York: McClure Co., 1907–8).

Scovel-1: James M. Scovel, "Personal Recollections of Abraham Lincoln," *Overland Monthly*, 18 (Nov. 1891): 497–506.

Scovel-2: James M. Scovel, "Side-Lights on Lincoln," *Overland Monthly*, 38 (Sept. 1901): 204–7.

Scovel-3: James M. Scovel, "Recollections of Lincoln and Seward," *Overland Monthly*, 38 (Oct. 1901): 265–71.

Sears: Stephen W. Sears, *George B. McClellan: The Young Napoleon* (New York: Ticknor & Fields, 1988).

Seaver: William J. Seaver, "Some Impressions of Abraham Lincoln in 1856," *Magazine of History*, 14 (No. 6, Dec. 1911): 242–47.

Senate Document 37: *Senate Documents*, 46 Congress, 1 session, Number 37 (Serial 1871).

Senate Report 108: *Senate Reports*, 37 Congress, 3 session, Number 108, Part I (Serial 1152).

Sermons: *Sermons Preached in Boston on the Death of Abraham Lincoln* (Boston: J. E. Tilton & Co., 1865).

Seward FW-1: Frederick W. Seward, *Seward at Washington, as Senator and Secretary of State: A Memoir of His Life, with Selections from His Letters, 1846-1861* (New York: Derby & Miller, 1891).

Seward FW-2: Frederick W. Seward, *Seward at Washington, as Senator and Secretary of State: A Memoir of His Life, with Selections from His Letters, 1861-1872* (New York: Derby & Miller, 1891).

Seward FW-3: Frederick W. Seward, *Reminiscences of a War-Time Statesman and Diplomat, 1830-1915* (New York: G. P. Putnam's Sons, 1916).

Seward Papers: Microfilm edition of the William H. Seward Papers, Rush Rees Library, University of Rochester.

Seward WHJr: William H. Seward, Jr., "Reminiscences of Lincoln," *Magazine of History*, 9 (Feb. 1909): 104–7.

Shaw: George W. Shaw, *Personal Reminiscences of Abraham Lincoln* (Moline, Ill.: Carlson Printing Co., 1924).

Sheridan: *Personal Memoirs of P. H. Sheridan* (2 vols.; New York: Charles L. Webster & Co., 1888).

Sherman: *Memoirs of General William T. Sherman, by Himself* (2 vols.; New York: D. Appleton & Co., 1875).

SHSP-ns: *Southern Historical Society Papers*, New Series.

Siegfried: André Siegfried, *Mes Souvenirs de la IIIe République: Mon Père et Son Temps, Jules Siegfried, 1836-1922* (Paris, 1922).

Simpson: Brooks D. Simpson, "Alexander McClure on Lincoln and Grant: A Questionable Account," *Lincoln Herald*, 95 (1993): 83–86.

Skelton: Oscar Douglas Skelton, *The Life and Times of Sir Alexander Tilloch Galt* (Toronto: Oxford University Press, 1920).

Smith G: Goldwin Smith, "President Lincoln," *Macmillan's Magazine*, 11 (Feb. 1865), 300–305.

Smith Papers: William Henry Smith Papers, Ohio Historical Society.

Smith WE: William E. Smith, *The Francis Preston Blair Family in Politics* (2 vols.; New York: Macmillan Co., 1933).

Speed: Joshua F. Speed, *Reminiscences of Abraham Lincoln and Notes of a Visit to California* (Louisville, Ky.: John P. Morton & Co., 1884).

Stanton HB: Henry B. Stanton, *Random Recollections* (New York: Harper & Brothers, 1887).

Stanton Papers: Microfilm edition of the Edwin M. Stanton Papers, Manuscript Division, Library of Congress.

Stanton RB: Robert Brewster Stanton, "Abraham Lincoln: Personal Memories of the Man," *Scribner's Magazine*, 68 (July 1920): 32-41.

Stanton RL: Robert Livingston Stanton, "Reminiscences of President Lincoln" (c. 1883), Robert Brewster Stanton Papers, New York Public Library.

Starr: Louis M. Starr, *Bohemian Brigade: Civil War Newsmen in Action* (New York: Alfred A. Knopf, 1954).

Stephens: Alexander H. Stephens, *A Constitutional View of the Late War Between the States* (2 vols.; Philadelphia: National Publishing Co., 1868-70).

Sterling: James T. Sterling, "How Lincoln 'Lost' His Inaugural Address," speech, Nov. 3, 1898, published in *Lincoln Herald*, 45 (1943): 23-25.

Stevens: Walter B. Stevens, *A Reporter's Lincoln* (St. Louis: Missouri Historical Society, 1916).

Stewart: George Rothwell Brown, ed., *Reminiscences of Senator William M. Stewart of Nevada* (New York: Neale Publishing Co., 1908).

Stewart Papers: Judd Stewart Papers, Huntington Library.

Stimmel: Smith Stimmel, *Personal Reminiscences of Abraham Lincoln* (Minneapolis: William H. M. Adams, 1928).

Stoddard-1: William O. Stoddard, *Inside the White House in War Times* (New York: Charles L. Webster & Co., 1890).

Stoddard-2: William O. Stoddard, Jr., ed., *Lincoln's Third Secretary: The Memoirs of William O. Stoddard* (New York: Exposition Press, 1955).

Stowe: Harriet Beecher Stowe, "Abraham Lincoln," *Watchman and Reflector*, re-published in *Littell's Living Age*, 80 (Feb. 6, 1864): 282-84.

Stradling: *His Talk with Lincoln: Being a Letter Written by James M. Stradling* (Boston: Houghton Mifflin Co., 1922).

Strong: Allan Nevins and Milton Halsey Thomas, eds., *The Diary of George Templeton Strong* (4 vols.; New York: Macmillan Co., 1952).

Sturgis Papers: Samuel D. Sturgis Papers, Wisconsin Historical Society.

Sturtevant: J[ulian] M. Sturtevant, Jr., ed., *Julian M. Sturtevant: An Autobiography* (New York: Fleming H. Revell Co., 1896).

Sumner Letters: Beverly Wilson Palmer, ed., *The Selected Letters of Charles Sumner* (2 vols.; Boston: Northeastern University Press, 1990).

Sumner Papers: Beverly Wilson Palmer, ed., The Papers of Charles Sumner, micro-film edition (Alexandria, Va.: Chadwyck-Healey, 1988).

Swett-1: Leonard Swett, "The Conspiracies of the Rebellion," *North American Review*, 144 (Feb. 1887): 179-89.

Swett-2: Leonard Swett, *Oration upon the Unveiling of the Statue of Abraham Lincoln in Lincoln Park, October 22, 1887* (n.p., n.d.).

Tarbell: Ida M. Tarbell, *The Life of Abraham Lincoln* (4 vols.; New York: Lincoln History Society, 1900, 1907).

Tarbell Papers: Ida M. Tarbell Papers, Pelletier Library, Allegheny College.

Teasdale: Thomas C. Teasdale, *Reminiscences and Incidents of a Long Life* (St. Louis: National Baptist Publishing Co., 1887).

Temple: Wayne C. Temple, "Lincoln as Seen by T. D. Jones," *Illinois Libraries*, 58 (June 1976): 447-56.

Thacher: George H. Thacher, "Lincoln and Meade After Gettysburg," *American Historical Review*, 32 (1926–27): 282–83.

Thomasson: Nelson Thomasson, "Recollections of Abraham Lincoln," read before the Illinois Commandery of the Loyal Legion, Feb. 3, 1927, pamphlet, Lincoln Room, University of Illinois Library, Urbana-Champaign.

Thompson: Joseph P. Thompson, "A Talk with President Lincoln," *Congregationalist*, Mar. 30, 1866, pp. 50–51.

Tinker: Charles A. Tinker, "A Telegrapher's Reminiscence," *Independent*, 47 (Apr. 4, 1895): 443–44.

Tree: Lambert Tree, "Lincoln among Lawyers," *Century Magazine*, 81 (Feb. 1911): 591–93.

Trumbull Papers: Lyman Trumbull Papers, Manuscript Division, Library of Congress.

Tuckerman: Charles K. Tuckerman, "Personal Recollections of Abraham Lincoln," *Magazine of American History*, 19 (Jan.–June 1888): 411–15.

Tyler: Moses Coit Tyler, "One of Mr. Lincoln's Old Friends," *Journal of the Illinois State Historical Society*, 28 (1935–36): 247–57, reprinted from the *Independent*, Mar. 12, 19, 1868.

Usher: John P. Usher, *President Lincoln's Cabinet* (Omaha, Neb., 1925).

Van Santvoord: Cornelius Van Santvoord, "A Reception by President Lincoln," *Century Magazine*, 25 (Feb. 1883): 612–14.

Viele-1: Egbert L. Viele, "A Trip with Lincoln, Chase and Stanton," *Scribner's Monthly*, 16 (Oct. 1878): 813–22.

Viele-2: Egbert L. Viele, "Lincoln as a Story-Teller," *Independent*, 47 (Apr. 4, 1895): 440–41.

Villard: *Memoirs of Henry Villard, Journalist and Financier, 1835-1900* (2 vols.; Boston: Houghton Mifflin & Co., 1904).

Voices: *Voices from the Pulpit of New York and Brooklyn: Our Martyr President, Abraham Lincoln* (New York: Tibbals & Whiting, 1865).

Volk: Leonard W. Volk, "The Lincoln Life-Mask and How It Was Made," *Century Magazine*, 23 (Dec. 1881): 223–28.

Wall: Alexander J. Wall, *A Sketch of the Life of Horatio Seymour, 1810-1886* (New York, 1929).

Wallace: *Lew Wallace: An Autobiography* (2 vols.; New York: Harper & Brothers, 1906).

Washburne Papers: Elihu B. Washburne Papers, Manuscript Division, Library of Congress.

Washington: John E. Washington, *They Knew Lincoln* (New York: E. P. Dutton & Co., 1942).

Weed SR: Samuel R. Weed, "Hearing the Returns with Mr. Lincoln," *New York Times Magazine*, Feb. 14, 1932, pp. 8–9, 21.

Weed T-1: Thurlow Weed, "President Lincoln as a Cabinet-Maker," *Appleton's Journal*, 3 (Jan. 16, 1870): 437–38.

Weed T-2: Thurlow Weed, "Mr. Lincoln and Three Friends in Council," *Galaxy*, 11 (Feb. 1871): 247–56.

Weed T-3: Harriet A. Weed, ed., *Autobiography of Thurlow Weed* (Boston: Houghton, Mifflin & Co., 1883).

Weik-1: Jesse W. Weik, "How Lincoln Was Convinced of General Scott's Loyalty," *Century Magazine*, 81 (Feb. 1911): 593–94.

Weik-2: Jesse W. Weik, *The Real Lincoln: A Portrait* (Boston: Houghton Mifflin Co., 1922).

Weik Papers: Jesse W. Weik Papers, Illinois State Historical Library.

Weldon: Lawrence Weldon, "Reminiscences of Lincoln as a Lawyer," an interview in *Independent*, 47 (Apr. 4, 1895): 450–52.

Welles-1: Howard K. Beale, ed., *Diary of Gideon Welles, Secretary of the Navy Under Lincoln and Johnson* (3 vols.; New York: W. W. Norton & Co., 1960).

Welles-2: Albert Mordell, ed., *Civil War and Reconstruction: Selected Essays by Gideon Welles* (New York: Twayne Publishers, 1959). Essays originally published in *The Galaxy*, 1870–73.

Welles-3: Gideon Welles, *Lincoln and Seward* (New York: Sheldon & Co., 1874).

Wentworth: M. Wentworth, "Mr. Lincoln and the Petitioners: A Record from the Executive Chamber," *Putnam's Magazine*, 16 (Nov. 1870): 527–36.

Whipple HB: H[enry] B. Whipple, "My Life Among the Indians," *North American Review*, 150 (Apr. 1890): 432–39.

Whipple W: Wayne Whipple, *The Story-Life of Lincoln* (Philadelphia: John C. Winston Co., 1908).

White: Horace White, *The Lincoln and Douglas Debates: An Address Before the Chicago Historical Society, February 17, 1914* (Chicago: University of Chicago Press, 1914).

Whitney-1: Henry C. Whitney, *Life on the Circuit with Lincoln* (Boston: Estes & Lauriat, 1892).

Whitney-2: Henry C. Whitney, *Lincoln the Citizen* (New York: Current Literature Publishing Co., 1907).

Williams F: [George] Forrester Williams, "General Sheridan's Bad Temper," *Independent* 53 (Oct. 10, 1901): 2397–2401.

Williams T: Talcott Williams, "Lincoln the Reader," *American Review of Reviews*, 61 (Feb. 1920): 193–96.

Wilson JF: James F. Wilson, "Some Memories of Lincoln," *North American Review*, 163 (Dec. 1896): 667–75.

Wilson JG-1: James Grant Wilson, "Recollections of Lincoln," *Putnam's Monthly*, 5 (Feb., Mar. 1909): 515–29, 670–75.

Wilson JG-2: James Grant Wilson, "Reminiscences of Abraham Lincoln," *Independent*, 74 (Feb. 20, 1913): 395–97.

Wilson RR-1: Rufus Rockwell Wilson, ed., *Lincoln Among His Friends: A Sheaf of Intimate Memories* (Caldwell, Idaho: Caxton Printers, 1942).

Wilson RR-2: Rufus Rockwell Wilson, ed., *Intimate Memories of Lincoln* (Elmira, N.Y.: Primavera Press, 1945).

Wilson WB: William Bender Wilson, *A Few Acts and Actors in the Tragedy of the Civil War in the United States* (Philadelphia, 1892).

Winchell: John M. Winchell, "Three Interviews with President Lincoln," *Galaxy*, 16 (July 1873): 33–41.

Winthrop: Robert C. Winthrop, Jr., *A Memoir of Robert C. Winthrop* (2nd ed.; Boston: Little, Brown & Co., 1897).

Wittenmyer: Annie Wittenmyer, *Under the Guns: A Woman's Reminiscences of the Civil War* (Boston: E. B. Stillings & Co., 1895).

Wolf S: Simon Wolf, *The Presidents I Have Known* (Washington, D.C.: Byron S. Adams Press, 1918).

Wolf WJ: William J. Wolf, *The Almost Chosen People: A Study of the Religion of Abraham Lincoln* (Garden City, N.Y.: Doubleday & Co., 1959).

Woods: Kate Tannatt Woods, wartime letter to her mother in *National Magazine*, 30 (Apr. 1909): 85–87.

Young: John Russell Young, *Men and Memories: Personal Reminiscences* (2 vols.; New York: F. T. Neely, 1901).

Zall: P. M. Zall, ed., *Abe Lincoln Laughing: Humorous Anecdotes from Original Sources by and About Abraham Lincoln* (Berkeley: University of California Press, 1982).

Zane: Charles S. Zane, "Lincoln As I Knew Him," *Sunset*, 29 (Oct. 1912): 430–38.

ACKNOWLEDGMENTS

The facilities of many institutions and the help of many persons made it possible to turn an idea, first set forth at Brown University in 1984, into the reality of this book. Our base of operations and primary source of materials was the Cecil H. Green Library at Stanford University. We thank the staffs of the circulation, reference, microform, special collections, and government documents departments, as well as the Stanford Law Library, and we are particularly grateful to James Knox for ordering certain acquisitions and to Sonia Moss and those assisting her in the work of arranging interlibrary loans. Because of Stanford's special library relationship with the University of California at Berkeley, we were able to borrow books from across the Bay by telephone, and we now express our thanks to the persons there who responded so quickly and so often to our requests.

In the search for appropriate materials, we paid visits to several libraries having notable Lincoln collections, and we now gratefully acknowledge their hospitality and contributions to our work. At the Huntington Library in San Marino, California, we had expert guidance from Paul M. Zall, the leading authority on Lincoln as a storyteller. He, Karen E. Kearns, and John H. Rhodehamel have also been generous in responding by mail to requests for specific items. At the John Hay Library of Brown University, Jennifer B. Lee and other members of the staff helped make research the pleasure that it can so often be. The same can be said of Thomas F. Schwartz (now Illinois State Historian), Cheryl Schnirring, and others at the Illinois State Historical Library in Springfield; and of John Hoffmann and Luann Matthews (of the Illinois Historical Survey and the Lincoln Room, respectively) at the University of Illinois Library in Urbana. At the Library of Congress, we made extensive use of books, periodicals, newspapers and manuscripts. The Manuscript Division, where we spent a good many days, has also lent much help through correspondence, and for that we thank James H. Hutson, Kathleen C. McDonough, and Charles J. Kelly. It has been our good fortune also to visit and make brief use of an outstanding private Lincoln collection at the home of Frank J. Williams near Providence, Rhode Island. We are grateful to him, not only for his hospitality at that time, but for the encouragement he, as longtime president of the Abraham Lincoln Association, lent this project from its inception.

The material gathered by us at Stanford and other places was supplemented by many items received through the mail, having been sent either voluntarily or in response to our specific requests. Our greatest debt of gratitude to any single person is the one owed to Michael Burlingame of Connecticut College, whose contributions have been so numerous and valuable that the book, one can truthfully say, would have been substantially poorer without them. We are also much indebted to Douglas L. Wilson, now of the Thomas Jefferson Memorial Foundation at Monticello, for texts of and expert advice on certain papers of William H.

Herndon; to Cullom Davis, director, and Dennis E. Suttles, William D. Beard, and Mark E. Steiner, staff members, of the Lincoln Legal Papers project for information concerning certain quotations of Lincoln as a lawyer; and to James Gilreath, Rare Book and Special Collections Division of the Library of Congress, for advice concerning the authenticity of a Lincoln signature. In addition to these correspondents and others already mentioned, we have good reason to thank the following persons and institutions: Daniel E. Pearson, president of the Lincoln Fellowship of Wisconsin; John K. Vandereedt, Civil Reference Branch of the National Archives in Washington; Margaret L. Moser and the Lawrence Lee Pelletier Library of Allegheny College; Ginger Shelley and the Lancaster County Historical Society in Lancaster, Pennsylvania; Joyce Ann Tracy and the American Antiquarian Society; Mary Robertson and the Yuba County Library in Marysville, California; Gary J. Arnold and the Ohio Historical Society; Faustino Avaloz, John Dougherty, and the Minnesota Historical Society; Muriel A. Sanford and the Raymond H. Fogler Library of the University of Maine; Edouard L. Desrochers of the library of Phillips Exeter Academy; Jean Ashton, Bernard R. Crystal, and the Rare Book and Manuscript Library, Butler Library, Columbia University; Bridget Burke and the Beinecke Rare Book and Manuscript Library, Yale University; Octavio Olvera and the University Library of the University of California at Los Angeles; the Chicago Historial Society.

We also thank Benjamin D. Paul for arranging a translation; Mark E. Neely, Jr., for his critical reading of the manuscript; and Norris Pope, John S. Feneron, and Eleanor P. Mennick of the Stanford University Press for their contributions to the shaping of an idea into a manuscript and the manuscript into this book.

INDEX

Library of Congress Cataloging-in-Publication Data

Recollected words of Abraham Lincoln / compiled and
  edited by Don E. Fehrenbacher and Virginia
  Fehrenbacher.
      p.   cm.
  Includes bibliographical references and index.
  ISBN 0-8047-2636-1 (cloth : alk. paper)
  I. Lincoln, Abraham, 1809–1865.   II. Fehrenbacher,
  Don Edward.   III. Fehrenbacher, Virginia.
  E457.99R43   1996
  973.7'092—dc20   95-37774
                                                      CIP

This book is printed on acid-free, recycled paper.

Original printing 1996
Last figure below indicates year of this printing:

05   04   03   02   01   00   99   98   97